PEARSON   ALWAYS LEARNING

Inventing Arguments

A Rhetoric and Reader for the University of Maryland's Academic Writing Program

Source material taken from:
Writing Arguments: A Rhetoric with Readings, Ninth Edition
by John D. Ramage, John C. Bean, and June Johnson

Ancient Rhetorics for Contemporary Students, Fifth Edition
by Sharon Crowley and Debra Hawhee

From Inquiry to Argument
by Linda McMeniman

Cover photo by John T. Consoli/University of Maryland.

Source material taken from:

Writing Arguments: A Rhetoric with Readings, Ninth Edition
by John D. Ramage, John C. Bean, and June Johnson
Copyright © 2012, 2010, 2007, 2004 by Pearson Education, Inc.
Upper Saddle River, New Jersey 07458

Ancient Rhetorics for Contemporary Students, Fifth Edition
by Sharon Crowley and Debra Hawhee
Copyright © 2011 by Pearson Education, Inc.
Published by Longman
New York, New York 10036

From Inquiry to Argument
by Linda McMeniman
Copyright © 1999 by Allyn & Bacon
Published by Pearson Education, Inc.
Boston, Massachusetts 02116

Pearson Learning Solutions, 501 Boylston Street, Suite 900, Boston, MA 02116
A Pearson Education Company
www.pearsoned.com

Printed in the United States of America

1 2 3 4 5 6 7 8 9 10 V092 17 16 15 14

000200010271915465

JH/CB

ISBN 10: 1-269-92475-3
ISBN 13: 978-1-269-92475-7

Contents

35   Argument Classics   643

SECTION ONE

Inventing Arguments

A Rhetoric and Reader for the University of Maryland's Academic Writing Program

Taken from *Writing Arguments: A Rhetoric with Readings*, Ninth Edition by John D. Ramage, John C. Bean, and June Johnson

PART ONE
Overview of Argument

1 Argument: An Introduction
2 Argument as Inquiry: Reading and Exploring

These stills from the film *Under the Same Moon* (2007) depict the painful separation and longing for connection of an immigrant mother in the United States and her young son, Carlitos, left behind in Mexico. The telephone booth and the furtive, precious calls symbolize the plight of families divided by economics and immigration policy. The film's appeals to our emotions are discussed in Michael Banks's exploratory essay in Chapter 2, pages 52–58.

Argument: An Introduction

At the outset of a book on argument, we ought to explain what an argument is. Instead, we're going to explain why no universally accepted definition is possible. Over the centuries, philosophers and rhetoricians have disagreed about the meaning of the term and about the goals that arguers should set for themselves. This opening chapter introduces you to some of these controversies.

We begin by asking what we mean by argument, suggesting what argument isn't as well as what it is. We then proceed to three defining features of argument: it requires writers or speakers to justify their claims, it is both a product and a process, and it combines elements of truth seeking and persuasion. Next, we explore more deeply the relationship between truth seeking and persuasion by asking questions about the nature of "truth" that arguments seek. Finally, we give you an example of a successful arguing process. Our goal is to show you various ways of thinking about argument as a way of helping you become a more powerful arguer yourself. In this chapter, you will learn to:

- Explain what argument is
- Describe the features of argument

What Do We Mean by Argument?

Let's begin by examining the inadequacies of two popular images of argument—fight and debate.

Argument Is Not a Fight or a Quarrel

To many, the word *argument* connotes anger and hostility, as when we say, "I just got in a huge argument with my roommate," or "My mother and I argue all the time." What we picture here is heated disagreement, rising pulse rates, and an urge to slam doors. Argument imagined as fight conjures images of shouting talk-show guests, flaming bloggers, or fist-banging speakers.

But to our way of thinking, argument doesn't imply anger. In fact, arguing is often pleasurable. It is a creative and productive activity that engages us at high levels of inquiry and critical thinking, often in conversation with people we like and respect. For your primary image of argument, we invite you to think not of a shouting match on cable news but of a small group of reasonable people seeking the best solution to a problem. We will return to this image throughout the chapter.

Argument Is Not Pro-Con Debate

Another popular image of argument is debate—a presidential debate, perhaps, or a high school or college debate tournament. According to one popular dictionary, *debate* is "a formal contest of argumentation in which two opposing teams defend and attack a given proposition." Although formal debate can develop critical thinking, its weakness is that it can turn argument into a game of winners and losers rather than a process of cooperative inquiry.

For an illustration of this weakness, consider one of our former students, a champion high school debater who spent his senior year debating the issue of prison reform. Throughout the year he argued for and against propositions such as "The United States should build more prisons" and "Innovative alternatives to prison should replace prison sentences for most crimes." We asked him, "What do you personally think is the best way to reform prisons?" He replied, "I don't know. I haven't thought about what I would actually choose."

Here was a bright, articulate student who had studied prisons extensively for a year. Yet nothing in the atmosphere of pro-con debate had engaged him in truth-seeking inquiry. He could argue for and against a proposition, but he hadn't experienced the wrenching process of clarifying his own values and taking a personal stand. As we explain throughout this text, argument entails a desire for truth; it aims to find the best solutions to complex problems. We don't mean that arguers don't passionately support their own points of view or expose weaknesses in views they find faulty. Instead, we mean that their goal isn't to win a game but to find and promote the best belief or course of action.

Arguments Can Be Explicit or Implicit

Before proceeding to some defining features of argument, we should note also that arguments can be either explicit or implicit. An *explicit* argument directly states its controversial claim and supports it with reasons and evidence. An *implicit* argument, in contrast, may not look like an argument at all. It may be a bumper sticker, a billboard, a poster, a photograph, a cartoon, a vanity license plate, a slogan on a T-shirt, an advertisement, a poem, or a song lyric. But like an explicit argument, it persuades its audience toward a certain point of view.

Consider the striking photograph in Figure 1.1—a baby wearing a bib labeled "POISON." This photograph enters a conversation about the safety of toys and other baby products sold in the United States. In recent years, fears about toy safety have come mostly from two sources: the discovery that many toys imported from China contained lead paint and the discovery that a substance used to make plastics pliable and soft—called *phthalates* (pronounced "thalates")—may be harmful. Phthalates have been shown to interfere with hormone production in rat fetuses and, based on other rodent studies, may produce some kinds of cancers and other ailments. Because many baby products contain phthalates—bibs, edges of cribs, rubber duckies, and any

FIGURE 1.1 An implicit argument against phthalates

number of other soft, rubbery toys—parents worry that babies can ingest phthalates by chewing on these toys.

The photograph of the baby and bib makes the argumentative claim that baby products are poisonous; the photograph implicitly urges viewers to take action against phthalates. But this photograph is just one voice in a surprisingly complex conversation. Is the bib in fact poisonous? Such questions were debated during a recent campaign to ban the sale of toys containing phthalates in California. A legislative initiative sparked intense lobbying from both child-advocacy groups and representatives of the toy industry. At issue were a number of scientific questions about the risk posed by phthalates. To what extent do studies on rats apply to humans? How much exposure to phthalates should be considered dangerous? (Experiments on rats used large amounts of phthalates—amounts that, according to many scientists, far exceed anything a baby could absorb by chewing on a toy.) Also at issue is the level of health risks a free market society should be willing to tolerate. The European Union, operating on the "precautionary principle," and citing evidence that such toys *might* be dangerous, has banned toys containing phthalates. The U.S. government sets less strict standards than does the European Union. A federal agency generally doesn't ban a substance unless it has been *proven* harmful to humans, not merely suspected of being harmful. In defense of free markets, the toy and chemical industries accused opponents of phthalates of using "junk science" to produce scary but inaccurate data.

Our point in summarizing the toxic toy controversy is to demonstrate the persuasive roles of both implicit and explicit arguments.

In contrast to the implicit argument made in Figure 1.1, Dr. Louis W. Sullivan, who was secretary of health and human services under the Clinton administration, makes an explicit argument in a letter to the governor of California. Sullivan opposes the bill banning phthalates, claiming that scientific agencies charged with public safety haven't found phthalates harmful. Instead, he supports an alternative "Green Chemistry Initiative" that would make public policy decisions based on "facts, not fear."

Let the Facts Decide, Not Fear: Ban AB 1108

LOUIS W. SULLIVAN, M.D.

Dear Governor Schwarzenegger:

As a physician and public servant who has worked in the field of medicine and public health all my life, I am writing to urge your veto of AB 1108, a bill that would ban the use of compounds used to make vinyl toys and childcare products soft and flexible. AB 1108 widely misses the mark on the most fundamental underpinning of all good public health policy—sound science.

AB 1108 ignores a recent, comprehensive review of the safety of vinyl toys conducted by the U.S. Consumer Product Safety Commission. The CPSC took a long, hard look at the primary softener used in children's toys and concluded that vinyl toys containing this compound are safe as used. In fact, its experts warned that using substitutes could make toys more brittle and less safe.

The CPSC's conclusions are reinforced by the findings of many scientific bodies around the globe—including the European Union's European Chemicals Bureau, the U.S. National Toxicology Program, and the U.S. Centers for Disease Control and Prevention. At a time when public officials are trying to deal with the serious issue of lead paint in toys imported from China, California lawmakers should not confuse the safety of these softening compounds in vinyl toys with that issue. Signing AB 1108 will do nothing to resolve the lead paint in toys issue.

California needs public health policies based on science. That's why I resoundingly support your Green Chemistry Initiative. This is a coordinated, comprehensive strategy for addressing possible risk from products—in a holistic, science-based fashion—that would serve the interests of California families and their children.

5   I urge you to reject AB 1108 and allow your health and safety experts, not legislators, to make judgments about the chemicals in our environment—based on facts, not fear.

Sincerely,

Louis W. Sullivan, M.D.
U.S. Secretary of Health & Human Services 1989–1993
President Emeritus, Morehouse School of Medicine

■ ■ ■   **FOR CLASS DISCUSSION** Implicit and Explicit Arguments

1. Any argument, whether implicit or explicit, tries to influence the audience's stance on an issue, moving the audience toward the arguer's claim. Arguments work on us psychologically as well as cognitively, triggering emotions as well as thoughts and ideas. How would you describe the differences in the way that the photograph with the bib labeled "poison" (Figure 1.1) and the letter from Sullivan "work on us"?

2. Assume that you are explaining implicit arguments to an international exchange student who is not yet familiar with U.S. politics and popular culture. Each of the implicit arguments in Figures 1.2–1.6 makes a claim on its audience, trying to get viewers to adopt the arguer's position, perspective, belief, or point of view on an issue. For each argument, answer the following questions for your new international friend:

   a. What conversation does this argument join? What is the issue or controversy? What is at stake?

   b. What is the argument's claim? That is, what value, perspective, belief, or position does the argument ask its viewers to adopt?

   c. What is an opposing or alternative view? What views is the argument pushing against?

   d. How does the argument try to do its work on the brains or hearts of the audience?

FIGURE 1.2 These colors don't run

FIGURE 1.3 These colors don't run the world

FIGURE 1.4 Assisted suicide isn't "natural"

FIGURE 1.5 The climate change controversy

FIGURE 1.6 Arizona tan block

The Defining Features of Argument

We turn now to examine arguments in more detail. (Unless we say otherwise, by *argument* we mean explicit arguments that attempt to supply reasons and evidence to support their claims.) This section examines three defining features of such arguments.

Argument Requires Justification of Its Claims

To begin defining argument, let's turn to a humble but universal site of disagreement: the conflict between a parent and a teenager over rules. In what way and in what circumstances do such conflicts constitute arguments?

Consider the following dialogue:

YOUNG PERSON (*racing for the front door while putting coat on*): Bye. See you later.

PARENT: Whoa! What time are you planning on coming home?

YOUNG PERSON (*coolly, hand still on doorknob*): I'm sure we discussed this earlier. I'll be home around 2 A.M. (*The second sentence, spoken very rapidly, is barely audible.*)

PARENT (*mouth tightening*): We did *not* discuss this earlier and you're *not* staying out till two in the morning. You'll be home at twelve.

At this point in the exchange, we have a quarrel, not an argument. Quarrelers exchange antagonistic assertions without any attempt to support them rationally. If the dialogue never gets past the "Yes-you-will/No-I-won't" stage, it either remains a quarrel or degenerates into a fight.

Let us say, however, that the dialogue takes the following turn:

YOUNG PERSON (*tragically*): But I'm *sixteen years old!*

Now we're moving toward argument. Not, to be sure, a particularly well-developed or cogent one, but an argument all the same. It's now an argument because one of the quarrelers has offered a reason for her assertion. Her choice of curfew is satisfactory, she says, *because* she is sixteen years old, an argument that depends on the unstated assumption that sixteen-year-olds are old enough to make decisions about such matters.

The parent can now respond in one of several ways that will either advance the argument or turn it back into a quarrel. The parent can simply invoke parental authority ("I don't care—you're still coming home at twelve"), in which case argument ceases. Or the parent can provide a reason for his or her view ("You will be home at twelve because your dad and I pay the bills around here!"), in which case the argument takes a new turn.

So far we've established two necessary conditions that must be met before we're willing to call something an argument: (1) a set of two or more conflicting assertions and (2) the attempt to resolve the conflict through an appeal to reason.

But good argument demands more than meeting these two formal requirements. For the argument to be effective, an arguer is obligated to clarify and support the reasons presented. For example, "But I'm sixteen years old!" is not yet a clear support for the assertion "I should be allowed to set my own curfew." On the surface, Young Person's argument seems absurd. Her parent, of all people, knows precisely how old she is. What makes it an argument is that behind her claim lies an unstated assumption—all sixteen-year-olds are old enough to set their own curfews. What Young Person needs to do now is to support that assumption.* In doing so, she must anticipate the sorts of questions the assumption will raise in the minds of her parent: What is the legal status of sixteen-year-olds? How psychologically mature, as opposed to chronologically mature, is Young Person? What is the actual track record of Young Person in being responsible? and so forth. Each of these questions will force Young Person to reexamine and clarify her assumptions about the proper degree of autonomy for sixteen-year-olds. And her responses to those questions should in turn force the parents to reexamine their assumptions about the dependence of sixteen-year-olds on parental guidance and wisdom. (Likewise, the parents will need to show why "paying the bills around here" automatically gives them the right to set Young Person's curfew.)

As the argument continues, Young Person and Parent may shift to a different line of reasoning. For example, Young Person might say: "I should be allowed to stay out until 2 A.M. because all my friends get to stay out that late." (Here the unstated assumption is that the rules in this family ought to be based on the rules in other families.) The parent might in turn respond, "But I certainly never stayed out that late when I was your age"—an argument assuming that the rules in this family should follow the rules of an earlier generation.

As Young Person and Parent listen to each other's points of view (and begin realizing why their initial arguments have not persuaded their intended audience), both parties find themselves in the uncomfortable position of having to examine their own beliefs and to justify assumptions that they have taken for granted. Here we encounter one of the earliest meanings of the term *to argue,* which is "to clarify." As an arguer begins to clarify her own position on an issue, she also begins to clarify her audience's position. Such clarification helps the arguer see how she might accommodate her audience's views, perhaps by adjusting her own position or by developing reasons that appeal to her audience's values. Thus Young Person might suggest an argument like this:

> I should be allowed to stay out until two on a trial basis because I need enough freedom to demonstrate my maturity and show you I won't get into trouble.

The assumption underlying this argument is that it is good to give teenagers freedom to demonstrate their maturity. Because this reason is likely to appeal to her parent's own values (the parent wants to see his or her daughter grow in maturity) and because it is tempered by the qualifier "on a trial basis" (which reduces

---

*Later in this text we will call the assumption underlying a line of reasoning its *warrant* (see Chapter 4).

some of the threat of Young Person's initial demands), it may prompt productive discussion.

Whether or not Young Person and Parent can work out a best solution, the preceding scenario illustrates how argument leads people to clarify their reasons and provide justifications that can be examined rationally. The scenario also illustrates two specific aspects of argument that we will explore in detail in the next sections: (1) Argument is both a process and a product. (2) Argument combines truth seeking and persuasion.

Argument Is Both a Process and a Product

As the preceding scenario revealed, argument can be viewed as a *process* in which two or more parties seek the best solution to a question or problem. Argument can also be viewed as a *product,* each product being any person's contribution to the conversation at a given moment. In an informal discussion, the products are usually short, whatever time a person uses during his or her turns in the conversation. Under more formal settings, an orally delivered product might be a short, impromptu speech (say, during an open-mike discussion of a campus issue) or a longer, carefully prepared formal speech (as in a PowerPoint presentation at a business meeting or an argument at a public hearing for or against a proposed city project).

Similar conversations occur in writing. Roughly analogous to a small-group discussion is an exchange of the kind that occurs regularly online through informal chat groups or more formal blog sites. In an online discussion, participants have more thinking time to shape their messages than they do in a real-time oral discussion. Nevertheless, messages are usually short and informal, making it possible over the course of several days to see participants' ideas shift and evolve as conversants modify their initial views in response to others' views.

Roughly equivalent to a formal speech would be a formal written argument, which may take the form of an academic argument for a college course; a grant proposal; an online posting; a guest column for the op-ed* section of a newspaper; a legal brief; a letter to a member of Congress; or an article for an organizational newsletter, popular magazine, or professional journal. In each of these instances, the written argument (a product) enters a conversation (a process)—in this case, a conversation of readers, many of whom will carry on the conversation by writing their own responses or by discussing the writer's views with others. The goal of the community of writers and readers is to find the best solution to the problem or issue under discussion.

Op-ed stands for "opposite-editorial." It is the generic name in journalism for a signed argument that voices the writer's opinion on an issue, as opposed to a news story that is supposed to report events objectively, uncolored by the writer's personal views. Op-ed pieces appear in the editorial-opinion section of newspapers, which generally features editorials by the resident staff, opinion pieces by syndicated columnists, and letters to the editor from readers. The term *op-ed* is often extended to syndicated columns appearing in newsmagazines, advocacy Web sites, and online news services.

Argument Combines Truth Seeking and Persuasion

In thinking about argument as a product, the writer will find herself continually moving back and forth between truth seeking and persuasion—that is, between questions about the subject matter (What is the best solution to this problem?) and about audience (What do my readers already believe or value? What reasons and evidence will most persuade them?). Back and forth she'll weave, alternately absorbed in the subject of her argument and in the audience for that argument.

Neither of the two focuses is ever completely out of mind, but their relative importance shifts during different phases of the development of a paper. Moreover, different rhetorical situations place different emphases on truth seeking versus persuasion. We could thus place arguments on a kind of continuum that measures the degree of attention a writer gives to subject matter versus audience. (See Figure 1.7.) At the far truth-seeking end of the continuum might be an exploratory piece that lays out several alternative approaches to a problem and weighs the strengths and weaknesses of each with no concern for persuasion. At the other end of the continuum would be outright propaganda, such as a political campaign advertisement that reduces a complex issue to sound bites and distorts an opponent's position through out-of-context quotations or misleading use of data. (At its most blatant, propaganda obliterates truth seeking; it will do anything, including the knowing use of bogus evidence, distorted assertions, and outright lies, to win over an audience.) In the middle ranges of the continuum, writers shift their focuses back and forth between truth seeking and persuasion but with varying degrees of emphasis.

As an example of a writer focusing primarily on truth seeking, consider the case of Kathleen, who, in her college argument course, addressed the definitional question "Is American Sign Language (ASL) a 'foreign language' for purposes of meeting the university's foreign language requirement?" Kathleen had taken two years of ASL at a community college. When she transferred to a four-year college, the chair of the foreign languages department at her new college would not allow her ASL proficiency to count for the foreign language requirement. ASL isn't a "language," the chair said summarily. "It's not equivalent to learning French, German, or Japanese."

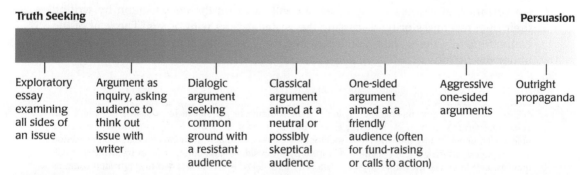

FIGURE 1.7 Continuum of arguments from truth seeking to persuasion

Kathleen disagreed, so she immersed herself in developing her argument. While doing research, she focused almost entirely on subject matter, searching for what linguists, neurologists, cognitive psychologists, and sociologists had said about the language of deaf people. Immersed in her subject matter, she was only tacitly concerned with her audience, whom she thought of primarily as her classmates and the professor of her argument class—people who were friendly to her views and interested in her experiences with the deaf community. She wrote a well-documented paper, citing several scholarly articles, that made a good case to her classmates (and the professor) that ASL is indeed a distinct language.

Proud of the big red A the professor had placed on her paper, Kathleen decided for a subsequent assignment to write a second paper on ASL—but this time aiming it directly at the chair of foreign languages and petitioning him to accept her ASL proficiency for the foreign language requirement. Now her writing task fell closer to the persuasive end of our continuum. Kathleen once again immersed herself in research, but this time focused not on subject matter (whether ASL is a distinct language) but on audience. She researched the history of the foreign language requirement at her college and discovered some of the politics behind it (an old foreign language requirement had been dropped in the 1970s and reinstituted in the 1990s, partly—a math professor told her—to boost enrollments in foreign language courses). She also interviewed foreign language teachers to find out what they knew and didn't know about ASL. She discovered that many teachers thought ASL was "easy to learn," so that accepting ASL would allow students a Mickey Mouse way to avoid the rigors of a "real" foreign language class. Additionally, she learned that foreign language teachers valued immersing students in a foreign culture; in fact, the foreign language requirement was part of her college's effort to create a multicultural curriculum.

This new understanding of her target audience helped Kathleen reconceptualize her argument. Her claim that ASL is a real language (the subject of her first paper) became only one section of her second paper, much condensed and abridged. She added sections showing the difficulty of learning ASL (to counter her audience's belief that learning ASL is easy), showing how the deaf community forms a distinct culture with its own customs and literature (to show how ASL would meet the goals of multiculturalism), and showing that the number of transfer students with ASL credits would be negligibly small (to allay fears that accepting ASL would threaten enrollments in language classes). She ended her argument with an appeal to her college's public emphasis (declared boldly in its mission statement) on eradicating social injustice and reaching out to the oppressed. She described the isolation of deaf people in a world where almost no hearing people learn ASL, and she argued that the deaf community on her campus could be integrated more fully into campus life if more students could "talk" with them. Thus the ideas included in her new argument—the reasons selected, the evidence used, the arrangement and tone—all were determined by her primary focus on persuasion.

Our point, then, is that all along the continuum, writers attempt both to seek truth and to persuade, but not necessarily with equal balance. Kathleen could not have written her second paper, aimed specifically at persuading the chair of foreign languages, if she hadn't first immersed herself in truth-seeking research that convinced her that ASL is indeed a distinct language. Nor are we saying that her second argument was better than her first. Both fulfilled their purposes and met the needs of their intended audiences. Both involved truth seeking and persuasion, but the first focused primarily on subject matter whereas the second focused primarily on audience.

Argument and the Problem of Truth

The tension that we have just examined between truth seeking and persuasion raises an ancient issue in the field of argument: Is the arguer's first obligation to truth or to winning the argument? And just what is the nature of the truth to which arguers are supposed to be obligated?

In Plato's famous dialogues from ancient Greek philosophy, these questions were at the heart of Socrates' disagreement with the Sophists. The Sophists were professional rhetoricians who specialized in training orators to win arguments. Socrates, who valued truth seeking over persuasion and believed that truth could be discovered through philosophic inquiry, opposed the Sophists. For Socrates, Truth resided in the ideal world of forms, and through philosophic rigor humans could transcend the changing, shadowlike world of everyday reality to perceive the world of universals where Truth, Beauty, and Goodness resided. Through his method of questioning his interlocutors, Socrates would gradually peel away layer after layer of false views until Truth was revealed. The good person's duty, Socrates believed, was not to win an argument but to pursue this higher Truth. Socrates distrusted rhetoricians because they were interested only in the temporal power and wealth that came from persuading audiences to the orator's views.

Let's apply Socrates' disagreement with the Sophists to a modern instance. Suppose your community is divided over the issue of raising environmental standards versus keeping open a job-producing factory that doesn't meet new guidelines for waste discharge. The Sophists would train you to argue any side of this issue on behalf of any lobbying group willing to pay for your services. If, however, you followed the spirit of Socrates, you would be inspired to listen to all sides of the dispute, peel away false arguments, discover the Truth through reasonable inquiry, and commit yourself to a Right Course of Action.

But what is the nature of Truth or Right Action in a dispute between jobs and the environment? The Sophists believed that truth was determined by those in power; thus they could enter an argument unconstrained by any transcendent beliefs or assumptions. When Socrates talked about justice and virtue, the Sophists could reply contemptuously that these were fictitious concepts invented by the weak to protect themselves from the strong. Over the years, the Sophists' relativist beliefs became so repugnant to people that the term *sophistry* became synonymous with trickery in argument.

However, in recent years the Sophists' critique of a transcendent Universal Truth has been taken seriously by many philosophers, sociologists, and other thinkers who doubt Socrates' confident belief that arguments, properly conducted, necessarily arrive at a single Truth. For these thinkers, as for the Sophists, there are often different degrees of truth and different kinds of truths for different situations or cultures. From this perspective, when we consider questions of interpretation or value, we can never demonstrate that a belief or assumption is true—not through scientific observation, not through reason, and not through religious revelation. We get our beliefs, according to these contemporary thinkers, from the shared assumptions of our particular cultures. We are condemned (or liberated) to live in a pluralistic, multicultural world with competing visions of truth.

If we accept this pluralistic view of the world, do we then endorse the Sophists' radical relativism, freeing us to argue any side of any issue? Or do we doggedly pursue some modern equivalent of Socrates' truth?

Our own sympathies are with Socrates, but we admit to a view of truth that is more tentative, cautious, and conflicted than his. For us, truth seeking does not mean finding the "Right Answer" to a disputed question, but neither does it mean a valueless relativism in which all answers are equally good. For us, truth seeking means taking responsibility for determining the "best answer" or "best solution" to the question for the good of the whole community when taking into consideration the interests of all stakeholders. It means making hard decisions in the face of uncertainty. This more tentative view of truth means that you cannot use argument to "prove" your claim, but only to make a reasonable case for your claim. One contemporary philosopher says that argument can hope only to "increase adherence" to ideas, not absolutely convince an audience of the necessary truth of ideas. Even though you can't be certain, in a Socratic sense, that your solution to the problem is the best one available, you must ethically take responsibility for the consequences of your claim and you must seek justice for stakeholders beyond yourself. You must, in other words, forge a personal stance based on your examination of all the evidence and your articulation of values that you can make public and defend.

To seek truth, then, means to seek the best or most just solution to a problem while observing all available evidence, listening with an open mind to the views of all stakeholders, clarifying and attempting to justify your own values and assumptions, and taking responsibility for your argument. It follows that truth seeking often means delaying closure on an issue, acknowledging the pressure of alternative views, and being willing to change one's mind. Seen in this way, learning to argue effectively has the deepest sort of social value: It helps communities settle conflicts in a rational and humane way by finding, through the dialectic exchange of ideas, the best solutions to problems without resorting to violence or to other assertions of raw power.

■ ■ ■ **FOR CLASS DISCUSSION** Role-Playing Arguments

On any given day, the media provides evidence of the complexity of living in a pluralistic culture. Issues that could be readily decided in a completely homogeneous culture raise questions in a society that has fewer shared assumptions. Choose one of the following cases as the subject for a "simulation game" in which class members present the points of view of the people involved.

Case 1: College Athletes Caught in Tangled Web

As the following newspaper excerpt shows, social networking Web sites such as Facebook create conflicts between free speech and the reputations of people and institutions in the public domain.

> College students across the country have been cited or disciplined for content they posted on social networking Web sites such as MySpace and Facebook, including such things as criticism of a student government candidate (at the University of Central Florida), complaints about the theater department (Cowley College in Kansas), or vulgar comments about a teaching assistant (Syracuse).
>
> "College administrators are very nervous about this huge new forum," said Greg Lukianoff, president of the Foundation for Individual Rights in Education.
>
> The most nervous of those might be coaches and athletic directors, whose student-athletes are under a more intense public spotlight than the general student body and who usually are required to adhere to more stringent policies and rules of conduct. One distasteful picture of a prominent football player on the Internet could be seen by anybody and might end up on the front page of a newspaper. It's why some athletic departments have stricter policies about such sites and restrict usage as part of individual team rules.

Your task: Imagine an open meeting on your campus on the issue of students' free speech rights versus the rights of your college or university and its athletic departments to establish rules and monitor students' online social network pages. Hold a meeting in which classmates play the following roles: (a) a student athlete who has been warned to remove from his Facebook profile a photograph of himself chugging beer at fraternity party; (b) students who are not on athletic teams but are concerned about institutionally imposed restrictions on students' freedom; (c) a faculty member who feels he has been libeled on a former student's Facebook page; (d) a women's basketball coach who forbids student athletes on her teams from having personal online social networking accounts; (e) a tennis coach who establishes clear team policies for postings on students' sites; (f) the athletic director, who is considering buying tracking technology to monitor athletes' online social networking pages; (g) a representative of the American Civil Liberties Union who supports student rights and free speech; and (h) the dean of students, who is concerned for the reputation of the institution and for the future well-being of students who might be embarrassed by current postings or endangered by disclosing too much personal information.

Case 2: Homeless Hit the Streets to Protest Proposed Ban

> The homeless stood up for themselves by sitting down in a peaceful but vocal protest yesterday in [name of city].
>
> About 50 people met at noon to criticize a proposed set of city ordinances that would ban panhandlers from sitting on sidewalks, put them in jail for repeatedly urinating in public, and crack down on "intimidating" street behavior.
>
> "Sitting is not a crime," read poster boards that feature mug shots of [the city attorney] who is pushing for the new laws. [. . .] "This is city property; the police want to tell us we can't sit here," yelled one man named R. C. as he sat cross-legged outside a pizza establishment.

Your task: Imagine a public hearing seeking reactions to the proposed city ordinance. Hold a mock hearing in which classmates play the following roles: (a) a homeless person; (b) an annoyed merchant; (c) a shopper who avoids places with homeless people; (d) a citizen advocate for the homeless; (e) the city attorney.

A Successful Process of Argumentation: The Well-Functioning Committee

We have said that neither the fist-banging speaker nor the college debate team represents our ideal image of argument. The best image for us, as we have implied, is a well-functioning small group seeking a solution to a problem. In professional life such small groups usually take the form of committees.

We use the word *committee* in its broadest sense to indicate all sorts of important work that grows out of group conversation and debate. The Declaration of Independence is essentially a committee document with Thomas Jefferson as the chair. Similarly, the U.S. Supreme Court is in effect a committee of nine judges who rely heavily, as numerous books and articles have demonstrated, on small-group decision-making processes to reach their judgments and formulate their legal briefs.

To illustrate our committee or small-group model for argument, let's briefly consider the workings of a university committee on which coauthor John Ramage once served, the University Standards Committee. The Arizona State University (ASU) Standards Committee plays a role in university life analogous to that of the Supreme Court in civic life. It's the final court of appeal for ASU students seeking exceptions to various rules that govern their academic lives (such as registering under a different catalog, waiving a required course, or being allowed to retake a course for the third time).

The issues that regularly come before the committee draw forth all the argument types and strategies discussed throughout this text. For example, the different argument claim types discussed in Part Four regularly surface during committee deliberations, as shown in the following list:

- **Definition issues:** Is math anxiety a "learning disability" for purposes of exempting a student from a math requirement?
- **Resemblance issues:** How is this case similar to a case from the same department that we considered last semester?
- **Cause/consequence issues:** What were the causes of this student's sudden poor performance during spring semester? What will be the consequences of approving or denying her appeal?
- **Evaluation issues:** What criteria need to be met before we allow a student to graduate under a previous catalog?
- **Proposal issues:** Should we make it a policy to allow course X to substitute for course Y in the General Studies requirements?

On any given day, the committee's deliberations show how dialogue can lead to clarification of thinking. On many occasions, committee members' initial views shift as they study the specifics of individual cases and listen to opposing arguments from their colleagues. What allows this committee to function as well as it does is the fundamental civility of its members and their collective concern that their decisions be just. Because of the importance of these decisions to students' lives, committee members are willing to concede a point to another member in the name of reaching a better decision and to view the deliberations as an ongoing process of negotiation rather than a series of win-lose debates.

To give you firsthand experience at using argument as a process of clarification, we conclude this chapter with an actual case that came before the University Standards Committee in the early 1990s, when Ramage was a member of the committee. We invite you to read the following letter, pretending that you are a member of the University Standards Committee, and then proceed to the exercises that follow.

Petition to Waive the University Mathematics Requirement

Standards Committee Members,

I am a 43-year-old member of the Pawnee Tribe of Oklahoma and a very nontraditional student currently pursuing Justice Studies at the Arizona State University (ASU) College of Public Programs. I entered college as the first step toward completion of my goal—becoming legal counsel for my tribe, and statesman.

I come before this committee in good faith to request that ASU suspend, in my special case, its mathematics requirement for undergraduate degree completion so I may enter the ASU college of Law during Fall 1993. The point I wish to make to this committee is this: I do not need algebraic skills; I will never use algebra in my intended profession; and, if forced to comply with ASU's algebra requirement, I will be needlessly prevented from graduating in time to enter law school next fall and face an idle academic year before my next opportunity in 1994. I will address each of these points in turn, but a few words concerning my academic credentials are in order first.

Two years ago, I made a vow of moral commitment to seek out and confront injustice. In September of 1990, I enrolled in college. Although I had only the benefit of a ninth grade education, I took the General Equivalency Diploma (GED) examination and placed in the top ten percent of those, nationwide, who took the test. On the basis of this score I was accepted into Scottsdale Community College (SCC). This step made me the first in my entire family, and practically in my tribe, to enter college. During my first year at SCC I maintained a 4.0 GPA, I was placed on the President's list twice, was active in the Honors Program, received the Honors Award of Merit in English Humanities, and was conferred an Honors Scholarship (see attached) for the Academic year of 1991–1992 which I declined, opting to enroll in ASU instead.

At the beginning of the 1991 summer semester, I transferred to ASU. I chose to graduate from ASU because of the courses offered in American Indian studies, an important field ignored by most other Universities but necessary to my commitment. At ASU I currently maintain a 3.6 GPA, although my cumulative GPA is closer to 3.9, I am a member of the Honors and Justice Colleges, was appointed to the Dean's List, and awarded ASU's prestigious Maroon and Gold Scholarship twice. My academic standing is impeccable. I will enter the ASU College of Law to study Indian and criminal law during the Fall of 1993—if this petition is approved. Upon successful completion of my juris doctorate I will return to Oklahoma to become active in the administration of Pawnee tribal affairs as tribal attorney and advisor, and vigorously prosecute our right to sovereignty before the Congress of the United States.

5   When I began my "college experience," I set a rigid time schedule for the completion of my goal. By the terms of that self-imposed schedule, founded in my belief that I have already wasted many productive years, I allowed myself thirty-five months in which to achieve my Bachelor of Science degree in Justice Studies, for indeed justice is my concern, and another thirty-six months in which to earn my juris doctorate—summa cum laude. Consistent with my approach to all endeavors, I fell upon this task with zeal. I have willingly assumed the burden of carrying substantial academic loads during fall, spring and summer semesters. My problem now lies in the fact that in order to satisfy the University's math requirement to graduate I must still take MAT-106 and MAT-117. I submit that these mathematics courses are irrelevant to my goals, and present a barrier to my fall matriculation into law school.

Upon consideration of my dilemma, the questions emerged: Why do I need college algebra (MAT-117)? Is college algebra necessary for studying American Indian law? Will I use college algebra in my chosen field? What will the University gain or lose, from my taking college algebra—or not? I decided I should resolve these questions.

I began my inquiry with the question: "Why do I need college algebra (MAT-117)?" I consulted Mr. Jim _____ of the Justice College and presented this question to him. He referred to the current ASU catalog and delineated the following answer: I need college algebra (1) for a minimum level of math competency in my chosen field, and (2) to satisfy the university math requirement in order to graduate. My reply to the first answer is this: I already possess ample math skills, both practical and academic; and, I have no need for algebra in my chosen field. How do I know this? During the spring 1992 semester at ASU I successfully completed introductory algebra (MAT-077), scoring the highest class grade on one test (see attached transcript and test). More noteworthy is the fact that I was a machine and welding contractor for fifteen years. I used geometry and algebra commonly in the design of many welded structures. I am proficient in the use of Computer Assisted Design (CAD) programs, designing and drawing all my own blueprints for jobs. My blueprints and designs are always approved by city planning departments. For example, my most recent job consisted of the manufacture, transportation and installation of one linear mile of anodized, aluminum handrailing at a luxury resort condo on Maui, Hawaii. I applied extensive use of math to calculate the amount of raw materials to order, the logistics of mass production and transportation for both men and materials from Mesa to Maui, the job site installation itself, and cash flow. I have successfully completed many jobs of this nature—all without a mathematical hitch. As to the application of math competency in my chosen field, I can guarantee this committee that there will not be a time in my practice of Indian law that I will need algebra. If an occasion ever occurs that I need algebra, I will hire a mathematician, just as I would an engineer if I need engineering, or a surgeon if I need an operation.

I then contacted Dr. _____ of the ASU Mathematics Department and presented him with the same question: "Why do I need college algebra?" He replied: (1) for a well rounded education; (2) to develop creative thinking; and (3) to satisfy the university math requirement in order to graduate. Responding to the first answer, I have a "well rounded education." My need is for a specific education in justice and American Indian law. In fact, I do not really need the degree to practice Indian law as representative of my tribe, just the knowledge. Regarding the second, I do not need to develop my creative thinking. It has been honed to a keen edge for many years. For example, as a steel contractor, I commonly create huge, beautiful and intricate structures from raw materials. Contracting is not my only experience in creative thinking. For twenty-five years I have also enjoyed the status of being one of this country's foremost designers and builders of racebikes. Machines I have designed and brought into existence from my imagination have topped some of Japan and Europe's best engineering efforts. To illustrate this point, in 1984 I rode a bike of my own design to an international victory over Honda, Suzuki, Laverda, BMW and Yamaha. I have excelled at creative thinking my entire life—I called it survival.

Expanding on the question of why I need college algebra, I contacted a few friends who are practicing attorneys. All responded to my question in similar manner. One, Mr. Billy _____, Esq., whose law firm is in Tempe, answered my two questions as follows: "When you attended law school, were there any courses you took which required algebra?" His response was "no." "Have you ever needed algebra during the many years of your practice?" Again, his response was "no." All agreed there was not a single occasion when they had need for algebra in their professional careers.

10   Just to make sure of my position, I contacted the ASU College of Law, and among others, spoke to Ms. Sierra _____. I submitted the question "What law school courses will I encounter in which I will need algebra?" The unanimous reply was, they knew of none.

I am not proposing that the number of credit hours I need for graduation be lowered. In fact, I am more than willing to substitute another course or two in its place. I am not trying to get out of anything hard or distasteful, for that is certainly not my style. I am seeking only to dispose of an unnecessary item in my studies, one which will prevent me from entering law school this fall—breaking my stride. So little holds up so much.

I agree that a young adult directly out of high school may not know that he needs algebraic skills. Understandably, he does not know what his future holds—but I am not that young adult. I claim the advantage. I know precisely what my future holds and that future holds no possibility of my needing college algebra.

Physically confronting injustice is my end. On reservations where government apathy allows rapacious pedophiles to pose as teachers; in a country where a million and a half American Indians are held hostage as second rate human beings whose despair results in a suicide, alcohol and drug abuse rate second to no other people; in prisons where helpless inmates are beaten like dogs by sadistic guards who should be the inmates—this is the realm of my chosen field—the disenfranchised. In this netherworld, algebra and justice exist independently of one another.

In summary, I am convinced that I do not need college algebra for a minimum level of math competency in my chosen field. I do not need college algebra for a well rounded education, nor to develop my creative thinking. I do not need algebra to take the LSAT. I do not need algebra for any courses in law school, nor will I for any purpose in the practice of American Indian law. It remains only that I need college algebra in order to graduate.

15   I promise this committee that ASU's integrity will not be compromised in any way by approving this waiver. Moreover, I assure this committee that despite not having a formal accreditation in algebra, I will prove to be nothing less than an asset to this University and its Indian community, both to which I belong, and I will continue to set a standard for integrity, excellence and perseverance for all who follow. Therefore, I ask this committee, for all the reasons described above, to approve and initiate the waiver of my University mathematics requirement.

[Signed] Gordon Adams

■ ■ ■   **FOR CLASS DISCUSSION** Responding to Adams's Argument

1. Before class discussion, decide how you would vote on this issue. Should this student be exempted from the math requirement? Write out the reasons for your decision.
2. Working in small groups or as a whole class, pretend that you are the University Standards Committee, and arrive at a group decision on whether to exempt this student from the math requirement.
3. After the discussion, write for five to ten minutes in a journal or notebook describing how your thinking evolved during the discussion. Did any of your classmates' views cause you to rethink your own? Class members should share with each other their descriptions of how the process of argument led to clarification of their own thinking.

We designed this exercise to help you experience argument as a clarifying process. But we had another purpose. We also designed the exercise to stimulate thinking about a problem we introduced at the beginning of this chapter: the difference between argument as clarification and argument as persuasion. Is a good argument necessarily a persuasive argument? In our opinion, this student's letter to the committee is a *good* argument. The student writes well, takes a clear stand, offers good reasons for his position, and supports his reasons with effective evidence. To what extent, however, is the letter a *persuasive* argument? Did it win its case? You know how you and your classmates stand on this issue. But what do you think the University Standards Committee at ASU actually decided during its deliberations?

We will return to this case in Chapter 4.

Conclusion

In this chapter we have explored some of the complexities of argument, showing you why we believe that argument is a matter not of fist banging or of win-lose debate but of finding, through a process of rational inquiry, the best solution to a problem or issue. What is our advice for you at the close of this introductory chapter? Briefly, to see the purpose of argument as truth seeking as well as persuasion. We suggest that throughout the process of argument you seek out a wide range of views, that you especially welcome views different from your own, that you treat these views respectfully, and that you see them as intelligent and rationally defensible. (Hence you must look carefully at the reasons and evidence on which they are based.)

Our goal in this text is to help you learn skills of argument. If you choose, you can use these skills, like the Sophists, to argue any side of any issue. Yet we hope you won't. We hope that, like Socrates, you will use argument for truth seeking and that you will consequently find yourself, on at least some occasions, changing your position on an issue while writing a rough draft (a sure sign that the process of arguing has complicated your views). We believe that the skills of reason and inquiry developed through the writing of arguments can help you get a clearer sense of who you are. If our culture sets you adrift in pluralism, argument can help you take a stand, to say, "These things I believe." In this text we will not pretend to tell you what position to take on any given issue. But as a responsible being, you will often need to take a stand, to define yourself, to say, "Here are the reasons that choice A is better than choice B, not just for me but for you also." If this text helps you base your commitments and actions on reasonable grounds, then it will have been successful.

For support in learning this chapter's content, follow this path in **MyCompLab:** Resources ⇒ Writing ⇒ Writing Purposes ⇒ Writing to Argue or Persuade. Review the instructions and multimedia resources about argument, and then complete the exercises and click on Gradebook to measure your progress.

Argument as Inquiry
Reading and Exploring

2

In the previous chapter we explained that argument is both a process and a product, both inquiry and persuasion. In this chapter, we focus on inquiry as the entry point into argumentative conversations. Although our social environment is rich with these conversations—think of the oral, visual, print, and hypertext arguments that surround us—argument in the early twenty-first century is often degraded into talk-show shouting matches or antagonistic sound bites and "talking points." This reductive trend has elicited the concern of many cultural critics, journalists, rhetoricians, scholars, and citizens. Journalist Matt Miller recently posed the questions, "Is it possible in America today to convince anyone of anything he doesn't already believe? . . . [A]re there enough places where this mingling of minds occurs to sustain a democracy?"* How can argument's role as a community's search for the best answers to disputed questions be emphasized? How can arguers participate in a "mingling of minds" and use argument productively to seek answers to problems?

We believe that the best way to reinvigorate argument is to approach the reading and writing of arguments as an exploratory process. To do so means to position ourselves as inquirers as well as persuaders, engaging thoughtfully with alternative points of view, truly listening to other perspectives, examining our own values and assumptions, and perhaps even changing our views. Rhetorician Wayne Booth proposes that when we enter an argumentative conversation, we should first ask, "When should I change my mind?" rather than, "How can I change your mind?"†

In this chapter, we present some practical strategies for reading and exploring arguments in an open-minded and sophisticated way. You will learn to play what rhetorician Peter Elbow calls the believing and doubting game, in which a thinker systematically stretches her thinking by willing herself to believe positions that she finds threatening and to doubt positions that she instinctively

---

*Matt Miller, "Is Persuasion Dead?" *New York Times* 4 June 2005, A29.
†Wayne Booth raised these questions in a featured session with Peter Elbow titled "Blind Skepticism vs. the Rhetoric of Assent: Implications for Rhetoric, Argument, and Teaching," presented at the CCCC annual convention, Chicago, Illinois, March 2002.

accepts.* The thinker's goal is to live with questions, to acknowledge uncertainty and complexity, and to resist settling for simple or quick answers. In this chapter, you will learn to:

- Use a variety of means to find complex, puzzling issues to explore
- Place a text in its rhetorical context
- Read to believe an argument's claims
- Read to doubt an argument's claims
- Think dialectically

Although we present these strategies separately here, as you become familiar with them you will use them automatically and often implement several at once. In this chapter, we show how one student, Michael Banks, jumped into the puzzling, complex problem of illegal immigration and used these strategies to guide his thoughtful exploration of various viewpoints and texts.

Finding Issues to Explore

The mechanisms by which you enter a controversy will vary, but most likely they will include reflecting on your experiences or reading. Typically, the process goes like this: Through reading or talking with friends, you encounter a contested issue on which you are undecided or a viewpoint with which you disagree. Your curiosity, confusion, or concern then prompts you to learn more about the issue and to determine your own stance. In this section we examine some strategies you can use to find issues worth exploring.

Do Some Initial Brainstorming

As a first step, make an inventory of issues that interest you. Many of the ideas you develop may become subject matter for arguments that you will write later in this course. The chart on page 27 will help you generate a productive list.

Once you've made a list, add to it as new ideas strike you and return to it each time you are given a new argumentative assignment.

Be Open to the Issues All around You

We are surrounded by argumentative issues. You'll start noticing them everywhere once you get attuned to them. You will be invited into argumentative conversations by posters, bumper stickers, blog sites, newspaper editorial pages, magazine articles, the sports section, movie reviews, song lyrics, and so forth. When you read or listen, watch for "hot spots"—passages or moments that evoke strong agreement, disagreement, or confusion. As an illustration of how arguments are all around us, try the following exercise on the issue of illegal immigration.

---

*Peter Elbow, *Writing without Teachers* (New York: Oxford University Press, 1973), 147–90.

Brainstorming Issues to Explore

What You Can Do	How It Works
Make an inventory of the communities to which you belong. Consider classroom communities; clubs and organizations; residence hall, apartment, neighborhood, or family communities; church/synagogue or work communities; communities related to your hobbies or avocations; your city, state, region, nation, and world communities.	Because arguments arise out of disagreements within communities, you can often think of issues for argument by beginning with a list of the communities to which you belong.
Identify controversies within those communities. Think both big and small: ▪ Big issue in world community: What is the best way to prevent destruction of rain forests? ▪ Small issue in residence hall community: Should quiet hours be enforced?	To stimulate thinking, use prompts such as these: ▪ People in this community frequently disagree about _____ . ▪ Within my work community, Person X believes _____ ; however, this view troubles me because _____ . ▪ In a recent residence hall meeting, I didn't know where I stood on _____ . ▪ The situation at _____ could be improved if _____ .
Narrow your list to a handful of problematic issues for which you don't have a position; share it with classmates. Identify a few issues that you would like to explore more deeply. When you share with classmates, add their issues to yours.	Sharing your list with classmates stimulates more thinking and encourages conversations. The more you explore your views with others, the more ideas you will develop. Good writing grows out of good talking.
Brainstorm a network of related issues. Any given issue is always embedded in a network of other issues. To see how open-ended and fluid an argumentative conversation can be, try connecting one of your issues to a network of other issues including subissues and side issues.	Brainstorm questions that compel you to look at an issue in a variety of ways. For example, if you explored the controversy over whether toys with phthalates should be banned (see Chapter 1), you might generate questions such as these about related issues: ▪ How dangerous are phthalates? ▪ Is the testing that has been done on rats adequate or accurate for determining the effects on humans? ▪ Is the European "precautionary principle" a good principle for the United States to follow? ▪ To what extent are controversies over phthalates similar to controversies over steroids, genetically modified foods, nitrites in cured meat, or mercury in dental fillings?

■ ■ ■ **FOR CLASS DISCUSSION** Responding to Visual Arguments about Immigration

Suppose, in your casual reading, you encounter some photos and political cartoons on the U.S. problems with illegal immigration (see Figures 2.1– 2.4). Working individually or in small groups, generate exploratory responses to these questions:

1. What claim is each cartoon or photo making?
2. What background information about the problems of illegal immigration do these cartoons and photos assume?
3. What network of issues do these visual texts suggest?
4. What puzzling questions do these visual texts raise for you?

FIGURE 2.1 Protest photo

FIGURE 2.2 Protest photo

FIGURE 2.3 Political cartoon on immigration and labor

FIGURE 2.4 Another political cartoon on immigrant labor

Explore Ideas by Freewriting

Freewriting is useful at any stage of the writing process. When you freewrite, you put fingers to keyboard (or pen to paper) and write rapidly *nonstop,* usually five to ten minutes at a stretch, without worrying about structure, grammar, or correctness. Your goal is to generate as many ideas as possible without stopping to edit your work. If you can't think of anything to say, write "relax" or "I'm stuck" over and over until new ideas emerge. Here is how Michael Banks did a freewrite in response to the cartoon in Figure 2.3.

Michael's Freewrite

This cartoon made me think about what jobs immigrant workers do. Come to think of it when I traveled with my dad on a business trip, all the chamber maids at the hotel were immigrants speaking Spanish. How ridiculous to think of replacing hotel housekeepers with robots! Yes, it's true that mechanization has taken away lots of jobs, but to think that all service jobs requiring low education could be easily done by machines is completely un-realistic. Relax think relax think relax. What other kinds of work do immigrants do? In my home region of Southern California a lot of the low pay work was done by Mexicans. My high school service group took free lunches to immigrants waiting for work in front of a Home Depot. It seemed that they would take any kind of job. Although lots of men were standing around, they seemed orderly and eager to work. Were these men illegal? The men who built the retaining wall in my neighbors' backyard and rolled out the sod lawn were immigrants and could have been illegal. Immigrants are willing to work hard. I wonder why there aren't enough jobs in Mexico. Why are we so dependent on immigrant labor? This low-skill work has to be done by someone. Why won't our homeless people or unemployed people in the United States take these low-skill jobs? Would American citizens take these jobs if they paid more? I can't help thinking that our whole economy would change if we cut way back on immigrant labor. Also all the efforts to limit immigration such as building the wall along the border have been super expensive and not effective. We can't build a wall over 1,900 miles long. Many of the ways we try to solve our immigration problem seem to be as out of touch as this cartoon.

Explore Ideas by Idea Mapping

Another good technique for exploring ideas is *idea mapping.* When you make an idea map, draw a circle in the center of a page and write some trigger idea (a broad topic, a question, or working thesis statement) in the center of the circle. Then record your ideas on branches and subbranches extending from the center circle. As long as you pursue one train of thought, keep recording your ideas on that branch. But when that line of thinking gives out, start a new branch. Often your thoughts will jump back and forth between branches. That's a major advantage of "picturing" your thoughts; you can see them as part of an emerging design rather than as strings of unrelated ideas.

Idea maps usually generate more ideas, though less well-developed ones, than freewrites. Figure 2.5 shows an idea map that student Michael Banks created on the issue of illegal immigration after class discussion of the photographs and cartoons in Figures 2.1–2.4.

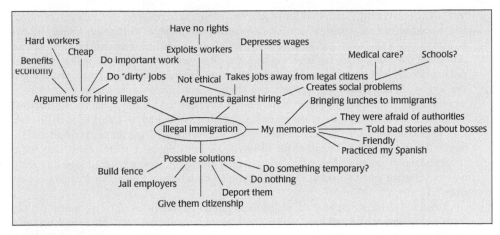

FIGURE 2.5 Michael's Idea map

Explore Ideas by Playing the Believing and Doubting Game

The believing and doubting game, a term coined by rhetorician Peter Elbow, is an excellent way to imagine views different from your own and to anticipate responses to those views.

- **As a believer, your role is to be wholly sympathetic to an idea.** You must listen carefully to the idea and suspend all disbelief. You must identify all the ways in which the idea may appeal to different audiences and all the reasons for believing the idea. The believing game can be difficult, even frightening, if you are asked to believe an idea that strikes you as false or threatening.

- **As a doubter, your role is to be judgmental and critical, finding fault with an idea.** The doubting game is the opposite of the believing game. You do your best to find counterexamples and inconsistencies that undermine the idea you are examining. Again, it is can be threatening to doubt ideas that you instinctively want to believe.

When you play the believing and doubting game with an assertion, simply write two different chunks, one chunk arguing for the assertion (the believing game) and one chunk opposing it (the doubting game). Freewrite both chunks, letting your ideas flow without censoring. Or, alternatively, make an idea map with believing and doubting branches. Here is how student writer Michael Banks played the believing and doubting game with an assertion about stopping illegal immigration: "Employers of illegal immigrants should be jailed."

Michael's Believing and Doubting Game

Believe: If we really want to stop illegal immigration, then we should jail employers who hire illegals. What draws illegal immigrants to this country is the money they can make, so if the government eliminated these jobs by jailing the employers then illegal immigration would stop. This would be just because employers of illegal immigrants benefit by not having to pay a fair wage and what's more they often do this hiring under the table so that they don't pay taxes. They are breaking laws and deserve to go to jail. By avoiding taxes and not providing medical insurance etc., they cost every American taxpayer more, and it is not fair to law abiding citizens. Employers also often exploit immigrant laborers, because they have nobody to be held accountable to. They also lower the wages of American workers. Their actions can cause rifts in communities already troubled by an influx of immigration. Like anybody else who supports illegal activity, employers of illegal immigration should be jailed. If employers faced charges for hiring illegal immigrants, it seems likely that there would be much less of a market for the services of immigrant workers. I could see this being a more effective way to combat illegal immigration than building fences or trying to deport them all.

Doubt: Jailing employers of illegal immigrants probably would stop some people from hiring undocumented immigrants, but I doubt it would be a reliable long-term solution. Especially for people who only hire a few immigrants at a time, it would likely be hard to prosecute them. Besides, I'm not convinced there is anything necessarily wrong with the employer's actions in hiring undocumented immigrants. If the government cannot enforce its own immigration laws, employers shouldn't be forced to do so for them. Many businesses, especially in agriculture, absolutely depend on good workers who will work long hours in hot fields to pick fruit and vegetables. Employers can't possibly be expected to do background checks on every employee. Moreover, if undocumented workers weren't available, the fruit wouldn't get picked. To send the employers to jail would mean to cause horrible disruption to much of our food supply. We are lucky to have these workers. The United States has a long history of people capitalizing on good business opportunities when the opportunity presents itself, and that's just what illegal immigrants are. It does not make sense to jail people for taking advantage of cheap and motivated labor.

Although Michael sees the injustice of paying workers substandard wages, he sees that much of our economy depends on this cheap labor. Playing the believing and doubting game has helped him articulate his dilemma and see the issue in more complex terms.

■ ■ ■ **FOR CLASS DISCUSSION** Playing the Believing and Doubting Game

Individual task: Choose one or more of the following controversial claims and play the believing and doubting game with it, through either freewriting or idea mapping. **Group task:** Working in pairs, in small groups, or as a whole class, share your results with classmates.

1. A student should report a fellow student who is cheating on an exam or plagiarizing an essay.
2. Women should be assigned to combat duty equally with men.
3. Athletes should be allowed to take steroids and human growth hormone under a doctor's supervision.
4. Illegal immigrants already living in the United States should be granted amnesty and placed on a fast track to U.S. citizenship.

■ ■ ■

Placing Texts in a Rhetorical Context

In the previous section, we suggested strategies for finding issues and entering argumentative conversations. Once you join a conversation, you will typically read a number of different arguments addressing your selected issue. The texts you read may be supplied for you in a textbook, anthology, or course pack, or you may find them yourself through library or Internet research. In this section and the ones that follow, we turn to productive strategies for reading arguments. We begin by explaining the importance of analyzing a text's rhetorical context as a preliminary step prior to reading. In subsequent sections, we explain powerful strategies for reading an argument—reading to believe, reading to doubt, and placing texts in conversation with each other through dialectic thinking.

As you read arguments on a controversy, try to place each text within its rhetorical context. It is important to know, for example, whether a blog that you are reading appears on Daily Kos (a liberal blog site) or on Little Green Footballs (a conservative blog site). In researching an issue, you may find that one article is a formal policy proposal archived on the Web site of an economics research institute, whereas another is an op-ed piece by a nationally syndicated columnist or a letter to the editor written by someone living in your community. To help you reconstruct a reading's rhetorical context, you need to understand the genres of argument as well as the cultural and professional contexts that cause people to write arguments. We'll begin with the genres of argument.

Genres of Argument

To situate an argument rhetorically, you should know something about its genre. A *genre* is a recurring type or pattern of argument such as a letter to the editor, a political cartoon, or the home page of an advocacy Web site. Genres are often categorized by recurring features, formats, and styles. The genre of any given argument helps determine its length, tone, sentence complexity, level of informality or formality, use of visuals, kinds of evidence, depth of research, and the presence or absence of documentation.

When you read arguments reprinted in a textbook such as this one, you lose clues about the argument's original genre. (You should therefore note the information about genre provided in our introductions to readings.) Likewise, you can lose clues about genre when you download articles from the Internet or from licensed databases such as Lexis-Nexis or ProQuest. When you do your own research, you therefore need to be aware of the original genre of the text you are reading: was this piece originally a newspaper editorial, a blog, an organizational white paper, a scholarly article, a student paper posted to a Web site, or something else?

In the chart on pages 34–36, we identify most of the genres of argument through which readers and writers carry on the conversations of a democracy.

Cultural Contexts: Who Writes Arguments and Why?

A democratic society depends on the lively exchange of ideas—people with different points of view creating arguments for their positions. Now that you know something about the genre of arguments, we ask you to consider who writes arguments and why.

Genres of Argument

Genre	Explanation and Examples	Stylistic Features
Personal correspondence	▪ Letters or e-mail messages ▪ Often sent to specific decision makers (complaint letter, request for an action)	▪ Style can range from a formal business letter to an informal note
Letters to the editor	▪ Published in newspapers and some magazines ▪ Provide a forum for citizens to voice views on public issues	▪ Very short (fewer than three hundred words) and time sensitive ▪ Can be summaries of longer arguments, but often focus in "sound bite" style on one point
Newspaper editorials and op-ed pieces	▪ Published on the editorial or op-ed ("opposite-editorial") pages ▪ Editorials promote views of the newspaper owners/editors ▪ Op-ed pieces, usually written by professional columnists or guest writers, range in bias from ultraconservative to socialist ▪ Often written in response to political events or social problems in the news	▪ Usually short (500–1,000 words) ▪ Vary from explicit thesis-driven arguments to implicit arguments with stylistic flair ▪ Have a journalistic style (short paragraphs) without detailed evidence ▪ Sources usually not documented
Articles in public affairs or niche magazines	▪ Usually written by staff writers or freelancers ▪ Appear in public affairs magazines such as *National Review* or *The Progressive* or in niche magazines for special-interest groups such as *Rolling Stone* (popular culture), *Minority Business Entrepreneur* (business), or *The Advocate* (gay and lesbian issues) ▪ Often reflect the political point of view of the magazine	▪ Often have a journalistic style with informal documentation ▪ Frequently include narrative elements rather than explicit thesis-and-reasons organization ▪ Often provide well-researched coverage of various perspectives on a public issue
Articles in scholarly journals	▪ Peer-reviewed articles published by nonprofit academic journals subsidized by universities or scholarly societies ▪ Characterized by scrupulous attention to completeness and accuracy in treatment of data	▪ Usually employ a formal academic style ▪ Include academic documentation and bibliographies ▪ May reflect the biases, methods, and strategies associated with a specific school of thought or theory within a discipline

Genre	Explanation and Examples	Stylistic Features
Legal briefs and court decisions	■ Written by attorneys or judges ■ "Friend-of-the-court" briefs are often published by stakeholders to influence appeals courts ■ Court decisions explain the reasoning of justices on civic cases (and often include minority opinions)	■ Usually written in legalese, but use a logical reasons-and-evidence structure ■ Friend-of-the-court briefs are sometimes aimed at popular audiences
Organizational white papers	■ In-house documents or PowerPoint presentations aimed at influencing organizational policy or decisions or giving informed advice to clients ■ Sometimes written for external audiences to influence public opinion favorable to the organization ■ External white papers are often posted on Web sites or sent to legislators	■ Usually desktop or Web published ■ Often include graphics and other visuals ■ Vary in style from the dully bureaucratic (satirized in *Dilbert* cartoons) to the cogent and persuasive
Blogs and postings to chat rooms and electronic bulletin boards	■ Web-published commentaries, usually on specific topics and often intended to influence public opinion ■ Blogs (Web logs) are gaining influence as alternative commentaries to the established media ■ Reflect a wide range of perspectives	■ Often blend styles of journalism, personal narrative, and formal argument ■ Often difficult to determine identity and credentials of blogger ■ Often provide hyperlinks to related sites on the Web
Public affairs advocacy advertisements	■ Published as posters, fliers, Web pages, or paid advertisements ■ Condensed verbal/visual arguments aimed at influencing public opinion ■ Often have explicit bias and ignore alternative views	■ Use succinct "sound bite" style ■ Employ document design, bulleted lists, and visual elements (graphics, photographs, or drawings) for rhetorical effect
Advocacy Web sites	■ Usually identified by the extension ".org" in the Web site address ■ Often created by well-financed advocacy groups such as the NRA (National Rifle Association) or PETA (People for the Ethical Treatment of Animals) ■ Reflect the bias of the site owner	■ Often contain many layers with hyperlinks to other sites ■ Use visuals and verbal text to create an immediate visceral response favorable to the site owner's views ■ Ethically responsible sites announce their bias and purpose in an "About Us" or "Mission Statement" link on the home page

(Continued)

Genre	Explanation and Examples	Stylistic Features
Visual arguments	■ Political cartoons, usually drawn by syndicated cartoonists ■ Other visual arguments (photographs, drawings, graphics, ads), usually accompanied by verbal text	■ Make strong emotional appeals, often reducing complex issues to one powerful perspective (see Chapter 9)
Speeches and PowerPoint presentations	■ Political speeches, keynote speeches at professional meetings, informal speeches at hearings, interviews, business presentations ■ Often made available via transcription in newspapers or on Web sites ■ In business or government settings, often accompanied by PowerPoint slides	■ Usually organized clearly with highlighted claim, supporting reasons, and transitions ■ Accompanying PowerPoint slides designed to highlight structure, display evidence in graphics, mark key points, and sometimes provide humor
Documentary films	■ Formerly nonfiction reporting, documentary films now range widely from efforts to document reality objectively to efforts to persuade viewers to adopt the filmmaker's perspective or take action ■ Usually cost less to produce than commercial films and lack special effects ■ Cover topics such as art, science, and economic, political, and military crises	■ Often use extended visual arguments, combined with interviews and voice-overs, to influence as well as inform viewers ■ The filmmaker's angle of vision may dominate, or his or her perspective and values may be more subtle

In reconstructing the rhetorical context of an argument, consider how any given writer is spurred to write by a motivating occasion and by the desire to change the views of a particular audience. In this section, we'll return to our example of illegal immigration. The following list identifies the wide range of writers, cartoonists, filmmakers, and others who are motivated to enter the conversation about immigration.

Who Writes Arguments about Immigration and Why?

■ **Lobbyists and advocacy groups.** Lobbyists and advocacy groups commit themselves to a cause, often with passion, and produce avidly partisan arguments aimed at persuading voters, legislators, government agencies, and other decision makers. They often maintain advocacy Web sites, buy advertising space in newspapers and magazines, and lobby legislators face-to-face. For example, the immigrant advocacy group La Raza defends immigrant rights, whereas the Federation for American Immigration Reform (FAIR) fights to end illegal immigration and rallies people to pressure businesses not to hire undocumented workers.

■ **Legislators, political candidates, and government officials.** Whenever new laws, regulations, or government policies are proposed, staffers do research and write white papers recommending positions on an issue. Often these are available on the Web. On the perplexing problem of illegal immigration, numerous staff researchers for legislators, political candidates, and government officials have produced white papers on the practicality of extending a wall along the U.S.-Mexican border, of beefing up border patrol to increase national security, and of offering temporary guest worker visas to immigrant laborers.

■ **Business professionals, labor union leaders, and bankers.** Business spokespeople often try to influence public opinion in ways that support corporate or business interests, whereas labor union officials support wage structures favorable to union members. Typically businesspeople produce "corporate image" advertisements, send white papers to legislators, or write op-ed pieces that frame issues from a business perspective, whereas labor unions produce arguments favorable to workers. Professionals that could profit from undocumented labor (fruit growers, winemakers, landscapers, construction companies, and so forth) or could be harmed by it (labor unions) are active participants in the public controversy.

■ **Lawyers and judges.** Immigration issues are frequently entangled in legal matters. Lawyers write briefs supporting their clients' cases. Sometimes lawyers or legal experts not directly connected to a case, particularly law professors, file "friend-of-the-court" briefs aimed at influencing the decision of judges. Finally, judges write court opinions explaining their decisions on a case. As more illegal immigrants are deported and others die trying to cross the border, more legal professionals are writing about these cases.

■ **Media commentators.** Whenever immigration issues are in the news, media commentators (journalists, editorial writers, syndicated columnists, bloggers, political cartoonists) write articles and blogs or op-ed pieces on the issue or produce editorial cartoons, filtering their arguments through the perspective of their own political views. For example, conservative commentator Lou Dobbs is known for his strong stand on keeping illegal immigrants out of the country.

■ **Professional freelance or staff writers.** Some of the most thoughtful analyses of public issues are composed by freelance or staff writers for public forum magazines such as *Atlantic Monthly, The Nation, Ms., The National Review, The New Yorker,* and many others. Arguments about immigration policy reform and immigrants' integration into American society surface whenever the topic seems timely to magazine editors.

■ **Think tanks.** Because today many political, economic, and social issues are very complex, policy makers and commentators often rely on research institutions or think tanks to supply statistical studies and in-depth investigation of problems. These think tanks range across the political spectrum, from conservative (the Hoover Institute, the Heritage Foundation) or libertarian (the Cato Institute) to the centrist or liberal (the Brookings Institution, the Pew Foundation, the Economic Policy Institute). They usually maintain many-layered Web sites that include background on research writers, recent publications, and archives of past publications, including policy statements and white papers. Recently the conservative Center for

Immigration Studies published articles on the cost to Americans of legal and illegal immigration; the Center for American Progress, a liberal think tank, outlined the important features for a reform of the U.S. immigration system.

- **Scholars and academics.** College professors play a public role through their scholarly research, contributing data, studies, and analyses to public debates. Scholarly research differs substantially from advocacy argument in its systematic attempt to arrive at the best answers to questions based on the full examination of relevant data. Much scholarship investigates the patterns of immigrant participation in American political life, the relationship between crime and immigration, possibilities of worker solidarity, and the cost of products and services if the United States were to raise the minimum wage substantially. Scholarly research is usually published in refereed academic journals rather than in popular magazines.

- **Independent and commercial filmmakers.** Testifying to the growing popularity of film and its power to involve people in issues, documentary filmmakers often reflect on issues of the day, and commercial filmmakers often embed arguments within their dramatic storytelling. The global film industry is adding international perspectives as well. Many recent documentary and dramatic films present the experiences of immigrants and undocumented workers and their struggle to fit into American society while preserving their cultural roots. For instance, the documentary film *Farmingville,* shown on PBS, follows the antagonism among immigrant day laborers, homeowners, and other residents of the town of Farmingville on Long Island, New York, and depicts the town debating the practicality of establishing a hiring site to remove day laborers from the streets.

- **Citizens and students.** Engaged citizens influence social policy through letters, contributions to advocacy Web sites, guest editorials for newspapers, blogs, and speeches in public forums. Students also write for university communities, present their work at undergraduate research conferences, and influence public opinion by writing to political leaders and decision makers. For example, students involved in a service-learning project tutoring children of immigrant laborers might write to spread their knowledge of immigrants' educational needs.

Analyzing Rhetorical Context and Genre

The background we have just provided about the writers and genres of argument will help you situate arguments in their rhetorical context. When you encounter any argumentative text, whether reprinted in a textbook or retrieved through your own library and Web research, use the following guide questions to analyze its rhetorical context:

Questions about Rhetorical Context and Genre

1. What genre of argument is this? How do the conventions of that genre help determine the depth, complexity, and even appearance of the argument?
2. Who is the author? What are the author's credentials and what is his or her investment in the issue?
3. What audience is he or she writing for?

4. What motivating occasion prompted the writing? The motivating occasion could be a current event, a crisis, pending legislation, a recently published alternative view, or another ongoing problem.
5. What is the author's purpose? The purpose could range from strong advocacy to inquiring truth seeker (analogous to the continuum from persuasion to truth seeking discussed in Chapter 1, page 14).
6. What information about the publication or source (magazine, newspaper, advocacy Web site) helps explain the writer's perspective or the structure and style of the argument?
7. What is the writer's angle of vision? By angle of vision, we mean the filter, lens, or selective seeing through which the writer is approaching the issue. What is left out from this argument? What does this author not see? (Chapter 5, pages 96–98, discusses how angle of vision operates in the selection and framing of evidence.)

This rhetorical knowledge becomes important in helping you select a diversity of voices and genres of argument when you are exploring an issue. Note how Michael Banks makes use of his awareness of rhetorical context in his exploratory paper on pages 52–58.

■ ■ ■ **FOR CLASS DISCUSSION** Placing Readings in Their Rhetorical Context
Find two recent arguments on the illegal immigration issue. Your arguments should (1) represent different genres and (2) represent different kinds of arguers (syndicated newspaper columnists, bloggers, freelance magazine writers, scholars, and so forth). You can find your arguments in any of these places:

- In magazines: news commentary/public affairs magazines or niche magazines
- On the Web: on Web sites for think tanks, advocacy organizations, or blogs
- In newspapers: local, regional, or national

For each argument, answer the "Questions about Rhetorical Context and Genre" on pages 38–39. Then share your findings with classmates. ■ ■ ■

Reading to Believe an Argument's Claims

Once you have established the rhetorical context of an argument, you are ready to begin reading. We suggest that you read arguments in the spirit of the believing and doubting game, beginning with "believing," in which you practice what psychologist Carl Rogers calls *empathic listening*. Empathic listening requires that you see the world through the author's eyes, temporarily adopt the author's beliefs and values, and suspend your skepticism and biases long enough to hear what the author is saying.

To illustrate what we mean by reading to believe, we will continue with our example of illegal immigration. As you may have discovered through prior experience, reading, and examining the cartoons and photos at the beginning of this chapter, this issue includes many related issues: Why do millions of foreigners risk their lives to come illegally to the United States? How can the United States reduce the number of illegal immigrants? What should the United States do about the people currently living in the United States illegally? Does the U.S. economy need the workforce represented by these undocumented workers? The following article, "Amnesty?" by Roman Catholic priest and professor of philosophy John F. Kavanaugh, appeared in the March 10, 2008, issue of *America,* a Jesuit publication that describes itself as "the only national Catholic weekly magazine in the United States." Please read this article carefully in preparation for the exercises and examples that follow.

Amnesty?
Let Us Be Vigilant and Charitable
JOHN F. KAVANAUGH

Let's call her María. She was illegally brought into the United States at the age of 2. Now 27, she is a vital member of her parish and has three young children. María was recently deported to Ciudad Juárez, where, in the last 15 years, 600 young women have been kidnapped, raped, murdered and buried in the desert. Luckily, she was able to find a way into the United States, again illegally, to be with her children. If she is discovered again, she will spend five years in a U.S. federal prison.

My Jesuit friend and neighbor, Dick Vogt, has told me of people like María and many others of the 12 to 14 million "undocumented aliens." She is not necessarily typical of the masses who have illegally entered this country. Some, no doubt, are drunks and dealers; many are incarcerated for other crimes than their immigrant status. But most have come at great risk to their lives, because their lives were already at risk from poverty and displacement. They want to make a living, form a family, and help their families back home.

The Catholic bishops of Mexico pointed out in January that the recent surge of immigration is a direct effect of the North American Free Trade Agreement. Open trade, while benefiting the most powerful and technologically advanced, has threatened poor farmers and their small rural communities. They cannot compete with heavily subsidized U.S.

and Canadian producers. It is this phenomenon that drives so many to leave their homeland for a livelihood in the United States, despite, as the bishops put it, "its anti-humane immigration program."

The U.S. bishops, witnessing everything from evictions in California to employment raids in Massachusetts, have stirred the consciences of their dioceses and taken stands in conscience of their own. The bishop of Oklahoma City and 10 of his pastors have publicly professed defiance of a punitive state law that makes felons of all who "aid, assist, or transport any undocumented person." The bishops of Missouri have expressed their alarm over politicians "who vie to see who can be tougher on illegal immigrants." Cognizant of the economic pressures on many families in rural Mexico, they call for a more compassionate, fair, and realistic reform of our immigration system, including education and humanitarian assistance to all children, "without regard to legal status."

5   There has been some resistance to the bishops' proposals and some resentment. It is reminiscent of the outrage directed by anti-immigrant groups toward last year's immigration reform bill, a very harsh measure that they nonetheless condemned for proposing what they called amnesty.

Some of the resentment is understandable. There are householders, especially on the border, who have had their land and yards trashed. Residents of some towns feel flooded with immigrants they cannot engage or manage. A few businesspersons who have refused to hire undocumented or cheaper labor have lost sales and customers.

But this does not explain the seething hostility that can be read in some nativist opinion columns and popular books or heard on radio talk shows: "They are criminals, felons; and that's that."

"They have broken the law." This is an interesting standard of ethics, justice or charity for a nation that sees itself as Judeo-Christian and humane. It is puzzling that we do not think of the Good Samaritan or of the "least of our brothers and sisters" in Matthew 25, or of the passage from Leviticus that the Missouri bishops quote: "The stranger who sojourns with you shall be to you as the native among you, and you shall love him as yourself."

As for making the law our bottom line, do Christians know how many times Jesus was in trouble with the law? Do they know that the natural law tradition, articulated in the work of Thomas Aquinas, holds an unjust law to be no law at all? Do they forget that our nation was founded upon an appeal to a higher law than positive law, an appeal shared by the labor movement, by Martin Luther King Jr., and by Elizabeth Cady Stanton and Susan B. Anthony?

10   A nation has every right to secure its borders. Unrestrained immigration will hurt our country, the immigrants, and their homeland. So let us indeed protect our borders (even though that will not solve the problem of those who enter legally and overstay their visa). Let us also honestly face the multiple causes of illegal immigration. As an excellent position paper from the Center for Concern notes, illegal immigration involves many factors: trade negotiation, the governments involved, the immigrants who break the law by entering our country, employers who take advantage of them, corporate leaders who profit from them, and consumers who benefit from lower food and service costs.

We must devise ways to offer legal status to anyone who contributes to our common good, whether as a future citizen or a temporary guest worker. If that means using the dirty word "amnesty," so be it.

As to those who sojourn in our midst, let us be vigilant if they are threats and charitable if they are friends. It would be a good, if unusual, move if our legislators had the imagination to call for citizen panels before which an illegal immigrant could request amnesty, leniency, and a path to citizenship based on his or her contribution to the community, solid employment record, faithful payment of taxes, family need, and crime-free record.

Instead of fearing some abstract horde of millions, we might see the faces of people like María and hear their stories. If we turn them away, we will have to face the fact that we are not so much a nation of Judeo-Christian values as a punitive and self-interested people hiding under the protection of lesser, human-made laws.

Summary Writing as a Way of Reading to Believe

One way to show that you have listened well to an article is to summarize its argument in your own words. A summary (also called an *abstract,* a *précis,* or a *synopsis*) presents only a text's major points and eliminates supporting details. Writers often incorporate summaries of other writers' views into their own arguments, either to support their own views or to represent alternative views that they intend to oppose. (When opposing someone else's argument, writers often follow the template "Although X contends that [summary of X's argument], I argue that _____.") Summaries can be any length, depending on the writer's purpose, but usually they range from several sentences to one or two paragraphs. To maintain your own credibility, your summary should be as neutral and fair to that piece as possible.

To help you write an effective summary, we recommend the following steps:

Step 1: *Read the argument for general meaning.* Don't judge it. Put your objections aside; just follow the writer's meaning, trying to see the issue from the writer's perspective. Try to adopt the writer's values and belief system. Walk in the writer's shoes.

Step 2: *Reread the article slowly, writing brief* does *and* says *statements for each paragraph (or group of closely connected paragraphs).* A *does* statement identifies a paragraph's function, such as "summarizes an opposing view," "introduces a supporting reason," "gives an example," or "uses statistics to support the previous point." A *says* statement summarizes a paragraph's content. Your challenge in writing *says* statements is to identify the main idea in each paragraph and translate that idea into your own words, most likely condensing it at the same time. This process may be easier with an academic article that uses long, developed paragraphs headed by clear topic sentences than with more informal, journalistic articles such as Kavanaugh's that use shorter, less developed paragraphs. What follows are *does* and *says* statements for the first six paragraphs of Kavanaugh's article:

Does/Says Analysis of Kavanaugh's Article

Paragraph 1: *Does:* Uses a vivid example to introduce the injustice of the current treatment of illegal immigrants. *Says:* The U.S. government is separating productive, long-term illegal immigrants from their families, deporting them, exposing them to dangerous conditions, and threatening them with felony charges.

Paragraph 2: *Does:* Puts the problem of illegal immigrants in a larger, international context. *Says:* Although some illegal immigrants are involved in criminal activities, most have been pushed here by poverty and loss of opportunity in their own countries and have come to the United States seeking a better life for themselves and their families.

Paragraph 3: *Does:* Further explores the reasons behind the increase in immigration rates. *Says:* Catholic bishops have spoken out against the North American Free Trade Agreement and corporate interests, which have sought their own trade benefits at the expense of poor farmers and rural communities.

Paragraph 4: *Does:* Presents a sketch of Catholic leaders protesting the recent crackdowns on illegal immigrants. *Says:* U.S. bishops are protesting recent punitive laws against illegal immigrants and advocating for "a more compassionate, fair, and realistic reform of our immigration system."

Paragraph 5: *Does:* Sketches some opposing views. *Says:* Anti-immigration groups and others object to humane treatment of illegal immigrants, seeing it as akin to amnesty.

Paragraph 6: *Does:* Recognizes the validity of some opposing views. *Says:* The problems of some groups of Americans, including homeowners living on the border and businesses trying not to hire illegally, need to be heard.

FOR CLASS DISCUSSION *Writing Does/Says Statements*

Working individually or in small groups, write *does* and *says* statements for the remaining paragraphs of Kavanaugh's article.

■ ■ ■

> **Step 3:** *Examine your does and says statements to determine the major sections of the argument.* Create a list of the major points (and subpoints) that must appear in a summary in order to represent that argument accurately. If you are visually oriented, you may prefer to make a diagram, flowchart, or scratch outline of the sections of Kavanaugh's argument.
>
> **Step 4:** *Turn your list, outline, flowchart, or diagram into a prose summary.* Typically, writers do this in one of two ways. Some start by joining all their *says* statements into a lengthy paragraph-by-paragraph summary and then prune it and streamline it. They combine ideas into sentences and then revise those sentences to make them clearer and more tightly structured. Others start with a one-sentence summary of the argument's thesis and major supporting reasons and then flesh it out with more supporting ideas. Your goal is to be as neutral and objective as possible by keeping your own response to the writer's ideas out of your summary. To be fair to the writer, you also need to cover all the writer's main points and give them the same emphasis as in the original article.
>
> **Step 5:** *Revise your summary until it is the desired length and is sufficiently clear, concise, and complete.* Your goal is to spend your words wisely, making every word count. In a summary of several hundred words, you will often need transitions to indicate structure and create a coherent flow of ideas: "Kavanaugh's second point is that...," or "Kavanaugh concludes by...." However, don't waste words with meaningless transitions such as "Kavanaugh goes on to say...." When you incorporate a summary into your own essay, you must distinguish that author's views from your own by using *attributive tags* (expressions such as "Kavanaugh asserts" or "according to Kavanaugh"). You must also put any directly borrowed wording in quotation marks. Finally, you must cite the original author using appropriate conventions for documenting sources.

What follows are two summaries of Kavanaugh's article—a one-paragraph version and a one-sentence version—by student writer Michael Banks. Michael's one-paragraph version illustrates the MLA documentation system in which page numbers for direct quotations are placed in parentheses after the quotation and complete bibliographic information is placed in a Works Cited list at the end of the paper.

Michael's One-Paragraph Summary of Kavanaugh's Argument

In his article "Amnesty?" from *America* magazine John F. Kavanaugh, a Jesuit priest and professor of philosophy at St. Louis University, questions the morality of the current U.S. treatment of undocumented immigrants and advocates for a frank dealing with "the multiple causes of illegal immigration" (39). He points out that most immigrants are not criminals but rather hard-working, family-oriented people. He attributes recent increases in immigration to the North American Free Trade Agreement and the poverty it causes among rural Mexican farmers. Kavanaugh reports that recently U.S. bishops have protested the "anti-humane" treatment of immigrants and called for "compassionate, fair, and realistic reform" (38). He also mentions the anti-immigration groups, residents on the border, and business owners who have resisted the bishops and any treatment that resembles "amnesty." Kavanaugh's piece culminates with his argument that a nation that identifies itself as "Judeo-Christian and humane" should follow biblical teaching, "higher law," and the courageous example of leaders such as Martin Luther King, Jr., in challenging unjust laws (39). Admitting that unrestrained immigration would help nobody, Kavanaugh exhorts the country to move constructively toward "legal status to anyone who contributes to our common good" (39) and suggests a radically new solution to the problem: a citizen panel for the review of an immigrant's legal status. He concludes by stating that turning away undocumented immigrants is an immoral act motivated by self-interest.

Work Cited

Kavanaugh, John F. "Amnesty?" *America* 10 Mar. 2008: 8. Rpt. in *Writing Arguments: A Rhetoric with Readings.* John D. Ramage, John C. Bean, and June Johnson. 9th ed. New York: Pearson Longman, 2012: 38–39. Print.

Michael's One-Sentence Summary of Kavanaugh's Argument

In his article in *America*, Jesuit professor of philosophy John F. Kavanaugh questions the morality of the current treatment of undocumented immigrants in the United States, arguing that in a Judeo-Christian nation anyone who contributes positively to their community should be afforded some level of legal status.

Practicing Believing: Willing Your Own Belief in the Writer's Views

Although writing an accurate summary of an argument shows that you have listened to it effectively and understood it, summary writing by itself doesn't mean that you have actively tried to enter the writer's worldview. Before we turn in the next section to doubting an argument, we want to stress the importance of believing it. Rhetorician Peter Elbow reminds us that before we critique a text, we should try to "dwell with" and "dwell in" the writer's ideas—play the believing game—in order to "earn" our right to criticize.* He asserts, and we agree, that this use of the believing game to engage with strange, threatening, or unfamiliar views can lead to a deeper understanding and may provide a new vantage point on our own knowledge, assumptions, and values. To believe a writer and dwell with his or her ideas, find places in the text that resonate positively for you, look for values and beliefs you hold in common (however few), and search for personal experiences and values that affirm his or her argument.

Reading to Doubt

After willing yourself to believe an argument, will yourself to doubt it. Turn your mental energies toward raising objections, asking questions, expressing skepticism, and withholding your assent. When you read as a doubter, you question the writer's logic,

---

*Peter Elbow, "Bringing the Rhetoric of Assent and the Believing Game Together—Into the Classroom," *College English,* 67.4 (March 2005), 389.

the writer's evidence and assumptions, and the writer's strategies for developing the argument. You also think about what is *not* in the argument by noting what the author has glossed over, unexplained, or left out. You add a new layer of marginal notes, articulating what is bothering you, demanding proof, doubting evidence, challenging the author's assumptions and values, and so forth. Writing your own notes helps you read a text actively, bringing your own voice into conversation with the author.

■ ■ ■ FOR CLASS DISCUSSION Raising Doubts about Kavanaugh's Argument

Return now to Kavanaugh's article and read it skeptically. Raise questions, offer objections, and express doubts. Then, working as a class or in small groups, list all the doubts you have about Kavanaugh's argument. **■ ■ ■**

Now that you have doubted Kavanaugh's article, compare your questions and doubts to some raised by student writer Michael Banks.

Michael's Doubts about Kavanaugh's Article

- Kavanaugh's introductory paragraph seems sensational. María's situation is disturbing, but I doubt that every deported immigrant is likely to be "kidnapped, raped, murdered, and buried in the desert" as he seems to be insinuating.

- His argument often seems to be based too much upon vague statements about the opposition. He talks about "some resentment," "some towns," "a few people," and "some hateful columns," but he doesn't provide specifics. He also doesn't provide any specific data about the effects of NAFTA, which seems like something he really should have provided.

- In his second paragraph, he says that María's story "is not necessarily typical of the masses who have illegally entered" the U.S. and that "many are incarcerated for other crimes than their immigrant status." However, he never considers the rate of criminal behavior of illegal immigrants in further detail. Are illegal immigrants more likely to commit crimes? This might be the start of an argument against him.

- His references to opinion columns and popular books and radio talk shows seem to suggest that the majority of opposition to immigration reform is simplistic and ignorant. He only pays lip service to a few "understandable" objections. There must be more to the opposition than this. It would be particularly interesting to find an ethical justification for an anti-immigration stance.

- Perhaps because he's a member of the Society of Jesus, he draws hardly any line at all between church and state. However, most U.S. citizens I know believe that government should be secular. This contrasts harshly with his notion that the U.S. self-identifies as "Judeo-Christian" and limits his audience to people who would probably already agree with him. If we remove religion from the equation, the capitalistic values behind NAFTA and immigration policy seem much more understandable. I would need to investigate the economic impact of illegal immigration. Who really benefits the most from it? Who's really harmed?

These are only some of the objections that might be raised against Kavanaugh's argument. The point here is that doubting as well as believing is a key part of the exploratory process and purpose. *Believing* takes you into the views of others so that you can expand your views and perhaps see them differently and modify or even change them. *Doubting* helps protect you from becoming overpowered by others' arguments and teaches you to stand back, consider, and weigh points carefully. It also leads you to new questions and points you might want to explore further.

Thinking Dialectically

This chapter's final strategy—thinking dialectically to bring texts into conversation with each other—encompasses all the previous strategies and can have a powerful effect on your growth as a thinker and arguer. The term *dialectic* is associated with the German philosopher Georg Wilhelm Friedrich Hegel, who postulated that each thesis prompts an opposing thesis (which he calls an "antithesis") and that the conflict between these views can lead thinkers to a new claim (a "synthesis") that incorporates aspects of both views. Dialectic thinking is the philosophical underpinning of the believing and doubting game, pushing us toward new and better ideas. As Peter Elbow puts it, "Because it's so hard to let go of an idea we are holding (or more to the point, an idea that's holding us), our best hope for leverage in learning to doubt such ideas is *to take on different ideas*."*

This is why expert thinkers actively seek out alternative views—not to shout them down but to listen to them. If you were an arbitrator, you wouldn't settle a dispute between A and B on the basis of A's testimony only. You would also insist on hearing B's side of the story (and perhaps also C's and D's if they are stakeholders in the dispute). Dialectic thinking means playing ideas against each other, creating a tension that forces you to keep expanding your perspective. It helps you achieve the "mingling of minds" that we discussed in the introduction to this chapter.

As you listen to differing views, try to identify sources of disagreement among arguers, which often fall into two categories: (1) disagreement about the facts of the case and (2) disagreement about underlying values, beliefs, or assumptions. We saw these disagreements in Chapter 1 in the conversation about phthalates in children's toys. At the level of facts, disputants disagreed about the amount of phthalates a baby might ingest when chewing a rubber toy or about the quantity of ingested phthalates needed to be harmful. At the level of values, disputants disagreed on the amount of risk that must be present in a free market economy before a government agency should ban a substance. As you try to determine your own position on an issue, consider what research you might have to do to resolve questions of fact; also try to articulate your own underlying values, beliefs, and assumptions.

Questions to Stimulate Dialectic Thinking

As you consider multiple points of view on an issue, try using the following questions to promote dialectic thinking:

---

*Peter Elbow, "Bringing the Rhetoric of Assent and the Believing Game Together—Into the Classroom," *College English* 67.4 (March 2005), 390.

Questions to Promote Dialectic Thinking

1. What would writer A say to writer B?
2. After I read writer A, I thought _____; however, after I read writer B, my thinking on this issue had changed in these ways: _____.
3. To what extent do writer A and writer B disagree about facts and interpretations of facts?
4. To what extent do writer A and writer B disagree about underlying beliefs, assumptions, and values?
5. Can I find any areas of agreement, including shared values and beliefs, between writer A and writer B?
6. What new, significant questions do these texts raise for me?
7. After I have wrestled with the ideas in these two texts, what are my current views on this issue?

Responding to questions like these—either through class discussion or through exploratory writing—can help you work your way into a public controversy. Earlier in this chapter you read John Kavanaugh's article expressing a Catholic, pro-immigrant, anti-corporate view of immigrants. Now consider an article expressing a quite different point of view, "Why Blame Mexico?" by freelance journalist Fred Reed, published in *The American Conservative* on March 10, 2008. We ask you to read the article and then use the preceding questions to stimulate dialectic thinking about Kavanaugh versus Reed.

■ ■ ■ **FOR CLASS DISCUSSION** Practicing Dialectic Thinking with Two Articles
Individual task: Freewrite your responses to the preceding questions, in which Kavanaugh is writer A and Reed is writer B. **Group task:** Working as a whole class or in small groups, share your responses to the two articles, guided by the dialectic questions. ■ ■ ■

Why Blame Mexico?

FRED REED

To grasp American immigration policy, one needs only remember that the United States frowns on smoking while subsidizing tobacco growers.

We say to impoverished Mexicans, "See this river? Don't cross it. If you do, we'll give you good jobs, drivers licenses, citizenship for your kids born here, school for said kids, public assistance, governmental documents in Spanish for your convenience, and a much better future. There is no penalty for getting caught. Now, don't cross this river, hear?"

How smart is that? We're baiting them. It's like putting out a salt lick and then complaining when

deer come. Immigrant parents would be irresponsible not to cross.

The problem of immigration, note, is entirely self-inflicted. The U.S. chose to let them in. It didn't have to. They came to work. If Americans hadn't hired them, they would have gone back.

We have immigration because we want immigration. Liberals favor immigration because it makes them feel warm and fuzzy and from a genuine streak of decency. Conservative Republican businessmen favor immigration, frequently *sotto voce*, because they want cheap labor that actually shows up and works.

It's a story I've heard many times—from a landscaper, a construction firm, a junkyard owner, a group of plant nurserymen. "We need Mexicans." You could yell "Migra!" in a lot of restaurants in Washington, and the entire staff would disappear out the back door. Do we expect businessmen to vote themselves out of business? That's why we don't take the obvious steps to control immigration. (A $1,000 a day fine for hiring illegals, half to go anonymously to whoever informed on the employer would do the trick.)

In Jalisco, Mexico, where I live, crossing illegally is regarded as casually as pirating music or smoking a joint and the coyotes who smuggle people across as a public utility, like light rail. The smuggling is frequently done by bribing the border guards, who are notoriously corrupt.

Why corrupt? Money. In the book *De Los Maras a Los Zetas,* by a Mexican journalist, I find an account of a tunnel he knew of that could put 150 illegals a day across the border. (I can't confirm this.) The price of passage is about $2,000 a person. That's $300,000 a day, tax-free. What does a border guard make? (And where can I find a shovel?) The author estimated that perhaps 40 tunnels were active at any given time. Certainly some are. A woman I know says she came up in a restaurant and just walked out the door. Let's hear it for Homeland Security.

There is much noise about whether to grant amnesty. The question strikes me as cosmetic. We are not going to round up millions of people and physically throw them across the border. Whether we should doesn't matter. It's fantasy. Too many people want them here or don't care that they are here or don't want to uproot families who have established new lives here. Ethnic cleansing is ugly.

Further, the legal Latino population is just starting to vote. A bumper crop of Mexican-American kids, possessed of citizenship, are growing headlong toward voting age. These people cannot be thrown out, even in principle.

People complain that Mexico doesn't seal the borders. Huh? Mexico is a country, not a prison. It has no obligation to enforce American laws that America declines to enforce. Then there was the uproar when some fast-food restaurant in the U.S. began accepting pesos. Why? Mexican border towns accept dollars. Next came outrage against Mexico because its consulates were issuing ID cards to illegals, which they then used to get drivers licenses. Why outrage? A country has every right to issue IDs to its citizens. America doesn't have to accept them. If it does, whose problem is that?

If you want to see a reasonable immigration policy, look to Mexico. You automatically get a 90-day tourist visa when you land. To get residency papers, you need two things apart from photographs, passport, etc. First, a valid tourist visa to show that you entered the country legally. Mexico doesn't do illegal aliens. Second, a demonstrable income of $1,000 a month. You are welcome to live in Mexico, but you are going to pay your own way. Sounds reasonable to me.

You want a Mexican passport? Mexico allows dual citizenship. You (usually) have to be a resident for five years before applying. You also have to speak Spanish. It's the national language. What sense does it make to have citizens who can't talk to anybody?

It looks to me as though America thoughtlessly adopted an unwise policy, continued it until reversal became approximately impossible, and now doesn't like the results. It must be Mexico's fault.

Three Ways to Foster Dialectic Thinking

In this concluding section, we suggest three ways to stimulate and sustain the process of dialectic thinking: Effective discussions in class, over coffee, or online; a reading log in which you make texts speak to each other; or a formal exploratory essay. We'll look briefly at each in turn.

Effective discussions Good, rich talk is one of the most powerful ways to stimulate dialectic thinking and foster a "mingling of minds." The key is to keep these discussions from being shouting matches or bully pulpits for those who like to dominate the airtime. Discussions are most productive if people are willing to express different points of view or to role-play those views for the purpose of advancing the conversation. Try Rogerian listening, in which you summarize someone else's position before you offer your own, different position. (See Chapter 7 for more explanation of Rogerian listening.) Probe deeply to discover whether disagreements are primarily about facts and evidence or about underlying values and beliefs. Be respectful of others' views, but don't hesitate to point out where you see problems or weaknesses. Good discussions can occur in class, in late-night coffee shops, or in online chat rooms or on discussion boards.

Reading Logs In our classes, we require students to keep reading logs or journals in which they use freewriting and idea mapping to explore their ideas as they encounter multiple perspectives on an issue. One part of a journal or reading log should include summaries of each article you read. Another part should focus on your own dialectic thinking as you interact with your sources while you are reading them. Adapt the questions for promoting dialectic thinking on page 47.

A Formal Exploratory Essay A formal exploratory essay tells the story of an intellectual journey. It is both a way of promoting dialectical thinking and a way of narrating one's struggle to negotiate multiple views. The keys to writing successful exploratory essays are: (1) choosing an issue to explore on which you don't have an answer or position (or on which you are open to changing your mind); (2) wrestling with an issue or problem by resisting quick, simple answers and by exploring diverse perspectives; and (3) letting your thinking evolve and your own stance on the issue grow out of this exploration.

Exploratory essays can be powerful thinking and writing experiences in their own right, but they can also be a valuable precursor to a formal argument. Many instructors assign a formal exploratory paper as the first stage of a course research project—what we might call a "thesis-seeking" stage. (The second stage is a formal argument that converts your exploratory thinking into a hierarchically organized argument using reasons and evidence to support your claim.) Although often used as part of a research project, exploratory essays can also be low-stakes reflective pieces narrating the evolution of a writer's thinking during a class discussion.

An exploratory essay includes these thinking moves and parts:

- The essay is opened and driven by the writer's issue question or research problem— not a thesis.
- The introduction to the essay presents the question and shows why it interests the writer, why it is significant, and why it is problematic rather than clear-cut or easy to resolve.
- The body of the essay shows the writer's inquiry process. It demonstrates how the writer has kept the question open, sincerely wrestled with different

views on the question, accepted uncertainty and ambiguity, and possibly redefined the question in the midst of his or her reading and reflection on multiple perspectives.

■ The body of the essay includes summaries of the different views or sources that the writer explored and often includes believing and doubting responses to them.

■ In the essay's conclusion, the writer may clarify his or her thinking and discover a thesis to be developed and supported in a subsequent argument. But the conclusion can also remain open because the writer may not have discovered his or her own position on the issue and may acknowledge the need or desire for more exploration.

One of the writing assignment options for this chapter is a formal exploratory paper. Michael Banks's exploratory essay on pages 52–58 shows how he explored different voices in the controversy over illegal immigration.

Conclusion

This chapter has focused on inquiry as a way to enrich your reading and writing of arguments. This chapter has offered five main strategies for deep reading: (1) Use a variety of questions and prompts to find an issue to explore; (2) place readings in their rhetorical context; (3) read as a believer; (4) read as a doubter; and (5) think dialectically. This chapter has also shown you how to summarize an article and incorporate summaries into your own writing, using attributive tags to distinguish the ideas you are summarizing from your own. It has explained why a reading's rhetorical context (purpose, audience, and genre) must be considered in any thoughtful response to an argument. Finally, it has emphasized the importance of dialectic thinking and has offered the exploratory essay as a way to encourage wrestling with multiple perspectives rather than seeking early closure.

WRITING ASSIGNMENT An Argument Summary or a Formal Exploratory Essay

Option 1: An Argument Summary   Write a 250-word summary of an argument selected by your instructor. Then write a one-sentence summary of the same argument. Use as models Michael Banks's summaries of John Kavanaugh's argument on immigration (pages 43 and 44).

Option 2: A Formal Exploratory Essay   Write an exploratory essay in which you narrate in first-person, chronological order the evolution through time of your thinking about an issue or problem. Rather than state a thesis or claim, begin with a question or problem. Then describe your inquiry process as you worked your way through sources or different views. Follow the guidelines for an exploratory paper shown on page 51. When you cite the sources you have considered, be sure to use attributive tags so that the reader can distinguish between your own ideas and those of the sources you have summarized. If

Organization Plan for an Exploratory Essay

Introduction (one to several paragraphs)	• Establish that your question is complex, problematic, and significant. • Show why you are interested in it. • Present relevant background on your issue. Begin with your question or build up to it, using it to end your introductory section.

Body section 1: First view or source	• Introduce your first source and show why you started with it. • Provide rhetorical context and information about it. • Summarize the source's content and argument. • Offer your response to this source, including both believing and doubting points. • Talk about what this source contributes to your understanding of your question: What did you learn? What value does this source have for you? What is missing from this source that you want to consider? Where do you want to go from here?

Body section 2: Second view or source	• Repeat the process with a new source selected to advance the inquiry. • Explain why you selected this source (to find an alternative view, pursue a subquestion, find more data, and so forth). • Summarize the source's argument. • Respond to the source's ideas. Look for points of agreement and disagreement with other sources. • Show how your cumulative reading of sources is shaping your thinking or leading to more questions.

Body sections 3, 4, 5, etc.	• Continue exploring views or sources.

Conclusion	• Wrap up your intellectual journey and explain where you are now in your thinking and how your understanding of your problem has changed. • Present your current answer to your question based on all that you have learned so far, or explain why you still can't answer your question, or explain what research you might pursue further.

you use research sources, use MLA documentation for citing ideas and quotations and for creating a Works Cited at the end.

Explanation and Organization

An exploratory essay could grow out of class discussion, course readings, field work and interviews, or simply the writer's role-playing of alternative views. In all cases, the purpose of an exploratory paper is not to state and defend a thesis. Instead, its purpose is to think dialectically about multiple perspectives, narrating the evolution through time of the writer's thought process. Many students are inspired by the open, "behind-the-scenes" feel of an exploratory essay. They enjoy taking readers on the same intellectual and emotional journey they have just traveled. A typical organization plan for an exploratory essay is shown on page 51. ■

Reading

What follows is Michael Banks's exploratory essay on the subject of illegal immigration. His research begins with the articles by Kavanaugh and Reed that you have already read and discussed. He then moves off in his own direction.

Should the United States Grant Legal Status to Undocumented Immigrant Workers?

MICHAEL BANKS (STUDENT)

Introduction shows the writer's interest and investment in the issue, which, in this case, began with personal experience.

Having grown up in the California Bay Area, I have long been aware of illegal immigration. In high school, I volunteered through a school program to deliver free lunches to Mexican workers waiting for day jobs at popular hiring sites such as local hardware stores. One time we even went out to one of the farm fields to deliver lunches, and some of the workers scattered when they saw us coming. Apparently they thought we were police or immigration officials. Although the relationships were not deep or lasting, I had the opportunity to talk with some of the workers in my stumbling high school Spanish, and they would tell me about some of their bad experiences such as employers who wouldn't pay them what was promised. They had no recourse to file a complaint because they lacked legal status. Our program supervisor often stressed the importance of recognizing the workers as friends or equals rather than as charity cases. I often wondered how they could work with such low wages and still live a dignified life. However, my experiences did not push me to consider deeply the reality of being an illegal immigrant.

With this background, I entered our class discussions sympathetic towards the immigrants. However, I also recognized that the cheap labor they provided allowed Americans to keep food prices affordable or to find workers for any kind of hard day-labor job such as landscaping or digging up a backyard septic system. I am still not sure whether illegal immigrants are taking away jobs that Americans want, but I do know that I and most of my college friends would not be willing to work low-paying summer jobs picking tomatoes or weeding lettuce. For this exploratory essay, I wanted to look more deeply into this complicated ethical and economic dilemma. I set for myself this question: What is the best way for the United States to handle the problem of illegal immigration?

My exploration began with an article that our instructor assigned to the whole class: "Amnesty?" from *America* magazine by John F. Kavanaugh, a Jesuit priest and professor of philosophy at St. Louis University. In this article, Kavanaugh questions the morality of the current U.S. treatment of undocumented immigrants. He points out that most immigrants are not criminals but rather hard-working, family-oriented people. He attributes recent increases in immigration to the North American Free Trade Agreement and the poverty it causes among rural Mexican farmers. He also notes that anti-immigration groups have a "seething hostility" (39) for these persons and strongly resist any granting of amnesty or legal status. Kavanaugh disagrees with these groups, arguing that a nation that identifies itself as "Judeo-Christian and humane" should follow biblical teaching, "higher law," and the courageous example of leaders such as Martin Luther King, Jr., in challenging unjust laws (39). Although admitting that unrestrained immigration would help nobody, Kavanaugh exhorts the country to give "legal status to anyone who contributes to our common good" (39). He recommends that a citizen panel be used to review an immigrant's status and make recommendations for amnesty.

I found Kavanaugh's article to be quite persuasive. This article could particularly inspire its Catholic readers, and I too had an easy time agreeing with much of what Kavanaugh says. In fact, he reminded me of the director of my high school outreach program. I like the argument that people who contribute to the community should not be labeled as "illegal" as if they are in the same category as thieves or welfare cheaters. But I wasn't yet convinced that the laws governing immigration were "unjust" in the same way that segregation laws were unjust. It seems to me that a country has the right to control who enters the country, but doesn't have the right to make certain people sit in the back of the bus. So the references to Martin Luther King's fighting unjust laws didn't quite connect with me. So I was still caught in the dilemma. Also, I saw some other major problems with Kavanaugh's argument. First, it may not be fair to apply Judeo-Christian ethics to everyone in the country, especially considering our Constitutional separation of church and state. His appeal to religious beliefs may be appropriate to persuade Christians to volunteer for a cause but not to change a secular nation's laws. Also, his solution of having a citizen panel seemed impractical, especially for handling the number of illegal immigrants. Finally, Kavanaugh doesn't address the economic side of this argument. He didn't help me see what the disadvantages would be to granting amnesty to millions of undocumented workers.

Writer moves to his next source and provides some rhetorical context, including information about the author.

5   My next article, which the class also read together, was from *The American Conservative* titled "Why Blame Mexico?" by Fred Reed. According to Reed's biographical sketch on the Web ("Fred on Everything: Biography"), Reed is an ex-marine, former scientist, wanderer and world traveler, former law-enforcement columnist for the *Washington Times,* and a freelance journalist currently living in Mexico. He is known for his provocative columns.

Writer summarizes the article.

Reed's article was hard to summarize because it jumps around and is very sarcastic. His overall view is best exemplified by his very first statement: "To grasp American immigration policy, one needs only remember that the United States frowns on smoking while subsidizing tobacco growers" (45). Reed argues that illegal immigration occurs not mainly because there are millions of impoverished Mexicans in need of work, but because liberals feel good about tolerating them and because "[c]onservative Republican businessmen favor immigration . . . because they want cheap labor that actually shows up and works" (45). Reed points out that Mexico itself is clear and consistent in its own immigration policies: Immigrants into Mexico must possess clear residency papers, must have regular monthly earnings, and must be fluent in Spanish. In contrast to Kavanaugh, who focuses on immigrants, Reed focuses on the Americans who hire them; without Americans wanting cheap labor, immigrants would have no reason to cross the border. He takes it for granted that illegal immigrants should not be given legal status. Reed offers no solutions for the tangled mess of U.S. treatment of illegal immigrants, but underscores the fact that it is this country's self-created problem.

Writer shows his dialectical thinking, as he weighs the ideas of this source against those in his first article. He explores points of disagreement between these two sources.

Writer shows how he is wrestling with the ideas in this source.

Reed's article pulled me back away from Kavanaugh's call for amnesty. It made me see more clearly the entangled economic issues. Many American citizens *want* a source of cheap labor. Reed, in contrast, wants to eliminate cheap labor. If we followed the logical path that Reed seems to propose, we'd start jailing employers in order to cut off the job supply. At this point in my research, the status quo seemed to be a better situation. If cheap labor is so important to America's economy and if a low paying job in the United States is better than no job, perhaps some kind of legal status other than amnesty and citizenship would help resolve the situation. My head was spinning because I could picture all my classmates who would disagree with my last sentence! At this point, I felt I needed to explore other approaches to this controversy.

The day after I read the Reed article, I was talking with a friend who suggested I watch a recent movie about immigration called *Under the Same*

Moon. I figured it would be a fun diversion, if nothing else, and rented it. The movie tells the tale of a nine-year-old boy, Carlitos, who lives with his grandmother until she dies and then sets out to cross the border illegally to find his mother, who has been working several jobs at once as an undocumented immigrant for four years in Los Angeles. The dramatic story— shown from the dual perspective of mother and son—highlights many of the dangers faced by the immigrants themselves: separation from family members and support networks, exploitation by border-crossing agencies, INS raids on job sites, and dangerous jobs such as picking pesticide-coated tomatoes, just to name a few. The main characters' immigrant laborer status also draws attention to the undeniable humanity of immigrants.

This film works powerfully to create sympathy for illegal immigrants but without the explicit religious coating provided by Kavanaugh. I cannot help but admire the sacrifices made by immigrant workers who leave behind children and family in order to try to provide a brighter future for their loved ones. In cases where immigrants are separated from their young children, granting these parents legal status could help unite families more quickly and could ease the great pain that comes with being separated while allowing them the opportunity to forge a better life. On the other hand, families would also be reunited if the parents were sent back to Mexico. The great sympathy I feel for illegal immigrants doesn't necessarily mean that granting amnesty and citizenship is the best solution. While the film evokes compassion for individual immigrants, it does not address the magnitude of the problem.

I had heard about a number of films about illegal immigration and immigrants' experiences and wanted to continue with another film, so I headed back to Blockbuster and asked one of the workers if he could point me towards a recent documentary on illegal immigration. What I came up with was *A Day Without a Mexican,* a mock documentary, or "mockumentary." The movie's plot imagines the complete disappearance of the entire Latino population in California, both legal and illegal. The state grinds to a complete halt, widespread panic occurs, and homes, restaurants, supermarkets, orchards, farms, schools, and construction services are completely dysfunctional. The story and structure of the film viciously satirize anti-immigrant organizations, the news media, the border patrol, and waffling politicians. I visited the movie's Web site to search for further information, as I was curious about its reception. The Latino audience saw this film as a hit; it took in the second best per screen average the weekend it was released in Southern California. According to the general sales manager of Televisa Cine, *A Day Without a Mexican*'s success "underscores that there is not only a broad Hispanic audience who wants to see this film, but also a significant crossover audience," while the director, Sergio Arau, and lead actress/screenwriter, Yareli Arizmendi, add "we still believe we can change the world one screen at a time" ("Missing José Found").

[Margin annotations:]

Writer explains his movement to his next source.

He summarizes the plot of the film.

Writer discusses and analyzes the ideas in the film by presenting believing and doubting points.

Writer mentions problems the source raises for him.

Writer explains his choice of another film.

A brief summary prepares for his discussion.

Writer presents some information about the rhetorical context of this film, including statements from the director and details about how it was first received.

Writer demonstrates 10
how he is grappling
with the issue of
illegal immigration
and how this film
complicates his
views.

The film's success at the box office suggests to me that Arau and Arizmendi have revealed the important truth that Latino immigration makes California a better place. The comic film works by exaggeration, but its image of a helpless California without immigrants is easy to believe. Since California, and presumably the rest of the country, relies so heavily upon its immigrants, it would make very little sense to create new immigration policies that made the status quo worse. Perhaps a solution might lie in somehow recognizing the worth of immigrants, as *A Day Without a Mexican* suggests is important, while maintaining the status quo of paying them wages lower than American standards. A moral dilemma remains, however, because this approach places economics above justice.

Writer takes stock of
his developing
views, sorting out
what he has learned
so far and what he is
currently thinking.

At this stage, I decided to review some of the possible "solutions" that I had encountered so far to the illegal immigration problem. One solution, based on our valuing the humanity of immigrants, is to offer them amnesty, legal status, and eventual citizenship. Another, based on our valuing the economic benefits of cheap labor, is to keep the status quo. Still another solution is to get rid of illegal aliens altogether either by deporting them or by jailing their employers and thus eliminating their source of income. None of these options appealed to me. In search of another approach, I decided to

He explains why he
thinks he needs to
continue exploring
the issue and
expand the diversity
of views he
examines.

head for the library to do more research. A friendly reference librarian suggested that I start with a couple of overview articles from *CQ Researcher*. These articles, which I just skimmed, provided some background information, statistical data on immigration, and summaries of different bills before Congress. I found my head swimming with so many little details that I began losing the big picture about an actual direction I wanted to go. However, one idea that kept emerging from the *CQ Researcher* was the possibility of

He narrates his
research path and
explains his selection
of sources.

guest worker programs. I decided I wanted to find out more about what these programs were. With the reference librarian's guidance, I used *Academic Search Complete* to find a number of articles on guest worker programs. I also entered "guest worker program" into Google and found a number of bloggers supporting or attacking guest worker programs.

Writer introduces his
next source and
summarizes it.

I focused first on an editorial, "That's Hospitality," from *The New Republic,* a news commentary magazine that is in the political center, neither dominantly liberal nor conservative. The editorial opposes a congressional bill that would establish a guest worker program wherein businesses could hire foreigners as "guest workers" for up to six years. These workers would be granted temporary legal status, but they would have to return to their home country when the six years were up. Although supporters of the bill called it "humane" and "compassionate," the editorial writer opposes it because it is "un-American." No other group of immigrants, the editorial states, has been treated this way—as second class transients who had no opportunity to make a full life in America. The article compares this proposed guest worker program to similar programs in Europe after WWII, where workers from Eastern Europe or Turkey came to countries like Germany or Netherlands and stayed but never assimilated.

What the article supports instead is an alternative bill that grants "temporary worker" status but allows workers to apply for a green card after six years and for citizenship after five more years.

Writer responds to this source and explains the current status of his thinking about his research question. He looks for points of agreement among this source and others he has consulted.

This article excited me because it seemed to promote a compromise that turned undocumented workers who were afraid of getting caught and deported into persons with legal status and with the hope of eventually becoming citizens. It shared the pro-immigrant spirit of Kavanaugh and *Under the Same Moon* but didn't directly undermine the economic benefits provided by cheap labor. Rather than offering direct amnesty, it specified a waiting period of at least eleven years before a person could apply for citizenship. Although this article did not specify how the United States might manage the volume and rate of people seeking guest worker and then citizen status, I thought that this proposal would be the position I would like to argue for in a later, persuasive paper.

Writer decides to continue exploring his question by looking at a source that opposes his preceding one. He gives information about the rhetorical context of this source, particularly about the blogger.

He summarizes the ideas in his blog.

Writer shows how this source has challenged the ideas in the preceding source, complicated the issue, and raised important questions for him.

But I decided next to look at the negative side of a guest worker program and was amazed at how many anti-immigration groups hated this bill. One provocative blog, "Guest Worker Program Illusion," is by a freelance writer, Frosty Woolridge, who maintains his own Web site aimed at combating "overpopulation and immigration." According to his blog site he has written hundreds of articles for seventeen national and two international magazines and has been an invited speaker on environmental issues at many universities. Woolridge favors strict border enforcement and deportation of anyone who has illegally entered the country. He sees all forms of guest worker programs as amnesty that will lead to overpopulation and an increasing welfare burden on middle-class Americans who try to provide services for the guest workers. He also argues that the guest workers will suppress wages for American workers. His strategy is to point out all the problems that the guest worker program will open up: Can the guest worker bring his or her family? Will children born to guest workers automatically be U.S. citizens? Must the states provide tax payer-supported schools and hospital services for the guest workers? If so, must the schools be bilingual? Will guest workers pay social security taxes and thus become eligible for social security? Will they be eligible for Workers Compensation if they get hurt on the job? Will their older children get in-state rates at public universities? Will their younger children be covered by child labor laws? Will they actually leave after six years or simply revert back to undocumented illegal status?

Although he has not fully worked out his answer to his research question, he sums up how his views have evolved. He explains how his reading and thinking have deepened and clarified his views on this issue.

15 All these problems raised by Woolridge were never mentioned in *The New Republic* editorial, and they severely dampened my spirits. As I end this exploratory paper, I still have a number of articles left to read and much left to learn, but I think I have a pretty good grasp of what the issues and disagreements are. I definitely think that the plan supporting a guest worker program with the chance of eventual citizenship is the best approach. But it has to be linked with other approaches also, including ways to improve the economies of Mexico and other Latin American countries so that poor people wouldn't have to come to the United States to find work. My hope is that

He sketches a path he might follow in further exploration of his question.

many of the objections raised by Woolridge are solvable. I have realized from my inquiry that my heart is with the immigrants and that I don't share Woolridge's desire to close America off from future immigration.

A Works Cited page in MLA format lists the sources consulted and discussed in this essay.

Works Cited

A Day Without a Mexican. Dir. Sergio Arau. Xenon Pictures, 2004. DVD.

Kavanaugh, John F. "Amnesty?" *America* 10 Mar. 2008: 8. Print.

"Missing José Found: Walks His Way to Box Office Success Throughout Southern California." *ADWAM News*. A Day Without a Mexican, n.d. Web. 12 July 2008.

Reed, Fred. "Why Blame Mexico?" *American Conservative* 10 Mar. 2008: 35. Print.

"That's Hospitality." *New Republic* 17 Apr. 2006: 7. *Academic Search Complete*. Web. 30 Aug. 2008.

Under the Same Moon. Dir. Patricia Riggen. Perf. Adrián Alonso, Kate del Castillo, and Eugenio Derbez. Twentieth Century Fox, 2008. DVD.

Woolridge, Frosty. "Guest Worker Program Illusion." *Newswithviews.com*. N.p., 2 Dec. 2005. Web. 22 May 2008.

PART TWO
Writing an Argument

This still from the *Tomb Raider* video game series features main character Lara Croft engaged in one of her typical combats with humans, beasts, or supernatural creatures. Lara, an adventurer and archeologist, represents both a sexualized and an empowered woman. Women and violent video games are the focus of student Carmen Tieu's argument developed in Chapters 3–5; however, Carmen explores gender roles from the perspective of a woman playing a "male" video game, *Halo.*

3

The Core of an Argument
A Claim with Reasons

In Part One we explained that argument combines truth seeking with persuasion. Part One, by highlighting the importance of exploration and inquiry, emphasizes the truth-seeking dimension of argument. The suggested writing assignments in Part One included a variety of exploratory tasks: freewriting, playing the believing and doubting game, and writing a formal exploratory essay. In Part Two we show you how to convert your exploratory ideas into a thesis-governed classical argument that uses effective reasons and evidence to support its claims. Each chapter in Part Two focuses on a key skill or idea needed for responsible and effective persuasion. In this chapter, you will learn to:

- Describe the key elements of classical argument
- Explain the rhetorical appeals
- Distinguish between issue and information questions and between genuine and pseudoarguments
- Describe the basic frame of an argument

The Classical Structure of Argument

Classical argument is patterned after the persuasive speeches of ancient Greek and Roman orators. In traditional Latin terminology, the main parts of a persuasive speech are the *exordium,* in which the speaker gets the audience's attention; the *narratio,* which provides needed background; the *propositio,* which is the speaker's claim or thesis; the *partitio,* which forecasts the main parts of the speech; the *confirmatio,* which presents the speaker's arguments supporting the claim; the *confutatio,* which summarizes and rebuts opposing views; and the *peroratio,* which concludes the speech by summing up the argument, calling for action, and leaving a strong, lasting impression. (Of course, you don't need to remember these tongue-twisting Latin terms. We cite them only to assure you that in writing a classical argument, you are joining a time-honored tradition that links back to the origins of democracy.)

Let's go over the same territory again using more contemporary terms. We provide an organization plan showing the structure of a classical argument on page 61, which shows these typical sections:

- **The introduction.** Writers of classical argument typically begin with an attention grabber such as a memorable scene, illustrative story, or startling statistic. They continue the introduction by focusing the issue—often

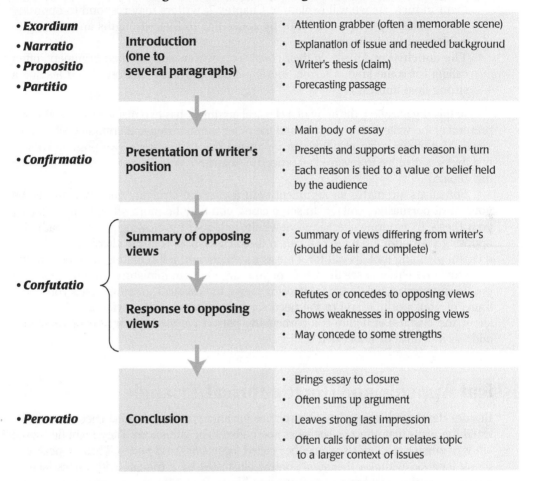

Organization Plan for an Argument with a Classical Structure

• *Exordium* • *Narratio* • *Propositio* • *Partitio*	**Introduction (one to several paragraphs)**	• Attention grabber (often a memorable scene) • Explanation of issue and needed background • Writer's thesis (claim) • Forecasting passage
• *Confirmatio*	**Presentation of writer's position**	• Main body of essay • Presents and supports each reason in turn • Each reason is tied to a value or belief held by the audience
• *Confutatio*	**Summary of opposing views**	• Summary of views differing from writer's (should be fair and complete)
	Response to opposing views	• Refutes or concedes to opposing views • Shows weaknesses in opposing views • May concede to some strengths
• *Peroratio*	**Conclusion**	• Brings essay to closure • Often sums up argument • Leaves strong last impression • Often calls for action or relates topic to a larger context of issues

by stating it directly as a question or by briefly summarizing opposing views—and providing needed background and context. They conclude the introduction by presenting their claim (thesis statement) and forecasting the argument's structure.

■ **The presentation of the writer's position.** The presentation of the writer's own position is usually the longest part of a classical argument. Here writers present the reasons and evidence supporting their claims, typically choosing reasons that tie into their audience's values, beliefs, and assumptions. Usually each reason is developed in its own paragraph or sequence of paragraphs. When a paragraph introduces a new reason, writers state the reason directly and then support it with evidence or a chain of ideas. Along the way, writers guide their readers with appropriate transitions.

■ **The summary and critique of alternative views.** When summarizing and responding to opposing views, writers have several options. If there are several opposing arguments, writers may summarize all of them together and then compose a single response, or they may summarize and respond to each argument in turn. As we will explain in Chapter 7, writers may respond to opposing views either by refuting them or by conceding to their strengths and shifting to a different field of values.

■ **The conclusion.** Finally, in their conclusion, writers sum up their argument, often calling for some kind of action, thereby creating a sense of closure and leaving a strong final impression.

In this organization, the body of a classical argument has two major sections—the one presenting the writer's own position and the other summarizing and critiquing alternative views. The organization plan and our discussion have the writer's own position coming first, but it is possible to reverse that order. (In Chapter 7 we consider the factors affecting this choice.)

For all its strengths, an argument with a classical structure may not always be your most persuasive strategy. In some cases, you may be more effective by delaying your thesis, by ignoring alternative views altogether, or by showing great sympathy for opposing views (see Chapter 7). Even in these cases, however, the classical structure is a useful planning tool. Its call for a thesis statement and a forecasting statement in the introduction helps you see the whole of your argument in miniature. And by requiring you to summarize and consider opposing views, the classical structure alerts you to the limits of your position and to the need for further reasons and evidence. As we will show, the classical structure is a particularly persuasive mode of argument when you address a neutral or undecided audience.

Classical Appeals and the Rhetorical Triangle

Besides developing a template or structure for an argument, classical rhetoricians analyzed the ways that effective speeches persuaded their audiences. They identified three kinds of persuasive appeals, which they called *logos, ethos,* and *pathos.* These appeals can be understood within a rhetorical context illustrated by a triangle with points labeled *message, writer or speaker,* and *audience* (see Figure 3.1). Effective arguments pay attention to all three points on this *rhetorical triangle.*

As Figure 3.1 shows, each point on the triangle corresponds to one of the three persuasive appeals:

■ *Logos* (Greek for "word") focuses attention on the quality of the message—that is, on the internal consistency and clarity of the argument itself and on the logic of its reasons and support. The impact of *logos* on an audience is referred to as its *logical appeal.*

■ *Ethos* (Greek for "character") focuses attention on the writer's (or speaker's) character as it is projected in the message. It refers to the credibility of the writer. *Ethos* is often conveyed through the writer's investment in his or her claim, through the fairness with which the writer considers alternative views, through the tone and style of the message, and even through the message's professional appearance on paper or screen, including correct grammar, flawless proofreading, and appropriate formats for citations and bibliography. In some cases, *ethos* is also a function of the writer's

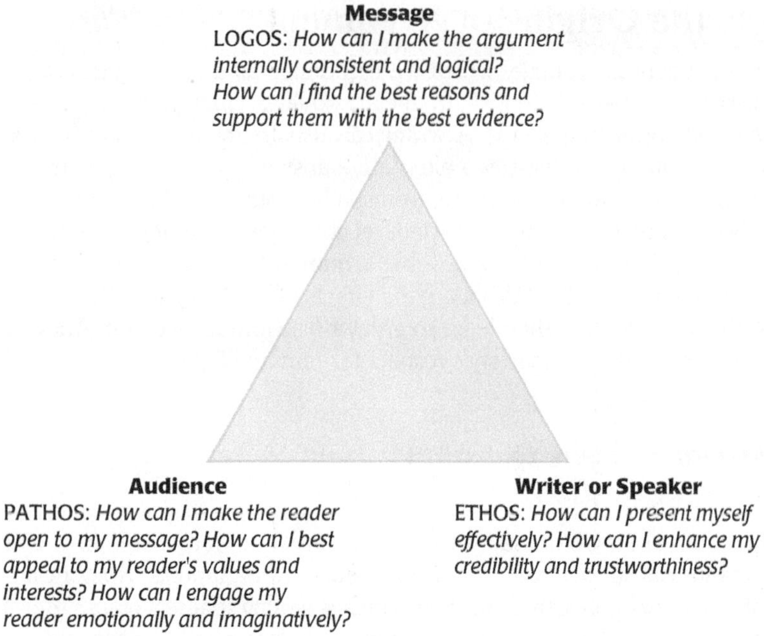

Message
LOGOS: *How can I make the argument*
internally consistent and logical?
How can I find the best reasons and
support them with the best evidence?

Audience
PATHOS: *How can I make the reader*
open to my message? How can I best
appeal to my reader's values and
interests? How can I engage my
reader emotionally and imaginatively?

Writer or Speaker
ETHOS: *How can I present myself*
effectively? How can I enhance my
credibility and trustworthiness?

FIGURE 3.1 The rhetotical triangle

reputation for honesty and expertise independent of the message. The impact of *ethos* on an audience is referred to as the *ethical appeal* or *appeal from credibility.*

■ ***Pathos*** (Greek for "suffering" or "experience") focuses attention on the values and beliefs of the intended audience. It is often associated with emotional appeal. But *pathos* appeals more specifically to an audience's imaginative sympathies—their capacity to feel and see what the writer feels and sees. Thus, when we turn the abstractions of logical discourse into a tangible and immediate story, we are making a pathetic appeal. Whereas appeals to *logos* and *ethos* can further an audience's intellectual assent to our claim, appeals to *pathos* engage the imagination and feelings, moving the audience to a deeper appreciation of the argument's significance.

A related rhetorical concept, connected to the appeals of *logos, ethos,* and *pathos,* is that of *kairos,* from the Greek word for "right time," "season," or "opportunity." This concept suggests that for an argument to be persuasive, its timing must be effectively chosen and its tone and structure in right proportion or measure. You may have had the experience of composing an argumentative e-mail and then hesitating before clicking the "send" button. Is this the right moment to send this message? Is my audience ready to hear what I'm saying? Would my argument be more effective if I waited for a couple of days? If I send this message now, should I change its tone and content? This attentiveness to the unfolding of time is what is meant by *kairos.* We will return to this concept in Chapter 6, when we consider *ethos* and *pathos* in more depth.

Given this background on the classical appeals, let's turn now to *logos*—the logic and structure of arguments.

Issue Questions as the Origins of Argument

At the heart of any argument is an issue, which we can define as a controversial topic area such as "the labeling of biotech foods" or "racial profiling," that gives rise to differing points of view and conflicting claims. A writer can usually focus an issue by asking an issue question that invites at least two alternative answers. Within any complex issue—for example, the issue of abortion—there are usually a number of separate issue questions: Should abortions be legal? Should the federal government authorize Medicaid payments for abortions? When does a fetus become a human being (at conception? at three months? at quickening? at birth?)? What are the effects of legalizing abortion? (One person might stress that legalized abortion leads to greater freedom for women. Another person might respond that it lessens a society's respect for human life.)

Difference between an Issue Question and an Information Question

Of course, not all questions are issue questions that can be answered reasonably in two or more differing ways; thus not all questions can lead to effective arguments. Rhetoricians have traditionally distinguished between *explication,* which is writing that sets out to inform or explain, and *argumentation,* which sets out to change a reader's mind. On the surface, at least, this seems like a useful distinction. If a reader is interested in a writer's question mainly to gain new knowledge about a subject, then the writer's essay could be considered explication rather than argument. According to this view, the following questions about teenage pregnancy might be called information questions rather than issue questions:

> How does the teenage pregnancy rate in the United States compare with the rate in Sweden? If the rates are different, why?

Although both questions seem to call for information rather than for argument, we believe that the second one would be an issue question if reasonable people disagreed on the answer. Thus, different writers might agree that the teenage pregnancy rate in the United States is seven times higher than the rate in Sweden. But they might disagree about why. One writer might emphasize Sweden's practical, secular sex-education courses, leading to more consistent use of contraceptives among Swedish teenagers. Another writer might point to the higher use of oral contraceptives among teenage girls in Sweden (partly a result of Sweden's generous national health program) and to less reliance on condoms for preventing pregnancy. Another might argue that moral decay in the United States or a breakdown of the traditional family is at fault. Thus, underneath the surface of what looks like a simple explication of the "truth" is really a controversy.

How to Identify an Issue Question

You can generally tell whether a question is an issue question or an information question by examining your purpose in relationship to your audience. If your relationship to your audience is that of teacher to learner, so that your audience hopes to gain new information, knowledge, or understanding that you possess, then your question is probably an information question. But if your relationship to your audience is that of advocate to decision maker or jury, so that your audience needs to make up its mind on something and is weighing different points of view, then the question you address is an issue question.

Often the same question can be an information question in one context and an issue question in another. Let's look at the following examples:

- **How does a diesel engine work?** (This is probably an information question, because reasonable people who know about diesel engines will probably agree on how they work. This question would be posed by an audience of new learners.)
- **Why is a diesel engine more fuel efficient than a gasoline engine?** (This also seems to be an information question, because all experts will probably agree on the answer. Once again, the audience seems to be new learners, perhaps students in an automotive class.)
- **What is the most cost-effective way to produce diesel fuel from crude oil?** (This could be an information question if experts agree and you are addressing new learners. But if you are addressing engineers and one engineer says process X is the most cost-effective and another argues for process Y, then the question is an issue question.)
- **Should the present highway tax on diesel fuel be increased?** (This is certainly an issue question. One person says yes; another says no; another offers a compromise.)

FOR CLASS DISCUSSION Information Questions versus Issue Questions
Working as a class or in small groups, try to decide which of the following questions are information questions and which are issue questions. Many of them could be either, depending on the rhetorical context. For such questions, create hypothetical contexts to show your reasoning.

1. What percentage of public schools in the United States are failing?
2. Which is more addictive, marijuana or alcohol?
3. What is the effect on children of playing first-person-shooter games?
4. Is genetically modified corn safe for human consumption?
5. Should a woman with newly detected breast cancer opt for a radical mastectomy (complete removal of the breast and surrounding lymph tissue) or a lumpectomy (removal of the malignant lump without removal of the whole breast)?

Difference between a Genuine Argument and a Pseudo-Argument

Although every argument features an issue question with alternative answers, not every dispute over answers is a rational argument. Rational arguments require two additional factors: (1) reasonable participants who operate within the conventions of reasonable behavior and (2) potentially sharable assumptions that can serve as a starting place or foundation for the argument. Lacking one or both of these conditions, disagreements remain stalled at the level of pseudo-arguments.

Pseudo-Arguments: Committed Believers and Fanatical Skeptics

A reasonable argument assumes the possibility of growth and change; disputants may modify their views as they acknowledge strengths in an alternative view or weaknesses in their own. Such growth becomes impossible—and argument degenerates to pseudo-argument—when disputants are fanatically committed to their positions. Consider the case of the fanatical believer and the fanatical skeptic.

From one perspective, committed believers are admirable persons, guided by unwavering values and beliefs. Committed believers stand on solid rock, unwilling to compromise their principles or bend to the prevailing winds. But from another perspective, committed believers can seem rigidly fixed, incapable of growth or change. When committed believers from two clashing belief systems try to engage in dialogue with each other, a truth-seeking exchange of views becomes difficult. They talk past each other; dialogue is replaced by monologue from within isolated silos. Once committed believers push each other's buttons on global warming, guns, health care, taxes, religion, or some other issue, each disputant resorts to an endless replaying of the same prepackaged arguments. Disagreeing with a committed believer is like ordering the surf to quiet down. The only response is another crashing wave.

In contrast to the committed believer, the fanatical skeptic dismisses the possibility of ever believing anything. Skeptics often demand proof where no proof is possible. So what if the sun has risen every day of recorded history? That's no proof that it will rise tomorrow. Short of absolute proof, which never exists, fanatical skeptics accept nothing. In a world where the most we can hope for is increased audience adherence to our ideas, the skeptic demands an ironclad, logical demonstration of our claim's rightness.

A Closer Look at Pseudo-Arguments: The Lack of Shared Assumptions

As we have seen, rational argument degenerates to pseudo-argument when there is no possibility for listening, learning, growth, or change. In this section, we look more closely at a frequent cause of pseudo-arguments: lack of shared assumptions.

Shared Assumptions and the Problem of Ideology As our discussion of committed believers suggests, reasonable argument is difficult when the disputants have differing "ideologies," which is an academic word for belief systems or worldviews. We all have our own ideologies. We all look at the world through a lens shaped by our life's experiences. Our beliefs and values are shaped by our family background, our friends, our culture, our particular time in history, our race or ethnicity, our gender or sexual orientation, our social class, our religion, our education, and so forth. Because we tend to think that our particular lens for looking at the world is natural and universal rather than specific to ourselves, we must be aware that persons who disagree with us may not share our deepest assumptions and beliefs. To participate in rational argument, we and our audience must seek *shared assumptions*—certain principles or values or beliefs that can serve as common ground.

The failure to find shared assumptions often leads to pseudo-arguments, particularly if one disputant makes assumptions that the other disputant cannot accept. Such pseudo-arguments often occur in disputes arising from politics or religion. For example, consider differences within the Christian community over how to interpret the Bible. Some Christian groups choose a straightforward, literal interpretation of the Bible as God's inerrant word while other groups read some passages metaphorically or mythically and focus on the paradoxes, historical contexts, and interpretive complexities of the Bible; still other Christian groups read it as an ethical call for social justice. Members of these different Christian groups may not be able to argue rationally about, say, evolution or gay marriage because they have very different ways of reading Biblical passages and invoking the authority of the Bible. Similarly, within other religious traditions, believers may also differ about the meaning and applicability of their sacred texts to scientific issues and social problems.

Similar disagreements about assumptions occur in the political arena as well. Our point is that certain religious or political beliefs or texts cannot be evoked for evidence or authority when an audience does not assume the belief's truth or does not agree on the way that a given text should be read or interpreted.

Shared Assumptions and the Problem of Personal Opinions Lack of shared assumptions also dooms arguments about purely personal opinions—for example, someone's claim that opera is boring or that pizza is better than nachos. Of course, a pizza-versus-nachos argument might be possible if the disputants assume a shared criterion about nutrition. For example, a nutritionist could argue that pizza is better than nachos because pizza provides more balanced nutrients per calorie. But if one of the disputants responds, "Nah, nachos are better than pizza because nachos taste better," then he makes a different assumption—"My sense of taste is better than your sense of taste." This is a wholly personal standard, an assumption that others are unable to share.

■ ■ ■ **FOR CLASS DISCUSSION** Reasonable Arguments versus Pseudo-Arguments
The following questions can all be answered in alternative ways. However, not all of them will lead to reasonable arguments. Try to decide which questions will lead to reasonable arguments and which will lead only to pseudo-arguments.

1. Are the *Star Wars* films good science fiction?
2. Is it ethically justifiable to capture dolphins and train them for human entertainment?
3. Should cities subsidize professional sports venues?
4. Is this abstract oil painting created by a monkey smearing paint on a canvas a true work of art?
5. Are nose rings and tongue studs attractive?

■ ■ ■

Frame of an Argument: A Claim Supported by Reasons

We said earlier that an argument originates in an *issue question,* which by definition is any question that provokes disagreement about the best answer. When you write an argument, your task is to take a position on the issue and to support it with reasons and evidence. The *claim* of your essay is the position you want your audience to accept. To put it another way, your claim is your essay's *thesis statement,* a one-sentence summary answer to your issue question. Your task, then, is to make a claim and support it with reasons.

What Is a Reason?

A *reason* (also called a *premise*) is a claim used to support another claim. In speaking or writing, a reason is usually linked to the claim with connecting words such as *because, since, for, so, thus, consequently,* and *therefore,* indicating that the claim follows logically from the reason.

Let us take an example. In one of our recent classes, students heatedly debated the ethics of capturing wild dolphins and training them to perform in marine parks or "swim with dolphins" programs. One student had recently seen the 2009 documentary *The Cove,* about the gory dolphin hunts in Japan in which dolphins are killed en masse by fishermen and some are captured for display in shows around the world. Another student cited the 1960s family show *Flipper,* featuring a dolphin working harmoniously with—and often saving—his human friends. One student commented that his sister fell in love with marine biology on a family vacation in Hawaii when she swam with a dolphin, gave signals for the dolphin's jump, and touched its rubbery skin during a "swim with dolphins" program. In response, a few students remarked that the only ethical way to experience dolphins is with a pair of binoculars from a boat. Here are the frameworks the class developed for two alternative positions on this issue:

One View

CLAIM: The public should not support the commercial use of captured dolphins.

REASON 1: Aquariums, marine parks, and "swim with dolphins" programs separate dolphins from their natural habitat and social groups.

REASON 2: The unnatural environment of aquariums, marine parks, and dolphin programs places great stress on dolphins.

REASON 3: Aquariums, marine parks, and dolphin programs are mainly big businesses driven by profit.

REASON 4: What these aquariums, marine parks, and "swim with" programs call "education about dolphins" is just a series of artificial, exploitive tricks taught through behavior modification.

REASON 5: Marine parks and programs create a commercial market for dolphins, which directly or indirectly encourages dolphin hunts and captures.

REASON 6: Marine parks and programs promote an attitude of human dominance over animals.

Alternative View

CLAIM: The public should continue to support aquariums, marine parks, and "swim with dolphins" programs.

REASON 1: These parks and programs observe accreditation standards for animal welfare, health, and nutrition, and monitor the well-being of their dolphins.

REASON 2: These marine parks and "swim with" programs enable scientists and veterinarians to study dolphin behavior in ways not possible with field studies in the wild.

REASON 3: While creating memorable family entertainment, these parks and programs provide environmental education and teach appreciation for dolphins.

REASON 4: Accredited programs do not endorse dolphin hunts and have self-sustaining breeding programs to avoid the need for dolphin hunts.

REASON 5: In their training of dolphins, these programs emphasize animal husbandry and animal enrichment to exercise dolphins' intelligence and abilities.

REASON 6: Marine parks and "swim with dolphins" programs support research and conservation.

Formulating a list of reasons in this way breaks your argumentative task into a series of subtasks. It gives you a frame for building your argument in parts. In the previous example, the frame for the argument opposing commercial use of dolphins suggests five different lines of reasoning a writer might pursue. A writer might use all five reasons or select only two or three, depending on which reasons would most persuade the intended audience. Each line of reasoning would be developed in its own separate section of the argument. For example, you might begin one section of your argument with the following sentence: "The public should not support these dolphin programs because they teach dolphins clownish tricks and artificial behaviors, which they pass off as 'education about dolphins.' " You would then provide examples of the tricks and stunts that dolphins are taught, explain how these contrast with dolphins' natural behaviors, and offer examples of erroneous facts or information about dolphins supplied by these programs. You might also need to support the underlying assumption that it is good for the public to acquire *real knowledge* about dolphins in the wild. (How one articulates and supports the underlying assumptions of an argument will be developed in Chapter 4 when we discuss warrants and backing.) You would then proceed in the same way for each separate section of your argument.

To summarize our point in this section, the frame of an argument consists of the claim (the thesis statement of the essay), which is supported by one or more reasons, which are in turn supported by evidence or sequences of further reasons.

■ ■ ■ **FOR CLASS DISCUSSION** Using Images to Support an Argument

In Chapter 1, we talked about implicit and explicit arguments and introduced you to some visual arguments. The photographs in Figures 3.2 and 3.3 are typical ways that dolphins are depicted in public discussions about dolphins. In groups or as a whole class, examine the photographs carefully and describe the image of dolphins that each photo is portraying. Then determine which claim, and more specifically, which reason or reasons, you think each image best supports. Which reason or reasons could each image be used to refute? Work out explanations for your thinking.

■ ■ ■

FIGURE 3.2 Typical photo from a "swim with dolphins" program

FIGURE 3.3 Jumping bottlenose dolphins

Expressing Reasons in Because Clauses

Chances are that when you were a child, the word *because* contained magical explanatory powers. Somehow *because* seemed decisive. It persuaded people to accept your view of the world; it changed people's minds. Later, as you got older, you discovered that *because* only introduced your arguments and that it was the reasons following *because* that made the difference. Still, *because* introduced you to the powers potentially residing in the adult world of logic.

Of course, there are many other ways to express the logical connection between a reason and a claim. Our language is rich in ways of stating *because* relationships:

- The public should not support marine parks and "swim with dolphins" programs because these programs place great stress on dolphins by separating them from their natural habitat and social groups.
- Marine parks and "swim with dolphin" programs place great stress on dolphins by separating them from their natural habitat and social groups. Therefore the public should not support the captivity of dolphins.
- Marine parks and "swim with dolphin" programs place great stress on dolphins by separating them from their natural habitat and social groups, so the public should not support these programs.
- One reason that the public should not support marine parks or "swim with dolphins" programs is that these programs place great stress on dolphins by separating them from their natural habitat and social groups.
- My argument that the public should not support marine parks and "swim with dolphins" programs is based mainly on the grounds that these programs place great stress on dolphins by separating them from their natural habitat and social groups.

Even though logical relationships can be stated in various ways, writing out one or more *because* clauses seems to be the most succinct and manageable way to clarify an argument for oneself. We therefore suggest that sometime in the writing process, you create a *working thesis statement* that summarizes your main reasons as because clauses attached to your claim.* Just when you compose your own working thesis statement depends largely on your writing process. Some writers like to plan out their whole argument from the start and often compose their working thesis statements with *because* clauses before they write their rough drafts. Others discover their arguments as they write. And sometimes it is a combination of both. For these writers, an extended working

---

*A working thesis statement opposing the commercial use of captured dolphins might look like this: *The public should not support the commercial use of captured dolphins because marine parks and "swim with dolphins" programs place great stress on dolphins by separating them from their natural habitat and social groups; because these parks and programs are mainly big businesses driven by profit; because they create inaccurate and incomplete educational information about dolphins; because they create a commercial market for dolphins that directly or indirectly encourages dolphin hunts and captures; and because they promote an attitude of human dominance over animals.* You might not put a bulky thesis statement like this into your essay; rather, a working thesis statement is a behind-the-scenes way of summarizing your argument so that you can see it whole and clear.

thesis statement is something they might write halfway through the composing process as a way of ordering their argument when various branches seem to be growing out of control. Or they might compose a working thesis statement at the very end as a way of checking the unity of the final product.

Whenever you write your extended thesis statement, the act of doing so can be simultaneously frustrating and thought provoking. Composing *because* clauses can be a powerful discovery tool, causing you to think of many different kinds of arguments to support your claim. But it is often difficult to wrestle your ideas into the *because* clause shape, which sometimes seems to be overly tidy for the complex network of ideas you are trying to work with. Nevertheless, trying to summarize your argument as a single claim with reasons should help you see more clearly what you have to do.

■ ■ ■ **FOR CLASS DISCUSSION** Developing Claims and Reasons

Try this group exercise to help you see how writing *because* clauses can be a discovery procedure. Divide into small groups. Each group member should contribute an issue that he or she would like to explore. Discussing one person's issue at a time, help each member develop a claim supported by several reasons. Express each reason as a *because* clause. Then write out the working thesis statement for each person's argument by attaching the *because* clauses to the claim. Finally, try to create *because* clauses in support of an alternative claim for each issue. Recorders should select two or three working thesis statements from the group to present to the class as a whole.   ■ ■ ■

Conclusion

This chapter has introduced you to the structure of classical argument, to the rhetorical triangle (message, writer or speaker, and audience), and to the classical appeals of *logos, ethos,* and *pathos.* It has also shown how arguments originate in issue questions, how issue questions differ from information questions, and how arguments differ from pseudo-arguments. At the heart of this chapter we explained that the frame of an argument is a claim supported by reasons. As you generate reasons to support your own arguments, it is often helpful to articulate them as *because* clauses attached to the claim.

In the next chapter we will see how to support a reason by examining its logical structure, uncovering its unstated assumptions, and planning a strategy of development.

WRITING ASSIGNMENT An Issue Question and Working Thesis Statements

Decide on an issue and a claim for a classical argument that you would like to write. Write a one-sentence question that summarizes the controversial issue that your claim addresses. Then draft a working thesis statement for your proposed argument. Organize the thesis as a claim with bulleted *because* clauses for reasons. You should have at least two reasons, but it is okay to have three or four. Also include an *opposing thesis statement*—that is, a claim with *because* clauses for an alternative position on your issue.

Recall that in Part One we emphasized exploratory writing as a way of resisting closure and helping you wrestle with multiple perspectives. Now we ask you to begin a process of closure by developing a thesis statement that condenses your argument into a claim with supporting reasons. However, as we emphasize throughout this text, drafting itself is an *exploratory process*. Writers almost always discover new ideas when they write a first draft; as they take their writing project through multiple drafts, their views may change substantially. Often, in fact, honest writers can change positions on an issue by discovering that a counterargument is stronger than their own. So the working thesis statement that you submit for this assignment may evolve substantially once you begin to draft.

In this chapter, as well as in Chapters 4 and 5, we will follow the process of student writer Carmen Tieu as she constructs an argument on violent video games. During earlier exploratory writing, she wrote about a classroom incident in which her professor had described video game playing as gendered behavior (overwhelmingly male). The professor indicated his dislike for such games, pointing to their antisocial, dehumanizing values. In her freewrite, Carmen described her own enjoyment of violent video games—particularly first-person-shooter games—and explored the pleasure that she derived from beating boys at *Halo 2*. She knew that she wanted to write an argument on this issue. What follows is Carmen's submission for this assignment.

Carmen's Issue Question and Working Thesis Statements

Issue Question: Should girls be encouraged to play first-person-shooter video games?

My claim: First-person-shooter (FPS) video games are great activities for girls

- because beating guys at their own game is empowering for girls
- because being skilled at FPS games frees girls from feminine stereotypes
- because they give girls a different way of bonding with males
- because they give girls new insights into a male subculture

Opposing claim: First-person-shooter games are a bad activity for anyone, especially girls,

- because they promote antisocial values such as indiscriminate killing
- because they amplify the bad, macho side of male stereotypes
- because they waste valuable time that could be spent on something constructive
- because FPS games could encourage women to see themselves as objects ■

For additional writing, reading, and research resources, go to www.mycomplab.com

4 The Logical Structure of Arguments

In Chapter 3 you learned that the core of an argument is a claim supported by reasons and that these reasons can often be stated as *because* clauses attached to a claim. In the present chapter we examine the logical structure of arguments in more depth. You will learn to:

- Explain the logical structure of argument
- Use the Toulmin system to analyze and plan arguments

An Overview of *Logos:* What Do We Mean by the "Logical Structure" of an Argument?

As you will recall from our discussion of the rhetorical triangle, *logos* refers to the strength of an argument's support and its internal consistency. *Logos* is the argument's logical structure. But what do we mean by "logical structure"?

Formal Logic versus Real-World Logic

First of all, what we *don't* mean by logical structure is the kind of precise certainty you get in a philosophy class in formal logic. Logic classes deal with symbolic assertions that are universal and unchanging, such as "If all ps are qs and if r is a p, then r is a q." This statement is logically certain so long as $p, q,$ and r are pure abstractions. But in the real world, $p, q,$ and r turn into actual things, and the relationships among them suddenly become fuzzy. For example, p might be a class of actions called "Sexual Harassment," while q could be the class called "Actions That Justify Dismissal from a Job." If r is the class "Telling Off-Color Stories," then the logic of our p–q–r statement suggests that telling off-color stories (r) is an instance of sexual harassment (p), which in turn is an action justifying dismissal from one's job (q).

Now, most of us would agree that sexual harassment is a serious offense that might well justify dismissal from a job. In turn, we might agree that telling off-color stories, if the jokes are sufficiently raunchy and are inflicted on an unwilling audience, constitutes sexual harassment. But few of us would want to say categorically that all people who tell off-color stories are harassing their listeners and ought to be fired. Most of us would want to know the particulars of the case before making a final judgment.

In the real world, then, it is difficult to say that *r*s are always *p*s or that every instance of a *p* results in *q*. That is why we discourage students from using the word *prove* in claims they write for arguments (as in "This paper will prove that euthanasia is wrong"). Real-world arguments seldom *prove* anything. They can only make a good case for something, a case that is more or less strong, more or less probable. Often the best you can hope for is to strengthen the resolve of those who agree with you or weaken the resistance of those who oppose you.

The Role of Assumptions

A key difference, then, between formal logic and real-world argument is that real-world arguments are not grounded in abstract, universal statements. Rather, as we shall see, they must be grounded in beliefs, assumptions, or values granted by the audience. A second important difference is that in real-world arguments, these beliefs, assumptions, or values are often unstated. So long as writer and audience share the same assumptions, it's fine to leave them unstated. But if these underlying assumptions aren't shared, the writer has a problem.

To illustrate the nature of this problem, consider one of the arguments we introduced in the last chapter.

> The public should not support marine parks and "swim with dolphins" programs because these programs separate dolphins from their natural habitat and social groups.

On the face of it, this is a plausible argument. But the argument is persuasive only if the audience agrees with the writer's assumption that it is wrong to separate wild animals from their natural habitats and social groups. What if you believed that confinement of wild animals is not always harmful or stressful to the animals, that the knowledge derived from the capture of wild animals enables humans to preserve the natural environment for these animals, and that the benefits to be gained from the captivity of a small number of wild animals outweigh the animals' loss of freedom? If this were the case, you might believe that dolphin programs have positive consequences so long as the marine parks strive to provide humane conditions for the animals, with minimal stress. If these were your beliefs, the argument wouldn't work for you because you would reject the underlying assumption. To persuade you with this line of reasoning, the writer would have to defend this assumption, showing why it is unwise or unethical to remove animals from their free and wild conditions.

The Core of an Argument: The Enthymeme

The previous core argument ("The public should not support marine parks and 'swim with dolphins' programs because these programs separate dolphins from their natural habitat and social groups") is an incomplete logical structure called an *enthymeme*. Its persuasiveness depends on an underlying assumption or belief that the audience must accept. To complete the enthymeme and make it effective, the audience must willingly supply a missing premise—in this case, that it is wrong to separate wild animals from their natural environments. The Greek philosopher Aristotle showed how successful enthymemes root the speaker's argument in assumptions, beliefs, or values held by the audience. The word *enthymeme* comes from the Greek *en* (meaning "in") and *thumos* (meaning "mind"). Listeners or readers must have in mind an assumption, belief, or value that lets them willingly supply the missing premise. If the audience is unwilling to supply the missing premise, then the argument fails. Our point is that successful arguments depend both on what the arguer says and on what the audience already has "in mind."

To clarify the concept of "enthymeme," let's go over this same territory again, this time more slowly, examining what we mean by "incomplete logical structure." The sentence "The public should not support marine parks and 'swim with dolphins' programs because these programs separate dolphins from their natural habitat and social groups" is an enthymeme. It combines a claim (the public should not support marine parks and "swim with dolphins" programs) with a reason expressed as a *because* clause (because these programs separate dolphins from their natural habitat and social groups). To render this enthymeme logically complete, the audience must willingly supply a missing assumption—that it is wrong to separate wild animals from their natural environments. If your audience accepts this assumption, then you have a starting place on which to build an effective argument. If your audience doesn't accept this assumption, then you must supply another argument to support it, and so on until you find common ground with your audience.

To sum up:

1. Claims are supported with reasons. You can usually state a reason as a *because* clause attached to a claim (see Chapter 3).
2. A *because* clause attached to a claim is an incomplete logical structure called an enthymeme. To create a complete logical structure from an enthymeme, the underlying assumption (or assumptions) must be articulated.
3. To serve as an effective starting point for the argument, this underlying assumption should be a belief, value, or principle that the audience grants.

Let's illustrate this structure by putting the previous example into schematic form.

> **ENTHYMEME**
>
> CLAIM The public should not support marine parks and "swim with dolphins" programs
>
> REASON because these programs seperate dolphins from their natural habitat and social groups.

Audience must supply this assumption —————↓

> **UNDERLYING ASSUMPTION**
> Wild animals should remain free in their natural habitats and social groups.

■ ■ ■ **FOR CLASS DISCUSSION** Identifying Underlying Assumptions

Working individually or in small groups, identify the unstated assumption that the audience must supply in order to make the following enthymemes persuasive.

Example

Enthymeme: Rabbits make good pets because they are gentle.

Underlying assumption: Gentle animals make good pets.

1. We shouldn't elect Joe as committee chair because he is too bossy.
2. Drugs should not be legalized because legalization would greatly increase the number of drug addicts.
3. Airport screeners should use racial profiling because doing so will increase the odds of stopping terrorists.
4. Racial profiling should not be used by airport screeners because it violates a person's civil rights.
5. We should strengthen the Endangered Species Act because doing so will preserve genetic diversity on the planet.
6. The Endangered Species Act is too stringent because it severely damages the economy.   ■ ■ ■

Adopting a Language for Describing Arguments: The Toulmin System

Understanding a new field usually requires us to learn a new vocabulary. For example, if you were taking biology for the first time, you'd have to learn dozens and dozens of new terms. Luckily, the field of argument requires us to learn a mere handful of new terms. A particularly useful set of argument terms, one we'll be using occasionally throughout the rest of this text, comes from philosopher Stephen Toulmin. In the 1950s, Toulmin rejected the prevailing models of argument based on formal logic in favor of a very audience-based courtroom model.

Toulmin's courtroom model differs from formal logic in that it assumes that (1) all assertions and assumptions are contestable by "opposing counsel" and that (2) all final "verdicts" about the persuasiveness of the opposing arguments will be rendered by a neutral third party, a judge or jury. As writers, keeping in mind the "opposing counsel" forces us to anticipate counterarguments and to question our assumptions. Keeping in mind the judge and jury reminds us to answer opposing arguments fully, without rancor, and to present positive reasons for supporting our case as well as negative reasons for disbelieving the opposing case. Above all else, Toulmin's model reminds us not to construct an argument that appeals only to those who already agree with us. In short, it helps arguers tailor arguments to their audiences.

The system we use for analyzing arguments combines Toulmin's language with Aristotle's concept of the enthymeme. It builds on the system you have already been practicing. We simply need to add a few key terms from Toulmin. The first term is Toulmin's *warrant,* the name we will now use for the underlying assumption that turns an enthymeme into a complete, logical structure as shown at the top of the next page.

Audience must accept this warrant

WARRANT
Wild animals should remain free in their natural habitats and social groups.

Toulmin derives his term *warrant* from the concept of "warranty" or "guarantee." The warrant is the value, belief, or principle that the audience has to hold if the soundness of the argument is to be guaranteed or warranted. We sometimes make similar use of this word in ordinary language when we say, "That is an unwarranted conclusion," meaning one has leaped from information about a situation to a conclusion about that situation without any sort of general principle to justify or "warrant" that move. Thus the warrant—once accepted by the audience—"guarantees" the soundness of the argument.

But arguments need more than claims, reasons, and warrants. These are simply one-sentence statements—the frame of an argument, not a developed argument. To give body and weight to our arguments and make them convincing, we need what Toulmin calls *grounds* and *backing*. Let's start with grounds. Grounds are the supporting evidence that causes an audience to accept your reason. Grounds are facts, data, statistics, causal links, testimony, examples, anecdotes—the blood and muscle that flesh out the skeletal frame of your enthymeme. Toulmin suggests that grounds are "what you have to go on" in an argument—the stuff you can point to and present before a jury. Here is how grounds fit into our emerging argument schema:

ENTHYMEME

CLAIM The public should not support marine parks and "swim with dolphins" programs

REASON because these programs separate dolphins from their natural habitat and social groups.

Grounds support the reason

GROUNDS

Evidence and arguments showing difference between dolphin behavior in the wild and in captivity and the stress caused by this difference:

• In the wild, dolphins swim in pods around forty miles a day in the open ocean whereas marine park tanks provide only a tiny fraction of that space.

• Evidence that the echoes from concrete pools, the music of dolphin shows, and the applause and noise of audiences are stressful and harmful

• Statistics about the excessive number of performances or about the levels of stress hormones produced in dolphins

In many cases, successful arguments require just these three components: a claim, a reason, and grounds. If the audience already accepts the unstated assumption behind the reason (the warrant), then the warrant can safely remain in the background, unstated and unexamined. But if there is a chance that the audience will question or doubt the warrant, then the writer needs to back it up by providing an argument in its support. *Backing* is the argument that supports the warrant. It may require no more than one or two sentences or as much as a major section in your argument. Its goal is to persuade the audience to accept the warrant. Here is how *backing* is added to our schema:

Backing supports the warrant

WARRANT

Wild animals should remain free in their natural habitats and social groups.

BACKING

Arguments showing why it is unwise, unethical, or otherwise wrong to separate wild animals from their natural environments:

• Examples of wild animals (those in aquariums and zoos) that do not thrive in artificially constructed environments, that don't live long, or that suffer psychological stress from confinement

• An ecological argument about the beauty of animals in the wild and of the complexity of the natural webs of which animals are a part

• A philosophical argument that humans shouldn't treat animals as instruments for their own enjoyment or profit

Toulmin's system next asks us to imagine how a resistant audience would try to refute our argument. Specifically, the adversarial audience might challenge our reason and grounds by arguing that dolphins in captivity are not as stressed as we claim (evidence provided by veterinarians, caretakers, or animal trainers verifying that most dolphins in captivity are in good health). Or the adversary might attack our warrant and backing by showing how the captivity of some wild animal might save the species from extinction or how animals are often saved from illness and predators by caring humans. An adversary might attack our philosophical or spiritual arguments by saying that the same reasoning, taken to its logical conclusion, would eliminate zoos and require all humans to become vegetarians or vegans. An adversary might even argue that dolphins enjoy being with humans and have the same capacity to be animal companions as dogs or cats.

In the case of the argument opposing dolphins in captivity, an adversary might offer one or more of the following rebuttals.

ENTHYMEME

CLAIM The public should not support marine parks and "swim with dolphins" programs

REASON because these programs separate dolphins from their natural habitat and social groups.

GROUNDS

Evidence and arguments showing stressful difference between dolphin behavior in the wild and in captivity:

• In the wild, dolphins swim in pods around forty miles a day in the open ocean whereas marine park tanks provide only a tiny fraction of that space.

• Evidence that the echoes from concrete pools, music of dolphin shows, and the applause and noise of audiences are stressful and harmful

• Statistics about the excessive number of performances or about the levels of stress hormones produced in dolphins

Writer must anticipate these attacks from skeptics

POSSIBLE CONDITIONS OF REBUTTAL

A skeptic can attack the reason and grounds

• Argument that these programs must observe strict accreditation standards for animal welfare, health, and nutrition

• Programs exercise dolphins' intelligence and abilities and build on their natural behaviors.

• Many dolphins in these programs have been bred in captivity, so they aren't "wild."

• The education and entertainment provided by these programs promote concern for dolphins.

WARRANT

Wild animals should remain free in their natural habitats and social groups.

BACKING

Arguments showing why it is unwise, unethical, or otherwise wrong to separate wild animals from their natural environments:

• Examples of wild animals (those in aquariums and zoos) that do not thrive in artificially constructed environments, that don't live long, or that suffer psychological stress from confinement

• An ecological argument about the beauty of animals in the wild and of the complexity of the natural webs of which animals are a part

• A philosophical argument that humans shouldn't treat animals as instruments for their own enjoyment or profit

POSSIBLE CONDITIONS OF REBUTTAL

A skeptic can attack the warrant and backing

• The natural habitat is not always the best environment for wild animals.

• Captivity may preserve a species or lengthen the lifespan of individual animals.

• Scientists have been able to conduct valuable studies of dolphins in captivity, which would have been impossible with dolphins in the wild.

As this example shows, adversarial readers can question an argument's reasons and grounds or its warrant and backing or sometimes both. Conditions of rebuttal remind writers to look at their arguments from the perspective of skeptics. The same principle can be illustrated in the following analysis of an argument that cocaine and heroin should be legalized.

ENTHYMEME

CLAIM Cocaine and heroin should be legalized

REASON because legalization would eliminate the black market in drugs.

GROUNDS

Statistical evidence and arguments showing how legalization would end the black market:

• Statistics and data showing the size of the current black market

• Examples, anecdotes, and facts showing how the black market works

• Causal explanation showing that selling cocaine and heroin legally in state-controlled stores would lower price and eliminate drug dealers

WARRANT

Eliminating the black market in drugs is good.

BACKING

Statistics and examples about the ill effects of the black market:

• The high cost of the black market to crime victims

• The high cost to taxpayers of waging the war against drugs

• The high cost of prisons to house incarcerated drug dealers

• Evidence that huge profits make drug dealing more attractive than ordinary jobs

CONDITIONS OF REBUTTAL
Attacking the reason and grounds

Arguments showing that legalizing cocaine and heroin would not eliminate the black market in drugs:

• Perhaps taxes on the drugs would keep the costs above black market prices.

• Perhaps new kinds of illegal designer drugs would be developed and sold on the black market.

CONDITIONS OF REBUTTAL
Attacking the warrant and backing

Arguments showing that the benefits of eliminating the black market are outweighed by the costs:

• The number of new drug users and addicts would be unacceptably high.

• The health and economic cost of treating addiction would be too high.

• The social costs of selling drugs legally in stores would bring harmful changes to our cultural values.

Toulmin's final term, used to limit the force of a claim and indicate the degree of its probable truth, is *qualifier*. The qualifier reminds us that real-world arguments almost never prove a claim. We may say things such as *very likely, probably,* or *maybe* to indicate the strength of the claim we are willing to draw from our grounds and warrant. Thus if there are exceptions to your warrant or if your grounds are not very strong, you will have to qualify your claim. For example, you might say, "Except for limited cases of scientific research, dolphins should not be held in captivity," or "With full awareness of the potential dangers, I suggest we consider the option of legalizing drugs as a way of ending the ill effects of the black market." In our future displays of the Toulmin scheme we will omit the qualifiers, but you should always remember that no argument is 100 percent persuasive.

■ ■ ■ **FOR CLASS DISCUSSION** Developing Enthymemes with the Toulmin Schema

Working individually or in small groups, imagine that you have to write arguments developing the six enthymemes listed in the For Class Discussion exercise on page 77. Use the Toulmin schema to help you determine what you need to consider when developing each enthymeme. We suggest that you try a four-box diagram structure as a way of visualizing the schema. We have applied the Toulmin schema to the first enthymeme: "We shouldn't elect Joe as committee chair because he is too bossy."

ENTHYMEME

CLAIM We shouldn't elect Joe as committee chair
REASON because he is too bossy.

GROUNDS

Evidence of Joe's bossiness:

• Examples of the way he dominates meetings—doesn't call on people, talks too much

• Testimony about his bossiness from people who have served with him on committees

• Anecdotes about his abrasive style

CONDITIONS OF REBUTTAL
Attacking the reason and grounds

Evidence that Joe is not bossy or is only occasionally bossy:

• Counterevidence showing his collaborative style

• Testimony from people who have liked Joe as a leader and claim he isn't bossy; testimony about his cooperativeness and kindness

• Testimony that anecdotes about Joe's bossiness aren't typical

---

WARRANT

Bossy people make bad committee chairs.

BACKING

Problems caused by bossy committee chairs:

• Bossy people don't inspire cooperation and enthusiam.

• Bossy people make others angry.

• Bossy people tend to make bad decisions because they don't incorporate advice from others.

CONDITIONS OF REBUTTAL
Attacking the warrant and backing

• Arguments that bossiness can be a good trait

  • Sometimes bossy people make good chairpersons.

  • Argument that this committee needs a bossy person who can make decisions and get things done

• Argument that Joe has other traits of good leadership that outweigh his bossiness

---

Using Toulmin's Schema to Determine a Strategy of Support

So far we have seen that a claim, a reason, and a warrant form the frame for a line of reasoning in an argument. Most of the words in an argument, however, are devoted to grounds and backing.

For an illustration of how a writer can use the Toulmin schema to generate ideas for an argument, consider the following case. In April 2005, the Texas house of representatives passed a bill banning "sexually suggestive" cheerleading. Across the nation, evening television show comics poked fun at the bill, while newspaper editorialists debated its wisdom and constitutionality. In one of our classes, however, several students, including one who had earned a high school varsity letter in competitive cheerleading, defended the bill by contending that provocative dance moves hurt the athletic image of cheerleading. In the following example, which draws on ideas developed in class discussion, we create a hypothetical student writer (we'll call her Chandale) who argues in defense of the Texas bill. Chandale's argument is based on the following enthymeme:

> The cheerleading bill to ban suggestive dancing is good because it promotes a view of female cheerleaders as athletes rather than exotic dancers.

Chandale used the Toulmin schema to brainstorm ideas for developing her argument. Here are her notes:

Chandale's Planning Notes Using the Toulmin Schema

Enthymeme: The cheerleading bill to ban suggestive dancing is good because it promotes a view of female cheerleaders as athletes rather than exotic dancers.

Grounds: First, I've got to use evidence to show that cheerleaders are athletes.

- Cheerleaders at my high school are carefully chosen for their stamina and skill after exhausting two-week tryouts.
- We begin all practices with a mile run and an hour of warm-up exercises—also expected to work out on our own for at least an hour on weekends and on days without practice.
- We learned competitive routines and stunts consisting of lifts, tosses, flips, catches, and gymnastic moves. This requires athletic ability! We'd practice these stunts for hours each week.
- Throughout the year cheerleaders have to attend practices, camps, and workshops to learn new routines and stunts.
- Our squad competed in competitions around the state.
- Competitive cheerleading is a growing movement across the country—University of Maryland has made it a varsity sport for women.
- Skimpy uniforms and suggestive dance moves destroy this image by making women eye candy like the Dallas Cowboys cheerleaders.

Warrant: It is a good thing to view female cheerleaders as athletes.

Backing: Now I need to make the case that it is good to see cheerleaders as athletes rather than as eye candy.

- Athletic competition builds self-esteem, independence, a powerful sense of achievement—contributes to health, strength, conditioning.
- Competitive cheerleading is one of the few sports where teams are made up of both men and women. (Why is this good? Should I use this?)
- The suggestive dance moves turn women into sex objects whose function is to be gazed at by men—suggests that women's value is based on their beauty and sex appeal.
- We are talking about HIGH SCHOOL cheerleading—very bad early influence on girls to model themselves on Dallas Cowboys cheerleaders or sexy MTV videos of rock stars.
- Junior high girls want to do what senior high girls do—suggestive dance moves promote sexuality way too early.

Conditions of Rebuttal: Would anybody try to rebut my reasons and grounds that cheerleading is an athletic activity?

- No. I think it is obvious that cheerleading is an athletic activity once they see my evidence.

- However, they might not think of cheerleading as a sport. They might say that the University of Maryland just declared it a sport as a cheap way to meet Title IX federal rules to have more women's sports. I'll have to make sure that I show this is really a sport.

- They also might say that competitive cheerleading shouldn't be encouraged because it is too dangerous—lots of serious injuries including paralysis have been caused by mistakes in doing flips, lifts, and tosses. If I include this, maybe I could say that other sports are dangerous also—and it is in fact danger that makes this sport so exciting.

Would anyone doubt my warrant and backing that it is good to see female cheerleaders as athletes?

- Yes, all those people who laughed at the Texas legislature think that people are being too prudish and that banning suggestive dance moves violates free expression. I'll need to make my case that it is bad for young girls to see themselves as sex objects too early.

The information that Chandale lists under "grounds" is what she sees as the facts of the case—the hard data she will use as evidence to support her contention that cheerleading is an athletic activity. The paragraph that follows shows how this argument might look when placed in written form.

First Part of Chandale's Argument

Although evening television show comedians have made fun of the Texas legislature's desire to ban "suggestive" dance moves from cheerleading routines, I applaud this bill because it promotes a healthy view of female cheerleaders as athletes rather than showgirls. I was lucky enough to attend a high school where cheerleading is a sport, and I earned a varsity letter as a cheerleader. To get on my high school's cheerleading squad, students have to go through an exhausting two-week tryout of workouts and instruction in the basic routines; then they are chosen based on their stamina and skill. Once on the squad, cheerleaders begin all practices with a mile run and an hour of grueling warm-up exercises and are expected to exercise on their own on weekends. As a result of this regimen, cheerleaders achieve and maintain a top level of physical fitness. In addition, to get on the squad, students must be able to do handstands, cartwheels, handsprings, high jumps, and the splits. Each year the squad builds up to its complex routines and stunts consisting of lifts, tosses, flips, catches, and gymnastic moves that only trained athletes can do. In tough competitions at the regional and state levels, the cheerleading squad demonstrates its athletic talent. This view of cheerleading as a competitive sport is also spreading to colleges. As reported recently in a number of newspapers, the University of Maryland has made cheerleading a varsity sport, and many other universities are following suit. Athletic performance of this caliber is a far cry from the sexy dancing that many high school girls often associate with cheerleading. By banning suggestive dancing in cheerleading routines, the Texas legislature creates an opportunity for schools to emphasize the athleticism of cheerleading.

As you can see, Chandale has plenty of evidence for arguing that competitive cheerleading is an athletic activity quite different from sexy dancing. But how effective is this argument as it stands? Is this all she needs? The Toulmin schema encourages writers to include—if needed for the intended audience—explicit support for their warrants as well as attention to conditions for rebuttal. Because the overwhelming national response to the Texas law was ridicule at the perceived prudishness of the legislators, Chandale decides to expand her argument as follows:

Continuation of Chandale's Argument

Whether we see cheerleading as a sport or as sexy dancing is an important issue for women. The erotic dance moves that many high school cheerleaders now incorporate into their routines show that they are emulating the Dallas Cowboys cheerleaders or pop stars on MTV. Our already sexually saturated culture (think of the suggestive clothing marketed to little girls) pushes girls and women to measure their value by their beauty and sex appeal. It would be far healthier, both physically and psychologically, if high school cheerleaders were identified as athletes. For women and men both, competitive cheerleading can build self-esteem, pride in teamwork, and a powerful sense of achievement, as well as promote health, strength, and fitness.

Some people might object to competitive cheerleading by saying that cheerleading isn't really a sport. Some have accused the University of Maryland of making cheerleading a varsity sport only as a cheap way of meeting Title IX requirements. But anyone who has watched competitive cheerleading, and imagined what it would be like to be thrown high into the air, knows instinctively that this is a sport indeed. In fact, other persons might object to competitive cheerleading because it is too dangerous, with potential for very severe injuries including paralysis. Obviously the sport is dangerous—but so are many sports, including football, gymnastics, diving, and trampoline. The danger and difficulty of the sport is part of its appeal. Part of what can make cheerleaders as athletes better role models for girls than cheerleaders as erotic dancers is the courage and training needed for success. Of course, the Texas legislators might not have had athleticism in mind when they banned suggestive dancing. They might only have been promoting their vision of morality. But at stake are the role models we set for young girls. I'll pick an athlete over a Dallas Cowboys cheerleader every time.

Our example suggests how a writer can use the Toulmin schema to generate ideas for an argument. For evidence, Chandale draws primarily on her personal experiences as a cheerleader/athlete and on her knowledge of popular culture. She also draws on her reading of several newspaper articles about the University of Maryland's making cheerleading a varsity sport. (In an academic paper rather than a newspaper editorial, she would need to document these sources through formal citations.) Although many arguments depend on research, many can be supported wholly or in part by your own personal experiences, so don't neglect the wealth of evidence from your own life when searching for data. A more detailed discussion of evidence in arguments occurs in Chapter 5.

■ ■ ■ **FOR CLASS DISCUSSION** Reasons, Warrants, and Conditions of Rebuttal

1. Working individually or in small groups, consider ways you could use evidence to support the stated reason in each of the following partial arguments.

   a. Another reason to oppose a state sales tax is that it is so annoying.

   b. Rap music has a bad influence on teenagers because it promotes disrespect for women.

   c. Professor X is an outstanding teacher because he (she) generously spends so much time outside of class counseling students with personal problems.

2. Now create arguments to support the warrants in each of the partial arguments in exercise 1. The warrants for each of the arguments are stated below.

a. Support this warrant: We should oppose taxes that are annoying.

b. Support this warrant: It is bad to promote disrespect for women.

c. Support this warrant: Time spent counseling students with personal problems is an important criterion for identifying outstanding teachers.

3. Using Toulmin's conditions of rebuttal, work out a strategy for refuting either the stated reasons or the warrants or both in each of the preceding arguments.

The Power of Audience-Based Reasons

As we have seen, both Aristotle's concept of the enthymeme and Toulmin's concept of the warrant focus on the arguer's need to create what we will now call "audience-based reasons." Whenever you ask whether a given piece of writing is persuasive, the immediate rejoinder should always be, "Persuasive to whom?" What seems like a good reason to you may not be a good reason to others. Finding audience-based reasons means finding arguments whose warrants the audience will accept—that is, arguments effectively rooted in your audience's beliefs and values.

Difference between Writer-Based and Audience-Based Reasons

To illustrate the difference between writer-based and audience-based reasons, consider the following hypothetical case. Suppose you believed that the government should build a dam on the nearby Rapid River—a project bitterly opposed by several environmental groups. Which of the following two arguments might you use to address environmentalists?

1. The government should build a dam on the Rapid River because the only alternative power sources are coal-fired or nuclear plants, both of which pose greater risk to the environment than a hydroelectric dam.

2. The government should build a hydroelectric dam on the Rapid River because this area needs cheap power to attract heavy industry.

Clearly, the warrant of argument 1 ("Choose the source of power that poses least risk to the environment") is rooted in the values and beliefs of environmentalists, whereas the warrant of argument 2 ("Growth of industry is good") is likely to make them wince. To environmentalists, new industry means more congestion, more smoke-stacks, and more pollution. However, argument 2 may appeal to out-of-work laborers or to the business community, to whom new industry means more jobs and a booming economy.

From the perspective of logic alone, arguments 1 and 2 are both sound. They are internally consistent and proceed from reasonable premises. But they will affect different audiences very differently. Neither argument proves that the government should build the dam; both are open to objection. Passionate environmentalists, for example, might counter argument 1 by asking why the government needs to build any power plant at all. They could argue that energy conservation would obviate the need for a new power plant. Or they might argue that building a dam would hurt the environment in ways unforeseen by dam supporters. Our point, then, isn't that argument 1 will persuade environmentalists. Rather, our point is that argument 1 will be more persuasive than argument 2 because it is rooted in beliefs and values that the intended audience shares.

Let's consider a second example by returning to Chapter 1 and student Gordon Adams's petition to waive his math requirement. Gordon's central argument, as you will recall, was that as a lawyer he would have no need for algebra. In Toulmin's terms, Gordon's argument looks like this:

ENTHYMEME	*Stated explicitly in Gordon's argument*
CLAIM I should be exempted from the algebra requirement	
REASON because in my chosen field of law I will have no need for algebra.	
GROUNDS	*Fully developed in Gordon's argument*
Testimony from lawyers and others that lawyers never use algebra	
WARRANT	*Left unstated in Gordon's argument*
General education requirements should be based on career utility (that is, if a course is not needed for a particular student's career, it shouldn't be required).	
BACKING	*Missing from Gordon's argument*
Arguments that career utility should be the chief criterion for requiring general education courses	

In our discussions of this case with students and faculty, students generally vote to support Gordon's request, whereas faculty generally vote against it. And in fact, the University Standards Committee rejected Gordon's petition, thus delaying his entry into law school.

Why do faculty and students differ on this issue? Mainly they differ because faculty reject Gordon's warrant that general education requirements should serve students' individual career interests. Most faculty believe that general education courses, including math, provide a base of common learning that links us to the past and teaches us modes of understanding useful throughout life.

Gordon's argument thus challenges one of college professors' most cherished beliefs—that the liberal arts and sciences are innately valuable. Further, it threatens his immediate audience, the committee, with a possible flood of student requests to waive other general education requirements on the grounds of their irrelevance to a particular career choice.

How might Gordon have created a more persuasive argument? In our view, Gordon might have prevailed had he accepted the faculty's belief in the value of the math requirement and argued that he had fulfilled the "spirit" of that requirement through alternative means. He could have based his argument on an enthymeme like this:

> I should be exempted from the algebra requirement because my experience as a contractor and inventor has already provided me with equivalent mathematical knowledge.

Following this audience-based approach, he would drop all references to algebra's uselessness for lawyers and expand his discussion of the mathematical savvy he acquired on the job. This argument would honor faculty values and reduce the faculty's fear of setting a bad precedent. Few students are likely to have Gordon's background, and those who do could apply for a similar exemption without threatening the system. Again, this argument might not have won, but it would have gotten a more sympathetic hearing.

■ ■ ■ **FOR CLASS DISCUSSION** Audience-Based Reasons
Working in groups, decide which of the two reasons offered in each instance would be more persuasive to the specified audience. Be prepared to explain your reasoning to the class. Write out the implied warrant for each *because* clause and decide whether the specific audience would likely grant it.

1. Audience: people who advocate a pass/fail grading system on the grounds that the present grading system is too competitive
   a. We should keep the present grading system because it prepares people for the dog-eat-dog pressures of the business world.
   b. We should keep the present grading system because it tells students that certain standards of excellence must be met if individuals are to reach their full potential.
2. Audience: young people ages fifteen to twenty-five
   a. You should become a vegetarian because an all-vegetable diet will help you lower your cholesterol.
   b. You should become a vegetarian because doing so will help eliminate the suffering of animals raised in factory farms.
3. Audience: conservative proponents of "family values"
   a. Same-sex marriages should be legalized because doing so will promote public acceptance of homosexuality.
   b. Same-sex marriages should be legalized because doing so will make it easier for gay people to establish and sustain long-term, stable relationships.   ■ ■ ■

Conclusion

Chapters 3 and 4 have provided an anatomy of argument. They have shown that the core of an argument is a claim with reasons that usually can be summarized in one or more *because* clauses attached to the claim. Often, it is as important to articulate and support the underlying assumptions in your argument (warrants) as it is to support the stated reasons because a successful argument should be rooted in your audience's beliefs and values. In order to plan an audience-based argument strategy, arguers can use the Toulmin schema, which helps writers discover grounds, warrants, and backing for their arguments and test them through conditions of rebuttal. Finally, we showed how the use of audience-based reasons helps you keep your audience in mind from the start whenever you design a plan for an argument.

WRITING ASSIGNMENT Plan of an Argument's Details

This assignment asks you to return to the working thesis statement that you created for the brief writing assignment in Chapter 3. From that thesis statement extract one of your enthymemes (your claim with one of your *because* clauses). Write out the warrant for your enthymeme. Then use the Toulmin schema to brainstorm the details you might use (grounds, backing, conditions of rebuttal) to convert your enthymeme into a fleshed-out argument. Use as your model Chandale's planning notes on pages 83–84.

Like the brief assignment for Chapter 3, this is a process-oriented brainstorming task aimed at helping you generate ideas for one part of your classical argument. You may end up changing your ideas substantially as you compose the actual argument. What follows is Carmen's submission for this assignment.

Carmen's Plan for Part of Her Argument

Enthymeme: First-person-shooter (FPS) video games are great activities for girls because playing these games gives girls new insights into male subculture.

Grounds: I've got to show the insights into male subculture I gained.

- The guys who play these video games are intensely competitive.
  - They can play for hours without stopping—intense concentration.
  - They don't multitask—no small talk during the games; total focus on playing.
  - They take delight in winning at all costs—they boast with every kill; they call each other losers.
- They often seem homophobic or misogynist.
  - They put each other down by calling opponents "faggot" and "wussy," or other similar names that are totally obscene.
  - They associate victory with being macho.

Warrant: It is beneficial for a girl to get these insights into male subculture.

Backing: How can I show these benefits?

- Although I enjoy winning at FPS games, as a girl I feel alienated from this male subculture.
- I'm glad that I don't feel the need to put everyone else down.
- It was a good learning experience to see how girls' way of bonding is very different from that of boys; girls tend to be nicer to each other rather than insulting each other.
- The game atmosphere tends to bring out these traits; guys don't talk this way as much when they are doing other things.

- This experience helped me see why men may progress faster than women in a competitive business environment—men seem programmed to crush each other and they devote enormous energy to the process.
- What else can I say? I need to think about this further.

Conditions of Rebuttal: Would anybody try to rebut my reasons and grounds?

- I think my evidence is pretty convincing that males put each other down, concentrate intensely, use homophobic or misogynist insults, etc.
- However, some guys may say, "Hey, I don't talk that way," etc.
- Maybe people would say that my sample is biased.

Would anyone try to rebut my warrant and backing?

- Skeptics may say that girls are just as mean to each other as guys are, but girls display their meanness in a different way. ■

 For additional writing, reading, and research resources, go to www.mycomplab.com

Using Evidence Effectively 5

In Chapters 3 and 4 we introduced you to the concept of *logos*—the logical structure of reasons and evidence in an argument—and showed you how an effective argument advances the writer's claim by linking its supporting reasons to one or more assumptions, beliefs, or values held by the intended audience. In this chapter, we turn to the uses of evidence in argument. By "evidence," we mean all the verifiable information a writer might use as support for an argument, such as facts, observations, examples, cases, testimony, experimental findings, survey data, statistics, and so forth. In Toulmin's terms, evidence is part of the "grounds" or "backing" of an argument in support of reasons or warrants.

In this chapter, we show you how to use evidence effectively. We begin by explaining some general principles for the persuasive use of evidence. Next we describe and illustrate various kinds of evidence and then present a rhetorical way to think about evidence, particularly the way writers select and frame evidence to support the writer's reasons while simultaneously guiding and limiting what the reader sees. By understanding the rhetorical use of evidence, you will better understand how to use evidence ethically, responsibly, and persuasively in your own arguments. We conclude the chapter by suggesting strategies to help you gather evidence for your arguments, including advice on conducting interviews and using questionnaires. You will learn to:

- Evaluate evidence for persuasiveness
- Select, frame, and use different types of evidence in a responsible, ethical manner
- Gather evidence from interviews, surveys, and questionnaires.

The Persuasive Use of Evidence

Consider a target audience of educated, reasonable, and careful readers who approach an issue with healthy skepticism, open-minded but cautious. What demands would such readers make on a writer's use of evidence? To begin to answer that question, let's look at some general principles for using evidence persuasively.

Apply the STAR Criteria to Evidence

Our open-minded but skeptical audience would first of all expect the evidence to meet what rhetorician Richard Fulkerson calls the STAR criteria:*

Sufficiency: Is there enough evidence?

Typicality: Is the chosen evidence representative and typical?

Accuracy: Is the evidence accurate and up-to-date?

Relevance: Is the evidence relevant to the claim?

Let's examine each in turn.

Sufficiency of Evidence How much evidence you need is a function of your rhetorical context. In a court trial, opposing attorneys often agree to waive evidence for points that aren't in doubt in order to concentrate on contested points. The more a claim is contested or the more your audience is skeptical, the more evidence you may need to present. If you provide too little evidence, you may be accused of *hasty generalization* (see Appendix), a reasoning fallacy in which a person makes a sweeping conclusion based on only one or two instances. On the other hand, if you provide too much evidence your argument may become overly long and tedious. You can guard against having too little or too much evidence by appropriately qualifying the claim your evidence supports.

> **Strong claim:** Working full time seriously harms a student's grade point average. (much data needed—probably a combination of examples and statistical studies)
>
> **Qualified claim:** Working full time often harms a student's grade point average. (a few representative examples may be enough)

Typicality of Evidence Whenever you select evidence, readers need to believe the evidence is typical and representative rather than extreme instances. Suppose that you want to argue that students can combine full-time work with full-time college and cite the case of your friend Pam, who pulled a straight-A grade average while working forty hours per week as a night receptionist in a small hotel. Your audience might doubt the typicality of Pam's case since a night receptionist can often use work hours for studying. What about more typical jobs, they'll ask, where you can't study while you work?

Accuracy of Evidence Evidence can't be used ethically unless it is accurate and up-to-date, and it can't be persuasive unless the audience believes in the writer's credibility. As a writer, you must be scrupulous in using the most recent and accurate evidence you can find. Faith in the accuracy of a writer's data is one function of *ethos*—the audience's confidence in the writer's credibility and trustworthiness (see Chapter 6, pages 113–114).

Relevance of Evidence Finally, evidence will be persuasive only if the reader considers it relevant to the contested issue. Consider the following student argument: "I deserve an A in this course because I worked exceptionally hard." The student then cites substantial evidence of how hard he worked—a log of study hours, copies of multiple drafts of papers, testimony from friends, and so forth. Such evidence is ample support for the claim "I

---

*Richard Fulkerson, *Teaching the Argument in Writing* (Urbana, IL: National Council of Teachers of English, 1996), 44–53. In this section, we are indebted to Fulkerson's discussion.

worked exceptionally hard" but is irrelevant to the claim "I deserve an A." Although some instructors may give partial credit for effort, the criteria for grades usually focus on the quality of the student's performance, not the student's time spent studying.

Use Sources That Your Reader Trusts

Another way to enhance the persuasiveness of your evidence is, whenever possible, to choose data from sources you think your readers will trust. Because questions of fact are often at issue in arguments, readers may be skeptical of certain sources. When you research an issue, you soon get a sense of who the participants in the conversation are and what their reputations tend to be. Knowing the political biases of sources and the extent to which a source has financial or personal investment in the outcome of a controversy will also help you locate data sources that both you and your readers can trust. Citing evidence from a peer-reviewed scholarly journal is often more persuasive than citing evidence found on an advocacy Web site. Similarly, citing a conservative magazine such as the *National Review* may be unpersuasive to liberal audiences, just as citing a Sierra Club publication may be unpersuasive to conservatives.

Rhetorical Understanding of Evidence

In the previous section we presented some general principles for effective use of evidence. We now want to deepen your understanding of how evidence persuades by asking you to consider more closely the rhetorical context in which evidence operates. We'll look first at the kinds of evidence used in arguments and then show you how writers select and frame evidence for persuasive effect.

Kinds of Evidence

Writers have numerous options for the kinds of evidence they can use in an argument, including personal-experience data, research findings, and hypothetical examples. To explain these options, we present a series of charts that categorize different kinds of evidence, illustrate how each kind might be worked into an argument, and comment on the strengths and limitations of each.

Data from Personal Experience One powerful kind of evidence comes from personal experience:

Example	Strengths and Limitations
Despite recent criticism that Ritalin is overprescribed for hyperactivity and attention-deficit disorder, it can often seem like a miracle drug. My little brother is a perfect example. Before he was given Ritalin, he was a terror in school. . . . [Tell the "before" and "after" story of your little brother.]	■ Personal-experience examples help readers identify with writer; they show writer's personal connection to the issue. ■ Vivid stories capture the imagination and appeal to *Pathos*. ■ Skeptics may sometimes argue that personal-experience examples are insufficient (writer is guilty of hasty generalization), not typical, or not adequately scientific or verifiable.

Data from Observation or Field Research You can also develop evidence by personally observing a phenomenon or by doing your own field research:

Example	Strengths and Limitations
The intersection at Fifth and Montgomery is particularly dangerous because pedestrians almost never find a comfortable break in the heavy flow of cars. On April 29, I watched fifty-seven pedestrians cross the street. Not once did cars stop in both directions before the pedestrian stepped off the sidewalk onto the street. [Continue with observed data about danger.]	▪ Field research gives the feeling of scientific credibility. ▪ It increases typicality by expanding database beyond example of one person. ▪ It enhances *ethos* of the writer as personally invested and reasonable. ▪ Skeptics may point to flaws in how observations were conducted, showing how data are insufficient, inaccurate, or nontypical.

Data from Interviews, Questionnaires, Surveys You can also gather data by interviewing stakeholders in a controversy, creating questionnaires, or doing surveys. (See pages 104–105 for advice on how to conduct this kind of field research.)

Example	Strengths and Limitations
Another reason to ban laptops from classrooms is the extent to which laptop users disturb other students. In a questionnaire that I distributed to fifty students in my residence hall, a surprising 60 percent said that they are annoyed by fellow students' sending e-mail, paying their bills, or surfing the Web while pretending to take notes in class. Additionally, I interviewed five students who gave me specific examples of how these distractions interfere with learning. [Report the examples.]	▪ Interviews, questionnaires, and surveys enhance the sufficiency and typicality of evidence by expanding the database beyond the experiences of one person. ▪ Quantitative data from questionnaires and surveys often increase the scientific feel of the argument. ▪ Surveys and questionnaires often uncover local or recent data not available in published research. ▪ Interviews can provide engaging personal stories, thus enhancing *pathos*. ▪ Skeptics can raise doubts about research methodology, questionnaire design, or typicality of interview subjects.

Data from Library or Internet Research For many arguments, evidence is derived from reading, particularly from library or Internet research. Part Five of this text helps you conduct effective research and incorporate research sources into your arguments:

Example	Strengths and Limitations
The belief that a high-carbohydrate–low-fat diet is the best way to lose weight has been challenged by research conducted by Walter Willett and his colleagues in the department of nutrition at the Harvard School of Public Health. Willett's research suggests that complex carbohydrates such as pasta and potatoes spike glucose levels, increasing the risk of diabetes. Additionally, some fats—especially monounsaturated and polyunsaturated fats found in nuts, fish, and most vegetable oils—help lower "bad" cholesterol levels (45).*	■ Researched evidence is often powerful, especially when sources are respected by your audience; writers can spotlight source's credentials through attributive tags. ■ Researched data may take the form of facts, examples, quotations, summaries of research studies, and so forth. ■ Skeptics might doubt the accuracy of facts, the credentials of a source, or the research design of a study. They might also cite studies with different results. ■ Skeptics might raise doubts about sufficiency, typicality, or relevance of your research data.

Testimony Writers frequently use testimony when direct data are either unavailable or highly technical or complex. Testimonial evidence can come from research or from interviews:

Example	Strengths and Limitations
Although the Swedish economist Bjorn Lomborg claims that acid rain is not a significant problem, many environmentalists disagree. According to David Bellamany, president of the Conservation Foundation, "Acid rain does kill forests and people around the world, and it's still doing so in the most polluted places, such as Russia" (qtd. in *BBC News*).	■ By itself, testimony is generally less persuasive than direct data. ■ Persuasiveness can be increased if source has impressive credentials, which the writer can state through attributive tags introducing the testimony. ■ Skeptics might undermine testimonial evidence by questioning credentials of source, showing source's bias, or quoting a countersource.

Statistical Data Many contemporary arguments rely heavily on statistical data, often supplemented by graphics such as tables, pie charts, and graphs. (See Chapter 9 for a discussion of the use of graphics in argument.)

Example	Strengths and Limitations
Americans are delaying marriage at a surprising rate. In 1970, 85 percent of Americans between ages twenty-five and twenty-nine were married. In 2010, however, only 45 percent were married (U.S. Census Bureau).	■ Statistics can give powerful snapshots of aggregate data from a wide database. ■ They are often used in conjunction with graphics (see pages 204–210). ■ They can be calculated and displayed in different ways to achieve different rhetorical effects, so the reader must be wary (see pages 102–103). ■ Skeptics might question statistical methods, research design, and interpretation of data.

*Parenthetical citations in this example and the next follow the MLA documentation system.

Hypothetical Examples, Cases, and Scenarios   Arguments occasionally use hypothetical examples, cases, or scenarios, particularly to illustrate conjectured consequences of an event or to test philosophical hypotheses:

Example	Strengths and Limitations
Consider what might happen if we continue to use biotech soybeans that are resistant to herbicides. The resistant gene, through cross-pollination, might be transferred to an ordinary weed, creating an out-of-control superweed that herbicides couldn't kill. Such a superweed could be an ecological disaster.	▪ Scenarios have strong imaginative appeal. ▪ They are persuasive only if they seem plausible. ▪ A scenario narrative often conveys a sense of "inevitability" even if the actual scenario is unlikely; hence rhetorical effect may be illogical. ▪ Skeptics might show the implausibility of the scenario or offer an alternative scenario.

Reasoned Sequence of Ideas   Sometimes arguments are supported with a reasoned sequence of ideas rather than with concrete facts or other forms of empirical evidence. The writer's concern is to support a point through a logical progression of ideas. Such arguments are conceptual, supported by linked ideas, rather than evidential. This kind of support occurs frequently in arguments and is often intermingled with evidentiary support.

Example	Strengths and Limitations
Embryonic stem cell research, despite its promise in fighting diseases, may have negative social consequences. This research encourages us to place embryos in the category of mere cellular matter that can be manipulated at will. Currently we reduce animals to this category when we genetically alter them for human purposes, such as engineering pigs to grow more human-like heart valves for use in transplants. Using human embryos in the same way—as material that can be altered and destroyed at will—may benefit society materially, but this quest for greater knowledge and control involves a reclassifying of embryos that could potentially lead to a devaluing of human life.	▪ These sequences are often used in causal arguments to show how causes are linked to effects or in definitional or values arguments to show links among ideas. ▪ They have great power to clarify values and show the belief structure on which a claim is founded. ▪ They can sketch out ideas and connections that would otherwise remain latent. ▪ Their effectiveness depends on the audience's acceptance of each link in the sequence of ideas. ▪ Skeptics might raise objections at any link in the sequence, often by pointing to different values or outlining different consequences.

Angle of Vision and the Selection and Framing of Evidence

You can increase your ability to use evidence effectively—and to analyze how other arguers use evidence—by becoming more aware of a writer's rhetorical choices when using evidence to support a claim. Where each of us stands on an issue is partly a function of our own critical thinking, inquiry, and research—our search for the best solution to a problem. But it is also partly a function of who we are as people—our values and beliefs as formed by the particulars of our existence such as our family history, education, gender and sexual orientation, age, class, and ethnicity. In other words, we don't enter the argumentative arena like disembodied computers arriving at our claims through a value-free calculus. We enter with our own ideologies, beliefs, values, and guiding assumptions.

These guiding assumptions, beliefs, and values work together to create a writer's "angle of vision." (Instead of "angle of vision," we could also use other words or metaphors such as *perspective, bias, lens,* or *filter*—all terms that suggest that our way of seeing the world is shaped by our values and beliefs.) A writer's angle of vision, like a

EXAMINING VISUAL ARGUMENTS

Angle of Vision

Because of nationally reported injuries and near-death experiences resulting from stage diving and crowd surfing at rock concerts, many cities have tried to ban mosh pits. Critics of mosh pits have pointed to the injuries caused by crowd surfing and to the ensuing lawsuits against concert venues. Meanwhile, supporters cite the almost ecstatic enjoyment of crowd-surfing rock fans who seek out concerts with "festival seating."

These photos display different angles of vision toward crowd surfing. Suppose you were writing a blog in support of crowd surfing. Which image would you include in your posting? Why? Suppose alternatively that you were blogging against mosh pits, perhaps urging local officials to outlaw them. Which image would you choose? Why?

Analyze the visual features of these photographs in order to explain how they are constructed to create alternative angles of vision on mosh pits.

Crowd surfing in a mosh pit

An alternative view of a mosh pit

lens or filter, helps determine what stands out for that writer in a field of data—that is, what data are important or trivial, significant or irrelevant, worth focusing on or worth ignoring.

To illustrate the concept of selective seeing, we ask you to consider how two hypothetical speakers might select different data about homeless people when presenting speeches to their city council. The first speaker argues that the city should increase its services to the homeless. The second asks the city to promote tourism more aggressively. Their differing angles of vision will cause the two speakers to select different data about homeless people and to frame these data in different ways. (Our use of the word *frame* derives metaphorically from a window frame or the frame of a camera's viewfinder. When you look through a frame, some part of your field of vision is blocked off, while the material appearing in the frame is emphasized. Through framing, a writer maximizes the reader's focus on some data, minimizes the reader's focus on other data, and otherwise guides the reader's vision and response.)

Because the first speaker wants to increase the council's sympathy for the homeless, she frames homeless people positively by telling the story of one homeless man's struggle to find shelter and nutritious food. Her speech focuses primarily on the low number of tax dollars devoted to helping the homeless. In contrast, the second speaker, using data about lost tourist income, might frame the homeless as "panhandlers" by telling the story of obnoxious, urine-soaked winos who pester shoppers for handouts. As arguers, both speakers want their audience to see the homeless from their own angles of vision. Consequently, lost tourist dollars don't show up at all in the first speaker's argument, whereas the story of a homeless man's night in the cold doesn't show up in the second speaker's argument. As this example shows, one goal writers have in selecting and framing evidence is to bring the reader's view of the subject into alignment with the writer's angle of vision. The writer selects and frames evidence to limit and control what the reader sees.

To help you better understand the concepts of selection and framing, we offer the following class discussion exercise to give you practice in a kind of controlled laboratory setting. As you do this exercise, we invite you to observe your own processes for selecting and framing evidence.

■ ■ ■ **FOR CLASS DISCUSSION** Creating an Angle of Vision by Selecting Evidence

Suppose that your city has scheduled a public hearing on a proposed ordinance to ban mosh pits at rock concerts. (See the Examining Visual Arguments feature on page 97, where we introduced this issue.) Among the possible data available to various speakers for evidence are the following:

- Some bands, such as Nine Inch Nails, specify festival seating that allows a mosh pit area.
- A female mosher writing on the Internet says: "I experience a shared energy that is like no other when I am in the pit with the crowd. It is like we are all a bunch of atoms bouncing off of each other. It's great. Hey, some people get that feeling from basketball games. I get mine from the mosh pit."

- A student conducted a survey of fifty students on her campus who had attended rock concerts in the last six months. Of the respondents, 80 percent thought that mosh pits should be allowed at concerts.
- Narrative comments on these questionnaires included the following:
  - Mosh pits are a passion for me. I get an amazing rush when crowd surfing.
  - I don't like to be in a mosh pit or do crowd surfing. But I love festival seating and like to watch the mosh pits. For me, mosh pits are part of the ambience of a concert.
  - I know a girl who was groped in a mosh pit, and she'll never do one again. But I have never had any problems.
  - Mosh pits are dangerous and stupid. I think they should be outlawed.
  - If you are afraid of mosh pits, just stay away. Nobody forces you to go into a mosh pit! It is ridiculous to ban them because they are totally voluntary. They should just post big signs saying, "City assumes no responsibility for accidents occurring in mosh pit area."
- A teenage girl suffered brain damage and memory loss at a 1998 Pearl Jam concert in Rapid City, South Dakota. According to her attorney, she hadn't intended to body surf or enter the mosh pit but "got sucked in while she was standing at its fringe."
- Twenty-four concert deaths were recorded in 2001, most of them in the area closest to the stage where people are packed in.
- A twenty-one-year-old man suffered cardiac arrest at a Metallica concert in Indiana and is now in a permanent vegetative state. Because he was jammed into the mosh pit area, nobody noticed he was in distress.
- In 2005, a blogger reported breaking his nose on an elbow; another described having his lip ring pulled out. Another blogger on the same site described having his lip nearly sliced off by the neck of a bass guitar. The injury required seventy-eight stitches. In May 2008, fifty people were treated at emergency rooms for mosh pit injuries acquired at a Bamboozle concert in New Jersey.
- According to a 2008 ABC news special, a company specializing in crowd management at rock festivals estimated "that 10,000 people have been injured in and around mosh pits in the last decade." The company said further "that the most injuries incurred from mosh pits aren't actually by the moshers but by innocent bystanders."

Tasks: Working individually or in small groups, complete the following tasks:

1. Compose two short speeches, one supporting the proposed city ordinance to ban mosh pits and one opposing it. How you use these data is up to you, but be able to explain your reasoning in the way you select and frame them. Share your speeches with classmates.
2. After you have shared examples of different speeches, explain the approaches that different classmates employed. What principle of selection was used? If arguers included evidence contrary to their positions, how did they handle it, respond to it, minimize its importance, or otherwise channel its rhetorical effect?

3. In the first task, we assigned you two different angles of vision—one supporting the ordinance and one opposing it. If you had to create your own argument on a proposal to ban mosh pits and if you set for yourself a truth-seeking goal—that is, finding the best solution for the problem of mosh pit danger, one for which you would take ethical responsibility—what would you argue? How would your argument use the list of data we provided? What else might you add?

Rhetorical Strategies for Framing Evidence

What we hope you learned from the preceding exercise is that an arguer consciously selects evidence from a wide field of data and then frames these data through rhetorical strategies that emphasize some data, minimize others, and guide the reader's response. Now that you have a basic idea of what we mean by framing of evidence, here are some strategies writers can use to guide what the reader sees and feels.

Strategies for Framing Evidence

- **Controlling the space given to supporting versus contrary evidence:** Depending on their audience and purpose, writers can devote most of their space to supporting evidence and minimal space to contrary evidence (or omit it entirely). Thus people arguing in favor of mosh pits may have used lots of evidence supporting mosh pits, including enthusiastic quotations from concert-goers, while omitting (or summarizing very rapidly) the data about the dangers of mosh pits.

- **Emphasizing a detailed story versus presenting lots of facts and statistics:** Often, writers can choose to support a point with a memorable individual case or with aggregate data such as statistics or lists of facts. A memorable story can have a strongly persuasive effect. For example, to create a negative view of mosh pits, a writer might tell the heartrending story of a teenager suffering permanent brain damage from being dropped on a mosh pit floor. In contrast, a supporter of mosh pits might tell the story of a happy music lover turned on to the concert scene by the rush of crowd surfing. A different strategy is to use facts and statistics rather than case narratives—for example, data about the frequency of mosh pit accidents, financial consequences of lawsuits, and so forth. The single-narrative case often has a more powerful rhetorical effect, but it is always open to the charge that it is an insufficient or nonrepresentative example. Vivid anecdotes make for interesting reading, but by themselves they may not be compelling logically. In contrast, aggregate data, often used in scholarly studies, can provide more compelling, logical evidence but sometimes make the prose wonkish and dense.

- **Providing contextual and interpretive comments when presenting data:** When citing data, writers can add brief contextual or interpretive comments that act as lenses over the readers' eyes to help them see the data from the writer's perspective. Suppose you want to support mosh pits, but also want to admit that mosh pits are dangerous. You could make that danger seem irrelevant or inconsequential by saying: "It is true that occasional mosh pit accidents happen, just as accidents happen in any kind of recreational activity such as swimming or weekend softball games." The concluding phrase frames the danger of mosh pits by comparing it to other recreational accidents that don't require special laws or regulations. The implied argument is this: banning mosh pits because of an occasional accident would be as silly as banning recreational swimming because of occasional accidents.

- **Putting contrary evidence in subordinate positions:** Just as a photographer can place a flower at the center of a photograph or in the background, a writer can place a piece of data in a subordinate or main clause of a sentence. Note how the structure of the following sentence minimizes emphasis on the rarity of mosh pit accidents: "Although mosh pit accidents are rare, the danger to the city of multimillion-dollar liability lawsuits means that the city should nevertheless ban them for reasons of fiscal prudence." The factual data that mosh pit accidents are rare is summarized briefly and tucked away in a subordinate *although* clause, while the writer's own position is elaborated in the main clause where it receives grammatical emphasis. A writer with a different angle of vision might say, "Although some cities may occasionally be threatened with a lawsuit, serious accidents resulting from mosh pits are so rare that cities shouldn't interfere with the desires of music fans to conduct concerts as they please."

- **Choosing labels and names that guide the reader's response to data:** One of the most subtle ways to control your readers' response to data is to choose labels and names that prompt them to see the issue as you do. If you like mosh pits, you might refer to the seating arrangements in a concert venue as "festival seating, where concertgoers have the opportunity to create a free-flowing mosh pit." If you don't like mosh pits, you might refer to the seating arrangements as "an accident-inviting use of empty space where rowdies can crowd together, slam into each other, and occasionally punch and kick." The labels you choose, along with the connotations of the words you select, urge your reader to share your angle of vision.

- **Using images (photographs, drawings) to guide the reader's response to data:** Another strategy for moving your audience toward your angle of vision is to include a photograph or drawing that portrays a contested issue from your perspective. You've already tried your hand at selecting mosh pit photographs that make arguments through their angle of vision. (See page 97.) Most people agree that the first photo supports a positive view of mosh pits. The crowd looks happy and relaxed (rather than rowdy or out of control), and the young woman lifted above the crowd smiles broadly, her body relaxed, her arms extended. In contrast, the second photo emphasizes muscular men (rather than a smiling and relaxed woman) and threatens danger rather than harmony. The crowd seems on the verge of turning ugly. (See Chapter 9 for a complete discussion of the use of visuals in argument.)

- **Revealing the value system that determines the writer's selection and framing of data:** Ultimately, how a writer selects and frames evidence is linked to the system of values that organize his or her argument. If you favor mosh pits, you probably favor maximizing the pleasure of concertgoers, promoting individual choice, and letting moshers assume the risk of their own behavior. If you want to forbid mosh pits, you probably favor minimizing risks, protecting the city from lawsuits, and protecting individuals from the danger of their own out-of-control actions. Sometimes you can foster connections with your audience by openly addressing the underlying values that you hope your audience shares with you. You can often frame your selected data by stating explicitly the values that guide your argument.

Special Strategies for Framing Statistical Evidence

Numbers and statistical data can be framed in so many ways that this category of evidence deserves its own separate treatment. By recognizing how writers frame numbers to support the story they want to tell, you will always be aware that other stories are also possible. Ethical use of numbers means that you use reputable sources for your basic data, that you don't invent or intentionally distort numbers for your own purposes, and that you don't ignore alternative points of view. Here are some of the choices writers make when framing statistical data:

- **Raw numbers versus percentages.** You can alter the rhetorical effect of a statistic by choosing between raw numbers and percentages. In the summer of 2002, many American parents panicked over what seemed like an epidemic of child abductions. If you cited the raw number of these abductions reported in the national news, this number, although small, could seem scary. But if you computed the actual percentage of American children who were abducted, that percentage was so infinitesimally small as to seem insignificant. You can apply this framing option directly to the mosh pit case. To emphasize the danger of mosh pits, you can say that twenty-four deaths occurred at rock concerts in a given year. To minimize this statistic, you could compute the percentage of deaths by dividing this number by the total number of people who attended rock concerts during the year, certainly a number in the several millions. From the perspective of percentages, the death rate at concerts is extremely low.

- **Median versus mean.** Another way to alter the rhetorical effect of numbers is to choose between the median and the mean. The mean is the average of all numbers on a list. The median is the middle number when all the numbers are arranged sequentially from high to low. In 2006 the mean annual income for retired families in the United States was $41,928—not a wealthy amount but enough to live on comfortably if you owned your own home. However, the median income was only $27,798, a figure that gives a much more striking picture of income distribution among older Americans. This median figure means that half of all retired families in the United States had annual incomes of $27,798 or less. The much higher mean income indicates that many retired Americans are quite wealthy. This wealth raises the average of all incomes (the mean) but doesn't affect the median.

- **Unadjusted versus adjusted numbers.** Suppose your boss told you that you were getting a 5 percent raise. You might be happy—unless inflation rates were running at 6 percent. Economic data can be hard to interpret across time unless the dollar amounts are adjusted for inflation. This same problem occurs in other areas. For example, comparing grade point averages of college graduates in 1970 versus 2012 means little unless one can somehow compensate for grade inflation.

■ **Base point for statistical comparisons.** In 2008, the stock market was in precipitous decline if one compared 2008 prices with 2007 prices. However, the market still seemed vigorous and healthy if one compared 2008 with 2002. One's choice of the base point for a comparison often makes a significant rhetorical difference.

■ ■ ■ **FOR CLASS DISCUSSION** Using Strategies to Frame Statistical Evidence

A proposal to build a new ballpark in Seattle, Washington, yielded a wide range of statistical arguments. All of the following statements are reasonably faithful to the same facts:

- The ballpark would be paid for by raising the sales tax from 8.2 percent to 8.3 percent during a twenty-year period.
- The sales tax increase is one-tenth of 1 percent.
- This increase represents an average of $7.50 per person per year—about the price of a movie ticket.
- This increase represents $750 per five-person family over the twenty-year period of the tax.
- For a family building a new home in the Seattle area, this tax will increase building costs by $200.
- This is a $250 million tax increase for the residents of the Seattle area.

How would you describe the costs of the proposed ballpark if you opposed the proposal? How would you describe the costs if you supported the proposal? ■ ■ ■

Gathering Evidence

We conclude this chapter with some brief advice on ways to gather evidence for your arguments. We begin with a list of brainstorming questions that may help you think of possible sources for evidence. We then provide suggestions for conducting interviews and creating surveys and questionnaires, since these powerful sources are often overlooked by students. For help in conducting library and Internet research—the most common sources of evidence in arguments—see Part Five: "The Researched Argument."

Creating a Plan for Gathering Evidence

As you begin contemplating an argument, you can use the following checklist to help you think of possible sources for evidence.

A Checklist for Brainstorming Sources of Evidence

■ What personal experiences have you had with this issue? What details from your life or the lives of your friends, acquaintances, or relatives might serve as examples or other kinds of evidence?

- What observational studies would be relevant to this issue?
- What people could you interview to provide insights or expert knowledge on this issue?
- What questions about your issue could be addressed in a survey or questionnaire?
- What useful information on this issue might encyclopedias, specialized reference books, or the regular book collection in your university library provide?
- What evidence might you seek on this issue using licensed database indexing sources for magazines, newspapers, and scholarly journals?
- How might an Internet search engine help you research this issue?
- What evidence might you find on this issue from reliable statistical resources such as U.S. Census Bureau data, the Centers for Disease Control, or *Statistical Abstract of the United States*?

Gathering Data from Interviews

Conducting interviews is a useful way not only to gather expert testimony and important data but also to learn about alternative views. To make interviews as productive as possible, we offer these suggestions.

- **Determine your purpose.** Consider why you are interviewing the person and what information he or she is uniquely able to provide.
- **Do background reading.** Find out as much as possible about the interviewee before the interview. Your knowledge of his or her background will help establish your credibility and build a bridge between you and your source. Also, equip yourself with a good foundational understanding of the issue so that you will sound informed and truly interested in the issue.
- **Formulate well-thought-out questions but also be flexible.** Write out beforehand the questions you intend to ask, making sure that every question is related to the purpose of your interview. However, be prepared to move in unexpected directions if the interview opens up new territory. Sometimes unplanned topics can end up being the most illuminating and useful.
- **Come well prepared for the interview.** As part of your professional demeanor, be sure to have all the necessary supplies (notepaper, pens, pencils, perhaps a tape recorder, if your interviewee is willing) with you.
- **Be prompt and courteous.** It is important to be punctual and respectful of your interviewee's time. In most cases, it is best to present yourself as a listener seeking clarity on an issue rather than an advocate of a particular position or an opponent. During the interview, play the believing role. Save the doubting role for later, when you are looking over your notes.
- **Take brief but clear notes.** Try to record the main ideas and be accurate with quotations. Ask for clarification of any points you don't understand.
- **Transcribe your notes soon after the interview.** Immediately after the interview, while your memory is still fresh, rewrite your notes more fully and completely.

When you use interview data in your writing, put quotation marks around any direct quotations. In most cases, you should also identify your source by name and indicate his or her title or credentials—whatever will convince the reader that this person's remarks are to be taken seriously.

Gathering Data from Surveys or Questionnaires

A well-constructed survey or questionnaire can provide lively, current data that give your audience a sense of the popularity and importance of your views. To be effective and responsible, however, a survey or questionnaire needs to be carefully prepared and administered, as we suggest in the following guidelines.

- **Include both closed-response questions and open-response questions.** To gain useful information and avoid charges of bias, you will want to include a range of questions. Closed-response questions ask participants to check a box or number on a scale and yield quantitative data that you can report statistically, perhaps in tables or graphs. Open-response questions elicit varied responses and often short narratives in which participants offer their own input. These may contribute new insights to your perspective on the issue.
- **Make your survey or questionnaire clear and easy to complete.** Consider the number, order, wording, and layout of the questions in your questionnaire. Your questions should be clear and easy to answer. The neatness and overall formal appearance of the questionnaire will also invite serious responses from your participants.
- **Explain the purpose of the questionnaire.** Respondents are usually more willing to participate if they know how the information gained from the questionnaire will benefit others. Therefore, it is a good idea to state at the beginning of the questionnaire how it will be used.
- **Seek a random sample of respondents in your distribution of the questionnaire.** Think out where and how you will distribute and collect your questionnaire to ensure a random sampling of respondents. For example, if a questionnaire about the university library went only to dorm residents, then you wouldn't learn how commuting students felt.
- **Convert questionnaires into usable data by tallying and summarizing responses.** Tallying the results and formulating summary statements of the information you gathered will yield material that might be used as evidence.

Conclusion

Effective use of evidence is an essential skill for arguers. In this chapter we introduced you to the STAR criteria and other strategies for making your data persuasive. We showed you various kinds of evidence and then examined how a writer's angle of vision influences the selection and framing of evidence. We also described framing strategies for emphasizing evidence, de-emphasizing it, and guiding your reader's response to it. Finally, we concluded with advice on how to gather evidence, including the use of interviews, surveys, and questionnaires.

WRITING ASSIGNMENT A Microtheme or a Supporting-Reasons Argument

Option 1: A Microtheme Write a one- or two-paragraph argument in which you support one of the following enthymemes, using evidence from personal experience, field observation, interviews, or data from a brief questionnaire or survey. Most of your microtheme should support the stated reason with evidence. However, also include a brief passage supporting the implied warrant. The opening sentence of your microtheme should be the enthymeme itself, which serves as the thesis statement for your argument. (Note: If you disagree with the enthymeme's argument, recast the claim or the reason to assert what you want to argue.)

1. Reading fashion magazines can be detrimental to teenage girls because such magazines can produce an unhealthy focus on beauty.
2. Surfing the Web might harm your studying because it causes you to waste time.
3. Service-learning courses are valuable because they allow you to test course concepts within real-world contexts.
4. Summer internships in your field of interest, even without pay, are the best use of your summer time because they speed up your education and training for a career.
5. Any enthymeme (a claim with a *because* clause) of your choice that can be supported without library or Internet research. (The goal of this microtheme is to give you practice using data from personal experience or from brief field research.) You may want to have your instructor approve your enthymeme in advance.

Option 2: A Supporting-Reasons Argument Write an argument that uses at least two reasons to support your claim. Your argument should include all the features of a classical argument except the section on summarizing and responding to opposing views, which we will cover in Chapter 7. This assignment builds on the brief writing assignments in Chapter 3 (create a thesis statement for an argument) and Chapter 4 (brainstorm support for one of your enthymemes using the Toulmin schema). We now ask you to expand your argument frame into a complete essay.

A *supporting-reasons argument* is our term for a classical argument without a section that summarizes and responds to opposing views. Even though alternative views aren't dealt with in detail, the writer usually summarizes an opposing view briefly in the introduction to provide background on the issue being addressed. Follow the explanations and organization chart for a classical argument as shown on page 61, but omit the section called "summary and critique of opposing views."

Like a complete classical argument, a supporting-reasons argument has a thesis-governed structure in which you state your claim at the end of the introduction, begin body paragraphs with clearly stated reasons, and use effective transitions throughout to keep your reader on track. In developing your own argument, place your most important, persuasive, or interesting reason last, where it will have the greatest impact on your readers. This kind of tightly organized structure is sometimes called a *self-announcing* or *closed-form* structure because the writer states his or her claim before beginning the body of the argument and forecasts the structure that is to follow. In contrast, an *unfolding* or *open-form* structure doesn't give away the writer's position until late in the essay. (We discuss delayed-thesis arguments in Chapter 7.)

In writing a self-announcing argument, students often ask how much of the argument to summarize in the thesis statement. Consider your options:

- You might announce only your claim:

   The public should not support the commercial use of captured dolphins.

- You might forecast a series of parallel reasons:

   There are several reasons why the public should not support the commercial use of captured dolphins.

- You might forecast the actual number of reasons:

   This paper presents four reasons why the public should not support the commercial use of captured dolphins.

- Or you might forecast the whole argument by including your *because* clauses with your claim:

   The public should not support the commercial use of captured dolphins because marine parks and "swim with dolphins" programs place direct stress on dolphins by separating them from their natural habitat and social groups; because they spread inaccurate and incomplete educational information about dolphins; because they create a commercial market for dolphins that directly or indirectly encourages dolphin hunts and captures; and because they promote an attitude of human dominance over animals.

This last thesis statement forecasts not only the claim, but also the supporting reasons that will serve as topic sentences for key paragraphs throughout the body of the paper.

No formula can tell you precisely how much of your argument to forecast in the introduction. However, these suggestions can guide you. In writing a self-announcing argument, forecast only what is needed for clarity. In short arguments, readers often need only your claim. In longer arguments, however, or in especially complex ones, readers appreciate your forecasting the complete structure of the argument (claim with reasons). ■

Reading

What follows is Carmen Tieu's supporting-reasons argument. Carmen's earlier explorations for this assignment are shown at the end of Chapters 3 and 4 (page 73 and page 89).

Why Violent Video Games Are Good for Girls

CARMEN TIEU (STUDENT)

It is ten o'clock P.M., game time. My entire family knows by now that when I am home on Saturday nights, ten P.M. is my gaming night when I play my favorite first-person-shooter games, usually *Halo 3,* on Xbox Live. Seated in my mobile chair in front of my family's 42-inch flat screen HDTV, I log onto Xbox Live. A small message in the bottom of the screen appears with the words "Kr1pL3r is online," alerting me that one of my male friends is online and already playing. As the game loads, I send Kr1pL3r a game invite, and he joins me in the pre-game room lobby.

In the game room lobby, all the players who will be participating in the match are chatting aggressively with each other: "Oh man, we're gonna own you guys so bad." When a member of the opposing team notices my gamer tag, "embracingapathy," he begins to insult me by calling me various degrading, gay-associated names: "Embracing apa-what? Man, it sounds so emo. Are you some fag? I bet you want me so bad. You're gonna get owned!" Players always assume from my gamer tag that I am a gay male, never a female. The possibility that I am a girl is the last thing on their minds. Of course, they are right that girls seldom play first-person-shooter games. Girls are socialized into activities that promote togetherness and talk, not high intensity competition involving fantasized shooting and killing. The violent nature of the games tends to repulse girls. Opponents of violent video games typically hold that these games are so graphically violent that they will influence players to become amoral and sadistic. Feminists also argue that violent video games often objectify women by portraying them as sexualized toys for men's gratification. Although I understand these objections, I argue that playing first-person-shooter games can actually be good for girls.

First, playing FPS games is surprisingly empowering because it gives girls the chance to beat guys at their own game. When I first began playing *Halo 2,* I was horrible. My male friends constantly put me down for my lack of skills, constantly telling me that I was awful, "but for a girl, you're good." But it didn't take much practice until I learned to operate the two joy sticks with precision and with quick instinctual reactions. While guys and girls can play many physical games together, such as basketball or touch football, guys will always have the advantage because on average they are taller, faster, and stronger than females. However, when it comes to video games, girls can compete equally because physical strength isn't required, just quick reaction time and manual dexterity—skills that women possess in abundance. The adrenaline rush that I receive from beating a bunch of testosterone-driven guys at something they supposedly excel at is exciting; I especially savor the look of horror on their faces when I completely destroy them.

Since female video gamers are so rare, playing shooter games allows girls to be freed from feminine stereotypes and increases their confidence. Culture generally portrays females as caring, nonviolent, and motherly beings who are not supposed to enjoy FPS games with their war themes and violent killings. I am in no way rejecting these traditional female values since I myself am a compassionate, tree-hugging vegan. But I also like to break these stereotypes. Playing video games offers a great way for females to break the social mold of only doing "girly" things and introduces them to something that males commonly enjoy. Playing video games with sexist males has also helped me become more outspoken. Psychologically, I can stand up to aggressive males because I know that I can beat them at their own game. The confidence I've gotten from excelling at shooter games may have even carried over into the academic arena because I am majoring in chemical engineering and have no fear whatsoever of intruding into the male-dominated territory of math and science. Knowing that I can beat all the guys in my engineering classes at *Halo* gives me that little extra confidence boost during exams and labs.

5   Another reason for girls to play FPS games is that it gives us a different way of bonding with guys. Once when I was discussing my latest *Halo 3* matches with one of my regular male friends, a guy whom I didn't know turned around and said, "You play *Halo*? Wow, you just earned my respect." Although I was annoyed that this guy apparently didn't respect women in general, it is apparent that guys will talk to me differently now that I can play video games. From a guy's perspective I can also appreciate why males find video games so addicting. You get joy from perfecting your skills so that your high-angle grenade kills become a thing of beauty. While all of these skills may seem trivial to some, the acknowledgment of my skills from other players leaves me with a perverse sense of pride in knowing that I played the game better than everyone else. Since I have started playing, I have also noticed that it is much easier to talk to males about lots of different subjects. Talking video games with guys is a great ice-breaker that leads to different kinds of friendships outside the realm of romance and dating.

Finally, playing violent video games can be valuable for girls because it gives them insights into a disturbing part of male subculture. When the testosterone starts kicking in, guys become blatantly homophobic and misogynistic. Any player, regardless of gender, who cannot play well (as measured by having a high number of kills and a low number of deaths) is made fun of by being called gay, a girl, or worse. Even when some guys finally meet a female player, they will also insult her by calling her a lesbian or an ugly fat chick that has no life. Their insults towards the girl will dramatically increase if she beats them because they feel so humiliated. In their eyes, playing worse than a girl is embarrassing because girls are supposed to be inept at FPS games. Whenever I play *Halo* better than my male friends, they often comment on how "it makes no sense that we're getting owned by Carmen."

When males act like such sexist jerks it causes one to question if they are always like this. My answer is no because I know, first hand, that when guys like that are having one-on-one conversations with a female, they show a softer side, and the macho side goes away. They don't talk about how girls should stay in the kitchen and make them dinner, but rather how they think it is cool that they share a fun, common interest with a girl. But when they are in a group of males their fake, offensive macho side comes out. I find this phenomenon troubling because it shows a real problem in the way boys are socialized. To be a real "man" around other guys, they have to put down women and gays in activities involving aggressive behavior where men are supposed to excel. But they don't become macho and aggressive in activities like reading and writing, which they think of as feminine. I've always known that guys are more physically aggressive than women, but until playing violent video games I had never realized how this aggression is related to misogyny and homophobia. Perhaps these traits aren't deeply ingrained in men but come out primarily in a competitive male environment. Whatever the cause, it is an ugly phenomenon, and I'm glad that I learned more about it. Beating guys at FPS games has made me a more confident woman while being more aware of gender differences in the way men and women are socialized. I joined the guys in playing *Halo,* but I didn't join their subculture of ridiculing women and gays.

For additional writing, reading, and research resources, go to www.mycomplab.com

Moving Your Audience
Ethos, Pathos, and Kairos

6

In Chapters 4 and 5 we focused on *logos*—the logical structure of reasons and evidence in argument. Even though we have treated *logos* in its own chapters, an effective arguer's concern for *logos* is always connected to *ethos* and *pathos* (see the rhetorical triangle introduced in Chapter 3, page 63). By seeking audience-based reasons—so that an arguer connects her message to the assumptions, values, and beliefs of her audience—she appeals also to *ethos* and *pathos* by enhancing the reader's trust and by triggering the reader's sympathies and imagination.

In this chapter, you will learn to:

- Use the persuasive appeals of *ethos*, *pathos*, and *kairos* to move your audience
- Improve the effectiveness of your arguments through deeper understanding of audience-based reasons

Ethos and *Pathos* as Persuasive Appeals: An Overview

At first, one may be tempted to think of *logos, ethos,* and *pathos* as "ingredients" in an essay, like spices you add to a casserole. But a more appropriate metaphor might be that of different lamps and filters used on theater spotlights to vary lighting effects on a stage. Thus if you switch on a *pathos* lamp (possibly through using more concrete language or vivid examples), the resulting image will engage the audience's sympathy and emotions more deeply. If you overlay an *ethos* filter (perhaps by adopting a different tone toward your audience), the projected image of the writer as a person will be subtly altered. If you switch on a *logos* lamp (by adding, say, more data for evidence), you will draw the reader's attention to the logical appeal of the argument. Depending on how you modulate the lamps and filters, you shape and color your readers' perception of you and your argument.

Our metaphor is imperfect, of course, but our point is that *logos, ethos,* and *pathos* work together to create an impact on the reader. Consider, for example, the different impacts of the following arguments, all having roughly the same logical appeal.

1. People should adopt a vegetarian diet because doing so will help prevent the cruelty to animals caused by factory farming.
2. If you are planning to eat chicken tonight, please consider how much that chicken suffered so that you could have a tender and juicy meal.

Commercial growers cram the chickens so tightly together into cages that they never walk on their own legs, see sunshine, or flap their wings. In fact, their beaks must be cut off to keep them from pecking each other's eyes out. One way to prevent such suffering is for more and more people to become vegetarians.

3. People who eat meat are no better than sadists who torture other sentient creatures to enhance their own pleasure. Unless you enjoy sadistic tyranny over others, you have only one choice: become a vegetarian.

4. People committed to justice might consider the extent to which our love of eating meat requires the agony of animals. A visit to a modern chicken factory—where chickens live their entire lives in tiny, darkened coops without room to spread their wings—might raise doubts about our right to inflict such suffering on sentient creatures. Indeed, such a visit might persuade us that vegetarianism is a more just alternative.

Each argument has roughly the same logical core:

ENTHYMEME

CLAIM People should adopt a vegetarian diet

REASON because doing so will help prevent the cruelty to animals caused by factory farming.

GROUNDS

• Evidence of suffering in commercial chicken farms, where chickens are crammed together and lash out at one another

• Evidence that only widespread adoption of vegetarianism will end factory farming

WARRANT

If we have an alternative to making animals suffer, we should use it.

But the impact of each argument varies. The difference between arguments 1 and 2, most of our students report, is the greater emotional power of argument 2. Whereas argument 1 refers only to the abstraction "cruelty to animals," argument 2 paints a vivid picture of chickens with their beaks cut off to prevent their pecking each other blind. Argument 2 makes a stronger appeal to *pathos* (not necessarily a stronger argument), stirring feelings by appealing simultaneously to the heart and to the head.

The difference between arguments 1 and 3 concerns both *ethos* and *pathos*. Argument 3 appeals to the emotions through highly charged words such as *torture, sadists,* and *tyranny*. But argument 3 also draws attention to its writer, and most of our students report not liking that writer very much. His stance is self-righteous and insulting. In contrast, argument 4's author establishes a more positive *ethos*. He establishes rapport by assuming his audience is committed to justice and by qualifying his argument with the conditional term *might.* He also invites sympathy for the chickens' plight—an appeal to *pathos*—by offering a specific description of chickens crammed into tiny coops.

Which of these arguments is best? They all have appropriate uses. Arguments 1 and 4 seem aimed at receptive audiences reasonably open to exploration of the issue, whereas arguments 2 and 3 seem designed to shock complacent audiences or to rally a group of True Believers. Even argument 3, which is too abusive to be effective in most instances, might work as a rallying speech at a convention of animal liberation activists.

Our point thus far is that *logos, ethos,* and *pathos* are different aspects of the same whole, different lenses for intensifying or softening the light beam you project onto the screen. Every choice you make as a writer affects in some way each of the three appeals. The rest of this chapter examines these choices in more detail.

How to Create an Effective *Ethos:* The Appeal to Credibility

The ancient Greek and Roman rhetoricians recognized that an argument would be more persuasive if the audience trusted the speaker. Aristotle argued that such trust resides within the speech itself, not in the prior reputation of the speaker. In the speaker's manner and delivery, tone, word choice, and arrangement of reasons, in the sympathy with which he or she treats alternative views, the speaker creates a trustworthy persona. Aristotle called the impact of the speaker's credibility the appeal from *ethos.* How does a writer create credibility? We suggest four ways:

- **Be knowledgeable about your issue.** The first way to gain credibility is to *be* credible—that is, to argue from a strong base of knowledge, to have at hand the examples, personal experiences, statistics, and other empirical data needed to make a sound case. If you have done your homework, you will command the attention of most audiences.
- **Be fair.** Besides being knowledgeable about your issue, you need to demonstrate fairness and courtesy to alternative views. Because true argument can occur only where people may reasonably disagree with one another, your *ethos* will be strengthened if you demonstrate that you understand and empathize with other points of view. There are times, of course, when you may appropriately scorn an opposing view. But these times are rare, and they mostly occur when you address audiences predisposed to your view. Demonstrating empathy to alternative views is generally the best strategy.
- **Build a bridge to your audience.** A third means of establishing credibility—building a bridge to your audience—has been treated at length in our earlier discussions of audience-based reasons. By grounding your argument in shared values and assumptions, you demonstrate your goodwill and enhance your image as a trustworthy person respectful of your audience's views. We mention audience-based reasons here to show how this aspect of *logos*—finding the reasons that are most rooted in the audience's values—also affects your *ethos* as a person respectful of your readers' views.

■ **Demonstrate professionalism.** Finally, you can enhance your *ethos* by the professionalism revealed in your manuscript itself: Appropriate style, careful editing and proofreading, accurate documentation, and adherence to the genre conventions expected by your audience all contribute to the image of the person behind the writing. If your manuscript is sloppy, marred by spelling or grammatical errors, or inattentive to the tone and style of the expected genre, your own credibility will be damaged.

How to Create *Pathos:* The Appeal to Beliefs and Emotions

Before the federal government outlawed unsolicited telephone marketing, newspapers published flurries of articles complaining about annoying telemarketers. Within this context, a United Parcel Service worker, Bobbi Buchanan, wanted to create sympathy for telemarketers. She wrote a *New York Times* op-ed piece entitled "Don't Hang Up, That's My Mom Calling," which begins as follows:

> The next time an annoying sales call interrupts your dinner, think of my 71-year-old mother, LaVerne, who works as a part-time telemarketer to supplement her social security income. To those Americans who have signed up for the new national do-not-call list, my mother is a pest, a nuisance, an invader of privacy. To others, she's just another anonymous voice on the other end of the line. But to those who know her, she's someone struggling to make a buck, to feed herself and pay her utilities—someone who personifies the great American way.

The editorial continues with a heartwarming description of LaVerne. Buchanan's rhetorical aim is to transform the reader's anonymous, depersonalized image of telemarketers into the concrete image of her mother: a "hardworking, first generation American; the daughter of a Pittsburgh steelworker; survivor of the Great Depression; the widow of a World War II veteran; a mother of seven, grandmother of eight, great-grandmother of three...." The intended effect is to alter our view of telemarketers through the positive emotions triggered by our identification with LaVerne.

By urging readers to think of "my mother, LaVerne" instead of an anonymous telemarketer, Buchanan illustrates the power of *pathos,* an appeal to the reader's emotions. Arguers create pathetic appeals whenever they connect their claims to readers' values, thus triggering positive or negative emotions depending on whether these values are affirmed or transgressed. Pro-life proponents appeal to *pathos* when they graphically describe the dismemberment of a fetus during an abortion. Proponents of improved women's health and status in Africa do so when they describe the helplessness of wives forced to have unprotected sex with husbands likely infected with HIV. Opponents of oil exploration in the Arctic National Wildlife Refuge (ANWR) do so when they lovingly describe the calving grounds of caribou.

Are such appeals legitimate? Our answer is yes, if they intensify and deepen our response to an issue rather than divert our attention from it. Because understanding is a matter of feeling as well as perceiving, *pathos* can give access to nonlogical, but not necessarily nonrational, ways of knowing. *Pathos* helps us see what is deeply at stake in an issue, what matters to the whole person. Appeals to *pathos* help readers walk in the writer's shoes. That is why arguments are often improved through the use of stories that make issues come alive or sensory details that allow us to see, feel, and taste the reality of a problem.

Appeals to *pathos* become illegitimate, we believe, when they confuse an issue rather than clarify it. Consider the case of a student who argues that Professor Jones ought to raise his grade from a D to a C, lest he lose his scholarship and be forced to leave college, shattering the dreams of his dear old grandmother. To the extent that students' grades should be based on performance or effort, the student's image of the dear old grandmother is an illegitimate appeal to *pathos* because it diverts the reader from rational to irrational criteria. The weeping grandmother may provide a legitimate motive for the student to study harder but not for the professor to change a grade.

Although it is difficult to classify all the ways that writers can create appeals from *pathos,* we will focus on four strategies: concrete language; specific examples and illustrations; narratives; and connotations of words, metaphors, and analogies. Each of these strategies lends "presence" to an argument by creating immediacy and emotional impact.

Use Concrete Language

Concrete language—one of the chief ways that writers achieve voice—can increase the liveliness, interest level, and personality of a writer's prose. When used in argument, concrete language typically heightens *pathos*. For example, consider the differences between the first and second drafts of the following student argument:

First Draft

People who prefer driving a car to taking a bus think that taking the bus will increase the stress of the daily commute. Just the opposite is true. Not being able to find a parking spot when in a hurry to be at work or school can cause a person stress. Taking the bus gives a person time to read or sleep, etc. It could be used as a mental break.

Second Draft (Concrete Language Added)

Taking the bus can be more relaxing than driving a car. Having someone else behind the wheel gives people time to chat with friends or cram for an exam. They can balance their checkbooks, do homework, doze off, read the daily newspaper, or get lost in a novel rather than foam at the mouth looking for a parking space.

In this revision, specific details enliven the prose by creating images that trigger positive feelings. Who wouldn't want some free time to doze off or to get lost in a novel?

Use Specific Examples and Illustrations

Specific examples and illustrations serve two purposes in an argument. They provide evidence that supports your reasons; simultaneously, they give your argument presence and emotional resonance. Note the flatness of the following draft arguing for the value of multicultural studies in a university core curriculum:

First Draft

Another advantage of a multicultural education is that it will help us see our own culture in a broader perspective. If all we know is our own heritage, we might not be inclined to see anything bad about this heritage because we won't know anything else. But if we study other heritages, we can see the costs and benefits of our own heritage.

Now note the increase in "presence" when the writer adds a specific example:

Second Draft (Example Added)

Another advantage of multicultural education is that it raises questions about traditional Western values. For example, owning private property (such as buying your own home) is part of the American dream. However, in studying the beliefs of American Indians, students are confronted with a very different view of private property. When the U.S. government sought to buy land in the Pacific Northwest from Chief Sealth, he is alleged to have replied:

> The president in Washington sends words that he wishes to buy our land. But how can you buy or sell the sky? The land? The idea is strange to us. If we do not own the freshness of the air and the sparkle of the water, how can you buy them?[. . .] We are part of the earth and it is part of us.[. . .] This we know: The earth does not belong to man, man belongs to the earth.

Our class was shocked by the contrast between traditional Western views of property and Chief Sealth's views. One of our best class discussions was initiated by this quotation from Chief Sealth. Had we not been exposed to a view from another culture, we would have never been led to question the "rightness" of Western values.

The writer begins his revision by evoking a traditional Western view of private property, which he then questions by shifting to Chief Sealth's vision of land as open, endless, and unobtainable as the sky. Through the use of a specific example, the writer brings to life his previously abstract point about the benefit of multicultural education.

Use Narratives

A particularly powerful way to evoke *pathos* is to tell a story that either leads into your claim or embodies it implicitly and that appeals to your readers' feelings and imagination. Brief narratives—whether true or hypothetical—are particularly effective as opening attention grabbers for an argument. To illustrate how an introductory narrative (either a story or a brief scene) can create pathetic appeals, consider the following first paragraph to an argument opposing jet skis:

> I dove off the dock into the lake, and as I approached the surface I could see the sun shining through the water. As my head popped out, I located my cousin a few feet away in a rowboat waiting to escort me as I, a twelve-year-old girl, attempted to swim across the mile-wide, pristine lake and back to our dock. I made it, and that glorious, summer day is one of my most precious memories. Today, however, no one would dare attempt that swim. Jet skis have taken over this small lake where I spent many summers with my grandparents. Dozens of whining jet skis crisscross the lake, ruining it for swimming, fishing, canoeing, rowboating,

and even waterskiing. More stringent state laws are needed to control jet skiing because it interferes with other uses of lakes and is currently very dangerous.

This narrative makes a case for a particular point of view toward jet skis by winning our identification with the writer's experience. She invites us to relive that experience with her while she also taps into our own treasured memories of summer experiences that have been destroyed by change.

Opening narratives to evoke *pathos* can be powerfully effective, but they are also risky. If they are too private, too self-indulgent, too sentimental, or even too dramatic and forceful, they can backfire on you. If you have doubts about an opening narrative, read it to a sample audience before using it in your final draft.

Use Words, Metaphors, and Analogies with Appropriate Connotations

Another way of appealing to *pathos* is to select words, metaphors, or analogies with connotations that match your aim. We have already described this strategy in our discussion of the "framing" of evidence (Chapter 5, pages 96–98). By using words with particular connotations, a writer guides readers to see the issue through the writer's angle of vision. Thus if you want to create positive feelings about a recent city council decision, you can call it "bold and decisive"; if you want to create negative feelings, you can call it "haughty and autocratic." Similarly, writers can use favorable or unfavorable metaphors and analogies to evoke different imaginative or emotional responses. A tax bill might be viewed as a "potentially fatal poison pill" or as "unpleasant but necessary economic medicine." In each of these cases, the words create an emotional as well as intellectual response.

■ ■ ■ **FOR CLASS DISCUSSION** Incorporating Appeals to *Pathos*

Outside class, rewrite the introduction to one of your previous papers (or a current draft) to include more appeals to *pathos*. Use any of the strategies for giving your argument presence: concrete language, specific examples, narratives, metaphors, analogies, and connotative words. Bring both your original and your rewritten introductions to class. In pairs or in groups, discuss the comparative effectiveness of these introductions in trying to reach your intended audience.

■ ■ ■

Using Images for Emotional Appeal

One of the most powerful ways to engage an audience emotionally is to use photos or other images. (Chapter 9 focuses exclusively on visual rhetoric—the persuasive power of images.) Although many written arguments do not lend themselves to visual illustrations, we suggest that when you construct arguments you consider the potential of visual support. Imagine that your argument were to appear in a newspaper, in a magazine, or on a Web site where space would be provided for one or two visuals. What photographs or drawings might help persuade your audience toward your perspective?

When images work well, they are analogous to the verbal strategies of concrete language, specific illustrations, narratives, and connotative words. The challenge in using visuals is to find material that is straightforward enough to be understood without elaborate explanations, that is timely and relevant, and that clearly adds impact to a specific part of your argument. As an example, suppose you are writing an argument supporting fund-raising efforts to help a third-world country that has recently experienced a natural catastrophe. To add a powerful appeal to *pathos,* you might consider incorporating into your argument the photograph shown in Figure 6.1 of the cleanup efforts in Port-au-Prince, Haiti, after the January 2010 earthquake. A photograph such as this one can evoke a strong emotional and imaginative response as well as make viewers think.

■ ■ ■ **FOR CLASS DISCUSSION** *Analyzing Images as Appeals to Pathos*
Working in small groups or as a whole class, share your responses to the following questions:

1. How would you describe the emotional/imaginative impact of Figure 6.1?
2. Many disaster-relief photos seek to convey the magnitude of the destruction and suffering, sometimes shockingly, by depicting destroyed buildings, mangled bodies, and images of human misery. How is your response to Figure 6.1 similar to or different from your response to commonly encountered close-up photographs of grief-stricken victims or to distance shots of widespread destruction? To what extent is Figure 6-1's story-with the woman carrying a basket juxtaposed against

FIGURE 6.1 Cleanup in Port-au-Prince, Haiti, after the 2010 earthquake

the enormous mechanical shovel—different from the more typical photographs of destroyed buildings or anguished faces?

Kairos: The Timeliness and Fitness of Arguments

To increase your argument's effectiveness, you need to consider not only its appeals to *logos, ethos,* and *pathos,* but also its *kairos*—that is, its timing, its appropriateness for the occasion. *Kairos* is one of those wonderful words adopted from another language (in this case, ancient Greek) that is impossible to define, yet powerful in what it represents. In Greek, *kairos* means "right time," "season," or "opportunity." It differs subtly from the ordinary Greek word for time, *chronos,* the root of our words "chronology" and "chronometer." You can measure *chronos* by looking at your watch, but you measure *kairos* by sensing the opportune time through psychological attentiveness to situation and meaning. To think *kairotically* is to be attuned to the total context of a situation in order to act in the right way at the right moment. By analogy, consider a skilled base runner who senses the right moment to steal second, a wise teacher who senses the right moment to praise or critique a student's performance, or a successful psychotherapist who senses the right moment to talk rather than listen in a counseling session. *Kairos* reminds us that a rhetorical situation is not stable and fixed, but evolves as events unfold or as audiences experience the psychological ebbs and flows of attention and care. Here are some examples that illustrate the range of insights contained by the term *kairos:*

- If you write a letter to the editor of a newspaper, you usually have a one- or two-day window before a current event becomes "old news" and is no longer interesting. An out-of-date letter will be rejected, not because it is poorly written or argued but because it misses its *kairotic* moment. (Similar instances of lost timeliness occur in class discussions: On how many occasions have you wanted to contribute an idea to class discussion, but the professor doesn't acknowledge your raised hand? When you finally are called on, the *kairotic* moment has passed.)

- Bobbi Buchanan's "Don't Hang Up, That's My Mom Calling," which we used to illustrate *pathos* (page 114), could have been written only during a brief historical period when telemarketing was being publicly debated. Moreover, it could have been written only late in that period, after numerous writers had attacked telemarketers. The piece was published in the *New York Times* because the editor received it at the right *kairotic* moment.

- A sociology major is writing a senior capstone paper for graduation. The due date for the paper is fixed, so the timing of the paper isn't at issue. But *kairos* is still relevant. It urges the student to consider what is appropriate for such a paper. What is the "right way" to produce a sociology paper at this moment in the history of the discipline? Currently, what are leading-edge versus trailing-edge questions in sociology? What theorists are now in vogue? What research methods would most impress a judging committee? How would a good capstone paper written in 2010 differ from one written a decade earlier?

As you can see from these examples, *kairos* concerns a whole range of questions connected to the timing, fitness, appropriateness, and proportions of a message within

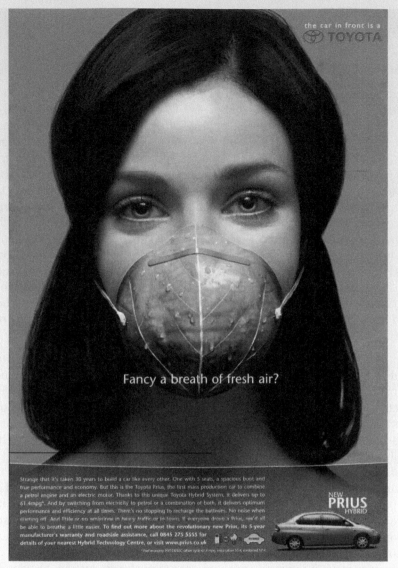

Logos, Ethos, Pathos, and *Kairos*

Increasing sales of Toyota's Prius, a hybrid car that runs on both electricity and gasoline, confirm that American consumers are willing to switch from SUVs to more energy-efficient cars. As this advertisement for the Prius shows, energy-efficient cars are connected to a constellation of issues, including the need to decrease carbon emissions because of pollution-caused health problems and environmental concern for cleaner energy.

How does this ad attempt to move its audience? Analyze the ad's visual and verbal appeals to *logos, ethos, pathos,* and *kairos.*

an evolving rhetorical context. There are no rules to help you determine the *kairotic* moment for your argument, but being attuned to *kairos* will help you "read" your audience and rhetorical situation in a dynamic way.

■ ■ ■ **FOR CLASS DISCUSSION** Analyzing an Argument from the Perspectives
of *Kairos, Logos, Ethos,* and *Pathos*

Your instructor will select an argument for analysis. Working in small groups or as a whole class, analyze the assigned argument first from the perspective of *kairos* and then from the perspectives of *logos, ethos,* and *pathos.*

1. As you analyze the argument from the perspective of *kairos,* consider the following questions:
   a. What is the motivating occasion for this argument? That is, what causes this writer to put pen to paper or fingers to keyboard?
   b. What conversation is the writer joining? Who are the other voices in this conversation? What are these voices saying that compels the writer to add his or her own voice? How was the stage set to create the *kairotic* moment for this argument?
   c. Who is the writer's intended audience and why?
   d. What is the writer's purpose? Toward what view or action is the writer trying to persuade his or her audience?
   e. To what extent can various features of the argument be explained by your understanding of its *kairotic* moment?
2. Now analyze the same argument for its appeals to *logos, ethos,* and *pathos.* How successful is this argument in achieving its writer's purpose?

■ ■ ■

How Audience-Based Reasons Enhance
Logos, Ethos, and *Pathos*

We conclude this chapter by returning to the concept of audience-based reasons that we introduced in Chapter 4. Audience-based reasons enhance *logos* because they are built on underlying assumptions (warrants) that the audience is likely to accept. But they also enhance *ethos* and *pathos* by helping the writer identify with the audience, entering into their beliefs and values. To consider the needs of your audience, you can ask yourself the following questions:

Questions for Analyzing Your Audience

What to Ask	Why to Ask It
1. *Who is your audience?*	Your answer will help you think about audience-based reasons.
	■ Are you writing to a single person, a committee, or the general readership of a newspaper, magazine, blog site, and so forth?

(Continued)

What to Ask	Why to Ask It
	■ Are your readers academics, professionals, fellow students, general citizens, or people with specialized background and interests? ■ Can you expect your audience to be politically and culturally liberal, middle of the road, conservative, or all over the map? What about their religious views? ■ How do you picture your audience in terms of social class, ethnicity, gender, sexual orientation, age, and cultural identity? ■ To what extent does your audience share your own interests and cultural position? Are you writing to insiders or outsiders with regard to your own values and beliefs?
2. *How much does your audience know or care about your issue?*	Your answer can especially affect your introduction and conclusion: ■ Do your readers need background on your issue or are they already in the conversation? ■ If you are writing to specific decision makers, are they currently aware of the problem you are addressing? If not, how can you get their attention? ■ Does your audience care about your issue? If not, how can you get them to care?
3. *What is your audience's current attitude toward your issue?*	Your answer will help you decide the structure and tone of your argument. ■ Are your readers already supportive of your position? Undecided? Skeptical? Strongly opposed? ■ What other points of view besides your own will your audience be weighing?
4. *What will be your audience's likely objections to your argument?*	Your answer will help determine the content of your argument and will alert you to extra research you may need. ■ What weaknesses will audience members find? ■ What aspects of your position will be most threatening to them and why? ■ How are your basic assumptions, values, or beliefs different from your audience's?
5. *What values, beliefs, or assumptions about the world do you and your audience share?*	Your answer will help you find common ground with your audience. ■ Despite different points of view on this issue, where can you find common links with your audience? ■ How might you use these links to build bridges to your audience?

To see how a concern for audience-based reasons can enhance *ethos* and *pathos,* suppose that you support racial profiling (rather than random selection) for determining who receives intensive screening at airports. Suppose further that you are writing a guest op-ed column for a liberal campus newspaper and imagine readers repulsed by the notion of racial profiling (as indeed you are repulsed too in most cases). It's important from the start that you understand and acknowledge the interests of those opposed to your position. The persons most likely targeted by racial profiling would be Middle Eastern males as well as black males with African passports, particularly those from African nations with large Islamic populations. These persons will be directly offended by racial profiling at airports. From the perspective of social justice, they can rightfully object to the racial stereotyping that lumps all people of Arabic, Semitic, or African appearance into the category "potential terrorists." Similarly, African Americans and Hispanics, who frequently experience racial profiling by police in U.S. cities, may object to further extension of this hated practice. Also, most political liberals, as well as many moderates and conservatives, may object to the racism inherent in selecting people for airport screening on the basis of ethnicity or country of origin.

What shared values might you use to build bridges to those opposed to racial profiling at airports? You need to develop a strategy to reduce your audience's fears and to link your reasons to their values. Your thinking might go something like this:

Problem: How can I create an argument rooted in shared values? How can I reduce fear that racial profiling in this situation endorses racism or will lead to further erosion of civil liberties?

Bridge-building goals: I must try to show that my argument's goal is to increase airline safety by preventing terrorism like that of 9/11/01. My argument must show my respect for Islam and for Arabic and Semitic peoples. I must also show my rejection of racial profiling as normal police practice.

Possible strategies:
- Stress the shared value of protecting innocent people from terrorism.
- Show how racial profiling significantly increases the efficiency of secondary searches. (If searches are performed at random, then we waste time and resources searching people who are statistically unlikely to be terrorists.)
- Argue that airport screeners must also use indicators other than race to select people for searches (for example, traits that might indicate a domestic terrorist).
- Show my respect for Islam.
- Show sympathy for people selected for searching via racial profiling and acknowledge that this practice would normally be despicable except for the extreme importance of airline security, which overrides personal liberties in this case.
- Show my rejection of racial profiling in situations other than airport screening— for example, stopping African Americans for traffic violations more often than whites and then searching their cars for drugs or stolen goods.
- Perhaps show my support of affirmative action, which is a kind of racial profiling in reverse.

These thinking notes allow you to develop the following plan for your argument.

- Airport screeners should use racial profiling rather than random selection to determine which people undergo intensive screening
  - because doing so will make more efficient use of airport screeners' time, increase the odds of finding terrorists, and thus lead to greater airline safety (*WARRANT: Increased airline safety is good;* or, at a deeper level, *The positive consequences of increasing airline safety through racial profiling outweigh the negative consequences.*)
  - because racial profiling in this specific case does not mean allowing it in everyday police activities nor does it imply disrespect for Islam or for Middle Eastern or African males (WARRANT: *Racial profiling is unacceptable in everyday police practices. It is wrong to show disrespect for Islam or Middle Eastern or African males.*)

As this plan shows, your strategy is to seek reasons whose warrants your audience will accept. First, you will argue that racial profiling will lead to greater airline safety, allowing you to stress that safe airlines benefit all passengers. Your concern is the lives of hundreds of passengers as well as others who might be killed in a terrorist attack. Second, you plan to reduce adversaries' resistance to your proposal by showing that the consequences aren't as severe as they might fear. Using racial profiling in airports would not justify using it in urban police work (a practice you find despicable) and it would not imply disrespect for Islam or Middle Eastern or African males. As this example shows, your focus on audience—on the search for audience-based reasons—shapes the actual invention of your argument from the start.

■ ■ ■ **FOR CLASS DISCUSSION** Planning an Audience-Based Argumentative Strategy

1. How does the preceding plan for an argument supporting racial profiling make appeals to *ethos* and *pathos* as well as to *logos*?
2. Working individually or in small groups, plan an audience-based argumentative strategy for one or more of the following cases. Follow the thinking process used by the writer of the racial-profiling argument: (1) state several problems that the writer must solve to reach the audience, and (2) develop possible solutions to those problems.

   a. An argument for the right of software companies to continue making and selling violent video games: aim the argument at parents who oppose their children's playing these games.

   b. An argument to reverse grade inflation by limiting the number of As and Bs a professor can give in a course: aim the argument at students who fear getting lower grades.

   c. An argument supporting the legalization of cocaine: aim the argument at readers of *Reader's Digest,* a conservative magazine that supports the current war on drugs.

■ ■ ■

Conclusion

In this chapter, we have explored ways that writers can strengthen the persuasiveness of their arguments by creating appeals to *ethos* and *pathos,* by being attentive to *kairos,* and by building bridges to their readers through audience-based reasons.

Arguments are more persuasive if readers trust the credibility of the writer and if the argument appeals to readers' hearts and imaginations as well as to their intellects. Sometimes images such as drawings or photographs may reinforce the argument by evoking strong emotional responses, thus enhancing *pathos*. Additionally, attentiveness to *kairos* keeps the writer attuned to the dynamics of a rhetorical situation in order to create the right message at the right time. Finally, all these appeals come together when the writer explicitly focuses on finding audience-based reasons.

WRITING ASSIGNMENT Revising a Draft for *Ethos, Pathos,* and Audience-Based Reasons

Part 1: Choose an argument that you have previously written or that you are currently drafting. Revise the argument with explicit focus on increasing its appeals to *ethos, pathos,* and *logos* via audience-based reasons and other strategies. Consider especially how you might improve *ethos* by building bridges to the audience or improve *pathos* through concrete language, specific examples, metaphors, or connotations of words. Finally, consider the extent to which your reasons are audience-based.

Or

Multimodal option: Imagine an argument that you have previously written or are currently drafting that could be enhanced with effective photographs or images. Revise your argument to include these images, perhaps creating a desktop published document that wraps text around visuals chosen to enhance *pathos*. Other multimodal possibilities include transforming your argument into a speech supported by PowerPoint images (see Chapter 14, pages 343–345), into a poster argument (see Chapter 9, page 203 and Chapter 14, page 326), or even into a podcast that includes music.

Part 2: Attach to your revision or transformed project a reflective letter explaining the choices you made in revising your original argument or in transforming it using a multimodal approach. Describe for your instructor the changes or transformations you made and explain how or why your new version enhances your argument's effectiveness at moving its audience. ■

For additional writing, reading, and research resources, go to www.mycomplab.com

7 Responding to Objections and Alternative Views

In the previous chapter we discussed strategies for moving your audience through appeals to *ethos, pathos,* and *kairos.* In this chapter we examine strategies for addressing opposing or alternative views—whether to omit them, refute them, concede to them, or incorporate them through compromise and conciliation. In this chapter, you will learn to:

- Make choices about an argument's structure, content, and tone depending on whether your audience is sympathetic, neutral, or resistant to your views
- Use argument as a collaborative, problem-solving communication to open up new channels of understanding between you and your audience

One-Sided, Multisided, and Dialogic Arguments

Arguments are said to be one-sided, multisided, or dialogic:

- *A one-sided argument* presents only the writer's position on the issue without summarizing and responding to alternative viewpoints.
- *A multisided argument* presents the writer's position, but also summarizes and responds to possible objections and alternative views.
- *A dialogic argument* has a much stronger component of inquiry in which the writer presents himself as uncertain or searching, the audience is considered a partner in the dialogue, and the writer's purpose is to seek common ground, perhaps leading to a consensual solution to a problem. (See our discussion in Chapter 1 of argument as truth seeking versus persuasion, pages 14–16.)

One-sided and *multisided* arguments often take an adversarial stance in that the writer regards alternative views as flawed or wrong and supports his own claim with a strongly persuasive intent. Although multisided arguments can be adversarial, they can also be made to feel *dialogic*, depending on the way the writer introduces and responds to alternative views.

At issue, then, is the writer's treatment of alternative views. Does the writer omit them (a one-sided argument), summarize them in order to rebut them (an adversarial kind of multisided argument), or summarize them in order to acknowledge their validity, value, and force (a more dialogic kind of multisided argument)? Each of these approaches can be appropriate for certain occasions, depending on your purpose, your confidence in your own stance, and your audience's resistance to your views.

How can one determine the kind of argument that would be most effective in a given case? As a general rule, one-sided arguments occur commonly when an issue is not highly contested. If the issue is highly contested, then one-sided arguments tend to strengthen the convictions of those who are already in the writer's camp, but alienate those who aren't. In contrast, for those initially opposed to a writer's claim, a multisided argument shows that the writer has considered other views, and thus reduces some initial hostility. An especially interesting effect can occur with neutral or undecided audiences. In the short run, one-sided arguments are often persuasive to a neutral audience, but in the long run, multisided arguments have more staying power. Neutral audiences who have heard only one side of an issue tend to change their minds when they hear alternative arguments. By anticipating and rebutting opposing views, a multisided argument diminishes the surprise and force of subsequent counterarguments. If we move from neutral to highly resistant audiences, adversarial approaches—even multisided ones—are seldom effective because they increase hostility and harden the differences between writer and reader. In such cases, more dialogic approaches have the best chance of establishing common ground for inquiry and consensus.

In the rest of this chapter we will show you how your choice of writing one-sided, multisided, or dialogic arguments is a function of how you perceive your audience's resistance to your views as well as your level of confidence in your own views.

Determining Your Audience's Resistance to Your Views

When you write an argument, you must always consider your audience's point of view. One way to imagine your relationship to your audience is to place it on a scale of resistance ranging from strong support of your position to strong opposition (see Figure 7.1). At the "Accord" end of this scale are like-minded people who basically agree with your position on the issue. At the "Resistance" end are those who strongly disagree with you, perhaps unconditionally, because their values, beliefs, or assumptions sharply differ from your own. Between "Accord" and "Resistance" lies a range of opinions. Close to your position will be those leaning in your direction but with less conviction than you have. Close to the resistance position will be those basically opposed to your view but willing to listen to your argument and perhaps willing to

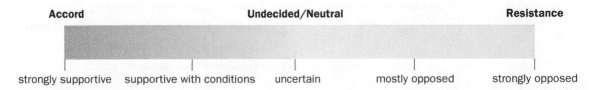

FIGURE 7.1 Scale of resistance

acknowledge some of its strengths. In the middle are those undecided people who are still sorting out their feelings, seeking additional information, and weighing the strengths and weaknesses of alternative views.

Seldom, however, will you encounter an issue in which the range of disagreement follows a simple line from accord to resistance. Often resistant views fall into different categories so that no single line of argument appeals to all those whose views are different from your own. You thus have to identify not only your audience's resistance to your ideas but also the causes of that resistance.

Consider, for example, the issues surrounding publicly financed sports stadiums. In one city, a ballot initiative asked citizens to agree to an increase in sales taxes to build a new retractable-roof stadium for its baseball team. Supporters of the initiative faced a complex array of resisting views (see Figure 7.2). Opponents of the initiative could be placed into four categories. Some simply had no interest in sports, cared nothing about baseball, and saw no benefit in building a huge, publicly financed sports facility. Another group loved baseball and followed the home team passionately, but was philosophically opposed to subsidizing rich players and owners with taxpayer money. This group argued that the whole sports industry needed to be restructured so that stadiums were paid for out of sports revenues. Still another group was opposed to tax hikes in general. It focused on the principle of reducing the size of government and of using tax revenues only for essential services. Finally, another powerful group supported baseball and supported the notion of public funding of a new stadium but opposed the kind of retractable-roof stadium specified in the initiative. This group wanted an old-fashioned, open-air stadium like Baltimore's Camden Yards or Cleveland's Jacobs Field.

Writers supporting the initiative found it impossible to address all of these resisting audiences at once. If a supporter of the initiative wanted to aim an argument at sports haters, he or she could stress the spinoff benefits of a new ballpark (for example, the new ballpark would attract tourist revenue, renovate a deteriorating downtown neighborhood, create jobs, make sports lovers more likely to vote for public subsidies of the arts, and so forth). But these arguments would be irrelevant to those who wanted

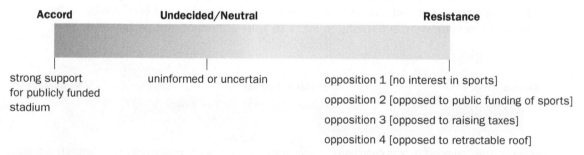

FIGURE 7.2 Scale of resistance, baseball stadium issue

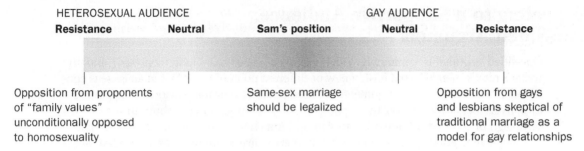

HETEROSEXUAL AUDIENCE   GAY AUDIENCE

Resistance   **Neutral**   **Sam's position**   **Neutral**   **Resistance**

Opposition from proponents   Same-sex marriage   Opposition from gays
of "family values"   should be legalized   and lesbians skeptical of
unconditionally opposed   traditional marriage as a
to homosexuality   model for gay relationships

FIGURE 7.3 Scale of resistance for same-sex-marriage issue

an open-air stadium, who opposed tax hikes categorically, or who objected to public subsidy of millionaires.

Another kind of complexity occurs when a writer is positioned between two kinds of resisting views. Consider the position of student writer Sam, a gay man who wished to argue that gay and lesbian people should actively support legislation to legalize same-sex marriage (see Figure 7.3). Most arguments that support same-sex marriage hope to persuade conservative heterosexual audiences, who tend to disapprove of homosexuality and stress traditional family values. But Sam imagined writing for a gay magazine such as the *Harvard Gay and Lesbian Review* or *The Advocate,* and he wished to aim his argument at liberal gay and lesbian activists who opposed traditional marriage on different grounds. These thinkers, critiquing traditional marriage for the way it stereotypes gender roles and limits the freedom of partners, argued that heterosexual marriage is not a good model for relationships in the gay community. These people constituted an audience 180 degrees removed from the conservative proponents of family values, who oppose same-sex marriage on moral and religious grounds.

In writing his early drafts, Sam was stymied by his attempt to address both audiences at once. Only after he blocked out the conservative "family values" audience and imagined an audience of what he called "liberationist" gays and lesbians was he able to develop a consistent argument. (You can read Sam's essay on pages 303–305.)

The baseball stadium example and the same-sex-marriage example illustrate the difficulty of adapting your argument to your audience's position on the scale of resistance. Yet doing so is important because you need a stable vision of your audience before you can determine an effective content, structure, and tone for your argument. As we showed in Chapter 4, effective content derives from choosing audience-based reasons that appeal to your audience's values, assumptions, and beliefs. As we show in the rest of this chapter, an effective structure and tone are often a function of where your audience falls on the scale of resistance. The next sections show how you can adjust your arguing strategy depending on whether your audience is supportive, neutral, or hostile.

Appealing to a Supportive Audience: One-Sided Argument

One-sided arguments commonly occur when an issue isn't highly contested and the writer's aim is merely to put forth a new or different point of view. When an issue is contested, however, one-sided arguments are used mainly to stir the passions of supporters—to convert belief into action by inspiring a party member to contribute to a senator's campaign or a bored office worker to sign up for a change-your-life weekend seminar.

Typically, appeals to a supportive audience are structured as one-sided arguments that either ignore opposing views or reduce them to "enemy" stereotypes. Filled with motivational language, these arguments list the benefits that will ensue from the reader's donations to the cause and the horrors just around the corner if the other side wins. One of the authors of this text recently received a fund-raising letter from an environmental lobbying group declaring, "It's crunch time for the polluters and their pals on Capitol Hill." The "corporate polluters" and "anti-environment politicians," the letter continues, have "stepped up efforts to roll back our environmental protections—relying on large campaign contributions, slick PR firms and well-heeled lobbyists to get the job done before November's election." This letter makes the reader feel part of an in-group of good guys fighting the big business "polluters." Nothing in the letter examines environmental issues from business's perspective or attempts to examine alternative views fairly. Because the intended audience already believes in the cause, nothing in the letter invites readers to consider the issues more thoroughly. Rather, the letter's goal is to solidify support, increase the fervor of belief, and inspire action. Most appeal arguments make it easy to act, ending with an 800 phone number to call, a Web site to visit, a tear-out postcard to send in, or a congressperson's address to write to.

Appealing to a Neutral or Undecided Audience: Classical Argument

The in-group appeals that motivate an already supportive audience can repel a neutral or undecided audience. Because undecided audiences are like jurors weighing all sides of an issue, they distrust one-sided arguments that caricature other views. Generally the best strategy for appealing to undecided audiences is the classically structured argument described in Chapter 3 (pages 60–62).

What characterizes the classical argument is the writer's willingness to summarize opposing views fairly and to respond to them openly—either by trying to refute them or by conceding to their strengths and then shifting to a different field of values. Let's look at these strategies in more depth.

Summarizing Opposing Views

The first step toward responding to opposing views in a classical argument is to summarize them fairly. Follow the *principle of charity,* which obliges you to avoid loaded, biased, or "straw man" summaries that oversimplify or distort opposing arguments, making them easy to knock over.

Consider the difference between an unfair and a fair summary of an argument. In the following example, a hypothetical supporter of genetically engineered foods intends to refute the argument of organic-food advocate Lisa Turner, who opposes all forms of biotechnology.

Unfair Summary of Turner's Argument

In a biased article lacking scientific understanding of biotechnology, natural-foods huckster Lisa Turner parrots the health food industry's party line that genetically altered crops are Frankenstein's monsters run amok. She ignorantly claims that consumption of biotech foods will lead to worldwide destruction, disease, and death, ignoring the wealth of scientific literature showing that genetically modified foods are safe. Her misinformed attacks are scare tactics aimed at selling consumers on overpriced "health food" products to be purchased at boutique organic-food stores.

Fair Summary of Turner's Argument

In an article appearing in a nutrition magazine, health food advocate Lisa Turner warns readers that much of our food today is genetically modified using gene-level techniques that differ completely from ordinary crossbreeding. She argues that the potential, unforeseen, harmful consequences of genetic engineering offset the possible benefits of increasing the food supply, reducing the use of pesticides, and boosting the nutritional value of foods. Turner asserts that genetic engineering is imprecise, untested, unpredictable, irreversible, and also uncontrollable because of animals, insects, and winds.

In the unfair summary, the writer distorts and oversimplifies Turner's argument, creating a straw man argument that is easy to knock over because it doesn't make the opponent's best case. In contrast, the fair summary follows the "principle of charity," allowing the strength of the opposing view to come through clearly.

■ ■ ■ **FOR CLASS DISCUSSION** Distinguishing Fair from Unfair Summaries
Working in small groups or as a whole class, analyze the differences between the two summaries.

1. What makes the first summary unfair? How can you tell?
2. In the unfair summary, what strategies does the writer use to make the opposing view seem weak and flawed? In the fair summary, how is the opposing view made strong and clear?
3. In the unfair summary, how does the writer attack Turner's motives and credentials? This attack is sometimes called an *ad hominem* argument ("against the person"—see Appendix for a definition of this reasoning fallacy) in that it attacks the arguer rather than the argument. How does the writer treat Turner differently in the fair summary?
4. Do you agree with our view that arguments are more persuasive if the writer summarizes opposing views fairly rather than unfairly? Why?   ■ ■ ■

Refuting Opposing Views

Once you have summarized opposing views, you can either refute them or concede to their strengths. In refuting an opposing view, you attempt to convince readers that its argument is logically flawed, inadequately supported, or based on erroneous assumptions. In refuting an argument, you can rebut (1) the writer's stated reason and grounds, (2) the writer's warrant and backing, or (3) both. Put in less specialized language, you can rebut a writer's reasons and evidence or the writer's underlying assumptions. Suppose, for example, that you wanted to refute this argument:

> We shouldn't elect Joe as committee chair because he is too bossy.

We can clarify the structure of this argument by showing it in Toulmin terms:

ENTHYMEME

CLAIM We shouldn't elect Joe as committee chair

REASON because he is too bossy.

WARRANT

Bossy people make bad committee chairs.

One way to refute this argument is to rebut the stated reason that Joe is too bossy. Your rebuttal might go something like this:

> I disagree that Joe is bossy. In fact, Joe is very unbossy. He's a good listener who's willing to compromise, and he involves others in decisions. The example you cite for his being bossy wasn't typical. It was a one-time circumstance that doesn't reflect his normal behavior. [The writer could then provide examples of Joe's cooperative nature.]

Or you could concede that Joe is bossy but rebut the argument's warrant that bossiness is a bad trait for committee chairs:

> I agree Joe is bossy, but that is just the trait we need now. This committee hasn't gotten anything done for six months and time is running out. We need a decisive person who can come in, get the committee organized, assign tasks, and get the job done.

Let's now illustrate these strategies in a more complex situation. Consider the controversy inspired by a *New York Times Magazine* article titled "Recycling Is Garbage." Its author, John Tierney, argued that recycling is not environmentally sound and that it is cheaper to bury garbage in a landfill than to recycle it. Tierney argued that recycling wastes money; he provided evidence that "every time a sanitation department crew picks up a load of bottles and cans from the curb, New York City loses money." In Toulmin's terms, one of Tierney's arguments is structured as shown on p. 131.

A number of environmentalists responded angrily to Tierney's argument, challenging either his reason, his warrant, or both. Those refuting the reason offered counterevidence showing that recycling isn't as expensive as Tierney claimed. Those refuting the warrant said that even if the costs of recycling are higher than the costs of burying wastes in a landfill, recycling still benefits the environment by reducing the amount of virgin materials taken from nature. These critics, in effect, offered a new warrant: We should dispose of garbage in the way that best saves the world's resources.

ENTHYMEME

CLAIM Recycling is bad policy

REASON because it costs more to recycle material than to bury it in a landfill.

GROUNDS

• Evidence of the high cost of recycling [Tierney says it costs New York City $200 more per ton for recyclables than trash.]

WARRANT

We should dispose of garbage in the least expensive way.

Strategies for Rebutting Evidence

Whether you are rebutting an argument's reasons or its warrant, you will frequently need to question a writer's use of evidence. Here are some strategies you can use:

- **Deny the truth of the data.** Arguers can disagree about the facts of a case. If you have reasons to doubt a writer's facts, call them into question.
- **Cite counterexamples and countertestimony.** You can often rebut an argument based on examples or testimony by citing counterexamples or countertestimony that denies the conclusiveness of the original data.
- **Cast doubt on the representativeness or sufficiency of examples.** Examples are powerful only if they are believed to be representative and sufficient. Many environmentalists complained that John Tierney's attack on recycling was based too largely on data from New York City and that it didn't accurately take into account more positive experiences of other cities and states. When data from outside New York City were examined, the cost-effectiveness and positive environmental impact of recycling seemed more apparent.
- **Cast doubt on the relevance or recency of the examples, statistics, or testimony.** The best evidence is up-to-date. In a rapidly changing universe, data that are even a few years out-of-date are often ineffective. For example, as the demand for recycled goods increases, the cost of recycling will be reduced. Out-of-date statistics will skew any argument about the cost of recycling.
- **Question the credibility of an authority.** If an opposing argument is based on testimony, you can undermine its persuasiveness if you show that a person being cited lacks current or relevant expertise in the field. (This is different from the *ad hominem* fallacy discussed in the Appendix because it doesn't attack the personal character of the authority but only the authority's expertise on a specific matter.)

- **Question the accuracy or context of quotations.** Evidence based on testimony is frequently distorted by being either misquoted or taken out of context. Often scientists qualify their findings heavily, but these qualifications are omitted by the popular media. You can thus attack the use of a quotation by putting it in its original context or by restoring the qualifications in its original source.
- **Question the way statistical data were produced or interpreted.** Chapter 5 provides fuller treatment of how to question statistics. In general, you can rebut statistical evidence by calling into account how the data were gathered, treated mathematically, or interpreted. It can make a big difference, for example, whether you cite raw numbers or percentages or whether you choose large or small increments for the axes of graphs.

Conceding to Opposing Views

In writing a classical argument, a writer must sometimes concede to an opposing argument rather than refute it. Sometimes you encounter portions of an argument that you simply can't refute. For example, suppose you support the legalization of hard drugs such as cocaine and heroin. Adversaries argue that legalizing hard drugs will increase the number of drug users and addicts. You might dispute the size of their numbers, but you reluctantly agree that they are right. Your strategy is thus not to refute the opposing argument but to concede to it by admitting that legalization of hard drugs will promote heroin and cocaine addiction. Having made that concession, your task is then to show that the benefits of drug legalization still outweigh the costs you've just conceded.

As this example shows, the strategy of a concession argument is to switch from the field of values employed by the writer you disagree with to a different field of values more favorable to your position. You don't try to refute the writer's stated reason and grounds (by arguing that legalization will *not* lead to increased drug usage and addiction) or the writer's warrant (by arguing that increased drug use and addiction is not a problem). Rather, you shift the argument to a new field of values by introducing a new warrant, one that you think your audience can share (that the benefits of legalization—eliminating the black market and ending the crime, violence, and prison costs associated with procurement of drugs—outweigh the costs of increased addiction). To the extent that opponents of legalization share your desire to stop drug-related crime, shifting to this new field of values is a good strategy. Although it may seem that you weaken your own position by conceding to an opposing argument, you may actually strengthen it by increasing your credibility and gaining your audience's goodwill. Moreover, conceding to one part of an opposing argument doesn't mean that you won't refute other parts of that argument.

Example of a Student Essay Using Refutation Strategy

The following extract from a student essay is the refutation section of a classical argument appealing to a neutral or undecided audience. In this essay, student writer Marybeth Hamilton argues for continued taxpayer support of First Place, an alternative public school for homeless children that also provides job counseling and mental health services for families. Because running First Place is costly and because it can accommodate only 4 percent of her city's homeless children, Marybeth recognizes that her audience may object to continued public funding. Consequently, to reach the neutral or skeptical members of her audience, she devotes the following portion of her argument to summarizing and refuting opposing views.

From "First Place: A Healing School for Homeless Children"

MARYBETH HAMILTON (STUDENT)

. . . As stated earlier, the goal of First Place is to prepare students for returning to mainstream public schools. Although there are many reasons to continue operating an agency like First Place, there are some who would argue against it. One argument is that the school is too expensive, costing many more taxpayer dollars per child than a mainstream school. I can understand this objection to cost, but one way to look at First Place is as a preventative action by the city to reduce the future costs of crime and welfare. Because all the students at First Place are at risk for educational failure, drug and alcohol abuse, or numerous other long-term problems, a program like First Place attempts to stop the problems before they start. In the long run, the city could be saving money in areas such as drug rehabilitation, welfare payments, or jail costs.

Others might criticize First Place for spending some of its funding on social services for the students and their families instead of spending it all on educational needs. When the city is already making welfare payments and providing a shelter for the families, why do they deserve anything more? Basically, the job of any school is to help a child become educated and have social skills. At First Place, students' needs run deep, and their entire families are in crisis. What good is it to help just the child when the rest of the family is still suffering? The education of only the child will not help the family out of poverty. Therefore, First Place helps parents look for jobs by providing job search help including assistance with résumés. They even supply clothes to wear to an interview. First Place also provides a parent support group for expressing anxieties and learning coping skills. This therapy helps parents deal with their struggles in a productive way, reducing the chance that they will take out their frustration on their child. All these "extras" are an attempt to help the family get back on its feet and become self-supporting.

Another objection to an agency like First Place is that the short-term stay at First Place does no long-term good for the student. However, in talking with Michael Siptroth, a teacher at First Place, I learned that the individual attention the students receive helps many of them catch up in school quite quickly. He reported that some students actually made a three-grade-level improvement in one year. This improvement definitely contributes to the long-term good of the student, especially in the area of self-esteem. Also, the students at First Place are in desperate situations. For most, any help is better than no help.

Thus First Place provides extended day care for the children so they won't have to be unsupervised at home while their parents are working or looking for work. For example, some homeless children live in motels on Aurora Avenue, a major highway that is overrun with fast cars, prostitutes, and drugs. Aurora Avenue is not a safe place for children to play, so the extended day care is important for many of First Place's students.

Finally, opponents might question the value of removing students from mainstream classrooms. Some might argue that separating children from regular classrooms is not good because it further highlights their differences from the mainstream children. Also, the separation period might cause additional alienation when the First Place child does return to a mainstream school. In reality, though, the effects are quite different. Children at First Place are sympathetic to each other. Perhaps for the first time in their lives, they do not have to be on the defensive because no one is going to make fun of them for being homeless; they are all homeless. The time spent at First Place is usually a time for catching up to the students in mainstream schools. When students catch up, they have one fewer reason to be seen as different from mainstream students. If the students stayed in the mainstream school and continued to fall behind, they would only get teased more.

5   First Place is a program that merits the community's ongoing moral and financial support. With more funding, First Place could help many more homeless children and their families along the path toward self-sufficiency. While this school is not the ultimate answer to the problem of homelessness, it is a beginning. These children deserve a chance to build their own lives, free from the stigma of homelessness, and I, as a responsible citizen, feel a civic and moral duty to do all I can to help them.

■ ■ ■ **FOR CLASS DISCUSSION** Refutation Strategies

1. Individually or in groups, analyze the refutation strategies that Marybeth employs in her argument.
   a. Summarize each of the opposing reasons that Marybeth anticipates from her audience.
   b. How does she attempt to refute each line of reasoning in the opposing argument? Where does she refute her audience's stated reasons? Where does she refute a warrant? Where does she concede to an opposing argument but then shift to a different field of values?
   c. How effective is Marybeth's refutation? Would you as a city resident vote for allotting more public money for this school? Why or why not?
2. Examine each of the following arguments, imagining how the enthymeme could be fleshed out with grounds and backing. Then attempt to refute each argument.

Suggest ways to rebut the reason or the warrant or both, or to concede to the argument and then switch to a different field of values.

a. Signing the Kyoto treaty (pledging that the United States will substantially lower its emission of greenhouse gases) is a bad idea because reducing greenhouse emissions will seriously harm the American economy.

b. Majoring in engineering is better than majoring in music because engineers make more money than musicians.

c. The United States should reinstitute the draft because doing so is the only way to maintain a large enough military to defend American interests in several different trouble spots in the world.

d. The United States should build more nuclear reactors because nuclear reactors will provide substantial electrical energy without emitting greenhouse gases.

e. People should be allowed to own handguns because owning handguns helps them protect their homes against potentially violent intruders.

Appealing to a Resistant Audience: Dialogic Argument

Whereas classical argument is effective for neutral or undecided audiences, it is often less effective for audiences strongly opposed to the writer's views or for arguments that lean toward the inquiry end of the argument continuum. Because resistant audiences hold values, assumptions, or beliefs widely different from the writer's, they are often unswayed by classical argument, which attacks their worldview too directly. Writers, too, may recognize that progress toward communication on some values-laden issues may require them to take a more open, problem-solving approach. On issues such as abortion, gun control, gay rights, or the role of religion in the public sphere, the distance between a writer and a resistant audience can be so great that dialogue seems impossible. In these cases the writer's goal may be simply to open dialogue by seeking common ground—that is, by finding places where the writer and audience agree. For example, pro-choice and pro-life advocates may never agree on a woman's right to an abortion, but they may share common ground in wanting to reduce teenage pregnancy. There is room, in other words, for conversation, if not for agreement.

Because of these differences in basic beliefs and values, the goal of dialogic argument is seldom to convert resistant readers to the writer's position. The best a writer can hope for is to reduce somewhat the level of resistance, perhaps by increasing the reader's willingness to listen as preparation for future dialogue. In this section and the next, we introduce you to two kinds of dialogic argument—delayed-thesis argument, which is particularly helpful at reducing the resistance of hostile audiences, and Rogerian argument, a communicating and thinking strategy that can enlarge the writer's as well as the readers's view of a conflicted issue.

Delayed-Thesis Argument as Both Exploration and Persuasion

Unlike a classical argument, a delayed-thesis argument assumes an exploratory approach to a subject. With some issues, you may want to convey that you are still thinking out your position, finding your way through a thicket of alternative views and the complexities of the issue. You yourself may be pulled in multiple directions and may have arrived at your position after pondering different views. In addition, your readers' resistance to your views means that they may be turned off if you forthrightly plunge into your claim and reasons. Under these rhetorical conditions, a delayed-thesis argument enables you to engage your audience in a dialogic exploration of the problem before you argue a thesis. Instead of declaring a claim and reasons early in the argument, you may work your way slowly to your claim, devoting a large part of the argument to examining different views and re-creating your own inquiry into the subject.

Let's look at an example of a delayed-thesis argument, examining its form and its emotional impact. (For another example of a delayed-thesis argument, see Ellen Goodman's commentary piece "Womb for Rent—for a Price" on pages 172–173.) The following op-ed piece by syndicated columnist Ross Douthat appeared in the *New York Times* during the public debates about the building of a Muslim community center near Ground Zero in lower Manhattan. Note how Douthat takes a nonthreatening tone and pulls readers into his exploration of the issue.

Islam in Two Americas

ROSS DOUTHAT

Writer frames the controversy as a conflict of American identities, two divergent ways that the country thinks of itself.

There's an America where it doesn't matter what language you speak, what god you worship or how deep your New World roots run. An America where allegiance to the Constitution trumps ethnic differences, language barriers and religious divides. An America where the newest arrival to our shores is no less American than the ever-so-great granddaughter of the Pilgrims.

But there's another America as well, one that understands itself as a distinctive culture, rather than just a set of political propositions. This America speaks English, not Spanish or Chinese or Arabic. It looks back to a particular religious heritage: Protestantism originally, and then a Judeo-Christian consensus that accommodated Jews and Catholics as well.

Writer establishes the problem and its timeliness and invites his readers to contemplate it with him.

These two understandings of America, one constitutional and one cultural, have been in tension throughout our history. They're in tension in the controversy over the Islamic mosque and cultural center scheduled to go up two blocks from ground zero.

Writer explores the problem from several perspectives, first, the inclusive constitutional America, which defends the right of all religious groups to worship as they please.

Writer shows his awareness of the problem's complexity by exploring the second perspective, the melting-pot America, which emphasizes its Judeo-Christian heritage.

Writer keeps the problem open as he examines how these two identities functioned in American history.

Writer finally presents his own viewpoint, his thesis-claim that Muslims should not build a community center near Ground Zero.

He briefly develops his claim.

He argues that by not building near Ground Zero, American Muslims would signal their disassociation from Islamic terrorist groups and their respect for the national pain caused by 9/11.

He sums up his argument by restating his thesis-claim in larger terms that leave readers with his thinking.

The first America views the project as the consummate expression of our nation's high ideals. "This is America," President Barack Obama intoned last week, "and our commitment to religious freedom must be unshakeable." The construction of the mosque, Mayor Michael Bloomberg told New Yorkers, is as important a test of the principle of religious freedom "as we may see in our lifetimes."

5 The second America begs to differ. It sees the project as an affront to the memory of 9/11, and a sign of disrespect for the values of a country where Islam has only recently become part of the public consciousness. And beneath these concerns lurks the darker suspicion that Islam in any form may be incompatible with the American way of life.

Both understandings of this country have wisdom to offer, and both have been necessary to the American experiment's success. During the great waves of 19th-century immigration, the insistence that new arrivals adapt to Anglo-Saxon culture was crucial to their swift assimilation.

The same was true in religion. The steady pressure to conform to American norms eventually persuaded the Mormons to abandon polygamy, smoothing their assimilation into the American mainstream. Nativist concerns about Catholicism's illiberal tendencies inspired American Catholics to prod their church toward a recognition of the virtues of democracy, making it possible for generations of immigrants to feel unambiguously Catholic and American.

So it is today with Islam. The first America is correct to insist on Muslims' absolute right to build and worship where they wish. But the second America is right to press for something more from Muslim Americans—particularly from figures like Feisal Abdul Rauf, the imam behind the mosque—than simple protestations of good faith.

Too often, American Muslim institutions have turned out to be entangled with ideas and groups that most Americans rightly consider beyond the pale. Too often, American Muslim leaders strike ambiguous notes when asked to disassociate themselves completely from illiberal causes.

10 For Muslim Americans to integrate fully into our national life, they'll need leaders who don't describe America as "an accessory to the crime" of 9/11 (as Rauf did shortly after the 2001 attacks), or duck questions about whether groups like Hamas count as terrorist organizations (as Rauf did in June). They'll need leaders whose antennas are sensitive enough to recognize that the quest for inter-religious dialogue is ill served by throwing up a high-profile mosque two blocks from the site of a mass murder committed in the name of Islam.

They'll need leaders, in other words, who understand that while the ideals of the first America protect the *e pluribus*, it's the demands the second America makes of new arrivals that help create the *unum*.

FIGURE 7.4 Marchers in support of the Islamic culture center at Ground Zero

In this delayed-thesis argument, Ross Douthat, a conservative columnist writing for the liberal *New York Times,* asks readers to think with him about the fierce clash of views over building a Muslim community center near Ground Zero. Douthat wants to reach typical *New York Times* readers, who are apt to support the Muslim project based on their liberal views of tolerance and religious freedom. As the photos taken during the protests show (see Figures 7.4–7.7), this proposal elicited powerful emotions. Douthat enters this public debate calmly, admits the legitimacy of different opposing views, and only toward the end of the argument states his own position.

If Douthat had chosen to write a classical argument, he would have declared his position in the first paragraph, perhaps with a thesis statement like this:

> Muslim Americans should not build their community center near Ground Zero because doing so represents disrespect for America's core cultural identity and insensitivity to Americans' national pain caused by Islamic terrorists.

With this thesis, readers would have no initial doubt where Douthat stands. However, this in-your-face thesis would activate the emotional objections of readers who support the Islamic community center and might prevent them from even reading the piece. In contrast, both liberal and conservative readers can get drawn into the building momentum of Douthat's delayed-thesis version and appreciate its subtlety and surprise.

FIGURE 7.5 People protesting the Islamic culture center at Ground Zero

Writing a Delayed-Thesis Argument

Clearly, where you place your claim can affect your argument's impact on its audience. We should note, however, that a delayed-thesis argument is not simply a classical argument turned upside down. Instead, it promotes dialogue with the audience rather than compels readers to accept the writer's views. It strives to enrich and complicate the discussion as well as present a view of an issue. It entails some risk to the writer because it leaves space only at the end of the argument for developing the writer's claim. However, it may lead the writer and readers to a deeper understanding of the issue, provide clarification, and promote further discussion.

Although there is no set form, the organization plan on page 143 shows characteristic elements often found in delayed-thesis arguments.

FIGURE 7.6 People protesting the Islamic culture center at Ground Zero

FIGURE 7.7 People defending the rights of Muslims

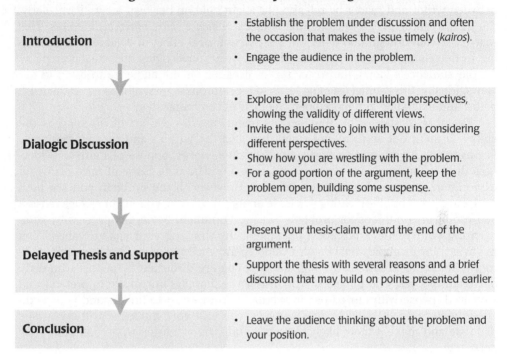

Organization Plan for a Delayed-Thesis Argument

Introduction	• Establish the problem under discussion and often the occasion that makes the issue timely (*kairos*). • Engage the audience in the problem.
Dialogic Discussion	• Explore the problem from multiple perspectives, showing the validity of different views. • Invite the audience to join with you in considering different perspectives. • Show how you are wrestling with the problem. • For a good portion of the argument, keep the problem open, building some suspense.
Delayed Thesis and Support	• Present your thesis-claim toward the end of the argument. • Support the thesis with several reasons and a brief discussion that may build on points presented earlier.
Conclusion	• Leave the audience thinking about the problem and your position.

A More Open-Ended Approach: Rogerian Argument

We now turn to a more complex kind of dialogic argument: *Rogerian argument.* All dialogic arguments emphasize problem solving, collaborative thinking, and negotiation with a resistant audience. But Rogerian argument, besides delaying its thesis, works to change the writer as well as the reader. Rogerian argument is named after psychotherapist Carl Rogers, who developed a communication strategy for helping people resolve differences.* The Rogerian strategy emphasizes "empathic listening," which Rogers defined as the ability to see an issue sympathetically from another person's perspective or "frame of reference." He trained people to withhold judgment of another person's ideas until after they had listened attentively to the other person, understood that person's reasoning, appreciated that person's values, and respected that person's humanity—in short, walked in that person's shoes. What Carl Rogers understood is that traditional methods of argumentation are threatening. Because Rogerian argument stresses the psychological as well as the logical dimensions of argument, it is particularly effective when dealing with emotion-laden issues.

---

*See Carl Rogers's essay "Communication: Its Blocking and Its Facilitation" in his book *On Becoming a Person* (Boston: Houghton Mifflin, 1961), 329–37. For a fuller discussion of Rogerian argument, see Richard Young, Alton Becker, and Kenneth Pike, *Rhetoric: Discovery and Change* (New York: Harcourt Brave, 1972).

With Rogerian communication, the writer tries to reduce the sense of difference between writer and reader by releasing her tight hold on her own views. Particularly, she tries to show that *both writer and resistant audience share many basic values.* This search for common ground often has the psychological effect of enlarging, complicating, or deepening the writer's own worldview. By acknowledging that she has empathy for the audience's views, the writer makes it easier for the audience to listen to her views. Ideally, this mutual listening leads to a compromise or synthesis or, at the least, better understanding and more open channels of communication.

Essential to successful Rogerian argument, besides the art of listening, is the ability to point out areas of agreement between the writer's and reader's positions. For example, if you, as a supporter of alternative energy, oppose offshore or wilderness drilling, and you are arguing with someone who is in favor of maximizing oil exploration, you are caught in an impasse. However, if the problem you are both confronting is that of increasing available energy resources, you might reduce tension and establish conditions for problem solving. You might begin this process by summarizing your reader's position sympathetically, stressing your shared values. You might say, for example, that you also value energy independence, that you appreciate recent advances in safe oil drilling, and that you are disturbed by people who deny our country's vast energy needs. You also agree that it is unrealistic to pretend that we can dispense with our oil needs overnight. Your effort to understand your audience's views and to build bridges between you and your audience will encourage dialogue and make it more likely that your audience will listen when you offer your perspective.

Rogers's communication strategies have been the subject of intense debate among scholars. On the one hand, some rhetoricians don't like the term "Rogerian *argument*," preferring instead "Rogerian *rhetoric*" or "Rogerian *communication*." These theorists say that Rogerian listening isn't a form of argument or persuasion at all. Rather, its goal is increased mutual understanding and enlarged perspectives on reality for both writer and audience. According to rhetorician Nathaniel Teich, Rogerian rhetoric seeks to foster discovery of others' perspectives and revision of both parties' worldviews.*

In contrast to this perspective, other scholars view Rogerian argument as a means of manipulating resistant audiences. According to this view, the best way to persuade a hostile audience is to adopt a nonthreatening tone and approach, treat the opponent's views sympathetically, and then lure the opponent into accepting your views. The problem with this perspective is that it is purely instrumental and reduces Rogerian argument to a technique, a clever means to an end.

Our view of Rogerian argument forges a middle path between these two perspectives. We emphasize argument as a process of inquiry and treat Rogerian argument as dialogic problem solving in which the writer negotiates with the audience in a mutual search for provisional solutions.

---

*For one of the most thorough analyes of Carl Rogers's influence on rhetoric and composition, see Nathaniel Teich's scholarly anthology *Rogerian Perspectives: Collaborative Rhetoric for Oral and Written Communication* (Norwood, NJ: Ablex Publishing Corporation, 1992).

Rogerian Argument as Growth for the Writer

One of the key features of Rogerian argument is the open relationship it establishes between the writer and the subject; it recasts argument as a process of growth for the writer. Because Rogerian argument asks the writer to listen to the opponent's views—views that the writer may find uncomfortable or threatening—it promotes inquiry and self-reflection, a more tentative and exploratory approach to the subject than the writer takes in classical argument or delayed-thesis argument. Rogerian argument urges writers to play Peter Elbow's "believing game," where the writer must try "to get inside the head of someone" who holds unwelcome ideas.* (See our discussion of the believing and doubting game in Chapter 2, pages 31–32.) This "dwelling in" unappealing ideas often compels writers to articulate their own values and to achieve a new understanding of them. Extending Elbow's strategy and emphasizing the connection between values and identity, rhetorician James Baumlin argues that Rogerian argument creates "a realm of plural selves or identities" in the process of taking on "another's beliefs and worldview" through role-playing.† Rogerian argument thus promotes a writer's self-examination and exploration of multiple perspectives on a problem. This double process of exploration and reflection can in turn lead to a change of mind or at least a deeper understanding of a problem.

Rogerian Argument as Collaborative Negotiation

A second key feature of Rogerian argument is its altered argumentative purpose and attitude toward the audience. In the absence of the possibility of persuading a resistant audience to accept the writer's views, the writer seeks different goals through a relationship with the audience. These goals include reducing antagonism toward those with different beliefs, initiating small steps in understanding, cultivating mutual respect, and encouraging further problem solving—in short, nurturing conditions for future exchanges. Thus Rogerian argument particularly lends itself to rhetorical situations involving complex, emotionally volatile issues. Rogerian argument is appropriate whenever writers are seeking to open up communication with a resistant audience and are themselves willing to work toward a synthesis of views.

Writing a Rogerian Argument

A major thrust of Rogerian argument is building bridges between writer and audience. Because Rogers's principles originated as a communication strategy between two parties in conversation, Rogerian argument most commonly takes the form of a letter or an open letter directed to a specific person or group. For example, the audience for a Rogerian argument might be a particular person whom the writer already knows, a

---

*For more suggestions on how to encourage empathic listening, see Elbow's "Bringing the Rhetoric of Assent and the Believing Game Together—and into the Classroom," *College English* 67.4 (March 2005), 389.
†For more discussion of the relationship between role-playing, understanding, and identity, see James S. Baumlin's "Persuasion, Rogerian Rhetoric, and Imaginative Play," *Rhetoric Society Quarterly* 17.1 (Winter 1987), 36.

speaker the writer has recently heard, or the author of an article that the writer has recently read. In all these cases, the writer is disturbed by the audience's views and hopes to open up dialogue. Rogerian argument will most likely include the features shown in the chart below, although not necessarily in any set form.

Organization Plan for a Rogerian Argument

Introduction	• Address the audience and identify the problem that you and your audience want to solve. • Possibly, show the timeliness (*kairos*) of the problem. • Try to establish a friendly or cordial relationship with the audience. • Possibly include information that shows your familiarity with the audience.
Summary of the Audience's Views	• Summarize the audience's views in a fair and neutral way that the audience would accept. • Show that you understand the audience's position. • Also show an understanding of, and respect for, the audience's values and beliefs; the goal of this "saying back" (Rogers's term) is to summarize these views in a way that will be entirely acceptable to the audience.
Common Ground	• Identify common ground you share with your audience. • Demonstrate your growth through empathic consideration of views that you would otherwise find threatening or unwelcome. • Show understanding of the audience's views by "indwelling" with them and perhaps by extending them to other situations through new examples. • Show how your views have been enlarged by empathic listening to the audience's ideas.
Contribution of New Points to the Negotiation	• Respectfully propose your own way of looking at this issue. • Through a respectful and inquiring tone, encourage the audience to listen and work with you to solve the problem.
Conclusion	• Possibly propose a synthesis of the two positions, discuss how both parties gain from an enlarged vision, or invite the audience to ongoing negotiation.

In the following example of a Rogerian argument, student writer Colleen Fontana responds to an article written by Robert A. Levy, a senior fellow for constitutional studies at the Cato Institute, a libertarian think tank. In this open letter, Colleen conducts a collaborative discussion directed toward solving the problem of gun violence.* Annotations in the margins indicate how Colleen is practicing Rogerian principles.

An Open Letter to Robert Levy in Response to His Article "They Never Learn"

COLLEEN FONTANA (STUDENT)

Dear Robert Levy,

Writer addresses the audience.

Writer identifies the problem, shows its current timeliness (*kairos*), and establishes a cordial relationship with the audience.

My recent interest in preventing gun violence led me to find your article "They Never Learn" in *The American Spectator* about the mass shooting at Virginia Tech in 2007. I was struck by the similarities between that incident and the recent shooting in Tucson, Arizona, where a young man gunned down U.S. Representative Gabrielle Giffords and nineteen others in a supermarket parking lot. Although your article came several years before this Arizona incident, we can see that gun violence remains an enduring issue. I have long struggled with the question of how we can reduce gun-related violence without detracting from an individual's right to own a gun. Your article shed new light on this question for me.

Summary: In neutral, fair terms, the writer summarizes the audience's previous argument, the article to which she is responding.

Your article stresses the need for something different from our nation's current gun policies. You assert that the solution lies, not in stricter gun control policies, but rather in "liberalized laws." According to you, Mr. Levy, it was primarily the existence of anti-gun laws on the Virginia Tech campus that prevented an armed citizen from saving the victims of the 2007 shooting. You comment that "gun control does not work. It just prevents weaker people from defending themselves against stronger predators." Your article gives detailed examples of studies that have substantiated that stricter gun laws have not resulted in lower murder rates. You also cite evidence that fewer crimes are likely to happen if the victim brandishes a gun, even if he or she never fires it. According to

---

*We are indebted to Doug Brent for his insight that Rogerian arguments can often be addressed to the author of an article that a reader finds disturbing. See "Rogerian Rhetoric: Ethical Growth Through Alternative Forms of Argumentation." In *Argument Revisited; Argument Redefined,* eds. Barbara Emmel, Paula Resch, and Deborah Tenney, (Thousand Oaks, CA: Sage, 1996), 81.

your article, stricter gun laws are doing nothing to help society, and your solution lies in relaxed laws, allowing more responsible citizens to carry concealed weapons.

Common ground: Writer identifies common values that she shares with her audience; she demonstrates empathic listening; she imagines instances where the audience's values make the most sense.

Living on a college campus myself, I identify immediately with your concern for preventing school shootings. I appreciate that you are concerned with the safety of the students and the public, and I agree that there exists a need for greater safety on school campuses. I also agree that current gun laws are not effective, as is shown by the number of gun-related deaths that happen annually. Even though such laws exist, they are not likely to stop "crazed fanatics undeterred by laws against murder," as you say, from committing certain crimes. I particularly agree with you when you discuss the right of self-defense. I struggle with laws that forbid carrying a gun because I believe in the right of self-defense. As you mentioned in your article, instances do occur in which civilians carrying guns have the ability to save themselves and others. Although I have not experienced this situation personally, I have read of brave acts of self-defense and intervention. For example, my research turned up an article by John Pierce on Minneapolis' *Examiner.com*, "It Takes a Gun to Stop a Gunman." In this article Pierce describes an occurrence in Richmond, Virginia, in July of 2009 where a store owner and several customers were saved from an armed robber by a civilian in the store who happened to be carrying a firearm. Even though Pierce is a long-time gun rights advocate and an NRA-certified instructor, the points he brought up were striking. If that civilian hadn't been carrying a gun in that store on that day, then everyone in the store might have been killed by the robber. This realization resonates with me. I imagine myself in that store, and I know I would have been quite grateful that he was carrying a weapon that saved my life. Reading this story has forced me to think of the responsibility many gun-owning citizens must feel—a responsibility to protect not only themselves but those around them as well. A similar event happened recently in New York where a person attempting to rob a jewelry shop was shot by the owner in an act of self-defense. His neighbors regard him as a hero (Kilgannon).

Writer moves respectfully to presenting her own questions and differing perspectives on the problem. Note her tone of negotiation and her willingness to engage in further discussion.

While I agree with you that self-defense is an important right and that armed citizens can sometimes prevent the death of innocent people, I wonder whether the possibility of allowing more guns in public through liberalized gun laws is the best solution. Is there a chance more guns in the hands of more people would foster a more danger-prone climate both from accidents and from sudden fits of rage? I was surprised to learn in a recent *New York Times* article by Charles M. Blow that for every ten people in America there are nine guns. Among major nations, according to a U.N. study, we have both the highest ratio of guns to people and the highest incidence of violence. If liberalizing gun ownership will lead to even more guns, then my concern is that there will be a higher chance of children finding a loaded gun in a parent's bed stand or of deaths caused by gang warfare or from momentary rage in an escalating fight between neighbors. Such danger could also exist on school campuses if guns were allowed. On a campus where drinking nurtures the party scene, I worry that rowdy people waving a gun perhaps as a joke might turn a party into a tragedy. Do you have any ideas, Mr. Levy, for reducing gun accidents or irresponsible use of firearms if they are widely available?

Writer expresses a second concern, one that Levy did not mention: assault weapons.

I found your point about owning a firearm for self-defense really thought provoking. But even if Virginia Tech had allowed guns on campus, what are the odds that an armed student or teacher would have been at the right place at the right time with an actual chance of shooting the gunman? Only in the movies are good guys and heroes *always* on the spot and capable of taking the right action to protect potential victims. Although I can really see your point about using handguns for self-defense, I don't think self-defense can be used as a justification for assault weapons or automatic weapons with large clips. If guns were freely allowed on campuses, perhaps massacres such as Virginia Tech might occur more often. Or is there a way to allow people to carry concealed handguns on campus but still to forbid rifles, shotguns, or other weapons more useful for massacres than for self-defense?

Writer concludes her letter with a reiteration of the mutual concerns she shares with her audience; she acknowledges how her perspectives have been widened by Levy's views; she seeks to keep the channel of communication open; and she expresses interest in further problem solving.

After reading your article I have more understanding of the arguments in favor of guns, and I continue to ponder the ethical and practical issues of gun control versus the right to self-defense. You have underscored for me the importance of our continuing to seek means of preventing these terrible massacres from happening in our nation's schools. You have also opened my eyes to the fact that no amount of enforcement of gun laws can deter determined people from using guns to harm others. I am not sure, however, that your proposal to eliminate gun control laws is the best solution, and I am hoping that you might be willing to consider some of my reasons for fearing guns, especially assault weapons and automatic weapons that can be fired like machine guns. Perhaps we could both agree that pursuing responsible gun ownership is a step in the right direction so that we reduce the number of accidents, keep guns away from children, and reduce access to guns capable of unleashing mass murder. I am hopeful that with our common concern over the current ineffectiveness of gun laws and the desire for safety in our schools, we can find a reasonable solution while still preserving the human right of self-defense.

Sincerely,

Colleen Fontana

Works Cited

Blow, Charles M. "Obama's Gun Play." *New York Times.* New York Times, 21 Jan. 2011. Web. 21 Mar. 2011.

Kilgannon, Cory. "After Shooting, Merchant Is Hero of Arthur Avenue." *New York Times.* New York Times, 12 Feb. 2011. Web. 21 Mar. 2011.

Levy, Robert A. "They Never Learn." *American Spectator.* American Spectator, 25 Apr. 2007. Web. 13 Mar. 2011.

Pierce, John. "It Takes a Gun to Stop a Gunman." *Examiner.com.* Clarity Digital Group, 15 July 2009. Web. 15 Mar. 2011.

■ ■ ■   **FOR CLASS DISCUSSION** Listening Empathically and Searching for Common Ground

A proposal to construct an Islamic community center near Ground Zero in Manhattan sparked intense emotional outbursts and public protests (the issue discussed in Ross Douthat's delayed-thesis argument "Islam in Two Americas" on pages 138–139). Protesters took different positions on this issue depending on their values and beliefs. Protesters even disagreed about what was at stake: Patriotism? Religious freedom? Respect for those who died when the World Trade Center towers collapsed? Anger at Muslims in general? The photos in Figures 7.4–7.7 portray some of these protesters and their views.

Working individually or in groups, choose the photo that represents the position on this controversy with which you most disagree. Then imagine that you are conducting a Rogerian discussion with the people in the photo and follow these thinking and writing steps:

1. What are your own views about the construction of an Islamic community center two blocks from Ground Zero? What's at stake for you in allowing or denying this proposal? Explore your own values.
2. Write a summary of the views you think the people in the photo hold. Write your summary in fair, neutral language that indicates your understanding and that would make your summary acceptable to the people you oppose.
3. Then write a common-grounds paragraph in which you go beyond summary to show your understanding of the values held by these people. Consider how these views might be valid. Demonstrate your empathy, and add an example of your own that shows how your views and those of the people in the photo could intersect.   ■ ■ ■

Conclusion

This chapter explains strategies for addressing alternative views. When intending to engage supportive audiences in a cause, writers often compose one-sided arguments. Neutral or undecided audiences generally respond most favorably to classical argument, which uses strong reasons in support of its claim while openly summarizing alternative views and responding to them through rebuttal or concession. Strongly resistant audiences typically respond most favorably to dialogic strategies, such as delayed-thesis or Rogerian argument, which seeks common ground with an audience, aims at reducing hostility, and takes a more inquiring or conciliatory stance. Rogerian argument, especially, envisions both writer and reader undergoing mutual change.

WRITING ASSIGNMENT   A Classical Argument or a Rogerian Letter

Option 1: A Classical Argument   Write a classical argument following the explanations in Chapter 3, pages 60–62, and using the guidelines for developing such an argument throughout Chapters 3–7. Depending on your instructor's preferences, this argument could be on a new issue, or it could be a final stage of an argument in progress throughout Part Two. This assignment expands the supporting-reasons assignment from Chapter 5 by adding sections that summarize opposing views and respond to them through refutation or concession. For an example of a classical argument, see " 'Half-Criminals' or Urban Athletes? A Plea for Fair Treatment of Skateboarders" by David Langley (pages 152–154).

Option 2: A Rogerian Letter   Write a Rogerian argument in the form of a letter addressed to a specific person, either someone you know, someone you have heard deliver a speech, or the author of an article that has disturbed you. As you generate ideas for your argument, take stock of what you know about your audience and summarize his or her views in a way that your audience would find satisfactory. As you explore what your audience values and believes in, also explore how your own values differ. Where do you agree with your audience? Under what conditions would you find your audience's values acceptable? Follow the suggestions in the chart that explains the elements of Rogerian argument on page 147 for determining a purpose and structure for your argument. Depending on the distance between your views and your audience's, your goal may be simply to plant in your audience a willingness to consider your perspective. For examples of Rogerian argument, see Colleen Fontana's "Open Letter to Robert Levy" on pages 147–150 and Rebekah Taylor's "Letter to Jim" on pages 154–155. Your instructor may ask you to attach a reflective response in which you describe how your experience of writing this Rogerian letter differed from your experience of writing classical arguments. ■

Readings

Our first student essay illustrates a classical argument. This essay grew out of a class discussion about alternative sports, conflicts between traditional sports and newer sports (downhill skiing versus snowboarding), and middle-age prejudices against groups of young people.

"Half-Criminals" or Urban Athletes? A Plea for Fair Treatment of Skateboarders

(A Classical Argument)

DAVID LANGLEY (STUDENT)

For skateboarders, the campus of the University of California at San Diego is a wide-open, huge, geometric, obstacle-filled, stair-scattered cement paradise. The signs posted all over campus read, "No skateboarding, biking, or rollerblading on campus except on Saturday, Sunday, and holidays." I have always respected these signs at my local skateboarding spot. On the first day of 1999, I was skateboarding here with my hometown skate buddies and had just landed a trick when a police officer rushed out from behind a pillar, grabbed me, and yanked me off my board. Because I didn't have my I.D. (I had emptied my pockets so I wouldn't bruise my legs if I fell—a little trick of the trade), the officer started treating me like a criminal. She told me to spread my legs and put my hands on my head. She frisked me and then called in my name to police headquarters.

"What's the deal?" I asked. "The sign said skateboarding was legal on holidays."

"The sign means that you can only *roll* on campus," she said.

But that's *not* what the sign said. The police officer gave one friend and me a warning. Our third friend received a fifty-dollar ticket because it was his second citation in the last twelve months.

5   Like other skateboarders throughout cities, we have been bombarded with unfair treatment. We have been forced out of known skate spots in the city by storeowners and police, kicked out of every parking garage in downtown, compelled to skate at strange times of day and night, and herded into crowded skateboard parks. However, after I was searched by the police and detained for over twenty minutes in my own skating sanctuary, the unreasonableness of the treatment of skateboarders struck me. Where are skateboarders supposed to go? Cities need to change their unfair treatment of skateboarders because skateboarders are not antisocial misfits as popularly believed, because the laws regulating skateboarding are ambiguous, and because skateboarders are not given enough legitimate space to practice their sport.

Possibly because to the average eye most skateboarders look like misfits or delinquents, adults think of us as criminal types and associate our skateboards with antisocial behavior. But this view is unfair. City dwellers should recognize that skateboards are a natural reaction to the urban environment. If people are surrounded by cement, they are going to figure out a way to ride it. People's different environments have always produced transportation and sports to suit the conditions: bikes, cars, skis, ice skates, boats, canoes, surfboards. If we live on snow, we are going to develop skis or snowshoes to move around. If we live in an environment that has flat panels of cement for ground with lots of curbs and stairs, we are going to invent an ingeniously designed flat board with wheels. Skateboards are as natural to cement as surfboards are to water or skis to snow. Moreover, the resulting sport is healthful, graceful, and athletic. A fair assessment of skateboarders should respect our elegant, nonpolluting means of transportation and sport, and not consider us hoodlums.

A second way that skateboarders are treated unfairly is that the laws that regulate skateboarding in public places are highly restrictive, ambiguous, and open to abusive application by police officers. My being frisked on the UCSD campus is just one example. When I moved to Seattle to go to college, I found the laws in Washington to be equally unclear. When a sign says "No Skateboarding," that generally means you will get ticketed if you are caught skateboarding in the area. But most areas aren't posted. The general rule then is that you can skateboard so long as you do so safely without being reckless. But the definition of "reckless" is up to the whim of the police officer. I visited the front desk of the Seattle East Precinct and asked them exactly what the laws against reckless skateboarding meant. They said that skaters are allowed on the sidewalk as long as they travel at reasonable speed and the sidewalks aren't crowded. One of the officers explained that if he saw a skater sliding down a handrail with people all around, he would definitely arrest the skater. What if there were no people around, I asked? The officer admitted that he might arrest the lone skater anyway and not be questioned by his superiors. No wonder skateboarders feel unfairly treated.

One way that cities have tried to treat skateboarders fairly is to build skateboard parks. Unfortunately, for the most part these parks are no solution at all. Most parks were designed by nonskaters who don't understand the momentum or gravity pull associated with the movement of skateboards. For example, City Skate, a park below the Space Needle in Seattle, is very appealing to the eye, but once you start to ride it you realize that the transitions and the verticals are all off, making it unpleasant and even dangerous to skate there. The Skate Park in Issaquah, Washington, hosts about thirty to fifty skaters at a time. Collisions are frequent and close calls, many. There are simply too many people in a small area. The people who built the park in Redmond, Washington, decided to make a huge wall in it for graffiti artists "to tag on" legally. They apparently thought they ought to throw all us teenage "half-criminals" in together. At this park, young teens are nervous about skating near a gangster "throwing up his piece," and skaters become dizzy as they take deep breaths from their workouts right next to four or five cans of spray paint expelling toxins in the air.

Of course, many adults probably don't think skateboarders deserve to be treated fairly. I have heard the arguments against skateboarders for years from parents, storeowners, friends, police officers, and security guards. For one thing, skateboarding tears up public and private property, people say. I can't deny that skating leaves marks on handrails and benches, and it does chip cement and granite. But in general skateboarders help the environment more than they hurt it. Skateboarding places are not littered or tagged up by skaters. Because skaters need smooth surfaces and because any small object of litter can lead to painful accidents, skaters actually keep the environment cleaner than the average citizen does. As for the population as a whole, skateboarders are keeping the air a lot cleaner than many other commuters and athletes such as boat drivers, car drivers, and skiers on ski lifts. In the bigger picture, infrequent repair of curbs and benches is cheaper than attempts to heal the ozone.

10   We skateboarders aren't going away, so cities are going to have to make room for us somewhere. Here is how cities can treat us fairly. We should be allowed to skate when others are present as long as we skate safely on the sidewalks. The rules and laws should be

clearer so that skaters don't get put into vulnerable positions that make them easy targets for tickets. I do support the opening of skate parks, but cities need to build more of them, need to situate them closer to where skateboarders live, and need to make them relatively wholesome environments. They should also be designed by skateboarders so that they are skater-friendly and safe to ride. Instead of being treated as "half-criminals," skaters should be accepted as urban citizens and admired as athletes; we are a clean population, and we are executing a challenging and graceful sport. As human beings grow, we go from crawling to walking; some of us grow from strollers to skateboards.

To illustrate a conciliatory or Rogerian approach to an issue, we show you student writer Rebekah Taylor's argument written in response to this assignment. Rebekah chose to write a Rogerian argument in the form of a letter. An outspoken advocate for animal rights on her campus, Rebekah addressed her letter to an actual friend, Jim, with whom she had had many long philosophical conversations when she attended a different college. Note how Rebekah "listens" empathically to her friend's position on eating meat and proposes a compromise action.

A Letter to Jim
(A Rogerian Argument)
REBEKAH TAYLOR (STUDENT)

Dear Jim,

I decided to write you a letter today because I miss our long talks. Now that I have transferred colleges, we haven't had nearly enough heated discussions to satisfy either of us. I am writing now to again take up one of the issues we vehemently disagreed on in the past—meat-based diets.

Jim, I do understand how your view that eating meat is normal differs from mine. In your family, you learned that humans eat animals, and this view was reinforced in school where the idea of the food pyramid based on meat protein was taught and where most children had not even heard of vegetarian options. Also, your religious beliefs taught that God intended humans to have ultimate dominion over all animals. For humans, eating meat is part of a planned cycle of nature. In short, you were raised in a family and community that accepted meat-based diets as normal, healthy, and ethically justifiable whereas I was raised in a family that cared very deeply for animals and attended a church that frequently entertained a vegan as a guest speaker.

Let me now briefly reiterate for you my own basic beliefs about eating animals. As I have shared with you, my personal health is important to me, and I, along with other vegetarians and vegans, believe that a vegetarian diet is much more healthy than a meat diet. But my primary motivation is my deep respect for animals. I have always felt an overpowering sense of compassion for animals and intense sorrow and regret for the injuries that humans inflict upon them. I detest suffering, especially when it is forced upon creatures that cannot speak out against it. These deep feelings led me to become a vegetarian at the age of 5. While lying in bed one night, I looked up at the poster of a silky-white harbor seal that had always hung on my wall. As I looked at the face of that seal, I made a connection between that precious animal on my wall and the animals that had been killed for the food I ate every day. In the dim glow of my Strawberry Shortcake night light, I promised those large, dark seal eyes that I would never eat animals again. Seventeen years have passed now and that promise still holds true. Every day I feel more dedicated to the cause of animal rights around the world.

I know very well that my personal convictions are not the same as yours. However, I believe that we might possibly agree on more aspects of this issue than we realize. Although we would not be considered by others as allies on the issue of eating meat, we do share a common enemy—factory farms. Although you eat animal products and I do not, we both share a basic common value that is threatened by today's factory farms. We both disapprove of the unnecessary suffering of animals.

5   Though we might disagree on the morality of using animals for food at all, we do agree that such animals should not be made to suffer. Yet at factory farms, billions of animals across the world are born, live, and die in horribly cramped, dark, and foul-smelling barns. None of these animals knows the feeling of fresh air, or of warm, blessed sunlight on their backs. Most do not move out of their tight, uncomfortable pens until the day that they are to be slaughtered. At these factory farms, animals are processed as if they were inanimate objects, with no regard for the fact that they do feel fear and pain.

It is because of our shared opposition to animal suffering that I ask you to consider making an effort to buy meat from small, independent local farmers. I am told by friends that all supermarkets offer such meat options. This would be an easy and effective way to fight factory farms. I know that I could never convince you to stop eating meat, and I will never try to force my beliefs on you. As your friend, I am grateful simply to be able to write to you so candidly about my beliefs. I trust that regardless of what your ultimate reaction is to this letter, you will thoughtfully consider what I have written, as I will thoughtfully consider what you write in return.

Sincerely,

Rebekah

For additional writing, reading, and research resources, go to www.mycomplab.com

PART THREE
Analyzing Arguments

This advocacy poster fuses three big contemporary public controversies: environmentalism, sustainability, and vegetarianism. What tactics does this poster use to appeal to viewers' emotions and dramatize its claim that meat eating is destroying the world? Chapters 8 and 9 provide guidance for conducting rhetorical analyses of verbal and visual texts that work in a complex way, as this one does.

157

8 Analyzing Arguments Rhetorically

In Part Two of this book, we explained thinking and writing strategies for composing your own arguments. Now in Part Three we show you how to use your new rhetorical knowledge to conduct in-depth analyses of other people's arguments. To analyze an argument rhetorically means to examine closely how it is composed and what makes it an effective or ineffective piece of persuasion. A rhetorical analysis identifies the text under scrutiny, summarizes its main ideas, presents some key points about the text's rhetorical strategies for persuading its audience, and elaborates on these points.

Becoming skilled at analyzing arguments rhetorically will have multiple payoffs for you.

In this chapter, you will learn to:

- Critically examine the rhetorical features of arguments
- Construct essays that analyze the rhetorical effectiveness of arguments

By themselves, rhetorical analyses are common assignments in courses in critical thinking and argument. Rhetorical analysis also plays a major role in constructing arguments. Writers often work into their own arguments summaries and rhetorical analyses of other people's arguments—particularly in sections dealing with opposing views. This chapter focuses on the rhetorical analysis of written arguments, and the next one (Chapter 9) equips you to analyze visual arguments.

Thinking Rhetorically about a Text

The suggested writing assignment for this chapter is to write your own rhetorical analysis of an argument selected by your instructor (see page 170). This section will help you get started by showing you what it means to think rhetorically about a text.

Before we turn directly to rhetorical analysis, we should reconsider the key word *rhetoric*. In popular usage, *rhetoric* often means empty or deceptive language, as in, "Well, that's just rhetoric." Another related meaning of *rhetoric* is decorative or artificial language. The Greek Stoic philosopher Epictetus likened rhetoric to hairdressers fixing hair*—a view that sees

---

*Chaim Perelman, "The New Rhetoric: A Theory of Practical Reasoning." In *Professing the New Rhetorics: A Sourcebook,* eds. Theresa Enos and Stuart C. Brown (Englewood Cliffs, NJ: Prentice Hall, 1994), 149.

rhetoric as superficial decoration. Most contemporary rhetoricians, however, adopt the larger view of rhetoric articulated by Greek philosopher Aristotle: the art of determining what will be persuasive in every situation. Contemporary rhetorician Donald C. Bryant has described rhetoric in action as "the function of adjusting ideas to people and of people to ideas."* Focusing on this foundational meaning of rhetoric, this chapter will show you how to analyze a writer's motivation, purpose, and rhetorical choices for persuading a targeted audience.

Most of the knowledge and skills you will need to write an effective rhetorical analysis have already been provided in Parts One and Two of the text. You have already learned how to place a text in its rhetorical context (Chapter 2), and from Chapters 3–7 you are already familiar with such key rhetorical concepts as audience-based reasons, the STAR criteria for evidence, and the classical appeals of *logos, ethos,* and *pathos.* This chapter prepares you to apply these argument concepts to the arguments you encounter.

■ ■ ■ **FOR CLASS DISCUSSION** An Initial Exercise in Rhetorical Analysis

In the following exercise, consider the strategies used by two different writers to persuade their audiences to act against climate change. The first is from the opening paragraphs of an editorial in the magazine *Creation Care: A Christian Environmental Quarterly.* The second is from the Web site of the Sierra Club, an environmental action group. Please study each passage and then proceed to the questions that follow.

Passage 1

As I sit down to write this column, one thing keeps coming to me over and over: "Now is the time; now is the time."

In the New Testament the word used for this type of time is *kairos.* It means "right or opportune moment." It is contrasted with *chronos,* or chronological time as measured in seconds, days, months, or years. In the New Testament *kairos* is usually associated with decisive action that brings about deliverance or salvation.

The reason the phrase, "Now is the time" kept coming to me over and over is that I was thinking of how to describe our current climate change moment.

The world has been plodding along in chronological time on the problem of climate change since around 1988. No more.

Simply put: the problem of climate change has entered *kairos* time; its *kairos* moment has arrived. How long will it endure? Until the time of decisive action to bring about deliverance comes—or, more ominously, until the time when the opportunity for decisive action has passed us by. Which will we choose? Because we do have a choice.

—Rev. Jim Ball, Ph.D., "It's *Kairos* Time for Climate Change: Time to Act," *Creation Care: A Christian Environmental Quarterly* (Summer 2008), 28.

---

*Donald C. Bryant, "Rhetoric: Its Functions and Its Scope." In *Professing the New Rhetorics: A Sourcebook,* eds. Theresa Enos and Stuart C. Brown (Englewood Cliffs, NJ: Prentice Hall, 1994), 282.

Passage 2

[Another action that Americans must take to combat global warming is to transition] to a clean energy economy in a just and equitable way. Global warming is among the greatest challenges of our time, but also presents extraordinary opportunities to harness home-grown clean energy sources and encourage technological innovation. These bold shifts toward a clean energy future can create hundreds of thousands of new jobs and generate billions of dollars in capital investment. But in order to maximize these benefits across all sectors of our society, comprehensive global warming legislation must auction emission allowances to polluters and use these public assets for public benefit programs.

Such programs include financial assistance to help low and moderate-income consumers and workers offset higher energy costs as well as programs that assist with adaptation efforts in communities vulnerable to the effects of climate change. Revenue generated from emissions allowances should also aid the expansion of renewable and efficient energy technologies that quickly, cleanly, cheaply, and safely reduce our dependence on fossil fuels and curb global warming. Lastly, it is absolutely vital that comprehensive global warming legislation not preempt state authority to cut greenhouse gas emissions more aggressively than mandated by federal legislation.

—Sierra Club, "Global Warming Policy Solutions," 2008, http://www.sierraclub.org/

Group task: Working in small groups or as a whole class, try to reach consensus answers to the following questions:

1. How do the strategies of persuasion differ in these two passages?
2. Explain these differences in terms of targeted audience and original genre.
3. How effective is each argument for its intended audience?
4. Would either argument be effective for readers outside the intended audience?

Questions for Rhetorical Analysis

Conducting a rhetorical analysis asks you to bring to bear on an argument your knowledge of argument and your repertoire of reading strategies. The chart of questions for analysis on pages 161–162 can help you examine an argument in depth. Although a rhetorical analysis will not include answers to all of these questions, using some of these questions in your thinking stages can give you a thorough understanding of the argument while helping you generate insights for your own rhetorical analysis essay.

An Illustration of Rhetorical Analysis

To illustrate rhetorical analysis in this section and in the student example at the end of the chapter, we will use two articles on reproductive technology, a subject that continues to generate arguments in the public sphere. By *reproductive technology* we mean scientific advances in the treatment of infertility such as egg and sperm donation, artificial insemination, in vitro fertilization, and surrogate motherhood. Our first article, from a decade ago, springs from the early and increasing popularity of these technological options. Our second article—to be used in our later student example—responds to the recent globalization of this technology.

Questions for Rhetorical Analysis

What to Focus On	Questions to Ask	Applying These Questions
The *kairotic* moment and writer's motivating occasion	■ What motivated the writer to produce this piece? ■ What social, cultural, political, legal, or economic conversations does this argument join?	■ Is the writer responding to a bill pending in Congress, a speech by a political leader, or a local event that provoked controversy? ■ Is the writer addressing cultural trends such as the impact of science or technology on values?
Rhetorical context: Writer's purpose and audience	■ What is the writer's purpose? ■ Who is the intended audience? ■ What assumptions, values, and beliefs would readers have to hold to find this argument persuasive? ■ How well does the text suit its particular audience and purpose?	■ Is the writer trying to change readers' views by offering a new interpretation of a phenomenon, calling readers to action, or trying to muster votes or inspire further investigations? ■ Does the audience share a political or religious orientation with the writer?
Rhetorical context: Writer's identity and angle of vision	■ Who is the writer and what is his or her profession, background, and expertise? ■ How does the writer's personal history, education, gender, ethnicity, age, class, sexual orientation, and political leaning influence the angle of vision? ■ What is emphasized and what is omitted in this text? ■ How much does the writer's angle of vision dominate the text?	■ Is the writer a scholar, researcher, scientist, policy maker, politician, professional journalist, or citizen blogger? ■ Is the writer affiliated with conservative or liberal, religious or lay publications? ■ Is the writer advocating a stance or adopting a more inquiry-based mode? ■ What points of view and pieces of evidence are "not seen" by this writer?
Rhetorical context: Genre	■ What is the argument's original genre? ■ What is the original medium of publication? How does the genre and the argument's place of publication influence its content, structure, and style?	■ How popular or scholarly, informal or formal is this genre? ■ Does the genre allow for in-depth or only sketchy coverage of an issue? ■ (See Chapter 2, pages 33–38, for detailed explanations of genre.)
ptr*Logos* of the argument**	■ What is the argument's claim, either explicitly stated or implied? ■ What are the main reasons in support of the claim? Are the reasons audience-based? ■ How effective is the writer's use of evidence? How is the argument supported and developed? ■ How well has the argument recognized and responded to alternative views?	■ Is the core of the argument clear and soundly developed? Or do readers have to unearth or reconstruct the argument? ■ Is the argument one-sided, multisided, or dialogic? ■ Does the argument depend on assumptions the audience may not share? ■ What evidence does the writer employ? Does this evidence meet the STAR criteria? (See pages 92–93.)

(Continued)

What to Focus On	Questions to Ask	Applying These Questions
Ethos of the argument	▪ What *ethos* does the writer project? ▪ How does the writer try to seem credible and trustworthy to the intended audience? ▪ How knowledgeable does the writer seem in recognizing opposing or alternative views and how fairly does the writer respond to them?	▪ If you are impressed or won over by this writer, what has earned your respect? ▪ If you are filled with doubts or skepticism, what has caused you to question this writer? ▪ How important is the character of the writer in this argument?
Pathos of the argument	▪ How effective is the writer in using audience-based reasons? ▪ How does the writer use concrete language, word choice, narrative, examples, and analogies to tap readers' emotions, values, and imaginations?	▪ What examples, connotative language, and uses of narrative or analogy stand out for you in this argument? ▪ Does this argument rely heavily on appeals to *pathos*? Or is it more brainy and logical?
Writer's style	▪ How do the writer's language choices and sentence length and complexity contribute to the impact of the argument? ▪ How well does the writer's tone (attitude toward the subject) suit the argument?	▪ How readable is this argument? ▪ Is the argument formal, scholarly, journalistic, informal, or casual? ▪ Is the tone serious, mocking, humorous, exhortational, confessional, urgent, or something else?
Design and visual elements	▪ How do design elements—layout, font sizes and styles, and use of color—influence the effect of the argument? (See Chapter 9 for a detailed discussion of these elements.) ▪ How do graphics and images contribute to the persuasiveness of the argument?	▪ Do design features contribute to the logical or the emotional/imaginative appeals of the argument? ▪ How would this argument benefit from visuals and graphics or some different document design?
Overall persuasiveness of the argument	▪ What features of this argument contribute most to making it persuasive or not persuasive for its target audience and for you yourself? ▪ How would this argument be received by different audiences? ▪ What features contribute to the rhetorical complexity of this argument? ▪ What is particularly memorable, disturbing, or problematic about this argument? ▪ What does this argument contribute to its *kairotic* moment and the argumentative controversy of which it is a part?	▪ For example, are appeals to *pathos* legitimate and suitable? Does the quality and quantity of the evidence help build a strong case or fall short? ▪ What specifically would count as a strength for the target audience? ▪ If you differ from the target audience, how do you differ and where does the argument derail for you? ▪ What gaps, contradictions, or unanswered questions are you left with? ▪ How does this argument indicate that it is engaged in a public conversation? How does it "talk" to other arguments you have read on this issue?

At this point, please read the following article, "Egg Heads" by Kathryn Jean Lopez, and then proceed to the discussion questions that follow. Lopez's article was originally published in the September 1, 1998, issue of the biweekly conservative news commentary magazine *National Review*.

Egg Heads

KATHRYN JEAN LOPEZ

Filling the waiting room to capacity and spilling over into a nearby conference room, a group of young women listen closely and follow the instructions: Complete the forms and return them, with the clipboard, to the receptionist. It's all just as in any medical office. Then they move downstairs, where the doctor briefs them. "Everything will be pretty much normal," she explains. "Women complain of skin irritation in the local area of injection and bloating. You also might be a little emotional. But, basically, it's really bad PMS."

This is not just another medical office. On a steamy night in July, these girls in their twenties are attending an orientation session for potential egg donors at a New Jersey fertility clinic specializing in in-vitro fertilization. Within the walls of IVF New Jersey and at least two hundred other clinics throughout the United States, young women answer the call to give "the gift of life" to infertile couples. Egg donation is a quietly expanding industry, changing the way we look at the family, young women's bodies, and human life itself.

It is not a pleasant way to make money. Unlike sperm donation, which is over in less than an hour, egg donation takes the donor some 56 hours and includes a battery of tests, ultrasound, self-administered injections, and retrieval. Once a donor is accepted into a program, she is given hormones to stimulate the ovaries, changing the number of eggs matured from the usual one per month up to as many as fifty. A doctor then surgically removes the eggs from the donor's ovary and fertilizes them with the designated sperm.

Although most programs require potential donors to undergo a series of medical tests and counseling, there is little indication that most of the young women know what they are getting themselves into. They risk bleeding, infection, and scarring. When too many eggs are matured in one cycle, it can damage the ovaries and leave the donor with weeks of abdominal pain. (At worst, complications may leave her dead.) Longer term, the possibility of early menopause raises the prospect of future regret. There is also some evidence of a connection between the fertility drugs used in the process and ovarian cancer.

5   But it's good money—and getting better. New York's Brooklyn IVF raised its "donor compensation" from $2,500 to $5,000 per cycle earlier this year in order to keep pace with St. Barnabas Medical Center in nearby Livingston, New Jersey. It's a bidding war. "It's obvious why we had to do it," says Susan Lobel, Brooklyn IVF's assistant director. Most New York–area IVF programs have followed suit.

Some infertile couples and independent brokers are offering even more for "reproductive material." The International Fertility Center in Indianapolis, Indiana, for instance, places ads in the *Daily Princetonian* offering Princeton girls as much as $35,000 per cycle. The National Fertility Registry, which, like many egg brokerages, features an online catalogue for couples to browse in, advertises $35,000 to $50,000 for Ivy League eggs. While donors are normally paid a flat fee per cycle, there have been reports of higher payments to donors who produce more eggs.

College girls are the perfect donors. Younger eggs are likelier to be healthy, and the girls themselves frequently need money—college girls have long been susceptible to classified ads offering to pay them for acting as guinea pigs in medical research. One 1998 graduate of the University of Colorado set up her own website to market her eggs. She had watched a television show on egg donation and figured it "seemed like a good thing to do"—especially since she had spent her money during the past year to help secure a country-music record deal. "Egg donation would help me with my school and music expenses while helping an infertile couple with a family." Classified ads scattered throughout cyberspace feature similar offers.

The market for "reproductive material" has been developing for a long time. It was twenty years ago this summer that the first test-tube baby, Louise Brown, was born. By 1995, when the latest tally was taken by the Centers for Disease Control, 15 percent of mothers in this country had made use of some form of assisted-reproduction technology in conceiving their children. (More recently, women past menopause have begun to make use of this technology.) In 1991 the American Society for Reproductive Medicine was aware of 63 IVF programs offering egg donation. That number had jumped to 189 by 1995 (the latest year for which numbers are available).

Defenders argue that it's only right that women are "compensated" for the inconvenience of egg donation. Brooklyn IVF's Dr. Lobel argues, "If it is unethical to accept payment for loving your neighbor, then we'll have to stop paying babysitters." As long as donors know the risks, says Glenn McGee of the University of Pennsylvania's Center for Bioethics, this transaction is only "a slightly macabre version of adoption."

10   Not everyone is enthusiastic about the "progress." Egg donation "represents another rather large step into turning procreation into manufacturing," says the University of Chicago's Leon

Kass. "It's the dehumanization of procreation." And as in manufacturing, there is quality control. "People don't want to say the word any more, but there is a strong eugenics issue inherent in the notion that you can have the best eggs your money can buy," observes sociology professor Barbara Katz Rothman of the City University of New York.

The demand side of the market comes mostly from career-minded baby-boomers, the frontiers women of feminism, who thought they could "have it all." Indeed they *can* have it all—with a little help from some younger eggs. (Ironically, feminists are also among its strongest critics; *The Nation*'s Katha Pollitt has pointed out that in egg donation and surrogacy, once you remove the "delusion that they are making babies for other women," all you have left is "reproductive prostitution.")

Unfortunately, the future looks bright for the egg market. Earlier this year, a woman in Atlanta gave birth to twins after she was implanted with frozen donor eggs. The same technology has also been successful in Italy. This is just what the egg market needed, since it avoids the necessity of coordinating donors' cycles with recipients' cycles. Soon, not only will infertile couples be able to choose from a wider variety of donor offerings, but in some cases donors won't even be needed. Young women will be able to freeze their own eggs and have them thawed and fertilized once they are ready for the intrusion of children in their lives.

There are human ovaries sitting in a freezer in Fairfax, Virginia. The Genetics and IVF Institute offers to cut out and remove young women's ovaries and cryopreserve the egg-containing tissue for future implantation. Although the technology was originally designed to give the hope of fertility to young women undergoing treatment for cancer, it is now starting to attract the healthy. "Women can wait to have children until they are well established in their careers and getting a little bored, sometime in their forties or fifties," explains Professor Rothman. "Basically, motherhood is being reduced to a good leisure-time activity."

Early this summer, headlines were made in Britain, where the payment of egg donors is forbidden, when an infertile couple traveled to a California clinic where the woman could be inseminated with an experimental hybrid egg. The egg was a combination of the recipient's and a donor's eggs. The clinic in question gets its eggs from a Beverly Hills brokerage, the Center for Surrogate Parenting and Egg Donation, run by Karen Synesiou and Bill Handel, a radio shock-jock in Los Angeles. Miss Synesiou recently told the London *Sunday Times* that she is "interested in redefining the family. That's why I came to work here."

15   The redefinition is already well under way. Consider the case of Jaycee Buzzanca. After John and Luanne Buzzanca had tried for years to have a child, an embryo was created for them, using sperm and an egg from anonymous donors, and implanted in a surrogate mother. In March 1995, one month before the baby was born, John filed for divorce. Luanne wanted child support from John, but he refused—after all, he's not the father. Luanne argued that John is Jaycee's father legally. At this point the surrogate mother, who had agreed to carry a baby for a stable two-parent household, decided to sue for custody.

Jaycee was dubbed "Nobody's Child" by the media when a California judge ruled that John was not the legal father nor Luanne the legal mother (neither one was genetically related to Jaycee, and Luanne had not even borne her). Enter Erin Davidson, the egg donor, who claims the egg was used without her permission. Not to be left out, the sperm donor jumped into the ring, saying that his sperm was used without his permission, a claim he later dropped. In March of this year, an appeals court gave Luanne custody and decided that John is the legal father, making

him responsible for child support. By contracting for a medical procedure resulting in the birth of a child, the court ruled, a couple incurs "the legal status of parenthood." (John lost an appeal in May.) For Jaycee's first three years on earth, these people have been wrangling over who her parents are.

In another case, William Kane left his girlfriend, Deborah Hect, 15 vials of sperm before he killed himself in a Las Vegas hotel in 1991. His two adult children (represented by their mother, his ex-wife) contested Miss Hect's claim of ownership. A settlement agreement on Kane's will was eventually reached, giving his children 80 percent of his estate and Miss Hect 20 percent. Hence she was allowed three vials of his sperm. When she did not succeed in conceiving on the first two tries, she filed a petition for the other 12 vials. She won, and the judge who ruled in her favor wrote, "Neither this court nor the decedent's adult children possess reason or right to prevent Hect from implementing decedent's pre-eminent interest in realizing his 'fundamental right' to procreate with the woman of his choice." One day, donors may not even have to have lived. Researchers are experimenting with using aborted female fetuses as a source of donor eggs.

And the market continues to zip along. For overseas couples looking for donor eggs, Bill Handel has the scenario worked out. The couple would mail him frozen sperm of their choice (presumably from the recipient husband); his clinic would use it to fertilize donor eggs, chosen from its catalogue of offerings, and reply back within a month with a frozen embryo ready for implantation. (Although the sperm does not yet arrive by mail, Handel has sent out embryos to at least one hundred international customers.) As for the young women at the New Jersey clinic, they are visibly upset by one aspect of the egg-donation process: they can't have sexual intercourse for several weeks after the retrieval. For making babies, of course, it's already obsolete.

■ ■ ■ **FOR CLASS DISCUSSION** Identifying Rhetorical Features

Working in groups, develop responses to the following questions:

1. How does Lopez appeal to *logos*? What is her main claim and what are her reasons? What does she use for evidence? What ideas would you have to include in a short summary?
2. What appeals to *pathos* does Lopez make in this argument? How well are these suited to the conservative readers of the *National Review*?
3. How would you characterize Lopez's *ethos*? Does she seem knowledgeable and credible? Does she seem fair to stakeholders in this controversy?
4. Choose an additional focus from the "Questions for Rhetorical Analysis" on pages 161–162 to apply to "Egg Heads." How does this question expand your understanding of Lopez's argument?
5. What strikes you as problematic, memorable, or disturbing in this argument?   ■ ■ ■

A Rhetorical Analysis of "Egg Heads"

Now that you have identified some of the rhetorical features of "Egg Heads," we offer our own notes for a rhetorical analysis of this argument.

Rhetorical Context As we began our analysis, we reconstructed the rhetorical context in which "Egg Heads" was published. In the late 1990s, a furious debate about egg donation rippled through college and public newspapers, popular journalism, Web sites, and scholarly commentary. This debate had been kicked off by several couples placing ads in the newspapers of the country's most prestigious colleges, offering up to $50,000 for the eggs of brilliant, attractive, athletic college women. Coinciding with these consumer demands, advances in reproductive technology provided an increasing number of complex techniques to surmount the problem of infertility, including fertilizing eggs in petri dishes and implanting them into women through surgical procedures. These procedures could use either a couple's own eggs and sperm or donated eggs and sperm. All these social and medical factors created the *kairotic* moment for Lopez's article and motivated her to protest the increasing use of these procedures. (Egg donation, surrogate motherhood, and the potential dehumanizing of commercial reproduction continue to be troubling and unresolved controversies across many genres, as you will see when you read Ellen Goodman's op-ed piece at the end of this chapter and student Zachary Stumps's rhetorical analysis of it.)

Genre and Writer When we considered the genre and writer of this article and its site of publication, we noted that this article appeared in the *National Review*, which describes itself as "America's most widely read and influential magazine and Web site for Republican/conservative news, commentary, and opinion." It reaches "an affluent, educated, and highly responsive audience of corporate and government leaders, the financial elite, educators, journalists, community and association leaders, as well as engaged activists all across America" (http://www.nationalreview.com). According to our Internet search, Kathryn Jean Lopez is known nationally for her conservative journalistic writing on social and political issues. Currently the editor of *National Review Online*, she has also published in the *Wall Street Journal,* the *New York Post*, and the *Washington Times.* This information told us that in her article "Egg Heads," Lopez is definitely on home territory, aiming her article at a conservative audience.

Logos Turning to the *logos* of Lopez's argument, we decided that the logical structure of Lopez's argument is clear throughout the article. Her claim is that egg donation and its associated reproductive advances have harmful, long-reaching consequences for society. Basically, she argues that egg donation and reproductive technology represent bad scientific developments for society because they are potentially harmful to the long-range health of egg donors and because they lead to an unnatural dehumanizing of human sexuality. She states a version of this last point at the end of the second paragraph: "Egg donation is a quietly expanding industry, changing the way we look at the family, young women's bodies, and human life itself" (page 163).

The body of her article elaborates on each of these reasons. In developing her reason that egg donation endangers egg donors, Lopez lists the risks but doesn't supply supporting evidence about the frequency of these problems: damage to the ovaries, persistent pain, early menopause, possible ovarian cancer, and even death. She supports her claim about "the expanding industry" by showing how the procedures have become commercialized. To show the popularity of these procedures as well as their commercial value, she quotes a variety of experts such as directors of in vitro clinics, fertility centers, bioethicists, and the American Society for Reproductive Medicine. She also cleverly bolsters her own case by showing that even liberal cultural critics agree with her views about the big ethical questions raised by the reproductive-technology business. In addition to quoting experts, Lopez has sprinkled impressive numbers and vivid examples throughout the body of her argument that give her argument momentum as it progresses from the potential harm to young egg donors to a number of case studies that depict increasingly disturbing ethical problems.

Pathos Much of the impact of this argument, we noted, comes from Lopez's appeals to *pathos*. By describing in detail the waiting rooms for egg donors at fertility clinics, Lopez relies heavily on pathetic appeals to move her audience to see the physical and social dangers of egg donation. She conveys the growing commercialism of reproductive technology by giving readers an inside look at the egg-donation process as these young college women embark on the multistep process of donating their eggs. These young women, she suggests in her title "Egg Heads," are largely unaware of the potential physical dangers to themselves and of the ethical implications and consequences of their acts. She asserts that they are driven largely by the desire for money. Lopez also appeals to *pathos* in her choice of emotionally loaded and often cynical language, which creates an angle of vision opposing reproductive technology: 'turning procreation into manufacturing'; 'reproductive prostitution'; "the intrusion of children in their lives"; 'motherhood . . . reduced to a good leisure-time activity'; "aborted female fetuses as a source of donor eggs"; and intercourse as an "obsolete" way to make babies (pages 164, 165).

Audience Despite Lopez's success at spotlighting serious medical and ethical questions, her lack of attention to alternative views and the alarmism of her language caused us to wonder: Who might find this argument persuasive and who would challenge it? What is noticeably missing from her argument—and apparently from her worldview—is the perspective of infertile couples hoping for a baby. Pursuing our question, we decided that a provocative feature of this argument—one worthy of deeper analysis—is the disparity between how well this argument is suited to its target audience and yet how unpersuasive it is for readers who do not share the assumptions, values, and beliefs of this primary audience.

To Lopez's credit, she has attuned her reasons to the values and concerns of her conservative readers of the *National Review*, who believe in traditional families, gender differences, and gender roles. Opposed to feminism as they understand it, this audience sanctions careers for women only if women put their families first. Lopez's choice of evidence and her orchestration of it are intended to play to her audience's fears that science has uncontrollably fallen into the hands of those who have little regard for the sanctity of the family or traditional motherhood. For example, in playing strongly to the values of her conservative readers, Lopez belabors the physical, social, and ethical dangers of egg donation, mentioning worst-case scenarios; however, these appeals to *pathos* will most likely strike other readers who do some investigating into reproductive technology as overblown. She emphasizes the commercialism of the process as her argument moves from college girls as egg donors to a number of sensationalist case studies that depict intensifying ethical ambiguity. In other words, both the *logos* and the *pathos* of her argument skillfully focus on details that tap her target audience's values and beliefs and feed that audience's fears and revulsion.

Use of Evidence For a broader or skeptical audience, the alarmism of Lopez's appeals to *pathos,* her use of atypical evidence, and her distortion of the facts weaken the *logos* and *ethos* of her argument. First, Lopez's use of evidence fails to measure up to the STAR criteria (that evidence should be sufficient, typical, accurate, and relevant). She characterizes all egg donors as young women seeking money. But she provides little evidence that egg donors are only out to make a buck. She also paints these young women as shortsighted, uninformed, and foolish. Lopez weakens her *ethos* by not considering the young women who have researched the process and who may be motivated, at least in part, by compassion for couples who can't conceive on their own. Lopez also misrepresents the people who are using egg donation, placing them all into two groups: (1) wealthy couples eugenically seeking designer babies with preordered special traits and (2) feminist career, women. She directs much of her criticism toward this latter group: "The demand side of the market comes mostly from career-minded baby-boomers, the frontierswomen of feminism, who thought they could 'have it all'" (page 164). However, readers who do a little research on their own, as we did, will learn that infertility affects one in seven couples; that it is often a male and a female problem, sometimes caused by an incompatibility between the husband's and the wife's reproductive material; and that most couples who take the big step of investing in these expensive efforts to have a baby have been trying to get pregnant for a number of years. Rather than being casual about having children, they are often deeply desirous of children and depressed about their inability to conceive. In addition, far from being the sure thing and quick fix that Lopez suggests, reproductive technology has a success rate of only 50 percent overall and involves a huge investment of time, money, and physical discomfort for women receiving donor eggs.

Another way that Lopez violates the STAR criteria is her choice of extreme cases. For readers outside her target audience, her argument appears riddled with straw man and slippery-slope fallacies. (See the Appendix, "Informal Fallacies," pages 349–356.) Her examples become more bizarre as her tone becomes more hysterical. Here are some specific instances of extreme, atypical cases:

- her focus on careerwomen casually and selfishly using the service of young egg donors
- the notorious case of Jaycee Buzzanca, dubbed "Nobody's Child" because her adoptive parents who commissioned her creation divorced before she was born
- the legal contest between a dead man's teen girlfriend and his ex-wife and adult children over his vials of sperm
- the idea of taking eggs from aborted female fetuses

By keeping invisible the vast majority of ordinary couples who go to fertility clinics out of last-hope desperation, Lopez uses extreme cases to create a "brave new world" intended to evoke a vehement rejection of these reproductive advances. These skeptical readers would offer the alternative view of the sad, ordinary couples of all ages sitting week after week in fertility clinics, hoping to conceive a child through the "miracle" of these reproductive advances and grateful to the young women who have contributed their eggs.

Concluding Points In short, we concluded that Lopez's angle of vision, although effectively in sync with her conservative readers of the *National Review,* exaggerates and distorts her case against these reproductive advances. Lopez's traditional values and slanting of the evidence undermine her *ethos,* limit the value of this argument for a wider audience, and compel that audience to seek out alternative sources for a more complete view of egg donation.

Conclusion

To analyze a text rhetorically means to determine how it works: what effect it has on readers and how it achieves or fails to achieve its persuasiveness. Assignments involving rhetorical analysis are present in courses across the curriculum, and analyzing texts rhetorically is a major step in constructing your own arguments. In this chapter, we showed you how to apply your understanding of argument concepts, such as the influence of genre and appeals to *logos, ethos,* and *pathos,* to examining the strength of verbal texts. We conclude with a student's rhetorical analysis written for the assignment in this chapter.

WRITING ASSIGNMENT   A Rhetorical Analysis

Write a thesis-driven rhetorical analysis essay in which you examine the rhetorical effectiveness of an argument specified by your instructor. Unless otherwise stated, direct your analysis to an audience of your classmates. In your introduction, establish the argumentative conversation to which this argument is contributing. Briefly summarize the argument and present your thesis highlighting two or more rhetorical features of the argument that you find central to the effectiveness or ineffectiveness of this argument. To develop and support your own points, you will need to include textual evidence in the form of examples or short quotations from the argument. Use attributive tags to distinguish your ideas from those of the writer of the argument. Use MLA documentation to cite points and quotations in your essay and in a Works Cited list at the end. Think of your rhetorical analysis as a way to shine a spotlight on important aspects of this argument and to make the argument understandable and interesting for your readers. A student paper written for this assignment is shown at the end of this chapter—Zachary Stumps's analysis of Ellen Goodman's "Womb for Rent."

Generating Ideas for Your Rhetorical Analysis

To develop ideas for your essay, you might follow these steps:

Step1	How to Do It
Familiarize yourself with the article you are analyzing.	Read your article several times. Divide it into sections to understand its structure.
Place the article in its rhetorical context.	Follow the strategies in Chapter 2 and use the "Questions for Rhetorical Analysis" on pages 161–162.
Summarize the article.	Follow the steps in Chapter 2 on pages 41–42. You may want to produce a longer summary of 150–200 words as well as a short, one-sentence summary.
Reread the article, identifying "hot spots."	Note hot spots in the article—points that impress you, disturb you, confuse you, or puzzle you.
Use the "Questions for Rhetorical Analysis" on pages 161–162.	Choose several of these questions and freewrite responses to them.
From your notes and freewriting, identify the focus for your analysis.	Choose several features of the article that you find particularly important and that you want to discuss in depth in your essay. Identify points that will bring something new to your readers and that will help them see this article with new understanding. You may want to list your ideas and then look for ways to group them together around main points.
Write a thesis statement for your essay.	Articulate your important points in one or two sentences, setting up these points clearly for your audience.

In finding a meaningful focus for your rhetorical analysis essay, you will need to create a focusing thesis statement that avoids wishy-washy formulas such as, "This argument has some strengths and some weaknesses." To avoid a vapid thesis statement, focus on the complexity of the argument, the writer's strategies for persuading the target audience, and the features that might impede its persuasiveness for skeptics. These thesis statements articulate how their writers see the inner workings of these arguments as well as the arguments' contributions to their public conversations.

> Lopez's angle of vision, although effectively in sync with her conservative readers of the *National Review*, exaggerates and distorts her case against these reproductive advances, weakening her *ethos* and the value of her argument for a wider audience. [This is the thesis we would use if we were writing a stand-alone essay on Lopez.]

> In his editorial "Why Blame Mexico?" published in *The American Conservative*, Fred Reed's irony and hard-hitting evidence undercut his desire to contrast the United States' hypocritical and flawed immigration policies with Mexico's successful ones.

> In his editorial "Amnesty?" in the Jesuit news commentary *America*, John F. Kavanaugh makes a powerful argument for his Catholic and religious readers; however, his proposal based on ethical reasoning may fail to reach other readers.

To make your rhetorical analysis of your article persuasive, you will need to develop each of the points stated or implied in your thesis statement using textual evidence, including short quotations. Your essay should show how you have listened carefully to the argument you are analyzing, summarized it fairly, and probed it deeply.

Organizing Your Rhetorical Analysis

A stand-alone rhetorical analysis can be organized as shown below. ■

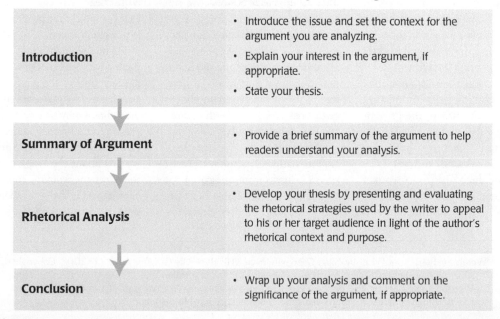

Organization Plan for a Rhetorical Analysis of an Argument

Introduction	• Introduce the issue and set the context for the argument you are analyzing. • Explain your interest in the argument, if appropriate. • State your thesis.
Summary of Argument	• Provide a brief summary of the argument to help readers understand your analysis.
Rhetorical Analysis	• Develop your thesis by presenting and evaluating the rhetorical strategies used by the writer to appeal to his or her target audience in light of the author's rhetorical context and purpose.
Conclusion	• Wrap up your analysis and comment on the significance of the argument, if appropriate.

Readings

Our first reading is by journalist Ellen Goodman, whose columns are syndicated in U.S. newspapers by the Washington Post Writers Group. This column, which appeared in 2008, is analyzed rhetorically by student Zachary Stumps in our second reading.

Womb for Rent—For a Price

ELLEN GOODMAN

BOSTON—By now we all have a story about a job outsourced beyond our reach in the global economy. My own favorite is about the California publisher who hired two reporters in India to cover the Pasadena city government. Really.

There are times as well when the offshoring of jobs takes on a quite literal meaning. When the labor we are talking about is, well, labor.

In the last few months we've had a full nursery of international stories about surrogate mothers. Hundreds of couples are crossing borders in search of lower-cost ways to fill the family business. In turn, there's a new coterie of international workers who are gestating for a living.

Many of the stories about the globalization of baby production begin in India, where the government seems to regard this as, literally, a growth industry. In the little town of Anand, dubbed "The Cradle of the World," 45 women were recently on the books of a local clinic. For the production and delivery of a child, they will earn $5,000 to $7,000, a decade's worth of women's wages in rural India.

5 But even in America, some women, including Army wives, are supplementing their income by contracting out their wombs. They have become surrogate mothers for wealthy couples from European countries that ban the practice.

This globalization of baby-making comes at the peculiar intersection of a high reproductive technology and a low-tech work force. The biotech business was created in the same petri dish as Baby Louise, the first IVF baby. But since then, we've seen conception outsourced to egg donors and sperm donors. We've had motherhood divided into its parts from genetic mother to gestational mother to birth mother and now contract mother.

We've also seen the growth of an international economy. Frozen sperm is flown from one continent to another. And patients have become medical tourists, searching for cheaper health care whether it's a new hip in Thailand or an IVF treatment in South Africa that comes with a photo safari thrown in for the same price. Why not then rent a foreign womb?

I don't make light of infertility. The primal desire to have a child underlies this multinational Creation, Inc. On one side, couples who choose surrogacy want a baby with at least half their own genes. On the other side, surrogate mothers, who are rarely implanted with their own eggs, can believe that the child they bear and deliver is not really theirs.

As one woman put it, "We give them a baby and they give us much-needed money. It's good for them and for us." A surrogate in Anand used the money to buy a heart operation for her son. Another raised a dowry for her daughter. And before we talk about the "exploitation" of the pregnant woman, consider her alternative in Anand: a job crushing glass in a factory for $25 a month.

10   Nevertheless, there is—and there should be—something uncomfortable about a free market approach to baby-making. It's easier to accept surrogacy when it's a gift from one woman to another. But we rarely see a rich woman become a surrogate for a poor family. Indeed, in Third World countries, some women sign these contracts with a fingerprint because they are illiterate.

For that matter, we have not yet had stories about the contract workers for whom pregnancy was a dangerous occupation, but we will. What obligation does a family that simply contracted for a child have to its birth mother? What control do—should—contractors have over their "employees" lives while incubating "their" children? What will we tell the offspring of this international trade?

"National boundaries are coming down," says bioethicist Lori Andrews, "but we can't stop human emotions. We are expanding families and don't even have terms to deal with it."

It's the commercialism that is troubling. Some things we cannot sell no matter how good "the deal." We cannot, for example, sell ourselves into slavery. We cannot sell our children. But the surrogacy business comes perilously close to both of these deals. And international surrogacy tips the scales.

So, these borders we are crossing are not just geographic ones. They are ethical ones. Today the global economy sends everyone in search of the cheaper deal as if that were the single common good. But in the biological search, humanity is sacrificed to the economy and the person becomes the product. And, step by step, we come to a stunning place in our ancient creation story. It's called the marketplace.

Critiquing "Womb for Rent—For a Price"

1. What is Goodman's main claim and what are her reasons? In other words, what ideas would you have to include in a short summary?
2. What appeals to *pathos* does Goodman make in this argument? How do these appeals function in the argument?
3. Choose an additional focus from the "Questions for Rhetorical Analysis" to apply to "Womb for Rent—For a Price." How does this question affect your perspective of Goodman's argument?
4. What strikes you as problematic, memorable, or disturbing in this argument?

Our second reading shows how student writer Zachary Stumps analyzed the Ellen Goodman article.

A Rhetorical Analysis of Ellen Goodman's "Womb for Rent—For a Price"

ZACHARY STUMPS (STUDENT)

Introduction provides context and poses issue to be addressed.

With her op-ed piece "Womb for Rent—For a Price," published in the *Seattle Times* on April 11, 2008 (and earlier in the *Boston Globe*), syndicated columnist Ellen Goodman enters the murky debate about reproductive technology gone global. Since Americans are outsourcing everything else, "Why not then rent a foreign womb?" (170) she asks. Goodman, a Pulitzer

Provides background
on Goodman

Prize–winning columnist for the Washington Post Writers Group, is known
for helping readers understand the "tumult of social change and its impact
on families," and for shattering "the mold of men writing exclusively about
politics" ("Ellen Goodman"). This op-ed piece continues her tradition of
examining social change from the perspective of family issues.

Summarizes the
op-ed piece

Goodman launches her short piece by asserting that one of the most recent
and consequential "jobs" to be outsourced is having babies. She explains how
the "globalization of baby production" (170) is thriving because it brings together the reproductive desires of people in developed countries and the bodily resources of women in developing countries like India. Briefly tracing how
both reproductive technology and medical tourism have taken advantage of
global possibilities, Goodman acknowledges that the thousands of dollars Indian women earn by carrying the babies of foreign couples represent a much
larger income than these women could earn in any other available jobs. After
appearing to legitimize this global exchange, however, Goodman shifts to her
ethical concerns by raising some moral questions that she says are not being
addressed in this trade. She concludes with a full statement of her claim that
this global surrogacy is encroaching on human respect and dignity, exploiting
business-based science, and turning babies into products.

Thesis paragraph

In this piece, Goodman's delay of her thesis has several rhetorical benefits: it gives Goodman space to present the perspective of poor women,
enhanced by her appeals to *pathos,* and it invites readers to join her journey
into the complex contexts of this issue; however, this strategy is also risky
because it limits the development of her own argument.

Develops first point
in thesis: use of
pathos in exploring
perspective of poor
women

Instead of presenting her thesis up front, Goodman devotes much of the first
part of her argument to looking at this issue from the perspective of foreign
surrogate mothers. Using the strategies of *pathos* to evoke sympathy for these
women, she creates a compassionate and progressively minded argument that
highlights the benefits to foreign surrogate mothers. She cites factual evidence
showing that the average job for a woman in Anand, India, yields a tiny "$25
a month" gotten through the hard work of "crushing glass in a factory" (170),
compared to the "$5,000 to $7,000" made carrying a baby to term (170). To
carry a baby to term for a foreign couple represents "a decade's worth of
women's wages in rural India" (170). Deepening readers' understanding of
these women, Goodman cites one woman who used her earnings to finance
her son's heart operation and another who paid for her daughter's dowry. In
her fair presentation of these women, Goodman both builds her own positive
ethos and adds a dialogic dimension to her argument by helping readers walk
in the shoes of otherwise impoverished surrogate mothers.

Develops second
point in thesis: the
complex contexts of
this issue—
outsourcing and
medical tourism

The second rhetorical benefit of Goodman's delayed thesis is that she 5
invites readers to explore this complex issue of global surrogacy with her before she declares her own view. To help readers understand and think through
this issue, she relates it to two other familiar global topics: outsourcing and

medical tourism. First, she introduces foreign surrogacy as one of the latest forms of outsourcing: "This globalization of baby-making comes at the peculiar intersection of a high reproductive technology and a low-tech work force" (170). Presenting these women as workers, she explains that women in India are getting paid for "the production and delivery of a child" (170) that is analogous to the production and delivery of sneakers or bicycle parts. Goodman also sets this phenomenon in the context of global medical tourism. If people can pursue lower-cost treatment for illnesses and health conditions in other countries, why shouldn't an infertile couple seeking to start a family not also have such access to these more affordable and newly available means? This reasoning provides a foundation for readers to begin understanding the many layers of the issue.

Shows how the delayed-thesis structure creates two perspectives in conflict

The result of Goodman's delayed-thesis strategy is that the first two-thirds of this piece seem to justify outsourcing surrogate motherhood. Only after reading the whole op-ed piece can readers see clearly that Goodman has been dropping hints about her view all along through her choice of words. Although she clearly sees how outsourcing surrogacy can help poor women economically, her use of market language such as "production," "delivery," and "labor" carry a double meaning. On first reading of this op-ed piece, readers don't know if Goodman's punning is meant to be catchy and entertaining or serves another purpose. This other purpose becomes clear in the last third of the article when Goodman forthrightly asserts her criticism of the commercialism of the global marketplace that promotes worldwide searching for a "cheaper deal": "humanity is sacrificed to the economy and the person becomes the product" (171). This is a bold and big claim, but does the final third of her article support it?

Restates the third point in his thesis: lack of space limits development of Goodman's argument

In the final five paragraphs of this op-ed piece, Goodman begins to develop the rational basis of her argument; however, the brevity of the op-ed genre and her choice not to state her view openly initially have left Goodman with little space to develop her own claim. The result is that she presents some profound ideas very quickly. Some of the ethically complex ideas she introduces but doesn't explore much are these:

- The idea that there are ethical limits on what can be "sold"
- The idea that surrogate motherhood might be a "dangerous occupation"
- The idea that children born from this "international trade" may be confused about their identities.

Discusses examples of ideas raised by Goodman but not developed

Goodman simply has not left herself enough space to develop these issues and perhaps leaves readers with questions rather than with changed views. I am particularly struck by several questions. Why have European countries banned surrogacy in developing countries and why has the United States not banned this practice? Does Goodman intend to argue that the United States should follow Europe's lead? She could explore more how this business of finding illiterate women to bear children for the wealthy continues to exploit third-world citizens much as sex tourism exploits women in the very same countries. It seems to perpetuate a tendency for the developed world to regard developing countries as a poor place of lawlessness where practices outlawed in the rest of the world (e.g., child prostitution, slave-like working conditions) are somehow tolerable. Goodman could have developed her argument more to state explicitly that a woman who accepts payment for bearing a baby becomes an indentured servant to the family. Yet another way to think of this issue is to see that the old saying of "a bun in the oven" is more literal than metaphoric when a woman uses her womb as a factory to produce children, a body business not too dissimilar to the commercialism of prostitution. Goodman only teases readers by mentioning these complex problems without producing an argument.

Conclusion

Still, although Goodman does not expand her criticism of outsourced surrogate motherhood or explore the issues of human dignity and rights, this argument does introduce the debate on surrogacy in the global marketplace, raise awareness, and begin to direct the conversation toward a productive end of seeking a responsible, healthy, and ethical future. Her op-ed piece lures readers into contemplating deep, perplexing ethical and economic problems and lays a foundation for readers to create an informed view of this issue.

Works Cited

Uses MLA format to list sources cited in the essay

"Ellen Goodman." *Postwritersgroup.com*. Washington Post Writer's Group, 2008. Web. 19 May 2008.

Goodman, Ellen. "Womb for Rent—For a Price." *Seattle Times* 11 Apr. 2008: B6. Rpt. in *Writing Arguments*. John D. Ramage, John C. Bean, and June Johnson. 9th ed. New York: Pearson Longman, 2012. Print.

For additional writing, reading, and research resources, go to www.mycomplab.com

Analyzing Visual Arguments

To see how images can make powerful arguments, consider the rhetorical persuasiveness of the "polar bear" marching in a small town parade (Figure 9.1). Sponsored by local environmentalists advocating action against global warming, the polar bear uses arguments from *logos* (drawing on audience knowledge that climate change threatens polar bears), *pathos* (evoking the bears' vulnerability), and *ethos* (conveying the commitment of the citizens group). Delighting children and adults alike, the bear creates a memorable environmental argument.

This chapter is aimed at increasing your ability to analyze visual arguments and use them rhetorically in your own work. In this chapter, you will learn to:

- Analyze visual arguments, including ads, posters, and cartoons
- Use visuals in your own arguments
- Display numeric data in graphs and charts

FIGURE 9.1 A visual argument about climate change

Understanding Design Elements in Visual Argument

To understand how visual images can produce an argument, you need to understand the design elements that work together to create a visual text. In this section we'll explain and illustrate the four basic components of visual design: use of type, use of space and layout, use of color, and use of images and graphics.

Use of Type

Type is an important visual element of written arguments. Variations in type, such as size, boldface, italics, or all caps, can direct a reader's attention to an argument's structure and highlight main points. In arguments designed specifically for visual impact, such as posters or advocacy advertisements, type is often used in eye-catching and meaningful ways. In choosing type, you need to consider the typeface or font style, the size of the type, and formatting options. The main typefaces or fonts are classified as serif, sans serif, and specialty type. Serif type has little extensions on the letters. (This text is set in serif type.) Sans serif type lacks these extensions. Specialty type includes script fonts and special symbols. In addition to font style, type comes in different sizes. It is measured in points, with 1 point equal to $\frac{1}{72}$ of an inch. Most text-based arguments consisting mainly of body text are written in 10- to 12-point type, whereas more image-based arguments may use a mixture of type sizes that interacts with the images for persuasive effect. Type can also be formatted using bold, italics, underlining, or shading for emphasis. Table 9.1 shows examples of type styles, as well as their typical uses.

The following basic principles for choosing type for visual arguments can help you tachieve your overall goals of readability, visual appeal, and suitability.

Table 9.1 Examples and Uses of Type Fonts

Font Style	Font Name	Example	Use
Serif fonts	Times New Roman Courier New Bookman Old Style	Use type wisely. Use type wisely. Use type wisely.	Easy to read; good for long documents, good for *body type,* or the main verbal parts of a document
Sans serif fonts	Arial Century Gothic	Use type wisely. Use type wisely.	Tiring to read for long stretches; good for *display type* such as headings, titles, slogans
Specialty fonts	Zapf Chancery Onyx MT	Use type wisely. Use type wisely.	Difficult to read for long stretches; effective when used sparingly for playful or decorative effect

Principles for Choosing Type for Visual Arguments

1. If you are creating a poster or advocacy advertisement, you will need to decide how much of your argument will be displayed in words and how much in images. For the text portions, choose *display type* (sans serif) or specialty fonts for titles, headings, and slogans, and *body or text type* (serif) for longer passages of text.
2. Make type functional and appealing by using only two or three font styles per document.
3. Use consistent patterns of type (similar type styles, sizes, and formats) to indicate relationships among similar items or different levels of importance.
4. Choose type to project a specific impression (a structured combination of serif and sans serif type to create a formal, serious, or businesslike impression; sans serif and specialty type to create a casual, informal, or playful impression, and so forth).

Besides these general principles, rhetorical considerations of genre and audience expectations should govern decisions about type. Text-based arguments in scholarly publications generally use plain, conservative fonts with little variation, whereas text-based arguments in popular magazines may use more variations in font style and size, especially in headings and opening leads. Visual arguments such as posters, fliers, and advocacy ads exploit the aesthetic potential of type.

Use of Space or Layout

A second component of visual design is layout, which is critical for creating the visual appeal of an argument and for conveying meaning. Even visual arguments that are mainly textual should use space very purposefully. By spacing and layout we mean all of the following points:

- Page size and type of paper
- Proportion of text to white space
- Proportion of text to image(s) and graphics
- Arrangement of text on page (space, margins, columns, size of paragraphs, spaces between paragraphs, justification of margins)
- Use of highlighting elements such as bulleted lists, tables, sidebars, boxes
- Use of headings and other means of breaking text into visual elements

In arguments that don't use visuals directly, the writer's primary visual concern is document design, in which the writer tries to meet the conventions of a genre and the expectations of the intended audience. For example, Julee Christianson's researched argument on pages 274–279 is designed to meet the document conventions of the American Psychological Association (APA). Note the use of a plain, conventional type-face (for easy reading); double spacing and one-inch margins (to leave room for editorial marking and notations); and special title page, headers, and page number locations (to meet expectations of readers familiar with APA documents—which all look exactly the same).

But in moving from verbal-only arguments to visual arguments that use visual elements for direct persuasive effect—for example, posters, fliers, or advocacy ads—creative use of layout is vital. Here are some ideas to help you think about the layout of a visual argument.

Principles for Laying Out Parts of a Visual Text

1. Choose a layout that avoids clutter and confusion by limiting how much text and how many visual items you put on a page.
2. Focus on creating coherence and meaning with layout.
3. Develop an ordering or structuring principle that clarifies the relationships among the parts.
4. Use layout and spacing to indicate the importance of items and to emphasize key ideas. Because Western readers read from left to right and top to bottom, top and center are positions that readily draw readers' eyes.

An Analysis of a Visual Argument Using Type and Spatial Elements

To illustrate the persuasive power of type and layout, we ask you to consider Figure 9.2, which shows an advocacy ad sponsored by a coalition of organizations aimed at fighting illegal drugs.

This ad, warning about the dangers of the drug Ecstasy, uses different sizes of type and layout to present its argument. The huge word "Ecstasy" first catches the reader's attention. The first few words at the top of the ad, exuding pleasure, lull the reader with the congruence between the pleasurable message and the playful type. Soon, however, the reader encounters a dissonance between the playful type and the meaning of the words: *dehydrate, hallucinate, paranoid,* and *dead* name unpleasant ideas. By the end of the ad, readers realize they have been led through a downward progression of ideas, beginning with the youth culture's belief that Ecstasy creates wonderfully positive feelings and ending with the ad's thesis that Ecstasy leads to paranoia, depression, and death. The playful informality of the font styles and the unevenly scattered layout of the type convey the seductiveness and unpredictability of the drug. The ad concedes that the first effects are "fall[ing] in love with the world" but implies that what comes next is increasingly dark and dangerous. At the end of the ad, in the lines of type near the bottom, the message and typestyle are congruent again. The question "Does that sound harmless to you?" marks a shift in type design and layout. The designer composed this section of the ad in conventional fonts centered on the page in a rational, businesslike fashion. This type design signals a metaphoric move from the euphoria of Ecstasy to the ordered structure of everyday reality, where the reader can now consider rationally the drug's harm. The information at the bottom of the ad identifies the ad's sponsors and gives both a Web address and a telephone number to call for more information about Ecstasy and other illegal drugs.

■ ■ ■ **FOR CLASS DISCUSSION** Comparing the Rhetorical Appeal of Two Advocacy Ads
This exercise asks you to examine Figure 9.3, an advocacy ad sponsored by Common Sense for Drug Policy, and to compare it to the ad in Figure 9.2. Figure 9.3 also

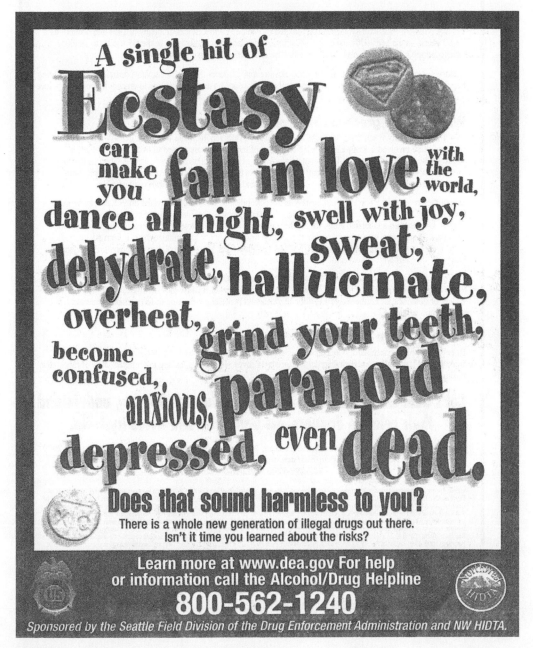

FIGURE 9.2 Advocacy advertisement warning against Ecstasy

What We Know About Ecstasy

What is Ecstasy?

Ecstasy, MDMA,[1] is a semi-synthetic drug patented by Merck Pharmaceutical Company in 1914 and abandoned for 60 years. In the late 1970s and early 1980s psychiatrists and psychotherapists in the US used it to facilitate psychotherapy.[2] In 1985 its growing recreational use caused the DEA to criminalize it.

Ecstasy's effects last 3 to 6 hours. It is a mood elevator that produces feelings of empathy, openness and well-being. People who take it at all night "rave" dances say they enjoy dancing and feeling close to others. It does not produce violence or physical addiction.[3]

What are the greatest risks from Ecstasy?

Death is a possibility when using MDMA. According to coroner reports, there were nine Ecstasy-related deaths (three of these involved Ecstasy alone) in 1998.[4] Some of these deaths are related to overheating. MDMA slightly raises body temperature. This is potentially lethal in hot environments where there is vigorous dancing and the lack of adequate fluid replacement.[5] Many of these tragic deaths were preventable with simple harm reduction techniques such as having free water available and rooms where people can rest and relax.

One of the recent risks associated with Ecstasy is the possibility of obtaining adulterated drugs that may be more toxic than MDMA. Some of the reported deaths attributed to Ecstasy are likely caused by other, more dangerous drugs.[6] Deaths from adulterated drugs are another consequence of a zero tolerance approach. While we do not encourage Ecstasy use, we recommend that the drug be tested for purity to minimize the risk from adulterated drugs by those who consume it.[7] However, MDMA itself has risks. For example, it raises blood pressure and heart rate. Persons with known cardiovascular or heart disease should not take MDMA.

Recent studies have indicated that individuals who have used MDMA may have decreased performance in memory tests compared to nonusers. These studies are presently controversial because they involved people who used a variety of other drugs. Furthermore, it is difficult to rule out possible pre-existing differences between research subjects and controls.[8]

What is a rave?

Raves are all-night dance parties popular with young people that feature electronic music. A variety of drug use, from alcohol to nicotine, and including ecstasy, occurs at raves. Hysteria is leading to criminalization of raves, thus pushing them underground and into less safe and responsible settings.

Let's deal with legal and illegal drugs knowledgeably, understand their relative dangers, act prudently and avoid hysteria.

Kevin B. Zeese, President, Common Sense for Drug Policy, 3220 N Street, NW #141, Washington, DC 20007
www.csdp.org * www.DrugWarFacts.org * www.AddictintheFamily.org * info@csdp.org
202-299-9780 * 202-518-4028 (fax)

1, 3 & 4 - methylenedioxymethamphetamine. 2 - Greer G. and Tolbert R., A Method of Conducting Therapeutic Sessions with MDMA. In Journal of Psychoactive Drugs 30 (1998) 4:371.379. For research on the therapeutic use of MDMA see: www.maps.org. 3 - Beck J. and Rosenbaum M., Pursuit of Ecstasy: The MDMA Experience. Albany: State University of New York Press, 1994. 4 - Drug Abuse Warning Network, Office of Applied Studies, Substance Abuse and Mental Health Services Administration, Report of March 21, 2000. (This was a special report because the published report only includes drugs where there were over 10 deaths.) 5 - C.M. Milroy; J.C. Clark; A.R.W. Forrest, Pathology of deaths associated with "ecstasy" and "eve" misuse, Journal of Clinical Pathology Vol 49 (1996) 149-153. 6 - Laboratory Pill Analysis Program, DanceSafe. For results visit www.DanceSafe.org. See also, Byard RW et al., Amphetamine derivative fatalities in South Australia—is "Ecstasy" the culprit?, American Journal of Forensic Medical Pathology, 998 (Sep) 19(3): 261-5. 7 - DanceSafe provides testing equipment and a testing service which can be used to determine what a substance is. See www.DanceSafe.org. 8 - E. Gouzoulis-Mayfrank; J. Daumann; F. Tuchtenhagen; S. Pelz; S. Becker; H.J. Kunert; B. Fimm; H. Sass; Impaired cognitive performance in drug-free users of recreational ecstasy (MDMA), by Journal Neurol Neurosurg Psychiatry Vol 68, June 2000, 719-725; K.I.Bolla; U.D.; McCann; G.A. Ricaurte; Memory impairment in abstinent MDMA ('Ecstasy') users, by Neurology Vol 51, Dec 1998, 1532-1537.

FIGURE 9.3 Common Sense for Drug Policy advocacy ad

focuses on the drug Ecstasy and also uses type and layout to convey its points. (This ad appeared in the liberal magazine *The Progressive.*) Individually or in groups, study this advocacy ad and then answer the following questions.

1. What is the core argument of this ad? What view of drug use and what course of action are this ad promoting? What similarities and differences do you see between the argument about Ecstasy in this ad and the ad in Figure 9.2?
2. What are the main differences in the type and layout of the two ads in Figures 9.2 and 9.3? To what extent do the ad makers' choices about type and layout match the arguments made in each ad?
3. How would you analyze the use of type and layout in Figure 9.3? How does this ad use typestyles to convey its argument? How does it use layout and spacing?
4. The ad in Figure 9.2 appeared in the weekly entertainment section of the *Seattle Times,* a newspaper with a large general readership, whereas the ad in Figure 9.3 appeared in a liberal news commentary magazine. In what ways is each ad designed to reach its audience?

Use of Color

A third important element of visual design is use of color, which can contribute significantly to the visual appeal of an argument and move readers emotionally and imaginatively. In considering color in visual arguments, writers are especially controlled by genre conventions. For example, academic arguments use color minimally, whereas popular magazines often use color lavishly. The appeal of colors to an audience and the associations that colors have for an audience are also important. For instance, the psychedelic colors of 1960s rock concert posters would probably not be effective in poster arguments directed toward conservative voters. Color choices in visual arguments often have crucial importance, including the choice of making an image black-and-white when color is possible. As you will see in our discussions of color throughout this chapter, makers of visual arguments need to decide whether color will be primarily decorative (using colors to create visual appeal), functional (for example, using colors to indicate relationships), realistic (using colors like a documentary photo), aesthetic (for example, using colors that are soothing, exciting, or disturbing), or some intentional combination of these.

Use of Images and Graphics

The fourth design element includes images and graphics, which can powerfully condense information into striking and memorable visuals; clarify ideas; and add depth, liveliness, and emotion to your arguments. A major point to keep in mind when using images is that a few simple images may be more powerful than complicated and numerous images. Other key considerations are (1) how you intend an image to work in your argument (for example, to convey an idea, illustrate a point, or evoke an emotional response) and (2) how you will establish the relationship between the image or graphic and the verbal text. Because using images and graphics effectively is especially challenging, we devote the rest of this chapter to explaining how images and graphics can be incorporated into visual arguments. We treat the use of photographs and draw-ings in the next main section and the use of quantitative graphics in the final section.

An Analysis of a Visual Argument Using All the Design Components

Before we discuss the use of images and graphics in detail, we would like to illustrate how all four of the design components—use of type, layout, color, and images—can reinforce and support each other to achieve a rhetorical effect. Consider the "Save the Children" advocacy ad from an April 2011 edition of *Newsweek* (Figure 9.4). This ad-vocacy ad highlights the design features of image, color, and layout, with type used to interpret and reinforce the message delivered by the other features. The layout of the page highlights the connection between the adorable baby on the left side of the page and the female health care worker on the right. The "story" of the ad is told in unob-trusive text (in small white font), which leads the readers' eyes from the baby's face to the heart of the health worker. Interestingly from a design perspective, a third figure, probably the baby's mother, is just partly visible in the form of a hands holding the baby. The text itself celebrates the effectiveness of this local health healer, identified by name: "To show you all of the seriously ill children that local health worker Khalada Yesmin helped save this year, we'd need 122 more pages." At the bottom of the page, text conveys the call to action in the form of memorable tag lines "HELP ONE. SAVE MANY"; and "See where the good goes at GoodGoes.org."

This advocacy ad works on readers by blending three themes—the universal ap-peal of babies; the beneficial effects of educating local workers, particularly, women; and the symbolic meaning of helping/healing hands—to convey how those of us in the developed world can provide aid that empowers people in developing countries to help themselves. These themes are portrayed through various visual strategies. In this ad, a baby, the health worker, and a third figure outside the frame of the photo (probably the baby's mother) sit on a woven mat, inside a structure. (Information on the Web site for "Save the Children" and the clothing of the people suggest that this scene takes place in Bangladesh.) The use of bright colors, creating a feeling of warmth and love, the arrangement of the figures, and the close-up shots of the baby and health worker draw viewers into the scene. The close-up, slightly low-angle shot accentuates faces, hands, feet and traditional clothing. The blurred background sug-gests palm trees and the doorway to a house. The building is, most likely, the home of the mother and baby, which the health worker is visiting on her rounds. The baby, wearing an orange-beaded blouse or smock, pink shorts or skirt, and a necklace of purple beads, sits and smiles alertly at the health worker, in dark clothing and a red headscarf, who is engrossed in taking the baby's temperature. She seems to be holding the thermometer under the baby's arm with one hand and holding a watch with the other. Her focus on her task conveys her expertise; she knows what she is doing, an idea reinforced by the caption, which tells us that this health worker, Khalada Yesmin, "has helped 122 sick children this year." This caption and the prominence of hands in this photo—Khalada Yesmin's hands, the baby's hand, and the mother's hands support-

FIGURE 9.4 Save the Children advocacy ad

ing the baby—accentuate the idea of direct, grassroots aid that is improving the lives of mothers and children in a community through compassion and knowledge. The slogans at the bottom of the ad "Help one. Save many" and "See where the good goes" extend this network of help to viewers of the ad. If we contribute money to the training and medical supplies of health workers like Khalada Yesmin, we will help expand the web of aid.

In choosing to make this ad portray a positive, upbeat scene of medical success, instead of portraying scenes of pneumonia, malaria, malnutrition, or other diseases that the "seriously ill" children mentioned suffer from, the designers of this ad gave a memorable embodiment to the ideas in the words "help," "save," and "good." Perhaps most importantly, unlike some global ads, this one empowers people in the developing world. Rather than depict them as victims or helpless people in backward countries, this ad shows them—through the image of Khalada Yesmin and the eagerness of the people she is helping—as primary agents in the improvements in their lives. Rather than take control and rush in to solve problems, viewers in developed countries are invited to contribute to this success, figuratively lending a hand through financial support.

The Compositional Features of Photographs and Drawings

Now that we have introduced you to the four major elements of visual design—type, layout, color, and images—we turn to an in-depth discussion of photographic images and drawings. Used with great shrewdness in product advertisements, photos and drawings can be used with equal shrewdness in posters, fliers, advocacy ads, and Web sites. When an image is created specifically for an argument, almost nothing is left to chance. Although such images are often made to seem spontaneous and "natural," they are almost always composed: designers consciously select the details of staging and composition as well as manipulate camera techniques (filters, camera angle, lighting) and digital or chemical development techniques (airbrushing, merging of images). Even news photography can have a composed feel. For example, public officials often try to control the effect of photographs by creating "photo ops" (photographing opportunities), wherein reporters are allowed to photograph an event only during certain times and from certain angles. Political photographs appearing in newspapers are often press releases officially approved by the politician's staff. (See the campaign photographs later in this chapter on pages 193–194) To analyze a photograph or drawing, or to create visual images for your own arguments, you need to think both about the composition of the image and about the camera's relationship to the subject. Because drawings produce a perspective on a scene analogous to that of a camera, design considerations for photographs can be applied to drawings as well. The following list of questions can guide your analysis of any persuasive image.

- **Type of photograph or drawing:** Is the image documentary-like (representing a real event), fictionlike (intending to tell a story or dramatize a scene), or conceptual (illustrating or symbolizing an idea or theme)? The two photos of mosh pits—a girl shown crowd surfing and an unruly, almost menacing mosh pit crowd (Chapter 5, page 97)—are documentary photos capturing real events in action. In contrast, the drawing of the lizards in the Earthjustice ad in Figure 9.5 is both a fictional narrative telling a story and a conceptual drawing illustrating a theme.

Just then, the three lizards came home and found Goldilocks eating their porridge...

IT'S JUST NOT THE SAME WITHOUT BEARS.

Once upon a time there were over 100,000 grizzly bears in the lower 48 states. Now, there are less than a thousand grizzly bears left. The health of the grizzly is dependent on vast, undisturbed, wild lands. When bears disappear, other species will follow. Bears are such an important part of our wilderness, history, and culture that it's hard to imagine a world without them in the picture.

Grizzly bears are a threatened species, protected by the Endangered Species Act. But some special interests are pushing the U.S. Fish and Wildlife Service to remove Yellowstone grizzlies from the endangered species list. Why? They want to open up wild lands around Yellowstone

National Park to destructive logging, mining, off-road vehicle use, and development.

You can help protect our wilderness and grizzly bears. Please take a moment to contact Secretary Bruce Babbitt, Department of Interior, 1849 C St. NW, Washington DC 20240, or email Bruce_Babbitt@os.doi.gov – Tell him to keep grizzly bears on the Endangered Species List and that grizzly bears need more protection, not less.

Earthjustice Legal Defense Fund is working tirelessly to protect the grizzly bears and the wilderness they stand for. If we all work together, the grizzly bears will live happily ever after.

HELP KEEP BEARS IN THE PICTURE

www.earthjustice.org

 EARTHJUSTICE
LEGAL DEFENSE FUND
1-800-584-6460

designed by Sustain

FIGURE 9.5 Earthjustice advocacy ad

- **Distance from the subject:** Is the image a close-up, medium shot, or long shot? Close-ups tend to increase the intensity of the image and suggest the importance of the subject; long shots tend to blend the subject into the background. In the baby photograph opposing phthalates in children's toys (Chapter 1, page 6), the effect of the baby's wearing a "poison" bib is intensified by the close-up shot without background. Contrast that close-up with the long shot shown in the photograph taken in Port-au-Prince, Haiti, after the 2010 earthquake (Chapter 6, page 118). The distance of the camera from the woman carrying a basket and the other huddled figures in the shadows makes them look small in contrast to the earth-moving machine brought in to grapple with the rubble of fallen buildings. While the photo captures the magnitude of the disaster, it also shows the woman carrying on with her life.

- **Orientation of the image and camera angle:** Is the camera (or artist) positioned in front of or behind the subject? Is it positioned below the subject, looking up (a low-angle shot)? Or is it above the subject, looking down (a high-angle shot)? Front-view shots, such as those of Carlitos and his mother in the stills from *Under the Same Moon* (page 3), tend to emphasize the persons being photographed. In contrast, rear-view shots often emphasize the scene or setting. A low-angle perspective tends to make the subject look superior and powerful, whereas a high-angle perspective can reduce the size—and by implication, the importance—of the subject. A level angle tends to imply equality. The high-angle shot of the girl in the mosh pit (page 97) emphasizes the superiority of the camera and the harmlessness of the mosh pit. In contrast, the low-angle perspective of the lizards in the Earthjustice advocacy ad in Figure 9.5 emphasizes the power of the lizards and the inferiority of the viewer.

- **Point of view:** Does the camera or artist stand outside the scene and create an objective effect as in the Haiti photograph on page 118? Or is the camera or artist inside the scene as if the photographer or artist is an actor in the scene, creating a subjective effect as in the drawing of the lizards in Figure 9.5?

- **Use of color:** Is the image in color or in black and white? Is this choice determined by the restrictions of the medium, (such as images designed to run in black and white in newspapers) or is it the conscious choice of the photographer or artist? Are the colors realistic or muted? Have special filters been used (a photo made to look old through the use of brown tints)? The bright colors in the lizard and Goldilocks drawing in Figure 9.5 resemble illustrations in books for children.

- **Compositional special effects:** Is the entire image clear and realistic? Is any portion of it blurred? Is it blended with other realistic or nonrealistic images (a car ad that blends a city and a desert; a body lotion ad that merges a woman and a cactus)? Is the image an imitation of some other famous image such as a classic painting (as in parodies)? The Earthjustice ad in Figure 9.5, the story of the polar bear in the Nissan Leaf ad in Figures 9.6–9.11, and the poster for the Wal-Mart movie in Figure 9.16 make visual associations with children's stories or other popular stories.

■ **Juxtaposition of images:** Are several different images juxtaposed, suggesting relationships between them? Juxtaposition can suggest sequential or causal relationships or can metaphorically transfer the identity of a nearby image or background to the subject (as when a bath soap is associated with a meadow). This technique is frequently used in public relations to shape viewers' perceptions of political figures, as when Barack Obama was photographed with a huge American flag at a campaign appearance (page 194) to counter Republican Party charges that he was not "American enough."

■ **Manipulation of images:** Are staged images made to appear real, natural, documentary-like? Are images altered with airbrushing? Are images actually composites of a number of images (for instance, using images of different women's bodies to create one perfect model in an ad or film)? Are images cropped for emphasis? What is left out? Are images downsized or enlarged?

■ **Settings, furnishings, props:** Is the photo or drawing an outdoor or indoor scene? What is in the background and foreground? What furnishings and props, such as furniture, objects in a room, pets, and landscape features, help create the scene? What social associations of class, race, and gender are attached to these settings and props? Note, for example, how the designers of *America's Army*, the army video game, used a few simple props to create a gritty, urban street fighting scene (Figure 9.17). The burned-out vehicle hull suggests the aftermath of days of street fighting, whereas the telephone or power poles in the middle of a narrow, deserted street suggest a poor city in a third-world country.

■ **Characters, roles, actions:** Does the photo or drawing tell a story? Are the people in the scene models? Are the models instrumental (acting out real-life roles) or are they decorative (extra and included for visual or sex appeal)? What are the facial expressions, gestures, and poses of the people? What are the spatial relationships of the figures? (Who is in the foreground, center, and background? Who is large and prominent?) What social relationships are implied by these poses and positions? In the "Save the Children" advocacy ad shown in Figure 9.4, the pose of the health worker and the baby—the health worker intently treating the baby and the baby happily trusting the health worker—tells the story of successful health care.

■ **Presentation of images:** Are images separated from each other in a larger composition or connected to each other? Are the images large in proportion to verbal text? How are images labeled? How does the text relate to the image(s)? Does the image illustrate the text? Does the text explain or comment on the image? For example, the poster advocating vegetarianism (page 157) effectively juxtaposes words and images. The top is dominated by a question: "Think you can be a meat-eating environmentalist?" The "answer" is the image of a world with a big bite taken out of it. The text beneath the image, "Think again . . .," makes sense only after the viewer has interpreted the image. In contrast, the coat hanger hook dominates the advocacy ad on page 313.

FIGURE 9.6 Nissan Leaf ad: Glacier melting and calving ice bergs

FIGURE 9.7 Nissan Leaf ad: Polar bear floating on shrinking sea ice

FIGURE 9.8 Nissan Leaf ad: Polar bear walking on railroad tracks

FIGURE 9.9 Nissan Leaf ad: Polar bear walking along a highway

FIGURE 9.10 Nissan Leaf ad: Polar bear walking through a suburb

FIGURE 9.11 Nissan Leaf ad: Polar bear hugging car owner

An Analysis of a Visual Argument Using Images

To show you how images can be analyzed, let's examine the advertisement for Nissan's new electric car, the Nissan Leaf. Stills for this television ad are shown in Figures 9.6–9.11. You can see the whole one-minute ad on YouTube, where the fluid sequence of frames gives the full effect. With this ad's debut during a National Football League broadcast in fall 2010, Nissan boldly entered the global controversy over global warming and climate change, casting the iconic polar bear and the Nissan Leaf owner as heroes in a dramatic narrative intended to portray environmental consciousness and responsible consumerism.

This ad links a series of images in a suspenseful story of a long journey culminating in a dramatic encounter. The ad begins with frames of dripping ice melt and a crumbling glacier crashing into the ocean. The next frame shows a polar bear lying on a small floating island of ice, succeeded by a long view of calved icebergs, fragments of the glacier. The camera follows the polar bear swimming, with views of its powerful body above and below the water, until it arrives on land. From there, the polar bear takes a long journey: walking through northern forests; sheltering in a concrete culvert under a train trestle; walking along a train track; padding along a country highway, where it growls at a passing diesel truck; sitting and observing the brilliant lights of a big city at night; traveling across a massive suspension bridge into the city; walking through the city; and finally, walking down a suburban street. In the final frames, a bright blue Nissan Leaf sits in the wide driveway of a comfortable suburban home. Suddenly, the polar bear appears from behind the Nissan Leaf and surprises its owner, who has just come out of his house dressed in a sports coat and carrying a briefcase, presumably heading out for his commute to his white-collar job. As the bear rises on its hind legs, towering above the man, the astonished owner is met not by an attack but by a bear hug: the bear's thank-you for the driver's act of environmental responsibility in buying this electric car. The final frame includes the only text of the ad, which invites viewers to check out the features of the Nissan Leaf on the Web site. A musical soundtrack accompanies the images, with the only other sounds the honk of the truck and the growl of the bear in response. Noticeably absent from this ad is any specific information about the car itself, such as its five-passenger carrying capacity, its zero emissions, and its hundred-mile distance per charge.

The ad uses visual narrative to convey both a causal and an ethical argument. Through vivid, memorable scenes—the glacier calving, the bear afloat, the bear swimming—the ad taps viewers' knowledge of recent scientific accounts of the increased rate of glacial melting and the vanishing sea ice. The ad argues that these events are real, immediate, and threatening. By implication, it argues that the high volume of carbon dioxide emissions from gasoline-powered vehicles—in other words, human actions—has caused this increased rate of melting and destruction of polar bears' habitat. It asks viewers to fill in the links in the causal chain: large amounts of carbon dioxide emissions from internal combustion engines in cars and trucks have contributed to an increase in temperatures, which has sped up the rate at which glaciers and sea ice are melting. This increased rate of melting has in turn decreased the number of seals who usually live on the sea ice and thus reduced the food supply of polar bears. The ad reminds viewers that polar bears are endangered and need human aid. The ad's ethical argument is that humans can help polar bears and the environment by buying electric Nissan Leafs.

The ad's effect is enhanced by its positive *ethos* and its powerful appeals to *pathos*. By making these causal links through bold images and a memorable story, Nissan has staked its claim as a leader in producing alternative-fuel vehicles. In our view, the ad makes brilliant use of visual images, drawing on the most famous environmental icons in the global warming debate: the melting glacier and the polar bear. (See the photograph of the parade polar bear at the beginning of this chapter on page 177.) While news reports of declining polar bear populations arouse concern in some people, numbers can be vague and abstract. Many more people will be stirred by the heroic character of the lone bear making a long journey. This visual narrative taps viewers' familiarity with other animal stories, often featured on Animal Planet and the Discovery Channel, that blend environmental education and entertainment. But the Nissan ad pushes further by creatively drawing on Disney-like, anthropomorphic movies in which a wild creature becomes a friend of humans. Any Inuit will testify that polar bears are intimidating and dangerous, but this ad constructs an environmental fantasy, eliciting viewers' compassion for the heroic bear. It creates a kind of inverted "call of the wild" narrative: Instead of a captured or domesticated animal finding its way back to its wilderness home, this wild creature, endowed with knowledge and filled with gratitude, courageously finds its way to civilization on a mission to thank the Nissan Leaf owner. The ad cultivates warm feelings toward the bear through juxtaposing its isolation against the background of our technologically transformed and urbanized environment—the diesel truck; the concrete culvert; the impressive bridge; the vast, illuminated city; the well-cultivated suburban neighborhood. The ad enhances the character of the bear by showing it take time to watch a delicately flitting butterfly and exchange a glance with a raccoon, a wild creature at home in the city. As viewers are engrossed with the travels of this bear, they wonder, "Where is it going? What will happen?" The genius of the ad is that it casts the bear as an ambassador of the threatened environment and makes viewers care about the bear. It also converts the Nissan Leaf owner into an environmental hero. The implied ethical argument is that the right moral action is to drive a Nissan Leaf and thus save the environment. Viewers, identifying with the awestruck Nissan owner, will feel, "I want to be an environmental hero, too."

In this sense, the ad follows a problem-solution scenario. Nissan has skillfully enlisted the main symbols of global warming in the service of promoting its new electric car. It has, of course, greatly oversimplified an environmental problem and skirted major issues such as the problem of producing the electricity necessary to charge the Nissan Leaf, the environmental costs of producing the cars themselves, and the drop-in-the-bucket effect of replacing only a tiny portion of gasoline cars with electric vehicles. However, the ad works by suppressing these concerns and implying instead that the individual consumer can make a substantial difference in saving the environment.

■ ■ ■ **FOR CLASS DISCUSSION** Analyzing Photos
Rhetorically

1. The techniques for constructing photos come
   into play prominently in news photography.
   In this exercise, we ask you to examine four
   photographs of American presidential candidates or presidents. Working individually or
   in groups, study the four photos in Figures
   9.12 through 9.15, and then answer the following questions:

   a. What camera techniques and composition
      features do you see in each photo?

   b. What do you think is the dominant
      impression of each photo? In other
      words, what is each photo's implicit
      argument?

2. In 2004, the photograph of the Democrat-
   ic candidate John Kerry (running against
   Republican George W. Bush) "backfired."
   Republicans reversed the intended impact
   of the photograph and used it to ridicule
   Kerry.

FIGURE 9.12 Presidential candidate John Kerry
windsurfing

   a. What is the intended effect of
      the Kerry photograph, which
      is from a windsurfing video
      showing Kerry zigzagging
      across the water?

   b. How might the Kerry photo-
      graph (and the windsurfing
      video) produce an unintended
      effect that opens the candidate
      to ridicule from the oppos-
      ing party? (Suggestion: Enter
      "Kerry windsurfing photo"
      into your Web search en-
      gine. For another example of
      a campaign photograph that
      backfired, search for "Michael
      Dukakis tank photo.")

3. President Bush and Vice-
   President Cheney nurtured their
   image as western men and

FIGURE 9.13 President Bush and Vice-President Cheney riding in a
track

FIGURE 9.14 Vice-presidential candidate Sarah Palin

FIGURE 9.15 Presidential candidate Barack Obama making a speech

ranchers, Bush from Texas and Cheney from Wyoming. How might this photo contribute to that image?

4. Sarah Palin, former Governor of Alaska, was John McCain's vice-presidential running mate in the 2008 election against Barak Obama and Joe Biden. In addition to portraying herself as a soccer mom and a family values advocate, Sarah Palin cultivates the image of rugged outdoors woman. How might this photo of Sarah Palin enhance her image? To what groups of voters would it most appeal?

5. The poster shown in Figure 9.16 is for the documentary film *Wal-Mart: The High Cost of Low Prices*, produced in 2005 by filmmaker and political activist Robert Greenwald. According to its Web site, the movie features "the deeply personal stories and everyday lives of families and communities struggling to survive in a Wal-Mart world."

Working individually or in groups, answer the following questions:

   a. What compositional features and drawing techniques do you see in this image? What is striking or memorable about the visual features?

   b. How would you state the argument made by this image?

   c. The effect of this image derives partly from what cultural analysts call "intertextuality." By this term, analysts mean the way that a viewer's reading of an image depends on familiarity with a network of "connected" images—in this case, familiarity with posters for Godzilla films from the 1950s as well as Wal-Mart's conventional use of the smiley face. How does this drawing use viewers' cultural knowledge of Godzilla and of smiley faces to create an image of Wal-Mart? Why is this monster wearing a suit? Why does it have five or more arms? Why is this monster destroying a suburb or housing area rather than a city of skyscrapers? In short, what does it retain of conventional Godzilla images, what does it change,

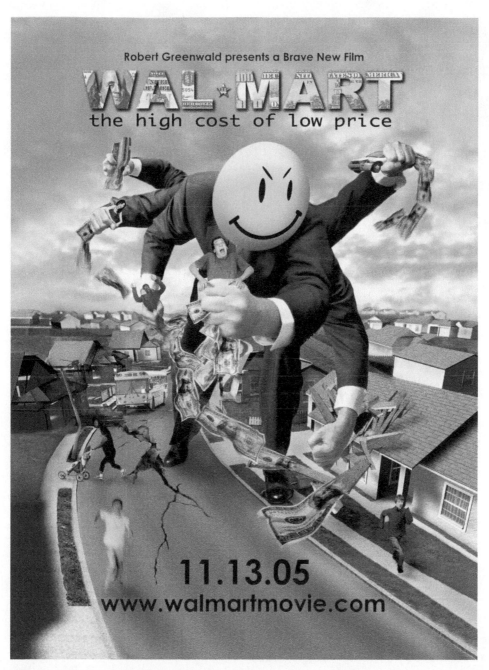

FIGURE 9.16 Poster for *Wal-Mart: The High Cost of Low Prices*

FIGURE 9.17 Urban assault scene, *America's Army* video game

and why? Similarly, how is the monster's smiley face similar to and different from the traditional Wal-Mart smiley face?

6. The images in Figures 9.17 and 9.18 are screen captures from the very popular PC action game *America's Army*, created by the U.S. Army. This "virtual soldiering" game, which is a free download from the Web site http://www.americasarmy.com, claims to "provide players with the most authentic military experience available."

a. In these screen captures from the game, what is the effect of the action's distance from the subject and the point of view of the viewer/player?

b. How do color and composition affect the visual appeal of these images?

c. What impressions do settings, characters, and roles convey?

d. Based on these two scenes from the game, why do you think this game has provoked heated public discussion? How effective do you think this game is as a recruitment device?

The Genres of Visual Argument

We have already mentioned that verbal arguments today are frequently accompanied by photographs or drawings that contribute to the text's persuasive appeal. For example, a verbal argument promoting U.N. action to help AIDS victims in Africa might be accompanied by a photograph of a dying mother and child. However, some genres of

FIGURE 9.18 Village scene, *America's Army* video game

argument are dominated by visual elements. In these genres, the visual design carries most of the argumentative weight; verbal text is used primarily for labeling, for focusing the argument's claim, or for commenting on the images. In this section we describe specifically these highly visual genres of argument.

Posters and Fliers

To persuade audiences, an arguer might create a poster designed for placement on walls or kiosks or a flier to be passed out on street corners. Posters dramatically attract and direct viewers' attention toward a subject or issue. They often seek to rally supporters, promote a strong stance on an issue, and call people to action. For example, during World War II, posters asked Americans to invest in war bonds and urged women to join the workforce to free men for active combat. During the Vietnam War, famous posters used slogans such as "Make Love, Not War" or "Girls say yes to boys who say no" to increase national resistance to the war.

The hallmark of an effective poster is the way it focuses and encodes a complex meaning in a verbal-visual text, often with one or more striking images. These images are often symbolic—for example, using children to symbolize family and home, a soaring bird to symbolize freedom, or three firefighters raising the American flag over the World Trade Center rubble on September 11, 2001, to symbolize American heroism, patriotism, and resistance to terrorism. These symbols derive potency from the values they share with their target audience. Posters tend to use words sparingly, either as slogans or as short, memorable directives. This terse verbal text augments the message encoded in an eye-catching, dominant image.

As an example of a contemporary poster, consider the poster on page 157, which is a call to stop eating red meat in order to protect the earth. This poster uses compositional special effects, depicting the earth from outer space against the backdrop of the Milky Way. The grain, color, and texture of pieces of red meat are superimposed over the continents of North and South America, where viewers expect to see the familiar greens and browns of Earth's surface. The impact of the poster is intensified by the big bite that has been taken out of Alaska, western Canada, and the West Coast of the United States. The substitution of meat for land and the presence of the bitten-out piece of the earth convey the message of immediate destruction. Framing this image of the earth on the top and bottom are a question and an imperative, phrased in casual but confrontational language: "Think you can be a meat-eating environmentalist? Think again!" The summary caption of the poster urges readers to become vegetarians. As you can see, this poster tries to shock and push readers toward a more radical environmentalism—one without meat.

Fliers and brochures often use visual elements similar to those in posters. An image might be the top and center attraction of a flier or the main focus of the front cover of a brochure. However, unlike posters, fliers and brochures offer additional space for verbal arguments, which often present the writer's claim supported with bulleted lists of reasons. Sometimes pertinent data and statistics, along with testimony from supporters, are placed in boxes or sidebars.

Public Affairs Advocacy Advertisements

Public affairs advocacy advertisements share with posters an emphasis on visual elements, but they are designed specifically for publication in newspapers and magazines and, in their persuasive strategies, are directly analogous to product advertisements. Public affairs advocacy ads are usually sponsored by a corporation or an advocacy organization and often have a more time-sensitive message than do posters and a more immediate and defined target audience. Designed as condensed arguments aimed at influencing public opinion on civic issues, these ads are characterized by their brevity, audience-based appeals, and succinct, "sound bite" style. Often, in order to sketch out their claim and reasons clearly and concisely, they employ headings and subheadings, bulleted lists, different sizes and styles of type, and a clever, pleasing layout on the page. They usually have an attention-getting slogan or headline such as "MORE KIDS ARE GETTING BRAIN CANCER. WHY?" or "STOP THE TAX REVOLT JUGGERNAUT!" And they usually include a call to action, whether it be a donation, a letter of protest to legislators, or an invitation to join the advocacy group.

The balance between verbal and visual elements in an advocacy advertisement varies. Some advocacy ads are verbal only, with visual concerns focused on document design (for example, an "open letter" from the president of a corporation appearing as a full-page newspaper ad). Other advocacy ads are primarily visual, using images and other design elements with the same shrewdness as advertisements. We looked closely at advocacy ads in this chapter when we examined the Ecstasy ads (Figures 9.2 and 9.3) and the Save the Children ad (Figure 9.4). These use text and images in different ways to present their messages.

As another example of a public affairs advocacy ad, consider the ad in Chapter 14, page 313, that attempts to counter the influence of the pro-life movement's growing campaign against abortion. As you can see, this ad is dominated by one stark image: a question mark formed by the hook of a coat hanger. The shape of the hook draws the reader's eye to the concentrated type centered below it. The hook carries most of the weight of the argument. Simple, bold, and harsh, the image of the hanger, tapping readers' cultural knowledge, evokes the dangerous scenario of illegal abortions performed crudely by nonmedical people in the dark backstreets of cities. The ad wants viewers to think of the dangerous last resorts that desperate women would have to turn to if they could not obtain abortions legally. The hanger itself creates a visual pun: As a question mark, it conveys the ad's dilemma about what will happen if abortions are made illegal. As a coat hanger, it provides the ad's frightening answer to the printed question—desperate women will return to backstreet abortionists who use coat hangers as tools.

■ ■ ■ **FOR CLASS DISCUSSION** Analyzing an Advocacy Ad Rhetorically

Reexamine the Earthjustice public affairs advocacy ad shown in Figure 9.5 on page 187. This ad defends the presence of grizzly bears in Yellowstone National Park as well as other wilderness areas in the Rocky Mountains. In our classes, this ad has yielded rich discussion of its ingenuity and complexity.

Working individually or in groups, conduct your own examination of this ad using the following questions:

1. What visual features of this ad immediately attract your eyes? What principles for effective use of type, layout, color, and image does this ad exemplify?
2. What is the core argument of this ad?
3. Why did Earthjustice use the theme of Goldilocks? How do the lizards function in this ad? Why does the ad *not* have any pictures of grizzlies or bears of any kind?
4. How would you design an advocacy ad for the preservation of grizzly bears? What visuals would you use? After discussing the Earthjustice advocacy ad, explore the rhetorical appeals of a product advertisement such as the one that appears in Chapter 6 on page 120. The designers of this Toyota ad have made key choices in the use of the main image, the woman with the face mask. How does this product ad work to convey its argument? Consider questions about its use of type, layout, and image; about the core of its argument; and about its appeals to *ethos, pathos,* and *kairos.*

Cartoons

An especially charged kind of visual argument is the editorial or political cartoon and its extended forms, the comic strip and the graphic novel. Cartoonist and author Will Eisner identifies the key elements of this art form as "design, drawing, caricature and writing" and describes how storytelling is broken up in "sequenced segments" called "panels or frames"* that the artist arranges to tell the story. Here we will focus on the political cartoon, which usually uses a single frame. British cartoonist Martin Rowson calls himself "a visual journalist" who employs "humor to make a journalistic point."† Political cartoons are often mini-narratives portraying an issue dramatically, compactly, and humorously. They employ images and a few well-chosen words to dramatize conflicts and problems. Using caricature, exaggeration, and distortion, a cartoonist distills an issue down to an image that boldly reveals the creator's perspective on an issue.

"Scrub that previous message Houston. There is no, I repeat no intelligent life on Mars."

FIGURE 9.19 *American Idol* Cartoon

The purpose of political cartoons is usually satire, or, as cartoonist Rowson says, "afflicting the comfortable and comforting the afflicted."‡ Because they are so condensed and are often connected to current affairs, political cartoons are particularly dependent on the audience's background knowledge of cultural and political events. When political cartoons work well, through their perceptive combination of image and words, they flash a brilliant, clarifying light on a perspective or open a new lens on an issue, often giving readers a shock of insight.

As an illustration, note the cartoon in Figure 9.19, which was posted on the cartoon Web site index http://www.cartoonstock.com. The setting of the cartoon takes place on Mars and features caricatures of an American astronaut and Martians. The cartoon focuses on the moment the astronaut realizes that the "intelligent life" he has discovered on Mars is sitting in front of a television broadcasting the popular reality show *American Idol*. The cartoon's comic science fiction narrative tells a "before

---

*Will Eisner explains the codes of comics as communication in *Comics & Sequential Art* (Tamarac, FL: Poorhouse Press, 1985), 38.

†"Biographies: Martin Rowson." *The British Cartoon Archive.* The British Cartoon Archives-University of Kent, n.d. Web. 2 June 2009.

‡"The Truth Told in Jest: Interview: Martin Rowson." *Morning Star.* Morning Star Online, 31 July 2007. Web. 6 June 2011.

I thought … but now I think" story: once, we wondered if there was life on Mars; then we encountered life-forms; then we realized that these beings are fascinated by *American Idol.* Through exaggeration, the cartoon humorously speaks to the vast global (and now interplanetary) range of television broadcasting as well as to the hyperbolic popularity of *American Idol.* Highlighting a social-cultural subject, it voices a biting critique of the quality of the show by asserting its low intellectual content, thus implying that anyone enamored of this show or habituated to watching it must not be very smart. A deeper question the cartoon suggests is "What impression of ourselves are we humans transmitting into space?"

■ ■ ■ **FOR CLASS DISCUSSION** Analyzing Cartoons

1. Cartoons can often sum up a worldview in a single image. The political cartoons in Chapter 2 on page 29 underscore the complexity of the economic role of illegal immigrants. The cartoons in Chapter 1 on page 10 respond to the gulf between those who accept and those who deny the problem of climate change and to the motivation behind Arizona's recent state law to control illegal immigration. What mini-narrative does each convey? What is each cartoon arguing? How does each cartoon use caricature, exaggeration, or distortion to convey its perspective?

2. Cartoons can provide insight into how the public is lining up on issues. Choose a current issue such as health care reform, dependence on foreign oil, the state of the job market, reduced government spending on public education, or identity theft. Then, using an online cartoon index such as Daryl Cagle's Professional Cartoonists Index (http://www.cagle.com) or a Web search of your own, find several cartoons that capture different perspectives on your issue. What is the mini-narrative, the main claim, and the use of caricature, exaggeration, or distortion in each? How is *kairos*, or timeliness, important to each cartoon?

Web Pages

So far we have only hinted at the influence of the World Wide Web in accelerating the use of visual images in argument. The hypertext design of Web pages, along with the Web's complex mix of text and image, has changed the way many writers think of argument. The home page of an advocacy site, for example, often has many features of a poster argument, with hypertext links to galleries of images on the one hand and to verbal arguments on the other. These verbal arguments themselves often contain photographs, drawings, and graphics. The strategies discussed in this chapter for analyzing and interpreting visual texts also apply to Web pages.

Constructing Your Own Visual Argument

The most common visual arguments you are likely to create are posters, fliers, and public affairs advocacy ads. You may also decide that in longer verbal arguments, the use of visuals or graphics could clarify your points while adding visual variety to your paper. The following guidelines will help you apply your understanding of visual elements to the construction of your own visual arguments.

Guidelines for Creating Visual Arguments

1. **Genre:** Determine where this visual argument is going to appear (on a bulletin board, passed out as a flier, imagined as a one-page magazine or newspaper spread, or as a Web page).

2. **Audience-based appeals:** Determine who your target audience is.
   - What values and background knowledge of your issue can you assume that your audience has?
   - What specifically do you want your audience to think or do after reading your visual argument?
   - If you are promoting a specific course of action (sign a petition, send money, vote for or against a bill, attend a meeting), how can you make that request clear and direct?

3. **Core of your argument:** Determine what clear claim and reasons will form the core of your argument; decide whether this claim and these reasons will be explicitly stated or implicit in your visuals and slogans.
   - How much verbal text will you use?
   - If the core of your argument will be largely implicit, how can you still make it readily apparent and clear for your audience?

4. **Visual design:** What visual design and layout will grab your audience's attention and be persuasive?
   - How can font sizes and styles, layout, and color be used in this argument to create a strong impression?
   - What balance and harmony can you create between the visual and verbal elements of your argument? Will your verbal elements be a slogan, express the core of the argument, or summarize and comment on the image(s)?

5. **Use of images:** If your argument lends itself to images, what photo or drawing would support your claim or have emotional appeal? (If you want to use more than one image, be careful that you don't clutter your page and confuse your message. Simplicity and clarity are important.)
   - What image would be memorable and meaningful to your audience? Would a photo image or a drawing be more effective?
   - Will your image(s) be used to provide evidence for your claim or illustrate a main idea, evoke emotions, or enhance your credibility and authority?

As an example of a poster argument, consider the "Heather's Life" poster in Figure 9.20, sponsored by Heather Lerch's parents and TxtResponsibly.org. This poster, which appears on the TxtResponsibily.org Web site, reaches out to young drivers and their parents, especially, and makes effective use of both images and text. The images at first puzzle and then shock (Heather looking happy and attractive at the top of the poster with her demolished car shown below). The connection between the images is made clear by the attention-grabbing text, which combines a causal narrative with a proposal/plea. This ad joins the national conversation about the dangers of distracted

FIGURE 9.20 Poster argument warning against texting while driving

driving and urges drivers to comply with new laws making it illegal to text and drive. TxtResponsibly.org invites viewers to contribute their consciousness-raising stories to its "Be a part of the solution" campaign.

■ ■ ■ **FOR CLASS DISCUSSION** Developing Ideas for a Poster Argument

This exercise asks you to do the thinking and planning for a poster argument to be displayed on your college or university campus. Working individually, in small groups, or as a whole class, choose an issue that is controversial on your campus (or in your town or city), and follow the Guidelines for Creating Visual Arguments on page 202 to envision the view you want to advocate on that issue. What might the core of your argument be? Who is your target audience? Are you representing a group, club, or other organization? What image(s) might be effective in attracting and moving this audience? Possible issues might be commuter parking; poor conditions in the computer lab; student reluctance to use the counseling center; problems with dorm life, financial aid programs, or intramural sports; ways to improve orientation programs for new students, work-study programs, or travel-abroad opportunities; or new initiatives such as study groups for the big lecture courses or new service-learning opportunities.

■ ■ ■

Using Information Graphics in Arguments

Besides images in the form of photographs and drawings, writers often use quantitative graphics to support arguments using numbers. In Chapter 5 we introduced you to the use of quantitative data in arguments. We discussed the persuasiveness of numbers and showed you ways to use them responsibly in your arguments. With the availability of spreadsheet and presentation programs, today's writers often create and import quantitative graphics into their documents. These visuals—such as tables, pie charts, and line or bar graphs—can have great rhetorical power by making numbers tell a story at a glance. In this section, we'll show you how quantitative graphics can make numbers speak. We'll also show you how to analyze graphics, incorporate them into your text, and reference them effectively.

How Tables Contain a Variety of Stories

Data used in arguments usually have their origins in raw numbers collected from surveys, questionnaires, observational studies, scientific experiments, and so forth. Through a series of calculations, the numbers are combined, sorted, and arranged in a meaningful fashion, often in detailed tables. Some of the tables published by the U.S. Census Bureau, for example, contain dozens of pages. The more dense the table, the more their use is restricted to statistical experts who pore over the data to analyze their meanings. More useful to the general public are midlevel tables contained on one or two pages that report data at a higher level of abstraction.

Consider, for example, Table 9.2, published by the U.S. Census Bureau and based on the 2010 census. This table shows the marital status of people age 15 and older, broken into gender and age groupings, in March 2010. It also provides comparative data on the "never married" percentage of the population in March 2010 and March 1970.

TABLE 9.2 Marital Status of People 15 Years and Over by Age and Sex: March 1970 and March 2010 (Numbers in thousands, except for percentages.)

Characteristic	Total	March 2010 — Number						Percent never married	March 1970 percent never married[a]
		Married spouse present	Married spouse absent	Separated	Divorced	Widowed	Never married		
Both Sexes									
Total 15 years old and over	242,047	120,768	3,415	5,539	23,742	14,341	74,243	30.7	24.9
15 to 19 years old	21,079	178	109	151	60	22	20,559	97.5	93.9
20 to 24 years old	21,142	2,655	202	309	195	17	17,765	84.0	44.5
25 to 29 years old	21,445	7,793	406	594	766	60	11,826	55.1	14.7
30 to 34 years old	19,623	10,896	337	632	1,447	72	6,239	31.8	7.8
35 to 44 years old	40,435	25,729	733	1,331	4,697	345	7,599	18.8	5.9
45 to 54 years old	44,373	28,619	703	1,295	6,951	1,080	5,725	12.9	6.1
55 to 64 years old	35,381	23,621	463	763	5,750	1,923	2,861	8.1	7.2
65 years old and over	38,569	21,276	461	465	3,875	10,823	1,668	4.3	7.6
Males									
Total 15 years old and over	117,686	60,384	1,789	2,352	9,981	2,974	40,206	34.2	28.1
15 to 19 years old	10,713	61	55	62	30	8	10,498	98.0	97.4
20 to 24 years old	10,677	946	86	123	49	3	9,469	88.7	54.7
25 to 29 years old	10,926	3,343	220	224	318	21	6,800	62.2	19.1
30 to 34 years old	9,759	5,143	188	246	593	28	3,561	36.5	9.4
35 to 44 years old	20,066	12,614	392	578	1,998	81	4,402	21.9	6.7
45 to 54 years old	21,779	14,280	367	539	3,063	284	3,246	14.9	7.5
55 to 64 years old	16,980	11,958	244	343	2,465	424	1,545	9.1	7.8
65 years old and over	16,786	12,039	237	237	1,464	2,124	685	4.1	7.5
Females									
Total 15 years old and over	124,361	60,384	1,626	3,187	13,760	11,368	34,037	27.4	22.1
15 to 19 years old	10,365	118	55	90	30	13	10,061	97.1	90.3
20 to 24 years old	10,465	1,708	116	185	146	14	8,296	79.3	35.8
25 to 29 years old	10,519	4,451	186	370	448	39	5,026	47.8	10.5
30 to 34 years old	9,864	5,753	150	386	854	44	2,678	27.1	6.2
35 to 44 years old	20,369	13,115	341	753	2,698	264	3,198	15.7	5.2
45 to 54 years old	22,594	14,339	337	756	3,889	794	2,479	11.0	4.9
55 to 64 years old	18,401	11,663	220	420	3,284	1,499	1,315	7.1	6.8
65 years old and over	21,783	9,238	224	227	2,412	8,700	983	4.5	7.7

[a]The 1970 percentages include 14-year-olds, and thus are for 14+ and 14–19.

Source: U.S. Census Bureau, *Current Population Survey,* March 2010 and March 1970.

Take a few moments to peruse the table and be certain you know how to read it. You read tables in two directions: from top to bottom and from left to right. Always begin with the title, which tells you what the table contains and includes elements from both the vertical and the horizontal dimensions of the table. In this case the vertical dimension presents demographic categories for people "15 years old and over" for both sexes, for males, and for females. Each of these gender categories is subdivided into age categories. The horizontal dimension provides information about "marital status." Seven of the columns give total numbers (reported in thousands) for March 2010. The eighth column gives the "percent never married" for March 2010, while the last column gives the "percent never married" for March 1970. To make sure you know how to read the table, pick a couple of rows at random and say to yourself what each number means. For example, the first row under "Both sexes" gives total figures for the entire population of the United States age 15 and older. In March 2010 there were 242,047,000 people age 15 and older (remember that the numbers are presented in thousands). Of these, 120,768,000 were married and living with their spouses. As you continue across the columns, you'll see that 3,415,000 people were married but not living with their spouses (a spouse may be stationed overseas or in prison; or a married couple may be maintaining a "commuter marriage" with separate households in different cities). Continuing across the columns, you'll see that 5,539,000 people were separated from their spouses, 23,742,000 were divorced, and 14,341,000 were widowed, and an additional 74,243,000 were never married. In the next-to-last column, the number of never-married people is converted to a percentage: 30.7 percent. Finally, the last column shows the percentage of never-married people in 1970: 24.9 percent. These last two columns show us that the number of unmarried people in the United States rose 5.8 percentage points since 1970.

Now that you know how to read the table, examine it carefully to see the kinds of stories it tells. What does the table show you, for example, about the percentage of married people age 25–29 in 1970 versus 2010? What does it show about different age-related patterns of marriage in males and females? By showing you that Americans are waiting much later in life to get married, a table like this initiates many causal questions for analysis and argument. What happened in American culture between 1970 and 2010 to explain the startling difference in the percentage of married people within, say, the 20–24 age bracket? In 2010 only 16 percent of people in this age bracket were married (we converted "unmarried" to "married" by subtracting 84 from 100). However, in 1970, 55.5 percent of people in this age bracket were married.

Using a Graph to Tell a Story

Table 9.2, as we have seen, tells the story of how Americans are postponing marriage. However, one has to tease out the story from the dense columns of numbers. To focus on a key story and make it powerfully immediate, you can create a graph.

Bar Graphs   Suppose you are writing an argument in which you want to show that the percentage of married women in the 20–29 age bracket has dropped significantly since 1970. You could tell this story through a bar graph (Figure 9.21).

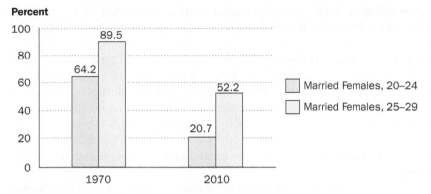

FIGURE 9.21 Percentage of married females ages 20–29, 1970 and 2010

Source: U.S. Census Bureau, *Current Population Survey,* March 2010.

Bar graphs use bars of varying length, extending either horizontally or vertically, to contrast two or more quantities. As with any graphic presentation, you must create a comprehensive title. In the case of bar graphs, titles tell readers what is being compared to what. Most bar graphs also have "legends," which explain what the different features on the graph represent. Bars are typically distinguished from each other by use of different colors, shades, or patterns of crosshatching. The special power of bar graphs is that they can help readers make quick comparisons.

Pie Charts   Another vivid kind of graph is a pie chart or circle graph, which depicts different percentages of a total (the pie) in the form of slices. Pie charts are a favorite way of depicting the way parts of a whole are divided up. Suppose, for example, that you wanted your readers to notice the high percentage of widows among women age 65 and older. To do so, you could create a pie chart (Figure 9.22) based on the data in the last row of Table 9.2. As you can see, a pie chart shows at a glance how the whole of something is divided into segments. However, the effectiveness of pie charts diminishes as you add more slices. In most cases, you'll begin to confuse readers if you include more than five or six slices.

Line Graphs   Another powerful quantitative graphic is a line graph, which converts numerical data into a series of

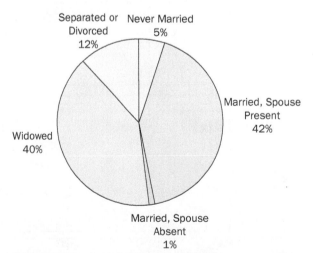

FIGURE 9.22 Marital status of females age 65 and older, 2010

Source: U.S. Census Bureau, *Current Population Survey,* March 2010.

points on a grid and connects them to create flat, rising, or falling lines. The result gives us a picture of the relationship between the variables represented on the horizontal and vertical axes.

Suppose you wanted to tell the story of the rising number of separated/divorced women in the U.S. population. Using Table 9.2, you can calculate the percentage of separated/divorced females in 2010 by adding the number of separated females (3,187,000) and the number of divorced females (13,760,000) and dividing that sum by the total number of females (124,361,000). The result is 13.6 percent. You can make the same calculations for 2000, 1990, 1980, and 1970 by looking at U.S. census data from those years (available on the Web or in your library). The resulting line graph is shown in Figure 9.23.

To determine what this graph is telling you, you need to clarify what's represented on the two axes. By convention, the horizontal axis of a graph contains the predictable, known variable, which has no surprises—what researchers call the "independent variable." In this case the horizontal axis represents the years 1970–2010 arranged predictably in chronological order. The vertical axis contains the unpredictable variable, which forms the graph's story—what researchers call the "dependent variable"—in this case, the percentage of separated or divorced females. The ascending curve tells the story at a glance.

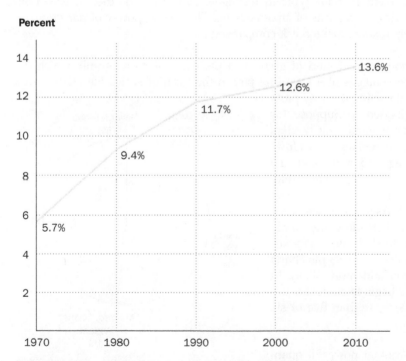

FIGURE 9.23 Percentage of females age 15 and older who were separated or divorced, 1970–2010

Source: U.S. Census Bureau, *Current Population Survey,* March 2010.

Note that with line graphs, the steepness of the slope (and hence the rhetorical effect) can be manipulated by the intervals chosen for the vertical axis. Figure 9.23 shows vertical intervals of 2 percent. The slope could be made less dramatic by choosing intervals of, say, 10 percent and more dramatic by choosing intervals of 1 percent.

Incorporating Graphics into Your Argument

Today, writers working with quantitative data usually use graphing software that automatically creates tables, graphs, or charts from data entered into the cells of a spreadsheet. For college papers, some instructors may allow you to make your graphs with pencil and ruler and paste them into your document.

Designing the Graphic When you design your graphic, your goal is to have a specific rhetorical effect on your readers, not to demonstrate all the bells and whistles available on your software. Adding extraneous data to the graph or chart or using such features as a three-dimensional effect can often distract from the story you are trying to tell. Keep the graphic as uncluttered and simple as possible and design it so that it reinforces the point you are making.

Numbering, Labeling, and Titling the Graphic In newspapers and popular magazines, writers often include graphics in boxes or sidebars without specifically referring to them in the text itself. However, in academic and professional workplace writing, graphics are always labeled, numbered, titled, and referred to directly in the text. By convention, tables are listed as "Tables," whereas line graphs, bar graphs, pie charts, or any other kinds of drawings or photographs are labeled as "Figures." Suppose you create a document that includes four graphics—a table, a bar graph, a pie chart, and a photograph. The table would be labeled as Table 1. The rest would be labeled as Figure 1, Figure 2, and Figure 3.

In addition to numbering and labeling, every graphic needs a comprehensive title that explains fully what information is being displayed. Look back over the tables and figures in this chapter and compare their titles to the information in the graphics. In a line graph showing changes over time, for example, a typical title will identify the information on both the horizontal and vertical axes and the years covered. Bar graphs also have a "legend" explaining how the bars are coded if necessary. When you import the graphic into your own text, be consistent in where you place the title—either above the graphic or below it.

Referencing the Graphic in Your Text Academic and professional writers follow a referencing convention called *independent redundancy*. The general rule is this: The graphic should be understandable without the text; the text should be understandable without the graphic; the text should repeat the most important information in the graphic. An example is shown in Figure 9.24.

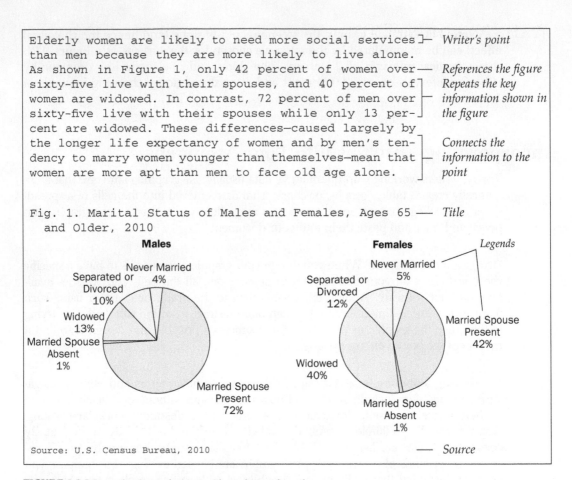

Elderly women are likely to need more social services ⎤— *Writer's point*
than men because they are more likely to live alone.
As shown in Figure 1, only 42 percent of women over— *References the figure*
sixty-five live with their spouses, and 40 percent of ⎤ *Repeats the key*
women are widowed. In contrast, 72 percent of men over ⎬ *information shown in*
sixty-five live with their spouses while only 13 per- ⎦ *the figure*
cent are widowed. These differences—caused largely by
the longer life expectancy of women and by men's ten- ⎤ *Connects the*
dency to marry women younger than themselves—mean that ⎬ *information to the*
women are more apt than men to face old age alone. ⎦ *point*

Fig. 1. Marital Status of Males and Females, Ages 65 —— *Title*
    and Older, 2010

Males

Never Married 4%
Separated or Divorced 10%
Widowed 13%
Married Spouse Absent 1%
Married Spouse Present 72%

Females   *Legends*

Never Married 5%
Separated or Divorced 12%
Married Spouse Present 42%
Widowed 40%
Married Spouse Absent 1%

Source: U.S. Census Bureau, 2010   —— *Source*

FIGURE 9.24 Example of a student text with a referenced graph

Conclusion

In this chapter we have explained the challenge and power of using visuals in arguments. We have examined the components of visual design—use of type, layout, color, and images—and shown how these components can be used for persuasive effect in arguments. We have also described the argumentative genres that depend on effective use of visuals—posters and fliers, advocacy advertisements, cartoons, and Web pages—and invited you to produce your own visual argument. Finally, we showed you that graphics can tell a numeric story in a highly focused and dramatic way. Particularly, we explained the functions of tables, bar graphs, pie charts, and line graphs, and showed you how to reference graphics and incorporate them into your own prose.

WRITING ASSIGNMENT A Visual Argument Rhetorical Analysis, a Visual Argument, or a Microtheme Using Quantitative Data

Option 1: Writing a Rhetorical Analysis of a Visual Argument Write a thesis-driven rhetorical analysis essay in which you examine the rhetorical effectiveness of a visual argument, either one of the visual arguments in this text or one specified by your instructor. Unless otherwise stated, direct your analysis to an audience of your classmates. In your introduction, establish the argumentative conversation to which this argument is contributing. Briefly summarize the argument and describe the visual text. Present your thesis, highlighting two or more rhetorical features of the argument that you find central to the effectiveness or ineffectiveness of this argument. To develop and support your own points, you will need to include visual features and details (such as color, design, camera angle, framing, and special effects) as well as short quotations from any verbal parts of the argument.

Option 2: Multimodal Assignment: A Poster Argument Working with the idea of a poster argument that you explored in For Class Discussion on page 204, use the visual design concepts and principles presented on page 202, your understanding of visual argument and the genre of poster arguments, and your own creativity to produce a poster argument that can be displayed on your campus or in your town or city. Try out the draft of your poster argument on people who are part of your target audience. Based on these individuals' suggestions for improving the clarity and impact of this visual argument, prepare a final version of your poster argument.

Option 3: Multimodal Assignment: Intertextual Visual Argument Often, visual arguments rely on what scholars call "intertextual associations." By "intertextual" (literally "between texts"), we mean that an image gets its power by drawing on ideas or emotions associated with other images that are part of our cultural background. A good example is the anti–Wal-Mart poster (Figure 9.16), in which the image of the smiley face corporate executive destroying a city depends for its effect on our cultural knowledge of Godzilla. Examples of frequently used intertextual images include the Statue of Liberty, the Uncle Sam "I Want You" recruitment poster, Adam and Eve in the garden with an apple or snake, Rosie the Riveter, the raising of the flag on Iwo Jima, and the Rodin sculpture *The Thinker*. Intertextual associations can also be drawn from fairy tales, legends, or popular culture, as in the Earthjustice poster's reference to Goldilocks and the Three Bears on page 187. For this assignment, create an idea for a poster or bumper sticker that would depend on an intertextual association for its persuasive effect. Think of an idea or behavior that you would like to promote and then link your persuasive purpose to an image from history, popular culture, or fairy tales that would speak to your audience and enliven your message. Finally, write a short reflection explaining the challenge of creating an intertextual visual argument. Possible ideas for an intertextual visual argument might include silencing cell phones in public places, buying local food, voting for a certain candidate, changing a school policy, supporting or criticizing skateboarders, admiring or mocking video game players, opposing Facebook addiction, defending an art form you value, supporting or criticizing car drivers who are angry at bikers, attacking employers' fixation on dress codes, and so forth.

Option 4: Multimodal Assignment: Cartoon Choose a controversial issue important to you and create a single-frame political cartoon that presents your perspective on the issue in a memorable way. Use the cartoon strategies of mini-narrative, caricature, exaggeration, distortion, and the interaction between image and text.

Option 5: A Microtheme Using a Quantitative Graphic Write a microtheme that tells a story based on data you select from Table 9.2 or from some other table provided by your instructor or located by you. Include in your microtheme at least one quantitative graphic (table, line graph, bar graph, pie chart), which should be labeled and referenced according to standard conventions. Use as a model the short piece shown in Figure 9.24 on page 210. ∎

For additional writing, reading, and research resources, go to www.mycomplab.com

PART FOUR

Arguments in Depth

Types of Claims

A shortage of body organs and long waiting lists have motivated some people to make personal appeals to the public on billboards like this one. In Chapter 13, a reading and the "Critiquing" exercise on pages 311–312 ask you to think about the evaluation and ethical issues involved in advertising for organs and in the selling and trading of body organs.

10 An Introduction to the Types of Claims

In Parts One, Two, and Three of this text, we showed how argument entails both inquiry and persuasion. We explained strategies for creating a compelling structure of reasons and evidence for your arguments (*logos*), for linking your arguments to the beliefs and values of your audience (*pathos*), and for establishing your credibility and trustfulness (*ethos*). We also explained how to do a rhetorical analysis of both verbal and visual texts.

Now in Part Four we examine arguments in depth by explaining five types of claims, each type having its own characteristic patterns of development and support. Because almost all arguments use one or more of these types of claims as "moves" or building blocks, knowing how to develop each claim type will advance your skills in argument. The claims we examine in Part Four are related to an ancient rhetorical concept called *stasis,* from a Greek term meaning "stand," as in "to take a stand on something." There are many competing theories of stasis, so no two rhetoricians discuss stasis in exactly the same way. But all the theories have valuable components in common.

In Part Four we present our own version of stasis theory, or, to use more ordinary language, our own approach to argument based on the types of claims.

In this chapter, which presents an overview of claim types, you will learn to:

■ Use strategies based on claim types to help you focus an argument, generate ideas for it, and structure it persuasively
■ Recognize how different claim types work together in hybrid arguments, thus increasing your flexibility as an arguer

An Overview of the Types of Claims

To appreciate what a study of claim types can do, imagine one of those heated but frustrating arguments in which the question at issue keeps shifting. Everyone talks at cross-purposes, each speaker's point unconnected to the previous speaker's. Suppose your heated discussion is about the use of steroids. You might get such a discussion back on track if one person says: "Hold it for a moment. What are we actually arguing about here? Are we arguing about whether steroids are a health risk or whether steroids should be banned from sports? These are two different issues. We can't debate both at once." Whether she recognizes it or not, this person is applying the concept of claim types to get the argument focused.

To understand how claim types work, let's return to the concept of stasis. A stasis is an issue or question that focuses a point of disagreement. You and your audience may agree on the answer to question A and so have nothing to argue about. Likewise you may agree on the answer to question B. But on question C you disagree. Question C constitutes a stasis where you and your audience diverge. It is the place where disagreement begins, where as an arguer you take a stand against another view. Thus you and your audience may agree that steroids, if used carefully under a physician's supervision, pose few long-term health risks but still disagree on whether steroids should be banned from sports. This last issue constitutes a stasis, the point where you and your audience part company.

Rhetoricians have discovered that the kinds of questions that divide people have classifiable patterns. In this text we identify five broad types of claims—each type originating in a different kind of question. The following chart gives you a quick overview of these five types of claims, each of which is developed in more detail in subsequent chapters in Part Four. It also shows you a typical structure for each type of argument. Note that the first three claim types concern questions of truth or reality, whereas the last two concern questions of value. You'll appreciate the significance of this distinction as this chapter progresses.

Claims about Reality, Truth, or the Way Things Are

Claim Type and Generic Question	Examples of Issue Questions	Typical Methods for Structuring an Argument
Definitional arguments: *In what category does this thing belong?* (Chapter 11)	■ Is sleep deprivation torture? ■ Is an expert video game player an athlete?	■ Create a definition that establishes criteria for the category. ■ Use examples to show how the contested case meets the criteria.
Resemblance arguments: *To what is this thing similar?* (Chapter 11)	■ Is opposition to gay marriage like opposition to interracial marriage? ■ Is steroid use to improve strength similar to LASIK surgery to improve vision?	■ Let the analogy or precedent itself create the desired rhetorical effect. [or] ■ Elaborate on the relevant similarities between the given case and the analogy or precedent.
Causal arguments: *What are the causes or consequences of this phenomenon?* (Chapter 12)	■ What are the causes of autism? ■ What might be the consequences of requiring a national ID card?	■ Explain the links in a causal chain going from cause to effect. [or] ■ Speculate about causes (consequences) or propose a surprising cause (consequence).

Claims about Values

Claim Type and Generic Question	Examples of Issue Questions	Typical Methods for Structuring an Argument
Evaluation and ethical arguments: *What is the worth or value of this thing?* (Chapter 13)	▪ Is behavior modification a good therapy for anxiety? ▪ Is it ethical to use steroids in sports?	▪ Establish the criteria for a "good" or "ethical" member of this class or category. ▪ Use examples to show how the contested case meets the criteria.
Proposal arguments: *What action should we take?* (Chapter 14)	▪ Should the United States enact a single-payer health care system? ▪ To solve the problem of prison overcrowding, should we legalize possession of drugs?	▪ Make the problem vivid. ▪ Explain your solution. ▪ Justify your solution by showing how it is motivated by principle, by good consequences, or by resemblance to a previous action the audience approves.

■ ■ ■   **FOR CLASS DISCUSSION** Identifying Types of Claims

Working as a class or in small groups, read the following questions and decide which claim type is represented by each. Sometimes the claim types overlap or blend together, so if the question fits two categories, explain your reasoning.

1. Should overnight camping be permitted in this state park?
2. Is taking Adderall to increase concentration for an exam a form of cheating?
3. Will an increase in gas taxes lead to a reduction in road congestion?
4. Is depression a learned behavior?
5. Were the terrorist attacks of September 11, 2001, more like Pearl Harbor (an act of war) or more like an earthquake (a natural disaster)?
6. How effective is acupuncture in reducing morning sickness?
7. Is acupuncture quackery or real medicine?
8. Should cities use tax dollars to fund professional sports arenas?
9. Are Mattel toy factories sweatshops?
10. Why are couples who live together before marriage more likely to divorce than couples who don't live together before marriage?

■ ■ ■

Using Claim Types to Focus an Argument and Generate Ideas: An Example

Having provided an overview of the types of claims, we now show you some of the benefits of this knowledge. First of all, understanding claim types will help you focus an argument by asking you to determine what's at stake between you and your audience.

Where do you and your audience agree and disagree? What are the questions at issue? Second, it will help you generate ideas for your argument by suggesting the kinds of reasons, examples, and evidence you'll need.

To illustrate, let's take a hypothetical case—one Isaac Charles Little (affectionately known as I. C. Little), who desires to chuck his contact lenses and undergo the new LASIK procedure to cure his nearsightedness. LASIK, or laser in-situ keratomileusis, is a surgical treatment for myopia. Sometimes known as "flap and zap" surgery, it involves using a laser to cut a thin layer of the cornea and then flattening it. It's usually not covered by insurance and is quite expensive.

I. C. Little has two different arguments he'd like to make: (1) he'd like to talk his parents into helping him pay for the procedure, and (2) he'd like to join with others who are trying to convince insurance companies that the LASIK procedure should be covered under standard medical insurance policies. In the discussions that follow, note how the five types of claims can help I. C. identify points of disagreement for each audience and simultaneously suggest lines of argument for persuading each one. Note, too, how the questions at issue vary for each audience.

Making the LASIK Argument to Parents

First imagine what might be at stake in I. C.'s discussions with his parents. Here is how thinking about claim types will help him generate ideas:

- **Definition argument:** Because I. C.'s parents will be concerned about the safety of LASIK surgery, the first stasis for I. C.'s argument is a question about categories: Is LASIK a safe procedure? I. C.'s mom has read about serious complications from LASIK and has also heard that ophthalmologists prefer patients to be at least in their midtwenties or older, so I. C. knows he will have to persuade her that the procedure is safe for twenty-year-olds.
- **Resemblance argument:** I. C. can't think of any resemblance questions at issue.
- **Causal argument:** Both parents will question I. C.'s underlying motivation for seeking this surgery. "Why do you want this LASIK procedure?" they will ask. (I. C.'s dad, who has worn eyeglasses all his life, will not be swayed by cosmetic desires. "If you don't like contacts," he will say, "just wear glasses.") Here I. C. needs to argue the good consequences of LASIK. Permanently correcting his nearsightedness will improve his quality of life and even his academic and professional options. I. C. decides to emphasize his desire for an active, outdoor life, and especially his passion for water sports, where his need for contacts is a serious handicap. He is even thinking of majoring in marine biology, so LASIK surgery would help him professionally. He says that wearing scuba equipment is easier without worrying about contact lenses or corrective goggles.
- **Evaluation argument:** When the pluses and minuses are weighed, is LASIK a good way to treat nearsightedness? Is it also a good way for his parents to spend family money? Would the results of the surgery be beneficial enough to justify

the cost and the risks? In terms of costs, I. C. might argue that even though the procedure is initially expensive (from $1,000 to $4,000), over the years he will save money by not needing glasses or contacts. The convenience of seeing well in the water and not being bothered by glasses or contacts while hiking and camping constitutes a major benefit. (Even though he thinks he'll look cooler without glasses, he decides not to mention the cosmetic benefits because his dad thinks wearing glasses is fine.)

- **Proposal argument:** Should I. C.'s parents pay for a LASIK procedure to treat their son's nearsightedness? (All the previous points of disagreement are subissues related to this overarching proposal issue.)

This example shows that writers often need to argue issues of reality and truth in order to make claims about values. In this particular case, I. C. would need to convince his parents (1) that the procedure is safe (definition argument), (2) that the consequences of the procedure would be beneficial recreationally and professionally (causal argument), and (3) that the benefits outweigh the costs (evaluation argument). Only then would I. C. be able to persuade his parents (4) that he should have LASIK surgery with their financial help (proposal claim). Almost all arguments combine subarguments in this way so that lower-order claims provide supporting materials for addressing higher-order claims.

Making the LASIK Argument to Insurance Companies

The previous illustration focused on parents as audience. If we now switch audiences, we can use our claim types to identify different questions at issue. Let's suppose I. C. wants to persuade insurance companies to cover the LASIK procedure. He imagines his primary audience as insurance company executives, along with the general public and state legislators, who may be able to influence them. Again, I. C. generates ideas by considering the claim types.

- **Definition argument:** For this audience the issue of safety is no longer relevant. (They share I. C.'s belief that LASIK is a safe procedure.) What's at stake is another definition issue: Should LASIK be considered "cosmetic surgery" (as insurance companies contend) or "medically justifiable surgery" (as I. C. contends)? This definitional question constitutes a major stasis. I. C. wants to convince his audience that LASIK belongs in the category of "medically justifiable surgery" rather than "cosmetic surgery." He will need to define "medically justifiable surgery" in such a way that LASIK can be included.
- **Resemblance argument:** Does LASIK more resemble a face-lift (not covered by insurance) or plastic surgery to repair a cleft palate (covered by insurance)?
- **Causal argument:** What will be the consequences to insurance companies and to the general public of making insurance companies pay for LASIK? Will there be an overwhelming crush of claims for LASIK surgery? Will there be a

corresponding decrease in claims for eye exams, contacts, and glasses? What will happen to the cost of insurance?

- **Evaluation argument:** Would it be good for society as a whole if insurance companies had to pay for LASIK?
- **Proposal argument:** Should insurance companies be required to cover LASIK?

As this analysis shows, the questions at issue change when you consider a different audience. Now the chief question at issue is definition: Is LASIK cosmetic surgery or medically justifiable surgery? I. C. does not need to argue that the surgery is safe (a major concern for his parents); instead he must establish criteria for "medically justifiable surgery" and then argue that LASIK meets these criteria. Again note how the higher-order issues of value depend on resolving one or more lower-order issues of reality and truth.

Note also that any of the claim type examples just described could be used as the major focus of an argument. If I. C. were not concerned about a values issue (his proposal claims), he might tackle only a reality/truth issue. He could, for example, focus an entire argument on a definition question about categories: "Is LASIK safe?" (an argument requiring him to research the medical literature). Likewise he could write a causal argument focusing on what might happen to optometrists and eyeglass manufacturers if the insurance industry decided to cover LASIK.

The key insight here is that when you develop an argument, you may have to work through issues of reality and truth before you can tackle a values issue and argue for change or action. Before you embark on writing an evaluation or proposal argument, you must first consider whether you need to resolve a lower-order claim based on reality and truth.

Hybrid Arguments: How Claim Types Work Together in Arguments

As the LASIK example shows, hybrid arguments can be built from different claim types. A writer might develop a proposal argument with a causal subargument in one section, a resemblance subargument in another section, and an evaluation subargument in still another section. Although the overarching proposal argument follows the typical structure of a proposal, each of the subsections follows a typical structure for its own claim type.

Some Examples of Hybrid Arguments

The examples on page 220 show how these combinations of claim types can play out in actual arguments. (For more examples of these kinds of hybrid arguments, see Chapter 14, pages 322–323, where we explain how lower-order claims about reality and truth can support higher-order claims about values.)

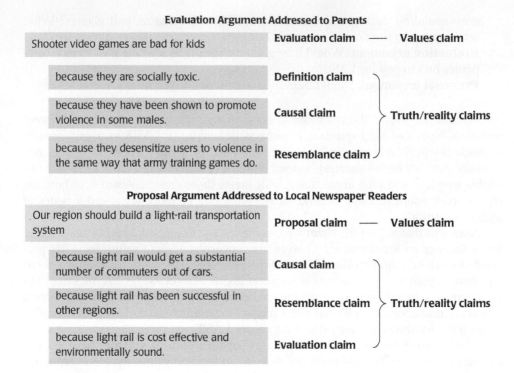

■ ■ ■ **FOR CLASS DISCUSSION** Exploring Different Claim Types and Audiences

1. Select an issue familiar to most members of the class—perhaps a current campus issue or an issue prominent in the local or national news—and generate possible issue questions and arguments using the claim types. Take as your models our discussion of I. C. Little's arguments about LASIK surgery. Consider how a writer or speaker might address two different audiences on this issue, with a different purpose for each audience.

2. The following is the table of contents for a "friend of the court" legal brief opposing a contested Missouri law outlawing sale of violent video games to minors. How would you classify the claims put forward in this brief?

   ■ What is the overarching claim of this legal brief? What claim type is it?

   ■ What are the claim types for major sections I, II, and III?

   ■ How might you recast section III's title to state its implied claim more explicitly

   ■ How does the "friend of the court" brief try to rebut the argument against violent video games shown in the example above?

No. 02-3010
In the
United States Court of Appeals for the Eighth Circuit
INTERACTIVE DIGITAL SOFTWARE ASS'N, et al.
Plaintiffs - Appellants,
v.
ST. LOUIS COUNTY, et al.

Defendants - Appellees

BRIEF *AMICI CURIAE* OF THIRTY-THREE MEDIA SCHOLARS
IN SUPPORT OF APPELLANTS, AND SUPPORTING REVERSAL

CONTENTS

An Extended Example of a Hybrid Argument

As the previous examples illustrate, different claim types often serve as building blocks for larger arguments. We ask you now to consider a more extended example. Read the following op-ed piece arguing the proposal claim that "the New York City Council should ban car alarms." Note how the reasons are different claim type subarguments that develop the overall proposal claim.

As you can see, the thesis of Friedman's op-ed piece is a proposal claim, and the article follows the typical problem-solution structure of proposal arguments. Although the whole argument follows a proposal shape, the individual pieces—the various subarguments that support the main argument—comprise different kinds of claim types with their own characteristic structures.

All That Noise for Nothing

AARON FRIEDMAN

Early next year, the New York City Council is supposed to hold a final hearing on legislation that would silence the most hated of urban noises: the car alarm. With similar measures having failed in the past, and with Mayor Michael R. Bloomberg withholding his support for the latest bill, let's hope the Council does right by the citizens it represents.

Every day, car alarms harass thousands of New Yorkers—rousing sleepers, disturbing readers, interrupting conversations and contributing to quality-of-life concerns that propel many weary residents to abandon the city for the suburbs. According to the Census Bureau, more New Yorkers are now bothered by traffic noise, including car alarms, than by any other aspect of city life, including crime or the condition of schools.

So there must be a compelling reason for us to endure all this aggravation, right? Amazingly, no. Many car manufacturers, criminologists and insurers agree that car alarms are ineffective. When the nonprofit Highway Loss Data Institute surveyed insurance-claims data from 73 million vehicles nationwide in 1997, they concluded that cars with alarms "show no overall reduction in theft losses" compared with cars without alarms.

There are two reasons they don't prevent theft. First, the vast majority of blaring sirens are false alarms, set off by passing traffic, the jostling of urban life or nothing at all. City dwellers quickly learn to disregard these cars crying wolf; a recent national survey by the Progressive Insurance Company found that fewer than 1 percent of respondents would call the police upon hearing an alarm.

5   In 1992, a car alarm industry spokesman, Darrell Issa (if you know his name that's because he would later spearhead the recall of Gov. Gray Davis in California), told the New York City Council that an alarm is effective "only in areas where the sound causes the dispatch of the police or attracts the owner's attention." In New York, this just doesn't happen.

Car alarms also fail for a second reason: they are easy to disable. Most stolen cars are taken by professional car thieves, and they know how to deactivate an alarm in just a few seconds.

Perversely, alarms can encourage more crime than they prevent. The New York Police Department, in its 1994 booklet "Police Strategy No. 5," explains how alarms (which "frequently go off for no apparent reason") can shatter the sense of civility that makes a community safe. As one of the "signs that no one cares," the department wrote, car alarms "invite both further disorder and serious crime."

I've seen some of my neighbors in Washington Heights illustrate this by taking revenge on alarmed cars: puncturing tires, even throwing a toaster oven through a windshield. False alarms enrage otherwise lawful citizens, and alienate the very people car owners depend on to call the police. In other words, car alarms work about as well as fuzzy dice at deterring theft while irritating entire neighborhoods.

The best solution is to ban them, as proposed by the sponsors of the City Council legislation, John Liu and Eva Moskowitz. The police could simply ticket or tow offending cars. This would be a great improvement over the current laws, which include limiting audible alarms to three minutes—something that has proved to be nearly impossible to enforce.

10   Car owners could easily comply: more than 50 car alarm installation shops throughout the city have already pledged to disable alarms at no cost, according to a survey by the Center for Automotive Security Innovation.

And there is a viable alternative. People worried about protecting their cars can buy what are called silent engine immobilizers. Many European cars and virtually every new General Motors and Ford vehicle use the technology, in which a computer chip in the ignition key communicates with the engine. Without the key, the only way to steal the car is to tow it away, something most thieves don't have the time for. In the meantime, the rest of us could finally get some sleep.

Margin annotations:
Humorous resemblance claim sums up problem

Main proposal claim, restated as evalution claim and supported by three criteria

Thus writers enlist other claim type subarguments in building main arguments. This knowledge can help you increase your flexibility and effectiveness as an arguer. In the following chapters in Part Four, we discuss each of the claim types in more detail, showing how they work and how you can develop skills and strategies for supporting each type of claim.

PEARSON

For additional writing, reading, and research resources, go to
www.mycomplab.com

Definition and Resemblance Arguments

11

Case 1 Is Our Love of Oil Like Adam and Eve's Love of the Apple?

This political cartoon by Pulitzer Prize–winning cartoonist Michael Ramirez uses a resemblance argument to link our desire for petroleum to Adam and Eve's desire for the apple. This analogy creates a thoughtful lens for viewing our love affair with SUVs and other gas-guzzling vehicles. Particularly, it raises questions like these: How was life during the era of cheap oil like Paradise? To what extent are Americans "seduced" by gasoline? Is the cartoonist correct in suggesting a theological dimension to the energy crisis?

"AS A MATTER OF FACT, WE JUST BOUGHT ANOTHER SUV...."

Case 2 Is a Frozen Embryo a Person or Property?

An infertile couple conceived several embryos in a test tube and then froze the fertilized embryos for future use. During the couple's divorce, they disagreed about the disposition of the embryos. The woman wanted to use the frozen embryos to try to get pregnant, and the man wanted to destroy them. When the courts were asked to decide what should be done with the embryos, several questions of definition arose: Should the frozen embryos be categorized as "persons," thus becoming analogous to children in custody disputes? Or should they be divided up as "property," with the man getting half and the woman getting the other half? Or should a new legal category be created for them that regards them as more than property but less than actual persons? The judge decided that frozen embryos "are not, strictly speaking, either 'persons' or 'property,' but occupy an interim category that entitles them to special respect because of their potential for human life."*

Arguments about definition or resemblance concern disputes about what category something belongs to, either directly by definition or indirectly or metaphorically through comparison or resemblance. They are among the most common argument types you will encounter. In this chapter you will learn to:

- Analyze questions about the category to which something belongs
- Use criteria-match reasoning to construct your own definition arguments
- Use reasoning about precedents or analogies to construct your own resemblance arguments

An Overview of Definition and Resemblance Arguments

Definition and resemblance arguments occur whenever you claim that a particular person, thing, act, or phenomenon should be identified with a certain category. Here are some examples:

Claims Involving Categories

Claim	This specific phenomenon . . .	. . . belongs to (or is similar to) this category
Piping loud rap music into a prison cell twenty-four hours a day constitutes torture.	Constant, loud rap music	Torture
Graffiti is often art, rather than vandalism.	Graffiti	Art (not vandalism)
Women's obsession with thinness serves the same cultural function as footbinding in ancient China.	Women's obsession with thinness	Footbinding in ancient China

Much is at stake when we place things into categories because the category that something belongs to can have real consequences. Naming the category that something belongs to makes an implicit mini-argument.

---

*See Vincent F. Stempel, "Procreative Rights in Assisted Reproductive Technology: Why the Angst?" *Albany Law Review* 62 (1999), 1187.

Consequences Resulting from Categorical Claims

To appreciate the consequences of categorical claims, consider the competing categories proposed for whales in the international controversy over commercial whaling. What category does a whale belong to? Some arguers might say that "whales are sacred animals," implying that their intelligence, beauty, grace, and power mean they should never be killed. Others might argue that "whales are a renewable food resource" like tuna, crabs, cattle, and chickens. This category implies that we can harvest whales for food the same way we harvest tuna for tuna fish sandwiches or cows for beef. Still others might argue that "whales are an endangered species"—a category that argues for the preservation of whale stocks but not necessarily for a ban on controlled hunting of individual whales. Each of these whaling arguments places whales in a separate, different category that implicitly urges the reader to adopt that category's perspective on whaling.

Significant consequences can also result from resemblance claims. Consider the way that media analysts tried to make sense of the September 11, 2001, terrorist attacks on the World Trade Center and the Pentagon by comparing them to different kinds of previous events. Some commentators said, "The September 11 attacks are like Timothy McVeigh's bombing of the Alfred P. Murrah Federal Building in Oklahoma City in 1995"—an argument that framed the terrorists as criminals who must be brought to justice. Others said, "The September 11 attacks are like the 1941 Japanese attack on Pearl Harbor"—an argument suggesting that the United States should declare war on some as-yet-to-be-defined enemy. Still others said, "The September 11 attacks are like an occasionally disastrous earthquake or an epidemic," arguing that terrorists will exist as long as the right conditions breed them and that it is useless to fight them using the strategies of conventional war. Under this analogy, the "war on terror" is a metaphorical war like the "war on poverty" or the "war against cancer." Clearly, each of these resemblance claims had high-stakes consequences. In 2001, the Pearl Harbor claim prevailed, and the United States went to war, first in Afghanistan and then in Iraq. Many critics of these wars continue to say that war is an inappropriate strategy for fighting the "disease of terrorism."

The Rule of Justice: Things in the Same Category Should Be Treated the Same Way

As you can see, the category we place something into—either directly through definition or indirectly through comparison—can have significant implications for people's actions or beliefs. To ensure fairness, philosophers refer to the *rule of justice,* which states that "beings in the same essential category should be treated in the same way." For example, the problem of how the courts should treat the users or sellers of marijuana depends on the category marijuana belongs to. Marijuana might be placed in the same category as tobacco and alcohol, in which case the possession and sale of marijuana would be legal but subject to regulation and taxes. Or marijuana could be placed in the same category as meth, cocaine, and heroin; in this case, it would be an illegal drug subject to criminal prosecution. Some states have placed marijuana in the same category as penicillin and insulin, making it a legal drug so long as it is obtained from a licensed dispensary with a doctor's prescription. Many states are not happy with any of these categories and are trying to define marijuana in some fourth way.

Such "rule of justice" issues occur regularly. Consider some more examples: Fans of first-person-shooter games have a stake in whether *Grand Theft Auto* or *Postal 2* is in the same category as a slasher film (in which case it is constitutionally protected free speech) or—as claimed by opponents of violent video games in a recent Supreme Court case—in the same category as pornography or even child pornography. If defined as child pornography, violent video games could be banned outright; if defined as pornography but not child pornography, their sale could be restricted to those eighteen and older. At a more familiar level, suppose your professor says that absence from an exam can be excused for emergencies only. How would you define "emergency"? Is attending your best friend's wedding an "emergency"? How about missing an exam because your

EXAMINING VISUAL ARGUMENTS

Claims about Categories (Definition or Resemblance)

When airport security introduced new, full-body X-ray scanners, persons who opted out of the scanner check were subject to "enhanced TSA pat downs." The topic of enhanced pat-downs became fodder for late-night comedy shows and cartoonists. In the first cartoon, Andy Marlette, cartoonist for the *Pensacola News Journal*, creates a resemblance argument comparing a grown male traveler upset by an enhanced pat-down to a child in a sex-abuse therapy session. In the second cartoon, Pat Begley, a cartoonist for Utah's *Salt Lake Tribune*, plays with definition arguments about waterboarding and rape. What is each cartoonist's attitude toward the TSA pat-downs? How does each cartoon work visually and conceptually to make its argument in the enhanced pat-down controversy?

car wouldn't start? Although your interests might be best served by a broad definition of emergency, your professor might prefer a narrow definition, which would permit fewer exemptions.

The rule of justice becomes especially hard to apply when we consider contested cases marked by growth or slow change through time. At what point does a child become an adult? When does a binge drinker become an alcoholic, an Internet poker player a compulsive gambler, or a fetus a human person? Although we may be able arbitrarily to choose a particular point and declare that "adult" means someone at least eighteen years old or that "human person" means a fetus at conception, or at three months, or at birth, in the everyday world the distinction between child and adult, between fetus and person, between Friday-night poker playing and compulsive gambling seems an evolution, not a sudden and definitive step. Nevertheless, our language requires an abrupt shift between categories. In short, applying the rule of justice often requires us to adopt a digital approach to reality (switches are either on or off, either a fetus is a human person or it is not), whereas our sense of life is more analogical (there are numerous gradations between on and off; there are countless shades of gray between black and white).

As we can see from the preceding examples, the promise of language to structure what psychologist William James called "the buzz and confusion of the world" into an orderly set of categories turns out to be elusive. In most category debates, an argument, not a quick trip to the dictionary, is required to settle the matter.

■ ■ ■ FOR CLASS DISCUSSION Applying the Rule of Justice

Suppose your landlord decides to institute a "no pets" rule. The rule of justice requires that all pets have to go—not just your neighbor's barking dog, but also Mrs. Brown's cat, the kids' hamster downstairs, and your own pet tarantula. That is, all these animals have to go, unless you can argue that some of them are not "pets" for purposes of the landlord's "no pets" rule.

1. Working in small groups or as a whole class, define *pets* by establishing the criteria an animal would have to meet to be included in the category "pets." Consider your landlord's "no pets" rule as the cultural context for your definition.
2. Based on your criteria, which of the following animals is definitely a pet that would have to be removed from the apartment? Based on your criteria, which animals could you exclude from the "no pets" rule? How would you make your argument to your landlord?
   - a German shepherd
   - a small housecat
   - a tiny, well-trained lapdog
   - a gerbil in a cage
   - a canary
   - a tank of tropical fish
   - a tarantula

Types of Definition Arguments

Unlike resemblance arguments, which assert that one phenomenon is like another, definition arguments make a more direct claim: they argue that a disputed phenomenon is (or is not) a member of a certain category. Because such disputes always depend on the category that something belongs to, they are sometimes called categorical arguments. Such arguments can be divided into two kinds:

1. **Simple categorical arguments,** in which the writer and an audience already agree on the definition of the category, and
2. **Definition arguments,** in which there is a dispute about the boundaries of the category and hence of its definition.

Simple Categorical Arguments

A categorical argument can be said to be "simple" if there is no disagreement about the definition of the category. For example, suppose you argue that regular milk is healthier than soy milk because soy milk is not calcium-rich. Your supporting reason ("soy milk is not calcium-rich") is a simple categorical claim. You assume that everyone agrees on what *calcium-rich* means; the point of contention is whether soy milk does or does not contain calcium.

As shown in the following chart, the basic procedure for supporting (or rebutting) a simple categorical claim is to supply examples and other data that show how the contested phenomenon fits or doesn't fit into the category:

Strategies for Supporting or Rebutting Simple Categorical Claims

Categorical Claim	Strategies for Supporting Claim	Strategies for Rebutting Claim
Joe is too bossy.	Show examples of his bossy behavior (for example, his poor listening skills, his shouting at people, or his making decisions without asking the committee).	Show counterexamples revealing his ability to listen and create community; reinterpret bossiness as leadership behavior, putting Joe in better light.
Low-carb diets are dangerous.	Cite studies showing the dangers; explain how low-carb diets produce dangerous substances in the body; explain their harmful effects.	Show design problems in the scientific studies; cite studies with different findings; cite counter examples of people who lost weight on low-carb diets with no bad health effects.
Little Green Footballs is a conservative blog.	Give examples of the conservative views it promotes; show the conservative leanings of pundits often cited on the blog.	Give examples from the blog that don't fit neatly into a conservative perspective.

■ ■ ■   **FOR CLASS DISCUSSION** Supporting and Rebutting Categorical Claims

Working individually or in small groups, consider how you would support the following categorical claims. What examples or other data would convince readers that the specified case fits within the named category? Then discuss ways you might rebut each claim.

1. Bottled water is environmentally unfriendly. [That is, bottled water belongs in the category of "environmentally unfriendly things."]
2. Nelly is a gangsta rapper.
3. Americans today are obsessed with their appearance. [That is, Americans belong in the category of "people obsessed with their appearance."]
4. Barack Obama is a centrist, not a socialist.
5. Competitive cheerleading is physically risky.

■ ■ ■

Definition Arguments

Simple categorical arguments morph into definition arguments whenever stakeholders disagree about the boundaries of a category. Suppose in the previous exercise that you had said about Nelly, "Well, that depends on how you define 'gangsta rapper.'" The need to define the term "gangsta rapper" adds a new layer of complexity to your arguments about Nelly. To understand full-blown definition arguments, one must distinguish between cases where definitions are *needed* and cases where definitions are *disputed*. Many arguments require a definition of key terms. If you are arguing, for example, that therapeutic cloning might lead to cures for various diseases, you would probably need to define *therapeutic cloning* and distinguish it from *reproductive cloning*. Writers regularly define key words for their readers by providing synonyms, by citing a dictionary definition, by offering their own definition, or by some other means.

In the rest of this chapter, we focus on arguments in which the meaning of a key term is disputed. Consider, for example, the environmental controversy over the definition of *wetland*. Section 404 of the federal Clean Water Act provides for federal protection of wetlands, but it leaves the task of defining *wetland* to administrative agencies and the courts. Currently, about 5 percent of the land surface of the contiguous forty-eight states is potentially affected by the wetlands provision, and 75 percent of this land is privately owned. Efforts to define *wetland* have created a battleground between pro-environment and pro-development (or pro–private property rights) groups. Farmers, homeowners, and developers often want a narrow definition of wetlands so that more property is available for commercial or private use. Environmentalists favor a broad definition in order to protect different habitat types and maintain the environmental safeguards that wetlands provide (control of water pollution, spawning grounds for aquatic species, floodwater containment, and so forth).

The problem is that defining *wetland* is tricky. For example, one federal regulation defines a wetland as any area that has a saturated ground surface for twenty-one consecutive days during the year. But how would you apply this law to a pine flatwood ecosystem that was wet for ten days this year but thirty days last year? And how should the courts react to lawsuits claiming that the regulation itself is either too broad or too narrow? One can see why the wetlands controversy provides hefty incomes for lawyers and congressional lobbyists.

The Criteria-Match Structure of Definition Arguments

As the wetlands example suggests, definition arguments usually have a two-part structure—(1) a definition part that tries to establish the boundaries of the category (What do we mean by *wetland*?) and (2) a match part that argues whether a given case meets that definition (Does this thirty-acre parcel of land near Swan Lake meet the criteria for a wetland?). To describe this structure, we use the term *criteria-match*. Here is an example:

> **Definition issue:** In a divorce proceeding, is a frozen embryo a "person" rather than "property"?
> **Criteria part:** What criteria must be met for something to be a "person"?
> **Match part:** Does a frozen embryo meet these criteria?

Developing the Criteria-Match Structure for a Definition Argument

To show how a definition issue can be developed into a claim with supporting reasons, let's look more closely at this example:

> **Definition issue:** For purposes of my feeling good about buying my next pair of running shoes, is the Hercules Shoe Company a socially responsible company?
> **Criteria part:** What criteria must be met for a company to be deemed "socially responsible"?
> **Match part:** Does the Hercules Shoe Company meet these criteria?

Let's suppose you work for a consumer information group that wishes to encourage patronage of socially responsible companies while boycotting irresponsible ones. Your group's first task is to define *socially responsible company*. After much discussion and research, your group establishes three criteria that a company must meet to be considered socially responsible:

> *Your definition:* A company is socially responsible if it (1) avoids polluting the environment, (2) sells goods or services that contribute to the well-being of the community, and (3) treats its workers justly.

The criteria section of your argument would explain and illustrate these criteria.

The match part of the argument would then try to persuade readers that a specific company does or does not meet the criteria. A typical thesis statement might be as follows:

> *Your thesis statement:* Although the Hercules Shoe Company is nonpolluting and provides a socially useful product, it is not a socially responsible company because it treats workers unjustly.

Toulmin Framework for a Definition Argument

Here is how the core of the preceding Hercules definition argument could be displayed in Toulmin terms. Note how the reason and grounds constitute the match argument while the warrant and backing constitute the criterion argument.

Toulmin Analysis of the Hercules Shoe Company Argument

ENTHYMEME

CLAIM The Hercules Shoe Company is not a socially responsible company

REASON because it treats workers unjustly.

GROUNDS

Evidence of unjust treatment:

- Evidence that the company manufactures its shoes in East Asian sweatshops

- Evidence of the inhumane conditions in these shops

- Evidence of hardships imposed on displaced American workers

CONDITIONS OF REBUTTAL
Attacking reasons and grounds

- Possible counter evidence that the shops maintain humane working conditions

- Possible questioning of statistical data about hardships on displaced workers

WARRANT

Socially responsible companies treat workers justly.

BACKING

- Arguments showing that just treatment of workers is right in principle and also benefits society

- Arguments that capitalism helps society as a whole only if workers achieve a reasonable standard of living, have time for leisure, and are not exploited

CONDITIONS OF REBUTTAL
Attacking warrant and backing

Justice needs to be considered from an emerging nation's standpoint:

- The wages paid workers are low by American standards but are above average by East Asian standards.

- Displacement of American workers is part of the necessary adjustment of adapting to a global economy and does not mean that a company is unjust.

As this Toulmin schema illustrates, the warrant and backing constitute the criteria section of the argument by stating and defending "just treatment of workers" as a criterion for a socially responsible company. The reason and grounds constitute the match section of the argument by arguing that the Hercules Shoe Company does not treat its workers justly. How much emphasis you need to place on justifying each criterion and supporting each match depends on your audience's initial beliefs. The conditions of rebuttal help you imagine alternative views and see places where opposing views need to be acknowledged and rebutted.

■ ■ ■ **FOR CLASS DISCUSSION** Identifying Criteria and Match Issues
Consider the following definition claims. Working individually or in small groups, identify the criteria issue and the match issue for each of the following claims.

> **Definition issue:** A Honda assembled in Ohio is (is not) an American-made car.
>
> **Criteria part:** What criteria have to be met before a car can be called "American made"?
>
> **Match part:** Does a Honda assembled in Ohio meet these criteria?

1. American Sign Language is (is not) a "foreign language" for purposes of a college graduation requirement.
2. The violence in *Grand Theft Auto* is (is not) constitutionally protected free speech.
3. Bungee jumping from a crane is (is not) a "carnival amusement ride" subject to state safety inspections.
4. For purposes of a state sales tax on "candy," a Twinkie is (is not) candy.
5. A skilled video game player is (is not) a true athlete. ■ ■ ■

Kinds of Definitions

In this section we discuss two methods of definition: Aristotelian and operational.

Aristotelian Definitions

Aristotelian definitions, regularly used in dictionaries, define a term by placing it within the next larger class or category and then showing the specific attributes that distinguish the term from other terms within the same category. For example, according to a legal dictionary, *robbery* is "the felonious taking of property" (next larger category) that differs from other acts of theft because it seizes property "through violence or intimidation." Legal dictionaries often provide specific examples to show the boundaries of the term. Here is one example:

> There is no robbery unless force or fear is used to overcome resistance. Thus, surreptitiously picking a man's pocket or snatching something from him without resistance on his part is *larceny,* but not robbery.

Many states specify degrees of robbery with increasingly heavy penalties. For example, *armed robbery* involves the use of a weapon to threaten the victim. In all cases, *robbery* is distinguished from the lesser crime of *larceny,* in which no force or intimidation is involved.

As you can see, an Aristotelian definition of a term identifies specific attributes or criteria that enable you to distinguish it from other members of the next larger class. We created an Aristotelian definition in our example about socially responsible companies. A socially responsible company, we said, is any company (next larger class) that meets three criteria: (1) it doesn't pollute the environment; (2) it creates goods or services that promote the well-being of the community; and (3) it treats its workers justly.

In constructing Aristotelian definitions, you may find it useful to employ the concept of accidental, necessary, and sufficient criteria.

- An *accidental criterion* is a usual but not essential feature of a concept. For example, armed robbers frequently wear masks, but wearing a mask is an accidental criterion because it has no bearing on the definition of *robbery.* In our example about socially responsible companies, "makes regular contributions to charities" might be an accidental criterion; most socially responsible companies contribute to charities, but some do not. And many socially irresponsible companies also contribute to charities—often as a public relations ploy.

- A *necessary criterion* is an attribute that *must* be present for something to belong to the category being defined. To be guilty of robbery rather than larceny, a thief must have used direct force or intimidation. The use of force is thus a necessary criterion for robbery. However, for a robbery to occur, another criterion must also be met: the robber must also take property from the victim.

- *Sufficient criteria* are all the criteria that must be present for something to belong to the category being defined. Together, the use of force plus the taking of property are *sufficient criteria* for an act to be classified as robbery.

Consider again our defining criteria for a "socially responsible" company: (1) the company must avoid polluting the environment; (2) the company must create goods or services that contribute to the well-being of the community; **and** (3) the company must treat its workers justly. In this definition, each criterion is necessary, but none of the criteria alone is sufficient. In other words, to be defined as socially responsible, a company must meet all three criteria at once, as the word *and* signals. It is not enough for a company to be nonpolluting (a necessary but not sufficient criterion); if that company makes a shoddy product or treats its workers unjustly, it fails to meet the other necessary criteria and can't be deemed socially responsible. Because no one criterion by itself is sufficient, all three criteria together must be met before a company can be deemed socially responsible.

In contrast, consider the following definition of *sexual harassment* as established by the U.S. Equal Employment Opportunity Commission in its 1980 guidelines:

Unwelcome sexual advances, requests for sexual favors, and other verbal or physical conduct of a sexual nature constitute sexual harassment when (1) submission to such conduct is made either explicitly or implicitly a term or condition of an individual's employment,

(2) submission to or rejection of such conduct by an individual is used as the basis for employment decisions affecting such individual, **or** (3) such conduct has the purpose or effect of unreasonably interfering with an individual's work performance or creating an intimidating, hostile, or offensive working environment.*

Here each of these criteria is sufficient, but none is necessary. In other words, an act constitutes sexual harassment if any one of the three criteria is satisfied, as the word *or* indicates.

■ ■ ■ **FOR CLASS DISCUSSION** Working with Criteria

Working individually or in small groups, try to determine whether each of the following is a necessary criterion, a sufficient criterion, an accidental criterion, or no criterion for defining the indicated concept. Be prepared to explain your reasoning and to account for differences in points of view.

Criterion	Concept to Be Defined
Presence of gills	Fish
Profane and obscene language	R-rated movie
Line endings that form a rhyming pattern	Poem
Disciplining a child by spanking	Child abuse
Diet that excludes meat	Vegetarian
Killing another human being	Murder
Good sex life	Happy marriage

■ ■ ■

Operational Definitions

In some rhetorical situations, particularly those arising in the physical and social sciences, writers need precise, *operational definitions* that can be measured empirically and are not subject to problems of context and disputed criteria. A social scientist studying the effects of television on aggression in children needs a precise, measurable definition of *aggression*. Typically, the scientist might measure "aggression" by counting the number of blows a child gives to an inflatable bobo doll over a fifteen-minute period when other play options are available. In our wetlands example, a federal authority created an operational definition of *wetland:* a wetland is a parcel of land that has a saturated ground surface for twenty-one consecutive days during the year.

---

*Quoted in Stephanie Riger, "Gender Dilemmas in Sexual Harassment Policies and Procedures," *American Psychologist* 46 (May 1991), 497–505.

Such operational definitions are useful because they are precisely measurable, but they are also limited because they omit criteria that may be unmeasurable but important. Thus, we might ask whether it is adequate to define a *superior student* as someone with a 3.5 GPA or higher or a *successful sex-education program* as one that results in a 25 percent reduction in teenage pregnancies. What important aspects of a superior student or a successful sex-education program are not considered in these operational definitions?

Conducting the Criteria Part of a Definition Argument

In constructing criteria to define your contested term, you can either research how others have defined your term or make your own definitions. If you take the first approach, you turn to standard or specialized dictionaries, judicial opinions, or expert testimony to establish a definition based on the authority of others. A lawyer defining a wetland based on twenty-one consecutive days of saturated ground surface would be taking the first approach, using federal regulation as his or her source. The other approach is to use your own critical thinking to make your own definition, thereby defining the contested term yourself. Our definition of a socially responsible company, specifying three criteria, is an example of an individual's own definition created through critical thinking. This section explains these approaches in more detail.

Approach 1: Research How Others Have Defined the Term

When you take this approach, you search for authoritative definitions acceptable to your audience yet favorable to your case. When the state of Washington tried to initiate a new sales tax on candy, lawyers and legislators wrestled with a definition. They finally created the following statute available to the public on a government Web site:

What Is the Definition of Candy?

"Candy" is a preparation of sugar, honey, or other natural or artificial sweeteners combined with chocolate, fruits, nuts, or other ingredients or flavorings in the form of bars, drops, or pieces. Candy does not require refrigeration, and does not include flour as an ingredient.

"Natural or artificial sweeteners" include, but are not limited to, high fructose corn syrup, dextrose, invert sugar, sucrose, fructose, sucralose, saccharin, aspartame, stevia, fruit juice concentrates, molasses, evaporated cane juice, and rice syrup.

"Flour" includes any flour made from a grain, such as wheat flour, rice flour, and corn flour.

Items that require "refrigeration," either before or after opening, are not candy. For example, popsicles, ice cream bars, and fruits in sweetened syrups are not candy.

This definition made it easy for state officials to exclude from the "candy tax" any snack food that contained flour. Thus Twinkies, Froot Loops cereal, and chocolate-covered pretzels were exempt from the tax. But considerable debate occurred over cough drops and halvah (a traditional dessert in India and Mediterranean countries). The state decided to exclude cough drops if the package contained a "drug facts" panel and a list of active ingredients. (Such cough drops were then classified as "over the counter drugs.") The state ruled that nut-butter halvah was taxable but that flour-based halvah was not taxable; even so, many kinds of halvah didn't fit neatly into these two categories.

Turning to established definitions is thus a first step for many definition arguments. Common sources of these definitions are specialized dictionaries such as *Black's Law Dictionary*, which form a standard part of the reference holdings of any library. Other sources of specialized definitions are state and federal appellate court decisions, legislative and administrative statutes, and scholarly articles examining a given definition conflict. Lawyers use this research strategy exhaustively in preparing court briefs. They begin by looking at the actual text of laws as passed by legislatures or written by administrative authorities. Then they look at all the court cases in which the laws have been tested and examine the ways courts have refined legal definitions and applied them to specific cases. Using these refined definitions, lawyers then apply them to their own case at hand.

If your research uncovers definitions that seem ambiguous or otherwise unfavorable to your case, you can sometimes appeal to the "original intentions" of those who defined the term. For example, if a scientist is dissatisfied with definitions of *wetlands* based on consecutive days of saturated ground surface, she might proceed as follows: "The original intention of Congress in passing the Clean Water Act was to preserve the environment." What Congress intended, she could then claim, was to prevent development of those wetland areas that provide crucial habitat for wildlife or that inhibit water pollution. She could then propose an alternative definition based on criteria other than consecutive days of ground saturation.

Approach 2: Create Your Own Extended Definition*

Often, however, you need to create your own definition of the contested term. An effective strategy is to establish initial criteria for your contested term by thinking of hypothetical cases that obviously fit the category you are trying to define and then by altering one or more variables until the hypothetical case obviously doesn't fit the category. You can then test and refine your criteria by applying them to borderline cases. For example, suppose you work at a homeless agency where you overhear street people discuss an incident that strikes you as potential "police brutality." You wonder whether you should write to your local paper to bring attention to the incident.

---

*The defining strategies and collaborative exercises in this section are based on the work of George Hillocks and his research associates at the University of Chicago. See George Hillocks Jr., Elizabeth A. Kahn, and Larry R. Johannessen, "Teaching Defining Strategies as a Mode of Inquiry: Some Effects on Student Writing," *Research in the Teaching of English* 17 (October 1983), 275–84. See also Larry R. Johannessen, Elizabeth A. Kahn, and Carolyn Calhoun Walter, *Designing and Sequencing Prewriting Activities* (Urbana, IL: NCTE, 1982).

A Possible Case of Police Brutality

Two police officers confront an inebriated homeless man who is shouting obscenities on a street corner. The officers tell the man to quiet down and move on, but he keeps shouting obscenities. When the officers attempt to put the man into the police car, he resists and takes a wild swing at one of the officers. As eyewitnesses later testified, this officer shouted obscenities back at the drunk man, pinned his arms behind his back in order to handcuff him, and lifted him forcefully by the arms. The man screamed in pain and was later discovered to have a dislocated shoulder. Is this officer guilty of police brutality?

To your way of thinking, this officer seems guilty: An inebriated man is too uncoordinated to be a threat in a fight, and two police officers ought to be able to arrest him without dislocating his shoulder. But a friend argues that because the man took a swing at the officer, the police were justified in using force. The dislocated shoulder was simply an accidental result of using justified force.

To make your case, you need to develop a definition of "police brutality." You can begin by creating a hypothetical case that is obviously an instance of "police brutality":

A Clear Case of Police Brutality

A police officer confronts a drunk man shouting obscenities and begins hitting him in the face with his police baton. *[This is an obvious incidence of police brutality because the officer intentionally tries to hurt the drunk man without justification; hitting him with the baton is not necessary for making an arrest or getting the man into the police car.]*

You could then vary the hypothetical case until it is clearly *not* an instance of police brutality.

Cases That Are Clearly Not Police Brutality

Case 1: The police officer handcuffs the drunk man, who, in being helped into the police car, accidentally slips on the curb and dislocates his arm while falling. *[Here the injury occurs accidentally; the police officer does not act intentionally and is not negligent.]*

Case 2: The police officer confronts an armed robber fleeing from a scene and tackles him from behind, wrestling the gun away from him. In this struggle, the officer pins the robber's arm behind his back with such force that the robber's shoulder is dislocated. *[Here aggressive use of force is justified because the robber was armed, dangerous, and resisting arrest.]*

Using these hypothetical cases, you decide that the defining criteria for police brutality are (1) *intention* and (2) use of *excessive force*—that is, force beyond what was required by the immediate situation. After more contemplation, you are convinced that the officer was guilty of police brutality and have a clearer idea of how to make your argument. Here is how you might write the "match" part of your argument:

Match Argument Using Your Definition

If we define police brutality as the *intentional* use of *excessive* force, then the police officer is guilty. His action was intentional because he was purposefully responding to the homeless man's drunken swing and was angry enough to be shouting obscenities back at the drunk (according to eyewitnesses). Second, he used excessive force in applying the handcuffs. A drunk man taking a wild swing hardly poses a serious danger to two police officers. Putting handcuffs on the drunk may have been justified, but lifting the man's arm violently enough to dislocate a shoulder indicates excessive force. The officer lifted the man's arms violently not because he needed to but because he was angry, and acting out of anger is no justification for that violence. In fact, we can charge police officers with "police brutality" precisely to protect us from being victims of police anger. It is the job of the court system to punish us, not the police's job. Because this officer acted intentionally and applied excessive force out of anger, he should be charged with police brutality.

The strategy we have demonstrated—developing criteria by imagining hypothetical cases that clearly do and do not belong to the contested category—gives you a systematic procedure for developing your own definition for your argument.

■ ■ ■ **FOR CLASS DISCUSSION** Developing a Definition

1. Suppose you wanted to define the concept of *courage.* Working in groups, try to decide whether each of the following cases is an example of courage:
   a. A neighbor rushes into a burning house to rescue a child from certain death and emerges, coughing and choking, with the child in his arms. Is the neighbor courageous?
   b. A firefighter rushes into a burning house to rescue a child from certain death and emerges with the child in her arms. The firefighter is wearing protective clothing and a gas mask. When a newspaper reporter calls her courageous, she says, "Hey, this is my job." Is the firefighter courageous?
   c. A teenager rushes into a burning house to recover a memento given to him by his girlfriend, the first love of his life. Is the teenager courageous?
   d. A parent rushes into a burning house to save a trapped child. The fire marshal tells the parent to wait because there is no chance that the child can be reached from the first floor. The fire marshal wants to try cutting a hole in the roof to reach the child. The parent rushes into the house anyway and is burned to death. Was the parent courageous?
2. As you make your decisions on each of these cases, create and refine the criteria you use.
3. Make up your own series of controversial cases, like those given previously for "courage," for one or more of the following concepts:
   a. cruelty to animals
   b. child abuse
   c. true athlete
   d. sexual harassment
   e. free speech protected by the First Amendment

Then, using the strategy of making up hypothetical cases that do and do not belong to each category, construct a definition of your chosen concept.   ■ ■ ■

Conducting the Match Part of a Definition Argument

In conducting a match argument, you need to supply examples and other evidence showing that your contested case does (does not) meet the criteria you established in your definition. In essence, you support the match part of your argument in much the same way you would support a simple categorical claim.

For example, if you were developing the argument that the Hercules Shoe Company is not socially responsible because it treats its workers unjustly, your match section would provide evidence of this injustice. You might supply data about the percentage of shoes produced in East Asia, about the low wages paid these workers, and about the working conditions in these factories. You might also describe the suffering of displaced American workers when Hercules closed its American factories and moved operations to Asia, where the labor is nonunion and cheap. The match section should also summarize and respond to opposing views.

Types of Resemblance Arguments

Whereas definition arguments claim that a particular phenomenon belongs to a certain category, resemblance arguments simply compare one thing to another. In general, there are two types of resemblance arguments:

1. **Arguments by analogy**, in which the arguer likens one thing to another by using a metaphor or imaginative comparison
2. **Arguments by precedent**, in which the arguer likens a current or proposed event or phenomenon to a previous event or phenomenon

We'll illustrate both types later in this section.

In both kinds of resemblance arguments, the arguer's intention is to transfer the audience's understanding of (or feelings about) the second thing back to the first. Thus when opponents of violent video games compare *Postal 2* to pornography, they intend to transfer the audience's disgust at pornography back to *Postal 2*'s particular kind of violence. The *logos* of resemblance arguments comes from their power to throw unexpected light on a contested phenomenon (seeing how gratuitous violence might be similar to pornography); the *pathos* comes from the audience's feelings, which are already attached to the second phenomenon (our disgust at exposing children to pornography). The risk of resemblance arguments is that the differences between the two things being compared are often so significant that the argument collapses under close examination.

Toulmin Framework for a Resemblance Argument

Like most other argument types, resemblance arguments can be analyzed using the Toulmin schema. Suppose you want to find a startling way to warn teenage girls away from excessive dieting. Simultaneously, you want to argue that excessive dieting is partially caused by a patriarchal construction of beauty that keeps women submissive and powerless. You decide to create a resemblance argument claiming that women's obsessive dieting is like footbinding in ancient China. This argument can be displayed in Toulmin terms as follows:

Toulmin Analysis of the Dieting Argument

ENTHYMEME

CLAIM Women's obsessive dieting in America serves the same harmful function as footbinding in ancient China

REASON because both practices keep women childlike, docile, dependent, and unthreatening to men.

GROUNDS

- Evidence that both practices make women childlike: The "perfect woman" is often made to seem childlike. (Men call beautiful women "dolls" or "babes.") Bound feet, covered with tiny slippers, are like children's feet; excessive dieting keeps women slim like pre-adolescent girls. (Fertility goddesses are fleshy; anorexia stops menstruation.)

- Evidence that both practices keep women weak or nonthreatening: Chinese women were physically maimed, unable to run or walk naturally. American women pursuing the ideal of thinness are psychologically maimed and often weakened by excessive dieting.

- Evidence that both practices make women satisfied with inferior positions in society so long as they are considered "pretty" or "beautiful": Footbinding indicated that the woman was upper class and didn't have to work. Dieting and pursuit of beauty (the expense of beauty products) reduce women's economic power.

POSSIBLE CONDITIONS OF REBUTTAL
Attacking the reason and grounds:

- Women who diet are concerned with health, not pursuit of beauty.

- Concern for healthy weight is "rational," not "obsessive."

- Thin women are often powerful athletes, not at all like Chinese victims of foot binding who can hardly walk.

- Dieting does not cause crippling deformity; a concern for beauty does not make a woman subordinate or satisfied with less pay.

- Dieting is a woman's choice—not something forced on her as a child.

WARRANT

Practices that are like ancient Chinese footbinding are bad.

BACKING

- Arguments that the subordinate position of women evidenced in both footbinding and obsession with weight is related to patriarchal construction of women's roles

- Arguments for why women should free themselves from patriarchal views

CONDITIONS OF REBUTTAL
Attacking the warrant and backing

- Perhaps arguments could be made that Chinese foot binding was not as repressive and patriarchal as the analogy implies (?). [We can't imagine a contemporary argument supporting footbinding.]

- Arguments supporting patriarchy and women's subordination

QUALIFIER: Perhaps the writer should say, *"Under certain conditions* obsessive dieting can even seem like Chinese footbinding."

For many audiences, the comparison of women's dieting to Chinese footbinding will have an immediate and powerful emotional effect perhaps causing them to see attitudes toward weight and food from a new, unsettling perspective. The analogy invites them to transfer their understanding of Chinese footbinding—which seems instantly repulsive and oppressive of women—to their understanding of obsessive concern for losing weight. Whereas social controls in ancient China were overt, the modern practice uses more subtle kinds of social controls, such as the influence of the fashion and beauty industry and peer pressure. But in both cases women feel forced to mold their bodies to a patriarchal standard of beauty—one that emphasizes soft curves, tiny waists, and daintiness rather than strength and power.

But this example also illustrates the dangers of resemblance arguments, which often ignore important differences or *disanalogies* between the terms of comparison. As the "conditions of rebuttal" show, there are many differences between dieting and foot-binding. For example, the practice of foot binding was not a conscious choice of young Chinese girls, who were forced to have their feet wrapped at an early age. Dieting, on the other hand, is something one chooses, and it may reveal a healthy and rational choice rather than an obsession with appearance. When the practice degenerates to anorexia or bulimia, it becomes a mental disease, not a physical deformity forced on a girl in childhood. Thus a resemblance argument is usually open to refutation if a skeptic points out important disanalogies.

We now turn to the two types of resemblance arguments: analogy and precedent.

Arguments by Analogy

A common kind of resemblance argument uses analogies—imaginative kinds of comparisons often with subtle persuasive effects. If you don't like your new boss, you can say that she's like a Marine drill sergeant, the cowardly captain of a sinking ship, or a mother hen. Each of these analogies suggests a different management style, clarifying the nature of your dislike while conveying an emotional charge.

Sometimes, as in the "My boss is like a Marine drill sergeant" example, arguers use short, undeveloped analogies for quick rhetorical effect. At other times, arguers develop extended analogies that carry a substantial portion of the argument. As an example of an extended analogy, consider the following excerpt from a professor's argument opposing a proposal to require a writing proficiency exam for graduation. In the following portion of his argument, the professor compares development of writing skills to the development of physical fitness.

> A writing proficiency exam gives the wrong symbolic messages about writing. It suggests that writing is simply a skill, rather than an active way of thinking and learning. It suggests that once a student demonstrates proficiency then he or she doesn't need to do any more writing.
>
> Imagine two universities concerned with the physical fitness of their students. One university requires a junior-level physical fitness exam in which students must run a mile in less than 10 minutes, a fitness level it considers minimally competent. Students at this university see the physical fitness exam as a one-time hurdle. As many as 70 percent of them can pass the exam with no practice; another 10–20 percent need a few months' training; and a few hopeless couch potatoes must go through exhaustive remediation.

After passing the exam, any student can settle back into a routine of TV and potato chips having been certified as "physically fit."

The second university, however, believing in true physical fitness for its students, is not interested in minimal competency. Consequently, it creates programs in which its students exercise 30 minutes every day for the entire four years of the undergraduate curriculum. There is little doubt which university will have the most physically fit students. At the second university, fitness becomes a way of life with everyone developing his or her full potential. Similarly, if we want to improve our students' writing abilities, we should require writing in every course throughout the curriculum.

Thus analogies have the power to get an audience's attention like virtually no other persuasive strategy. But seldom are they sufficient in themselves to provide full understanding. At some point, with every analogy, you need to ask yourself, "How far can I legitimately go with this? At what point are the similarities between the two things I am comparing going to be overwhelmed by their dissimilarities?" Analogies are useful attention-getting devices, but they can conceal and distort as well as clarify.

If you choose to make an analogy argument, you will need to focus on the points of comparison that serve your purposes. In the preceding case, the writer's purpose is to argue that the goal of a writing program is to help students develop their full abilities as writers rather than meet minimalist standards. To keep this focus, the writer avoids the disanalogies between the two elements. (For example, writing requires the use of intellect and may differ substantially from physical fitness, which requires muscles and endurance.) Typically, then, in developing an analogy, writers keep the audience's attention only on the relevant similarities.

■ ■ ■ **FOR CLASS DISCUSSION** Developing Analogies

The following exercise will help you clarify how analogies function in the context of arguments. Working individually or in small groups, think of two analogies for each of the following topics. One analogy should urge readers toward a positive view of the topic; the other should urge a negative view. Write each of your analogies in the following one-sentence format:

_____ is like _____ : A, B, C . . . (in which the first term is the contested topic being discussed; the second term is the analogy; and A, B, and C are the points of comparison).

Example

Topic: Cramming for an exam
Negative analogy: Cramming for an exam is like pumping iron for ten hours straight to prepare for a weight-lifting contest: exhausting and counterproductive.
Positive analogy: Cramming for an exam is like carbohydrate loading before a big race: it gives your brain a full supply of facts and concepts, all fresh in your mind.

1. Using spanking to discipline children
2. Using racial profiling for airport security
3. Using steroids to increase athletic performance
4. Paying college athletes
5. Eating at fast-food restaurants

■ ■ ■

Arguments by Precedent

A second kind of resemblance argument uses precedent for its persuasive force. An argument by precedent tries to show that a current situation is like a past situation and that therefore a similar action or decision should be taken or reached. You can refute a precedence argument by showing that the present situation differs substantially from the past situation.

Precedence arguments are very common. For example, during the debate about health care reform in the first year of Barack Obama's presidency, supporters of a single-payer, "Medicare-for-all" system pointed to Canada as a successful precedent. Supporters said that since a single-payer system was successful in Canada, it would also be successful in the United States. But opponents also used the Canadian precedent to attack a single-payer system. They pointed to problems in the Canadian system as a reason to reject a Medicare-for-all system in the United States.

A good example of an extended precedence argument can be found in an article entitled "The Perils of Ignoring History: Big Tobacco Played Dirty and Millions Died. How Similar Is Big Food?"* The authors argue that the food-processing industry is trying to avoid government regulations by employing the same "dirty tricks" used earlier by Big Tobacco. The authors show how Big Tobacco hired lobbyists to fight regulation, how it created clever advertising to make cigarette smoking seem cool, and how it sponsored its own research to cast doubt on data linking nicotine to lung cancer or asthma to secondhand smoke. The researchers argue that Big Food is now doing the same thing. Through lobbying efforts, coordinated lawsuits, and public relations campaigns, Big Food resists labeling ingredients in food products, casts doubt on scientific evidence about possible carcinogens in processed foods, and uses advertising to create a local, "family farm" image for Big Food. The researchers use this precedence argument to call for stricter government oversight of Big Food.

■ ■ ■   **FOR CLASS DISCUSSION** Using Claims of Precedent

1. Consider the following claims of precedent, and evaluate how effective you think each precedent might be in establishing the claim. How would you develop the argument? How would you cast doubt on it?
   a. To increase alumni giving to our university, we should put more funding into our football program. When University X went to postseason bowls for three years in a row, alumni donations to building programs and academics increased by 30 percent. We can expect the same increases here.
   b. Postwar democracy can be created successfully in Afghanistan because it was created successfully in Germany and Japan following World War II.
2. Advocates for "right to die" legislation legalizing active euthanasia under certain conditions often point to the Netherlands as a country where acceptance of euthanasia works effectively. Assume for the moment that your state legislature is considering a law legalizing euthanasia. Assume further that you are a research

---

*Kelly D. Brownell and Kenneth E. Warner, "The Perils of Ignoring History: Big Tobacco Played Dirty and Millions Died. How Similar Is Big Food?" *The Milbank Quarterly* 87.1 (2009), 259–294.

assistant working for a legislator who hasn't made up her mind how to vote on the issue. She has asked you to research the arguments for and against euthanasia based on the experience of the Netherlands. Working in small groups, make a list of research questions you would want to ask. Your long-range rhetorical goal is to use your research to support (or attack) the legalization of euthanasia.

WRITING ASSIGNMENT   A Definition Argument

The assignment for this chapter focuses on definition disputes about categories. Write an essay in which you argue that a borderline or contested case fits (or does not fit) within a given category. In the opening of your essay, introduce the borderline case you will examine and pose your definition question. In the first part of your argument, define the boundaries of your category (criteria) by reporting a definition used by others or by developing your own extended definition. In the second part of your argument (the match), show how your borderline case meets (or doesn't meet) your definition criteria.

Exploring Ideas

Ideally, in writing this argument you will join an ongoing conversation about a definition issue that interests you. What cultural and social issues that concern you involve disputed definitions? In the public arena, you are likely to find numerous examples simply by looking through news stories—for example, the disputes about defining "candy" in the Washington State sales tax controversy, about the definition of "torture" in interrogating terrorist suspects, or about definitions of "pornography" that might include ultra-violent video games. Often you can frame your own definition issues even if they aren't currently in the news. Is using TiVo to avoid TV commercials a form of theft? Is spanking a form of child abuse? Are cheerleaders athletes? Is flag burning protected free speech? Is a person who downloads instructions for making a bomb a terrorist? Are today's maximum-security prisons "cruel and unusual punishment"? Is Wal-Mart a socially responsible company? Can a model or beauty pageant winner (or a man) be a feminist?

If you have trouble discovering a local or national issue that interests you, you can create fascinating definition controversies among your classmates by asking whether certain borderline cases are "true" or "real" examples of some category: Are highly skilled video game players (race car drivers, synchronized swimmers, marbles players) true athletes? Is a gourmet chef (skilled furniture maker, tagger) a true artist? Is a chiropractor (acupuncturist, naturopathic physician) a "real doctor"? Working as a whole class or in small groups inside or outside class, create an argumentative discussion on one or more of these issues. Listen to the various voices in the controversy, and then write out your own argument.

You can also stimulate definition controversies by brainstorming borderline cases for such terms as *courage* (Is mountain climbing an act of courage?), *cruelty to animals* (Are rodeos [zoos, catch-and-release trout fishing, use of animals for medical research] cruelty to animals?), or *war crime* (Was the American firebombing of Tokyo in World War II a war crime?).

As you explore your definition issue, try to determine how others have defined your category. If no stable definition emerges from your search, create your own definition by deciding what criteria must be met for a contested case to fit within your category. Try using the strategy for creating criteria that we discussed on pages 237–238 with reference to police brutality. Once you have determined your criteria, freewrite for five or ten minutes, exploring whether your contested case meets each of the criteria.

Identifying Your Audience and Determining What's at Stake

Before drafting your argument, identify your targeted audience and determine what's at stake. Consider your responses to the following questions:

- What audience are you targeting? What background do they need to understand your issue? How much do they already care about it?
- Before they read your argument, what stance on your issue do you imagine them holding? What change do you want to bring about in their views?

Organization Plan 1: Definition Argument with Criteria and Match in Separate Sections

Introduce the issue and state your claim.	• Engage reader's interest in your definition issue and show why it is controversial or problematic. • Show what's at stake. • Provide background information needed by your audience. • State your claim.
Present your criteria.	• State and develop criterion 1. • State and develop criterion 2. • Continue with the rest of your criteria. • Anticipate and respond to possible objections to the criteria.
Present your match argument.	• Consider restating your claim for clarity. • Argue that your case meets (does not meet) criterion 1. • Argue that your case meets (does not meet) criterion 2. • Continue with the rest of your match argument. • Anticipate and respond to possible objections to the match argument.
Conclude.	• Perhaps sum up your argument. • Help reader return to the "big picture" of what's at stake. • End with something memorable.

- What will they find new or surprising about your argument?
- What objections might they raise? What counterarguments or alternative points of view will you need to address?
- Why does your argument matter? Who might be threatened or made uncomfortable by your views? What is at stake?

Organizing a Definition Argument

As you compose a first draft of your essay, you may find it helpful to know typical structures for definition arguments. There are two basic approaches, as shown in Organization Plans 1 and 2. You can either discuss the criteria and the match separately or interweave the discussion.

Questioning and Critiquing a Definition Argument

A powerful way to stimulate global revision of a draft is to role-play a skeptical audience. The following questions will help you strengthen your own argument or rebut

Organization Plan 2: Definition Argument with Criteria and Match Interwoven

Introduce the issue and state your claim.	• Engage reader's interest in your definition issue and show why it is problematic or controversial.
	• Show what's at stake.
	• Provide background information needed by your audience.
	• State your claim.
Present series of criterion-match arguments.	• State and develop criterion 1 and argue that your case meets (does not meet) the criterion.
	• State and develop criterion 2 and argue that your case meets (does not meet) the criterion.
	• Continue with the rest of your criterion-match arguments.
Respond to possible objections to your argument.	• Anticipate and summarize possible objections.
	• Respond to the objections through rebuttal or concession.
Conclude.	• Perhaps sum up your argument.
	• Help reader return to the "big picture" of what's at stake.
	• End with something memorable.

the definition arguments of others. In critiquing a definition argument, you need to appreciate its criteria-match structure because you can question your criteria argument, your match argument, or both.

Questioning Your Criteria

- Could a skeptic claim that your criteria are not the right ones? Could he or she offer different criteria or point out missing criteria?
- Could a skeptic point out possible bad consequences of accepting your criteria?
- Could a skeptic cite unusual circumstances that weaken your criteria?
- Could a skeptic point out bias or slant in your definition?

Questioning Your Match

- Could a skeptic argue that your examples or data don't meet the STAR criteria (see Chapter 5, pages 92–93) for evidence?
- Could a skeptic point out counterexamples or alternative data that cast doubt on your argument?
- Could a skeptic reframe the way you have viewed your borderline case? ∎

Our first reading, by student writer Arthur Knopf, grew out of his research into agricultural subsidies and the nutritional content of foods. It was written for the assignment on page 245.

Is Milk a Health Food?

ARTHUR KNOPF (STUDENT)

If asked to name a typical health food, most of us would put milk high on our lists. We've all seen the "Got Milk?" ads with their milk-mustached celebrities or the dairy product campaigns entitled "Milk, It Does a Body Good" or "Body By Milk." These ads, featuring well known athletes or trim celebrities, argue visually that milk helps you grow fit and strong. But if you define "health food" based on science rather than on marketing claims, and if you include in your definition of health food concerns for the planet as well as for individual bodies, then milk might not fit the category of health food at all.

My first criterion for a "health food" is that the food should have a scientifically supported health benefit with minimal risks. Based on the food pyramid from the United States Department of Agriculture (USDA), milk at first glance seems to fit this criterion. On the *MyPyramid* Web site the dairy group (milk, yogurt, cheese) is one of the essential components of a healthy diet (United States Dept. of Agriculture). All elements of the milk group provide calcium, which is important for healthy bones and the prevention of osteoporosis. Dairy products also provide important vitamins. But the Web site entry under the dairy group specifies in a footnote, "Choose fat-free or low-fat milk, yogurt, and cheese." One cup of whole milk, according to the Web site, contains 70 more calories than a cup of skim milk (147 calories compared to 83). The extra 70 calories are potentially harmful saturated fats and sugar, linked to heart disease and obesity. We can say then that "non-fat milk" fits my first criterion for a health food, but that the rest of the milk group may not.

So how do dairy products in general get listed as essential ingredients on the food pyramid rather than just low fat milk or yogurt? The answer to this question brings us to my second criterion for a health food: Potentially unhealthy aspects of the food should be widely disclosed, not hidden by marketing. Because we are bombarded daily by conflicting nutrition claims, many people turn to the U.S. government for neutral, unbiased information. But the place of dairy products on the USDA food pyramid may be itself a result of marketing. The USDA's mandate isn't directly to promote health, but to promote agriculture and to help farmers flourish economically. In recommending three servings of dairy products per day, the food pyramid serves the interests of dairy farmers by promoting the whole class of dairy products, not just skim milk. According to the Environmental Working Group's Farm Subsidies Database, the USDA spent $4.8 billion in dairy subsidies between 1995 and 2009 ("Dairy Program Subsidies"). All these policies invest public dollars to create a steady consumption of dairy products and fundamentally depend on the premise that dairy products are good for us.

As we have seen, skim milk may be good for us but dairy products in general are more problematic. When the fat in whole milk is removed to make skim milk, it is not thrown away. It is used to make high calorie, high fat products like cheese and ice cream. Revealing its true ambivalence to public nutrition, the USDA warns against saturated fats in its food pyramid site while simultaneously working with companies like Domino's Pizza, to increase the amount of cheese in their products. According to the *New York Times* (Moss), the USDA helped Domino's create a pizza with 40 percent more cheese and paid for a $12 million ad campaign to promote it. The *New York Times* further writes that Americans now consume almost three times as much cheese as we did in 1970. At a time of a national obesity epidemic, the promotion of dairy products either directly or indirectly introduces high calorie, high saturated fat foods into our diet while making many persons think they are eating healthfully.

5   Finally, I would like to suggest a third criterion for health food. A true health food should be good not only for our bodies but also for the earth. Milk, as it is currently produced in the United States, clearly does not meet this criterion. According to environmental writer Jim Motavalli, both "the front and rear ends of a cow" compete with coal plant smokestacks and vehicle tail pipes as "iconic" causes of global warming and environmental degradation (27). Drawing on statistical sources from both the United Nations and the USDA, Motavalli states that livestock in the United States consume 90 percent of the soy crop and more than 70 percent of the corn and grain crops—foods that could otherwise be used for people and could be grown in a more environmentally friendly way. Not only do cattle consume much of the world's grain supply, the need to clear space for grazing contributes to the destruction of rain forests. The other end of the cow, says Motavalli, is equally destructive. While chewing their cuds, cows directly emit methane gas (according to Motavalli, methane has a greenhouse effect 23 times more potent than carbon dioxide) and the concentration of their manure in factory farm sludge ponds produces ammonia, nitrous oxide, and additional methane. According to Motavalli, cows produce a staggering amount of manure ("five tons of waste for every U.S. citizen" [27]), producing 18 percent of the world's greenhouse gases—more than all of the world's cars, trains, and planes (27). Motavalli also cites additional health risks posed by cows, including dangers of disease from unsafe processing of manure and from antibiotic-resistant bacteria (half of the world's antibiotics are given to cattle instead of humans [28]).

In sum, there is no doubt that skim milk, along with low fat yogurt and cheese, is a vital source of bone-building calcium and belongs on our list of health foods. But for most people, "milk" evokes dairy products in general, all of which we tend to associate with health. What we don't picture is the extra sugar and saturated fat in whole milk and cheese nor the environmental dangers of the dairy and livestock industries in general. From the perspective of the earth, perhaps dairy products should not be considered a health food at all.

Works Cited

"Dairy Program Subsidies." *Farm Subsidies Database*. Environmental Working Group, Jan. 2009. Web. 21 Jan. 2011.

Moss, Michael. "While Warning about Fat, U.S. Pushes Cheese Sales." *New York Times*. New York Times, 6 Nov. 2010. Web. 2 Jan. 2011.

Motavalli, Jim. "The Meat of the Matter: Our Livestock Industry Creates More Greenhouse Gas than Transportation Does." *Environmental Magazine* July–Aug. 2008: 29–31. *Academic Search Complete*. Web. 11 Jan. 2011.

United States. Dept. of Agriculture. *MyPyramid.gov: Steps to a Healthier You*. Jan. 2011. Web. 20 Jan. 2011.

Critiquing "Is Milk a Health Food?"

1. Identify the following features of Arthur's essay: (1) his implied definition of "health food"; (2) his criteria for determining whether a borderline case is a health food; (3) his "match" arguments showing whether milk fits each of the criteria.
2. Do you agree with Arthur's criterion that a true health food ought to be good for the planet as well as good for the body?
3. Based on Arthur's argument, do you think the inclusion of dairy products in the USDA's recommendations for a healthy diet is still justified? Visit the USDA's new nutrition Web site, www.choosemyplate.gov. Would you suggest changes to these USDA recommendations? If so, what and why?

The second reading, by student Kathy Sullivan, was also written for the definition assignment on page 245. The definition issue that she addresses—"Are the Menasee photographs obscene?"—was a local controversy in the state of Washington when the state liquor control board threatened to revoke the liquor license of a Seattle gay bar, the Oncore, unless it removed a series of photographs that the board deemed obscene.

Oncore, Obscenity, and the Liquor Control Board

KATHY SULLIVAN (STUDENT)

In early May, Geoff Menasee, a Seattle artist, exhibited a series of photographs with the theme of "safe sex" on the walls of an inner city, predominantly homosexual restaurant and lounge called the Oncore. Before hanging the photographs, Menasee had to consult with the Washington State Liquor Control Board because, under the current state law, art work containing material that may be considered indecent has to be approved by the board before it can be exhibited. Of the almost thirty photographs, six were rejected by the board because they partially exposed "private parts" of the male anatomy. Menasee went ahead and displayed the entire series of photographs, placing Band-Aids over the "indecent" areas, but the customers continually removed the Band-Aids.

The liquor control board's ruling on this issue has caused controversy in the Seattle community. The *Seattle Times* has provided news coverage, and a "Town Meeting" segment was filmed at the restaurant. The central question is this: Should an establishment that caters to a predominantly homosexual clientele be enjoined from displaying pictures promoting "safe sex" on the grounds that the photographs are obscene?

Before I can answer this question, I must first determine whether the art work should truly be classified as obscene. To make that determination, I will use the definition of obscenity in *Black's Law Dictionary:*

> Material is "obscene" if to the average person, applying contemporary community standards, the dominant theme of material taken as a whole appeals to prurient interest, if it is utterly without redeeming social importance, if it goes substantially beyond customary limits of candor in description or representation, if it is characterized by patent offensiveness, and if it is hard core pornography.

An additional criterion is provided by Pember's *Mass Media Laws:* "A work is obscene if it has a tendency to deprave and corrupt those whose minds are open to such immoral influences (children for example) and into whose hands it might happen to fall" (394). The art work in question should not be prohibited from display at predominantly homosexual establishments like the Oncore because it does not meet the above criteria for obscenity.

First of all, to the average person applying contemporary community standards, the predominant theme of Menasee's photographs is not an appeal to prurient interests. The first element in this criterion is "average person." According to Rocky Breckner, manager of the Oncore, 90 percent of the clientele at the Oncore is made up of young white homosexual males. This group therefore constitutes the "average person" viewing the exhibit. "Contemporary community standards" would ordinarily be the standards of the Seattle community. However, this art work is aimed at a particular group of people—the homosexual community. Therefore, the "community standards" involved here are those of the gay community rather than the city at large. Since the Oncore is not an art museum or gallery, which attracts a broad spectrum of people, it is appropriate to restrict the scope of "community standards" to that group who voluntarily patronize the Oncore.

5   Second, the predominant theme of the photographs is not "prurient interest" nor do the photographs go "substantially beyond customary limits of candor." There are no explicit sexual acts found in the photographs; instead, their theme is the prevention of AIDS through the practice of safe sex. Homosexual displays of affection could be viewed as "prurient interest" by the larger community, but same-sex relationships are the norm for the group at whom the exhibit is aimed. If the exhibit were displayed at McDonald's or even the Red Robin it might go "substantially beyond customary limits of candor," but it is unlikely that the clientele of the Oncore would find the art work offensive. The manager stated that he received very few complaints about the exhibit and its contents.

Nor is the material pornographic. The liquor control board prohibited the six photographs based on their visible display of body parts such as pubic hair and naked buttocks, not on the basis of sexual acts or homosexual orientation. The board admitted that the photographs depicted no explicit sexual acts. Hence, it can be concluded that they did not consider the suggestion of same-sex affection to be hard-core pornography. Their sole objection was that body parts were visible. But visible genitalia in art work are not necessarily pornographic. Since other art work, such as Michelangelo's sculptures, explicitly depict both male and female genitalia, it is arguable that pubic hair and buttocks are not patently offensive.

It must be conceded that the art work has the potential of being viewed by children, which would violate Pember's criterion. But once again the incidence of minors frequenting this establishment is very small.

But the most important reason for saying these photographs are not obscene is that they serve an important social purpose. One of *Black*'s criteria is that obscene material is "utterly without redeeming social importance." But these photographs have the explicit purpose of promoting safe sex as a defense against AIDS. Recent statistics reported in the *Seattle Times* show that AIDS is now the leading cause of death of men under forty in the Seattle area. Any methods that can promote the message of safe sex in today's society have strong redeeming social significance.

Those who believe that all art containing "indecent" material should be banned or covered from public view would most likely believe that Menasee's work is obscene. They would disagree that the environment and the clientele should be the major determining factor when using criteria to evaluate art. However, in the case of this exhibit I feel that the audience and the environment of the display are factors of overriding importance. Therefore, the exhibit should have been allowed to be displayed because it is not obscene.

Critiquing "Oncore, Obscenity, and the Liquor Control Board"

1. Kathy Sullivan here uses authoritative definitions for *obscenity*. Based on the definitions of *obscenity* in *Black's Law Dictionary* and Pember's *Mass Media Laws,* what criteria for obscenity does Kathy use?
2. How does she argue that the Menasee photographs do *not* meet the criteria?
3. Working as a whole class or in small groups, share your responses to the following questions: (a) If you find Kathy's argument persuasive, which parts were particularly influential or effective? (b) If you are not persuaded, which parts of her argument do you find weak or ineffective? (c) How does Kathy shape her argument to meet the concerns and objections of her audience? (d) How might a lawyer for the liquor control board rebut Kathy's argument?

Our last readings are a political cartoon and a letter to the editor written in response to that cartoon. The cartoon, by Pulitzer Prize winner Clay Bennett, makes a resemblance argument linking laws against gay marriage to earlier laws against interracial marriage. The occasion for the cartoon was a California Supreme Court decision legalizing gay marriage in California. The cartoon first appeared in the *Chattanooga Times Free Press* on June 18, 2008, and was reprinted in the *Seattle Times.* The responding letter to the editor, by Beth Reis, appeared in the *Seattle Times* on June 20, 2008.

Just Emancipated

CLAY BENNETT

Toon Offensive

BETH REIS

Don't get me wrong. I'm excited about California recognizing same-sex couples' right to marriage equality. I was a plaintiff in a Washington state marriage lawsuit. But the cartoon car with the words "just emancipated" on it, equating this development to the ending of slavery, especially on Juneteenth—the anniversary of the freeing of slaves after generations of brutality, forced labor, and families being separated and sold—is so offensive!

Yes, I feel a little more equal under the law this week. Yes, it matters that some people are now first class citizens, entitled to the same rights and held to the same responsibilities as other couples. Yes, the word *marriage* is honorable and understandable and right.

But, please: How is that like outlawing slavery, exactly 146 years ago today? How is it like 143 years ago, when Texans were told that for the last three years they'd been enslaved illegally and were actually free? How is it like being told, nearly a century later, that they could finally vote?

I am proud to be gay, but not at all proud to have this week's small victory equated with the emancipation of slaves and the enfranchisement of their descendants.

Critiquing "Just Emancipated" and "Toon Offensive"

1. How does the cartoon use an analogy to praise the California gay marriage decision? What is the cartoon's implied claim?
2. How does Beth Reis's letter to the editor point out disanalogies as a method of refuting the cartoon's argument?
3. One strategy often used to support the legalization of same-sex marriage is to point out its similarities to earlier court decisions legalizing interracial marriages. What are the analogies and disanalogies between interracial marriage and same-sex marriage?
4. Analyze Beth Reis's rhetorical appeals to *logos*, *ethos*, and *pathos*.

For additional writing, reading, and research resources, go to www.mycomplab.com

Causal Arguments

12

Case 1 What Causes Global Warming?

One of the early clues linking global warming to atmospheric carbon dioxide (CO_2) came from side-by-side comparisons of graphs plotting atmospheric carbon dioxide and global temperatures over time. These graphs show that increases in global temperature parallel increases in the percentage of carbon dioxide in the atmosphere. However, the graphs show only a correlation, or link, between increased carbon dioxide and higher average temperature. To argue that an increase in CO_2 could *cause* global warming, scientists needed to expalin the links in a causal chain. They could do so by comparing the earth to a greenhouse. Carbon dioxide, like glass in a greenhouse, lets some of the earth's heat radiate into space but also reflects some of it back to the earth. The higher the concentration of carbon dioxide, the more heat is reflected back to the earth.

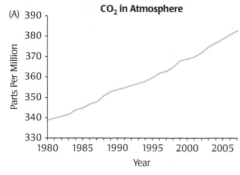

(A)

Source: Data from Dr. Pieter Tans, NOAA/ESRL

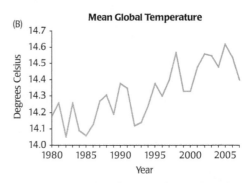

(B)

Source: Data from NASA Goddard Institute for Space Studies Surface Temperature Analysis

Case 2 What Has Caused the Crime Rate to Decline Since the Early 1990s?

Beginning in the 1990s, the crime rate in the United States dropped precipitously. For example, the number of murders in New York City decreased from 2,245 in 1990 to 494 in 2007. Similar reductions for all kinds of crime, ranging from murders to assaults to auto thefts, were reported across the nation. What caused this sudden and unexpected decline?

Many causal theories were debated in social science journals and the popular media. Among the proposed causes were innovative policing strategies, increased incarceration of criminals, an aging population, tougher gun control laws, a strong economy, and more police officers. However, economist Steven Levitt proposed that the primary cause was *Roe v. Wade,* the 1973 Supreme Court decision that legalized abortion.* According to Levitt's controversial theory, the crime rate began dropping because the greatest source of criminals—unwanted children entering their teens and twenties—were largely absent from the cohort of young people coming of age in the 1990s and 2000s; they had been aborted rather than brought up in the crime-producing conditions of unstable families, poverty, and neglect.

We encounter causal issues all the time. What are the causes of global warming? What caused the sudden decline in the U.S. crime rate beginning in the 1990s? Why did rap music become popular? Why are white teenage girls seven times as likely to smoke as African American teenage girls? Why do couples who live together before marriage have a higher divorce rate than those who don't? In addition to asking causal questions like these, we pose consequence questions as well: What might be the consequences of legalizing heroin and other hard drugs, of closing our borders to immigrants, or of overturning *Roe v. Wade*? What have been the consequences—expected or unexpected—of the invasion of Iraq or the emerging popularity of YouTube? What might be the consequences—expected or unexpected—of aggressively combating global warming as opposed to adapting to it? Often, arguments about causes and consequences have important stakes because they shape our view of reality and influence government policies and individual decisions.

In this chapter, you will learn to:

- Analyze causal methods and mechanisms
- Use causal reasoning to construct your own causal arguments

An Overview of Causal Arguments

Typically, causal arguments try to show how one event brings about another. When causal investigation focuses on material objects—for example, one billiard ball striking another—the notion of causality appears fairly straightforward. But when humans become the focus of a causal argument, the nature of causality becomes more vexing. If we say that something happened that "caused" a person to act in a certain way, what do we mean? Do we mean that she was "forced" to act in a certain way, thereby negating her free will (as in, an undiagnosed brain tumor caused her to act erratically), or do we mean more simply that she was "motivated" to act in a certain way (as in, her anger at her parents caused her to act erratically)? When we argue about causality in human

*Steven D. Levitt and Stephen J. Dubner, "Where Have All the Criminals Gone?" In *Freakonomics: A Rogue Economist Explores the Hidden Side of Everything* (New York: HarperCollins, 2005), 117–44.

beings, we must guard against confusing these two senses of "cause" or assuming that human behavior can be predicted or controlled in the same way that nonhuman behavior can. A rock dropped from a roof will always fall at thirty-two feet per second squared, and a rat zapped for turning left in a maze will always quit turning left. But if we raise interest rates, will consumers save more money? If so, how much? This is the sort of question we debate endlessly.

Kinds of Causal Arguments

Arguments about causality can take a variety of forms. Here are three typical kinds:

- **Speculations about possible causes.** Sometimes arguers speculate about possible causes of a phenomenon. For example, whenever a shooter opens fire on innocent bystanders (as in the 2011 attempted assassination of Arizona Representative Gabrielle Giffords in a Tucson parking lot), social scientists, police investigators, and media commentators begin analyzing the causes. One of the most heavily debated shooting incidents occurred in 1999 at Columbine High School in Littleton, Colorado, when two male students opened fire on their classmates, killing thirteen people, wounding twenty-three others, and then shooting themselves. Figure 12.1 illustrates some of the proposed theories for the Columbine shootings. What was at stake was not only our desire to understand the sociocultural sources of school violence but also our desire to institute policies to prevent future school shootings. If a primary cause is the availability of guns, then we might push for more stringent gun control laws. But if the primary cause is the disintegration of the traditional family, the shooters'

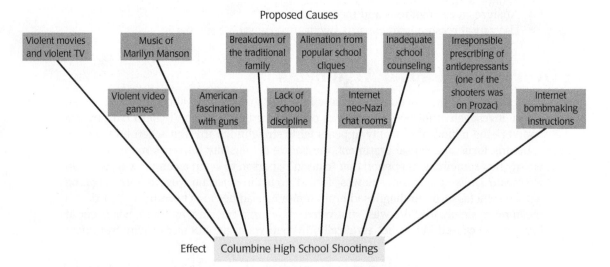

FIGURE 12.1 Speculation about possible causes: Columbine High School massacre

alienation from high school cliques, or the dangerous side effects of Prozac, then we might seek different solutions.

■ **Arguments for an unexpected or surprising cause.** Besides sorting out possible causes of a phenomenon, sometimes arguers try to persuade readers to see the plausibility of an unexpected or surprising cause. This was the strategy used by syndicated columnist John Leo, who wanted readers to consider the role of violent video games as a contributing cause to the Columbine massacre.* After suggesting that the Littleton killings were partly choreographed on video game models, Leo suggested the causal chain shown in Figure 12.2.

■ **Predictions of consequences.** Still another frequently encountered kind of causal argument predicts the consequences of current, planned, or proposed actions or events. Consequence arguments have high stakes because we often judge actions on whether their benefits outweigh their costs. As we will see in Chapter 14, proposal arguments usually require writers to predict the consequences of a proposed action, do a cost/benefit analysis, and persuade readers that no unforeseen negative consequences will result. Just as a phenomenon can have multiple causes, it can also have multiple consequences. Figure 12.3 shows the consequence arguments considered by environmentalists who propose eliminating several dams on the Snake River in order to save salmon runs.

Many youngsters are left alone for long periods of time (because both parents are working).

↓

They play violent video games obsessively.

↓

Their feelings of resentment and powerlessness "pour into the killing games."

↓

The video games break down a natural aversion to killing, analogous to psychological techniques employed by the military.

↓

Realistic touches in modern video games blur the "boundary between fantasy and reality."

↓

Youngsters begin identifying not with conventional heroes but with sociopaths who get their kicks from blowing away ordinary people ("pedestrians, marching bands, an elderly woman with a walker").

↓

Having enjoyed random violence in the video games, vulnerable youngsters act out the same adrenaline rush in real life.

FIGURE 12.2 Argument for a surprising cause: Role of violent video games in the Columbine massacre

Toulmin Framework for a Causal Argument

Because causal arguments can involve lengthy or complex causal chains, they are often harder to summarize in *because* clauses than are other kinds of arguments. Likewise, they are not as likely to yield quick analysis through the Toulmin schema.

---

*John Leo, "Kill-for-Kicks Video Games Desensitizing Our Children," *Seattle Times* 27 April 1999, B4.

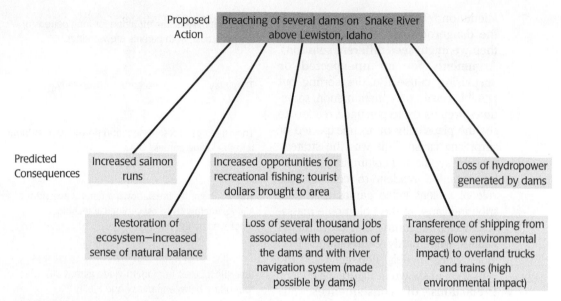

FIGURE 12.3 Predictions of consequences: Breaching dams on the Snake River

Nevertheless, a causal argument can usually be stated as a claim with *because* clauses. Typically, a *because* clause pinpoints one or two key elements in the causal chain rather than summarizes every link. John Leo's argument linking the Columbine massacre to violent video games could be summarized in the following claim with a *because* clause:

> Violent video games may have been a contributing cause to the Littleton massacre because playing these games can make random, sociopathic violence seem pleasurable.

Once stated as an enthymeme, the argument can be analyzed using Toulmin's schema. It is easiest to apply Toulmin's schema to causal arguments if you think of the grounds as the observable phenomena at any point in the causal chain and the warrants as the shareable assumptions about causality that join links together.

Toulmin Analysis of the Violent Video Games Argument

ENTHYMEME

CLAIM Violent video games may have been a contributing cause to the Columbine school shooting

REASON because playing these games can make random, sociopathic violence seem pleasurable.

Qualifiers

GROUNDS

- Evidence that the killers, like many young people, played violent video games

- Evidence that the games are violent

- Evidence that the games involve random, sociopathic violence (not good guys versus bad guys) such as killing ordinary people—marching bands, little old ladies, etc.

- Evidence that young people derive pleasure from these games

CONDITIONS OF REBUTTAL
Attacking the reason and grounds

- Perhaps the killers didn't play violent video games.

- Perhaps the video games are no more violent than traditional kids' games such as cops and robbers.

- Perhaps the video games do not feature sociopathic killing.

WARRANT

If young people derive pleasure from random, sociopathic killing in video games, they can transfer this pleasure to real life, thus leading to the Columbine shooting.

BACKING

- Testimony from psychologists

- Evidence that violent video games desensitize people to violence

- Analogy to military training in which video games are used to "make killing a reflex action"

- Evidence that the distinction between fantasy and reality becomes especially blurred for unstable young people

CONDITIONS OF REBUTTAL
Attacking the warrant and backing

- Perhaps kids are fully capable of distinguishing fantasy from reality.

- Perhaps the games are just fun with no transference to real life.

- Perhaps the games are substantially different from military training games.

■ ■ ■   **FOR CLASS DISCUSSION** Developing Causal Chains

1. Working individually or in small groups, create a causal chain to show how the item on the left could help lead to the item on the right.

   a. High price of oil   Redesign of cities

   b. Invention of the automobile   Changes in sexual mores

   c. Invention of the telephone   Loss of sense of community
                                                           in neighborhoods

   d. Origin of rap in the black urban   The popularity of rap spreads from
      music scene   urban black audiences to white
                                                           middle-class youth culture

   e. Development of way to prevent   Liberalization of euthanasia laws
      rejections in transplant operations

2. For each of your causal chains, compose a claim with an attached *because* clause summarizing one or two key links in the causal chain—for example, "The high price of oil is causing homeowners to move from the suburbs into new high-density urban communities because the expense of gasoline is making people value easy access to their work."

■ ■ ■

Two Methods for Arguing that One Event Causes Another

One of the first things you need to do when preparing a causal argument is to note exactly what sort of causal relationship you are dealing with—a onetime phenomenon, a recurring phenomenon, or a puzzling trend. Here are some examples.

Kind of Phenomenon	Examples
Onetime phenomenon	<ul><li>2007 collapse of a freeway bridge in Minneapolis, Minnesota</li><li>Firing of a popular teacher at your university</li><li>Your friend's sudden decision to join the army</li></ul>
Recurring phenomenon	<ul><li>Eating disorders</li><li>Road rage</li><li>Someone's tendency to procrastinate</li></ul>
Puzzling trend	<ul><li>Rising popularity of extreme sports</li><li>Declining audience for TV news</li><li>Increases in diagnosis of autism</li></ul>

With recurring phenomena or with trends, one has the luxury of being able to study multiple cases, often over time. You can interview people, make repeated observations, or study the conditions in which the puzzling phenomenon occurs. But with a onetime occurrence, one's approach is more like that of a detective than a scientist.

EXAMINING VISUAL ARGUMENTS

A Causal Claim

This ad campaign, "Kill a Child, Destroy a Family," from the Pedestrian Council of Australia, makes a causal argument against careless driving. How does the ad work visually to suggest the links in a causal chain? Place into your own words the argument implied by this ad. You can see the other ads in the campaign online. Why do you think this ad campaign won awards for its effective advocacy?

Because one can't repeat the event with different variables, one must rely only on the immediate evidence at hand, which can quickly disappear.

Having briefly stated these words of caution, let's turn now to two main ways that you can argue that one event causes another.

First Method: Explain the Causal Mechanism Directly

The most convincing kind of causal argument identifies every link in the causal chain, showing how an initiating cause leads step by step to an observed effect. A causes B, which causes C, which causes D. In some cases, all you have to do is fill in the missing links. In other cases—when your assumptions about how one step leads to the next may seem questionable to your audience—you have to argue for the causal connection with more vigor.

A careful spelling out of each step in the causal chain is the technique used by science writer Robert S. Devine in the following passage from his article "The Trouble with Dams." Although the benefits of dams are widely understood (they produce pollution-free electricity while providing flood control, irrigation, barge transportation, and recreational boating), the negative effects are less commonly known and understood. In this article, Devine tries to persuade readers that dams have serious negative consequences. In the following passage, he explains how dams reduce salmon flows by slowing the migration of smolts (newly hatched, young salmon) to the sea.

Causal Argument Describing a Causal Chain

Such transformations lie at the heart of the ongoing environmental harm done by dams. Rivers are rivers because they flow, and the nature of their flows defines much of their character. When dams alter flows, they alter the essence of rivers.

Consider the erstwhile river behind Lower Granite (a dam on Idaho's Snake River). Although I was there in the springtime, when I looked at the water it was moving too slowly to merit the word "flow"—and Lower Granite Lake isn't even one of the region's enormous storage reservoirs, which bring currents to a virtual halt. In the past, spring snowmelt sent powerful currents down the Snake during April and May. Nowadays hydropower operators of the Columbia and Snake systems store the runoff behind the dams and release it during the winter, when demand—and the price—for electricity rises. Over the ages, however, many populations of salmon have adapted to the spring surge. The smolts used the strong flows to migrate, drifting downstream with the current. During the journey smolts' bodies undergo physiological changes that require them to reach salt water quickly. Before dams backed up the Snake, smolts coming down from Idaho got to the sea in six to twenty days; now it takes from sixty to ninety days, and few of the young salmon reach salt water in time. The emasculated current is the single largest reason that the number of wild adult salmon migrating up the Snake each year has crashed from predevelopment runs of 100,000–200,000 to what was projected to be 150–75 this year.*

Smolts use the river flow to reach the sea.
↓
Dams restrict the flow of the river.
↓
Before development, a trip that took 6 to 20 days now takes 60 to 90 days.
↓
Migrating smolts undergo physiological changes that demand quick access to salt water.
↓
Lengthened migration time kills the smolts.

This tightly constructed passage connects various causal chains to explain the decline of salmon runs.

Describing each link in the causal chain—and making each link seem as plausible as possible—is the most persuasive means of convincing readers that a specific cause leads to a specific effect.

Second Method: Infer Causal Links Using Inductive Reasoning

If we can't explain a causal link directly, we often employ a reasoning strategy called *induction*. Through induction we infer a general conclusion based on a limited number of specific cases. For example, if on several occasions you got a headache after drinking red wine but not after drinking white wine, you would be likely to conclude inductively that red wine causes you to get headaches, although you

*Robert S. Devine, "The Trouble with Dams," *Atlantic* (August 1995), 64–75. The example quotation is from page 70.

can't explain directly how it does so. However, because there are almost always numerous variables involved, inductive reasoning gives only probable truths, not certain ones.

Three Ways of Thinking Inductively When your brain thinks inductively, it sorts through data looking for patterns of similarity and difference. In this section we explain three ways of thinking inductively: looking for a common element, looking for a single difference, and looking for correlations.

1. **Look for a common element.** One kind of inductive thinking places you on a search for a common element that can explain recurrences of the same phenomenon. For example, psychologists attempting to understand the causes of anorexia have discovered that many anorexics (but not all) come from perfectionist, highly work-oriented homes that emphasize duty and responsibility. This common element is thus a suspected causal factor leading to anorexia.

2. **Look for a single difference.** Another approach is to look for a single difference that may explain the appearance of a new phenomenon. When infant death rates in the state of Washington shot up in July and August 1986, one event making these two months different stood out: increased radioactive fallout over Washington from the April Chernobyl nuclear meltdown in Ukraine. This single difference led some researchers to suspect radiation as a possible cause of the increase in infant deaths.

3. **Look for correlations.** Still another method of induction is *correlation,* which means that two events or phenomena tend to occur together but doesn't imply that one causes the other. For example, there is a correlation between nearsightedness and intelligence. (That is, in a given sample of nearsighted people and people with normal eyesight, the nearsighted group will have a somewhat higher mean IQ score.) But the direction of causality isn't clear. It could be that high intelligence causes people to read more, thus ruining their eyes (high intelligence causes nearsightedness). Or it could be that nearsightedness causes people to read more, thus raising their intelligence (nearsightedness causes high intelligence). Or it could be that some unknown phenomenon, perhaps a gene, is related to both nearsightedness and intelligence. So keep in mind that correlation is not causation—it simply suggests possible causation.

Beware of Common Inductive Fallacies that Can Lead to Wrong Conclusions Largely because of its power, informal induction can often lead to wrong conclusions. You should be aware of two common fallacies of inductive reasoning that can tempt you into erroneous assumptions about causality. (Both fallacies are treated more fully in the Appendix.)

- **Post hoc fallacy:** The *post hoc, ergo propter hoc* fallacy ("after this, therefore because of this") mistakes sequence for cause. Just because event A regularly precedes event B doesn't mean that event A causes event B. The same reasoning that tells us that flipping a switch causes the light to go on can make us believe that low levels of radioactive fallout from the Chernobyl nuclear disaster caused a sudden rise in infant death rates in the state of Washington. The nuclear disaster clearly preceded the rise in death rates. But did it clearly *cause* it? Our point is that precedence alone is no proof of causality and that we are guilty of this fallacy whenever we are swayed to believe that one thing causes another just because it comes first.

■ **Hasty generalization:** The *hasty generalization* fallacy occurs when you make a generalization based on too few cases or too little consideration of alternative explanations: You flip the switch, but the lightbulb doesn't go on. You conclude—too hastily—that the lightbulb has burned out. (Perhaps the power has gone off or the switch is broken.) How many trials does it take before you can make a justified generalization rather than a hasty generalization? It is difficult to say for sure.

Both the *post hoc* fallacy and the hasty generalization fallacy remind us that induction requires a leap from individual cases to a general principle and that it is always possible to leap too soon.

■ ■ ■ **FOR CLASS DISCUSSION** Developing Plausible Causal Chains Based on Correlations

Working individually or in small groups, develop plausible causal chains that may explain the relationship between the following pairs of phenomena:

a. A person who registers a low stress level on an electrochemical stress meter — does daily meditation

b. A white female teenager — is seven times as likely to smoke as a black female teenager

c. A person who grew up in a house with two bathrooms — is likely to have higher SAT scores than a person who grew up in a one-bathroom home

d. A person who buys lots of ashtrays — is more likely to develop lung cancer

e. A member of the National Rifle Association — supports the death penalty

■ ■ ■

Glossary of Terms Encountered in Causal Arguments

Because causal arguments are often easier to conduct if writer and reader share a few specialized terms, we offer the following glossary for your convenience.

■ **Fallacy of oversimplified cause.** One of the great temptations is to look for *the* cause of something, as if a phenomenon had only one cause rather than multiple causes. For example, in recent years the number of persons in the United States sending out Christmas cards has declined substantially. Many commentators attribute the decline to the increasing use of Facebook, which keeps old friends in touch year-round, eliminating the need for holiday "family letters." But there may be other causes also, such as a decline in the number of nuclear families, fewer networks of long-term friends, or generational shifts away from older traditions. When you make a causal argument, be especially careful how you use words such as *all, most, some, the,* or *in part*. For example, to say that *all* the decline in Christmas cards is caused by Facebook is to make a universal statement about Facebook as *the* cause. An argument will be stronger and more accurate if the arguer makes a less sweeping statement: *Some* of the cause for the decline in Christmas cards can be attributed to Facebook. Arguers sometimes deliberately mix up these quantifiers to misrepresent and dismiss opposing views.

■ **Immediate and remote causes.** Every causal chain extends backward indefinitely into the past. An immediate cause is the closest in time to the event being examined. Consider the causes for the release of nuclear contaminants around the Fukushima nuclear power plant following the 2011 earthquake off the coast of Japan. The immediate cause was loss of power to the water pumps that cooled the reactor's fuel rods, causing the rods to overheat and partially melt. A slightly less immediate cause (several days earlier) was the earthquake-produced tsunami that had swept away the diesel fuel tanks needed to run the backup generators. These immediate causes can be contrasted with a remote cause—in this case, a late-1960s design decision that used backup diesel generators to power the water pumps in case of an electrical power loss to the reactor facility. Still more remote causes were the economic and regulatory systems in the late 1960s that led to this particular design.

■ **Precipitating and contributing causes.** These terms are similar to *immediate* and *remote* causes but don't designate a temporal link going into the past. Rather, they refer to a main cause emerging out of a background of subsidiary causes. If, for example, a husband and wife decide to separate, the *precipitating cause* may be a stormy fight over money, after which one of the partners (or both) says, "I've had enough." In contrast, *contributing causes* would be all the background factors that are dooming the marriage—preoccupation with their careers, disagreement about priorities, in-law problems, and so forth. Note that contributing causes and the precipitating cause all coexist at the same time.

■ **Constraints.** Sometimes an effect occurs because some stabilizing factor—a *constraint*—is removed. In other words, the presence of a constraint may keep a certain effect from occurring. For example, in the marriage we have been discussing, the presence of children in the home may be a constraint against divorce; as soon as the children graduate from high school and leave home, the marriage may well dissolve.

■ **Necessary and sufficient causes.** A *necessary cause* is one that has to be present for a given effect to occur. For example, fertility drugs are necessary to cause the conception of septuplets. Every couple who has septuplets must have used fertility drugs. In contrast, a *sufficient cause* is one that always produces or guarantees a given effect. Smoking more than a pack of cigarettes per day is sufficient to raise the cost of one's life insurance policy. This statement means that if you are a smoker, no matter how healthy you appear to be, life insurance companies will always place you in a higher risk bracket and charge you a higher premium. In some cases, a single cause can be both necessary and sufficient. For example, lack of ascorbic acid is both a necessary and a sufficient cause of scurvy. (Think of those old-time sailors who didn't eat fruit for months.) It is a necessary cause because you can't get scurvy any other way except through absence of ascorbic acid; it is a sufficient cause because the absence of ascorbic acid always causes scurvy.

■ ■ ■   **FOR CLASS DISCUSSION** Brainstorming Causes and Constraints

The terms in the preceding glossary can be effective brainstorming tools for thinking of possible causes of an event. For the following events, try to think of as many causes as possible by brainstorming possible *immediate causes, remote causes, precipitating causes, contributing causes,* and *constraints:*

1. Working individually, make a list of different kinds of causes/constraints for one of the following:
   a. Your decision to attend your present college
   b. An important event in your life or your family (a job change, a major move, etc.)
   c. A personal opinion you hold that is not widely shared
2. Working as a group, make a list of different kinds of causes/constraints for one of the following:
   a. Why women's fashion and beauty magazines are the most frequently purchased magazines in college bookstores
   b. Why American students consistently score below Asian and European students in academic achievement
   c. Why the number of babies born out of wedlock has increased dramatically in the last thirty years

■ ■ ■

WRITING ASSIGNMENT   A Causal Argument

Choose an issue about the causes or consequences of a trend, event, or other phenomenon. Write an argument that persuades an audience to accept your explanation of the causes or consequences of your chosen phenomenon. Within your essay you should examine alternative hypotheses or opposing views and explain your reasons for rejecting them. You can imagine your issue either as a puzzle or as a disagreement. If a puzzle, your task will be to create a convincing case for an audience that doesn't have an answer to your causal question already in mind. If a disagreement, your task will be more overtly persuasive because your goal will be to change your audience's views.

Exploring Ideas

Arguments about causes and consequences abound in public, professional, or personal life, so you shouldn't have difficulty finding a causal issue worth investigating and arguing.

In response to a public controversy over why there are fewer women than men on science and math faculties, student writer Julee Christianson argued that culture, not biology, is the primary cause (see pages 274–279). Student writer Carlos Macias, puzzled by the ease with which college students are issued credit cards, wrote a researched argument disentangling the factors leading young people to bury themselves in debt (see pages 283–286). Other students have focused on causal issues such as these: Why do kids join gangs? What are the consequences of mandatory drug testing (written by a student who has to take amphetamines for narcolepsy)? What has happened since 1970 to cause young people to delay getting married? (This question was initiated by the student's interest in the statistical table in Chapter 9, page 205.)

If you have trouble finding a causal issue to write about, you can often create provocative controversies among your classmates through the following strategies:

- **Make a list of unusual likes and dislikes.** Think about unusual things that people like or dislike. You could summarize the conventional explanations that people give for an unusual pleasure or aversion and then argue for a surprising or unexpected cause. What attracts people to extreme sports? How do you explain the popularity of the tricked-out Cadillac Escalade as a dream car for urban youth?

- **Make a list of puzzling events or trends.** Another strategy is to make a list of puzzling phenomena and then try to explain their causes. Start with onetime events (a curriculum change at your school, the sudden popularity of a new app). Then list puzzling recurring events (failure of knowledgeable teenagers to practice safe sex). Finally, list some recent trends (growth of naturopathic medicine, increased interest in tattoos). Engage classmates in discussions of one or more of the items on your list. Look for places of disagreement as entry points into the conversation.

- **Brainstorm consequences of a recent or proposed action.** Arguments about consequences are among the most interesting and important of causal disputes. If you can argue for an unanticipated consequence of a real or proposed action, whether good or bad, you can contribute importantly to the conversation. What might be the consequences, for example, of placing "green taxes" on coal-produced electricity; of legalizing marijuana; of overturning *Roe v. Wade;* or of requiring national public service for all young adults?

Identifying Your Audience and Determining What's at Stake

Before drafting your argument, identify your targeted audience and determine what's at stake. Consider your responses to the following questions:

- What audience are you targeting? What background do they need to understand your issue? How much do they already care about it?
- Before they read your argument, what stance on your issue do you imagine them holding? What change do you want to bring about in their views?

- What will they find new or surprising about your argument?
- What objections might they raise? What counterarguments or alternative points of view will you need to address?
- Why does your argument matter? Who might be threatened or made uncomfortable by your views? What is at stake?

Organizing a Causal Argument

At the outset, it is useful to know some of the standard ways that a causal argument can be organized. Later, you may decide on a different organizational pattern, but the standard ways shown in Organization Plans 1, 2, and 3 on pages 271–272 will help you get started.

Plans 2 and 3 are similar in that they examine numerous possible causes or consequences. Plan 2, however, tries to establish the relative importance of each cause or consequence, whereas Plan 3 aims at rejecting the causes or consequences normally assumed by the audience and argues for an unexpected, surprising cause or consequence. Plan 3 can also be used when your purpose is to change your audience's mind about a cause or consequence.

Questioning and Critiquing a Causal Argument

Knowing how to question and critique a causal argument will help you anticipate opposing views in order to strengthen your own. It will also help you rebut another person's causal argument. Here are some useful questions to ask:

- When you explain the links in a causal chain, can a skeptic point out weaknesses in any of the links?
- If you speculate about the causes of a phenomenon, could a skeptic argue for different causes or arrange your causes in a different order of importance?
- If you argue for a surprising cause or a surprising consequence of a phenomenon, could a skeptic point out alternative explanations that would undercut your argument?
- If your argument depends on inferences from data, could a skeptic question the way the data were gathered or interpreted? Could a skeptic claim that the data weren't relevant (for example, research done with lab animals might not apply to humans)?
- If your causal argument depends on a correlation between one phenomenon and another, could a skeptic argue that the direction of causality should be reversed or that an unidentified, third phenomenon is the real cause?

Organization Plan 1: Argument Explaining Links in a Causal Chain

Introduce the issue and state your claim.	• Engage reader's interest in your causal issue and show why it is controversial or problematic. • Show what's at stake. • State your claim.
Explain the links in the chain going from cause to effect.	• Explain the links and their connections in order. • Anticipate and respond to possible objections if needed.
Conclude.	• Perhaps sum up your argument. • Return to the "big picture" of what's at stake. • End with something memorable.

Organization Plan 2: Argument Proposing Multiple Causes or Consequences of a Phenomenon

Introduce the issue and state your claim.	• Engage reader's interest in your causal issue and show why it is problematic or controversial. • Show what's at stake. • State your claim.
Propose relative contributions of different causes of a phenomenon or relative importance of different consequences.	• Describe the first possible cause or consequence and explain your reasoning. • Continue with the rest of your causes or consequences. • Arrange causes or consequences in increasing order of importance, significance, or surprise.
Respond to possible objections to your argument (if needed).	• Anticipate and summarize possible objections. • Respond through rebuttal or concession.
Conclude.	• Perhaps sum up your argument. • Return to the "big picture" of what's at stake. • End with something memorable.

Organization Plan 3: Argument Proposing a Surprising Causes or Consequence

Introduce the issue and state your claim.	• Engage reader's interest in your causal issue and show why it is problematic or controversial. • Show what's at stake. • State your claim.

Reject commonly assumed causes or consequences.	• Describe the first commonly assumed cause or consequence and show why you don't think the explanation is adequate. • Continue with the rest of your commonly assumed causes or consequences.

Argue for your surprising cause or consequence.	• Describe your surprising cause or consequence. • Explain your causal reasoning. • Anticipate and respond to possible objections if needed.

Conclude.	• Perhaps sum up your argument. • Return to the "big picture" of what's at stake. • End with something memorable.

Our first reading, by student Julee Christianson, was written in response **READINGS**
to the assignment in this chapter. Julee was entering an intense public
debate about the underrepresentation of women on prestigious math
and science faculties, a controversy initiated by Lawrence Summers, then president of
Harvard, who suggested the possibility of a genetic cause for this phenomenon. A furious reaction ensued. The Web site of the Women in Science and Engineering Leadership Institute has extensive coverage of the controversy, including Summers' original
speech.

Julee's argument illustrates the format and documentation system for a paper following the guidelines of the American Psychological Association (APA).

Why Lawrence Summers Was Wrong: Culture Rather than Biology

Explains the Underrepresentation of Women in Science and Mathematics

Julee Christianson

December 8, 2008

Why Lawrence Summers Was Wrong: Culture Rather
than Biology Explains the Underrepresentation of
Women in Science and Mathematics

In 2005, Harvard University's president, Lawrence H. Summers, gave a controversial speech that suggested that the underrepresentation of women in tenured positions in math and science departments is partly caused by biological differences. In his address, Summers proposed three hypotheses explaining why women shy away from math and science careers. First, he gave a "high-powered job hypothesis" that stated that women naturally want to start a family and therefore will not have the time or desire to commit to the high-stress workload required for research in math and science. His second hypothesis was that genetic differences between the sexes cause more males than females to have high aptitude for math and science. Lastly, he mentioned the hypothesis that women are underrepresented because of discrimination, but he dismissed discrimination as an insignificant factor. It was Summers's second hypothesis about biological differences that started a heated national debate. The academic world seems split over this nature/nurture issue. Although there is some evidence that biology plays a role in determining math ability, I argue that culture plays a much larger role, both in the way that women are socialized and in the continued existence of male discrimination against women in male-dominated fields.

Evidence supporting the role of biology in determining math ability is effectively presented by Steven Pinker (2005), a Harvard psychologist who agrees with Summers. In his article "The Science of Difference: Sex Ed," Pinker focuses extensively on Summers's argument. According to Pinker, "in many traits, men show greater variance than women, and are disproportionately found at both the low and high ends of the distribution" (p. 16). He explains that males and females have similar average scores on math tests but that there are more males than females in the top and the bottom percentiles. This greater variance means that there are disproportionately more male than female math geniuses (and math dunces) and thus more male than female candidates for top math and science positions at major research universities. Pinker explains this greater variance through evolutionary biology: men can pass on their genes to dozens of offspring, whereas women can pass on their genes to only a few. Pinker also argues that men and women have different brain structures that result in different kinds of thinking. For example, Pinker cites research that shows that on average men are better at mental rotation of figures and mathematical word problems, while women are better at remembering locations, doing mathematical calculations, reading faces, spelling, and using language. Not only do males and females think differently, but they release different hormones. These hormones help shape gender because males release more testosterone and females more estrogen, meaning that men are more aggressive and apt to take risks, while women "are more solicitous to their children" (p. 16). One example Pinker uses to support his biological hypothesis is the case of males born with abnormal genitals and raised as females. These children have more testosterone than normal female children, and many times they show characteristically male interests and behavior. Pinker uses these cases as evidence that no matter how a child is raised, the child's biology determines the child's interests.

Although Pinker demonstrates that biology plays some role in determining math aptitude, he almost completely ignores the much larger role of discrimination and socialization in shaping the career paths of women. According to an editorial from Nature Neuroscience ("Separating," 2005), "[t]he evidence to support [Summers's] hypothesis of 'innate difference' turns out to be quite slim" (p. 253). The editorial reports that intercultural studies of the variance between boys' and girls' scores on math tests show significant differences between countries. For example, in Iceland girls outscore boys on math tests. The editorial also says that aptitude tests are not very good at predicting the future success of students and that the "SATs tend to underpredict female and over-predict male academic performance" (p. 253). The editorial doesn't deny that men and women's brains work differently, but states that the differences are too small to be blamed for the under-representation of women in math and science careers.

If biology doesn't explain the low number of women choosing math and science careers, then what is the cause? Many believe the cause is culture, especially the gender roles children are taught at a very young age. One such believer is Deborah L. Rhode (1997), an attorney and social scientist who specializes in ethics and gender, law, and public policy. Rhode describes the different gender roles females and males are expected to follow from a very young age. Gender roles are portrayed in children's books and television shows. These gender roles are represented by male characters as heroes and problem solvers, while the female characters are distressed damsels. Another example of gender roles is that only a very small number of these shows and books portray working mothers or stay-at-home fathers. Rhodes also discusses how movies and popular music, especially rap and heavy metal, encourage violence and objectify women. As girls grow up, they face more and more gender stereotypes from toys to magazines. Parents give their boys interactive, problem-solving toys such as chemistry sets and telescopes, while girls are left with dolls. Although more organizations such as the Girl Scouts of America,

WHY LAWRENCE SUMMERS WAS WRONG   4

who sponsor the Website (Girls Go Tech.org) are trying to interest girls in science and math and advertise careers in those fields to girls, the societal forces working against this encouragement are also still pervasive. For example, magazines for teenage girls encourage attracting male attention and the importance of looks, while being smart and successful is considered unattractive. Because adolescents face so many gender stereotypes, it is no wonder that these stereotypes shape the career paths they choose later in life. The gender roles engraved in our adolescents' minds cause discrimination against women later in life. Once women are socialized to see themselves as dependent and not as smart as males, it becomes very difficult to break away from these gender stereotypes. With gender bias so apparent in our society, it is hard for females to have high enough self-confidence to continue to compete with males in many fields.

The effect of socialization begins at a very early age. One study (Clearfield & Nelson, 2006) shows how parents unconsciously send gendered messages to their infants and toddlers. This study examined differences in mothers' speech patterns and play behaviors based on the gender of infants ranging from six months to fourteen months. Although there was no difference in the actual play behavior of male and female infants, the researchers discovered interesting differences in the way mothers interacted with daughters versus sons. Mothers of daughters tended to ask their daughters more questions, encouraging social interaction, whereas mothers of sons were less verbal, encouraging their sons to be more independent. The researchers concluded that "the mothers in our study may have been teaching their infants about gender roles through modeling and reinforcement....Thus girls may acquire the knowledge that they are 'supposed' to engage in higher levels of interaction with other people and display more verbal behavior than boys....In contrast, the boys were reinforced for exploring on their own" (p. 136).

One of the strongest arguments against the biological hypothesis comes from a transgendered Stanford neurobiologist, Ben A. Barres (2006), who has been a scientist first as a woman and then as a man. In his article "Does Gender Matter?" Barres states that "there is little evidence that gender differences in [mathematical] abilities exist, are innate or are even relevant to the lack of advancement of women in science" (p. 134). Barres provides much anecdotal evidence of the way women are discriminated against in this male-dominated field. Barres notes that simply putting a male name rather than a female name on an article or résumé increases its perceived value. He also describes research showing that men and women do equally well in gender-blind academic competitions but that men win disproportionately in contests where gender is revealed.

APA

WHY LAWRENCE SUMMERS WAS WRONG   5

As Barres says, "The bar is unconsciously raised so high for women and minority candidates that few emerge as winners" (p. 134). In one study reported by Barres, women applying for a research grant needed more than twice the productivity of men in order to be considered equally competent. As a female-to-male transgendered person, Barres has personally experienced discrimination when trying to succeed in the science and math fields. When in college, Barres was told that her boyfriend must have done her homework, and she later lost a prestigious fellowship competition to a male even though she was told her application was stronger and she had published "six high-impact papers," while the man that won published only one. Barres even notices subtle differences, such as the fact that he can now finish a sentence without being interrupted by a male.

   Barres urges women to stand up publicly against discrimination. One woman he particularly admires as a strong female role model is MIT biologist Nancy Hopkins, who sued the MIT administration for discrimination based on the lesser amount of lab space allocated to female scientists. The evidence from this study was so strong that even the president of MIT publicly admitted that discrimination was a problem (p. 134). Barres wants more women to follow Hopkins's lead. He believes that women often don't realize they are being discriminated against because they have faith that the world is equal. Barres explains this tendency as a "denial of personal disadvantage" (p. 134). Very few women will admit to seeing or experiencing discrimination. Until discrimination and sexism are addressed, women will continue to be oppressed.

   As a society, we should not accept Lawrence Summers's hypothesis that biological differences are the reason women are not found in high-prestige tenured jobs in math and science. In fact, in another generation the gap between men and women in math and science might completely disappear. In 2003–2004, women received close to one-third of all doctorates in mathematics, up from 15 percent of doctorates in the early 1980s ("American Mathematical Society," 2005). Although more recent data are not yet available, the signs point to a steadily increasing number of women entering the fields of math, science, and engineering. Blaming biology for the lack of women in these fields and refusing to fault our culture is taking the easy way out. Our culture can change.

WHY LAWRENCE SUMMERS WAS WRONG   6
References

American Mathematical Society. (2005, July 6). *Women in Mathematics: Study shows gains*. Retrieved from http://www/ams.org/news?news_id=489

Barres, B. A. "Does gender matter?" *Nature* 44.7 (2006): 133–36. doi:10.1038/442133a

Clearfield, M. W., and Nelson, N. M. (2006). Sex differences in mothers' speech and play behavior with 6-, 9-, and 14-month-old infants. *Sex Roles* 54.1–2 : 127–37. doi:.10.1007/s11199-005-8874-1

Pinker, S. (2005 February 14). The science of difference: Sex ed. *New Republic.* 232, 15–17.

Rhode, D. L. (1997) *Speaking of sex: The denial of gender inequality.* Cambridge, MA: Harvard University Press.

Separating science from stereotype. [Editorial]. (2005) *Nature Neuroscience* 8(3) 253. doi:10.1038/nn0305-253

Summers. L. H. (2005 January 14). Remarks at NBER conference on diversifying the science and engineering workforce. Retrieved from http://designintelligences.wordpress.com/lawrence-h-summers-remarks-at-nber-conference/

APA

Critiquing "Why Lawrence Summers Was Wrong"

1. The controversy sparked by Harvard President Lawrence Summers' remarks was a highly politicized version of the classic nature/nurture problem. Liberal commentators claimed that women were underrepresented in science because of cultural practices that discouraged young girls from becoming interested in math and science and that blocked women Ph.D.s from advancing in their scientific careers. In contrast, conservative commentators—praising Summers' courage for raising a politically incorrect subject—took the "nature" side of this argument by citing studies pointing to innate cognitive differences between human males and females. How would you characterize Christianson's position in this controversy?

2. How does Christianson handle opposing views in her essay?

3. Do you regard Christianson's essay as a valuable contribution to the controversy over the reasons for the low numbers of women in math and science? Why or why not?

4. How would you characterize Christianson's *ethos* as a student writer in this piece? Does her *ethos* help convince you that her argument is sound? Explain.

Our second reading, by evolutionary biologist Olivia Judson of Imperial College in London, was published as an op-ed piece in the *New York Times*. In this causal argument, a distinguished scientist looks at the scientific evidence bearing on Summers' remarks.

Different but (Probably) Equal

OLIVIA JUDSON

Hypothesis: males and females are typically indistinguishable on the basis of their behaviors and intellectual abilities.

This is not true for elephants. Females have big vocabularies and hang out in herds; males tend to live in solitary splendor, and insofar as they speak at all, their conversation appears mostly to consist of elephant for "I'm in the mood, I'm in the mood . . . "

The hypothesis is not true for zebra finches. Males sing elaborate songs. Females can't sing at all. A zebra finch opera would have to have males in all the singing roles.

And it's not true for green spoon worms. This animal, which lives on the sea floor, has one of the largest known size differences between male and female: the male is 200,000 times smaller. He

spends his whole life in her reproductive tract, fertilizing eggs by regurgitating sperm through his mouth. He's so different from his mate that when he was first discovered by science, he was not recognized as being a green spoon worm; instead, he was thought to be a parasite.

5   Is it ridiculous to suppose that the hypothesis might not be true for humans either?

No. But it is not fashionable—as Lawrence Summers, president of Harvard University, discovered when he suggested this month that greater intrinsic ability might be one reason that men are over-represented at the top levels of fields involving math, science, and engineering.

There are—as the maladroit Mr. Summers should have known—good reasons it's not fashionable. Beliefs that men are intrinsically better at this or that have repeat-edly led to discrimination and prejudice, and then they've been proved to be nonsense. Women were thought not to be world-class musicians. But when American symphony orchestras introduced blind auditions in the 1970s—the musician plays behind a screen so that his or her gender is invisible to those listening—the number of women offered jobs in professional orchestras increased.

Similarly, in science, studies of the ways that grant applications are evaluated have shown that women are more likely to get financing when those reading the applica-tions do not know the sex of the applicant. In other words, there's still plenty of work to do to level the playing field; there's no reason to suppose there's something inevi-table about the status quo.

All the same, it seems a shame if we can't even voice the ques-tion. Sex differences are fascinat-ing—and entirely unlike the other biological differences that distin-guish other groups of living things

10 (like populations and species). Sex differences never arise in isolation, with females evolving on a moun-taintop, say, and males evolving in a cave. Instead, most genes—and in some species, all genes—spend equal time in each sex. Many sex differences are not, therefore, the result of *his* having one gene while *she* has another. Rather, they are attributable to the way particu-lar genes behave when they find themselves in *him* instead of *her*.

The magnificent difference between male and female green spoon worms, for example, has nothing to do with their having different genes: each green spoon worm larva could go either way. Which sex it becomes depends on whether it meets a female dur-ing its first three weeks of life. If it meets a female, it becomes male and prepares to regurgitate; if it doesn't, it becomes female and settles into a crack on the sea floor.

What's more, the fact that most genes occur in both males and females can generate interesting sexual tensions. In male fruit flies, for instance, variants of genes that confer particular success—which on Mother Nature's abacus is the number of descendants you have—tend to be detrimental when they occur in females, and vice versa. Worse: the bigger the advantage in one sex, the more detrimental those genes are in the other. This means that, at least for fruit flies, the same genes that make a male a Don Juan would also turn a fe-male into a wallflower; conversely,

the genes that make a female a knockout babe would produce a clumsy fellow with the sex appeal of a cake tin.

But why do sex differences ap-pear at all? They appear when the secret of success differs for males and females: the more divergent the paths to success, the more ex-treme the physiological differenc-es. Peacocks have huge tails and strut about because peahens prefer males with big tails. Bull elephant seals grow to five times the mass of females because big males are bet-ter at monopolizing the beaches where the females haul out to have sex and give birth.

Meanwhile, the crow-like jack-daw has (as far as we can tell) no obvious sex differences and appears to lead a life of devoted monoga-my. Here, what works for him also seems to work for her, though the female is more likely to sit on the eggs. So by studying the differ-ences—and similarities—among men and women, we can poten-tially learn about the forces that have shaped us in the past.

And I think the news is good. We're not like green spoon worms or elephant seals, with males and females so different that aspiring to an egalitarian society would be ludicrous. And though we may not be jackdaws either—men and women tend to look different, though even here there's over-lap—it's obvious that where there are intellectual differences, they are so slight they cannot be pre-judged.

15 The interesting questions are, is there an average intrinsic difference? And how extensive is the variation? I would love to know if the averages are the same but the underlying variation is different—with members of one sex tending to be either superb or dreadful at particular sorts of thinking while members of the other are pretty good but rarely exceptional.

Curiously, such a result could arise even if the forces shaping men and women have been identical. In some animals—humans and fruit flies come to mind—males have an X chromosome and a Y chromosome while females have two Xs. In females, then, extreme effects of genes on one X chromosome can be offset by the genes on the other. But in males, there's no hiding your X. In birds and butterflies, though, it's the other way around: females have a Z chromosome and a W chromosome, and males snooze along with two Zs.

The science of sex differences, even in fruit flies and toads, is a ferociously complex subject. It's also famously fraught, given its malignant history. In fact, there was a time not so long ago when I would have balked at the whole enterprise: the idea there might be intrinsic cognitive differences between men and women was one I found insulting. But science is a great persuader. The jackdaws and spoon worms have forced me to change my mind. Now I'm keen to know what sets men and women apart—and no longer afraid of what we may find.

Critiquing "Different but (Probably) Equal"

1. What parts of Judson's article tend to support the "nurture" view that cultural practices account for women's underrepresentation in math and science? What parts tend to support the "nature" view?
2. Judson's argument relies heavily on analogies between humans and the animal world. In your own words, explain why the green spoon worm and the jackdaw (crow) are important to Judson's argument. Why does she say that the interesting questions involve "average intrinsic difference" and the extensiveness of "variation"?
3. How would you characterize Judson's *ethos* in this article? Pay particular attention to the narrative embedded in the last paragraph—her claim that she is no longer afraid of what we might find. How important is it that we know the author is a woman?

Our final causal argument, by student writer Carlos Macias, examines the phenomenon of credit card debt among college students. Note how Macias intermixes personal experiences and research data in order to make his case.

"The Credit Card Company Made Me Do It!"—The Credit Card Industry's Role in Causing Student Debt

CARLOS MACIAS (STUDENT)

One day on spring break this year, I strolled into a Gap store. I found several items that I decided to buy. As I was checking out, the cute female clerk around my age, with perfect hair and makeup, asked if I wanted to open a GapCard to save 10 percent on all purchases I made at Gap, Banana Republic, and Old Navy that day. She said I would also earn points toward Gap gift certificates in the future. Since I shop at the Gap often enough, I decided to take her up on her offer. I filled out the form she handed me, and within seconds I—a jobless, indebted-from-student-loans, full-time college student with no substantial assets or income whatsoever—was offered a card with a $1000 credit line. Surprised by the speed at which I was approved and the amount that I was approved for, I decided to proceed to both Banana Republic and Old Navy that day to see if there was anything else I might be interested in getting (there was). By the end of the day, I had rung up nearly $200 in purchases.

I know my $200 shopping spree on credit is nothing compared to some of the horror stories I have heard from friends. One of my friends, a college sophomore, is carrying $2000 on a couple of different cards, a situation that is not unusual at all. According to a May 2005 study by Nellie Mae, students with credit cards carry average balances of just under $3000 by the time they are seniors ("Undergraduate"2). The problem is that most students don't have the income to pay off their balances, so they become hooked into paying high interest rates and fees that enrich banks while exploiting students who have not yet learned how to exercise control on their spending habits.

Who is to blame for this situation? Many people might blame the students themselves, citing the importance of individual responsibility and proclaiming that no one forces students to use credit cards. But I put most of the blame directly on the credit card companies. Credit cards are enormously profitable; according to a *New York Times* article, the industry made $30 billion in pretax profits in 2003 alone (McGeehan). Hooking college students on credit cards is essential for this profit, not only because companies make a lot of money off the students themselves, but because hooking students on cards creates a habit that lasts a lifetime. Credit card companies' predatory lending practices—such as using exploitive advertising, using credit scoring to determine creditworthiness, disguising the real cost of credit, and taking advantage of U.S. government deregulation—are causing many unwitting college students to accumulate high levels of credit card debt.

First of all, credit card companies bombard students with highly sophisticated advertising. College students, typically, are in an odd "in-between" stage where they are not necessarily teens anymore, provided for by their parents, but neither are they fully adults, able to provide entirely for themselves. Many students feel the pressures from family, peers and themselves to assume adult roles in terms of their dress and jobs, not relying on Mom or Dad for help. Card companies know about these pressures. Moreover, college students are easy to target because they are concentrated on campuses and generally consume the same media. I probably get several mailings a month offering me a preapproved credit card. These advertisements are filled with happy campus scenes featuring students wearing just the right clothes, carrying their books in just the right backpack, playing music on their iPods or opening their laptop computers. They also appeal to students' desire to feel like responsible adults by emphasizing little emergencies that college students can relate to such as car breakdowns on a road trip. These advertisements illustrate a point made by a team of researchers in an article entitled "Credit Cards as Lifestyle Facilitators": The authors explain how credit card companies want consumers to view credit cards as "lifestyle facilitators" that enable "lifestyle building" and "lifestyle signaling" (Bernthal, Crockett, and Rose). Credit cards make it easy for students to live the lifestyle pictured in the credit card ads.

5   Another contributing cause of high credit card debt for college students is the method that credit card companies use to grant credit—through credit scoring that does not consider income. It was credit scoring that allowed me to get that quadruple-digit credit line at the Gap while already living in the red. The application I filled out never asked my income. Instead, the personal information I listed was used to pull up my credit score, which is based on records of outstanding debts and payment history. Credit scoring allows banks to grant credit cards based on a person's record of responsibility in paying bills rather than on income. According to finance guru Suze Orman, "Your FICO [credit] score is a great tool to size up how good you will be handling a new loan or credit card" (21). Admittedly, credit scoring has made the lending process as a whole much fairer, giving individuals such as minorities and women the chance to qualify for credit even if they have minimal incomes. But when credit card companies use credit scoring to determine college students' creditworthiness, many students are unprepared to handle a credit line that greatly exceeds their ability to pay based on income. In fact, the Center for Responsible Lending, a consumer advocacy organization in North Carolina, lobbied Congress in September 2003 to require credit card companies to secure proof of adequate income for college-age customers before approving credit card applications ("Credit Card Policy Recommendations"). If Congress passed such legislation, credit card companies would not be able to as easily take advantage of college students who have not yet learned how to exercise control on their spending habits. They would have to offer students credit lines commensurate to their incomes. No wonder these companies vehemently opposed this legislation.

Yet another contributing cause of high levels of credit card debt is the high cost of having this debt, which credit card companies are especially talented at disguising. As credit card debt increases, card companies compound unpaid interest, adding it to the balance that must be repaid. If this balance is not repaid, they charge interest on unpaid interest. They add exorbitant fees for small slip-ups like making a late payment or exceeding the credit limit. While these costs are listed on statements when first added to the balance, they quickly vanish into the "New Balance" number on all subsequent statements, as if these fees were simply past purchases that have yet to be repaid. As the balance continues to grow, banks spike interest rates even higher. In his 2004 article

"Soaring Interest Is Compounding Credit Card Pain for Millions," Patrick McGeehan describes a "new era of consumer credit, in which thousands of Americans are paying millions of dollars each month in fees that they did not expect . . . lenders are doubling or tripling interest rates with little warning or explanation." These rate hikes are usually tucked into the pages of fine print that come with credit cards, which many consumers are unable to fully read, let alone understand. Usually, a credit card company will offer a very low "teaser rate" that expires after several months. While this industry practice is commonly understood by consumers, many do not understand that credit card companies usually reserve the right to raise the rate at any time for almost any reason, causing debt levels to rise further.

Admittedly, while individual consumers must be held accountable for any debt they accumulate and should understand compound and variable interest and fees, students' ignorance is welcomed by the credit card industry. In order to completely understand how the credit card industry has caused college students to amass high amounts of credit card debt, it is necessary to explain how this vicious monster was let loose during banking deregulation over the past 30 years. In 1978, the Supreme Court opened the floodgates by ruling that the federal government could not set a cap on interest rates that banks charged for credit cards; that was to be left to the states. With Uncle Sam no longer protecting consumers, Delaware and South Dakota passed laws that removed caps on interest rates, in order to woo credit card companies to conduct nationwide business there (McGeehan). Since then, the credit card industry has become one of the most profitable industries ever. Credit card companies were given another sweet deal from the U.S. Supreme Court in 1996, when the Court deregulated fees. Since then, the average late fee has risen from $10 or less, to $39 (McGeehan). While a lot of these fees and finance charges are avoidable if the student pays the balance in full, on time, every month, for college students who carry balances for whatever reason, these charges are tacked on, further adding to the principal on which they pay a high rate of compounded interest. (Seventy-nine percent of the students surveyed in the Nellie Mae study said that they regularly carried a balance on their cards [8].) Moreover, the U.S. government has refused to step in to regulate the practice of universal default, where a credit card company can raise the rate they charge if a consumer is late on an unrelated bill, like a utility payment. Even for someone who pays his or her bills in full, on time, 99% of the time, one bill-paying slip-up can cause an avalanche of fees and frustration, thanks to the credit card industry.

Credit card companies exploit college students' lack of financial savvy and security. It is no secret that most full-time college students are not independently wealthy; many have limited means. So why are these companies so willing to issue cards to poor college students? Profits, of course! If they made credit cards less available to struggling consumers such as college students, consumers would have a more difficult time racking up huge balances, plain and simple. It's funny that Citibank, one of the largest, most profitable credit card companies in the world, proudly exclaims "Live richly" in its advertisements. At the rate that it and other card companies collect interest and fees from their customers, a more appropriate slogan would be "Live poorly."

Works Cited

Bernthal, Matthew J., David Crockett, and Randall L. Rose. "Credit Cards as Lifestyle Facilitators." *Journal of Consumer Research* 32.1 (2005): 130–45. *Research Library Complete.* Web. 18 June 2005.

"Credit Card Policy Recommendations." *Center for Responsible Lending.* Center for Responsible Lending, Sept. 2003. Web. 18 June 2005.

McGeehan, Patrick. "Soaring Interest Is Compounding Credit Card Pain for Millions." *New York Times.* New York Times, 21 Nov. 2004. Web. 3 July 2005.

Nellie Mae. "Undergraduate Students and Credit Cards in 2004: An Analysis of Usage Rates and Trends." *Nellie Mae.* SLM Corporation, May 2005. Web. 3 July 2005.

Orman, Suze. *The Money Book for the Young, Fabulous and Broke.* New York: Riverhead, 2005. Print.

Critiquing 'The Credit Card Company Made Me Do It!'

1. How effective is Macias's argument that the predatory practices of banks and credit card companies are the primary cause of credit card debt among college students?

2. Suppose that you wanted to join this conversation by offering a counterview with a thesis something like this: "Although Macias is partially correct that banks and credit card companies play a role in producing credit card debt among college students, he underestimates other important factors." What would you emphasize as the causes of credit card debt? How would you make your case?

PEARSON
mycomplab

For additional writing, reading, and research resources, go to
www.mycomplab.com

Evaluation and Ethical Arguments

13

Case 1 What Is the Value of Immigrants?

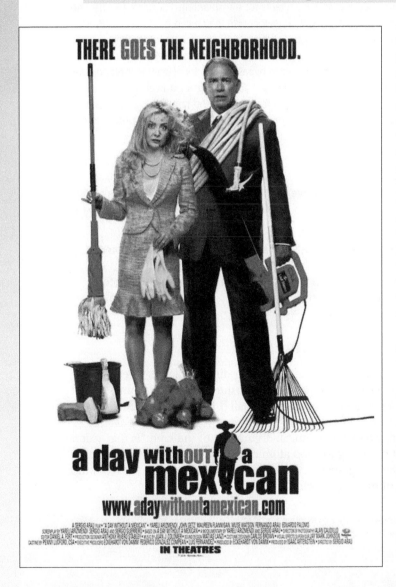

As we explored in Chapter 2, the United States has been embroiled in an ongoing controversy over the influx of illegal immigrants, mostly from Mexico and Central America. While some Americans want to offer citizenship as soon as possible to these immigrants, others want to close off the border between Mexico and the United States and to reduce the number of undocumented workers through deportation or through a crackdown on employers. This marketing image for the movie *A Day without a Mexican* makes a humorous evaluation argument in favor of Mexican immigrants. It argues that the labor provided by immigrants is valuable—so valuable, in fact, that Californians could hardly endure a day without them. The image of the wealthy white couple having to do their own housekeeping, yard work, and tomato picking is an ironic reminder that the standard of living many Americans take for granted depends on the cheap labor of immigrants.

> ### Case 2 What Is a "Good Organ" for a Transplant? How Can an Ill Person Ethically Find an Organ Donor?
>
> In the United States some 87,000 sick people have been waiting as long as six years for an organ transplant, with a portion of these dying before they can find a donor. The problem of organ shortages raises two kinds of evaluation issues. First, doctors are reevaluating the criteria by which they judge a "good organ"—that is, a good lung, kidney, or liver suitable for transplanting. Formerly, people who were elderly or obese or who had engaged in risky behaviors or experienced heart failure or other medical conditions were not considered sources of good organs. Now doctors are reconsidering these sources as well as exploring the use of organs from pigs. Second, the shortage of organs for donation has raised numerous ethical issues: Is it ethical for people to bypass the national waiting list for organs by advertising on billboards and Web sites (see the billboard advertising for a liver on page 213)? Is it morally right for people to sell their organs? Is it right for patients and families to buy organs or in any way remunerate living organ donors? Some states are passing laws that allow some financial compensation to living organ donors.

In our roles as citizens and professionals, we are continually expected to make difficult evaluations and to persuade others to accept them. In this chapter, you will learn to:

■ Analyze questions about the worth or value of something by using a criteria-match thinking strategy
■ Analyze ethical questions from the perspective of principles or consequences
■ Use these analytical tools to make your own evaluation or ethical arguments

An Overview of Evaluation Arguments

In this chapter we explain strategies for conducting two different kinds of evaluation arguments. First, we examine categorical evaluations of the kind "Is this thing a good member of its class?"* (Is Ramon a good committee chair?) In such an evaluation, the writer determines the extent to which a given something possesses the qualities or standards of its class. Second, we examine ethical arguments of the kind "Is this action right (wrong)?" (Was it right or wrong to drop atomic bombs on Hiroshima and Nagasaki in World War II?) In these arguments, the writer evaluates a given act from the perspective of some system of morality or ethics.

---

*In addition to the term *good*, a number of other evaluative terms involve the same kind of thinking—*effective, successful, workable, excellent, valuable,* and so forth.

Criteria-Match Structure of Categorical Evaluations

A categorical evaluation uses a criteria-match structure similar to the structure we examined in definition arguments (see Chapter 11). A typical claim-with-reasons frame for an evaluation argument has the following structure:

> This thing/phenomenon is/is not a good member of its class because it meets (fails to meet) criteria A, B, and C.

The main conceptual difference between an evaluation argument and a definition argument is the nature of the contested category. In a definition argument, one argues whether a particular thing belongs within a certain category. (Is this swampy area a *wetland?*) In an evaluation argument, we know what category something belongs to. For example, we know that this 2002 Ford Escort is a *used car.* For an evaluation argument, the question is whether this 2002 Ford Escort is a *good used car.* Or, to place the question within a rhetorical context, is this Ford Escort a *good used car for me to buy for college?*

Toulmin Framework for an Evaluation Argument

As an illustration of the criteria-match structure of an evaluation argument, let's continue with the Ford Escort example. Suppose you get in a debate with Parent or Significant Other about the car you should buy for college. Let's say that Parent or Significant Other argues that the following criteria are particularly important: (1) initial value for the money, (2) dependability, (3) safety, and (4) low maintenance costs. (Note: You would strenuously reject these criteria if you were looking for a muscle car, coolness, or driving excitement. This is why establishing criteria is a crucial part of evaluation arguments.) A Toulmin analysis of how Parent or Significant Other might make the case for "initial value for the money" is shown on page 290. Note how the warrant is a criterion while the stated reason and grounds assert that the specific case meets the criterion.

As the Toulmin analysis shows, Parent or Significant Other needs to argue that getting high value for the initial money is an important consideration (the criterion argument) and that this 2002 Ford Escort meets this criterion better than competing choices (the match argument). If you can't see yourself driving a Ford Escort, you've got to either argue for other criteria (attack the warrant) or accept the criterion but argue that the Ford Escort's projected maintenance costs undermine its initial value (attack the reason and grounds).

Conducting a Categorical Evaluation Argument

Now that you understand the basic criteria-match structure of a categorical evaluation, let's look at some thinking strategies you can use to develop your criteria and to argue whether the thing you are evaluating meets the criteria.

Toulmin Analysis of the Ford Escort Argument

ENTHYMEME

CLAIM The Ford Escort is a good used car for you at college

REASON because it provides the most initial value for the money.

GROUNDS

- Evidence that Escorts are dependable
- Evidence that Escorts are not in very high demand, so you can get a 2002 Escort for $5,000 less than a 2002 Honda Civic with the same mileage
- Evidence that a 2002 Civic for the same price would have double the miles
- Low initial mileage means years of dependable use without large repair bills.

CONDITIONS OF REBUTTAL
Attacking the reason and grounds

A 2002 Escort is not as great a value as it seems:

- My research suggests there are high maintenance costs after 60,000 miles.
- The initial savings may be blown on high repair costs.

WARRANT

High value for the initial money is an important criterion for buying your college car.

BACKING

Arguments showing why it is important to get high value for the money:

- Money saved on the car can be used for other college expenses.
- Buying in this thrifty way meets our family's image of being careful shoppers.

CONDITIONS OF REBUTTAL
Attacking the warrant and backing

Other criteria are more important to me:

- Great handling and acceleration
- The fun of driving
- The status of having a cool car

Developing Your Criteria

To help you develop your criteria, we suggest a three-step thinking process:

1. Place the thing you are evaluating in the smallest relevant category so that you don't compare apples to oranges.
2. Develop criteria for your evaluation based on the purpose or function of this category.
3. Determine the relative weight of your criteria.

Let's look at each of these steps in turn.

Step 1: Place the Thing You Are Evaluating in the Smallest Relevant Category

Placing your contested thing in the smallest category is a crucial first step. Suppose, for example, that you want one of your professors to write you a letter of recommendation for a summer job. The professor will need to know what kind of summer job. Are you applying to become a camp counselor, a law office intern, a retail sales clerk, or a tour guide at a wild animal park in your state? Each of these jobs has different criteria for excellence. Or to take a different example, suppose that you want to evaluate e-mail as a medium of correspondence. To create a stable context for your evaluation, you need to place e-mail in its smallest relevant category. You may choose to evaluate e-mail as medium for business communication (by contrasting e-mail with direct personal contact, phone conversations, or postal mail), as a medium for staying in touch with high school friends (in contrast, say, to text messaging or Facebook), or as a medium for carrying on a long-distance romance (in contrast, say, to old-fashioned "love letters"). Again, criteria will vary across these different categories.

By placing your contested thing in the smallest relevant class, you avoid the apples-and-oranges problem. That is, to give a fair evaluation of a perfectly good apple, you need to judge it under the class "apple" and not under the next larger class, "fruit," or a neighboring class such as "orange." And to be even more precise, you may wish to evaluate your apple in the class "eating apple" as opposed to "pie apple" because the latter class is supposed to be tarter and the former class juicier and sweeter.

Step 2: Develop Criteria for Your Evaluation Based on the Purpose or Functions of This Category Suppose that the summer job you are applying for is tour guide at a wild animal park in your state. The functions of a tour guide are to drive the tour buses, make people feel welcome, give them interesting information about the wild animals in the park, make their visit pleasant, and so forth. Criteria for a good tour guide would thus include reliability and responsibility, a friendly demeanor, good speaking skills, and knowledge of the kinds of animals in the wild animal park. In our e-mail example, suppose that you want to evaluate e-mail as a medium for business communication. The purpose of this class is to provide a quick and reliable means of communication that increases efficiency, minimizes misunderstandings, protects the confidentiality of internal communications, and so forth. Based on these purposes, you might establish the following criteria:

A good medium for business communication:

- Is easy to use, quick, and reliable
- Increases employee efficiency
- Prevents misunderstandings
- Maintains confidentiality where needed

Step 3: Determine the Relative Weight of Your Criteria In some evaluations all the criteria are equally important. However, sometimes a phenomenon to be evaluated is strong in one criterion but weak in another—a situation that forces the evaluator to decide which criterion takes precedence. For example, the supervisor interviewing candidates for tour guide at the wild animal park may find one candidate who is very knowledgeable about the wildlife but doesn't have good speaking skills. The supervisor would need to decide which of these two criteria gets more weight.

EXAMINING VISUAL ARGUMENTS

An Evaluation Claim

This photograph of Stephen Colbert and Jon Stewart of *The Colbert Report* and *The Daily Show* was taken at the October 30, 2010 "Rally to Restore Sanity 'or Fear,'" on the Washington D.C. National Mall, an event that drew thousands of people. The event followed by two months the "Restoring Honor Rally" led by conservative Fox News talk show celebrity Glenn Beck on August 28, 2010. Political commentators debated whether the Colbert and Stewart rally was simply a satirical entertainment mocking the Beck rally or whether it was serious political activism supporting the liberal left. If your goal was to portray this event as serious political activism, would this photograph be a good image to accompany your argument? What criteria would you establish for selecting a photograph to support your argument that Colbert and Stewart are effective political activists and not simply entertainers?

Making Your Match Argument

Once you've established and weighed your criteria, you'll need to use examples and other evidence to show that the thing being evaluated meets or does not meet the criteria. For example, your professor could argue that you would be a good wildlife park tour guide because you have strong interpersonal skills (based on your work on a college orientation committee), that you have good speaking skills (based on a speech you gave in the professor's class), and that you have quite a bit of knowledge about animals and ecology (based on your major in environmental science).

In our e-mail example, you might establish the following working thesis:

> Despite its being easy to learn, quick, and reliable, e-mail is not an effective medium for business communication because it reduces worker efficiency, leads to frequent misunderstandings, and often lacks confidentiality.

You could develop your last three points as follows:

- **E-mail reduces worker efficiency.** You can use personal anecdotes and research data to show how checking e-mail is addictive and how it eats into worker time (one research article says that the average worker devotes ten minutes of every working hour to reading and responding to e-mail). You might also show how e-mail frequently diverts workers from high-priority to low-priority tasks. Some research even suggests that workers don't relax as much away from work because they are always checking their e-mail.

- **E-mail leads to misunderstandings.** Because an e-mail message is often composed rapidly without revision, e-mail can cause people to state ideas imprecisely, to write something they would never say face-to-face, or to convey an unintended tone. Without the benefits of tone of voice and body language available in face-to-face conversation, e-mail can be easily misread. You could give a personal example of a high-consequence misunderstanding caused by e-mail.

- **E-mail often lacks confidentiality.** You could provide anecdotal or research evidence of cases in which a person clicked on the "reply to all" button rather than the "reply" button, sending a message intended for one person to a whole group of people. Stories also abound of employers who snoop through employees' e-mail messages or workers who forward e-mails without permission from the sender. Perhaps most troubling is the way that e-mail messages are archived forever, so that messages that you thought were deleted may show up years later in a lawsuit.

As these examples illustrate, the key to a successful match argument is to use sufficient examples and other evidence to show how your contested phenomenon meets or does not meet each of your criteria.

■ ■ ■   **FOR CLASS DISCUSSION** Developing Criteria and Match Arguments

The following small-group exercise can be accomplished in one or two class hours. It gives you a good model of the process you can go through in order to write your own categorical evaluation.

1. Choose a specific controversial person, thing, or event to evaluate (your school's computer services help desk, the invite-a-professor-to-lunch program in your dormitory, Harvey's Hamburger Haven). To help you think of ideas, try brainstorming controversial members of the following categories: *people* (athletes, political leaders, musicians, clergy, entertainers, businesspeople); *science and technology* (weapons systems, word-processing programs, spreadsheets, automotive advancements, treatments for diseases); *media* (a newspaper, a magazine or journal, a TV program, a radio station, a Web site, an advertisement); *government and world affairs* (an economic policy, a Supreme Court decision, a law or legal practice, a government custom or practice, a foreign policy); *the arts* (a movie, a book, a building, a painting, a piece of music); *your college or university* (a course, a teacher, a textbook, a curriculum, an administrative policy, the financial aid system); *the world of work* (a job, a company operation, a dress policy, a merit pay system, a hiring policy, a supervisor); or any other categories of your choice.
2. Place your controversial person or thing within the smallest relevant class, thus providing a rhetorical context for your argument and showing what is at stake. Do you want to evaluate Harvey's Hamburger Haven in the broad category of *restaurants,* in the narrow category of *hamburger joints,* or in a different narrow category such as *late-night study places*? If you are evaluating a recent film, are you evaluating it as *a chick flick,* as a possible *Academy Award nominee,* or as a *political filmmaking statement?*
3. Make a list of the purpose or function of that class, and then list the criteria that a good member of that class would need to have in order to accomplish the purpose or function. (What is the purpose or function of a computer services help desk, a late-night study place, or a chick flick? What criteria for excellence can you derive from these purposes or functions?)
4. If necessary, rank your criteria from most to least important. (For a late-night study place, what is more important: good ambience, Wi-Fi availability, good coffee, or convenient location?)
5. Provide examples and other evidence to show how your contested something matches or does not match each of your criteria. (As a late-night study place, Carol's Coffee Closet beats out Harvey's Hamburger Haven. Although Harvey's Hamburger Haven has the most convenient location, Carol's Coffee Closet has Wi-Fi, an ambience conducive to studying, and excellent coffee.)

An Overview of Ethical Arguments

A second kind of evaluation argument focuses on moral or ethical issues, which can often merge or overlap with categorical evaluations. For example, many apparently straightforward categorical evaluations can turn out to have an ethical dimension. Consider again the criteria for buying a car. Most people would base their evaluations on cost, safety, comfort, and so forth. But some people may feel morally obligated to buy the most fuel-efficient car, to buy an American car, or not to buy a car from a manufacturer whose labor policies they find morally repugnant. Depending on how large a role ethical considerations play in the evaluation, we may choose to call this an ethical argument based on moral considerations rather than a categorical evaluation based on the purposes of a class or category.

As the discussion so far has suggested, disagreements about an ethical issue often stem from different systems of values that make the issue irresolvable. It is precisely this problem—the lack of shared assumptions about value—that makes it so important to confront issues of ethics with rational deliberation. The arguments you produce may not persuade others to your view, but they should make others think seriously about it, and they should help you work out more clearly the reasons and warrants for your own beliefs. By writing about ethical issues, you see more clearly what you believe and why you believe it. Although the arguments demanded by ethical issues require rigorous thought, they force us to articulate our most deeply held beliefs and our richest feelings.

Major Ethical Systems

When we are faced with an ethical issue, we must move from arguments of good or bad to arguments of right or wrong. The terms *right* and *wrong* are clearly different from the terms *good* and *bad* when the latter terms mean, simply, "effective" (meets purposes of class, as in "This is a good laptop") or "ineffective" (fails to meet purposes of class, as in "This is a bad cookbook"). But *right* and *wrong* often also differ from what seems to be a moral use of the terms *good* and *bad*. We may say, for example, that sunshine is good because it brings pleasure and that cancer is bad because it brings pain and death, but that is not quite the same thing as saying that sunshine is "right" and cancer is "wrong." It is the problem of "right" and "wrong" that ethical arguments confront.

For example, from a nonethical standpoint, you could say that certain people are "good terrorists" in that they fully realize the purpose of the class "terrorist": they cause great anguish and damage with a minimum of resources, and they bring much attention to their cause. However, if we want to condemn terrorism on ethical grounds, we have to say that terrorism is wrong. The ethical question is not whether a person fulfills the purposes of the class "terrorist," but whether it is wrong for such a class to exist.

There are many schools of ethical thought—too many to cover in this brief overview—so we'll limit ourselves to two major systems: arguments from consequences and arguments from principles.

Consequences as the Base of Ethics

Perhaps the best-known example of evaluating acts according to their ethical consequences is utilitarianism, a down-to-earth philosophy that grew out of nineteenth-century British philosophers' concern to demystify ethics and make it work in the practical world. Jeremy Bentham, the originator of utilitarianism, developed the goal of the greatest good for the greatest number, or "greatest happiness," by which he meant the most pleasure for the least pain. John Stuart Mill, another British philosopher, built on Bentham's utilitarianism by using predicted consequences to determine the morality of a proposed action.

Mill's consequentialist approach allows you readily to assess a wide range of acts. You can apply the principle of utility—which says that an action is morally right if it produces a greater net value (benefits minus costs) than any available alternative action—to virtually any situation, and it will help you reach a decision. Obviously, however, it's not always easy to make the calculations called for by this approach because, like any prediction of the future, an estimate of consequences is conjectural. In particular, it's often very hard to assess the long-term consequences of any action. Too often, utilitarianism seduces us into a short-term analysis of a moral problem simply because long-term consequences are difficult to predict.

Principles as the Base of Ethics

Any ethical system based on principles will ultimately rest on moral tenets that we are duty bound to uphold, no matter what the consequences. Sometimes the moral tenets come from religious faith—for example, the Ten Commandments. At other times, however, the principles are derived from philosophical reasoning, as in the case of German philosopher Immanuel Kant. Kant held that no one should ever use another person as a means to his own ends and that everyone should always act as if his acts are the basis of universal law. In other words, Kant held that we are duty bound to respect other people's sanctity and to act in the same way that we would want all other people to act. The great advantage of such a system is its clarity and precision. We are never overwhelmed by a multiplicity of contradictory and difficult-to-quantify consequences; we simply make sure we are following (or not violating) the principles of our ethical system and proceed accordingly.

Constructing an Ethical Argument

To show you how to conduct an ethical argument, let's now apply these two strategies to an example. In general, you can conduct an ethical evaluation by using the frame for either a principles-based argument or a consequences-based argument or a combination of both.

> **Principles-Based Frame:** An act is right (wrong) because it follows (violates) principles A, B, and C.
>
> **Consequences-Based Frame:** An act is right (wrong) because it will lead to consequences A, B, and C, which are good (bad).

To illustrate how these frames might help you develop an ethical argument, let's use them to develop arguments for or against capital punishment.

Constructing a Principles-Based Argument

A principles-based argument looks at capital punishment through the lens of one or more guiding principles. Kant's principle that we are duty bound not to violate the sanctity of other human lives could lead to arguments opposing capital punishment. One might argue as follows:

> *Principles-based argument opposing capital punishment:* The death penalty is wrong because it violates the principle of the sanctity of human life.

You could support this principle either by summarizing Kant's argument that one should not violate the selfhood of another person or by pointing to certain religious systems such as Judeo-Christian ethics, where one is told, "Vengeance is mine, saith the Lord" or "Thou shalt not kill." To develop this argument further, you might examine two exceptions in which principles-based ethicists may allow killing—self-defense and war—and show how capital punishment does not fall in either category.

Principles-based arguments can also be developed to support capital punishment. You may be surprised to learn that Kant himself—despite his arguments for the sanctity of life—supported capital punishment. To make such an argument, Kant evoked a different principle about the suitability of the punishment to the crime:

> There is no sameness of kind between death and remaining alive even under the most miserable conditions, and consequently there is no equality between the crime and the retribution unless the criminal is judicially condemned and put to death.

Stated as an enthymeme, Kant's argument is as follows:

> *Principles-based argument supporting capital punishment:* Capital punishment is right because it follows the principle that punishments should be proportionate to the crime.

In developing this argument, Kant's burden would be to show why the principle of proportionate retribution outweighs the principle of the supreme worth of the individual. Our point is that a principles-based argument can be made both for and against capital punishment. The arguer's duty is to make clear what principle is being evoked and then to show why this principle is more important than opposing principles.

Constructing a Consequences-Based Argument

Unlike a principles-based argument, which appeals to certain guiding maxims or rules, a consequences-based argument looks at the consequences of a decision and measures the positive benefits against the negative costs. Here is the frame that an arguer might use to oppose capital punishment on the basis of negative consequences:

> *Consequences-based argument opposing capital punishment:* Capital punishment is wrong because it leads to the following negative consequences:

- The possibility of executing an innocent person
- The possibility that a murderer who may repent and be redeemed is denied that chance
- The excessive legal and political costs of trials and appeals
- The unfair distribution of executions so that one's chances of being put to death are much greater if one is a minority or is poor

To develop this argument, the reader would need to provide facts, statistics, and other evidence to support each of the stated reasons.

A different arguer might use a consequences-based approach to support capital punishment:

Consequences-based argument supporting capital punishment: Capital punishment is right because it leads to the following positive consequences:

- It may deter violent crime and slow down the rate of murder.
- It saves the cost of lifelong imprisonment.
- It stops criminals who are menaces to society from committing more murders.
- It helps grieving families reach closure and sends a message to victims' families that society recognizes their pain.

It should be evident, then, that adopting an ethical system doesn't lead to automatic answers to one's ethical dilemmas. A system offers a way of proceeding—a way of conducting an argument—but it doesn't relieve you of personal responsibility for thinking through your values and taking a stand. When you face an ethical dilemma, we encourage you to consider both the relevant principles and the possible consequences the dilemma entails. In many arguments, you can use both principles-based and consequences-based reasoning as long as irreconcilable contradictions don't present themselves.

■ ■ ■ **FOR CLASS DISCUSSION** Developing Ethical Arguments

Working as individuals or in small groups, construct an ethical argument (based on principles, consequences, or both) for or against the following actions:

1. Eating meat
2. Buying a hybrid car
3. Legalizing assisted suicide for the terminally ill
4. Selling organs
5. Generating state revenue through lotteries

■ ■ ■

Common Problems in Making Evaluation Arguments

When conducting evaluation arguments (whether categorical or ethical), writers can bump up against recurring problems that are unique to evaluation. In some cases these problems complicate the establishment of criteria; in other cases they complicate the match argument. Let's look briefly at some of these common problems.

- **The problem of standards—what is commonplace versus what is ideal:** In various forms, we experience the dilemma of the commonplace versus the ideal all the time. Is it fair to get a ticket for going seventy miles per hour on a sixty-five-mile-per-hour freeway when most of the drivers go seventy miles per hour or faster? (Does what is *commonplace*—going seventy—override what is *ideal*—obeying the law?) Is it better for high schools to pass out free contraceptives to students because students are having sex anyway (what's *commonplace*), or is it better not to pass them out in order to support abstinence (what's *ideal*)?

- **The problem of mitigating circumstances:** This problem occurs when an arguer claims that unusual circumstances should alter our usual standards of judgment. Ordinarily, it is fair for a teacher to reduce a grade if you turn in a paper late. But what if you were up all night taking care of a crying baby? Does that count as a *mitigating circumstance* to waive the ordinary criterion? When you argue for mitigating circumstances, you will likely assume an especially heavy burden of proof. People assume the rightness of usual standards of judgment unless there are compelling arguments for abnormal circumstances.

- **The problem of choosing between two goods or two bads:** Often an evaluation issue forces us between a rock and a hard place. Should we cut pay or cut people? Put our parents in a nursing home or let them stay at home, where they have become a danger to themselves? In such cases one has to weigh conflicting criteria, knowing that the choices are too much alike—either both bad or both good.

- **The problem of seductive empirical measures:** The need to make high-stakes evaluations has led many people to seek quantifiable criteria that can be weighed mathematically. Thus we use grade point averages to select scholarship winners, student evaluation scores to decide merit pay for teachers, and combined scores of judges to evaluate figure skaters. In some cases, empirical measures can be quite acceptable, but they are often dangerous because they discount important nonquantifiable traits. The problem with empirical measures is that they seduce us into believing that complex judgments can be made mathematically, thus rescuing us from the messiness of alternative points of view and conflicting criteria.

- **The problem of cost:** A final problem in evaluation arguments is cost. Something may be the best possible member of its class, but if it costs too much, we have to go for second or third best. We can avoid this problem somewhat by placing items into different classes on the basis of cost. For example, a Mercedes will exceed a Kia on almost any criterion, but if we can't afford more than a Kia, the comparison is pointless. It is better to compare a Mercedes to a Lexus and a Kia to an equivalent Ford. Whether costs are expressed in dollars, personal discomfort, moral repugnance, or some other terms, our final evaluation of an item must take cost into account.

WRITING ASSIGNMENT   An Evaluation or Ethical Argument

Write an argument in which you try to change your readers' minds about the value, worth, or ethics of something. Choose a phenomenon to be evaluated that is controversial so that your readers are likely at first to disagree with your evaluation or at least to be surprised by it. Somewhere in your essay you should summarize alternative views and either refute them or concede to them (see Chapter 7).

Exploring Ideas

Evaluation issues are all around us. Think of disagreements about the value of a person, thing, action, or phenomenon within the various communities to which you belong—your dorm, home, or apartment community; your school community, including clubs or organizations; your academic community, including classes you are currently taking; your work community; and your city, state, national, and world communities. For further ideas, look at the categories listed in the For Class Discussion exercise on pages 293–294. Once you have settled on a controversial thing to be evaluated, place it in its smallest relevant category, determine the purposes of that category, and develop your criteria. If you are making an ethical evaluation, consider your argument from the perspective of both principles and consequences.

Identifying Your Audience and Determining What's at Stake

Before drafting your argument, identify your targeted audience and determine what's at stake. Consider your responses to the following questions:

- What audience are you targeting? What background do they need to understand your issue? How much do they already care about it?
- Before they read your evaluation argument, what stance on your issue do you imagine them holding? What change do you want to bring about in their view?
- What will they find new or surprising about your argument?
- What objections might they raise? What counterarguments or alternative points of view will you need to address?
- Why does your evaluation matter? Who might be threatened or made uncomfortable by your views? What is at stake?

Organizing an Evaluation Argument

As you write a draft, you may find useful the following prototypical structures for evaluation arguments shown in Organization Plans 1 and 2 on pages 301 and 302. Of course, you can always alter these plans if another structure better fits your material.

Questioning and Critiquing a Categorical Evaluation Argument

Here is a list of questions you can use to critique a categorical evaluation argument:

Will a skeptic accept my criteria? Many evaluative arguments are weak because the writers have simply assumed that readers will accept their criteria. Whenever your audience's acceptance of your criteria is in doubt, you will need to argue for your criteria explicitly.

Will a skeptic accept my general weighting of criteria? Another vulnerable spot in an evaluation argument is the relative weight of the criteria. How much anyone weights a given criterion is usually a function of his or her own interests relative to your contested something. You should always ask whether some particular group might have good reasons for weighting the criteria differently.

Organization Plan 1: Criteria and Match in Separate Sections

Introduce the issue and state your claim.	• Engage reader's interest in your evaluation issue and show why it is controversial or problematic. • Show what's at stake. • Provide background information needed by your audience. • State your claim.
Present your criteria.	• State and develop criterion 1. • State and develop criterion 2. • Continue with the rest of your criteria. • Anticipate and respond to possible objections to the criteria.
Present your match argument.	• Consider restating your claim for clarity. • Argue that your case meets (does not meet) criterion 1. • Argue that your case meets (does not meet) criterion 2. • Continue with the rest of your match argument. • Anticipate and respond to possible objections to the match argument.
Conclude.	• Perhaps sum up your argument. • Help reader return to the "big picture" of what's at stake. • End with something memorable.

Will a skeptic accept my criteria but reject my match argument? The other major way of testing an evaluation argument is to anticipate how readers may object to your stated reasons and grounds. Will readers challenge you by showing that you have cherry-picked your examples and evidence? Will they provide counterexamples and counterevidence?

Organization Plan 2: Criteria and Match Interwoven

Introduce the issue and state your claim.	• Engage reader's interest in your evaluation issue and show why it is controversial or problematic. • Show what's at stake. • Provide background information needed by your audience. • State your claim.
Present series of criterion-match arguments.	• State and develop criterion 1 and argue that your case meets (does not meet) the criterion. • State and develop criterion 2 and argue that your case meets (does not meet) the criterion. • Continue with the rest of your criterion-match arguments.
Respond to possible objections to your argument.	• Anticipate and summarize possible objections. • Respond to the objections through rebuttal or concession.
Conclude.	• Perhaps sum up your argument. • Help reader return to the "big picture" of what's at stake. • End with something memorable.

Critiquing an Ethical Argument

Ethical arguments can be critiqued through appeals to consequences or principles. If an argument appeals primarily to principles, it can be vulnerable to a simple cost analysis. What are the costs of adhering to this principle? There will undoubtedly be some, or else there would be no real argument. If the argument is based strictly on consequences, we should ask whether it violates any rules or principles, particularly such commandments as the Golden Rule—"Do unto others as you would have others do unto you"—which most members of our audience adhere to. By failing to mention these alternative ways of thinking about ethical issues, we undercut not only our argument but our credibility as well. ■

Our first reading, by student writer Sam Isaacson, was written for the assignment on page 299. It joins a conversation about whether the legalization of same-sex marriage would be good for our society. However, Isaacson, a gay writer, limits the question to whether legalization of same-sex marriage would be *good for the gay community*. Earlier in this text (see Chapter 7, page 129), we discussed Isaacson's rhetorical choices as he considered the audience for his essay. Isaacson's decision was to address this paper to the readers of a gay magazine such as *Harvard Gay and Lesbian Review* or *The Advocate*.

READINGS

Would Legalization of Gay Marriage Be Good for the Gay Community?

SAM ISAACSON (STUDENT)

For those of us who have been out for a while, nothing seems shocking about a gay pride parade. Yet at this year's parade, I was struck by the contrast between two groups—the float for the Toys in Babeland store (with swooning drag queens and leather-clad, whip-wielding, topless dykes) and the Northwest chapters of Integrity and Dignity (Episcopal and Catholic organizations for lesbians and gays), whose marchers looked as conservative as the congregation of any American church.

These stark differences in dress are representative of larger philosophical differences in the gay community. At stake is whether or not we gays and lesbians should act "normal." Labeled as deviants by many in straight society, we're faced with various opposing methods of response. One option is to insist that we are normal and work to integrate gays into the cultural mainstream. Another response is to form an alternative gay culture with its own customs and values; this culture would honor deviancy in response to a society which seeks to label some as "normal" and some as "abnormal." For the purposes of this paper I will refer to those who favor the first response as "integrationists" and those who favor the second response as "liberationists." Politically, this ideological clash is most evident in the issue of whether legalization of same-sex marriage would be good for the gay community. Nearly all integrationists would say yes, but many liberationists would say no. My belief is that while we must take the objections of the liberationists seriously, legalization of same-sex marriage would benefit both gays and society in general.

Let us first look at what is so threatening about gay marriage to many liberationists. Many liberationists fear that legalizing gay marriage will reinforce current social pressures that say monogamous marriage is the normal and right way to live. In straight society, those who choose not to marry are often viewed as self-indulgent, likely promiscuous, and shallow—and it is no coincidence these are some of the same stereotypes gays struggle against. If gays begin to marry, married life will be all the more the norm and subject those outside of marriage to even greater marginalization. As homosexuals, liberationists argue, we should be particularly sensitive to the tyranny of the majority. Our sympathies should lie with the deviants—the transsexual, the fetishist, the drag queen, and the leather-dyke. By choosing marriage, gays take the easy route into "normal" society; we not only abandon the sexual minorities of our community, we strengthen society's narrow notions of what is "normal" and thereby further confine both straights and gays.

Additionally, liberationists worry that by winning the right to marry, gays and lesbians will lose the distinctive and positive characteristics of gay culture. Many gay writers have commented on how as a marginalized group, gays have been forced to create different forms of relationships that often allow for a greater and often more fulfilling range of life experiences. Writer Edmund White, for instance, has observed that there is a greater fluidity in the relationships of gays than straights. Gays, he says, are more likely than straights to stay friends with old lovers, are more likely to form close friendships outside the romantic relationship, and are generally less likely to become compartmentalized into isolated couples. It has also been noted that gay relationships are often characterized by more equality and better communication than are straight relationships. Liberationists make the reasonable assumption that if gays win the right to marry, they will be subject to the same social pressure to marry that straights are subject to. As more gays are pressured into traditional life patterns, liberationists fear the gay sensibility will be swallowed up by the established attitudes of the broader culture. All of society would be the poorer if this were to happen.

5   I must admit that I concur with many of the arguments of the liberationists that I have outlined above. I do think if given the right, gays would feel social pressure to marry; I agree that gays should be especially sensitive to the most marginalized elements of society; and I also agree that the unique perspectives on human relationships that the gay community offers should not be sacrificed. However, despite these beliefs, I feel that legalizing gay marriage would bring valuable benefits to gays and society as a whole.

First of all, I think it is important to put the attacks the liberationists make on marriage into perspective. The liberationist critique of marriage claims that marriage in itself is a harmful institution (for straights as well as gays) because it needlessly limits and normalizes personal freedom. But it seems clear to me that marriage in some form is necessary for the well-being of society. Children need a stable environment in which to be raised. Studies have shown that children whose parents divorce often suffer long-term effects from the trauma. Studies have also shown that people tend to be happier in stable long-term relationships. We need to have someone to look after us when we're old, when we become depressed, when we fall ill. All people, gay or straight, parents or nonparents, benefit from the stabilizing force of marriage.

Second, we in the gay community should not be too quick to overlook the real benefits that legalizing gay marriage will bring. We are currently denied numerous legal rights of marriage that the straight community enjoys: tax benefits, insurance benefits, inheritance rights, and the right to have a voice in medical treatment or funeral arrangements for a dying partner.

Further, just as important as the legal impacts of being denied the right to marriage is the socially symbolic weight this denial carries. We are sent the message that while gay sex in the privacy of one's home will be tolerated, gay love will not be respected. We are told that it is not important to society whether we form long-term relationships or not. We are told that we are not worthy of forming families of our own. By gaining the same recognitions by the state of our relationships and all the legal and social weight that recognition carries, the new message will be that gay love is just as meaningful as straight love.

Finally, let me address what I think is at the heart of the liberationist argument against marriage—the fear of losing social diversity and our unique gay voice. The liberationists are wary of society's normalizing forces. They fear that if gays win the right to marry, gay relationships will simply become imitations of straight relationships—the richness gained through the gay experience will be lost. I feel, however, this argument unintentionally plays into the hands of conservatives. Conservatives argue that marriage is, by definition, the union between man and woman. As a consequence, to the broad culture gay marriage can only be a mockery of marriage. As gays and lesbians we need to argue that conservatives are imposing arbitrary standards on what is normal and not normal in society. To fight the conservative agenda, we must suggest instead that marriage is, in essence, a contract of love and commitment between two people. The liberationists, I think, unwittingly feed into conservative identification and classification by pigeonholing gays as outsiders. Reacting against social norms is simply another way of being held hostage by them.

10   We need to understand that the gay experience and voice will not be lost by gaining the right to marry. Gays will always be the minority by simple biological fact and this will always color the identity of any gay person. But we can only make our voice heard if we are seen as full-fledged members of society. Otherwise we will remain an isolated and marginalized group. And only when we have the right to marry will we have any say in the nature and significance of marriage as an institution. This is not being apologetic to the straight culture, but is a demand that we not be excluded from the central institutions of Western culture. We can help merge the fluidity of gay relationships with the traditionally more compartmentalized married relationship. Further, liberationists should realize that the decision *not* to marry makes a statement only if one has the ability to choose marriage. What would be most radical, most transforming, is two women or two men joined together in the eyes of society.

Critiquing "Would Legalization of Gay Marriage Be Good for the Gay Community?"

1. Who is the audience that Sam Isaacson addresses in this argument?
2. Ordinarily when we think of persons opposing gay marriage, we imagine socially conservative heterosexuals. However, Sam spends little time addressing the antigay marriage arguments of straight society. Rather, he addresses the antimarriage arguments made by "liberationist" gay people. What are these arguments? How well does Sam respond to them?
3. What are the criteria Sam uses to argue that legalizing gay marriage would be good for the gay community?
4. How persuasive do you think Sam's argument is to the various audiences he addresses?

Our second reading, by student writer Christopher Moore, grew out of class discussions about what constitutes a "good news media" and about whether today's college students are informed about the news.

Information Plus Satire:
Why *The Daily Show* and *The Colbert Report* Are Good Sources of News for Young People

CHRISTOPHER MOORE (STUDENT)

Media commentators often complain that college-age students, along with much of the older population, are uninformed about the news. Fewer people today read mainstream newspapers or watch network news than in the past. Hard-core news junkies often get their news online from blog sites or from cable news. Meanwhile, less informed people use social networking tools like Twitter and Facebook for instant, unofficial news, often about popular culture or their favorite celebrities. Another possible source of news is *The Daily Show* and *The Colbert Report.* By presenting information and entertainment together, these shows attract a young audience, especially college-age students who shy away from newspapers or news networks like Fox or CNN. But are these actually good news sources? I will argue that they are, especially for a young audience, because they cover each day's important news and because their satire teaches viewers how to read the news rhetorically. The content on these shows provides up-to-date news stories and compels consumers to recognize that all news has an angle of vision demanding thoughtful processing, not simply blind consumption.

The first thing a good news source does is keep consumers up-to-date on the most important worldwide news. Since *The Daily Show* and *The Colbert Report* both air every weekday except Friday, they constantly present viewers with up-to-date news. Furthermore, all broadcasts are available online, as well as archived—if you missed Tuesday's episode, it's easy to backtrack so that you can stay current. Content published in these shows is trimmed to about 22 minutes (to allow for commercial time), so only the most pertinent information is presented. Consider, for example, the content published in January and February of 2011, which focused almost exclusively on the revolutions in Egypt and the volatile political climate in Tunisia. In these episodes, the shows pulled information from different news sources, both liberal and conservative, showing clips, news anchor commentary, or primary sources just the way other news sources do. In one episode during the turmoil in the Middle East, Stewart interviewed CNN reporter Anderson Cooper, who had just returned from reporting on the revolution from inside Egypt. Viewers watching Stewart might have had more insight into the controversial issues surrounding these revolutions than watchers of network news.

Skeptics, however, may argue that *The Daily Show* and *The Colbert Report* aren't providing real news but just satire. After all, the shows air on Comedy Central. Yet even a satirist needs material to satirize, and these satires always focus on current events, politics, or social trends. Moreover, watching *The Daily Show* offers deeper coverage than many network news programs because it focuses on what is most significant or important in the news. Whereas network news broadcasts tend to move quickly toward sports, weather, humanitarian "feel good" stories, or "breaking news" such as fires, robberies, or traffic accidents, Stewart and Colbert keep their satirical focus on major events with social or political significance.

The satirical methods used by Stewart and Colbert lead to my second and most important reason that *The Daily Show* and *The Colbert Report* are good sources of news: The satire teaches audiences how to "read" the news rhetorically. Unlike conventional news sources, the satire in these two shows unmasks the way that traditional news is packaged and framed, encouraging viewers to be skeptical of news. The satire in these shows functions by pointing out a news source's angle of vision, which promotes specific ideologies and presents news with an agenda. Consider the satirical character played by Stephen Colbert, who presents at one moment a far-right conservative ideology, only to compromise these beliefs at the next moment. His dramatization helps viewers see how rhetorical strategies create an angle of vision. For example, in an interview with Julian Assange, the founder of WikiLeaks, Colbert told his audience that he would show two versions of the interview: one of the unaltered footage and one that deliberately edited the footage to serve an agenda. Network news programs often employ the same tactics as Colbert, but in a much more subtle fashion. Editing may be one strategy, but opinion show hosts like Bill O'Reilly and other conservative news commentators employ a variety of tactics, like selective interviewing, cherry-picking news topics, following "fair and balanced" news with tacit conservative thinking, or any number of other methods. Showing the two versions of Colbert's interview is just one example that reminds viewers that information can be manipulated, presented out of context, edited, or reshaped. Foregrounding these strategies helps viewers criticize and analyze the news they digest.

5   The satire on these shows also points out the absurdities and pretensions of politicians, media commentators, and other public figures. An episode that discussed the Wisconsin labor protests in early 2011 focused on newly elected Republican Governor Scott Walker's decision to slash union benefits and collective bargaining rights to cover deficits in the state budget. When protestors took to the streets, Stewart showed clips from CNN, MSNBC and CBS, that called these protests "inspired by" or "having strong parallels to" revolutionary political action in Egypt or Cairo. However, Stewart rejected this comparison. He pointed out that "no citizens have died, no reporters have been abused, and Republican Governor Scott Walker was elected with 52 percent of the vote—dictators like Mubarak typically hold about 92 percent favor." Stewart's point, in other words, is that comparing two dissimilar things, as traditional news media had done, is unjust to both the Wisconsin protestors and the Tunisian and Egyptian rebels. It belittles those Tunisians or Egyptians who had the courage to raise their voices against dictators just as it distorts the very different political and economic issues and motivations at work in Wisconsin.

Satire also points out inconsistencies in news reporting, or the logical pitfalls into which politicians regularly stumble. In a skit in which Jon Stewart interviewed a conservative political candidate, he exposed inconsistencies in ideological views about when life begins.

On the abortion issue, the candidate argued that life begins at conception, but on constitutional issues of citizenship, he argued that life begins at birth. Stewart took these two conflicting Republican ideologies and used a humorous either/or fallacy to show their inconsistency. Stewart argued that Obama was conceived by his mother in Hawaii. Therefore, if pro-life Republicans believe life begins at conception, then logically Obama is a natural citizen of Hawaii. Either Obama is a citizen, or life does not begin at conception, contradicting the fundamental right-to-life belief. Arguments like these help show how poorly constructed arguments or logical fallacies are common tools of news media for political discussions, facilitating a certain agenda or ideological perspective.

Viewers of *The Daily Show* or *The Colbert Report* will not get the same kind of news coverage that they would get from reading hard-copy news or an online newspaper, but they learn a healthy skepticism about the objective truthfulness of news. To many young people, entering a discussion on current affairs can be intimidating. Both Stephen Colbert and Jon Stewart make it easier for younger audiences to analyze the rhetorical dimension of news stories, thus allowing the viewer to see bias and angle of vision. The use of satire is a means of allowing entertainment and information to mingle together on a critical level. These approaches to delivering news are energizing, providing an alternative to lackluster news sources that can make us feel like we're drowning in a sea of information. The conservative Fox News commentator Bill O'Reilly once called my generation "a bunch of stone slackers" who sit at home unengaged in politics and watching *The Daily Show* and *The Colbert Report*. Yeah, right. But I wonder, where did he get his information?

Critiquing "Information Plus Satire"

1. Christopher Moore's first criterion for a good news source is that it should keep viewers up-to-date with significant and important news rather than with ephemeral events like traffic accidents or celebrity divorces. Do you agree with Moore that *The Daily Show* and *The Colbert Report* keep viewers up-to-date with important news?

2. Moore's second criterion is the thought-provoking claim that a good news source teaches viewers to read the news rhetorically. What does he mean by reading the news rhetorically? How does he make his case? Are you persuaded?

3. Much of Christopher Moore's argument is topical in that it refers to events happening at the time he was drafting his essay (for example, the references to revolutions in Egypt or the release of government documents on WikiLeaks). One of his topical events concerns the "birther movement"—claims made by "birthers" that Barack Obama was born in Kenya rather than in Hawaii and therefore was constitutionally ineligible to be president. (Several months after Moore's essay was written, Obama released his long-form Hawaiian birth certificate, reducing the impact of the "birther movement.") How does this additional background information help you understand Moore's paragraph on "inconsistencies in ideological views on when life begins" (paragraph 6).

Our third reading is a political cartoon by Adey Bryant, a self-taught British cartoonist. In this whimsical visual argument, Bryant reinforces one of the environmental complaints against wind energy—the danger posed to migrating birds.

Well, It Bloody Wasn't There Last Year!

ADEY BRYANT

"Well, it bloody wasn't there last year!"

Critiquing "Well, It Bloody Wasn't There Last Year!"

1. Through the use of image and text, political cartoons can powerfully condense a complex argument into a brief statement with a claim and an implied line of reasoning. In your own words, what is the claim and implied supporting argument made by this cartoon?
2. How do the drawing, action, and words call attention to this drawback of wind energy?
3. What background knowledge about wind energy do readers need to possess before they understand this cartoon?

Our final readings are a guest opinion piece and a subsequent letter to the editor, both appearing in the *New York Times* in March 2011. The op-ed piece is by Christian Longo, a prisoner on death row in the Oregon State Penitentiary, convicted of the gruesome murder of his wife and three children. Longo's op-ed sparked wide debate in the blogosphere—partly because of the ethical issues raised by his argument and partly because of his bizarre history: he fled to Mexico after his crime and stole the identity of a *New York Times* reporter. In prison, Longo founded the organization GAVE (Gifts of Anatomical Value from Everyone). The responding letter to the editor (one of four that appeared in the *New York Times* on March 13, 2011) is by Dr. Kenneth Prager, a professor of clinical medicine and chairman of the Medical Ethics Committee at New York–Presbyterian Hospital/Columbia University Medical Center.

Giving Life after Death Row

CHRISTIAN LONGO

Salem, Ore. Eight years ago I was sentenced to death for the murders of my wife and three children. I am guilty. I once thought that I could fool others into believing this was not true. Failing that, I tried to convince myself that it didn't matter. But gradually, the enormity of what I did seeped in; that was followed by remorse and then a wish to make amends.

I spend 22 hours a day locked in a 6 foot by 8 foot box on Oregon's death row. There is no way to atone for my crimes, but I believe that a profound benefit to society can come from my circumstances. I have asked to end my remaining appeals, and then donate my organs after my execution to those who need them. But my request has been rejected by the prison authorities.

According to the United Network for Organ Sharing, there are more than 110,000 Americans on organ waiting lists. Around 19 of them die each day. There are more than 3,000 prisoners on death row in the United States, and just one inmate could save up to eight lives by donating a healthy heart, lungs, kidneys, liver and other transplantable tissues.

There is no law barring inmates condemned to death in the United States from donating their organs, but I haven't found any prisons that allow it. The main explanation is that Oregon and most other states use a sequence of three drugs for lethal injections that damages the organs. But Ohio and Washington use a larger dose of just one drug, a fast-acting barbiturate that doesn't destroy organs. If states would switch to a one-drug regimen, inmates' organs could be saved.

5   Another common concern is that the organs of prisoners may be tainted by infections, H.I.V. or hepatitis. Though the prison population does have a higher prevalence of such diseases than do non-prisoners, thorough testing can easily determine whether a prisoner's organs are healthy. These tests would be more reliable than many given to, say, a victim of a car crash who had signed up to be a donor; in the rush to transplant organs after an accident, there is less time for a full risk analysis.

There are also fears about security—that, for example, prisoners will volunteer to donate organs as part of an elaborate escape scheme. But prisoners around the country make hospital trips for medical reasons every day. And in any case, executions have to take place on prison grounds, so the organ removal would take place 10 there as well.

Aside from these logistical and health concerns, prisons have a moral reason for their reluctance to allow inmates to donate. America has a shameful history of using prisoners for medical experiments. In Oregon, for example, from 1963 to 1973, many inmates were paid to "volunteer" for research into the effects of radiation on testicular cells. Some ethicists believe that opening the door to voluntary donations would also open the door to abuse. And others argue that prisoners are simply unable to make a truly voluntary consent.

But when a prisoner initiates a request to donate with absolutely no enticements or pressure to do so, and if the inmate receives the same counseling afforded every prospective donor, there is no question in my mind that valid organ-donation consent can be given.

I am not the only condemned prisoner who wants the right to donate his organs. I have discussed this issue with almost every one of the 35 men on Oregon's death row, and nearly half of them expressed a wish to have the option of donating should their appeals run out.

I understand the public's apprehension. And I know that it could look as if what I really want are extra privileges or a reduction in my sentence. After all, in a rare and well-publicized case last December, Gov. Haley Barbour of Mississippi released two sisters who had been sentenced to life in prison so that one could donate a kidney to the other. But I don't expect to leave this prison alive. I am seeking nothing but the right to determine what happens to my body once the state has carried out its sentence.

If I donated all of my organs today, I could clear nearly 1 percent of my state's organ waiting list. I am 37 years old and healthy; throwing my organs away after I am executed is nothing but a waste.

And yet the prison authority's response to my latest appeal to donate was this: "The interests of the public and condemned inmates are best served by denying the petition."

Many in the public, most inmates, and especially those who are dying for lack of a healthy organ, would certainly disagree.

A Death Row Donation of Organs?

KENNETH PRAGER

The most important argument against carrying out Mr. Longo's altruistic wish to donate his organs for transplantation after he is executed is an ethical one. This would come too close to violating what ethicists call the dead-donor rule, which states that a person must never be killed for the purpose of removing organs for transplant.

Although his execution would be punishment for a quadruple

homicide, its linkage to organ removal would be too close to pass ethical muster. It would be reminiscent of an egregious violation of human rights, as when the Chinese executed scores of prisoners and harvested their organs to fuel a lucrative trade in organ transplants.

Moreover, the exploitation of prisoners for the ostensibly laudable reason of furthering medical knowledge should give us further pause before trying to wring benefit from an act of execution.

Organ donation from dead patients will always be a sensitive moral enterprise. We must not risk ethically sullying this practice by harvesting organs from executed prisoners.

Critiquing "Giving Life after Death Row" and "A Death Row Donation of Organs?"

1. Longo's proposal to allow organ donation from executed prisoners is supported by both categorical evaluation arguments and ethical arguments. How does Longo make the categorical case that his organs will be healthy? How does he make the ethical case that it is right for executed prisoners to be able to donate their organs? Besides his appeals to *logos*, how does he also try to create appeals to *ethos* and *pathos*?

2. What opposing arguments does Longo address? How well does he refute these opposing arguments?

3. In his responding letter to the editor, what objection does Kenneth Prager make to Longo's proposal? How do Longo's op-ed and Prager's response illustrate the ethical conflict between arguments from principle and arguments from consequences?

For additional writing, reading, and research resources, go to www.mycomplab.com

Proposal Arguments

14

Case 1 Should the Supreme Court Overturn *Roe v. Wade?*

Among the most heated debates in the United States is whether the due process and privacy protections of the Fourteenth Amendment can be extended to a woman's right to an abortion. The right-to-life movement has intensified its efforts to restrict access to abortions at the state level and to overturn *Roe v. Wade* in the U.S. Supreme Court. Meanwhile, pro-choice advocates such as Planned Parenthood have vigorously defended a woman's right to an abortion. Both sides make effective use of visual arguments. Right-to-life groups

When your right to an abortion is taken away, what are you going to do

Reproductive rights are under attack. The Pro-Choice Public Education Project. It's pro-choice or no choice.
1(688) 253-CHOICE or www.protect.choice.org

313

frequently use posters showing ultrasound images of unborn babies (often not using the word "fetus"). The poster on the previous page, sponsored by Planned Parenthood, features a starkly black question mark that on second look is seen to be made from a coat hanger. It makes an implied proposal claim ("Abortion should remain legal") and supports it with a consequence argument: If abortions are outlawed, women will have abortions anyway—using coat hangers instead of medically safe procedures. The image of the coat hanger (reminiscent of horror stories about abortions prior to *Roe v. Wade*) appeals simultaneously to *logos* and *pathos*.

Case 2 How Should the United States Reduce Its Dependence on Foreign Oil?

In 2010, the United States imported approximately 70 percent of its oil, much of it from the Middle East. Not only did this dependency threaten our economy and harm the environment, it also threatened national security. Conservatives often propose solving this problem through more drilling of domestic oil, particularly in offshore sites and in the Arctic National Wildlife Refuge. Liberals and environmentalists, meanwhile, pin their hopes on conservation and renewable sources such as wind and solar energy. Almost everyone is nervous about nuclear power, which has the advantage of not promoting global warming but carries enormous risk, as shown when radioactivity escaped from the Fukushima nuclear plant after Japan's 2011 earthquake and tsunami. With no large-scale technological solutions in sight, concerned citizens have proposed dozens of ideas for reducing domestic consumption of oil. Among the proposals are the following: placing a "green tax" on gasoline; requiring auto manufacturers to increase the fuel efficiency of their fleets; giving tax credits for buying a fuel-efficient car; increasing incentives for carpooling or taking public transportation; increasing the cost of parking; subsidizing hybrid or all-electric cars; charging different gas prices at the pump, with higher prices for less fuel-efficient cars; promoting telecommuting; and rebuilding cities so that housing is closer to worksites.

Although proposal arguments are the last type of argument we examine, they are among the most common arguments that you will encounter or be called on to write. In this chapter, you will learn to:

- Develop proposal arguments using a typical problem-solution-justification structure
- Use the claim-types strategy and the stock issues strategy to develop supporting reasons for your proposal argument
- Use words and images to create a one-page advocacy poster or advertisement

An Overview of Proposal Arguments

The essence of proposal arguments is that they call for action. In reading a proposal, the audience is enjoined to make a decision and then to act on it—to *do* something. Proposal arguments are sometimes called *should* or *ought* arguments because those helping verbs express the obligation to act: "We *should* do this [action]" or "We *ought* to do this [action]."

For instructional purposes, we will distinguish between two kinds of proposal arguments even though they are closely related and involve the same basic arguing strategies. The first kind we will call *practical proposals,* which propose an action to solve some kind of local or immediate problem. A student's proposal to change the billing procedures for scholarship students would be an example of a practical proposal, as would an engineering firm's proposal for the design of a new bridge being planned by a city government. The second kind we will call *policy proposals,* in which the writer offers a broad plan of action to solve major social, economic, or political problems affecting the common good. An argument that the United States should adopt a national health insurance plan or that the electoral college should be abolished would be an example of a policy proposal.

The primary difference is the narrowness versus breadth of the concern. *Practical* proposals are narrow, local, and concrete; they focus on the nuts and bolts of getting something done in the here and now. They are often concerned with the exact size of a piece of steel, the precise duties of a new person to be hired, or a close estimate of the cost of paint or computers to be purchased. *Policy* proposals, in contrast, are concerned with the broad outline and shape of a course of action, often on a regional, national, or even international issue. What government should do about overcrowding of prisons would be a problem addressed by policy proposals. How to improve the security alarm system for the county jail would be addressed by a practical proposal.

Learning to write both kinds of proposals is valuable. Researching and writing a *policy* proposal is an excellent way to practice the responsibilities of citizenship, which require the ability to understand complex issues and to weigh positive and negative consequences of policy choices. In your professional life, writing *practical* proposals may well be among your most important duties on the job. Effective proposal writing is the lifeblood of many companies and also constitutes one of the most powerful ways you can identify and help solve problems.

The Structure of Proposal Arguments

Proposal arguments, whether practical proposals or policy proposals, generally have a three-part structure: (1) description of a problem, (2) proposed solution, and (3) justification for the proposed solution. In the justification section of your proposal argument, you develop *because* clauses of the kinds you have practiced throughout this text.

Toulmin Framework for a Proposal Argument

The Toulmin schema is particularly useful for proposal arguments because it helps you find good reasons and link them to your audience's beliefs, assumptions, and values. Suppose that your university is debating whether to banish fraternities and sororities. Suppose further that you are in favor of banishing the Greek system. One of your arguments is that eliminating the Greek system will improve your university's academic reputation. The chart on page 317 shows how you might use the Toulmin schema to make this line of reasoning as persuasive as possible.

Special Concerns for Proposal Arguments

In their call for action, proposal arguments entail certain emphases and audience concerns that you don't generally face with other kinds of arguments. Let's look briefly at some of these special concerns.

- **The need for presence**. To persuade people to *act* on your proposal, particularly if the personal or financial cost of acting is high, you must give your argument presence as well as intellectual force. By *presence* we mean an argument's ability to grip your readers' hearts and imaginations as well as their intellects. You can give presence to an argument through appeals to *pathos* such as effective use of details, provocative statistics, dialogue, illustrative narratives, and compelling examples that show the reader the seriousness of the problem you are addressing or the consequences of not acting on your proposal.
- **The need to overcome people's natural conservatism**. Another difficulty with proposals is the innate conservatism of all human beings, whatever their political persuasion, as suggested by the popular adage "If it ain't broke, don't fix it." The difficulty of proving that something needs fixing is compounded by the fact that frequently the status quo appears to be working. So sometimes when writing a proposal, you can't argue that what we have is bad, but only that what we could have would be better. Often, then, a proposal argument will be based not on present evils but on the evils of lost potential. And getting an audience to accept lost potential may be difficult indeed, given the inherently abstract nature of potentiality.
- **The difficulty of predicting future consequences**. Further, most proposal makers will be forced to predict consequences of their proposed action. As the "law of unintended consequences" suggests, few major decisions lead neatly to their anticipated results without surprises along the way. So when we claim that our proposal will lead to good consequences, we can expect our audience to be skeptical.
- **The problem of evaluating consequences**. A final problem for proposal writers is the difficulty of evaluating consequences. In government and industry, managers often use a *cost-benefit analysis* to reduce all consequences to a single-scale comparison, usually money. Although this scale may work well in some circumstances, it can lead to grotesquely inappropriate conclusions in other situations. Just how does one balance the environmental benefits of high gasoline prices against the suffering of drivers who can't afford to get to work or the benefits of pollution-free nuclear power against the costs of a potential nuclear accident? Also, what will be a cost for one group will often be a benefit for others. For example, if Social Security benefits are cut, current workers will have smaller retirement incomes, but the savings can be used to reduce the national debt.

Toulmin Analysis of the Greek System Argument

ENTHYMEME

CLAIM Our university should eliminate the Greek system

REASON because doing so will improve our university's academic reputation.

GROUNDS

Evidence that eliminating the Greek system will improve our academic reputation:

- Excessive party atmosphere of some Greek houses emphasizes social life rather than studying—we are known as a party school.

- Last year the average GPA of students in fraternities and sororities was lower than the GPA of non-Greek students.

- New pledges have so many house duties and initiation rites that their studies suffer.

- Many new students think about rush more than about the academic life.

CONDITIONS OF REBUTTAL
Attacking the reason and grounds

- Many of the best students are Greeks. Last year's highest-GPA award went to a sorority woman, and several other Greeks won prestigious graduate school scholarships.

- Statistics on grades are misleading. Many houses had a much higher average GPA than the university average. Total GPA was brought down by a few rowdy houses.

- Many other high-prestige universities have Greek systems.

- There are ways to tone down the party atmosphere on campus without abolishing the Greek system.

- Greeks contribute significantly to the community through service projects.

WARRANT

It is good for our university to achieve a better academic reputation.

BACKING

- The school would attract more serious students, leading to increased prestige.

- Campus would be more academically focused and attract better faculty.

- Losing the "party-school" reputation would put us in better light for taxpayers and legislators.

- Students would graduate with more skills and knowledge.

CONDITIONS OF REBUTTAL
Attacking the warrant and backing

- No one will argue that it is not good to have a strong academic reputation.

- However, skeptics may say that eliminating sororities and fraternities won't improve the university's academic reputation but will hurt its social life and its wide range of living options.

These, then, are some of the general difficulties facing someone who sets out to write a proposal argument. Although these difficulties may seem daunting, the rest of this chapter offers strategies to help you overcome them and produce a successful proposal.

Developing a Proposal Argument

Writers of proposal arguments must focus in turn on three main phases or stages of the argument: showing that a problem exists, explaining the proposed solution, and offering a justification.

Convincing Your Readers that a Problem Exists

There is one argumentative strategy generic to all proposal arguments: calling your reader's attention to a problem. In some situations, your intended audience may already be aware of the problem and may have even asked for solutions. In such cases, you do not need to develop the problem extensively or motivate your audience to solve it. But in most situations, awakening your readers to the existence of a problem—a problem they may well not have recognized before—is your first important challenge. You must give your problem presence through anecdotes, telling statistics, or other means that show readers how the problem affects people or otherwise has important stakes. Your goal is to gain your readers' intellectual assent to the depth, range, and potential seriousness of the problem and thereby motivate them to want to solve it.

Typically, the arguer develops the problem in one of two places in a proposal argument—either in the introduction prior to the presentation of the arguer's proposal claim or in the body of the paper as the first main reason justifying the proposal claim. In the second instance the writer's first *because* clause has the following structure: "We should do this action *because* it addresses a serious problem."

Here is how one student writer gave presence to a proposal, addressed to the chair of the mathematics department at her school, calling for redesign of the first-year calculus curriculum in order to slow its pace. She wants the chair to see the problem from her perspective.

Example Passage Giving Presence to a Problem

For me, who wants to become a high school math teacher, the problem with introductory calculus is not its difficulty but its pace. My own experience in the Calculus 134 and 135 sequence last year showed me that it was not the learning of calculus that was difficult for me. I was able to catch on to the new concepts. My problem was that it went too fast. Just as I was assimilating new concepts and feeling the need to reinforce them, the class was on to a new topic before I had full mastery of the old concept. . . . Part of the reason for the fast pace is that calculus is a feeder course for computer science and engineering. If prospective engineering students can't learn the calculus rapidly, they drop out of the program. The high dropout rate benefits the Engineering School because they use the math course to weed out an overabundance of engineering applicants. Thus the pace of the calculus course is geared to the needs of the engineering curriculum, not to the needs of someone like me, who wants to be a high school mathematics teacher and who believes that my own difficulties with math—combined with my love for it—might make me an excellent math teacher.

By describing the fast pace of the math curriculum from the perspective of a future math teacher rather than an engineering student, this writer brings visibility to a problem.

What before didn't look like a problem (it is good to weed out weak engineering majors) suddenly became a problem (it is bad to weed out future math teachers). Establishing herself as a serious student genuinely interested in learning calculus, she gave presence to the problem by calling attention to it in a new way.

Showing the Specifics of Your Proposal

Having decided that there is a problem to be solved, you should lay out your thesis, which is a proposal for solving the problem. Your goal now is to stress the feasibility of your solution, including costs. The art of proposal making is the art of the possible. To be sure, not all proposals require elaborate descriptions of the implementation process. If you are proposing, for example, that a local PTA chapter buy new tumbling mats for the junior high gym classes, the procedures for buying the mats will probably be irrelevant. But in many arguments the specifics of your proposal—the actual step-by-step methods of implementing it—may be instrumental in winning your audience's support.

You will also need to show how your proposal will solve the problem either partially or wholly. Sometimes you may first need to convince your reader that the problem is solvable, not something intractably rooted in "the way things are," such as earthquakes or jealousy. In other words, expect that some members of your audience will be skeptical about the ability of any proposal to solve the problem you are addressing. You may well need, therefore, to "listen" to this point of view in your refutation section and to argue that your problem is at least partially solvable.

In order to persuade your audience that your proposal can work, you can follow any one of several approaches. A typical approach is to lay out a causal argument showing how one consequence will lead to another until your solution is effected. Another approach is to turn to resemblance arguments, either analogy or precedent. You try to show how similar proposals have been successful elsewhere. Or, if similar things have failed in the past, you try to show how the present situation is different.

The Justification: Convincing Your Readers that Your Proposal Should Be Enacted

The justification phase of a proposal argument will need extensive development in some arguments and minimal development in others, again depending on your particular problem and the rhetorical context of your proposal. If your audience already acknowledges the seriousness of the problem you are addressing and has simply been waiting for the right solution to come along, then your argument will be successful so long as you can convince your audience that your solution will work and that it won't cost too much. Such arguments depend on the clarity of your proposal and the feasibility of its being implemented.

But what if the costs are high? What if your readers don't think the problem is serious? What if they don't appreciate the benefits of solving the problem or the bad consequences of not solving it? In such cases you have to develop persuasive reasons for enacting your proposal. You may also have to determine who has the power to act on your proposal and apply arguments directly to that person's or agency's immediate interests. You need to know to whom or to what your power source is beholden or responsive and what values your power source holds that can be appealed to. You're looking, in short, for the best pressure points.

Proposal Arguments as Advocacy Posters or Advertisements

A frequently encountered kind of proposal argument is the one-page newspaper or magazine advertisement often purchased by advocacy groups to promote a cause. Such arguments also appear as Web pages or as posters or fliers. These condensed advocacy arguments are marked by their bold, abbreviated, tightly planned format. The creators of these arguments know they must work fast to capture our attention, give presence to a problem, advocate a solution, and enlist our support. Advocacy advertisements frequently use photographs, images, or icons that appeal to a reader's emotions and imagination. In addition to images, they often use different type sizes and styles. Large-type text in these documents frequently takes the form of slogans or condensed thesis statements written in an arresting style. To outline and justify their solutions, creators of advocacy ads often put main supporting reasons in bulleted lists and sometimes enclose carefully selected facts and quotations in boxed sidebars. To add an authoritative *ethos,* the arguments often include fine-print footnotes and bibliographies. (For more detailed discussion of how advocacy posters and advertisements use images and arrange text for rhetorical effect, see Chapter 9 on visual argument.)

Another prominent feature of these condensed, highly visual arguments is their appeal to the audience through a direct call for a course of action: go to an advocacy Web site to find more information on how to support the cause; cut out a postcardlike form to send to a decision maker; vote for or against the proposition or the candidate; write a letter to a political representative; or donate money to a cause.

An example of a student-produced advocacy advertisement is shown in Figure 14.1. Here student Lisa Blattner joins a heated debate in her city on whether to close down all-ages dance clubs. Frustrated because the evening dance options for under-twenty-one youth were threatened in Seattle, Lisa directed her ad toward the general readership of regional newspapers, with the special intention of reaching adult voters and parents. Lisa's ad uses three documentary-like, emotionally loaded, and disturbing photographs to give immediacy and presence to the problem. The verbal text in the ad states the proposal claim and provides three reasons in support of the claim. Notice how the reasons also pick up the ideas in the three photo images. The final lines of text memorably reiterate the claim and call readers to action. The success of this ad derives from the collaboration of layout, photos, and verbal text in conveying a clear, direct argument.

**What Is Left for Teenagers to Do When the Teen Ordinance
Bans Them from Dance Clubs?**

Take Ecstasy   Drink at Places with   Roam the Streets
at Raves   No Adult Supervision

Is There an Answer to These Problems?

**Yes! Through your support of the All Ages Dance Ordinance,
teens will have a safe place to go where:**

• **No hard drugs, like ecstasy and cocaine, are present**
• **Responsible adults are watching over everyone**
• **All of their friends can hang out in one place indoors, instead
  of outside with drug dealers, criminals, and prostitutes**

Give Your Child a Safe Place to Have Fun at Night

**Let the Seattle City Committee Know
That You Support the
All Ages Dance Ordinance**

FIGURE 14.1 Student advocacy advertisement

Now that you have been introduced to the main elements of a proposal argument, including condensed visual arguments, we explain in the next two sections two
invention strategies you can use to generate persuasive reasons for a proposal argument and to anticipate your audience's doubts and reservations. We call these the
"claim type strategy" and the "stock issues strategy."

Using the Claim Types Strategy to Develop a Proposal Argument

In Chapter 10 we explained how claim type theory can help you generate ideas for an argument. Specifically, we explained how evaluation and proposal claims often depend for their supporting reasons on claims about category, cause, or resemblance. This fact leads to a powerful idea-generating strategy based on arguments from category (which also includes argument from principle), on arguments from consequences, or on arguments from resemblance. This "claim types" strategy is illustrated in the following chart:

Explanation of Claim Types Strategy for Supporting a Proposal Claim

Claim Type	Generic Template	Example from Biotechnology Issue
Argument from principle or category	We should do this action ■ because doing so adheres to this good principle [or] ■ because this action belongs to this good category	We should support genetically modified foods ■ because doing so values scientific reason over emotion [or] ■ because genetically modified foods are safe
Argument from consequences	■ because this action will lead to these good consequences	■ because biotech crops can reduce world hunger ■ because biotech crops can improve the environment by reducing use of pesticides
Argument from resemblance	■ because this action has been done successfully elsewhere [or] ■ because this action is like this other good action	■ because genetic modification is like natural crossbreeding that has been accelerated [or] ■ because genetic modification of food is like scientific advancements in medicine

Before we give you some simple strategies for using this approach, let's illustrate it with another example.

Insurance companies should pay for long-term psychological counseling for anorexia (proposal claim)

■ because paying for such counseling is a demonstration of commitment to women's health. (principle/category)

■ because paying for such counseling may save insurance companies from much more extensive medical costs at a later date. (consequence)

■ because paying for anorexia counseling is like paying for alcoholism or drug counseling, which is already covered by insurance. (resemblance)

Note how each of these supporting reasons appeals to the value system of the audience. The writer hopes to show that covering the cost of counseling is within the class of things that the audience already values (commitment to women's health), will lead to consequences desired by the audience (reduced long-term costs), and is similar to something the audience already values (drug and alcohol counseling). The claim types strategy for generating ideas is easy to apply in practice. The following chart shows you how.

Suggestions for Applying the Claim Types Strategy to Your Proposal

Claim Type	Your Goal	Thinking Strategy
Argument from principle or category	Show how your proposed action follows a principle valued by your audience or belongs to a category valued by your audience.	■ Think of how your proposed action adheres to a rule or principle. ■ Use this template: "because doing this action is" and then fill in the blank with a noun or adjective: *kind, just, loving, courageous, merciful, legal, fair, democratic, constitutional, an act of hope, an illustration of the golden rule, faithful to the principle of limited government.* ■ If you are opposing a proposal, search for negative rather than positive principles/categories.
Argument from consequences	Show how your proposed action will lead to consequences valued by your audience.	■ Brainstorm consequences of your proposal and identify those that the audience will agree are good. ■ If you are opposing a proposal, search for negative consequences.
Argument from resemblance	Show how your proposed action has been done successfully elsewhere or is like another action valued by your audience.	■ Brainstorm places or times when your proposal (or something similar to it) has been done successfully. ■ Brainstorm analogies that compare your proposed action to something the audience already values. ■ If you are opposing a proposal, think of places or times where similar actions have failed or construct a negative analogy.

■ ■ ■ **FOR CLASS DISCUSSION** Generating Ideas Using the Claim Types Strategy

1. Working individually or in small groups, use the strategies of principle/category, consequence, and resemblance to create *because* clauses that support each of the following claims. Try to have at least one *because* clause from each of the categories, but generate as many reasons as possible. Don't worry about whether any individual reason exactly fits the category. The purpose is to stimulate thinking, not fill in the slots.

Example

Congress should not pass gun control laws (proposal claim)

- because the Second Amendment guarantees the right to own guns (principle or category)
- because owning a gun allows citizens to protect themselves, their homes, and their loved ones from intruders (consequence)
- because laws to ban guns will be as ineffective as laws to ban alcohol during Prohibition (resemblance)

   a. Marijuana should be legalized.

   b. Division I college athletes should receive salaries.

   c. High schools should pass out free contraceptives.

   d. Violent video games should be made illegal.

   e. Parents should be heavily taxed for having more than two children.

2. Repeat the first exercise, taking a different position on each issue.

Using the "Stock Issues" Strategy to Develop a Proposal Argument

Another effective way to generate ideas for a proposal argument is to ask yourself a series of questions based on the "stock issues" strategy. Suppose, for example, you wanted to develop the following argument: "In order to solve the problem of students who won't take risks with their writing, the faculty should adopt a pass/fail method of grading in all writing courses." The stock issues strategy invites the writer to consider "stock" ways (that is, common, usual, frequently repeated ways) that such arguments can be conducted.

Stock issue 1: *Is there really a problem here that needs to be solved?* Is it really true that a large number of student writers won't take risks in their writing? Is this problem more serious than other writing problems such as undeveloped ideas, lack of organization, and poor sentence structure? This stock issue invites the writer to convince her audience that a true problem exists. Conversely, an opponent to the proposal may argue that a true problem does not exist.

Stock issue 2: *Will the proposed solution really solve this problem?* Is it true that a pass/fail grading system will cause students to take more risks with their writing? Will more interesting, surprising, and creative essays result from pass/fail grading? Or will students simply put less effort into their writing? This stock issue prompts a supporter to demonstrate that the proposal will solve the problem; in contrast, it prompts the opponent to show that the proposal won't work.

Stock issue 3: *Can the problem be solved more simply without disturbing the status quo?* An opponent of the proposal may agree that a problem exists and that the proposed solution might solve it. However, the opponent may say, "Are there not less radical ways to solve this problem? If we want more creative and risk-taking student essays, can't we just change our grading criteria so that we reward risky papers and penalize conventional ones?" This stock issue prompts supporters to show that *only* the proposed solution will solve the problem and that no minor tinkering with the status quo will be adequate. Conversely, opponents will argue that the problem can be solved without acting on the proposal.

Stock issue 4: *Is the proposed solution really practical? Does it stand a chance of actually being enacted?* Here an opponent to the proposal may agree that the proposal would work but contends that it involves pie-in-the-sky idealism. Nobody will vote to change the existing system so radically; therefore, it is a waste of our time to debate it. Following this prompt, supporters would have to argue that pass/fail grading is workable and that enough faculty members are disposed to it that the proposal is worth debating. Opponents may argue that the faculty is so traditional that pass/fail has utterly no chance of being accepted, despite its merits.

Stock issue 5: *What will be the unforeseen positive and negative consequences of the proposal?* Suppose we do adopt a pass/fail system. What positive or negative consequences may occur that are different from what we at first predicted? Using this prompt, an opponent may argue that pass/fail grading will reduce the effort put forth by students and that the long-range effect will be writing of even lower quality than we have now. Supporters would try to find positive consequences—perhaps a new love of writing for its own sake rather than for the sake of a grade.

■ ■ ■ **FOR CLASS DISCUSSION** Brainstorming Ideas for a Proposal
The following collaborative task takes approximately two class days to complete. The exercise takes you through the process of creating a proposal argument.

1. In small groups, identify and list several major problems facing students in your college or university.
2. Decide among yourselves which are the most important of these problems and rank them in order of importance.
3. Take your group's number one problem and explore answers to the following questions. Group recorders should be prepared to present their group's answers to the class as a whole:
    a. Why is the problem a problem?
    b. For whom is the problem a problem?
    c. How will these people suffer if the problem is not solved? (Give specific examples.)
    d. Who has the power to solve the problem?
    e. Why hasn't the problem been solved up to this point?
    f. How can the problem be solved? (That is, create a proposal.)
    g. What are the probable benefits of acting on your proposal?
    h. What costs are associated with your proposal?
    i. Who will bear those costs?

  j. Why should this proposal be enacted?

  k. Why is it better than alternative proposals?

4. As a group, draft an outline for a proposal argument in which you

  a. describe the problem and its significance.

  b. propose your solution to the problem.

  c. justify your proposal by showing how the benefits of adopting that proposal outweigh the costs.

5. Recorders for each group should write their group's outline on the board and be prepared to explain it to the class.

EXAMINING VISUAL ARGUMENTS

A Proposal Claim

This advocacy poster, sponsored by the Endangered Wildlife Trust, presents a photograph of a dead baby albatross on a beach on Midway Island, a main nesting ground for albatrosses. The photo is part of environmental photographer Chris Jordan's 2009 exhibit "Midway: Message from the Gyre." In this exhibit, Jordan exposes the effects of increasing volumes of ocean garbage on albatrosses, who mistake the garbage for food. What policy proposal is the Endangered Wildlife Trust making in this poster? What action is it asking people to take? The colorful, plastic-filled carcass of the baby albatross creates a complex appeal to *pathos* in its effort to give presence to the problem. How does the verbal text help to interpret this appeal while driving home the *logos* of the argument?

WRITING ASSIGNMENT   A Proposal Argument

Option 1: A Practical Proposal Addressing a Local Problem Write a practical proposal offering a solution to a local problem. Your proposal should have three main sections: (1) description of the problem, (2) proposed solution, and (3) justification. Proposals are usually accompanied by a *letter of transmittal*—a one-page business letter that introduces the proposal to its intended audience and provides some needed background about the writer.

Document design is important in practical proposals, which are aimed at busy people who have to make many decisions under time constraints. An effective design helps establish the writer's *ethos* as a quality-oriented professional and helps make the reading of the proposal as easy as possible. For a student example of a practical proposal, see Megan Johnson's argument on pages 332–335.

Option 2: A Policy Proposal as a Guest Editorial Write a two- to three-page policy proposal suitable for publication as a feature editorial in a college or city newspaper or in a publication associated with a particular group, such as a church newsletter or employee bulletin. The voice and style of your argument should be aimed at readers of your chosen publication. Your editorial should have the following features:

1. The identification of a problem (Persuade your audience that this is a genuine problem that needs solving; give it presence.)
2. A proposal for action that will help alleviate the problem
3. A justification of your solution (the reasons why your audience should accept your proposal and act on it)

Option 3: A Researched Argument Proposing Public Policy Write an eight- to twelve-page proposal argument as a formal research paper, using researched data for development and support. In business and professional life, this kind of research proposal is often called a *white paper*, which recommends a course of action internally within an organization or externally to a client or stakeholder. An example of a researched policy proposal is student writer Juan Vazquez's "Why the United States Should Adopt Nuclear Power" on pages 336–340.

Option 4: Multimedia Project: A One-Page Advocacy Advertisement Using the strategies of visual argument discussed in Chapter 9 and on pages 320–321 of this chapter, create a one-page advocacy advertisement urging action on a public issue. Your advertisement should be designed for publication in a newspaper or for distribution as a poster or flier. An example of a student-produced advocacy advertisement is shown in Figure 14.1 on page 321.

Option 5: Multimedia Project: A Proposal Speech with Visual Aids Deliver a proposal argument as a prepared but extemporaneous speech of approximately five to eight minutes, supported with visual aids created on presentation software such as PowerPoint. Your speech should present a problem, propose a solution, and justify the solution with reasons and evidence. Use visual aids to give "presence" to the problem and to enhance appeals to *logos*, *ethos*, and *pathos*. Good aids use visual strategies to create encapsulated visual arguments; they are not simply bullet point outlines of your speech. Sandy Wainscott's speech outline and selected PowerPoint slides (pages 343–345) illustrate this genre.

Exploring Ideas

Because *should* or *ought* issues are among the most common sources of arguments, you may already have ideas for proposal issues. To think of ideas for practical proposals, try making an idea map of local problems you would like to see solved. For initial spokes, try trigger words such as the following:

- Problems at my university (dorms, parking, registration system, financial aid, campus appearance, clubs, curriculum, intramural program, athletic teams)
- Problems in my city or town (dangerous intersections, ugly areas, inadequate lighting, parks, police policy, public transportation, schools)
- Problems at my place of work (office design, flow of customer traffic, merchandise display, company policies)
- Problems related to my future career, hobbies, recreational time, life as a consumer, life as a homeowner

If you can offer a solution to the problem you identify, you may make a valuable contribution to some phase of public life.

To find a topic for policy proposals, stay in touch with the news, which will keep you aware of current debates on regional and national issues. Also, visit the Web sites of your congressional representatives to see what issues they are currently investigating and debating. You might think of your policy proposal as a white paper for one of your legislators.

Once you have decided on a proposal issue, we recommend you explore it by trying one or more of the following activities:

- Explore ideas by using the claim types strategy (see pages 322–324).
- Explore ideas by using the "stock issues" strategy (see pages 324–325).
- Explore ideas using the eleven questions (a–k) on pages 325–326.

Identifying Your Audience and Determining What's at Stake

Before drafting your argument, identify your targeted audience and determine what's at stake. Consider your responses to the following questions:

- What audience are you targeting? What background do they need to understand your problem? How much do they already care about it? How could you motivate them to care?
- After they read your argument, what stance do you imagine them holding? What change do you want to bring about in their view or their behavior?
- What will they find uncomfortable or threatening about your proposal? Particularly, what costs will they incur by acting on your proposal?

- What objections might they raise? What counterarguments or alternative solutions will you need to address?
- Why does your proposal matter? What is at stake?

Organizing a Proposal Argument

When you write your draft, you may find it helpful to have at hand an organization plan for a proposal argument. The plan on page 330 shows a typical structure for a proposal argument. In some cases, you may want to summarize and rebut opposing views before you present the justification for your own proposal.

Designing a One-Page Advocacy Advertisement

As an alternative to a traditional written argument, your instructor may ask you to create a one-page advocacy advertisement. The first stage of your invention process should be the same as that for a longer proposal argument. Choose a controversial public issue that needs immediate attention or a neglected issue about which you want to arouse public passion. As with a longer proposal argument, consider your audience in order to identify the values and beliefs on which you will base your appeal.

When you construct your argument, the limited space available demands efficiency in your choice of words and in your use of document design. Your goal is to have a memorable impact on your reader in order to promote the action you advocate. The following questions may help you design and revise your advocacy ad:

1. How could photos or other graphic elements establish and give presence to the problem?
2. How can type size, typestyle, and layout be used to present the core of your proposal, including the justifying reasons, in the most powerful way for the intended audience?
3. Can any part of this argument be presented as a memorable slogan or catchphrase? What key phrases could highlight the parts or the main points of this argument?
4. How can document design clarify the course of action and the direct demand on the audience this argument is proposing?
5. How can use of color enhance the overall impact of your advocacy argument? (Note: One-page advertisements are expensive to reproduce in color, but you might make effective use of color if your advocacy ad were to appear as a poster or Web page.)

Designing PowerPoint Slides or Other Visual Aids for a Speech

In designing visual aids, your goal is to increase the persuasive effect of your speech rather than to demonstrate your technical wizardry. A common mistake with Power-Point presentations is to get enamored with the program's bells and whistles. If you find yourself thinking about special effects (animations, fade-outs, flashing letters) rather than about "at a glance" visual appeals to *logos* or *pathos*, you may be on the wrong track. Another common mistake is to use slides simply to project a bullet point outline of your speech. Our best advice in designing slides is thus to "think visual argument."

Organization Plan for a Proposal Argument

Introduce and develop the problem.	• Engage readers' interest in your problem. • Provide background, including previous attempts to solve the problem. • Give the problem "presence" by showing who is affected and what is at stake. • Argue that the problem is solvable (optional).
Present your proposed solution to the problem.	• First, state your proposal concisely to serve as your thesis statement or claim. • Then, explain the specifics of your proposal.
Justify your proposed solution through a series of supporting reasons.	• Restate your claim and forecast your supporting reasons. • Present and develop reason 1. • Present and develop reason 2. • Present and develop additional reasons.
Respond to objections or to alternative proposals.	• Anticipate and summarize possible objections or alternative ways to solve the problem. • Respond appropriately through rebuttal or concession.
Conclude.	• Sum up your argument and help readers return to the "big picture" of what's at stake. • Call readers to action. • End with something memorable.

In terms of visual argument, effective presentation slides can usually be placed in three design categories:

- Slides using images (photographs, drawings) to enhance *pathos* or to create snapshot visual clarity of a concept (*logos*)
- Slides using graphs or other visual displays of numbers to make numeric arguments
- Slides using bulleted (all-text) subpoints for evidence

All the strategies for visual arguments discussed in Chapter 9 and in this chapter under "Proposal Arguments as Advocacy Posters or Advertisements" (pages 320–321) apply equally to presentation slides.

In most cases, the "title" of the slide should put into words the "take-away point" of the slide—a verbal summary of the slide's visual argument. Most rhetoricians suggest that the title of a slide be a short sentence that makes a point rather than just a topic phrase.

Topic as Title (Weak)	Point as Title (Strong)
Coal and the Environment	Burning Coal Produces Dangerous Greenhouse Gases
The Effect of Money on Happiness	More Money Doesn't Mean More Happiness

Student writer Sandy Wainscott tried to follow these principles in her speech and accompanying PowerPoint slides, shown on pages 343–345. ■

Questioning and Critiquing a Proposal Argument

As we've suggested, proposal arguments need to overcome the innate conservatism of people, the difficulty of anticipating all the consequences of a proposal, and so forth. What questions, then, can we ask about proposal arguments to help us anticipate these problems?

Will a skeptic deny that my problem is really a problem? Be prepared for skeptics who aren't bothered by your problem, who see your problem as limited to a small group of people, or who think you are exaggerating.

Will a skeptic doubt the effectiveness of my solution? A skeptic might agree that your problem is indeed important and worth solving, but will not be convinced that your solution will work. For these skeptics, you'll need to provide evidence that your solution is feasible and workable. Also be prepared for skeptics who focus on the potential negative or unintended consequences of your proposed solution.

Will a skeptic think my proposal costs too much? The most commonly asked question of any proposal is simply, "Do the benefits of enacting the proposal outweigh the costs?" Be wary of the (understandable) tendency to underestimate the costs and exaggerate the benefits of a proposal. Honesty will enhance your *ethos.*

Will a skeptic suggest counterproposals? Once you've convinced readers that a problem exists, they are likely to suggest solutions different from yours. It only makes sense to anticipate alternative solutions and to work out ways to argue why your solution is better. And who knows, you may end up liking the counterproposal better and changing your mind about what to propose!

Our first reading, by student writer Megan Johnson, is a practical proposal **READINGS**
addressing the problem of an inequitable meal plan on her campus—one
that she claims discriminates against women. As a practical proposal, it uses headings and
other elements of document design aimed at giving it a finished and professional appearance. When sent to the intended audience, it is accompanied by a single-spaced letter of
transmittal following the conventional format of a business letter.

A Practical Proposal

MEGAN JOHNSON (STUDENT)

Ms. Jane Doe

Vice-President for Budgeting and Finance

Certain University

Certain City

Certain State, Zip

Dear Ms. Doe:

Enclosed is a proposal that addresses our university's minimum meal plan requirements for students living on campus. My proposal shows the problems associated with this
requirement and suggests a workable solution for the university.

The enclosed proposal suggests a modest plan for allowing students to use their campus
cards to purchase items off campus. Currently, students are required to purchase a minimum meal plan of $1,170, even though women eat less than men and often have to donate
unspent meal funds back to the university. This proposal would give students the option to
spend some of their meal plan money off campus. The benefits of my plan include more
fairness to women students, fewer incentives toward binge eating, more opportunities for
student bonding, and better relations with the nearby business community.

Through web research, I have discovered that other universities have systems in place
similar to what I am proposing. I hope that my proposal is received well and considered as
a workable option. A change in the minimum meal plan requirement might make our university a more desirable option for more prospective students as well as ultimately benefit
the general welfare of the current student body.

Thank you for your time.

Sincerely,
Megan Johnson (Student)

A Proposal to Allow Off-Campus Purchases with a Meal Card
Submitted by Megan Johnson (Student)

Problem

The problem with this university's required meal plan is that it is too large for many students, particularly women. For example, at the end of Winter Quarter, my final balance on my meal card was $268.50, all of which, except for $100, I had to donate back to the university. As the current system stands, students have to purchase a minimum meal plan for living on campus. The minimum meal plan totals $1,170 per quarter. During the academic year an amount of $100 may be rolled into the next quarter. At the end of the quarter any remaining funds, excluding the $100, will be removed from the meal plan. Therefore, if students do not spend the money on their meal plans, it will be wasted. As a woman, I am frustrated about having to decide whether to give my money back to the university or to use up my meal card by binge eating at the end of each quarter.

Proposed Solution

I propose that our university create a system in which students are able to use their campus meal plans at local businesses off campus such as local drug stores, grocery stores, and restaurants. As I will note later in this proposal, other universities have such a system, so the technical difficulties should be easy to solve. Basically, the card works as a debit card loaded with the amount of money the student places on the card. Local businesses would swipe a student's card the same way as the on-campus food service currently does, deducting the current charge against the amount still available on the card. It would probably be possible to limit the total number of dollars available for spending off campus.

Justification

My proposal would allow on-campus residential students to use some of their meal plan money on groceries, on non-food related items such as toiletries, or on an occasional off-campus meal at a local restaurant. This proposal would resolve the problem of gender bias in the current system, promote opportunities for more bonding among students, and ultimately help create a healthier student body. Moreover, it would show the university's commitment to its students' welfare.

First of all, the current meal plan policy tends to discriminate against women. All students on campus are required to have a minimum meal plan, even though men and women have clearly different eating habits. Men tend to eat much more than women and frequently have to add money to their meal plans to get through the quarter. In contrast, many women, like myself, don't use up their prepaid amounts. For example, my friend James ran out of his meal plan by the eighth week of the quarter whereas my roommate Blaire still had over $400 left on her card at the end of the quarter. She and I, like many other women, will have to donate our money back to the school. Therefore, women often feel cheated out of their money while men do not. It is discriminatory to require all students, regardless of gender, to have the same minimum meal plan. However, if the university is going to require all students to have the same minimum meal plan, then the university needs to give women

more options to spend their money on things other than food purchased in the school dining halls.

5   In addition, my proposal would create more opportunities for bonding. For example, it
would allow persons who love to cook, such as me, to use the residence hall kitchens to create "home-cooked meals" for floor mates, thus creating more friendships among students.
Personally, I have had the pleasure of helping create such bonds among the women on my
floor by cooking a "family dinner" in our floor's kitchen. The aroma of the roasted chicken
and homemade mashed potatoes drew the students on the fifth floor into the lounge. After our shared dinner, it seemed as if our floor felt more comfortable being around each
other in a more family-like way. I think that cooking on campus gives students a sense of
comfort that they do not get when they go to the dining halls and have food pre-made for
them. While I would love to cook dinner for my floor more often, the bottom line is that
ingredients are too expensive to pay for on my regular credit card when I have already
purchased from the university more food than I can eat. If the school were to implement a
system where we could use a portion of our meal plans off campus, students would be able
to buy groceries from local stores and to put to better use the kitchens already built into the
residence halls.

       In addition to creating closer bonds between students, an off-campus option for our
meal cards would help women eat more healthfully. The current system promotes bad eating habits causing women to overeat or even to binge in order to use up their extra meal
plan money. For example, with the left over money on my card at the end of Fall Quarter,
I bought cases of energy drinks which are filled with high fructose corn syrup and other
empty calories. As another example, my friend Amber purchases multiple meals such as
pizza and a burger for dinner because she doesn't want to waste her money. Overeating is
obviously unhealthy and could eventually lead to an increase in obesity or eating disorders.
However, if students were able to use their meal card off campus, they could buy items
such as shampoo or other toiletries, which would be more beneficial for women than overeating to avoid losing money.

       Despite all these benefits of a new meal plan system, some administrators might be
skeptical of the benefits and focus on the drawbacks instead. The biggest drawback is the
potential loss of revenue to food services. As it is now, women help subsidize food costs
for men. Without that subsidy, the food service might not be able to break even, forcing
them to raise food costs for everyone. I don't have the financial expertise to know how to
compute these costs. Clearly, however, other universities have thought about these issues
and decided that allowing students to spend some of their food money off campus was a
benefit worth providing for students. For example, the University of Texas, the University
of Minnesota, and the University of Florida allow their meal cards to be used as debit cards
at local businesses. As stated on their website, the University of Texas has a system called
Bevo Bucks in which students can "purchase food, goods and services at participating locations, both on and off campus" by loading money onto their ID cards. Also according to
the University of Minnesota's website, students have a system called FlexDine connected
to their ID cards. FlexDine gives students the "convenience . . . [to eat] at PAPA JOHN's
for residence hall residents." If other schools can implement off campus use of dining

cards, then the plan is feasible. It might also be possible to limit the number of dollars that could be spent each quarter off campus in order to assure a minimum level of revenue for the food service.

Even if my proposal would be costly in terms of lost revenue to the food service, the benefits of my plan might still outweigh the costs. A revised meal card system might become a recruiting point for prospective students because they would feel as if the university is more personalized to fit the students' needs rather than just the university's needs. My proposal might help prospective students see how close the students at our university are and might draw more students to apply here. (Our website and view books could even include pictures of students' cooking in the resident hall kitchens or eating at a local restaurant.) Moreover local off-campus businesses would welcome the opportunity for more student customers and might offer special promotions for students. A new meal card system might even improve the relationship between the university and the surrounding community.

Based on all these reasons, I believe that the university community as a whole would benefit if my proposal were enacted. The new plan would be especially appreciated by women students, many of whom now subsidize the food costs of men. In addition, the new system would bring students closer together by encouraging more creative use of the residence hall kitchens for community meals and by reducing the incentive toward binge eating at the end of each quarter. Finally, if other universities can use this system then our university should be able to use it as well. Although the food service may lose money to local businesses, the university would ultimately benefit by creating a more flexible and attractive meal option—especially for women—and by showing administrative concern for student welfare.

Critiquing "A Proposal to Allow Off-Campus Purchases with a University Meal Card"

1. In your own words, summarize briefly the problem that Megan Johnson addresses, her proposed solution, and her justifying reasons.
2. Megan addresses her proposal to Ms. Jane Doe, an administrator who has the power to change policy. To what extent does Megan develop audience-based reasons that resonate for this audience of university administrators? How effectively does she anticipate and respond to objections her audience might raise?
3. How does Megan establish a positive *ethos* in this argument? To what extent does she appeal to *pathos* as well as *logos*?
4. How effective is Megan's proposal?

Our second reading, by student writer Juan Vazquez, is a researched public policy proposal written in response to the option 3 assignment on page 327. Vazquez's argument is based on library and Internet research he conducted into the problem of fossil fuels and climate change. It is formatted as a formal research paper using the documentation style of the Modern Language Association (MLA).

Vazquez 1

Juan Vazquez

Professor Bean

English 210

15 July 2008

Why the United States Should Adopt Nuclear Power

Thousands of studies conducted by scientists to measure climate change over the last one hundred years have accumulated substantial evidence that global warming is occurring unequivocally. According to the NASA *Earth Observatory* web site, greenhouse gas emissions caused the average surface temperature of the Earth to increase by 0.6 to 0.9 degrees Celsius between 1906 and 2006. If fossil fuel energy continues to be burned relentlessly, scientists are predicting that the average surface temperatures could rise between 2°C and 6°C by the end of the twenty-first century (Riebeek). A prevalent consensus among scientists is that humans are a major culprit in global warming by burning fossil fuels such as coal and petroleum, with coal-fired power plants being one of the major problems. Lately, discussion has focused on what governments in developed countries can do to tackle climate change.

One solution, advocated by scientist William Sweet writing for the magazine *Discover*, is that the United States should expand its long-ignored nuclear power industry. However, many people—especially environmentalists—are afraid of nuclear power and believe that we can solve global warming through other alternatives. Despite these fears and counter-arguments, I believe that Sweet is right about nuclear energy. The United States should as quickly as possible phase out coal-burning power plants and replace them with nuclear power and other green technologies.

Before we look at the advantages of nuclear power, it is important to see why many people are opposed to it. First, opponents argue that nuclear power plants aren't safe. They regularly cite the Three Mile Island accident in 1979 and the disastrous Chernobyl meltdown in 1986. A more exhaustive list of recent small scale but worrisome nuclear accidents is provided by an editorial from the *Los Angeles Times,* which describes how a July 2007 magnitude 6.8 earthquake in Japan "caused dozens of problems at the world's biggest nuclear plant, leading to releases of radioactive elements into the air and ocean and an indefinite shutdown" ("No to Nukes"). Opponents also argue that nuclear plants are attractive terrorist targets. A properly placed explosive could spew radioactive material over wide swathes of densely populated areas. Nuclear power plants also provide opportunities for terrorists to steal plutonium for making their own nuclear weapons.

Second, while agreeing that nuclear power plants don't produce greenhouse gases, opponents remind us that radioactive waste cannot be stored safely and that radioactive waste remains hazardous for tens of thousands of years. The heavy walled concrete containers used to enclose nuclear waste will eventually develop cracks. If the planned disposal facility at Yucca Mountain, Nevada—where wastes would be stored in concrete and steel containers deep underground—ever becomes operational, it would ease the waste issue for the United States but would not eliminate it. The dangerous nuclear waste would still have to be trucked to Nevada, and even the Nevada site might not be completely impervious to earthquake damage or to the possibility that future generations would dig it up accidentally.

Finally, opponents claim that nuclear power plants are extremely expensive and the process of building them is extremely slow so that this method won't provide any short-term solutions for climate change. According to the "No to Nukes" editorial from the *Los Angeles Times,* the average nuclear plant is estimated to cost about $4 billion, making nuclear-generated energy about 25% to 75% more expensive than old-fashioned coal. At the same time, the regulatory process for building nuclear power plants is slow and unpredictable, making investors hesitant about supplying the capital needed. Opponents of nuclear energy argue that these high costs and long waiting period would make it impossible to launch a massive construction of nuclear power plants that would have an immediate impact on global warming.

So in the face of these risks, why should we support Sweet's proposal for expanding nuclear technology? One answer is that some of the fears about nuclear plants are overstated, fabricated, or politicized. It is true that in the past there have been accidents at nuclear power plants, but improvements in technology make such disasters in the future very unlikely. According to Sweet, changes in the design of nuclear reactors in the United States make them "virtually immune to the type of accident that occurred at Chernobyl in April 1986" (62). Furthermore, Sweet points out, the oft-cited Three Mile Island accident didn't injure a single person and led to a better regulatory system that makes new reactors much safer than old ones. According to Sweet, today's "coal fired power plants routinely kill tens of thousands of people in the United States each year by way of lung cancer, bronchitis, and other ailments; the U.S. nuclear economy kills virtually no one in a normal year" (62). In addition, management of power plants has improved. As for the fear of terrorist threats and nuclear proliferation, these concerns have been blown out of proportion. As Sweet argues, if any terrorists are seeking to produce bombs, their access to plutonium will not depend on how many nuclear power plants the U.S. is building. Because nuclear power plants must be housed within concrete containment barriers to prevent damage from earthquakes, hurricanes, and floods, they are also resistant to terrorist attacks. A study carried out by the Electric Power Research Institute and reported in a major study of nuclear power by scientists from MIT showed that an airplane crashing into a U.S. nuclear power plant would not breech the containment barriers (*Future of Nuclear Power* 50). Moreover, nuclear scientists say that the safe containment of nuclear waste is not a technical problem but a political problem.

Although nuclear reactors are not risk free, they are much safer for people's health and for the environment than are coal-fired plants with their pollution-spewing greenhouse gases. According to the MIT study on nuclear power, since the first commercial nuclear reactor was built in the United States in 1957 (there are now currently 100 nuclear reactors in the United States), there has been only one accident that caused core damage (Three Mile Island). Using statistical analysis, the researchers estimate that the current safety regulations and design specifications will limit core damage frequency to about 1 accident per 10,000 reactor-per-years. They also believe that the technology exists to reduce the rate of serious accidents to 1 in 100,000 reactor-years (*Future of Nuclear Power* 48). The benefits of nuclear power for reducing global warming therefore outweigh the real but very low risks of using nuclear energy.

As to the problem of nuclear power's expense, it is true that nuclear plants are more expensive than coal plants, but it is important to understand that the high initial cost of building a nuclear power plant is being compared to the artificially low cost of coal power. If we were to tax coal-burning plants through a cap and trade system so that coal plants would have to pay for social and environmental costs of pollution and production of greenhouse gases, nuclear power would become more competitive. As Sweet argues, we need a tax or equivalent trading scheme that would increase the cost of coal-generated electricity to encourage a switch from cheap coal to more environmentally friendly nuclear power plants.

Nuclear power plants are not the perfect or sole alternative to burning coal to generate energy, but they are certainly the most effective for combating global warming. Without nuclear power plants, we can't generate enough electricity to meet U.S. demands while also reducing carbon emissions. There are other alternatives such as wind technology, but this is also more expensive than coal and not nearly as reliable as nuclear power. Wind turbines only generate energy about a third of the time, which would not be enough to meet peak demands, and the problem of building enough wind towers and creating a huge distribution system to transmit the power from remote windy regions to cities where the power is needed is overwhelming. Currently wind power generates less than 1% of the nation's electricity whereas nuclear power currently generates 20 percent (Sweet). According to Jesse Ausubel, head of the Program for the Human Environment at Rockefeller University, "To reach the scale at which they would contribute importantly to meeting global energy demand, renewable sources of energy such as wind, water, and biomass cause serious environmental harm. Measuring renewables in watts per square meter, nuclear has astronomical advantages over its competitors."

To combat global warming we need to invest in strategies that could make a large difference fairly quickly. The common belief that we can slow global warming by switching to fluorescent light bulbs, taking the bus to work, and advocating for wind or solar energy is simply wrong. According to science writer Matt Jenkins, the climate problem is solvable. "But tackling it is going to be a lot harder than you've been led to believe" (39). Jenkins summarizes the work of Princeton researchers Stephen Pacala and Robert Socolow, who have identified a "package of greenhouse gas reduction measures" (44), each measure of which they call a "stabilization wedge." Each wedge would reduce carbon gas emissions by one gigaton. Pacala and Socolow have identified 15 possible stabilization wedges and have shown that adopting 7 of these wedges will reduce carbon emissions to the levels needed to halt global warming. One of Pacala and Socolow's wedges could be achieved by raising the fuel economy of 2 billion cars from 30 mpg to 60 mpg (Jenkins 44). Another wedge would come from building 50 times more wind turbines than currently exist in the world or 700 times more solar panels. In contrast, we could achieve a wedge simply by doubling the number of nuclear power plants in the world. Nuclear power is clearly not the only solution to climate change. In Pacala and Socolow's scheme, it is at most one-seventh of the solution, still forcing us to take drastic measures to conserve energy, stop the destruction of rain forests, develop clean-burning coal, and create highly fuel-efficient automobiles. But nuclear energy produces the quickest, surest, and most dramatic reduction of the world's carbon footprint. If we do not take advantage of its availability, we will need to get equivalent carbon-free power from other sources, which may not be possible and will certainly be more expensive. Therefore expanded use of nuclear technology has to be part of the solution to stop global warming. We should also note that other countries are already way ahead of us in the use of nuclear technology. France gets almost 80% of its electricity from nuclear power and Sweden almost 50% ("World Statistics"). These countries have accepted the minimal risks of nuclear power in favor of a reduced carbon footprint and a safer environment.

In sum, we should support Sweet's proposal for adopting nuclear power plants as a major national policy. However, there are other questions that we need to pursue. Where are we going to get the other necessary wedges? Are we going to set gas mileage requirements of 60 mpg on the auto industry? Are we going to push research and development for ways to burn coal cleanly by sequestering carbon emissions in the ground? Are we going to stop destruction of the rain forests? Are we going to fill up our land with wind towers to get one more wedge? If all these questions make climate change seem unsolvable, it will be even more difficult if we cannot factor in nuclear technology as a major variable in the equation.

Works Cited

Ausubel, Jesse H. "Renewable and Nuclear Heresies." Canadian Nuclear Association. Ottowa, CA. 10 Mar. 2005. Plenary Address. *Nuclear Green.* Web. 20 June 2008.

The Future of Nuclear Power: An Interdisciplinary MIT Study. Massachusetts Institute of Technology, 29 July 2003. Web. 20 June 2008.

Jenkins, Matt. "A Really Inconvenient Truth." *Miller McClune* April-May 2008: 38-49. Print.

"No to Nukes." Editorial. *Los Angeles Times.* Los Angeles Times, 23 July 2007. Web. 1 July 2008.

Riebeek, Holli. "Global Warming." *Earth Observatory.* NASA, 11 May 2007. Web. 18 June 2008.

Sweet, William. "Why Uranium Is the New Green." *Discover* Aug. 2007: 61-62. Print.

"World Statistics: Nuclear Energy around the World." *Resources and Stats.* Nuclear Energy Institute, 2008. Web. 19 June 2008.

Critiquing "Why the United States Should Adopt Nuclear Power"

1. What are Juan Vazquez's major reasons for building more nuclear power plants? Which of these reasons do you feel is most persuasive?
2. What are your own major objections to building more nuclear power plants? Do you have any objections that Vazquez fails to summarize?
3. To what extent does Vazquez respond persuasively to your objections? Which of his refutations of the anti-nuke arguments is weakest?
4. How effective is Vazquez's use of audience-based reasons? How would you evaluate his overall appeal to *logos, ethos,* and *pathos*?

Our third reading is the one-page paid advocacy advertisement on page 342. This is the second in a series of ads produced by the Center for Children's Health and the Environment, located at Mount Sinai School of Medicine in New York. The ads were intended to work in concert with the organization's Web site, http:// www.childenvironment.org, which provides backup documentation including access to the scientific studies on which the ads' arguments are based. All the ads can be downloaded as PDF files from the Web site. The ads' purpose is to call public attention to environmental dangers to children and to urge public action.

Critiquing the Advocacy Ad from the Center for Children's Health and the Environment

1. A difficulty faced by many proposal writers is awakening the audience to the existence of the problem. The doctors and researchers who founded the Center for Children's Health and the Environment felt that a series of full-page newspaper ads was the best way to awaken the public to a problem that Americans either denied or didn't know existed.

   a. In your own words, what is the problem that this proposal addresses?
   b. How does the ad give presence to the problem?

2. How does this ad use the strategies of visual argument (use of images, arrangement of text, type size, and so forth) discussed in Chapter 9? The ad makers probably had available thousands of pictures to use in this ad. Why did they choose this photograph? Try to reconstruct the thinking of the ad makers when they decided on their use of type sizes and fonts. How is the message in different parts of the ad connected to the visual presentation of the words?

3. How effective is the verbal argument of this advertisement? Why does it place "Toxic chemicals appear linked to rising rates of some cancers" in boldface type at the beginning of the text?

4. Most of this ad is devoted to presentation of the problem. What does the ad actually propose?

5. Overall, how effective do you find this advocacy advertisement? If you were thumbing through a newspaper, would you stop to read this ad? If so, what would hook you?

More kids are getting brain cancer.
Why?

Toxic chemicals appear linked to rising rates of some cancers.

As scientists and physicians, we've seen a drop in the death rates of many adult and childhood cancers because of earlier detection and better treatment. But we are also seeing a disturbing rise in the reported *incidence* of cancer among young children and adolescents, especially brain cancer, testicular cancer, and acute lymphocytic leukemia. In fact, after injuries and violence, cancer is the leading cause of death in our children.

The increase in childhood cancers may be explained in part by better detection or better access to medical care. But evidence suggests the rise in these childhood cancers, as well as in cancers like non-Hodgkin's lymphoma and multiple myeloma among adults, may also be partially explained by exposure to chemicals in the environment, chemicals found in many products, from paints and pesticides to dark-colored hair dyes.

What We Know

Pound for pound, kids are exposed to more toxic chemicals in food, air, and water than adults, because children breathe twice as much air, eat three to four times more food, and drink as much as two to seven times more water. Recent epidemiologic studies have shown that as children's exposures to home and garden pesticides increase, so does their risk of non-Hodgkin's lymphoma, brain cancer, and leukemia. Yet, right now, you can go to your hardware store and buy lawn pesticides, paint thinner and weed killers, all containing toxic chemicals linked to these diseases.

In both children and adults, the incidence rate for non-Hodgkin's lymphoma has increased thirty percent since 1950. The disease has been linked to industrial chemicals, chemicals found in agricultural, home, and garden pesticides, as well as dark hair dyes.

Studies have shown that Vietnam veterans and chemical workers exposed to Agent Orange, a phenoxy herbicide, are especially at risk for non-Hodgkin's lymphoma. American farmers who use phenoxy herbicides have an increased risk of the cancer. A Swedish study showed that among the general population, the risk of non-Hodgkin's lymphoma rises with increased exposure to these herbicides. And, a study in Southern California found that children of parents who use home pesticides have seven times the risk of non-Hodgkin's lymphoma. Multiple myeloma, a bone marrow cancer, is also associated with toxic chemicals. Its incidence has tripled since 1950. Farmers are especially at risk: a recent analysis of thirty-two studies worldwide showed "consistent, positive findings" of an association between farming and multiple myeloma.

What We Can Do

There is much that parents can do to protect their children from carcinogenic chemicals, beginning with the elimination of many pesticides both outside and in the home. And, of course, the cessation of smoking. There are more suggestions on our website, www.childenvironment.org.

But more needs to be done. As a society, we've done much to protect people, especially children, from the toxic chemicals in cigarettes. But too many toxic chemicals are being marketed without adequate testing. We should demand that new chemicals undergo the same rigorous testing as medicines before being allowed on the market. And we should phase out those chemicals linked with a wide range of health problems from neurological impairment to cancer in children.

A summary of the supporting scientific evidence, and a list of scientific endorsers, can be found at www.childenvironment.org.

Center for Children's Health and the Environment

MOUNT SINAI SCHOOL OF MEDICINE

Box 1043, One Gustave Levy Place, New York, NY 10029 • **www.childenvironment.org**

Our fourth reading, by student Sandy Wainscott, illustrates option 5, a proposal speech supported by visual aids. We have reproduced Sandy's outline for her speech, along with six of her ten PowerPoint slides. Her final slide was a bibliography of the sources she used in her speech. Note how she has constructed her slides as visual arguments supporting a point (stated in the slide title) as opposed to using her slides to reproduce her speech outline.

Why McDonald's Should Sell Meat and Veggie Pies: A Proposal to End Subsidies for Cheap Meat

SANDY WAINSCOTT (STUDENT)

Introduction: McDonald's hamburgers are popular because they're satisfying and pretty darn cheap. It's quite amazing, when you think about it, that McDonald's can sell a double cheeseburger on their 99 cent menu. The average American wage earner can buy this burger after just 3 minutes of work. But I will argue that the hamburger is cheap because the American taxpayer subsidizes the cost of meat. Uncle Sam pays agribusiness to grow feed corn while not requiring agribusiness to pay the full cost for water or for cleaning up the environmental damage caused by cattle production. If meat producers had to recover the true cost of their product, the cost of meat would be substantially higher, but there would be offsetting benefits: a healthier environment, happier lives for cows and chickens, and healthier diets for all of us.

1. Meat is cheap partly because
   a. U.S. taxpayers give farmers money to grow feed corn, which is fed to cows
   b. U.S. taxpayers provide farmers with cheap water
2. Keeping meat cheap creates significant costs to our health, to the environment, and to animals
   a. Cheap meat threatens health
      (i) Factory-style farms significantly reduce effectiveness of antibiotics
      (ii) Antibiotic-resistant pathogens are potentially huge killers
      (iii) Factory farms are likely sources of new swine and bird flus
      (iv) Meat-related food poisoning harms millions of people per year with thousands of deaths
   b. Cheap meat threatens the environment
      (i) Factory farms create 130 times more sewage than humans
         (1) This sewage is not treated
         (2) It is held in open-air lagoons and releases large amounts of ammonium nitrate into the atmosphere and water supply

FIGURE 14.2 Sandy's title slide

FIGURE 14.3 Slide using Sandy's humorous drawing to illustrate a point

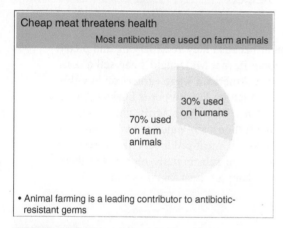

FIGURE 14.4 Slide using graphic for support

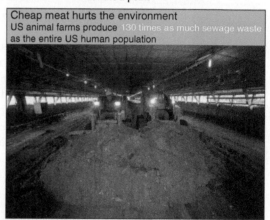

FIGURE 14.5 Slide using photograph for support

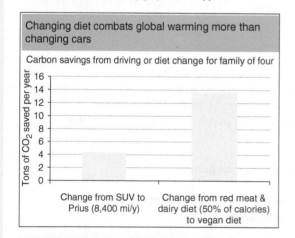

FIGURE 14.6 Slide using graphic for support

FIGURE 14.7 Slide using photograph for support

      (ii) Animal farming contributes more to global warming than all forms of human transportation combined
- (1) Most people think the way to combat global warming is by changing our driving habits (driving fuel-efficient cars, carpooling, taking the bus) or doing more conservation (fluorescent light bulbs, insulation, recycling)
- (2) More impact would be achieved by reducing amount of meat in our diets

    (iii) Animal farming uses much of the world's land and water
- (1) Cattle consume 14 times more calories in grain than they produce in meat
- (2) 80% of grain produced in the U.S. is eaten by livestock, not people
- (3) It requires 125 times as much water to produce a calorie of beef as a calorie of potatoes
- (4) The amount of land required to grow the plants to feed the animals leads to deforestation

  c. Cheap meat requires cruelty to animals
- (1) 98% of egg-laying hens in the U.S. spend their entire lives in stacked 9'' × 9'' × 9'' cages
- (2) Cruel conditions also exist for pigs and cows

Conclusion: If we quit giving farmers taxpayer subsidies and required them to pay for the pollution they cause, the cost of meat would be much higher—but with great benefits to our health and to our environment. A restaurant like McDonald's would likely adjust its menus. McDonald's would move the burger off its 99 cent menu and replace it with something like a meat pie, a similarly warm, quick, and satisfying choice, but with a lower proportion of meat than a burger. In a fair market, we should have to pay more for a hamburger than for a meat pie or a stir fry. But we would have the benefit of a healthier earth.

Critiquing "Why McDonald's Should Sell Meat and Veggie Pies: A Proposal to End Subsidies for Cheap Meat"

1. Although it is common to design PowerPoint slides that use topics and bullets to reproduce the speaker's outline, most public speaking experts prefer the approach that Sandy takes in this speech. She uses photographs, drawings, and graphics to create a visual argument that reinforces rather than simply reproduces the verbal message of her speech. How do her slides operate visually to create arguments from both *logos* and *pathos*?

2. Note that the top heading of each slide is a complete sentence making a point rather than a topic phrase without a subject and verb. For example, Figure 14.5 might have had the heading "Cost to Environment" or "Cheap Meat and the Environment." Do you agree with most experts, who would say that the complete sentence version ("Cheap meat hurts the environment") is more effective? Why or why not?

3. How effective do you find Sandy's speech?

Our final reading appeared in the *Wall Street Journal* on February 19, 2011. The authors are both professors of entomology at Wageningen University in the Netherlands. In 2007, Marcel Dicke was awarded the NWO-Spinoza award, often called the Dutch Nobel Prize. He gives speeches (summaries of which are available on the Web) arguing that humans should eat insects rather than meat as one solution to the environmental degradation caused by the meat industry. Coauthor Arnold Van Huis coordinates a research consortium of scientists investigating the nutritional value of insects. He also gives cooking classes featuring bug recipes.

The Six-Legged Meat of the Future

MARCEL DICKE AND ARNOLD VAN HUIS

At the London restaurant Archipelago, diners can order the $11 Baby Bee Brulee: a creamy custard topped with a crunchy little bee. In New York, the Mexican restaurant Toloache offers $11 chapulines tacos: two tacos stuffed with Oaxacan-style dried grasshoppers.

Could beetles, dragonfly larvae and water bug caviar be the meat of the future? As the global population booms and demand strains the world's supply of meat, there's a growing need for alternate animal proteins. Insects are high in protein, B vitamins and minerals like iron and zinc, and they're low in fat. Insects are easier to raise than livestock, and they produce less waste. Insects are abundant. Of all the known animal species, 80% walk on six legs; over 1,000 edible species have been identified. And the taste? It's often described as "nutty."

Worms, crickets, dung beetles—to most people they're just creepy crawlers. To Brooklyn painter and art professor Marc Dennis, they're yummy ingredients for his Bug Dinners.

The vast majority of the developing world already eats insects. In Laos and Thailand, weaverant pupae are a highly prized and nutritious delicacy. They are prepared with shallots, lettuce, chilies, lime and spices and served with sticky rice. Further back in history, the ancient Romans considered beetle larvae to be gourmet fare, and the Old Testament mentions eating crickets and grasshoppers. In the 20th century, the Japanese emperor Hirohito's favorite meal was a mixture of cooked rice, canned wasps (including larvae, pupae and adults), soy sauce and sugar.

Will Westerners ever take to insects as food? It's possible. We are entomologists at Wageningen University, and we started promoting insects as food in the Netherlands in the 1990s. Many people laughed—and cringed—at first, but interest gradually became more serious. In 2006 we created a "Wageningen—City of Insects" science festival to promote the idea of eating bugs; it attracted more than 20,000 visitors.

Over the past two years, three Dutch insect-raising companies, which normally produce feed for animals in zoos, have set up special production lines to raise locusts and mealworms for human consumption. Now those insects are sold, freeze-dried, in two dozen retail food outlets that cater to restaurants. A few restaurants in the Netherlands have already placed insects on the menu, with locusts and mealworms (beetle larvae) usually among the dishes.

Insects have a reputation for being dirty and carrying diseases—yet less than 0.5% of all known insect species are harmful to people, farm animals or crop plants. When raised under hygienic conditions—eating bugs

straight out of the backyard generally isn't recommended—many insects are perfectly safe to eat.

Meanwhile, our food needs are on the rise. The human population is expected to grow from six billion in 2000 to nine billion in 2050. Meat production is expected to double in the same period, as demand grows from rising wealth. Pastures and fodder already use up 70% of all agricultural land, so increasing livestock production would require expanding agricultural acreage at the expense of rain forests and other natural lands. Officials at the United Nations Food and Agriculture Organization recently predicted that beef could become an extreme luxury item by 2050, like caviar, due to rising production costs.

Raising insects for food would avoid many of the problems associated with livestock. For instance, swine and humans are similar enough that they can share many diseases. Such co-infection can yield new disease strains that are lethal to humans, as happened during a swine fever outbreak in the Netherlands in the late 1990s. Because insects are so different from us, such risks are accordingly lower.

Insects are also cold-blooded, so they don't need as much feed as animals like pigs and cows, which consume more energy to maintain their body temperatures. Ten pounds of feed yields one pound of beef, three pounds of pork, five pounds of chicken and up to six pounds of insect meat.

Insects produce less waste, too. The proportion of livestock that is not edible after processing is 30% for pork, 35% for chicken, 45% for beef and 65% for lamb. By contrast, only 20% of a cricket is inedible.

Raising insects requires relatively little water, especially as compared to the production of conventional meat (it takes more than 10 gallons of water, for instance, to produce about two pounds of beef). Insects also produce far less ammonia and other greenhouse gases per pound of body weight. Livestock is responsible for at least 10% of all greenhouse gas emissions.

Raising insects is more humane as well. Housing cattle, swine or chickens in high densities causes stress to the animals, but insects like mealworms and locusts naturally like to live in dense quarters. The insects can be crowded into vertical stacked trays or cages. Nor do bug farms have to be restricted to rural areas; they could sprout up anywhere, from a suburban strip mall to an apartment building. Enterprising gourmets could even keep a few trays of mealworms in the garage to ensure a fresh supply.

The first insect fare is likely to be incorporated subtly into dishes, as a replacement for meat in meatballs and sauces. It also can be mixed into prepared foods to boost their nutritional value—like putting mealworm paste into a quiche. And dry-roasted insects can be used as a replacement for nuts in baked goods like cookies and breads.

We continue to make progress in the Netherlands, where the ministry of agriculture is funding a new $1.3 million research program to develop ways to raise edible insects on food waste, such as brewers' grain (a byproduct of beer brewing), soyhulls (the skin of the soybean) and apple pomace (the pulpy remains after the juice has been pressed out). Other research is focusing on how protein could be extracted from insects and used in processed foods.

Though it is true that intentionally eating insects is common only in developing countries, everyone already eats some amount of insects. The average person consumes about a pound of insects per year, mostly mixed into other foods. In the U.S., most processed foods contain small amounts of insects, within limits set by the Food and Drug Administration. For chocolate, the FDA limit is 60 insect fragments per 100 grams. Peanut butter can have up to 30 insect parts per 100 grams, and fruit juice can have five fruit-fly eggs and one or two larvae per 250 milliliters (just over a cup). We also use many insect products to dye our foods, such as the red dye cochineal in imitation crab sticks, Campari and candies. So we're already some of the way there in making six-legged creatures a regular part of our diet.

Not long ago, foods like kiwis and sushi weren't widely known or available. It is quite likely that in 2020 we will look back in surprise at the era when our menus didn't include locusts, beetle larvae, dragonfly larvae, crickets and other insect delights.

Critiquing "The Six-Legged Meat of the Future"

1. On page 316 we note that a problem faced by all proposal writers is "the need to overcome people's natural conservatism." Their readers' natural conservatism is a major constraint for co-authors Dicke and Van Huis ("Hey, I've never eaten bugs before! If four-legged meat was good enough for my parents, it's good enough for me!") How do the authors use the appeals of *logos, ethos,* and *pathos* to try to overcome this natural conservatism?

2. Although this journalistic piece does not have a tightly closed-form structure with transitions and because clauses marking each reason, it still provides a logical progression of separate reasons in support of eating insects. Convert this argument into a bulleted list of because clauses in support of the claim "Westerners should eat insects as a major source of protein."

3. Are you persuaded by this argument? Would you try some mealworm spaghetti or a handful of fried crickets? Why or why not?

For additional writing, reading, and research resources, go to www.mycomplab.com

Informal Fallacies

In this appendix, we look at ways of assessing the legitimacy of an argument within a real-world context of probabilities rather than within a mathematical world of certainty. Whereas formal logic is a kind of mathematics, the informal fallacies addressed in this appendix are embedded in everyday arguments, sometimes making fallacious reasoning seem deceptively persuasive, especially to unwary audiences. We begin by looking at the problem of conclusiveness in arguments, after which we give you an overview of the most commonly encountered informal fallacies.

The Problem of Conclusiveness in an Argument

In real-world disagreements, we seldom encounter arguments that are absolutely conclusive. Rather, arguments are, to various degrees, "persuasive" or "nonpersuasive." In the pure world of formal logic, however, it is possible to have absolutely conclusive arguments. For example, an Aristotelian syllogism, if it is validly constructed, yields a certain conclusion. Moreover, if the first two premises (called the "major" and "minor" premises) are true, then we are guaranteed that the conclusion is also true. Here is an example:

Valid Syllogism

Major premise: All ducks are feathered animals.

Minor premise: Quacko is a duck.

Conclusion: Therefore Quacko is a feathered animal.

This syllogism is said to be valid because it follows a correct form. Moreover, because its premises are true, the conclusion is guaranteed to be true. However, if the syllogism follows an incorrect form (and is therefore invalid), we can't determine whether the conclusion is true.

Invalid Syllogism

Major premise: All ducks are feathered animals.

Minor premise: Clucko is a feathered animal.

Conclusion: Therefore Clucko is a duck.

In the valid syllogism, we are guaranteed that Quacko is a feathered animal because the minor premise states that Quacko is a duck and the major premise places ducks within the larger class of feathered animals. But in the invalid syllogism, there is no guaranteed conclusion. We know that Clucko is a feathered animal but we can't know whether he is a duck. He may be a duck, but he may also be a buzzard or a chicken. The invalid syllogism thus commits a "formal fallacy" in that its form doesn't guarantee the truth of its conclusion even if the initial premises are true.

From the perspective of real-world argumentation, the problem with formal logic is that it isn't concerned with the truth of premises. For example, the following argument is logically valid even though the premises and conclusion are obviously untrue:

Valid Syllogism with Untrue Major and Minor Premises

Major premise: The blood of insects can be used to lubricate lawn mower engines.

Minor premise: Vampires are insects.

Conclusion: Therefore the blood of vampires can be used to lubricate lawn mower engines.

Even though this syllogism meets the formal requirements for validity, its argument is ludicrous.

In this appendix, therefore, we are concerned with "informal" rather than "formal" fallacies because informal fallacies are embedded within real-world arguments addressing contestable issues of truth and value. Disputants must argue about issues because they can't be resolved with mathematical certainty; any contestable claim always leaves room for doubt and alternative points of view. Disputants can create only more or less persuasive arguments, never conclusive ones.

An Overview of Informal Fallacies

The study of informal fallacies remains the murkiest of all logical endeavors. It's murky because informal fallacies are as unsystematic as formal fallacies are rigid and systematized. Whereas formal fallacies of logic have the force of laws, informal fallacies have little more than explanatory power. Informal fallacies are quirky; they identify classes of less conclusive arguments that recur with some frequency, but they do not contain formal flaws that make their conclusions illegitimate no matter what the terms may say. Informal fallacies require us to look at the meaning of the terms to determine how much we should trust or distrust the conclusion. In evaluating arguments with informal fallacies, we usually find that arguments are "more or less" fallacious, and determining the degree of fallaciousness is a matter of judgment.

Knowledge of informal fallacies is most useful when we run across arguments that we "know" are wrong, but we can't quite say why. They just don't "sound right." They look reasonable enough, but they remain unacceptable to us. Informal fallacies are a sort of compendium of symptoms for arguments flawed in this way. We must be careful, however, to make sure that the particular case before us "fits" the descriptors for the fallacy that seems to explain its problem. It's much easier, for example, to find informal fallacies in a hostile argument than in a friendly one simply because we are more likely to expand the limits of the fallacy to make the disputed case fit.

In arranging the fallacies, we have, for convenience, put them into three categories derived from classical rhetoric: *pathos, ethos,* and *logos.* Fallacies of *pathos* rest on flaws in the way an argument appeals to the audience's emotions and values. Fallacies of *ethos* rest on flaws in the way the argument appeals to the character of opponents or of sources and witnesses within an argument. Fallacies of *logos* rest on flaws in the relationship among statements in an argument.

Fallacies of Pathos

Argument to the People (Appealing to Stirring Symbols) This is perhaps the most generic example of a *pathos* fallacy. Arguments to the people appeal to the fundamental beliefs, biases, and prejudices of the audience in order to sway opinion through a feeling of solidarity among those of the group. Thus a "Support Our Troops" bumper sticker, often including the American flag, creates an initial feeling of solidarity among almost all citizens of goodwill. But the car owner may have the deeper intention of actually meaning "support our president" or "support the war in _____." The stirring symbol of the flag and the desire shared by most people to support our troops is used fallaciously to urge support of a particular political act. Arguments to the people often use visual rhetoric, as in the soaring eagle used in Wal-Mart corporate ads or images of happy families in marketing advertisements.

Appeal to Ignorance This fallacy persuades an audience to accept as true a claim that hasn't been proved false or vice versa. "Jones must have used steroids to get those bulging biceps because he can't prove that he hasn't used steroids." Appeals to ignorance are particularly common in the murky field of pseudoscience. "UFOs (ghosts, abominable snowmen) do exist because science hasn't proved that they don't exist." Sometimes, however, it is hard to draw a line between a fallacious appeal to ignorance and a legitimate appeal to precaution: "Genetically modified organisms must be dangerous to our health because science hasn't proved that they are safe."

Appeal to Popularity—Bandwagon To board the bandwagon means (to use a more contemporary metaphor) to board the bus or train of what's popular. Appeals to popularity are fallacious because the popularity of something is irrelevant to its actual merits. "Living together before marriage is the right thing to do because most couples are now doing it." Bandwagon appeals are common in advertising where the claim that a product is popular substitutes for evidence of the product's excellence. There are times, however, when popularity may indeed be relevant: "Global warming is probably caused by human activity because a preponderance of scientists now hold this position." (Here we assume that scientists haven't simply climbed on a bandwagon themselves, but have formed their opinions based on research data and well-vetted, peer-reviewed papers.)

Appeal to Pity Here the arguer appeals to the audience's sympathetic feelings in order to support a claim that should be decided on more relevant or objective grounds. "Honorable judge, I should not be fined $200 for speeding because I was distraught from hearing news of my brother's illness and was rushing to see him in the hospital." Here the argument is fallacious because the arguer's reason, while evoking sympathy, is not a relevant justification for speeding (as it might have been, for instance, if the arguer had been rushing an injured person to the emergency room). In many cases, however, an arguer can legitimately appeal to pity, as in the case of fund-raising for victims of a tsunami or other disaster.

Red Herring This fallacy's funny name derives from the practice of using a red herring (a highly odiferous fish) to throw dogs off a scent that they are supposed to be tracking. It refers to the practice of throwing an audience offtrack by raising an unrelated or irrelevant point. "Debating a gas tax increase is valuable, but I really think there should be an extra tax on SUVs." Here the arguer, apparently uncomfortable with the gas tax issue, diverts the conversation to the emotionally charged issue of owning SUVs. A conversant who noted how the argument has gotten offtrack might say, "Stop talking, everyone. The SUV question is a red herring; let's get back to the topic of a gas tax increase."

Fallacies of Ethos

Appeal to False Authority Arguers appeal to false authority when they use famous people (often movie stars or other celebrities) to testify on issues about which these persons have no special competence. "Joe Quarterback says Gooey Oil keeps his old tractor running sharp; therefore, Gooey Oil is a good oil." Real evidence about the quality of Gooey Oil would include technical data about the product rather than testimony from an actor or hired celebrity. However, the distinction between a "false authority" and a legitimate authority can become blurred. Consider the Viagra ads by former senator Bob Dole during the first marketing years of this impotence drug. As a famous person rather than a doctor, Dole would seem to be a false authority. But Dole was also widely known to have survived prostate cancer, and he may well have used Viagra. To the extent a person is an expert in a field, he or she is no longer a "false authority."

Ad Hominem Literally, *ad hominem* means "to the person." An *ad hominem* argument is directed at the character of an opponent rather than at the quality of the opponent's reasoning. Ideally, arguments are supposed to be *ad rem* ("to the thing"), that is, addressed to the specifics of the case itself. Thus an *ad rem* critique of a politician would focus on her voting record, the consistency and cogency of her public statements, her responsiveness to constituents, and so forth. An *ad hominem* argument would shift attention from her record to features of her personality, life circumstances, or the company she keeps. "Senator Sweetwater's views on the gas tax should be discounted because her husband works for a huge oil company" or "Senator Sweetwater supports tax cuts for the wealthy because she is very wealthy herself and stands to gain." But not all *ad hominem* arguments are *ad hominem* fallacies. Lawyers, for example, when questioning expert witnesses who give damaging testimony, often make an issue of their honesty, credibility, or personal investment in an outcome.

Poisoning the Well This fallacy is closely related to *ad hominem.* Arguers poison the well when they discredit an opponent or an opposing view in advance. "Before I yield the floor to the next speaker, I must remind you that those who oppose my plan do not have the best interests of working people in their hearts."

Straw Man The straw man fallacy occurs when you oversimplify an opponent's argument to make it easier to refute or ridicule. Rather than summarizing an opposing view fairly and completely, you basically make up the argument you wish your opponent had made because it is so much easier to knock over, like knocking over a straw man or scarecrow in a corn field. See pages 130–131 for a fuller discussion of the straw man fallacy.

Fallacies of *Logos*

Hasty Generalization This fallacy occurs when someone makes a broad generalization on the basis of too little evidence. Generally, the evidence needed to support a generalization persuasively must meet the STAR criteria (sufficiency, typicality, accuracy, and relevance) discussed in Chapter 5 (pages 92–93). But what constitutes a sufficient amount of evidence? The generally accepted standards of sufficiency in any given field are difficult to determine. The Food and Drug Administration (FDA), for example, generally proceeds cautiously before certifying a drug as "safe." However, if people are harmed by the side effects of an FDA-approved drug, critics often accuse the FDA of having made a hasty generalization. At the same time, patients eager to have access to a new drug and manufacturers eager to sell a new product may lobby the FDA to quit "dragging its feet" and get the drug to market. Hence, the point at which a hasty generalization passes over into the realm of a prudent generalization is nearly always uncertain and contested.

Part for the Whole Sometimes called by its Latin name *pars pro toto,* this fallacy is closely related to hasty generalization. In this fallacy, arguers pick out a part of the whole or a sample of the whole (often not a typical or representative part or sample) and then claim that what is true of the part is true for the whole. If, say, individuals wanted to get rid of the National Endowment for the Arts (NEA), they might focus on several controversial programs funded by the NEA and use them as justification for wiping out all NEA programs. The flip side of this fallacy occurs when an arguer picks only the best examples to make a case and conveniently forgets about examples that may weaken the case.

Post Hoc, Ergo Propter Hoc The Latin name of this fallacy means "after this, therefore because of this." The fallacy occurs when a sequential relationship is mistaken for a causal relationship. (See Chapter 12, pages 265–266), where we discuss this fallacy in more depth.) For example, you may be guilty of this fallacy if you say, "Cramming for a test really helps because last week I crammed for my psychology test and I got an A on it." When two events occur frequently in conjunction with each other, we've got a good case for a causal relationship. But until we can show how one causes the other and until we have ruled out other causes, we cannot be certain that a causal relationship is occurring. For example, the A on your psych test may have been caused by something other than your cramming. Maybe the exam was easier, or perhaps you were luckier or more mentally alert. It is often difficult to tell when a *post hoc* fallacy occurs. When the New York police department changed its policing tactics in the early 1990s, the crime rate plummeted. Many experts attributed the declining crime rate to the new policing tactics, but some critics proposed other explanations. (See pages 256–257, Case 2, where economist Steven Levitt attributes the declining crime rate to the legalization of abortion in the 1970s.)

Begging the Question—Circular Reasoning Arguers beg the question when they provide a reason that simply restates the claim in different words. Here is an example: "Abortion is murder because it is the intentional taking of the life of a human being." Because "murder" is defined as "the intentional taking of the life of a human being," the argument is circular. It is tantamount to saying, "Abortion is murder because it is murder." In the abortion debate, the crucial issue is whether a fetus is a "human being" in the legal sense. So in this case the arguer has fallaciously "begged the question" by assuming from the start that the fetus is a legal human being. The argument is similar to saying, "That person is obese because he is too fat."

False Dilemma—Either/Or This fallacy occurs when an arguer oversimplifies a complex issue so that only two choices appear possible. Often one of the choices is made to seem unacceptable, so the only remaining option is the other choice. "It's my way or the highway" is a typical example of a false dilemma. Here is a more subtle one: "Either we allow embryonic stem cell research, or we condemn people with diabetes, Parkinson's disease, or spinal injuries to a life without a cure." Clearly, there may be other options, including other approaches to curing these diseases. A good extended example of the false dilemma fallacy is found in sociologist Kai Erikson's analysis of President Truman's decision to drop the A-bomb on Hiroshima. His analysis suggests that the Truman administration prematurely reduced numerous options to just two: either drop the bomb on a major city, or sustain unacceptable losses in a land invasion of Japan. Erikson, however, shows there were other alternatives.

Slippery Slope The slippery slope fallacy is based on the fear that once we put a foot on a slippery slope heading in the wrong direction, we're doomed to slide right out of sight. The controlling metaphor is of a slick mountainside without places to hold on rather than of a staircase with numerous stopping places. Here is an example of a slippery slope: "Once we allow medical use of marijuana, we'll eventually legalize it for everyone, after which we're on a slippery slope toward social acceptance of cocaine and heroin." Slippery slope arguments are frequently encountered when individuals request exceptions to bureaucratic rules: "Look, Blotnik, no one feels worse about your need for open-heart surgery than I do. But I still can't let you turn this paper in late. If I were to let you do it, then I'd have to let everyone turn in papers late." Slippery slope arguments can be very persuasive—and often rightfully so because every slippery slope argument isn't necessarily a slippery slope fallacy. Some slopes really are slippery. The slippery slope becomes a fallacy when we forget that we can often dig a foothold into the slope and stop. For example, we can define procedures for exceptions to rules so that Blotnik can turn in his paper late without allowing everyone to turn in a paper late. Likewise, a state could legalize medical use of marijuana without legalizing it for everyone.

False Analogy In Chapter 11 on definition and resemblance arguments, we explained that no analogy is perfect (see our discussion of analogies on pages 242–243). Any two things being compared are similar in some ways and different in other ways. Whether an analogy is persuasive or false often depends on the audience's initial degree of skepticism. For example, people opposed to gun control may find the following argument persuasive: "Banning guns on the basis that guns accidentally kill people is like banning cars on the basis that cars accidentally kill people." In contrast, supporters of gun control are likely to call this argument a false analogy on the basis of dissimilarities between cars and guns. (For example, they might say that banning cars would be far more disruptive on our society than would be banning guns.) Just when a persuasive analogy turns into a false analogy is difficult to say.

Non Sequitur The name of this fallacy means "it does not follow." *Non sequitur* is a catchall term for any claim that doesn't follow from its premises or is supported by irrelevant premises. Sometimes the arguer seems to make an inexplicably illogical leap: "Genetically modified foods should be outlawed because they are not natural." (Should anything that is not natural be outlawed? In what way are they not natural?) At other times there may be a gap in the chain of reasons: "Violent video games have some social value because the army uses them for recruiting." (There may be an important idea emerging here, but too many logical steps are missing.) At still other times an arguer may support a claim with irrelevant reasons: "I should not receive a C in this course because I currently have a 3.8 GPA." In effect, almost any fallacy could be called a *non sequitur* because fallacious reasoning always indicates some kind of disconnect between the reasons and the claim.

Loaded Label or Definition Sometimes arguers try to influence their audience's view of something by creating a loaded label or definition. For example, people who oppose the "estate tax" (which calls to mind rich people with estates) have relabeled it the "death tax" in order to give it a negative connotation without any markers of class or wealth. Or to take another example, proponents of organic foods could create definitions like the following: "Organic foods are safe and healthy foods grown without any pesticides, herbicides, or other unhealthy additives." "Safe" and "healthy" are evaluative terms used fallaciously in what purports to be a definition. The intended implication is that nonorganic foods are not safe and healthy.

■ ■ ■ **FOR CLASS DISCUSSION** Persuasive or Fallacious?

Working individually or in small groups, determine the potential persuasiveness of each of the following argument cores. If fleshed out with supporting evidence, how persuasive do each of these arguments promise to be? If any argument seems doomed because of one or more of the fallacies discussed in this appendix, identify the fallacies and explain how they render the argument nonpersuasive. In your discussion, remember that it is often hard to determine the exact point where fallacious reasoning begins to kick in, especially when you consider different kinds of audiences. So in each case, consider also variations in audience. For which audiences would any particular argument appear potentially fallacious? Which audiences would be more likely to consider the argument persuasive?

1. Either we legalize marijuana or we watch a steady increase in the number of our citizens who break the law.
2. Smoking must cause lung cancer because a much higher percentage of smokers get lung cancer than do nonsmokers.
3. Smoking does not cause cancer because my grandfather smoked two packs per day for fifty years and died in his sleep at age ninety.
4. Society has an obligation to provide housing for the homeless because people without adequate shelter have a right to the resources of the community.
5. Based on my observations of the two renters in our neighborhood, I have concluded that people who own their own homes take better care of them than those who rent. [This arguer provided detailed evidence about the house-caring practices of the two renters and of the homeowners in the neighborhood.]
6. Intelligent design must qualify as a scientific theory because hundreds of scientists endorse it.
7. If we pass legislation requiring mandatory registration of handguns, we'll open the door to eventual confiscation of hunting rifles.
8. Those who support gun control are wrong because they believe that no one should have the right to defend himself or herself in any situation.
9. Most other progressive nations have adopted a program of government-provided health insurance. Therefore it is time for the United States to abandon its present employer-funded insurance system and adopt federally funded universal health insurance.
10. You should discount Dr. Smith's objections to federally funded health care because as a doctor he may face a loss of some income. ■ ■ ■

SECTION TWO
Rhetoric Supplement

Inquiry and Argument 15

Taken from *From Inquiry to Argument* by Linda McMeniman

Read the following selection carefully, then respond as indicated below:

> Imagine that you enter a parlor. You come late. When you arrive, others have long preceded you, and they are engaged in a heated discussion, a discussion too heated for them to pause and tell you exactly what it is about. In fact, the discussion had already begun long before any of them got there, so that no one present is qualified to retrace for you all the steps that had gone before. You listen for a while until you decide that you have caught the tenor of the argument; then you put in your oar. Someone answers; you answer him; another comes to your defense; another aligns himself against you. . . . However, the discussion is interminable. The hour grows late, you must depart. And you do depart, with the discussion still in progress.
>
> —Kenneth Burke, *The Philosophy of Literary Form*

Writer's Journal

In your notebook, write informally to explain the meaning of the passage. Then describe its effects on you and express any other responses you may have. Strive for an entry of at least 150 words.

From Inquiry . . .

Let's begin with the term *inquiry,* a simple word, one we all know how to use. If you examine the following uses of *inquiry* (and its relative, *to inquire*), some may strike you as more appropriate than others:

1. Sal inquired about the penalty for late payment of his gas bill.
2. Judith made an inquiry as to the location of the restroom.
3. The House of Representatives began an inquiry into the states' enforcement of highway traffic laws.
4. The counterman inquired what flavor ice cream I wanted.

If you discuss your responses with classmates, you might discover you agree—that in sentences 1 and 3 *inquiry* works well, but that in 2 and 4 it seems artificial or awkward. In these sentences, you may prefer *asked* as less grand, less affected. Or perhaps you disagree because you can envision a scene or context for sentences 2 and 4 that calls for a special, more elevated word than *ask*. You can agree, however, that the word *inquiry* and the act of *inquiring* are not about asking just any question; an inquiry is more self-conscious, more intentional.

A look in the dictionary reveals that the word *inquiry* shares the same Latin root as *question: quaerere,* meaning "to seek." The prefix *in* serves as an intensifier, so we might say that inquire is built from its roots to mean "to seek intensely." In the actual definition, an inquiry is said to be a "question or query" or "a close examination of some matter in a quest for information or truth."

I like this last definition because the phrase "quest for information or truth" reflects the deepest purpose of academic life, the discovery of explanations that will endure—at least until the next inquiry. And "close examination" implies study and research, processes that flow beneath and animate all the teaching and talking, paper writing and e-mailing, reading and note taking that form the day-to-day activities in higher education.

But this definition doesn't tell us much about the context of inquiry or about its inspiration. Why bother to inquire? What creates the need to know?

The Motives for Inquiry

Consider a time when you made an intensive search for knowledge. Make a list of such times. Do these occasions have anything in common? What motivated your need to know?

Often, the search for information or "truth" results from a problem, an impending decision, a conflict between possible choices, or some other controversial situation. The need may be immediate and practical. Perhaps someone whose father has developed cataracts wants information about eye disease in order to understand possible treatments.

Or the need may be to plan for the future. A student may be about to make the life-altering decision to attend college and so collects and studies many college catalogues in order to make the most appropriate choice. A county might study traffic patterns over the course of the workday and workweek so that future road improvements can be planned.

Or the necessary information may be more abstract: solving a societal problem such as a rise in high school dropout rates requires analyzing and perhaps conducting numerous studies of adolescent behavior, the educational system, family dynamics, and so forth.

So an inquiry implies certain things: a problem, dilemma, or controversial issue, first of all, and a community that has a stake in resolving that problem.

The Context of Inquiry

Such a community can be official, such as a township, a civic or professional group, or a university. But many communities or groups of people linked by a common interest or situation are informal and unofficial. Cliques in a high school, recreational groups such as golfers or quilters, and fans of the ballet or progressive jazz are examples. Any group that uses discourse—that is, any form of written or spoken communication—to maintain itself, articulate and solve group problems, and otherwise assist its own cohesiveness and identity is called a **discourse community**. Members of discourse communities—and we are all members of several—base their interactions with each other on the discourse expectations of the group. The discourse community is an active collaborator in any member's use of language, providing a vocabulary and expected styles of discussing and handling issues of concern and even limiting or defining acceptable topics. Such a community has conventions for discussing, analyzing, and proving ideas and for addressing conflicts.

A high school clique may evolve a trademark vocabulary that reaffirms its identity and may develop customary ways of discussing academic work, friendships, romances, and other topics. Inside jokes can be cued with a few words, and greeting or parting may involve signature phrases or gestures. To a certain extent, any member's behavior and talk, both subject and style, will be based on the group's expectations.

ACTIVITY 1

Identifying Discourse Communities

A town-council meeting will also be characterized by a customary discourse. Some characteristics of its discourse will be common to town-council meetings throughout the United States, for local government officials and politically active citizens constitute an informal national discourse community. Most likely, the discussion will be sprinkled with technical terms or jargon derived from various professional domains: the law, real estate, health and public safety, and so on. The discourse will be generally polite and somewhat formal but probably will include informal segments in which humorous asides and little in-jokes lighten the mood. Discourse will follow an agenda, the shape of which may be mandated by law or determined by custom. Proceedings will follow parliamentary procedure to a greater or lesser extent. Decisions will be made by the head official or the council through voice vote, secret ballot, or consensus as local law requires or as is customary.

It is fair to say that any inquiry a person conducts occurs within the web of a discourse community, and it involves interaction with that community. Individual inquiries require dialogue, perhaps oral, perhaps written. How a problem is defined, how study and research are performed, and what counts as a result or solution are all determined by our linguistic and social environment. Discourse communities limit their members to the discourse formulations within them; but discourse communities also open pathways for members by providing conventions of wording and expression and patterns of thought out of which understanding is built.

ACTIVITY 2

Exploring Discourse Communities

ACTIVITY 3

Recognizing Discourse Communities

As Gregory Clark writes, "Using language is necessarily an act of collaboration through which we create the meaning we share, a socially constructed meaning that is inherently incomplete".

The Civic and Academic Discourse Communities

Two broad discourse communities that encompass specialized and regional discourse communities are the academic and the civic discourse communities.

The Civic Discourse Community The civic discourse community is the broad discourse community of U.S. public life and includes all of us who communicate with each other about the issues and topics of the day, either interpersonally or through reading newspapers and magazines, listening to radio or television news, and so on.

Strictly defined, *civic* means pertaining to citizenship, but in an expanded sense civic refers to everything affecting the community in which people live, including issues national, local, and international, and topics directly and indirectly governmental. The topics of the chitchat that hums around us—about the sensational murder trial, the latest crime statistics, shocking infant mortality rates, the search for effective treatments for AIDS and cancer—and the goings-on of our lawmakers in Congress all come under the banner of civic issues.

In a free society, discourse about issues is a part of the democratic process. As political science professor John Nelson writes, "The relationship of politics to rhetoric [effective language use] is especially intimate in the domestic policies of America and other representational democracies. . . . To ask about the legitimacy of governors, laws, and policies in a representational polity is largely to ask how well it communicates public opinions to public officials, how well the officials communicate public needs to citizens, and how well the citizens communicate among themselves about public problems." In a sense, democracy comes down to communication. As a result, orienting people to take an interest in and function well in the national and local civic discourse communities is an important goal of education.

Civic discourse also encompasses the information and ideas flowing to us via the mass media. But the civic discourse community is not a creation of the mass media; there was a civic discourse community before there was CNN or television or the *New York Times*. Civic discourse has always been assisted by the media, whether printed one-page broadsides sold for a penny on the streets of colonial Philadelphia or presidential debates broadcast by national networks or extremist diatribes uploaded to an Internet forum. But civic discourse goes on among individuals and in public arenas, in meetings of town councils and parent-teacher organizations, student councils and boards of trustees. This discourse community, although broad in its inclusiveness, does foster conventional, accepted ways of thinking, discussing, analyzing, and ultimately approving or discrediting ideas that affect everyone within it.

The Academic Discourse Community The academic discourse community is sometimes called "academia"; others refer to it, not so approvingly, as "the ivory tower." Sarcasm aside, the academic discourse community is a national, even international, one that shares many characteristics with the civic. But, in addition to discussion and analysis, the academic discourse community mandates research and the active or conscious creation of new perspectives, new connections between ideas, and new ways of looking at the world—that is, new knowledge.

The local academic discourse community that you, your classmates, professors, and other college staff members belong to has its own specific characteristics, many of which are shared by people at other colleges and universities around the country and even around the world. Within any academic institution, there are smaller discourse communities, the academic disciplines. Like the academic discourse community as a whole, your college's academic departments are local sites of larger discourse communities of each discipline. Within each, there will be customary types of problems and controversies and expectations about how inquiry is conducted and what form the outcomes of inquiry will take.

For example, you can imagine how different the research conducted by an English major on the topic "symbolism in Stephen Crane's novels" would be from that of a psychology major assigned to write about recent research on infants' reactions to sweet, salt, and bitter tastes. An education major preparing a case study of a dyslexic child would conduct a different inquiry and write quite a different paper than a biology major assigned to do a laboratory experiment and write a lab report. If you at are the beginning of your college experience, you are a member-in-training of academia, and you may be somewhat unsure of the language expectations this community has. This book focuses on the expectations of the broad academic community rather than the requirements of specific disciplines.

ACTIVITY 4

Exploring Academic Discourse

The academic discourse community has a somewhat stronger emphasis than the civic on the written word, in that texts in libraries have been the major medium of interaction among scholars within a field. Although today many researchers turn to the World Wide Web or the Internet for some of their research, the outcome is still printed text read privately. Oral and public discourse does occur in academia, of course, not only in the college lecture hall and discussion classroom but in disciplinary conferences, forums, public lectures, and, increasingly, online in electronic forums. Academia is and will likely remain a text-oriented culture in which writing is a fundamental aspect of issue discovery, problem solving, and knowledge creation. Understanding and using well the modes of inquiry and discussion common to the academic disciplines are necessary for success in college.

. . . To Argument

Taken in its everyday sense, the word argument may imply a battle: my side versus your side, "us" against "them," often a fruitless banging of heads that can be ended only with an insult or a begrudging remark like "everyone's entitled to an opinion." Our day-to-day experience with argument is often strongly oppositional and intensely frustrating.

Within the academic and civic discourse communities, argument refers to the building and presenting of a developed case in support of a position on an issue or controversy. When people analyze and evaluate the results of their quests for truth and knowledge—their inquiries—and formulate a position convincingly for presentation to others, they engage in argument. We often become interested in a controversy in midstream, like a person entering the parlor where Burke's unending conversation is going on. Arguments are already flowing, and so our inquiry must begin with understanding the arguments that have already been made.

Disputes over ideas raise new questions and inspire new inquiries, resulting in a landscape of understandings, possible truths, and perspectives. Arguments themselves weave in and out of the inquiry process and usually don't boil down to a simple pro and con or "us" against "them." In fact, the win-lose mind-set can cause people to overlook the range and complexity of viewpoints on an issue. Besides the form of argument that defends an opinion, our common discourse includes other argumentative forms in which negotiation or reconciliation between oppositional views is sought and in which inquiry and the posing of questions are prominent.

Consulting the dictionary on argument is informative. There we learn that the root of the word is *arg,* meaning "to shine, white, or the shining or white metal, silver." The Latin word *arguere* based on this root means "to make clear, or demonstrate" ("Arg-"). Knowing about these related roots helps me get a feel for the goal of argument: to come up in clear water after diving in deep, to achieve some clarity about important issues.

Arguments can open minds, encourage complexity of opinions, and advance the appreciation of evidence, but they don't always change minds. As we shall see, many factors underlie a person's choice of opinion, and not all of them are easily addressable in an argument. (Section 2 will address some of these factors.) If argument's goal is converting readers, then most arguments are failures. But when argument is seen as a mode of participation in our discourse community, as a vehicle for personal and intellectual growth, and as a means to encourage and validate new options, perspectives, and solutions, then argument can be a vital and exciting process.

With the discourse community in mind, we can put aside those images of raised voices and pounded tables and see argumentation in a more positive light: as a means of participation in the larger intellectual forum of our society. In addition, in its testing of our ideas, argument can provide personal growth and intellectual maturing that is lifelong and ever-complicating. Argument, then, is an honorable and productive activity that seasons our own perspective and makes a responsible contribution to our society.

ACTIVITY 5

Exploring Real-Life Arguments

The Elements of Argument

Argument in the broadest sense is an ancient discipline—a form of discourse cultivated by the ancient Greeks and Romans and passed down through the centuries as a means of engaging and advancing ideas and activating support. The writings that have come down to us about argument, from Aristotle through Cicero and Quintilian, provide terminology and strategies about argumentation that are still in use today. This is so even though the ancient rhetoricians (that is, specialists in effective language use) concentrated on oral rather than written language because oratory was then the major component of civic discourse. The ancients associated argumentation with citizenship; it was considered a communal activity designed to promote good civic policy as well as a method for testing ideas, philosophical, ethical, political, or otherwise. As one scholar in the field puts it, the "Greeks and Romans invented and developed rhetoric . . . specifically for their politics."

Formal argumentation involves more than batting around ideas in a free-for-all. Rather, in argumentation, a person presents a position, also called a **claim**, **assertion**, or **proposition**. A claim can clarify facts, explain causes (of problems), promote a value, or advocate a solution, policy, or change. An argumentative claim asserts the most believable or best position to hold on an issue or policy. What is most believable or best will necessarily be determined by the standards of the discourse community in which the argument occurs—and even then a debate frequently occurs over which standards should hold sway. The argumentative writer's goal is to set out the claim in a manner most convincing to the members of the discourse community being addressed.

Argument today includes a broad field of methods, techniques, and perspectives on how meaning is attached to events and situations, how viewpoints are articulated, developed, and lent credence—that is, supportability. But many expectations about argumentative discourse hold true throughout academic and many civic discourse communities:

1. Ideas are valued on the basis of evidence.
2. Ideas build on the ideas and evidence of others, as acquired through research.
3. Arguers will be knowledgeable about the major relevant ideas on a subject of controversy.

Expectations about Evidence   In the civic and academic discourse communities, whether an idea has value or not is usually determined by whether it is supportable—that is, whether there is evidence for it. This may seem so obvious that it might go without saying, and it often does. But requiring ideas to be backed up in order to be valued is a basic assumption that is especially strong in the academic and, to some extent, the civic discourse communities.

In our culture, as a result of our Greek and Roman heritage, the test of whether a claim should be believed lies in the reasonableness of the analysis and evidence. Logic, explored in depth by the ancients, is one of the ways such credence is achieved. Factual information also comes into play in creating a reasonable claim. But there is no formula for reasonableness, no one definition or standard. Rather, reasonableness encompasses a broad spectrum of qualities, including logicality of ideas, depth and breadth of evidence, coherence with similar historical events or cases, practical concerns for fairness and effectiveness of consequences, and comprehensiveness. Philosopher Richard Rorty claims that reasonableness is a state of mind: "to be rational is simply to discuss any topic—religious, literary or scientific—in a way which [avoids] dogmatism, defensiveness and righteous indignation."

The term *evidence* may remind you of a court of law, and to some extent this image is appropriate. Evidence for an argument must be weighed and evaluated, just as in a courtroom.

Not all evidence is "created equal." There are different types, and not all types work to support every claim or work well in different discourse communities. Some evidence, for example, is factual. Facts include the results of scientific research and experimentation; data acquired by taking surveys of people's opinions or living conditions; details gathered by observation; information about events, people, and so forth recorded in public records, documents, or news reports. Examples, which are individual factual cases, also weigh in as evidence.

But only some claims call for facts as evidence. Sometimes explanations and analyses are offered as support for belief in a claim. In an argument against zoos, for example, a person might explain how different the behavior of a wild gorilla is from that of a captive, leading to the assertion that the educational value of watching a gorilla in a zoo is negligible.

Analytic evidence might take the form of discussions of causes and effects; comparisons or contrasts with similar situations, events, or issues in history, politics, culture, or nature; processes or procedures. And whether evidence is logically applied remains another concern.

People argue about what evidence should be acceptable to answer questions raised about civic and social issues. Should a dramatic or extraordinary example alter one's perspective? Does, for example, the televised trial of a scandalous murder case accurately inform us of the ways our justice system works most of the time? To what extent can statistics be relied on as a determinant of truth? If the SAT test scores of U.S. students have been declining since the 1960s, and television became almost universal in U.S. households in the 1950s, should television be blamed for the decline in student ability? Should SAT scores be accepted as a reliable measure or definition of how educated our students are?

As you can see from these questions, even the idea of what is reasonable is subject to inquiry and debate.

Expectations about Research A second convention within both the civic and academic discourse communities is the expectation that ideas will build on other ideas. For most arguers of claims, supporting evidence comes through research in printed or multimedia sources and is borrowed from other analysts, experiments, or researchers. The discourse community assumes that research will be done accurately and thoroughly, that it will be focused and analytic, and that other thinkers and writers who contribute to the understanding gained will be acknowledged.

In our culture generally, ideas are perceived as "owned." People who formally present ideas to the discourse community—in print or via a recordable medium—are held accountable for them. When anyone refers to, discusses, or incorporates the ideas or articulated knowledge of another, it is conventional to acknowledge the original source. In civic discourse, such acknowledgment is usually informal, often just a mention of a commentator's or writer's name or an author's book title. In the academic discourse community, however, the procedures for acknowledgment of ideas are codified into formal documentation rules that members of each discipline are expected to follow.

When Al Gore appears on *Larry King Live* to talk about the environment, his discourse represents his distillation of everything he's read and heard about the subject; his book, *Earth in the Balance,* acknowledges his debts in notes. Gore's handling of sources reflects an academic seriousness and respect for others' ideas. When a student jots down Gore's televised words and quotes them in a paper, she will acknowledge her debt to Gore, but not to all the influences on his thinking.

Attributing ideas to their authors, either formally or informally, suggests ownership, but technically and in a legal sense ideas cannot be owned—that is, they cannot be copyrighted or registered with the federal government as the property of a particular person. Only the specific expression of ideas can be legally tied to a person through copyright. So a poem, a newspaper opinion piece, or a film review can be copyrighted. Reviewer Janet Maslin's opinion of the film *The English Patient* cannot be copyrighted, but her review—the actual words—can be. But the convention of acknowledgment is more inclusive than legal copyright. Any idea or information borrowed from someone who has formally presented ideas, either in published words or "for the record" on electronic media, must be acknowledged as originating in that source.

Expectations about Coverage   Both the academic and civic discourse communities expect that arguers will, to some extent, possess a command of pertinent evidence and other relevant arguments on all sides of the issue in question. The civic discourse community is more lenient on this requirement, but, still, in most contexts, an informed arguer is a more believable one. Depending on the context, it may be important to be knowledgeable about the most recent discussions and evidence on the issue or about the well-known, controversial, or classic arguments about the topic, and most likely to show awareness of positions opposed to your own.

In the academic discourse community, arguers are expected to present a complete view of the issue—that is, to review and engage the important ideas and viewpoints about the topic. Many academic disciplines expect their full members—graduate students and professors—to "review the literature"—that is, to identify all the relevant claims and evidence on the topic—before going on to build their own arguments. It is expected that new understandings and interpretations will build on previous arguments and defend against possible objections by providing disqualifying reasoning or evidence.

Academic writers strive for complete, encyclopedic coverage of a controversy, but expectations for undergraduate students are not so stringent. In responding to college assignments, students should determine what the expectations of coverage are and then limit coverage of the controversy or issue accordingly. Time, if nothing else, should force you to both read selectively and present a relevant sampling of other writers' positions.

Classical argumentation provides for the consideration of alternate viewpoints in the refutation stage of an argument. Refutation is a catchall for a variety of ways of dealing with opposing claims. A writer might simply acknowledge the existence of differing points of view; maintain the priority or special relevance of his or her own view; briefly discount other views; accept a qualified or partial version of an opposing view; or identify and thoroughly critique flaws in opposing arguments. Some writers even structure or develop their own presentation of evidence through the refutation of differing views.

Beyond refutation, there are other ways of interacting with different viewpoints. Striving for a middle ground or writing to establish common ground is one technique for using arguments to advance solutions to current societal problems. Writing to foster negotiation between differing views or adopting a "Rogerian," or noncombative, stance are other ways people work with multiple viewpoints. And using an inquiry perspective, in which questions are identified instead of answered, can also be a constructive approach to competing claims.

The Subject of Argument

Not everything is fair game for argumentation. Statements or assertions of personal preferences and tastes, for example, are just that—personal. No one can argue with you about your love of Cherry Garcia ice cream or your enjoyment of *The X Files*. Such tastes are unarguable. However, the healthfulness of a Cherry Garcia—based diet or the artistic merits of a television series are suitable topics for argument because such arguments involve establishing a common standard of value or merit and comparing the specific choice—Cherry Garcia or *The X Files*—to these standards. Personal tastes become arguable when objective criteria can be established. Wine lovers, for example, have a system of taste analysis that removes the subjectivity from wine tasting and provides a standard for discussion and debate.

Assertions that proclaim accepted facts are usually deemed unsuitable for argument. Consider the following claims:

Automobile seatbelts save lives.

Vitamin C is a requirement for good health.

Dyslexia can seriously affect a student's ability to learn.

At one time, all these claims were hypothetical, but as research was conducted, these assertions have come to be considered facts.

Sometimes "facts" may turn out to be less than proven, or they may be alleged to be less than certain. Hence, although most people accept as a fact that smoking is unhealthful, some in the cigarette industry mounted the argument that smoking has nothing to do with cancer and heart attacks and is not addicting. Likewise, it's hard to argue with the facts that show the dangers of motorcycling bareheaded, yet motorcyclists have risen up to contest these facts and have mobilized to get helmet laws changed.

Legitimate and well-positioned arguments against "facts" sometimes do occur. After all, at one time, it was considered a fact that the sun revolved around the earth, and someone had to contest this idea to establish the reality. Within the discourse community of particular academic disciplines, for example, arguments do occur over facts. In history and science, new discoveries or reinterpretations of existing evidence may cause an argument over whether to revise a "fact," or something previously thought to be true. New discoveries of fossils and bones cause frequent revisions of the facts about when and where and how humans developed.

In many academic fields, there are areas where the facts are constantly uncertain or where debate rages over what the facts are. "Is there life elsewhere in the universe?" is a factual question that remains open to debate because science just has not accumulated enough evidence. More down-to-earth facts can also be uncertain. The authorship of a book sometimes attributed to Mikhail Bakhtin is uncertain, for it was published under the name of Bakhtin's less important colleague, V.N. Voloshinov, at a time when Bakhtin was in danger of imprisonment for his ideas. *Marxism* is either a collaboration between Bakhtin and Voloshinov, wholly by Bakhtin, or by Voloshinov under Bakhtin's influence, depending on which Bakhtin scholar you read.

Finally, it is difficult to argue over assertions of belief that are based on faith, tradition, or membership. The disciplines of philosophy and religious studies have developed modes of inquiry and debate about such matters as whether God, devils, angels, and so forth exist, but outside such specialized study assertions about religious matters are nearly unarguable.

16 Exigence

Academic Writing Program, University of Maryland

What Is "Exigence," and Why Do I Need to Know?

How many times have you written something—or read something—that just didn't seem to have much of a reason for being (aside, perhaps, from getting a grade in a class)? Although this problem certainly arises outside the classroom, it plagues the writing most students do in school. Perhaps your research paper leaves the impression of being unrelated to anyone or anything in the "real world," or your essay just doesn't seem to go anywhere or do anything important. We can probably all think of times when a reader's most honest response to our writing would reasonably have been "So what? Why should I care about this?"

Writing that fails to answer the "so what?" question lacks what is known as **exigence**. That is, it fails to convey the urgency, importance, usefulness, timeliness, or interest of its subject for its particular audience. Readers are likely to become bored because they find the writing pointless. Isn't that the last thing we want our readers, including our professors, to think? On the other hand, writing that establishes exigence gives its readers a genuine reason to keep reading.

Kairos and *Chronos* and Exigence

In Ancient Greece, there were two different concepts of time. *Chronos* expressed quantifiable, linear, time; it's the source of our word "chronological," for example. But they also conceived a term that expressed a sense of circumstance or situation. That word, *kairos*, is more akin to a sense of quality of time rather than quantity of time. We might think of it more in the sense of "the right time" or a "window of opportunity." And it is to this sense of *kairos* that exigence refers. When something has exigence, it is taking advantage of the right time, the right place, of a sense of urgency or advantage or appropriateness.

Intrinsic and Extrinsic Exigence

Writers must always be conscious of exigence as they compose, but because exigence is related to the audience and the situation, it often seems to exist outside of the writer's control. There are, in other words, situations that seem to have an **extrinsic** sense of exigence; the situation itself presents all the urgency and appropriateness, seeming to demand a response. For example, if there is a terrible natural catastrophe in, say, California, we expect the President to make some remarks about it. In that case, it seems to be the situation that calls for a response. Not only does it call for a response, but it calls for a certain kind of response. We can imagine what we would deem appropriate or inappropriate for the President to say in such a situation. In the workplace, assigned work provides the exigence for writing a report or a memo. In these cases, the exigence comes from the situation; so long as you attend to the subject at hand, you will have established the exigence for your discourse for that audience. (While this kind of situation might seem to "naturally" demand a response, the idea that a situation in endowed with essential exigence is thought by many to be questionable; instead, they suggest that there are social or situational reasons why we expect certain responses, why some things seem to "be" news and others are not).

In contrast to situations with a strong sense of extrinsic exigence, other situations seem to need to have exigence created for them. That will be the case with most of your writing. While indeed you are responding to a situation outside of your own making—that is, you are responding to a requirement set up by the instructor of your course—beyond that exigence you should also consider creating a sense of urgency and need for your writing. We refer to the author creating the exigence as a situation of **intrinsic** exigence; that is, the exigence is created within the composition rather than in the situation outside of the writing. How do you fashion such an opening, such a sense of urgency or demand for your argument? By showing your readers that a problem exists, that there is a situation that demands their attention, that you will discuss something they will find interesting and applicable to their lives.

Can You Give Me an Example?

Let's start with a typical example from *The Washington Post*. When the paper runs a story evaluating twenty brands of bottled water, the writer of the article may begin by explaining, "Since last week, when the federal government released studies showing that tap water in forty states is polluted, there has been a run on bottled water. What are the better brands?" Why does a story about bottled water begin this way? With his lead-in, the writer has shown the audience that his story addresses a problem that may affect them: much tap water is polluted, so they are probably changing to bottled water right now—shouldn't they know which is the best buy? Thus, the writer creates exigence for his story.

In academic writing, a writer might begin by referencing past works written on a topic, or with a review of the literature, or a review of what past scholars have said, on a given topic. The writer does this to establish exigence in the scholarly debate on the topic: people in the field are talking about it, and the writer is adding a new dimension to the conversation. An article in *College Composition and Communication* on using technology in the classroom aimed at an audience of writing teachers and scholars, for example, might begin by referring to recent articles on the topic published in journals of the field. The writer might then show what his article adds to the conversation about teaching with technology. Or, a writer might show that no one else has talked about a topic, and create exigence that shows how this new view adds to the field. For example, an article in a history journal on a lesser-known historical figure might begin by showing how this figure has been ignored in past scholarship and then by establishing the importance of this figure to understanding a particular point in history. Writers publishing in scholarly journals provide exigence that shows how their work is adding to the academic conversations in the field.

Now let's look back at the opening paragraphs of this discussion of exigence. You will find that we began by identifying a need or problem that affects our audience: students. We assumed that as students, you would find this problem pressing enough to read about our proposed solution. If you felt that this discussion was worth reading, for a reason other than passing a quiz, perhaps we have proven our point?

In these cases, the writers have taken steps to create an impression of exigence *for their readers,* even though the writers themselves naturally believe that the problems they are addressing are obviously both real and pressing. The point is that writers must begin with language that leads readers to believe that they should care.

When Do I Establish Exigence? Do I Just Need a Catchy Introduction?

Exigence should be apparent throughout a paper, and the first place it would appear is the introduction. When a reader finds that she has something at stake in a particular argument, issue, or decision, she will read on. In the first several sentences, it is essential to pull your reader in with a brief and clear picture of how your topic is relevant to her experience or self-interest.

Since you only have a few moments to catch a reader's attention, you should try to establish exigence early on. But readers may continue asking "So what?" as they read; if your writing continues to provide an answer to this question, they will continue reading. Thus, establishing exigence goes beyond writing a clever or captivating introduction. Solid exigence should reside behind your thesis statement, and every other statement in your text, because it keeps your readers' needs in mind. It is a factor guiding your selection of information to include and information to discard. It is a factor determining the order in which information is disclosed, and the way your writing is introduced and concluded. Exigence tells the writer and the reader what the importance behind the work is, providing focus and giving a sense of force or drive behind the words.

Let's consider the possible differences between a catchy introduction and the establishment of exigence. An introduction to a paper arguing for research funds for cystic fibrosis could be a sad story about a child with cystic fibrosis. The story could be a pathetic appeal to readers which could provide the "hook" that encourages them to continue reading past the first paragraph or two. In fact, the story could be an important supporting argument for your thesis. But it may not be enough to convince readers that they have a stake in the issue. What would be enough? Maybe the articulation of a problem marked by an urgency: thousands of children each year are born with this debilitating disease.

This brings us to a very important distinction in persuasive writing. There is a subtle difference between compelling your readers to read and persuading your readers to hold a position or to change their minds or to act for change. For the writing you do in this class, then, think of your interesting introduction and your established exigence as two separate things that work together. But remember that your argument needs both an interesting introduction to engage readers and established exigence to convince them that they have a stake in the issue about which you are writing.

17 Using the Five Canons of Rhetoric as Steps in the Process of Writing

Academic Writing Program, University of Maryland

Have you ever had the experience of sitting with a blank sheet of paper (or a blank computer screen) before you and being unable to make any progress on a writing task that you are trying to accomplish? Does it seem that there are just too many things to think about? That you don't know where to start? As surprising as it might sound, even experienced writers feel this way sometimes. There's no shame in admitting it: writing is hard work. Effectively putting thoughts down on paper requires great effort and careful consideration; you must think about what you want to say, what order you want to say it in, what wording or style you want to use. It can often seem overwhelming.

Classical rhetoricians, who wanted to systematize the process of writing speeches, developed a pattern for steps in the writing process, so that speech writers could proceed in an organized fashion and consider everything necessary for composing a good speech. This pattern became known as the "parts" or **canons** of rhetoric. One influential version of this pattern included five canons: invention, arrangement, style, memory, and delivery. This structure can also be adapted to other types of composition besides speeches, as long as we keep in mind the distinctions between composing oral speeches and composing typewritten papers.

Invention: Generating Arguments

Of all the steps in the writing process, invention is probably the hardest—and the most important. Invention is the crucial first step of determining what to put in your paper. One reason it can be so hard to figure out what we want to say is that we often take for granted that good writing has to be "original" in the sense of saying something the likes of which has never been said before. When taken to an extreme, this notion almost makes it seem as if good writing appears magically out of thin air. In reality, good writing can indeed be original, but classical rhetoricians recognized that real originality has less to do with trying to produce something from nothing, and more to do with working with what you already have and making it better. After all, when entrepreneurs "invent" a new tool or labor-saving device, they work with materials that are already available; they don't just magically create something from nothing. Similarly, classical rhetoricians imagined "invention" as a process of "finding" ideas that already exist—appropriately enough, since the word "invent" really means "come upon" or "find." Thinking about writing in this way can make the writing process less intimidating, since you're no longer under pressure to come up with something absolutely new. It doesn't mean that there's no room for originality or creativity. On the contrary, some of the most original and creative writing owes a great deal to ideas and writings that came before it.

So how exactly do you go about "inventing" an argument? There are several options available. You may already be familiar with the method called **brainstorming**, in which you jot down a list of words, phrases, or ideas on a sheet of paper as they come to you, not worrying (at least at first) whether everything fits together neatly; this process can give you a place to start. There's also the technique known as **freewriting**, in which you try to write continuously for a set period of time, not worrying about things like grammar and sentence structure. Using methods such as these, you may come up with some things that you may eventually choose not to include in the final draft of your paper, but the more material that you can generate using invention exercises, the more potential material you will have to choose from when you are deciding what belongs and what doesn't.

Arrangement: Organizing Arguments

So you've figured out what you want to say. Does it matter what order you say it in? With respect to argumentative writing, we can definitely say yes. The order in which you present your material can have a significant impact on the success or failure of your writing. To take one example, let's say you have three main points, two of which the audience might find strongly convincing, but one of which is weaker and less convincing. Should you save the best for last, and therefore present the weakest point first? That might cause your audience to lose interest early on, thinking that all your points will be as ineffective as the first one. Or do you leave the weakest point for last? That might be problematic too, since the last point is often the one most likely to be remembered by the reader, and you don't want the reader to walk away dwelling on your weakest point. In such a situation, many experts recommend a sort of "sandwich" structure in which the weakest point comes in between the two stronger ones. The point is that when you write your own papers, you must make decisions about how best to organize your material, keeping in mind the audience and purpose of your writing.

In addition to thinking about how to present your main points, it's also necessary to consider how to begin and end the paper, as well as what other structural features your paper might need. Papers that jump right into their main points with no background or context are generally not successful or even interesting to readers, since readers need to know why the topic is important before they can make sense of what a writer is arguing about that topic. The same goes for papers that end too suddenly. For this reason, a very basic pattern of writing arrangement consists of an introduction, body (where the main points are explained in detail), and conclusion. For longer papers (such as the final paper that you will write this semester), you will learn about an expanded version of the basic arrangement pattern. This version, called the "parts of a full argument," is especially helpful when you have more than a few sentences of background information, and when you must think about how to organize both your own supporting points and your refutation of opposing points. In the end, it's important to keep in mind that usually there is no single correct way to set up a paper. Instead, a different range of options is available in each case, and you as the writer must decide which option is best for the audience you are trying to reach and the purpose you are trying to achieve.

Style: Expressing Arguments

How you say something can be as important as what you say. Language can be a tricky thing, because it presents us with a seemingly endless range of potential problems. Some words have more than one meaning, and you want your readers to be clear about what meaning you intend. Different words can have the same meaning; or, more likely, they have meanings that are very similar but with slightly different connotations, and you will need to think carefully about which is the right one to use in a given situation.

To add to the complexity, no single variety of any language can be used in all possible situations. The language appropriate to a formal event would be inappropriate in a more casual context. The style a writer uses on a particular occasion may be influenced by things like dialect, slang, jargon, and colloquialisms, or it may be carefully crafted to be as neutral as possible. We have all probably wished at one time or another that language were simple, that there were only one single, correct word for each object or idea, so that there would never be any confusion or ambiguity. It might seem as if that would make writing (and indeed, all communication) much easier.

Looked at another way, however, the complexity of language presents us with a great opportunity. Different forms of language exist both because people themselves are different and because the same people can use different forms of language depending on the situation. Thus, the complexities inherent in language are best seen from a rhetorical perspective as possibilities available for a given audience and situation. The study of style, the consideration of how best to express one's own ideas to a specific audience in a particular situation, is empowering because it gives us the chance to make choices for ourselves, to choose our words just as we choose our method of organization. How formal should you be? What tone do you want to express in your writing? Will your audience understand jargon if you use it? Does your audience expect conciseness, or does the complexity of your content require you to present some information in two or three different ways?

To help you think about these and other stylistic issues, a number of language skills are built into the writing curriculum. Practicing these skills can help you develop your own written style, enabling you to make choices about emphasizing ideas in different ways, using figures of speech to create patterns and support your arguments, and combining sentences so that your writing flows more smoothly. In essence, style is about learning what options are available, so that you can use your own creativity to make the most effective choices in your writing.

Memory: Storing Arguments

Since classical rhetoricians were concerned primarily with composing speeches that would be delivered before an audience (and in an era without teleprompters), they devoted a considerable amount of thought to techniques that would help speakers memorize their points and arguments so that they could deliver them without having to look at notes. Such techniques often included mnemonic devices and "tricks" to aid memorization. For the composition of typewritten papers, memorization for oral delivery usually does not play a prominent role, but memory—in the sense of where typewritten arguments are *stored*—is still important. Think of what we mean when we talk about a computer's "memory," for example. Today, a number of technologies are available that allow us to store documents with ease, and it is to our advantage to make use of them. It goes without saying that you should save a copy of a paper that you are working on. But it pays to save *multiple* copies of really important documents (including ones that will be turned in for a grade), since accidents happen—files can be corrupted, disks can get erased, hard drives can crash, flash drives can get lost, and so on. To be on the safe side, you may even want to take the precaution of saving your paper to an email attachment that is stored in your email system; that way, even if your own hardware fails at some point, you still have a version of your paper on email that you can access. You may also find it helpful to deliberately save multiple versions of a single paper. For example, it's difficult to undo a major change to your draft if you don't have an earlier version saved. So you should consider at least saving a file copy of your rough draft and a separate copy of your final draft, so that you can access both versions electronically if you decide that it's useful to do so. Not only can using these labor-saving techniques help you out of potentially disastrous computer malfunctions, but they can also make the overall writing process flow more smoothly.

Delivery: Publishing and Formatting Arguments

"Delivery" originally referred to the act of delivering speeches orally before a live audience. Being an effective speaker usually means speaking loudly enough and at the right speed so that the audience can easily hear and follow the speech, enunciating clearly and according to the audience's standards for public speech, and perhaps using gestures to emphasize a point. But even in writing, delivery is important. For writing, we can think of delivery in two aspects: how an argument is transmitted to an audience, and how a typewritten argument is formatted.

When a speech is delivered orally before a live audience, the audience simply hears it as the speaker delivers it. But if your argument is typewritten, how would your audience physically receive it? For example, if you imagined writing your paper to "every citizen of the United States," how would you ensure that every citizen in the country could read your argument? It's obviously impractical to imagine mailing a copy of your argument to everyone in the country. Could you have it published in a venue in which everyone could read it? You might imagine having it published in a widely-read newspaper or magazine, but realistically, there's no newspaper or magazine that is read by *every* person in the country. How about publishing it online? Even then, it is worth considering that some American citizens don't have access to the internet.

In many cases, thinking about issues like these can prompt you to reconsider your audience, to narrow it down in order to make your argument more effective. For example, even if you are writing about an issue with a national scope—say, what to do about illegal immigration—that doesn't mean that your argument should be written to every citizen of the U.S. Your argument is more likely to be successful if you focus. For example, if you decide that you want to focus on the effect of the immigration debate on American presidential campaigns, then you could write your paper to scholars of government and politics, and emphasize the aspects of the issue that are most interesting to them. Since they are experts in political science, they would be able to put your argument to better use in advancing the national debate on immigration and politics than the "average" American citizen would; many of the latter might not only disagree with what you're arguing, they might even lack interest in the political side of the issue. By choosing to deliver your argument by having it published in a political science journal (such as *The Journal of Politics*), or even by imagining that you would distribute copies to your instructor and fellow students in the Government and Politics course that you're taking this semester, you can use the concept of delivery to narrow your audience and be more confident that the audience will be interested in your scholarly approach to the topic.

Thinking about where you would publish your argument is helpful for conceptualizing your audience, but within the context of ENGL 101, you will be designing your papers so that a special set of overhearers—your instructor and (in draft workshops) your fellow students—can read it. Thus, your paper must be formatted so that these readers can understand your argument. Formatting requirements that might seem minor are really a matter of audience expectation. For example, consider how your experience of reading a textbook, such as this one, would change if it were printed in tiny type, in a strange script or Old English style font, or, worse, if it were handwritten. Would you bother to read it? Would you even be able to read it? This is why most teachers have standard requirements for what papers should look like. For example, double-spacing your papers and leaving one-inch margins allows your teacher to make comments on your paper that will help you understand both what you did well and what you could improve on. Page numbers help readers find their way around the paper. And using a clear, standard format for citing your sources helps readers track down additional information and helps you establish yourself as a valid participant in a public or scholarly debate.

Other seemingly minor issues with potentially substantial impact also relate to delivery and format. Printing problems can happen to anybody, but when a writer turns in a paper with printing that obviously hasn't been aligned correctly, or that is far too light because of ink problems, it makes the paper—and the writer—look bad. If you submitted such a document to an audience other than your teacher (if, for example, you submitted a resume with that problem to potential employers), your readers wouldn't be inclined to take it seriously, and there is no reason why your teacher is obligated to do so, either. That's why you should print out your paper ahead of time so that you can correct any printing problems that may arise. And don't fall into the habit of handing in your paper as a jumble of loose sheets; you should staple your paper together (or at the very least paper-clip it) so that your teacher doesn't have to keep track of loose paper. Finally, perhaps the most important part of delivery is turning in your paper when it's due. Even the most brilliant argument cannot achieve its intended purpose if it's not delivered at the right time.

For these reasons, you will be expected to follow formatting guidelines in your papers. Your teacher will include information about formatting requirements on his or her course policies.

Seeing the Parts of Rhetoric as a Whole

This five-part pattern is a useful tool, but it should be used with flexibility. Ideally, an orderly writing process would treat invention first, then arrangement, then style, then memory, and finally delivery. But in reality, good writers keep all of them in mind throughout the composing process. In the middle of considering arrangement, you may discover that your paper seems unbalanced and that you need to add another main point, which sends you back to the invention process to find more material. Also, the parts can overlap; arrangement and style can be closely related, especially when you consider the layout of sentences within a paragraph. The parts of rhetoric, then, are not meant to be rigid and inhibiting. Instead, they are simply terms and concepts for things that writers need to think about under any circumstances. They give you a way of structuring the process of writing; just keep in mind that this structure can be adaptable and open-ended.

18 Invention—Generating Ideas with Stasis Theory

Academic Writing Program, University of Maryland

One way to invent something to say is to think about the kinds of questions people might ask about a subject. Just as classical rhetorical theory offers a system for the process of writing, it also offers a system for inventing or analyzing what's at issue in any debate. This system is called **stasis theory**. Stasis theory can help you come up with ways to argue and it can help you understand the ways others are arguing. The term *stasis* comes from a Greek term that means "a stand," as in "taking a stand." For the Greeks, who literally pictured their arguments, the arguer envisioned where "to stand" in a particular debate. The best translation here might be "issue," as in understanding what is "at issue" in a controversy. That's a phrase you might hear in a news report covering a topic; the reporter, having introduced the topic and offered some information, might begin to delineate "what's at issue" in the topic by saying what various participants or factions in the debate think and what kinds of questions come up in the matter. When you are thinking about a topic for a composition, it can be useful to imagine yourself as a reporter looking at some problem and beginning to think about what's at issue, where the controversies are, where you may take a stand.

Stasis theory presents us with categories or questions to pose in understanding a debate or understanding where there is debate or disagreement in an issue. There are many theories about how many categories of the stases there are; some theorists use slightly different categories than the ones we have included here. In general, the stases and the questions they pose are these:

Stasis	Questions
Conjecture (or fact/ definition, or essence/ existence)	Did it happen? Does it exist? What is it? How is it defined?
Cause/Effect	How did it get this way? What caused this to happen? What are/will be the effects of this?

Value	Is it a good or bad thing?
	Is it right or wrong, honorable or dishonorable?
	Is it better or worse, more or less desirable than any alternatives?
	Should it be sought out or avoided?
Action	What should we do about this?
	What actions are possible?
	What proposals shall we make about it?
Jurisdiction	Who should handle this matter?
	Who has the right to decide this matter?

Staking a Claim with Stasis Theory

Perhaps you want to write about an experience you had with the police last year. One day, you were driving home from a friend's house, and you saw police lights flashing in your rearview mirror. You were pulled over, and the white police officer looked at you suspiciously and asked to see your license. Too afraid to ask what this was about, you just complied. Later that night, you heard that a crime had been committed not far from where you were stopped, and the suspect was vaguely described as a young African American man. You too are a young African American man. When you tell the story to some friends, they say that you were stopped for DWB—driving while black.

How can you begin inquiry into this experience? There's no doubt that it occurred—you were definitely stopped. But what other possible questions arise here. Think about stasis theory. What can you call what happened to you—was it routine police work? racial profiling? Why did it happen? Was it a good or bad thing it happened? Was it reasonable or unreasonable? Should you do something about it? What could be done about it? Is it up to you as an individual to do something about it, or should you look to others to respond? If you use these questions from stasis theory, you can find what about the issue interests you and focus on that in your inquiry.

Or perhaps one of the experiences you cherish most from your childhood was listening to stories from your grandmother. She told stories about everything—about when she was a small girl on a farm during the Great Depression, about when your dad was born, stories she made up, stories she heard herself as a young girl. But how can you write about this in terms of an argument of inquiry? Again, you might use the questions from stasis theory to help you think about whether there are any issues to consider here. Again, there's no disputing that this happened, but you can again think about definitions—were the stories your grandmother told you just stories, or could they be considered folklore? Why do we tell stories? Is it to pass along values, or just for entertainment? What effect did these stories have on you? What effect does storytelling have on children (or cultures) in general? Is hearing stories a good thing? Is it better for children to hear stories from family than, say, to watch television or see movies? Should we encourage the telling of stories among families? How should we encourage storytelling? Who should do such encouraging, if we agree it should be done?

19 Writing a Rhetorical Analysis

Academic Writing Program, University of Maryland

One of the best ways to engage a text rhetorically is to look at how an author utilizes the rhetorical appeals to persuade his or her audience. This may be done either by looking at a single persuasive text or by looking at two persuasive texts that tackle the same topic. To demonstrate how a rhetorical analysis might be written, we have chosen to discuss two arguments on the topic of gay straight alliance clubs from the April 14, 2000 issue of *CQ Researcher*.

At Issue: Should High Schools Permit "Gay-Straight Alliance" Clubs?

Yes

Jim Anderson
Communications Director, Gay, Lesbian and Straight Education Network

WRITTEN FOR *THE CQ RESEARCHER*

Considerable media attention has been paid over the past few months, to gay-straight alliance (GSA) controversies in Utah, Louisiana and Orange County, Calif. In each instance, school boards either considered or took action to prevent students from exercising their federally protected right under the Equal Access Act.

While these battles and controversies have been intriguing, it is, perhaps, more interesting to consider the stories that have not made the news.

Little attention has been paid to the approximately 700 gay-straight alliances that are currently meeting in high schools from coast-to-coast. These school communities accepted or embraced the students and their efforts, and not as a result of judicial mandate. Instead, they recognized their professional, if not moral, responsibility to do so.

Should other high schools permit the creation of gay-straight alliances? To answer the question, we need to define gay-straight alliances and to discuss why students are forming them in such numbers. A gay-straight alliance is formed by lesbian, gay, bisexual and transgender (LGBT) students and their straight classmates. These students join together to support one another and to address concerns about the misinformation and ignorance that too often result in anti-gay harassment or violence at school.

Their concerns are well-founded. Studies by the federal Centers for Disease Control and Prevention (CDC) show that lesbian, gay and bisexual students are more than four times as likely as their heterosexual classmates to be threatened with or injured by a weapon while at school.

The Gay, Lesbian and Straight Education Network found similarly disturbing trends. In a recent national survey, we found that 61 percent of LGBT students experience verbal harassment, 27 percent physical harassment and 14 percent outright physical assault while at school.

This harassment and isolation may negatively affect students' self-esteem and school performance. Such experiences may explain why national mainstream organizations such as the American Counseling Association and the National Association of Social Workers have recently endorsed gay-straight alliances.

Every student is entitled to a supportive, safe and affirming learning environment. With this goal in mind, we urge schools not only to permit gay-straight alliances but also to encourage and foster their existence.

No

Peter LaBarbera
Senior Analyst, Family Research Council

WRITTEN FOR *THE CQ RESEARCHER*
School districts should not allow the formation of gay-straight alliances on their campuses. These groups, where they already exist, have become de facto homosexuality booster clubs—causing unnecessary divisions and distractions and subjecting the entire student body to one-sided propaganda. Moreover, they are part of a movement that promotes radical identities and dangerous sexual practices to vulnerable, confused teens.

The gay-straight alliances are part of an ingenious strategy by pro-homosexuality and transsexuality groups like the Gay, Lesbian and Straight Education Network (GLSEN) to inject their unhealthy sexual and gender ideologies into the classroom. Students rally around the "rights" of gay, bi or even trans (transgender) classmates who, it is true, are ostracized and sometimes mistreated by their peers.

But while GLSEN and other groups have artfully "spun" the issue of youth homosexuality into one of "discrimination," it is really about behavior and parents' rights to guide their children's moral decisions.

In Massachusetts, taxpayers subsidize the formation of gay-straight alliances—there are now 185—through state grants for GSA projects.

Across the country, educators are wasting valuable school time by allowing GSAs to promote extreme notions to the entire student body. Students rarely get to hear the other side of the debate, and they fear expressing their opposition to homosexuality because of the schools' politically correct embrace of homosexuality.

The National Education Association, the American Civil Liberties Union, GLSEN and their allies promote GSAs in the name of school "safety." But schools shouldn't promote homosexual identities to troubled kids when studies show that homosexual males have drastically shorter life spans. This is due to the risky sexual behavior that flourishes in the promiscuous "gay" world. At a March conference sponsored by GLSEN's Boston affiliate, speakers from the state's Education Department approvingly discussed "queer sex" acts to an audience made up mostly of students ages 14–21.

Parents must resist an agenda that uses schools' authority to confirm impressionable youth in harmful lifestyles. As one former homosexual has noted, "From every medical and health aspect—up to and including the probability of becoming infected with AIDS—it is tragic, even criminal, to lead a child into homosexuality because he or she showed some degree of confusion in adolescence."

Rhetorical Analysis—Understanding the Appeals

Quick, which of the two arguments is more convincing? Jim Anderson's in favor of high schools permitting gay straight alliance clubs or Peter LaBarbera's opposing high schools' decisions to allow gay straight alliance clubs? The answer you arrive at by performing a rhetorical analysis could be that either author's argument is stronger for its intended audience. Your goal in the rhetorical analysis is to assess each author's effectiveness in using the three rhetorical appeals and to conclude that one author's argument is more effective overall for its intended audience because of the way that author uses one, two, or all three rhetorical appeals.

Before we proceed, we must identify each author's intended audience. Although both writers, Jim Anderson and Peter LaBarbera, composed their arguments for the *CQ Researcher*, and their audiences share certain traits, it is also clear from reading the two arguments that the authors have two very different audiences in mind. What traits do the two authors' audiences share? We can determine these by looking at the authors' joint publication choice: the *CQ Researcher*. *CQ Researcher* is published weekly in print, and offered forty-four times a year online to libraries, universities, and researchers who subscribe, and it attempts to give in depth coverage to a single topic each issue. In addition to each edition featuring a bibliography, each edition features a pair of opposing arguments from politicians, academics, or people connected by their vocations to the issue. Both Anderson's and LaBarbera's audiences, therefore, are interested in topics of debate, either because they are politically minded or because they are pursuing research on a particular topic: in this case, gay-straight alliance clubs. Anderson's and LaBarbera's audiences are also similar in that they would be made up of adults voting-age and older and would include all races and both genders. There is, however, an important characteristic that differentiates the two authors' intended audiences: degree of partisanship. Whereas Jim Anderson, who supports gay-straight alliance clubs in high schools, attempts to convince those who are neutral and perhaps slightly opposed to his position as well as supporters, Peter LaBarbera is addressing exclusively those who support his position. LaBarbera's choice is problematic, given the fact that the readers of the *CQ Researcher* cover every pole of the liberal to conservative spectrum.

He will have to be careful to avoid offending those who disagree with his position. Now we are ready for the next stage of the rhetorical analysis: an evaluation of each author's use of the rhetorical appeals.

Let's begin by comparing the two authors' extrinsic ethos. Extrinsic ethos refers to the credibility that an author possesses outside of the argumentative text itself. Jim Anderson is the Communications Director of the Gay, Lesbian and Straight Education Network. Based upon his position and his organizational affiliation, what level of credibility should we attach to Anderson outside of the argument? The nature of his position and his role as director of communications leads us to conclude both that he is trained and well educated and that he is frequently called upon to communicate with the press and the public. This suggests strong extrinsic ethos. His organizational affiliation, in contrast, points to exactly what position he will be taking: supporting gay-straight alliance clubs. Although this does not necessarily translate as weak extrinsic ethos, it does mean that Anderson will have to work to convince a neutral or opposing audience that he is not biased. Peter LaBarbera is the Senior Analyst for the Family Research Council, a conservative think tank. Even if you did not know that the Family Research Council is a conservative think tank, the phrase "family research" should clue you in to what stand LaBarbera will be taking on the question of whether high schools should permit gay-straight alliance clubs. Similarly to Anderson, LaBarbera will have to work to convince a neutral or opposing audience that he is not biased in terms of character. LaBarbera's title and position indicates that he is an expert in tabulating, compiling, and assessing data. In this regard, LaBarbera's extrinsic ethos is strong.

In order to grasp Jim Anderson's intrinsic ethos, we need to ask a series of questions. Is he fair-minded? Does he cite knowledgeable authorities and provide outside evidence to back his claims? Does he treat the opposing side with respect? Anderson succeeds in all three of these endeavors, and avoids alienating an opposing audience, because he is careful to build his credibility slowly, over the course of his entire argument. He uses the first three paragraphs to set up the question that he asks in the opening sentence of the fourth paragraph: "Should other high schools permit the creation of gay straight alliances?" (321) By asking this question overtly, he is suggesting to an opposing audience that support for gay straight alliance clubs is not a foregone conclusion and that it is a stance that must be carefully considered before being defended. He proceeds to justify a need for a definition of gay-straight alliance clubs and offers a warrant for why those clubs have become necessary (victimization of gay students). He then calls upon the statistical findings of two national organizations, one of which is his own: the federal Centers for Disease Control and Prevention and the Gay, Lesbian and Straight Education Network. Finally, after invoking the support of the American Counseling Association and the National Association of Social Workers, he makes an ethical plea: "Every student is entitled to a supportive, safe, and affirming learning environment" (321). Once he has presented a full defense of gay straight alliance clubs, he is comfortable stating the position that he would like his audience to take: "not only to permit gay straight alliances but also to encourage and foster their existence" (321).

Peter LaBarbera's intrinsic ethos, in contrast, is poor, not because of the position he is taking but because of the way he addresses the opposing side. His overriding disrespect for the proponents of gay straight alliance clubs can be seen in two different ways: through his use of language and characterization, and through his use of quotation marks. Consider the diction or word choice that LaBarbera incorporates in the opening sentence of the second paragraph: "The gay-straight alliances are part of an ingenious strategy by pro-homosexuality and transsexuality groups like the Gay, Lesbian and Straight Education Network (GLSEN) to inject their unhealthy sexual and gender ideologies into the classroom" (321). In choosing words like "ingenious" to describe the opponents' method, "inject" to describe how organizations supporting gay rights get their information into the classrooms, and "unhealthy" to describe the "ideologies" that organizations like GLSEN promote, LaBarbera risks alienating both readers who have not yet made up their mind about gay straight alliance clubs and supporters of gay civil rights. LaBarbera's use of quotation marks presents an even greater chance that he will lose the support of an opposing or neutral audience. Consider the first instance where LaBarbera uses quotation marks. LaBarbera writes:

> Students rally around the "rights" of gay, bi, or even trans (transgender) classmates, who, it is true, are ostracized and sometimes mistreated by their peers. (321)

Any credibility that LaBarbera might gain by the concession that he makes at the end of the sentence (that gays are "sometimes mistreated") is undermined by his decision to put quotation marks around the word *rights*. The reader may wonder, "Does LaBarbera believe that gays, bisexuals, and transsexuals do not deserve rights?" On multiple occasions later in LaBarbera's argument, he uses quotation marks in a manner that calls into question whether he respects his opposing audience. For example, he writes that "GLSEN and other groups have artfully `spun' the issue of youth homosexuality into one of `discrimination'" (321). Does he not believe that what gays face is discrimination? Each instance where LaBarbera comes across as unnecessarily antagonistic may solidify a neutral or opposing reader's opinion that LaBarbera disrespects the opposing side. The end result is that LaBarbera may lose credibility in all but the staunchest supporter's mind.

Ethos is not the only measure of whether a piece of persuasive writing is weak or strong. In fact, "many rhetoricians . . . have considered pathos the strongest of the appeals." Whereas in terms of ethos, Anderson's argument is stronger, in terms of pathos, LaBarbera's argument is stronger. LaBarbera excels in making the audience fear for the morality of students. One way in which he does this is by identifying gay straight alliance clubs as a threat. LaBarbera concludes his opening paragraph by suggesting that "[gay straight alliance clubs] are part of a movement that promotes radical identities and dangerous sexual practices to vulnerable, confused teens" (321). Even if we disagree with LaBarbera's stance, we must recognize the emotional impact of his word choices: "a movement," "radical identities," "dangerous sexual practices," and "vulnerable, confused teens." Each phrase asks LaBarbera's audience to feel the same concern that he feels regarding the implementation of gay straight alliance clubs. Jim Anderson, on the other hand, does not take full advantage of the fact that he is making an argument that is based upon empathizing (and sympathizing) with the plight of gay and bisexual students, who are "more than four times as likely as their heterosexual classmates to be threatened with or injured by a weapon while at school" (321). Although Anderson provides a statistic, he could have also made the statistic personal by identifying one such victim of anti-gay or anti-bisexual harassment by name if that person was willing.

In terms of logos, Anderson and LaBarbera adopt completely different strategies; and it is up to you to make the case that one of the strategies is more successful. Anderson begins by giving a context for an argument on the topic of gay straight alliance clubs. He then proceeds to offer a definition of gay straight alliances that suggests the twofold purpose of such organizations is to open up communication between homosexuals and heterosexuals and to help spread awareness of the obstacles that many gay students face. He waits until the final sentence of his argument to state the position that he would like his audience to take (in support of gay straight alliances), but not until he makes an assertion that few teachers and parents would disagree with: "Every student is entitled to a supportive, safe, and affirming learning environment" (321). LaBarbera, in contrast, opens with the thesis or position that he wants his audience to support: "School districts should not allow the formation of gay straight alliances on their campuses" (321). He proceeds to attach as much negativity and long-term risk as he can to the effect of high schools allowing gay straight alliance clubs to form.

Ultimately, if you conclude in your rhetorical analysis that Jim Anderson's argument supporting gay straight alliance clubs is stronger, you are most likely building your case on Anderson's effective use of ethos, whereas if you conclude that LaBarbera's argument opposing gay straight alliance clubs is more persuasive you are building your case both on LaBarbera's substantial use of pathos and on the fact that his intended audience supports his position.

Rhetorical Analysis and Stasis Theory— Determining What's at Issue in a Text

You already know something about **stasis theory**, about the categories of questions for thinking about what is at issue in a topic. When you do rhetorical analysis, particularly of a persuasive text, it's important to know what arguments are being made, and one way to recognize the arguments is to think of what kinds of issues are being discussed.

Determining "what's at issue" in a debate is crucial to understanding the topic, proceeding with research, and finding a solution. But arguers rarely stop to identify the kind of issue they are debating. Imagine two educators disagreeing over whether a national school exit test should come at the end of the eighth or twelfth grades. They will probably not stop to tell their audience, "The issue we are debating here concerns what course of action to take." Yet the reader analyzing their arguments needs to have a general system for describing what kind of issue is being addressed.

The first four stases are "hierarchical", meaning they build on each other and there must be agreement in an earlier stasis before there can be agreement in a later one. So, for example, before two historians can agree about the **causes** of terrorism, they must agree not only that terrorism exists (a matter of **conjecture**) but also on how to **define** it. Similarly, before two policy analysts can agree on a proposal of how to deal with terrorism, they must agree that it exists (**fact**), on how exactly it should be **defined**, on what **causes** and **effects** it has, and on its **value**. Then they can debate a plan of **action**. The stasis of **jurisdiction** stands outside this hierarchy but it can relate to any of the other questions. Thus before the policy that the analysts working for the executive branch agree upon can be implemented, it must be agreed that it is the executive branch that has a right to make such decisions.

First Stasis: Conjecture (or Fact and Definition)

The questions in this stasis concern the existence, nature, and attributes of subjects. Arguments about whether something existed or exists, happened or is happening belong in this stasis. Some disagreements concern how or whether a potential "fact" can be verified, and some disagreements go deeper and question whether the status of "fact" is even possible in some cases.

Identifying facts can depend on prior definitions. We saw this with the recent recategorization of Pluto. Because there was disagreement on what constituted a planet, there was disagreement about which bodies in space should be categorized as planets. Once the definition was changed, the categorization was changed.

There are other instances when arguers agree on some set of "facts" but disagree on how they should be labeled or characterized. For example, we may agree that a friend of ours has taken a car, but disagree on whether to call that fact "borrowing" or "stealing."

Second Stasis: Cause

If we agree that something exists or happened, we may next naturally question what brought it about. Causes are usually matters of probable argument rather than factual demonstration when people are involved, since it is usually impossible to recreate human events in order to test a causal hypothesis, while controlling all the potentially influential variables.

Predictions—forecasts of what will happen—are essentially questions about cause since our speculations about what might happen depend on what causes we think could bring about a certain effect, whether we think those causes are likely to occur, and whether we agree upon what kinds of effects a certain event might cause.

Third Stasis: Value (or Quality or Evaluation)

Many perspectives can gather around questions of quality and value. What quality does the thing have? Is it good or bad of its kind, beautiful or ugly, moral or immoral, or at any of the fine gradations between these extremes? These disagreements can also concern what kind of evaluation to make in the first place. Should a person, a politician for example, be judged only in one area of performance, or for character overall? Should a work of art be evaluated morally, or only aesthetically?

Often participants in a discussion about values find they actually share the same values but disagree over how to weight or order them according to importance in a given case. They must use some key value to help them create a hierarchy of other values from most to least important.

Fourth Stasis: Action

If we agree that a situation exists and we evaluate it negatively, we next naturally ask what, if anything, can be done about it. (In fact, one argumentative strategy pushes to action as the issue under debate, as though agreement existed on the preceding issues. Rebuttal then requires moving the issue back down the stases.)

There can be many different arguments over what the best possible course of action might be. Thus arguments in this stasis frequently concern feasibility and trade-offs. We can often agree on what should be done ideally, but not on what is actually possible given the available resources. We can also debate who has the authority or responsibility to take action; in fact, some arguments for courses of action spend much of their time trying to "create" an audience that will act.

We can also agree that a situation exists and evaluate it positively, concurring that we'd like to see the situation maintained (although others might argue against us). Maintaining the *status quo* and arguing that we *should* maintain it also belong within the action stasis.

Questions of Jurisdiction

During an argument in any of the preceding stases, but particularly in questions of evaluation and action, someone may challenge someone else's right to conduct or even to participate in the discussion. Does a particular group have the right to make decisions about the issue? Is one group interfering in another's domain? How do we determine the appropriate forum in which to conduct the argument?

Jurisdictional arguments can be raised in many kinds of controversies. Is it America's right to evaluate China's human rights policies? Do certain powers belong to Congress, to the States, or to the people? Who has the right to decide what a person can do with his or her body? Because such questions do not directly tackle the arguments advanced within the four stases outlined above, they form a separate stasis. Jurisdiction, however, does not follow the first four stases in sequential order. Instead, it is a kind of underlying stasis which attempts to shift the conversation to a different forum or to redistribute the authority for making decisions about the subject. It is ultimately a question of who can debate and who can decide.

The Rhetoric of "Setting an Issue"

Classifying an issue according to its stasis is a useful stage in the arts of inquiry, discussion, and argument. Arguers making or responding to a case can try to set or change the issue to their advantage.

The order of the stases (from fact and definition to cause, to value, to action) is an important feature of the system since it reveals the consequences of setting an issue in a certain stasis. Setting an issue in the third or fourth stasis, for example, frequently assumes agreement in the first or second; in some situations that agreement may be unwarranted. An arguer may propose action for a situation that the audience has yet to identify as a problem. The audience is pressured to see the situation as a problem, however, simply because a solution has been proposed. Similarly, in some situations and with some audiences, arguing in the first or second stasis will immediately create agreement in the third or fourth. For example, a case for the disappearance of a certain species of fish (first stasis) will function with some very receptive audiences as a call to action (fourth stasis). So setting the issue in a particular stasis can be a powerful rhetorical strategy.

Let's look at the pair of articles from *CQ Researcher*. The way they are presented underscores the point here about stasis theory: the whole section is titled "AT ISSUE". What is "at issue" in the overriding question "Should high schools permit 'gay-straight' alliance clubs?" In which stasis is that question? That's pretty simple—should it be done is a question of **action**. But are the articles only discussing action? Let's consider them with more depth.

Jim Anderson's "yes" argument begins with points that related to the fact/definition stasis: he points out that there has been "considerable media attention" to this subject, and that school boards have considered or taken action. He doesn't dispute anything there, he just says what has happened. He makes a point that is in the stasis of fact/ definition, but it's not a controversial point, as far as he is concerned.

He then goes on to say that what is more interesting is what hasn't made the news (paragraph two), and that's the "approximately 700 gay-straight alliance" clubs that are already meeting. Again, he's making a point about the existence of these clubs, but that's not what's controversial. He notes that "These school communities accepted or embraced the students and their efforts, and not as a result of judicial mandate. Instead, they recognized their professional, if not moral, responsibility to do so." In terms of the stases, he's suggesting *why* schools formed these clubs (that's a point about cause/effect), and saying that the cause was professional and/or moral duty. That last part sounds a lot like value, and it's a good example of how cause/effect and value are very intertwined. He's stating the idea that forming these clubs was morally right. Certainly someone could interject their own perspective here and say no, they are not, but Anderson is not arguing this point—he makes this move and believes his audience agrees, because he doesn't argue this point.

Then, in paragraph four, he raises the question of whether there should be more of these clubs in other high schools. We can see there that he has moved to action after making some presumptions about existence, cause and value. But then he makes an interesting move. From that question about action—"Should other high schools permit the creation of gay-straight alliances"—he jumps back to the definition stasis and the causal stasis, saying that "To answer the question, we need to define gay-straight alliances and to discuss why students are forming them in such numbers.' What's the rhetorical effect of the way he is arranging these arguments so far?

Anderson offers a definition of these alliances in the rest of paragraph four. Is the definition particularly controversial? Would we say he is making an argument with this definition? Why or why not? Is his definition of the alliances purely definitional, or does he pull in elements of cause/effect and value as well? How does he do this? Why might he be doing it?

In the next three paragraphs, Anderson builds his argument with arguments from various authorities, using statistics to make his case. All of these are examples of arguments that state the existence of threats and harassment, which point out arguments in cause/effect stasis: the statistics prove that these threats exist, and these threats have an effect ("This harassment and isolation may negatively affect students' self-esteem and school performance"). He also makes subtle value arguments here—the affects are negative, the trends are disturbing.

Anderson ends the argument with a clear statement of action, dependent on a sentence that has to do with fact/definition, cause, and value: "Every student is entitled [the idea that students are entitled to something harkens back to the idea that our rights exist] to a supportive, safe and affirming learning environment" [the implication is that such an environment will have an effect on students; furthermore, the implication is that it will be a positive affect]. Based on arguments of fact/definition, cause/effect and value, Anderson makes his argument: yes, these clubs should exist.

If we think about it, it makes sense that any argument about an action should be made on points about cause/effect and value—we generally decide that we want to do things because we believe they will have positive effects. We have coffee in the morning because we believe it will have an effect (it will caffeinate us) and that effect will be good (it will make us alert). Anderson has used the hierarchy of the stases—whether consciously or not—to establish this argument about an action he favors. The extent to which he goes into each point has to do with the constraints of his rhetorical situation: his audience, the genre, the source, the limitations of space.

Exercise

Look at Peter LaBarbera's "no" argument about gay-straight alliance clubs. Does he, like Anderson, make arguments in other stases to construct his point that the clubs should not be permitted in high schools? How can you compare their arguments using the way each constructs points in the various stases? Does LaBarbera use one stasis more than others to make his point?

20 Stasis Theory— Identifying the Issues and Joining the Debate

Academic Writing Program, University of Maryland

Without a sense of what is at issue in a disagreement, it can be difficult to decide where to begin one's own argument or to determine what even counts as arguable within a particular discourse. In his book *Political Communication*, Dan Hahn suggests that one reason there is apathy in American politics is because it is hard to find one's way into a debate:

> Anybody who has ever arrived late to a cocktail party knows how difficult it is to catch up. Every conversation you try to join is confusing. You don't know what has already been said, so you don't know what you should say. Sometimes you plunge in, only to have somebody say, "Yes, that was what Bill was saying a few minutes ago." After a few such embarrassing incidents, you learn either to keep your mouth shut or to change the subject as soon as you enter the group.
>
> Unfortunately, those are also the two options most people take when becoming aware of politics. Nobody bothers to explain what the societal conversation has already covered (although history courses try to do so). Nobody brings you "up to snuff" on the nature of the controversies, what the various sides are, and why people on those sides take the positions they do. All too many people conclude that politics is too complicated and give up.[1]

Perhaps you have felt this way when reading about a topic. Stasis theory offers a system for finding your way in, for getting "up to snuff" on a debate. The stases are like sorting bins for issues and questions. No matter what the subject, the issues can be put into one or more of the five categories described below. (Note that, collectively, the categories are called **stases**; each individual category is called a **stasis**.) If you keep these categories in mind while you read about a subject, you will find it easier to identify the separate issues in the discourse about it. Later, as you begin to fashion your own arguments, knowing where people tend to agree and disagree will assist you in knowing how to start and how to rebut counterarguments that assume agreement where it does not, in fact, exist.

[1] Hahn, Dan F. *Political Communication: Rhetoric, Government, and Citizens.* 2nd ed. State College, PA: Strata Publishing, Inc.: 2003.

As you prepare your stasis grid, you can use stasis theory to both anticipate debates and to recognize them when you see them.

The Stases in a Debate

We often wonder how the stases will help us as writers once we have figured out what to write about. Since we know the stases work as sorting bins to classify different types of arguments, and we know how to decide which stasis applies to our opposing arguments, we can use this to devise a thesis that confronts our opposition in the right mode. But do the stases have any use to us as writers after we've formulated our thesis? The answer is an emphatic "yes!"

To understand how they are useful, we must first understand how the stases function differently in a large, multi-faceted debate as opposed to their use in our own individual arguments. In a large debate, we can trace the stases through the issues by posing them as a series of questions:

- Does X exist? How do we define X?
- What causes X? What are the consequences of X?
- Is X therefore a good thing or bad thing? Are the benefits of X worth the costs?
- What should we do about X? Should we implement X?
- Who decides any of these questions about X?

In doing this, we can map the arc of the debate, identify the points at which opposing sides are in disagreement, and decide where we, as participants, should intervene in the debate. For example, we may map the debate over same-sex marriage:

- How do we define marriage?
- What are the consequences of applying or ignoring that definition?
- Are the benefits of these consequences worth the costs?
- Should we legalize same-sex marriage?
- Who should make this decision—states, the federal government, a popular vote?

The Stases in Your Argument

When you as a writer sit down to say your piece about this issue, you may realize a couple of things. First, you may notice that the two major parties in the debate don't agree in any of the stases, so even though the debate is bogged down in definitional issues, the public discourse is centered on action. Second, you may notice that in order to establish your action claims, you must first establish your value claims, which in turn rely on the answer to the cause and consequence questions, which themselves require a definition to work from. Each question depends on the answer reached in the previous stasis.

Suddenly, you have to tackle five major questions instead of one, but fortunately, they're already organized into a logical sequence for you. Thus, in constructing your own argument, you can use the procedure of moving through the stases as an organizational technique. Depending on your position, then, a basic outline might look like one of these:

Definition:	Marriage, a love bond between two consenting adults, is a fundamental right.
Consequence:	By denying same-sex partners marriage, we are consequently withholding their human rights.
Evaluation:	These human rights are more important than archaic traditions based on procreation.
Action (thesis):	We should legalize same-sex marriage.

-or-

Definition:	Marriage is a procreative bond and a privilege.
Consequence:	By extending these rights to same-sex couples, we de-emphasize the role of parenting and break down the family structure.
Evaluation:	Upholding traditional family structures is more important than granting special rights to couples whose bond is not for the purpose of procreation.
Action (thesis):	We should reserve marriage for heterosexual couples.

Notice that taking this debate through the stases in both your own position and the opposing position or positions is also useful for invention. Here, for example, someone supporting same-sex marriage would notice that by starting with marriage as primarily procreative in purpose, the opposing side potentially paints itself into a corner, unless it is willing to stipulate that infertile heterosexuals cannot properly marry. Since few opponents of same-sex marriage are willing to go that far, the supporter now has a useful point of refutation. Someone opposing same-sex marriage, on the other hand, would notice that the definition they start with may lead them to a position they do not in fact hold, and therefore will want to modify their definition.

You will surely find that your argument is more complex than this: perhaps your definitional argument will require a few paragraphs, and your evaluation argument may require a few more. You may want to add a jurisdiction component to your action argument, or propose a compromise that bridges more than one position. Still, by following the shape of the larger debate using the stases, you will find that the logic of your argument follows more smoothly, and, if well managed, more convincingly.

When you read through your research, you may notice that individual authors often work through these stases, even though an author's thesis will focus on one stasis. As you read the articles you have found for your writing project, try to locate each article's thesis, identify its stasis, and then work backwards. Ask yourself whether the author builds an argument by using the conclusions drawn in the previous stasis. By analyzing how other authors work through the stases, you may well find yourself devising a claim structure for your own argument.

SECTION THREE

Style: Composition and Ornament

Taken from *Ancient Rhetorics for Contemporary Students*, Fifth Edition by Sharon Crowley and Debra Hawhee

Style: Composition and Ornament

21

Cicero holds that, while invention and arrangement are within the reach of anyone of good sense, eloquence belongs to the rhetor alone. . . . The verb eloqui *means the production and communication to the audience of all that the rhetor has conceived . . . and without this power all the preliminary accomplishments of rhetoric are as useless as a sword that is kept permanently concealed within its sheath.*

—Quintilian, *Institutes* VIII Pr. 14–15

Ancient rhetoricians devoted an entire canon of their art to the study of unusual uses or arrangements of words. They called this canon "style" (*lexis* or "words," in Greek; *elocutio* or "speaking out" in Latin). Defined as persuasive or extraordinary uses of language, style can be distinguished from grammar, which is the study of ordinary uses of language.

No one knows for sure when style emerged as the third canon of rhetoric. From earliest times, of course, poets and singers had used unusual words and patterns in their work. Here, for example, are some lines from the *Iliad*, which is usually dated from the eighth century BCE—that is, two hundred years prior to Gorgias' trip to Athens during the sixth century BCE:

> Ah, Hektor,
> this harshness is no more than just. Remember, though, your spirit's like
> an ax-edge whetted sharpthat goes through timber, when a good ship-
> wright hews out a beam: the tool triples his power.
> That is the way your heart is in your breast. (III 58–62)

When he compared Hector's heart to an axe used by a strong shipbuilder, the poet employed a figure later called a **simile,** wherein two unlike things are placed together so that the attributes of one are transferred to the other. Notice how the simile adds meaning to the picture of Hector that the poet is painting; we learn from it that, like the strokes of an axe wielded by a strong man, Hector's courage is tireless, regular, and strong. As Quintilian remarked, such uses of language make things even more intelligible than does clarity alone (VIII ii 11).

Historians of rhetoric usually credit Gorgias with the discovery that extraordinary uses of language were persuasive in prose as well as poetry. Here, for example, is the opening passage of Gorgias' "Encomium to Helen":

> Fairest ornament to a city is a goodly army and to a body beauty and to a soul wisdom and to an action virtue and to speech truth, but their opposites are unbefitting. Man and woman and speech and deed and city and object should be honored with praise if praiseworthy but on the unworthy blame should be laid; for it is equal error and ignorance to blame the praiseworthy and to praise the blameworthy.

The first sentence shows careful attention to **sentence composition** in its use of balanced phrases ("to a body beauty" and so on). Both sentences contain examples of **antithesis,** wherein contrary or contradictory ideas are expressed in phrases that are grammatically alike ("to blame the praiseworthy and to praise the blameworthy," for example).

Stylistic ornament is still widely used. For instance, to bolster their claim that children can learn civility around the dinner table, Laurie David and Carleton Kendrick suggest that parents "load up our children's dinner plates with healthy home-cooked food and generous portions of kindness, respect, empathy and conversation. Let's answer our president's call and feed our children what they need to become our next generation of compassionate, civil citizens." Here food is a **metaphor** for civility. It is almost commonplace these days to speak of electronic gadgets as having brains or hearts, which can create the figure called **personification** by the ancients. Advertisements for the iPad, for example, describe it with adjectives such as "playful," "literary," "artful," "friendly," and "productive" to imbue the product with human qualities.

Ancient teachers of rhetoric argued that rhetorical language ought to be clear, of course, but they also maintained that it ought to touch the emotions as well. Teachers helped their students achieve stylistic excellence by teaching them about as many unusual uses of language as they could isolate and classify, by asking them to imitate famous authors, and to practice by composing their own examples of various **schemes** or **figures** (Greek *schemata;* Latin *figura,* "shape"). Ancient rhetoricians isolated four qualities of style that permitted them to distinguish a persuasive style from a less effective one. Although there was some disagreement about which qualities ought to be included in a list of stylistic excellences, in the main ancient authors agreed that a good style ought to manifest correctness, clearness, appropriateness, and ornament. Once we have discussed these four features of style, we will turn to stylistic flourishes that can enhance a rhetor's character or voice—that is, her ethos.

Correctness

The Greek and Latin words for correctness were *hellenismos* and *latinitas,* respectively. Sometimes translated as "purity," correctness meant that rhetors should use words that were current and should adhere to the grammatical rules of whatever language they wrote. In Greek and Latin, meaning depended to a great degree on word endings;

nouns had different endings depending on their case, number, and gender, whereas verb endings indicated such things as tense and mood. Thus, the achievement of correctness in one of those languages was a more complex and interesting task than it is in English, which depends primarily on word order for its meanings.

Ancient rhetoricians ordinarily left instruction in correctness (and sometimes clarity as well) to the elementary school teachers, who were grammarians and students of literature. Cicero wrote in *De Oratore* that "the rules of correct Latin style . . . are imparted by education in childhood and fostered by a more intensive and systematic study of literature, or else by the habit of daily conversation in the family circle, and confirmed by books and by reading the old orators and poets" (III xii 48). Interestingly enough, Cicero agreed in this with the contemporary linguists, who argue that native speakers of any language internalize a good many of its grammatical rules while they are learning it. Because native speakers of a language have an intuitive grasp of its grammar, the correctness rules that trouble people today usually involve conventional niceties of written language such as spelling, punctuation, and some outdated rules of grammar and usage. These features of correctness govern choices that can be made while **editing**.

Clarity

Clarity is the English word most often used for the Greek *sapheneia,* although it is sometimes translated "lucidity" (from Latin *lucere,* "to shine"), or "perspicuity" (from Latin *perspicere,* "to see through"). The Latin terms demonstrate that clarity once connoted language that let meanings "shine through" it, like light through a window. As we noted earlier, however, rhetoricians like Gorgias were suspicious about the capacity of language to transfer meaning clearly from rhetors to audiences. For most ancient teachers, clarity simply meant that rhetors should use words in their ordinary or usual everyday senses unless they had some compelling reason to do otherwise.

According to Quintilian, rhetors could avoid the obligation to be clear only if they were compelled to refer to obscenities, unseemly behavior, or trivial matters. In any of these cases, they could resort to **circumlocution** (Greek *periphrasis,* "speaking around"), a more roundabout means of references. Terms like *restroom* or *powder room* are circumlocutions for *toilet;* it is a circumlocution to say that "Henry and the company decided to part ways" when Henry was fired. Clarity can also be obscured by the use of obsolete, technical, new or colloquial words. Obsolete words are those that are no longer in popular use (*motored* for *drove*). Technical language (that is, jargon) is used by specialists in a profession or discipline (for example, *valorize* and *abjection* from current talk among academics). Quintilian also advised against the practice of coining of new words (**neologism**) because new words are not familiar to those who hear or read them. He told a funny story about a speaker who, in his anxiety to give a formal tone to his talk, used the phrase "Iberian grass" to refer to the plant known as "Spanish broom" (VIII I 2–3). The problem with "Iberian grass" was that the phrase puzzled everyone who heard it, which is, we must admit, an offense against clarity.

Colloquial words are used in a very specific locale or culture. For example, *with it,* originally from the Beat culture of the 1950s, is colloquial and now obsolete as well. So are the "in" terms from the 1970s—*groovy* and *far out.* However, other colloquial terms, such as *hip* and *cool,* are amazingly tenacious: *hip* was "cool" in the sixties, whereas *cool* was "hip" in the fifties and the seventies; *cool* is still in popular use today, although *hot* seemed to be gaining on it for awhile.

As Quintilian said, the best course is to call things by the names people ordinarily use, unless for some reason the name would puzzle an audience or give offense. In other words, rhetors should always use language that is familiar to their audiences, even if this language is colloquial or jargon ridden. A rhetor who addresses an audience that uses a dialect should use it if she is comfortable doing so. Former president Jimmy Carter, who was raised in Georgia, uses a Southern dialect of English. When he campaigned in the South, he told his audiences that they should elect him to have someone in the presidency who had no accent! Likewise, a rhetor who addresses astronomers or software engineers should use whatever jargon is currently in vogue within that group because jargon is ordinarily invented as a means of attaining precision—that is, clarity. A rhetor who is addressing teachers or bosses should try to use language that is familiar to those audiences. If this means learning a technical vocabulary, so be it.

Appropriateness: Kairos and Style

Once we move past correctness and clarity, we are working in more truly rhetorical realms of style—appropriateness and ornament.[1] Oddly enough, these realms are not often treated in contemporary composition textbooks, whose authors are more anxious that writers be correct and clear than that they be persuasive.

Appropriateness probably derives from the Greek rhetorical notion *to prepon,* meaning to say or do whatever is fitting in a given situation. Perhaps it is also descended from Gorgias' notion of **kairos,** seizing the right moment to speak, the moment when listeners are ready to hear. Cicero upheld appropriateness or propriety as the most important rule of thumb for effective rhetoric when he wrote that "the universal rule, in oratory as in life, is to consider propriety" (*Orator* xxi 71). But for Cicero, propriety was not something that can be made into a list of hard and fast rules. Cicero defined propriety as "what is fitting and agreeable to an occasion or person; it is important often in actions as well as in words, in the expression of the face, in gesture and in gait" (xxii, 74). So Cicero favored a situational propriety, one that comes closer to the Greek notion of *kairos.* The mythical figure Kairos was often depicted balancing on some object—be it a razorblade or a ball or a wheel. Achieving a balanced style is one of the challenges rhetors often face. Cicero was well aware of this challenge as a central concern for rhetoric. He wrote: "When a case presents itself in which the full force of eloquence can be expended, then the orator will display his powers more fully; then we will rule and sway men's minds, and move them as he will, that is as the nature of the case and the exigency of the occasion demand" (xxxv, 125).

Cicero was not the only ancient rhetorician who expressed a concern for propriety in rhetoric. Even Plato, who was skeptical about the value of rhetoric, emphasized the importance of using an appropriate style. In Plato's *Phaedrus,* the character Socrates tells Phaedrus that when a rhetor supplements an awareness of the audience with "a knowledge of the times for speaking and for keeping silence, and has also distinguished the favorable occasions (*kairous*) for brief speech or pitiful speech or intensity and all the classes of speech which he has learned, then, and not till then, will his art be fully and completely finished" (272–73). For Plato, then, attention to *kairos*—the nature of the subject matter, the general attitudes and backgrounds of the audience—helped the rhetor make decisions about an appropriate style. A young aspiring rhetor like Phaedrus, for example, might steer clear of using hyperbole (exaggeration of a case) in front of Socrates, the teacher of reason, for it would be in Phaedrus' best interest to establish himself as a reasonable rhetor.

Like ethical proof, attention to kairos in style requires sensitivity to community standards of behavior because appropriateness is dictated by the standards of the community in which we live. In our culture, for example, people do not generally pick their noses in public because the community defines this as inappropriate behavior. The community dictates the standards of rhetorical appropriateness as well. When ancient teachers of rhetoric counseled their students to use an appropriate style, they generally meant that a style should be suited to subject, occasion, and audience. This meant that rhetors had to understand the standards of behavior required by the occasion for which they composed a piece of discourse. Because every occasion for writing or speaking differs from the next, it is very difficult to generate rules to govern appropriateness. Cicero underscored this difficulty in *De Oratore:*

> different styles are required by deliberative speeches, panegyrics, lawsuits and lectures, and for consolation, protest, discussion and historical narrative, respectively. The audience is also important—whether it is the lords or the commons or the bench; a large audience or a small one or a single person, and their personal character; and consideration must be given to the age, station and office of the speakers themselves, and to the occasion, in peace time or during a war, urgent or allowing plenty of time. (III iv 211–12)

In other words, the achievement of an appropriate style requires rhetors to pay attention to the conventional rules for verbal behavior in a given context, rules that have been laid down by their culture. If a rhetor has been asked to give a eulogy (a funeral speech), for example, her language should be dignified and subdued because our culture dictates dignified and subdued behavior on such occasions. If, on the other hand, she writes lyrics for country music, dignified and subdued won't cut it because the style of country music is down-home and informal.

Ancient teachers distinguished three very general levels of style that were appropriate to various rhetorical settings: grand, middle, and plain.[2] According to the author of *ad Herennium,* discourse was composed in the grand style "if to each idea are applied the most ornate words that can be found for it, whether literal or figurative; if impressive thoughts are chosen . . . and if we employ figures of thought and figures of diction which have grandeur" (IV viii 11). He supplied us with a fine example of the grand style, which we quote in part:

> Who of you, pray, jury members, could devise a punishment drastic enough for him who has plotted to betray the fatherland to our enemies? What offence can compare with this crime, what punishment can be found commensurate with this offence? Upon those who had done violence to a freeborn youth, outraged the mother of a family, wounded, or—basest crime of all—slain a man, our ancestors exhausted the catalogue of extreme punishments; while for this most savage and impious villainy they bequeath no specific penalty. In other wrongs, indeed, injury arising from another's crime extends to one individual, or only to a few; but the participants in this crime are plotting, with one stroke, the most horrible catastrophes for the whole body of citizens. O such men of savage hearts! O such cruel designs! O such human beings bereft of human feeling! (IV viii 12)

In keeping with our author's definition of the grand style, this passage concerns a lofty issue—treachery—and uses a great deal of ornament. It opens with two **rhetorical questions,** a figure in which a rhetor asks a question to which she doesn't really expect an answer. In fact, asking the question actually provides an opportunity to say more damning things about the traitors. The second rhetorical question also contains an *antistrophe* ("turning about"), the repetition of the same or similar words in successive clauses. Rather than referring to Rome by name, the speaker employs an **epithet**—fatherland—which is also a pun that reminds listeners about their dependent relationship on the state ("father" and "patriotism" have the same root, "*patria*" in Latin). There are several examples of **isocolon** (balanced clauses), and the final passionate outbursts are examples of **apostrophe** ("turning away") to address absent persons or some abstraction—"O such cruel designs."

The middle style does not use ordinary prose, but it is more relaxed than the grand style. Cicero said that "all the ornaments are appropriate" to this style, especially metaphor and its relatives (*Orator* xxvi 91–96). A rhetor using the middle style develops arguments in leisurely fashion and as fully as possible, and uses as many commonplaces as can be worked into the argument without drawing attention to their presence. The author of *ad Herennium* also provided an example of the middle style:

> men of the jury, you see against whom we are waging war—against allies who have been wont to fight in our defence, and together with us to preserve our empire by their valor and zeal. Not only must they have known themselves, their resources, and their manpower, but their nearness to us and their alliance with us in all affairs enabled them no less to learn and appraise the power of the Roman people in every sphere. When they had resolved to fight against us, on what, I ask you, did they rely in presuming to undertake the war, since they understood that much the greater part of our allies remained faithful to duty, and since they saw that they had at hand no great supply of soldiers, no competent commanders, and no public money—in short, none of the things needful for carrying on the war? (IV ix 13)

Here the rhetor used ordinary everyday language and loose sentence construction. Although there are fewer ornaments than in the grand style, a few do appear: there is a fairly complex **isocolon** in the second sentence ("their resources, and their manpower, but their nearness to and their alliance with us"). "On what, I ask you" is another example of a rhetorical question.

According to the author of *ad Herennium,* the plain or simple style uses the "most ordinary speech of every day," almost as though it were conversation (IV x 14). Cicero elaborated on this bare description of the plain style, noting that it is "stripped of ornament" and "to the point, explaining everything and making every point clear rather than impressive" (*Orator* v 20). Usually the plain style employs straightforward narrative ("this happened and then this") or simple exposition of the facts, and it uses **loose** rather than **periodic** sentences.

Once again, rhetors should choose the level of style that is appropriate to their ethos, their subject matter, their audience and the occasion. The grand style is certainly appropriate for ceremonial functions like weddings, funerals, and inaugurations. The plain style is appropriate when clarity is the main goal dictated by the occasion, whereas the middle style is appropriate for almost any discourse that will be published.

Ornament

The last, and most important, of the excellences of style is ornament. Under this heading, ancient rhetoricians discussed uses of language that were unusual or extraordinary. They divided their study of ornament into three broad categories: **figures of speech** (Latin *figurae verborum*), **figures of thought** (*figurae sententiarum*), and **tropes** (Greek *tropoi,* "turns"). Ancient grammarians and rhetoricians argued endlessly over the definitions and distinctions among these three sorts of ornament, and modern scholars haven't done much better at making sense out of the categories. As ancient rhetoric matured, the confusion grew. In some scholarly traditions, ornaments like **climax** and **antithesis** were classed under more than one heading (sometimes as figures, sometimes as tropes), whereas others, like **metaphor** and epithet, were often discussed both as single words (diction) and in terms of their effects in groups of words (composition).

Contemporary rhetors don't need to keep the categories straight because discussions of figures and tropes no longer have to be memorized as they did in Aristotle's time. However, rhetoricians should be able to distinguish among figures of language, figures of thought, and tropes. So, with Quintilian's help, we try to distinguish among these ancient categories.

Generally, a figure is any form of expression where "we give our language a conformation other than the obvious and ordinary" (IX i 4). Sometimes Quintilian seems to mean the term *figure* literally; a figure is any piece of language that has a remarkable or artful shape. He likened the changes in language or meaning brought about by the use of figures to the changes in the shape of the body that came about "by sitting, lying down on something or looking back" (IX i 11). That is, use of a figure changes the shape of language, just as a change in posture or position changes the shape of the body. There are two kinds of figures. Figures of thought involve artful changes in ideas, feelings, or conceptions; these figures depart from ordinary patterns of moving an argument along (17). Figures of language, on the other hand, involve unusual patternings of language, such as repetition or juxtaposition of similar words or constructions.

A trope is any substitution of one word or phrase for another. Grammatically speaking, a trope can transfer words or phrases from their proper place to another. This kind of grammatical trope is rare. Winston Churchill used it when he said, "This is a kind of impertinence up with which I will not put." Here Churchill substituted an unusual word order for the ordinary pattern to make fun of the traditional grammatical rule that says prepositions may not appear at the end of sentences. Rhetorically speaking, a trope transfers the usual signification of a word or phrase to another, as in "My love is like a red, red rose." Here the poet (Robert Burns) transferred the meanings associated with roses (fragile, thorny, blooming briefly) to his love.

We review the ornaments of style in keeping with the ancient spirit of *copia*. Cicero wrote to his friend Trebatius, "as I have a guest with such a ravenous appetite for this feast of learning, I shall provide such an abundance that there may be something left from the banquet, rather than let you go unsatisfied" (*Topics* IV 25). Rhetors can study and practice using figures and tropes to enlarge their linguistic repertoire, and thus to have them at hand whenever their use is appropriate to occasion, subject, audience, and ethos. But there are yet other reasons for their use. Quintilian argued that ornament, carefully deployed, contributes not a little to the furtherance of our case as well. For when our audience find it a pleasure to listen, their attention and their readiness to believe what they hear are both alike increased, while they are generally filled with delight, and sometimes even transported by admiration (VIII iii 5). A carefully chosen metaphor can make an argument clearer and more striking; a nicely balanced antithesis can lend emphasis to a point. Thus ornament enhances persuasion; indeed, it can also aid clarity.

Sentence Composition

We begin with ancient advice about sentence structure because an understanding of ancient terms for parts of sentences is necessary to an understanding of figurative language. The ancient term for a sentence was **period** (Greek *periodos,* "a way around"). Modern scholars think that the ancient conception of a period as a whole made up of parts or **members** may derive from an analogy to the human body, which also has a main part—its trunk—from which the limbs or members branch off. In any case, ancient rhetoricians called any stretch of words that could stand on its own a "period," giving a sense of completeness (this is the source of our use of the term *period* to name a piece of punctuation that marks the end of a sentence). An ancient period is equivalent to a modern punctuated sentence: in other words, a period is any unit of prose that begins with a capital letter and ends with some mark of terminal punctuation (period, question mark, or exclamation point).

To grasp ancient thought about periods, it is helpful to think of any period as having a main part on which all the other parts depend—just like a tree or a human body. The main part of a period is meaningful all by itself, but this is usually not true of its members or branches.

> John loves Mary. (MAIN PART)
> John loves Mary | even though he barely knows her.
> (MAIN PART) | (MEMBER)

The stretches of language on either side of the | are logically different, because the left-hand one makes sense all by itself, whereas the one on the right is needs more information to make complete sense.

Some periods consist only of one main part, with no additional members: "John loves Mary." It is also possible to string several main parts into a single period: "John loves Mary; Mary loves Fred; Fred despises everyone." Each section of this period is meaningful by itself. (Traditional grammarians call this a **compound sentence.** The ancients did not use this terminology, however). It is also possible to add several kinds of dependent structures to the main part of any sentence. As the name implies, dependent structures are not meaningful by themselves. (Traditional grammarians call any sentence that has a main part and one or more dependent parts a **complex sentence.**) Ancient rhetoricians recognized two kinds of dependent structures: **colons** and **commas.**

Quintilian defined a colon (Latin membrum, "part" or "limb") as any expression that was rhythmically complete but meaningless if detached from the rest of the sentence. The author of *ad Herennium* gave these examples of colons:

> On the one hand you were helping your enemy
> and on the other you were hurting your friend (IV xix 26).

Colons not always equivalent to English clauses. Nevertheless, the structure known in English as a dependent or subordinate clause is a colon. Hence, English speakers use the terms *semicolon* and *colon* to refer to punctuation marks that set off internal parts of sentences.

A comma (Latin *articulus,* "part jointed on") referred to any set of words set apart by pauses (whence our term for the mark of punctuation, the comma, which serves that very function in English sentences). Demetrius of Phaleron called a comma a "chip" because it was a piece cut or hacked off from a longer member (*On Style* I i 9). Quintilian defined it as an expression lacking rhythmical completeness, or a portion of a colon (IX iv 122). A comma can consist of a single word, as in these examples from the *ad Herennium:*

> By your vigour, voice, looks you have tarried your adversaries.
> You have destroyed your enemies by jealousy, injuries, influence, perfidy.

In the first example, *voice* is a comma; in the second, *injuries* and *influence* are commas. In modern prose, commas are usually set off by punctuation. Because commas are very short, the English word *phrase* is usually a satisfactory translation.

Isocrates was widely regarded throughout antiquity as a master of artful composition. We use a sentence from his "Helen" to illustrate the ancient terms of composition:

> And although the Trojans might have rid themselves of the misfortunes which encompassed them by surrendering Helen, and the Greeks might have lived in peace for all time by being indifferent to her fate, neither so wished; on the contrary, the Trojans allowed their cities to be laid waste and their land to be ravaged, so as to avoid yielding Helen to the Greeks, and the Greeks chose rather, remaining in a foreign land to grow old there and never to see their own again, than, leaving her behind, to return to their fatherland (50–51).

This is a very long sentence (94 words) even by ancient standards. And yet it is still readable, because Isocrates (and his translator) paid careful attention to rhythm, internal punctuation, and the placement and balance of its parts. We graph the sentence to indicate its parts and their relations:

> And although
>
> the Trojans might have rid themselves of the misfortunes which encompassed them by surrendering Helen (COLON)
>
> and
>
> the Greeks might have lived in peace for all time by being indifferent to her fate (COLON)
>
> neither [the Trojans or Greeks] so wished (FIRST MAIN PART)
>
> on the contrary (COMMA)
>
> the Trojans allowed their cities to be laid waste and their land to be ravaged
>
> (FIRST HALF SECOND MAIN PART)
>
> so as to avoid yielding Helen to the Greeks (COLON)
>
> and
>
> the Greeks chose (SECOND HALF SECOND MAIN PART)
>
> remaining in a foreign land to grow old there and never to see their own again
>
> rather than
>
> leaving her behind to return to their fatherland (COLON).

Traditional grammarians would call this a **compound-complex sentence** because it has two main parts, and each of these has dependent clauses attached. An ancient rhetorician, however, would have noticed the artful placement of the carefully balanced colons, as well as the rhythms built into the entire period. To appreciate these, you may have to read the sentence aloud.

You can best appreciate the rhetorical effects of the other examples we provide for ancient figures of language if you read them aloud as well because they are intended to please the ear as well as the eye. Indeed, we recommend that you get into the habit of reading your own prose aloud to determine whether it has rhythm and shape. Reading aloud sometimes indicates the places where internal punctuation is needed, as well.

Paratactic and Periodic Styles

Ancient rhetoricians distinguished two types of sentences, which they called loose and periodic. Greek terms for a loose sentence can be translated "running" or "strung-on" or "continuous." Aristotle defined a style made up of loose sentences as having "no natural stopping-places." This style "comes to a stop only because there is no more to say of that subject" (III ix 9). He seems to have meant that the parts of a loose sentence are simply tacked onto one another. If we accept Aristotle's definition, a style made up of loose sentences might most accurately be called **paratactic** (Greek *parataxis*, "placed alongside"). A paratactic style gives the impression that the rhetor placed utterances somewhat carelessly side by side, just as they occurred to her. (The preceding sentence is an example).

Later rhetoricians recommended this style for use in conversation and informal letters because of its simplicity and naturalness. They refined their discussions of the paratactic style to suggest that loosely constructed sentences also observe the ordinary or usual word order of the language in which they are written (as this very sentence does, or did, until we added this parenthesis). Paratactic style is frequently used in electronic mail, for this medium is fast, casual, and conducive to "chat" rather than to formal decrees. Because the paratactic style observes the natural word order of a language, its use does not constitute a figure unless a rhetor uses it to achieve some artistic effect, such as an impression of carelessness or breathlessness.

Aristotle thought that the paratactic style was unpleasant to read "because it goes on indefinitely—one always likes to sight a stopping-place in front of one. That explains why runners, just when they have reached the goal, lose their breath and strength, whereas before, when the end is in sight, they show no signs of fatigue" (*Rhetoric* III xi 1409a). For this reason, Aristotle preferred a style where units of speech were more carefully demarcated and set off from one another. Like the rhetoricians who would later apply his terminology to all sentences, he called a unit of this kind a "period," and he defined it as "a portion of speech that has in itself a beginning and end, being at the same time not too big to be taken in at a glance" (35). Aristotle wrote that periods satisfied readers because they reached definite conclusions, and they were easier to remember, too. A periodic sentence, then, has an obvious structure; ordinarily its main part does not come at the beginning, as in a loose sentence. Its meaning may be distributed among several of its parts, as it is in the example from Isocrates, where the two main parts of the sentence are sandwiched between two groups of paired colons.

Later rhetoricians dictated that rhetors should postpone the sense of the period until readers reached its final member, but this restriction was not usually a part of classical lore about style. In this example from Gorgias' "Helen," the main part of the period is placed last: "Who it was and why and how he sailed away, taking Helen as his love, I shall not say" (5). Hellenistic rhetoricians also dictated that periods could contain as few as one member or as many as four. Of course it is possible to write sentences that contain an infinite number of members, but ancient rhetoricians generally cautioned against such excess.

A style becomes periodic when readers have the sense that sentences are carefully constructed and satisfactorily "rounded off." Because the periodic style was appropriate to the most dignified and important occasions, most teachers also cautioned their students to use periodic sentences sparingly.

Figurative Language

In general, a paratactic style does not employ many figures of language because it is structurally simple by definition. This is not true of the periodic style, however. Ancient rhetoricians compiled endless lists of variations on the use and arrangements of the basic parts of the period: these variations are the figures of language. Quintilian wrote that this group of figures has "one special merit, that they relieve the tedium of every-day stereotyped speech and save us from commonplace language" (IX iii 3–4). When they are used sparingly, they serve as a seasoning to any style. We have divided the figures of language into two broad categories: those that interrupt normal word order, and those that repeat words or structures for effect.

Figures That Interrupt Normal Word Order Here is a periodic sentence from Gorgias' "Defense of Palamedes": "If then the accuser, Odysseus, made his accusation through good will toward Greece, either clearly knowing that I was betraying Greece to the barbarians or imagining somehow that this was the case, he would be best of men" (Sprague 55). We graph the sentence to show off its elegant balance:

> If then the accuser made his accusation through good will toward Greece
>
>   either
>
>   knowing clearly that I was betraying Greece to the barbarians
>
>   or
>
>   imagining somehow that this was the case
>
> he [Odysseus] would be the best of men.

Notice that Gorgias delayed the sense of the sentence until the very end (Odysseus is the best of men—if his motives are honest). The periodic structure keeps readers in suspense, heightening their curiosity about the author's opinion of Odysseus.

Later on, Gorgias used a sentence constructed on similar lines to state another possibility: "But if he has put together this allegation out of envy or conspiracy or knavery, just as in the former case he would be the finest of men, so in this he would be the worst of men."

> But if he has put together this allegation out of envy or conspiracy or knavery
>
>   just as
>
> in the former case he would be the finest of men
>
>   so
>
> in   this   he would be the worst of men.

Again, the author's judgement of Odysseus' motives is postponed to the very end of the sentence. Taken together, the two sentences create an antithesis that works across several sentences.

Here is a periodic sentence from the nineteenth century written by Ralph Waldo Emerson in his essay "Nature": "Crossing a bare common, in snow puddles, at twilight, under a clouded sky, without having in my thoughts any occurrence of special good fortune, I have enjoyed a perfect exhilaration."

> Crossing the common
> > in snow puddles
> > at twilight
> > under a clouded sky
> > without . . . good fortune
> I have enjoyed a perfect exhilaration.

Emerson postponed the point of the sentence (his achievement of perfect exhilaration) until its end, thus keeping readers in suspense and yet giving them the satisfaction of a firm closure when it finally arrives. He also used grammatically balanced commas (each is a prepositional phrase) inside a longish colon ("crossing . . . fortune") to build up suspense.

Here is a third example, a beautiful periodic sentence written by Alice Walker: "Wrapped in his feathered cape, his winged boots, he sent his soul flying to Zede while holding his body, his thought, his attentions on Carlotta, whom he did not cease to love" (*The Temple of My Familiar*, 24).

> Wrapped in his feathered cape
> > his winged boots
> he sent his soul flying   to Zede
> > while holding
> > > his body
> > > his thought
> > > his attentions on Carlotta, whom he did not cease to love.

Walker used parallel commas to emphasize her character's divided loyalties, which she reveals to readers only at the conclusion of the period.

News writers occasionally use periodic sentences as well. This one appeared in a reflective essay on the history of racism in America, written by Jeffrey Gettleman: "Yet even at the height of segregation, when working-class whites clubbed black demonstrators in the streets of Birmingham and Atlanta, some white leaders were willing to question the old ways" ("Southern"). The juxtaposition of the two contrasting but balanced comments about whites, with the second, more unexpected, clause coming last, demonstrates the force that a good period sentence can convey.

Rhetors can also interrupt normal word order by inserting a word or phrase inside a colon or period, as in this example, again composed by Gettleman, in an article about Somalia: "But confidence in the government—never very high—is rapidly bleeding away" ("The New Somalia"). Quintilian called this figure *interpositio,* but it is still known in English by its Greek name, **parenthesis** ("a statement alongside another"). As the interpolation in the previous sentence demonstrates, a parenthetical statement decreases distance because it suddenly discloses the author's presence—as though she were speaking behind her hand. Parenthetical statements may appear between commas, like this, but they are more often punctuated by dashes—as we have done here—or with parentheses (as illustrated here). The novelist Robert Graves made interesting use of an almost wholly parenthetical style in the opening passage of his novel, *I Claudius:*

> I, Tiberius Claudius Drusus Nero Germanicus This-that-and-the-other (for I shall not trouble you yet with all my titles) who was once, and not so long ago either, known to my friends and relatives and associates as "Claudius the Idiot, or "That Claudius," or "Claudius the Stammerer," or "Clau-Clau-Claudius" or at best as "poor Uncle Claudius," am now about to write this strange history of my life. (1961, 3)

The parenthetical asides nearly swamp the main part of this sentence, inserted as they are between "I" and "am now about to write." Graves used them to suggest an important feature of Claudius' character: even though he wasn't very well organized, he was a stickler for detail.

Rhetors can interrupt normal word order in a number of other ways. The ancients gave such interruptions the generic name of **hyperbaton** (a sudden turn). A rhetor can attach a descriptive comma, as follows: "Mary, though reputed to be in love with John, is actually quite fond of Fred." The interpolated comma is an **appositio** ("putting off from," apposition in English), a phrase that interrupts the main part of the period to modify it or to add commentary about it. Or she can use an apostrophe to call on her audience or someone else: "I am, heaven help me, lost." In a very long sentence, it is sometimes helpful to sum up with an interrupter: "Invention, arrangement, style, memory and delivery—these, the five canons of rhetoric—are all that occupy me now." The ancients called this figure **metabasis,** a summarizing transition.

Ancient rhetoricians also identified a pair of figures having to do with the use of connecting words between colons: **asyndeton** (no connectors) and **polysyndeton** (many connectors). Using the first figure, a rhetor eliminates connectors that ordinarily appear between colons or commas, as in this example from Cicero: "I ordered those against whom information was laid, to be summoned, guarded, brought before the senate: they were led into the senate" (quoted by Quintilian IX iii 50). Cicero eliminated the *ands* that would ordinarily connect coordinate commas to give an impression of haste and vigor. Compare his version to a version that inserts connecting *ands:* "I ordered those against whom information was laid to be summoned and guarded and brought before the senate, and they were led into the senate."

Gorgias used the opposing figure in the opening passage of his "Helen":

> Fairest ornament to a city is a goodly army and to a body beauty and to a soul wisdom and to an action virtue and to speech truth, but their opposites are unbefitting. Man and woman and speech and deed and city and object should be honored with praise if praiseworthy but on the unworthy blame should be laid; for it is equal error and ignorance to blame the praiseworthy and to praise the blameworthy.

Here both sentences contain examples of **polysyndeton,** where the rhetor employs more conjunctions ("and" in this case) than are required by either grammar or sense.

This figure enabled Gorgias to stretch out a series of words or phrases, thus calling attention to each item in the series and giving the whole a leisurely pace. To grasp the rhetorical effect of polysyndeton compared to that of asyndeton, compare Gorgias' versions to a revision that substitutes punctuation for *and:*

> Fairest ornament to a city is a goodly army; to a body beauty; to a soul wisdom; to an action virtue; to a speech truth. Man, woman, speech, deed, city, object, should be honored.

Figures of Repetition   Repetition is a means of calling attention to words and ideas that are important; hence rhetors should not be afraid to repeat words that are central to their arguments. Artful repetition was available to speakers of Greek and Latin in single words. Rhetors could simply repeat a word to call attention to it, as Demosthenes is said to have done when asked what was the most important part of rhetoric. He replied: "Delivery, delivery, delivery." Gertrude Stein used repetition to make fun of poetic metaphors about roses: "A rose is a rose is a rose." Nikki Giovanni, a poet and distinguished professor of English at Virginia Tech delivered the following eulogy at a memorial for those slain in the terrible killings on that campus in 2007:

> We are Virginia Tech.
> We are sad today and we will be sad for quite awhile.
> We are not moving on; we are embracing our mourning.
> We are Virginia Tech.
> We are strong enough to stand tall tearlessly;
> We are brave enough to bend to cry
> And sad enough to know we must laugh again.
> We are Virginia Tech.
> We do not understand this tragedy. We know we did nothing to deserve it, but neither does the child in Africa dying of AIDS; neither do the invisible children walking the night away to avoid being captured by a rogue army; neither does the baby elephant watching his community be devastated for ivory; neither does the Mexican child looking for fresh water; neither does a Appalachian infant killed in the middle of the night in his crib in the home his father built with his own hands being run over by a boulder because the land was destabilized. No one deserves a tragedy.
> We are Virginia Tech.
> The Hokie Nation embraces our own and reaches out with open heart and hand to those who offer their hearts and minds. We are strong and brave and innocent and unafraid. We are better than we think, and not quite what we want to be. We are alive to the imagination and the possibility we will continue to invent the future through our blood and tears, through all this sadness. We are the Hokies.
> We will prevail!
> We will prevail!
> We will prevail!
> We are Virginia Tech.

Giovanni borrows a popular sports chant to use as a rallying cry. In the context of the memorial, the repetition of the chant serves to remind all who are listening that Virginia Tech is a tight-knit community. Giovanni also repeats sentence structures, as in the many clauses beginning with "neither." If you want to feel the full effect of her use of repetition, you should listen to the recording, which can be found at americanrhetoric.com.

Another means of repeating words is **synomyny** ("the same name"), that is, using words that are similar in meaning as a means of repeating an important point: "Call it treason, betrayal, sedition, or villainy—it is one." The author of *ad Herennium* gave these examples: "You have impiously beaten your father; you have criminally laid hands upon your parent" and "You have overturned the republic from its roots; you have demolished the state from its foundations" (IIV xxviii 38). A thesaurus can help when a rhetor wants to pile up similar words to create the figure of synonymy. A thesaurus should never be used to avoid repeating words, though; to do this is to commit the rhetorical sin of circumlocution. As the ancient rhetoricians repeatedly pointed out, repetition is not necessarily a bad thing. Artfully used, it constitutes a figure. A thesaurus supplies lists of words that are similar to one another (synonyms). But synonyms are not pure equivalents, despite their Greek name. No two words mean exactly the same thing, because meaning depends on context and use. Students who use a thesaurus to avoid repetition or to find words that "sound fancier" than the ones they ordinarily use, then, are misusing it, and they run the risk as well of saying something they don't mean.

There is another class of figures of language that use artful synonymy and exploit other similarities between words as well. These are now known generically as **puns.** Puns allow rhetors to repeat something in an artful and often funny way: "He told the sexton and the sexton tolled the bell." The punch lines of shaggy dog stories were funny because they punned on some sober maxim: "Don't hatchet your counts before they chicken"; "People who live in grass houses shouldn't stow thrones." A practice currently in vogue is to give businesses punning names, such as "Shear Madness" for a barber shop or "The Great Impasta" for Italian restaurants. Ancient puns often do not survive translation, because the pun depends on some similarity in word shape or sound. Quintilian quoted this one from the Roman poet Ovid: "Cur ego non dicam, Furia, te furiam?" ("Furia, why should I not call you a fury?"); and this one, which does survive translation, from *ad Herennium:* "Nam amari iucundum sit, si curetur ne quid insit amari" ("To be dear to you would bring me joy—if only I take care it shall not in anguish cost me dear"; IV xiv 21; *Institutes* IX iii 69–70).

According to Quintilian, puns belong to the class of figures that "attracts the ear of the audience and excites their attention by some resemblance, equality or contrast or words" (IX iii 66). The ancient term for pun was "**paronomasia,**" which the author of *ad Herennium* defined as "the figure in which, by means of a modification of sound, or change of letters, a close resemblance to a given verb or noun is produced, so that similar words express dissimilar things" (IV xxi 29). Generally, puns exploit accidental resemblances among words, as in "You can pay for school, but you can't buy class" from "Swagger Like Us" by T. I. and Jay-Z. There are many varieties of this figure, but all have to do with using words that are similar to others, either in sound, shape, meaning, or function. In short, puns can exploit almost any accidental resemblance among the shapes, functions, sounds, spellings, or meanings of words.

When editors of *The Atlantic* asked readers to help them coin a word "to describe the moment of undignified vulnerability that people in airport security lines experience when they have to take off their shoes," they were flooded with puns about socks and shoes, including "insockurity," "sole-baring," "shoemiliation," "disshoeveled," "pedanoia," "footwary," and "unshoddenfreude." The winner, as it turns out, was "toeing the line" ("Word Fugitives," *The Atlantic* July/August 2007, p. 160). Quintilian thought that this form of the figure was a "poor trick even when employed in jest" (*Institutes* I xiii 73ff). Along with Quintilian, we often roll our eyes at puns.

Using ***antanaclasis*** ("bending back"), the rhetor repeats a word in two different senses: "I would leave this place, should the Senate give me leave" (*ad Herennium* IV xiv 21). "If we don't hang together, we'll hang separately" (Ben Franklin). Using ***homoioteleuton*** ("same ending"), the rhetor repeats words having similar endings: "You dare to act dishonorably, you strive to talk despicably; you live hatefully, you sin zealously, you speak offensively" (*ad Herennium* IV xx 28). This figure had more uses in Greek and Latin than it does in English, where only a few parts of speech, such as the adverbs illustrated here, have similar endings—"Bieber Fever" notwithstanding.

Using **zeugma** and its relatives, the rhetor ties a number of commas or colons to the same verb. Quintilian quoted this example from Cicero: "Lust conquered shame, boldness fear, madness reason" (*"Pro Cluentio"* vi 15; *Institutes* IX iii 62). Modern rhetoricians like to cite Alexander Pope's use of zeugma in "The Rape of the Lock," whose heroine's confused values are such that she would just as soon "stain her honor, or her new brocade." Here is another zeugma from Pope, about Queen Anne:

> Here thou, great Anna! whom three realms obey
> Dost sometimes counsel take—and sometimes tea.

Pope's juxtaposition of the heavily political and the slightly domestic is funny (and it was possibly even funnier when *obey* actually rhymed with *tea*). Because zeugma turns the same verb in different directions, it useful for dealing with complex issues. This feature, combined with its inherent economy, makes zeugma a favorite for writers. Here is a tagline from an article about the beverage Four Loko:

> "The alcoholic beverage with a caffeine kick briefly captured the hearts—and livers—of America's youth." ("The Rise and Fall")

Zeugma appears in another headline, this one again from the sportswriter Tom Boswell covering golf:

> "Opportunity, and Paradise, Lost at Open"

One of us composed this zeugma after watching the film *The Social Network:*

> Mark Zuckerberg made a mess, and a bundle, with Facebook.

Another set of figures also depends on repetition of words, but this group requires the composition of periods having two or more members. Rhetors using these figures repeat words that appear in similar positions in each of several members of a period. For example, words can be repeated at the beginning of successive colons expressing either similar or different ideas (**anaphora** or **epanaphora**, literally "carrying back"): "To you must go the credit for this, to you are thanks due, to you will this act of yours bring glory" (*ad Herennium* IV xiii 19). President Barack Obama used anaphora in his acceptance speech for the Nobel Peace Prize: "But it is also incumbent upon all of us to insist that nations like Iran and North Korea do not game the system. Those who claim to respect international law cannot avert their eyes when those laws are flouted. Those who care for their own security cannot ignore the danger of an arms race in the Middle East or East Asia. Those who seek peace cannot stand idly by as nations arm themselves for nuclear war." (http://www.americanrhetoric.com/speeches/barackobama/barackobamanobelprizespeech.htm)

Here the repetition of sentences beginning with "Those who," as well as the parallel sentence structure, alert listeners and readers to the necessity of paying close attention to world affairs.

Rhetors can also repeat the last word in successive phrases (**epiphora**): "It was by the justice of the Roman people that the Carthaginians were conquered, by its force of arms that they were conquered, by its generosity that they were conquered." Or they can combine epanaphora and epiphora to get **symploke** ("tied together"): "One whom the Senate has condemned, one whom the Roman people has condemned, one whom universal public opinion has condemned, would you by your votes acquit such a one?" (xiv 20). Note also that this example postpones the rhetorical question, which carries the sense of the sentence, until the very end.

Yet another figure of language links colons or commas together by repeating words in each member (**anadiplosis**, "repeating two pieces"). Here is an example from *ad Herennium:* "You now even dare to come into the sight of these citizens, traitor to the fatherland? Traitor, I say, to the fatherland, you dare come into the sight of these citizens?" (IV xxviii 38). In a more complex use of anadiplosis, the rhetor repeats the last word of one member as the first word of the next. Here is a wonderful example from the journalist Tom Wolfe's *The Kandy-Kolored Tangerine-Flake Streamline Baby:*

> And there they have it, the color called Landlord's Brown, immune to time, flood, tropic heat, arctic chill, punk rumbles, slops, blood, leprotic bugs, cockroaches the size of mice, mice the size of rats, rats the size of Airedales and lumpenprole tenants. (286)

Just when this very long sentence threatens to lose itself in a chaotic list, Wolfe brings some order to it by employing anadiplosis—he ends one item in the series with the word that begins the next. Here is another example of anadiplosis, this time from Amy Chua: "What Chinese parents understand is that nothing is fun until you're good at it. To get good at anything you have to work, and children on their own never want to work, which is why it is crucial to override their preferences." Interestingly, this use of anadiplosis also creates an **enthymeme**.

When a period has a series of members that become increasingly important, it displays a figure called **climax** (Greek "ladder"). The author of the *ad Herennium* defined climax as "the figure in which the speaker passes to the following word only after advancing by steps to the preceding one" (IV xxiv 34). He gave this example: "Now what remnant of the hope of liberty survives, if those men may do what they please, if they can do what they may, if they dare do what they can, if they do what they dare, and if you approve what they do?" Here is another example, from Demosthenes' *On the Crown* (179), quoted by the author of the *ad Herennium* and by Quintilian as well: "I did not say this and then fail to make the motion; I did not make the motion and then fail to act as an ambassador; I did not act as an ambassador and then fail to persuade the Thebans" (IV xxv 34; IX iii 55–56).

Strictly speaking, climax uses anadiplosis, as all of these examples do. A less strict application of the figure refers to any placement of phrases or clauses in order of their increasing importance. An eighteenth-century rhetorician named George Campbell quoted this example of climax from the "Song of Solomon":

> My beloved spake and said to me, Arise, my love, my fair, and come away; for lo, the winter is past, the rain is over and gone, the flowers appear on the earth, the time of the singing of birds is come, and the voice of the turtle is heard in our land; the fig-tree putteth forth her green figs, and the vines, with the tender grape, perfume the air. Arise, my love, my fair, and come away. (Ch.II v 10–13)

Campbell noted that the poet begins with negative phrases indicating that winter has passed, and moves toward positive indications of the coming of spring, arranged in order of their increasing importance (*Philosophy of Rhetoric* III i 1). Rhetoricians sometimes recommend that whole discourses feature the movement of climax, saving their most important or most persuasive point for last.

Commas or colons themselves can have ornamental effects when two or more that are similarly structured are repeated within a single period. This figure is called *isocolon* in Greek and **parallelism** in English. Here is a famous example from Abraham Lincoln's "Gettysburg Address": "The world will little note nor long remember what we say here, but it can never forget what they did here." We graph this sentence to illustrate the balanced colons a little more clearly:

The world will	little note	what we say here,
	nor long remember	
but it	can never forget	what they did here.

In parallelism, verbs should be balanced against verbs, prepositional phrases against prepositional phrases, and so on. Some ancient authors claimed that the members of an isocolon should have a similar number of syllables, so that the parallelism between them was nearly perfect. Here is an example from *ad Herennium:*

| The father was meeting death | in | battle; |
| the son was planning marriage | at | his home. (IV xx 27) |

Here is a modern example of parallelism, written by the nineteenth-century feminist Elizabeth Cady Stanton:

> I should feel exceedingly diffident to appear before you at this time, having never before spoken in public, were I not nerved by a sense of right and duty, did I not feel the time had fully come for the question of woman's wrongs to be laid before the public, did I not believe that woman herself must do this work; for woman alone can understand the height, the depth, the length, and the breadth of her own degradation. (Speech at the Seneca Falls Convention, 1848)

Cady Stanton repeated the phrase "did I not" in successive colons to emphasize her urgent reasons for violating taboo against women speaking in public. She also used asyndeton to yoke the parallel commas in the last colon, thus vigorously and forcefully expressing the seriousness of women's situation.

When the parallel members express logically contrary thoughts, the figure is called an **antithesis** ("counter statement"). In classical rhetorical theory, an antithesis occurred when either words or their meanings were opposed to one another. The author of the *ad Alexandrum* differentiated these two kinds of antithesis as follows: "Let the rich and prosperous give to the poor and needy" (opposition in terms only); "I nursed him when he was ill, but he has caused me a very great deal of harm" (opposition in meaning; 26 1435b). But the author *of ad Herennium* included any use of opposites or contraries under this figure. He illustrated its use with this jingling example:

> When all is calm, you are confused; when all is in confusion, you are calm. In a situation requiring all your coolness, you are on fire; in one requiring all you ardor, you are cool. When there is need for you to be silent, you are uproarious; when you should speak, you grow mute. Present, you wish to be absent; absent, you are eager to return. In peace, you demand war; in war, you yearn for peace. In the Assembly, you talk of valor; in battle, you cannot for cowardice endure the trumpet's sound. (IV xv 21)

All ancient authorities credit Gorgias with the invention of antithesis, and its preference for stating balanced contraries is consonant with Sophistic thought. In this example, from his "Helen," Gorgias combined antithesis with the figure of thought known as division: "For either by will of Fate and decision of the gods and vote of Necessity did she do what she did, or by force reduced or by words seduced or by love possessed" (6).

John F. Kennedy's use of antithesis is perhaps the most famous by an American: "Ask not what your country can do for you; ask what you can do for your country." This kind of antithesis—where the actual words are reversed—is called **chiasmus** (arranged crosswise; in the shape of the greek letter *chi,* which looks like an X). Sometimes a chiasmus uses more than two words, like this impressive example from novelist Richard Powers: "Data survive all hope of learning, but hope must learn how to survive the data" (88). Note the crisscross pattern in the language here:

data : hope : learning   ::   hope : learn : data

An even more complex use of antithesis appears in the figure called ***antimetabole*** ("thrown over against"). Here the rhetor expresses contrasting ideas in juxtaposed structures. Here are two examples from *ad Herennium:* "A poem ought to be a painting that speaks; a painting ought to be a silent poem"; "If you are a fool, for that reason you should be silent; and yet, although you should be silent, you are not for that reason a fool" (IV xxxviii 39). The best-known modern example was made popular by John Dean of Watergate fame: "When the going gets tough, the tough get going." During the 2008 Republican National Convention, vice-presidential candidate Sarah Palin used antimetabole to characterize her running mate, Senator John McCain: "In politics, there are some candidates who use change to promote their careers. And then there are those, like John McCain, who use their careers to promote change." Not to be outdone, the next evening Senator McCain offered up an antimetabole of his own: "We were elected to change Washington, and we let Washington change us."

Figures of Thought

In *De Oratore* and *Orator,* Cicero classed virtually all ornament under the head of figures of thought. This seems appropriate because these figures (*sententia* in Latin) are the most rhetorical of the ornaments of style. By this we mean two things: first of all, the *sententia* are arguments in themselves; that is, they can function as proofs. Second, they can enhance a rhetor's *ethos* or appeal to an audience's emotions (*pathos*). As Quintilian noted, the figures of thought "lend credibility to our arguments and steal their way secretly into the minds of the judges" (IX i 19–20). Perhaps because they are so highly rhetorical, so obviously calling attention to themselves as artifice and to rhetoric as performance, the figures of thought are not often discussed by modern rhetoricians. This was not true of ancient authorities, however. Quintilian treated only those figures of thought that "depart from the direct method of statement," and he still managed to discriminate well over a dozen (IX ii 1). We have divided our discussion of the *sententia* among figures that call attention to the rhetor, figures that stimulate the emotions of an audience, and figures drawn from the argument itself.

Figures of Thought That Enhance Ethos   This group of figures allows rhetors to call attention to the fact that they are manipulating the flow of the discourse. As such, they strengthen the rhetor's ethos; in most cases, their use decreases distance between the rhetor and an audience as well. Rhetors may use these figures to emphasize a point or to draw attention away from something, to hesitate, apologize, interrupt, attack opponents, make promises.

Rhetors often use questions (Latin *interrogatio*) to draw attention to important points. Quintilian gave the following example: "How long, Cataline, will you abuse our patience?" (IX 11 7–8). Notice that the effect of this question relies on an unspoken statement: "You have abused our patience a long time, Cataline." Rhetors can also ask a question to which it is impossible or difficult to reply: "How can this be?" Or we may ask questions to belittle or besmirch the character of the person to whom it is addressed ("What would you have me do, you who have cut off my options?"), to excite pity ("Where will I go, what can I do?"), or to embarrass an opponent ("Can't you hear the cries of your victims?"; IX ii 9–10).

Today, the best-known figure of this group is the rhetorical question: "Do you really expect me to respond to such an outrageous accusation?" or "Who can tell the depths to which this treachery has sunk?" Here, of course, the rhetor does not expect a reply; indeed, she expects the audience to fill in the response for themselves, in the first case with "no," and in the second with the name of the person she hopes will be blamed for the treachery. Variations on rhetorical questioning include **hypophora** or *subjectio,* when the rhetor asks what can be said in favor of those who oppose her ("Who, indeed, can support those who discriminate against the helpless poor?") or inquires what can possibly be said against her case ("On what grounds, my friends, can you object to so honorable a cause as mine?"). Use of this figure gives rhetors an opportunity to question the opinions or practices of those who oppose them or to anticipate and answer objections that might be made to their positions. Insofar as it allows rhetors to anticipate and answer objections that might be made to their positions, this figure is useful in refutation.

Asking a question to get information is not a figure; for a question to constitute a figure, it must be used to emphasize a point. Rhetors should also guard against using questions to which they don't know the answers. Audiences can usually discern when a rhetor is asking questions to avoid committing herself. The only effective rhetorical question, after all, is one to which the answer is so obvious that everyone, including the audience, can supply its answer. This figure depends for its effect on an audience's feeling that it is participating in the construction of the argument.

The author of *ad Herennium* mentions another *sententia* that depends on questioning. He calls it **reasoning by question and answer** (*ratiocinatio,* reasoning) wherein the rhetor inserts a question between successive affirmative statements. We quote a portion of his rather long illustration of this device. (The passage also displays several prejudicial commonplaces about women's characters, prejudices that have not entirely disappeared):

> When our ancestors condemned a woman for one crime, they considered that by this single judgement she was convicted of many transgressions. How so? Judged unchaste, she was also deemed guilty of poisoning. Why? Because, having sold her body to the basest passion, she had to live in fear of many persons. Who are these? Her husband, her parents, and the others involved, as she sees, in the infamy of her dishonor. And what then? Those whom she fears so much she would inevitably wish to destroy. Why inevitably? Because no honorable motive can restrain a woman who is terrified by the enormity of her crime, emboldened by her lawlessness, and made heedless by the nature of her sex. (IV xvi 23)

The use of *ratiocinatio* allowed the rhetor to repeat his charges. The repetitions hammer home the accusations, thus making them seem tenable whether they are or not. The device also calls attention to the ways in which the successive statements connect to each other, thus heightening the impression that the rhetor is proceeding rationally.

The author of *ad Herennium* pointed out that not all uses of interrogation are impressive or elegant. It is so when the points against the adversaries' cause have been summed up, and it reinforces the argument that has just been delivered, as follows: "So when you were doing and saying and managing all this, were you, or were you not, alienating and estranging from the republic the sentiments of our allies? And was it, or was it not, needful to employ someone to thwart these designs of your and prevent their fulfillment?" (IV xv 22). Fans of courtroom drama will easily recognize this device, which contemporary attorneys often use in their summations. The "were you or were you not" construction allows the person using it to repeat statements that may or may not be true without having to commit to them.

Anticipation (Greek *prolepsis,* "to take before") is a generic name given to any figure of thought wherein a rhetor foresees and replies to possible objections to his arguments. For example, a rhetor may anticipate that some point or points in his argument will seem weak or dishonorable to his audience. Here, for example, is the Reverend Al Sharpton, explaining why he visited the man who had assaulted him with a knife:

> I decided to visit my attacker in jail. This was by far the most difficult thing I had to do—to look directly in the face of a man who tried to kill me. I told him I did it for me, not for him. To be clear, I am not seeking credit for a noble act. Nor do I claim to be above feeling anger or understanding the frustrations that can stem from issues of race.

Sharpton apparently anticipated criticism of his act as self-seeking, or racebaiting, and he uses anticipation to dispel those readings before they can occur.

Rhetors may also state that they will not speak or write about something all the while they are actually doing so (***paralepsis,*** "to take alongside of"). Here is an example: "I will not here list all the negative effects of violent rhetoric: its divisiveness, its disruptiveness, its ugliness, the danger to it poses to innocent bystanders."

A closely related figure is **hesitation** or indecision (Latin *dubitatio,* "doubt"). Using this figure, a rhetor pretends to be unable to decide "where to begin or end, or to decide what especially requires to be said or not to be said at all" (*Institutes* IX ii 19). A rhetor may express indecision over a word choice, for example: "Conservatives label pro-choice positions as 'anti-family,' but I am not sure that this is the most informative way to characterize those who favor abortion rights." Using *dubatio,* a rhetor may point out that an issue is so vast that it can't be covered satisfactorily in the time or space allotted. Or she may express hesitation or doubt about introducing unpleasant or distasteful matters: "Most people are so sensitive about racism that I hesitate even to discuss it." Quintilian remarked that this figure lends "an impression of truth to our statements." Rhetors who use it can depict themselves as people who are sensitive to nuance and to the feelings of audiences as well.

Another similar figure of thought is **correction**, where a rhetor replaces a word or phrase he had used earlier with a more precise one. The author of *ad Herennium* gave this example of *correctio:* "After the men in question had conquered—or rather had been conquered, for how shall I call that a conquest which has brought more disaster than benefit to the conquerors?" (IV xxvi 36). The rhetor's reconsideration makes him seem thoughtful and intelligent. In this example, the use of correction also emphasizes the point that the action being discussed can be read in more than one way. Here is another example: "I refer to hateful speech. However, things would be clearer if this practice were known by its rightful name—racism."

Figures of Thought That Involve Audience   Quintilian mentioned a set of figures of thought that involve the audience in the argument. He discussed these under the general heading of communication. In these figures, the rhetor addresses the audience, taking them into her confidence: "No reasonable person can doubt the severe consequences of this practice." One form of this figure is **concession,** where the rhetor concedes a disputed point, or leaves a disputed point up to the audience to decide: "Of course I am aware that hateful speech hurts those it is aimed against. Nevertheless, the hurt felt by some does not justify the regulation of all." In **suspension,** the rhetor raises expectations that something bad or sensational will be mentioned, and then mentions something much worse. Quintilian gave this example from Cicero: "What think you? Perhaps you expect to hear of some theft or plunder?" (IX ii 22). Cicero then went on to discuss serious crimes against the state.

The opposite of suspension is **paradox** ("contrary opinion"), where the rhetor raises expectations and then mentions something trivial. The headlines on supermarket tabloids are paradoxes in this sense. In modern rhetoric, paradox has a different but related meaning. A paradox is any statement that seems self-contradictory, but in some sense may be true: "There are none so credulous as unbelievers."

A related figure of thought is **oxymoron,** where contradictory terms are yoked together, usually as adjective and noun: "cold heat," "eloquent silence." A favorite example of oxymoron comes from a professor of philosophy: "This passage in Heidegger is clearly opaque."

The author of *ad Herennium* discussed a figure of thought called **parrhesia** (frankness of speech). This figure occurs "when, talking before those to whom we owe reverence or fear, we yet exercise our right to speak out, because we seem justified in reprehending them, or persons dear to them, for some fault" (IV xxxvi 48). For example: "The university administration has tolerated hateful speech on this campus, and so to some extent they are to blame for its widespread use." An opposing figure is **litotes (understatement)**, where a rhetor diminishes some feature of the situation that is obvious to all. The author of *ad Herennium* gave this example from the defense of a very wealthy person: "his father left him a patrimony that was—I do not wish to exaggerate— not the smallest" (IV xxxviii 50). Using litotes, the rhetor avoids stating the exact extent of the rich man's holdings, and the audience is led to admire her tact as well. Modern rhetoricians define litotes as any statement that denies its contrary statement: "She was not unmindful of my wishes." But the figure occurs in any deliberate understatement of a state of affairs wherein more is understood than is said: "Nuclear weapons are dangerous." Sometimes litotes is not deliberate, as when an American president brushed off "the vision thing" as inappropriate to his administration.

Figures of Thought That Arouse Emotion   According to Quintilian, "the figures best adapted for intensifying emotion consist chiefly in simulation" (IX ii 26). This group of figures requires more inventiveness from a rhetor than any other because their persuasive quality depends on skill in creating convincing fictions. As Quintilian remarked, such devices make a great demand on our powers of eloquence. For with things that are false and incredible by nature there are but two alternatives: either they will move our hearers with exceptional force because they are beyond the truth, or they will be regarded as empty nothings because they are not the truth (IX ii 33). This group of sententia includes **personification**, *enargeia*, **irony**, and *ethopoeia*.

Personification or impersonation "consists in representing an absent person as present, or in making a mute thing or one lacking form articulate" (*ad Herennium* IV liii 66). We may represent someone who has died as though she were present: "If my mother were alive, she would wash his mouth out with soap." We can represent animals or nature as having human qualities, as the poet John Milton did in this passage from *Paradise Lost:*

> Earth felt the wound, and Nature from her seat
> Sighing through all her Works gave signs of woe. (IX, 529–30)

The advantage of this figure, according to Quintilian, is that we can display the inner thoughts of others as though they were present. He cautioned, however, that people and things must be represented credibly.

Enargeia is usually translated "ocular demonstration" or "vivid demonstration." Used as a figure, an enargeia paints a picture of a scene so vividly that it seems to be happening right in front of the audience. This is usually done by appealing to the sense of sight. Here is Mitch Landrieu, mayor of New Orleans, speaking at a ceremony marking the fifth anniversary of Hurricane Katrina:

> We must think back and remember, to what seems like so long ago. The days and the moments that have been etched into our memories flood back to us like the rising water.
> Oppressive heat, pitch black nights, confusion and fear—it all rushes back, a torrent of sights, of sounds, of smells.
> An abandoned, but not empty city, still and eerily silent. People stranded, trapped by the rising water, tattered white sheets waving at the sky, screams from the roof tops filled with anguish: "We are still alive!"
> The hum of a boat's motor, the silence of a corpse laying face down in the water, a man holding his dog, standing motionless—there were no words.
> A woman in a tattered dress clutching a clock, because it was the only thing she had left. She wouldn't let it go. She said she didn't "have nothin'." She said she didn't "know nothin'." But at least she knew what time it was.
> Tented emergency rooms hastily erected in the blazing sun in the shadow of the Convention Center. Makeshift beds on the Super Dome floor, wet and close; children crying, hope fading. Three thousand souls stuck in a sweltering shed in the Port of St. Bernard, waiting.

> People, like apparitions, defiantly emerging from the water—head first, shoulders second—holding a black garbage bag filled with the only things that they had left. Some people made it out. Others did not.
>
> Vera Smith lay dead on the corner of Magazine and Jackson. For days the street was her grave, a thin, white sheet covering her frail body; a simple epitaph written in black permanent marker, "Here lies Vera. God help us."
>
> Grandmas and grandpas died in storm battered hospitals and nursing homes. They were left on cots in a crowded chapel that became a makeshift morgue. In a city where everything broke down, in a time where nothing was just or fair, they were part of "the greatest generation" who saved the world, and we could not save them.

Mayor Landrieu paints a vivid picture of the aftermath of the hurricane by using visual and olfactory details to bring the experience to mind. As a result, the enargeia jogs the memories of those who lived through the hurricane, and, for those who were not present, sharply conveys the terror and despair that was felt by the residents of New Orleans.

The next figure, irony, is probably more often used today that any other figure. Simply defined, **irony** occurs when an audience understands the opposite of what is expressed: someone says, "Nice day, huh?" when it is windy and snowing; another asks, "Hot enough for you?" when everyone is suffering from the heat. When a friend flubs an answer in class and we give him the "thumbs-up" sign, that's an ironic gesture. But irony can be extremely complex. As Quintilian put it, in this figure,

> the meaning, and sometimes the whole aspect of our case, conflicts with the language and the tone of voice adopted; nay, a man's whole life may be colored with irony, as was the case with Socrates, who was called an ironist because he assumed the role of an ignorant man lost in wonder at the wisdom of others. (IX ii 46)

Irony abounds in contemporary political rhetoric: "My opponent is an honorable woman, I am sure"; "the party of moral values is the party that brought us Watergate, the savings-and-loan scandals and the Iran-Contra affair." Sometimes irony rebounds on its users. When a politician labels his opponent a draft dodger, the situation becomes ironic if the politician himself somehow escaped mandated military service. If this is discovered, his figure can backfire on him.

Irony has made a comeback in the era of Jon Stewart and Stephen Colbert. Colbert's schtick, where he poses as a conservative, is replete with irony. This can become extremely funny, as it did when Colbert addressed the White House Correspondents' dinner in 2006. Here is his take on President George W. Bush's approval numbers:

> Now, I know there are some polls out there saying this man has a 32 percent approval rating. But guys like us, we don't pay attention to the polls. We know that polls are just a collection of statistics that reflect what people are thinking in "reality." And reality has a well-known liberal bias. . . . Sir, pay no attention to the people who say the glass is half empty, because 32 percent means it's two-thirds empty. There's still some liquid in that glass, is my point. But I wouldn't drink it. The last third is usually backwash. (DailyKos.com 4/30/06)

Colbert uses irony to remind his audience that the president is not very popular, all the while seeming to say the contrary.

Irony finds a home on T-shirts such as the one that says, "Ironic Hipster Shirt." The T-shirts reading "F*** censorship" are also ironic because, well, they display censorship in action. Then there are the ironic T-shirts that read "[Insert Ironic Phrase Here]." Irony is very difficult to pull off in lengthier or more distant forms of writing such as memos and letters, yet *The Onion* manages to produce ironic essays and videos nearly every day, while authors and commenters on blogs often use the phrase IMHO when the opinion expressed is anything but humble.

Ethopoeia, or character portrayal, consists in "representing and depicting in words clearly enough for recognition the bodily form of some person" (*ad Herennium* IV xlix 63). The author gave this example: "the ruddy, short, bent man, with white and rather curly hair, blue-grey eyes, and a huge scar on his chin." But character portrayal may deal with a person's qualities, as well as her physical characteristics. The author of *ad Herennium* portrayed a rich man by depicting his habits:

> That person there . . . thinks it admirable that he is called rich. . . . once he has propped his chin on his left hand he thinks that he dazzles the eyes of all with the gleam of his jewelry and the glitter of his gold. . . . When he turns to his slave boy here, his only one . . . he calls him now by one name, now by another, and now by a third . . . so that unknowing hearers may think he is selecting one slave from among many. (IV xlix 63)

It is not difficult to update this sketch: simply put a Rolex on the man's arm and substitute a personal secretary or a bodyguard for the slave. We have met this kind of *ethopoeia* before, in the character sketches of Theophrastus, and also in the *progymnasmata* by the same name. Quintilian treated this figure as a kind of imitation, where the rhetor copies or emulates someone's words or deeds. He recommended the use of *ethopoeia* because of its charm and variety. He also pointed out that depictions of character, because they seem natural and spontaneous, can make an audience more receptive to a rhetor's ethos (IX ii 59), or the *ethos* of the person being described.

Here is Rick Perlstein's description of Richard Nixon as he appeared on television in his famous debate with John F. Kennedy during the election of 1960:

> when the close-up was on Nixon, you could write a book: the discomfited fluttering of the eyelids (it made him look fey), the deeply etched lines of his jowls (one side was deeper than the other; the dimple in his tie was also off-center), the shadow of beard that bled through when he tilted his chin at the angle he used for emphasis on key points. There had been a time when Richard Nixon had known how to take advantage of his awkwardness—to make a face like Kennedy's stand in for every smooth, slick superior who had eve done an ordinary Joe wrong. . . . Not this time. (56)

It is possible that Nixon's appearance at this debate cost him the presidency. At any rate, Perlstein's ethopoeia shows how an audience might infer clues to a person's character from his haggard and disheveled appearance.

Figures of Thought Borrowed from Invention and Arrangement   Quintilian disapproved of the practice of borrowing figures from invention or arrangement, and so he refused to treat them. In Book IX of the *Institutes,* he huffed: "I will pass by those authors who set no limit to their craze for inventing technical terms and even include among figures what really comes under the head of arguments" (iii 99). Most ancient rhetoricians were not as fastidious as Quintilian, however. For example, the author of the *ad Herennium* treated **reasoning by contraries** (enthymeme or conclusio) as a figure of thought. As you can see from the Greek term for this figure, it is borrowed from invention. In the *ad Herennium,* reasoning by contraries is a figure when the rhetor uses one of two opposite statements to prove the other, as in the following: "A faithless friend cannot be an honorable enemy"; or "George has never spoken the truth in private, and so he cannot be expected to refrain from lying in public." This figure resembles an enthymeme because it draws a conclusion (George will lie in public) from a statement that is not open to question (George lies to his friends). The author of *ad Herennium* liked it because of its "brief and complete rounding-off," and so he recommended that it be completed in one unbroken period (IV xviii 26).

Other figures of thought repeat on the sentence level the parts of arrangement suggested for whole discourses. Cicero was particularly fond of these as a means of helping the audience keep track of the progress of the argument. Along with other ancient rhetoricians, he recommended that complex topics be divided into parts, and a reason for accepting the parts be attached to each (divisio). Here is an example from *ad Herennium:* "If you are an upright man, you have not deserved reproach; if a wicked man, you will be unmoved" (IV xl 52). In this case, the rhetor divides alternatives into only two (the man is either upright or wicked); this allows the rhetor to select from among many characteristics that might be chosen and thus to control the audience's response to the man. This figure is closely related to **distribution** (diairesis, distributio), where the rhetor divides up possibilities and distributes them among different areas. Here is an example from *ad Herennium:* "The Senate's function is to assist the state with counsel; the magistracy's is to execute, by diligent activity, the Senate's will; the people's to choose and support by its votes the best measures and the most suitable men" (IV xxxv 47). The distribution makes this political arrangement seem fair and equitable.

Accumulation (*frequentatio*) is another figure of thought based on arrangement. Here the rhetor gathers together points that are scattered about and lists them all together. This has the effect of making a shaky conclusion seem more evident or reasonable. Interestingly enough, accumulation is forbidden in courtroom argument. In many cases, prosecutors are not allowed to introduce an accused person's past offenses into their argument on the grounds that a person should be tried only for the crime with which he is currently charged. This practice testifies to the rhetorical power of accumulation: although juries or judges might not be impressed by the evidence assembled to substantiate one instance of a crime, they are more likely to be impressed by evidence that testifies to the commission of a series of like or related crimes. Television uses a combination of images and speech to create the effect of accumulation, as when, for example, a sportscaster calls an NBA game a "dunkfest" while the rolling clips show twelve different slam dunks from the game. The accumulated images reinforce the credibility of the term. Accumulation can also be used to create **enargeia.**

Cicero and the author of *ad Herennium* also treated **transitions** as figures of thought (*Orator* xl 137; IV xxvi 35). A transition is any word or phrase that connects pieces of discourse. Cicero recommended that rhetors use transition to announce what is about to be discussed when introducing a topic (*propositio*) and sum up when concluding a topic (*enumeratio*); if both are used together, they constitute a smooth transition between topics. Using transition, a rhetor can briefly recall what has just been said and briefly announce what will follow.

Now that we have concluded our discussion of figures, we move to an analysis of tropes (hint: this sentence is a transition).

Tropes

Neither ancient nor modern rhetoricians have ever been able to agree about what distinguishes this class of ornament from figures. It is probably safe to say that tropes are characterized by the substitution of one word or phrase for another, but even this distinction does not clearly demarcate tropes from some figures of language, such as **synonomy** or puns. However, even though ancient rhetoricians could not agree about the definition of a trope, they knew one when they saw one. With the notable exception of Aristotle, who was ambivalent about every ornament except **metaphor,** major rhetoricians used a list of ten tropes that remained more or less standard throughout antiquity. The ten are: *onomatopoeia, antonomasia,* **metonymy,** *periphrasis, hyperbaton,* **hyperbole, synecdoche, catachresis,** metaphor, and **allegory.**

Onomatopeia   According to the author of the *ad Herennium,* the rhetor who uses *onomatopeia* ("making a new name") assigns a new word to "a thing which either lacks a name or has an inappropriate name" (IV xxx 42). This trope could be used either for imitative purposes, as illustrated by words like *roar, bellow, murmur, hiss* (*sibulus* in Latin), or for expressiveness. To exemplify this second use of *onomatopeia,* the author coined a Latin word, *fragor,* which his modern translator renders as *hullabaloo:* "After this creature attacked the republic, there was a hullabaloo among the first men of the state." (The 1960s gave us another *onomatopeia* for a hullabaloo—*hootenanny*). Readers who have been paying attention will notice that *onomatopeia* bears a close resemblance to **neologism**—the coining of new words—a practice that was condemned by Quintilian as "scarcely permissible to a Roman." That quintessential Roman, Julius Caesar, warned us to "avoid, as you would a rock, an unheard-of and unfamiliar word" (notice the nice analogy here). Nonetheless, ancient rhetoricians agreed that *onomatopeia* was the means by which language was invented, as their ancestors found names for things by emulating the noises those things characteristically made (*Institutes* VIII vi 31).

Antonomasia   In the trope called *antonomasia* ("another name"; Latin *pronominatio*), a rhetor substitutes a descriptive phrase for someone's proper name (or vice versa).

When Quintilian referred to Cicero as "the prince of Roman orators," he used *antonomasia* (VIII vi 30). The author of *ad Herennium* suggested that, rather than naming the Gracchi, whose reputations were contested, a rhetor could more effectively refer to them as "the grandsons of Africanus" because Africanus' reputation was impeccable (IV xxxi 42). *Antonomasia* appears frequently in contemporary rhetoric. Athletes acquire nicknames like "The Big Aristotle," "King James," and "Mr. Excitement." Red-haired snowboarder Shaun White is called "The Flying Tomato," and one of us earned herself the epithet "Dr. Collision" on the ultimate frisbee field. But the contemporary popularity of this trope is not limited to sports. In 2006, President George W. Bush called himself the "The Decider." Elvis is "the King," and in an article about rock-and-roll star Little Richard, music writer Bob Mehr begins with a whole collection of *antonomasiai:* "Before he was the Originator, the Innovator, the Emancipator, before he could claim his throne as the King, Queen or Quasar of Rock 'n' Roll, Little Richard stood before a microphone in a cramped New Orleans studio and delivered his masterwork" (90). The rhetorical effects of this trope are obvious. It not only suggests that someone is so well known that her name need not be used, thus cementing group loyalty; it also provides a rhetor with an opportunity to characterize the person she speaks or writes about in either positive or negative terms.

Metonomy   Metonomy, "altered name," names something with a word or phrase closely associate with with it: "the White House" for the president of the United States or "the Kremlin" for the leadership of the former Union of Socialist Soviet Republics. The maxim "The pen is mightier than the sword" is a metonomy where *pen* stands for persuasive language and *sword* for war. We refer to the works of an author by her name: "Morrison" or "McEwan" stand in for novels written by Toni Morrison or Ian McEwan. We use metonymy when we say, "I like The Black Eyed Peas" to mean that we like their music.

Periphrasis   We have already met the figure called *periphrasis* ("circling speech") under its Latin name of circumlocution. Quintilian defined uses of this figure as "whatever might have been expressed with greater brevity, but is expanded for purposes of ornament" (VIII vi 61). He gave this poetic example from Virgil's *Aeneid:* "Now was the time/When the first sleep to weary mortals comes/Stealing its way, the sweetest boon of heaven" (ii 268). Virgil did not simply say "night arrived." Rather, he embroidered on this simple observation to achieve the effect of calmness that sleep brings.

   Quintilian worried that rhetors would use this figure simply to fill up space, or to impress:

> some rhetors introduce a whole host of useless words; for, in their eagerness to avoid ordinary methods of expression, and allured by false ideals of beauty they wrap up everything in a multitude of words simply and solely because they are unwilling to make a direct and simple statement of the facts. (VIII ii 17)

A contemporary rhetorician named Richard Lanham argues persuasively that much contemporary American prose is written in what he calls "the Official Style." He gives this example:

> The history of Western psychological thought has long been dominated by philosophical considerations as to the nature of man. These notions have dictated corresponding considerations of the nature of the child within society, the practices by which children were to be raised, and the purposes of studying the child. (*Revising Prose* 1992: 10)

In essence, this passage says that psychologists are interested in human nature and that this interest has led them to investigate childhood and child-rearing practices. In other words, users of the official style do exactly what Quintilian warned against—they pile up more words and phrases than are necessary to achieve an impressive effect. There is a big difference between using words to enhance an effect or to call attention to a point, and simply failing to notice them.

Hyperbaton   *Hyperbaton* is the transposition of a word to somewhere other than its usual place: "Backward run sentences, until reels the mind" (a parody of the erstwhile style of *Time* magazine). Strictly speaking, *hyperbaton* is a figure of language because its effect depends on a change in normal word order. But, as Quintilian noted, it can be called a trope when "the meaning is not complete until the two words have been put together" (VIII vi 66). Winston Churchill supposedly employed hyperbaton to make fun of a persnickety editor who forbade him to place a preposition at the end of a sentence: "This is the sort of bloody nonsense up with which I will not put." We parody our own writing by imposing a hyperbaton on the first sentence of this paragraph: "Hyperbaton is the transposition, to somewhere other than its usual place, of a word."

Hyperbole   Quintilian defined hyperbole ("thrown above"; "excess") as "an elegant straining of the truth" (VIII vi 67), and gives this wonderful example from Cicero: "Vetto gives the name of farm to an estate which might easily be hurled from a sling, though it might well fall through the hole in the hollow sling, so small is it" (73). Aristotle gave these examples: speaking of a man with a black eye, "You would have thought him a basket of mulberries"; and of a skinny man, "he has legs like parsley" (*Rhetoric* III xi 1413a). In other words, hyperbole is exaggeration used for effect. People often use hyperbole to describe extreme weather conditions. During a Midwestern July heat wave, one of us heard this hyperbole: "Hotter than the hinges on the gates of hell." It has become almost commonplace for weather forecasters to hyperbolize winter weather events, using labels such as "snowmageddon" and "snowpocalypse" to describe or anticipate them. Sportscasters, especially color commentators, often use hyperbole to create excitement. When someone makes a long-range three pointer, for instance, the sportscaster might yell, "From the parking lot!" or engaging in even more exaggerated hyperbole, he might say the shot came "From Downtown!" Hyperbole has made it into e-mail, instant messages, and text messages. Although LOL is often not hyperbole, ROTFL usually is: a person can't typically type or text while rolling on the floor.

Synecdoche   In synecdoche ("to receive together") rhetors substitute the part for the whole (or vice versa) or cause for effect (or vice versa). Quintilian wrote that this figure occurred most commonly with numbers, as in "The Roman won the day," where "the Roman" refers to an entire army. The author of *ad Herennium* gave this example of synecdoche: "Were not those nuptial flutes reminding you of his marriage?" (the flutes stand for the whole ceremony). Like hyperbole, this trope is common in everyday speech. We say "give me a hand," where *hand* refers to help or assistance, and we use the phrase "400 head" to refer to 400 animals. Here is James Wolcott, having fun with synecdoche in a short piece about professional football: "Dennis Perrin and Ioz are squaring off over the upcoming Jets–Steelers battlegame galactica—the most titanic clash since last week's megasaurus grudge match, in which Rex Ryan's Toes of Fury sent Bill Belichek's Scowling Hoodie into the fjord mists of playoff elimination."

Catachresis   Catachresis ("to use against") is "the inexact use of a like and kindred word in place of the precise and proper one" (*ad Herennium* IV xxxiii 45). The author gave these examples: "the power of man is short," "small height," "long wisdom," "mighty speech." In these examples adjectives are misapplied to nouns: we ordinarily speak of human power as limited rather than short; of wisdom as enduring rather than long and so on. Quintilian defined this trope more narrowly as "the practice of adapting the nearest available term to describe something for which no actual term exists" (VIII vi 34). The Latin name for catachresis is "abuse," and novice rhetors might be wise to avoid it.

Metaphor   A metaphor transfers or substitutes one word for another. The Greek people have always taken metaphor seriously, it seems. If you visit modern Greece, you might notice that a transfer truck bears the label *metaphoros*. Some metaphors are so common in our daily speech that we no longer think about their metaphoric quality: we say that a disappointed lover "struck out" or "never got to first base," borrowing metaphors from baseball. When someone has exhausted all her alternatives, we say that she is "at the end of her rope," borrowing a grisly metaphor from executions. We say that the abortion question presents us with a thicket of difficult issues, borrowing a metaphor from nature. Truly striking metaphors appear in poetry. Here are two examples from a poem by Emily Dickinson:

> There is no frigate like a book
> To take us lands away,
> Nor any coursers like a page
> Of prancing poetry.

Dickinson compared a book to a ship and its pages to a pair of horses. In prose these comparisons don't make much sense, but they work beautifully in Dickinson's poem to evoke images and emotions.

Aristotle, like other ancient rhetoricians, was more interested in metaphor than he was in other tropes or figures, and metaphor has received more attention from modern rhetoricians and literary critics than has any other trope or figure. In the *Poetics*,

Aristotle defined metaphor as the movement of a name from its own genus or species to another genus or species (XXI 7 1457b). In the *Rhetoric,* he noted that metaphors borrowed from something greater in the same genus or species were complimentary, whereas those borrowed from something worse could be used to denigrate the person or thing to whom it was applied. Thus, pirates can be called "entrepreneurs" or "businesspeople," whereas someone who has made a mistake can be accused of criminal behavior (III ii 1405a). Humans often get compared to other species because of some shared characteristic that the rhetor wants to highlight: humans can be as stubborn as donkeys or as wily as foxes.

Aristotle classed metaphors among those tropes and figures he called witty or urbane sayings, and he developed a theory about why metaphors give us pleasure. They do so, he wrote, "because metaphors help us to learn new things, and learning is naturally pleasurable to humans" (x 1410b). In other words, because metaphors express ideas in new or unusual ways, they help us to see things in new ways. He suggested that metaphors be taken from two sources: those that are beautiful, either in sound or effect, and those that appealed to the senses (ii 1405b). It would not do, he wrote, to substitute "red-fingered" or even "purple-fingered" for Homer's "rosy-fingered dawn." He told a funny story about Simonides, who at first declined to write a poem for a man who had won a mule race, on the ground that he did not want to celebrate half-asses. When the man paid enough, however, Simonides accepted the commission and wrote "Hail, daughters of storm-footed mares!"

Aristotle gave many examples of successful metaphors: citizens are like a ship's captain who is strong but deaf; ungrateful neighbors are like children who accept candy but keep on crying; orators are like babysitters who eat the baby's food and then moisten the baby's lips with their saliva (iv, 1406b, 1407a).

Sometimes a metaphor can launch and sustain an argument. For example, after several people were shot in Tucson, Arizona (among them Congresswoman Gabrielle Giffords), commentators saw a connection between the shooting and one of Sarah Palin's campaign ads. Here, Dean Rader shows how the metaphoric connection was made:

> Readers who may have arrived at this story only recently may not know that Ms. Palin's political action committee (PAC) has "targeted" Ms. Giffords' Arizona district for conservative activism. To visually denote this, a "crosshairs"—two lines that intersect in the middle to denote aim or the focus of sight—was placed over three congressional districts in Arizona and around the country.
>
> Some critics of the former Alaska governor have made a direct link between the signifier (crosshair) and what is, perhaps, its main signified (shooting). That is, the crosshairs planted the seed to shoot the representative of the district targeted by the bullseye.
>
> Supporters of Ms. Palin defend her use of the crosshairs icon because for them it is not a violent signifier; merely a symbol of "focus." Opponents, and even some supporters, like *The View*'s Elisabeth Hasselbeck, on the other hand, have leveled harsh criticism at Palin for use of a signifier that connotes hunting, shooting, killing. Hasselbeck herself noted the map "looks like an al Qaeda Christmas card."

In other words, words that were meant metaphorically (*targets, crosshairs*) can also be read literally, to encourage actual targeting and shooting. In this way, metaphors can become a means of invention. All tropes can, for that matter.

Quintilian distinguished several kinds of metaphor. In one of these, a rhetor substitutes one living thing for another: "He is a lion"; "Scipio was continually barked at by Cato" (VIII vi 9). In another kind, inanimate things may be substituted for animate, and vice versa. Quintilian thought this was most impressive when an inanimate object is spoken of as though it were alive, as in Cicero's "What was that sword of yours doing, Tubero?", or "The dam decided to collapse at that moment." Aristotle would have classed both of these kinds of metaphor under the head of species-to-species, where a rhetor substitutes the name of one particular for another. Aristotle and Quintilian both named metaphors that substitute a part for a whole, or vice versa, as a separate class, but modern rhetoricians label such metaphors as synecdoches (for example, "Jane Doe" to represent all women).

In the *Poetics* Aristotle writes, "In some cases of analogy no current term exists" (XXXI 1458a). The example he gives is this: "To release seed is to 'sow,' while the sun's release of fire lacks a name" (XXI 1458a). Aristotle also treated **analogy** as a kind of metaphor. In analogy, rhetors compare a relationship rather than items. Aristotle cited Pericles' saying that the young men killed in a recent war had vanished from Athens as though someone had taken Spring from the year (III x 1411a). Analogies frequently come in handy when a physician questions a patient about his pain—"Does the pain feel like more like needles or a knife?"

Allegory   A metaphor becomes an **allegory** (literally "speaking otherwise") when it is sustained throughout a long passage. One of the most well-known allegories is Plato's allegory of the cave in book VII of *The Republic,* where the darkness of the cave is made analogous to those who don't know philosophy. Allegory is still popular and useful. Many critics saw it at work in James Cameron's film, *Avatar.* Thomas Eddlam explains:

> The use of Avatars in the attack on the Na'vi also makes a perfect allegory to the Indian wars of America's settlement. Many times the colonists sought the aid of native tribes in order to subdue other more assertive tribes, and the Avatars could be compared to the tribes friendly to the colonists, who were later disposed of in subsequent wars. Divide and conquer was the strategy in the displacement of native Americans, but on Pandora the biological links between the natives makes the issue much more difficult.

Other critics saw an allegorical allusion in the film to the environmental devastation wreaked on Iraq and Afghanistan by American wars in those countries.

Voice and Rhetorical Distance

Rhetors can create a character within a discourse, and that such self-characterizations are persuasive. Ancient rhetoricians realized that very subtle ethical effects were available through the manipulation of certain features of style. Here is Hermogenes of

Tarsus, for example, on how to convey an appearance of anger by means of word choice:

> Rough and vehement diction and coined words are indicative of anger, especially in sudden attacks on your opponent, where unusual words that seem to be coined on the spur of the moment are quote suitable, words such as "iamb-eater or "pen-pusher." All such words are suitable since they seem to have been dictated by emotion. (*On Types of Style* 359)

Contemporary rhetoricians give the name "voice" to this self-dramatization in style.[3] Of course, voice is a metaphor in that it suggests that all rhetorical situations, even those that use written or electronic media, mimic the relation of one person speaking to another. Written or electronic discourse that creates a lively and accessible voice makes reading more interesting. Like the characters of style, the repertoire of possible voices is immense: there are cheerful voices, gloomy ones, stuffy ones, homey ones, sincere ones, angry ones—the list is endless.

Voices affect the rhetorical distance that can seem to exist between rhetors and their audiences. Once again, the term *distance* is a metaphor representing the degree of physical and social distance that exists between people speaking to one another. But even in written or electronic discourse rhetors can narrow or widen the rhetorical distance between themselves and their audiences by means of stylistic choice. When creating a voice, rhetors should consider the situation for which they are composing: how much distance is appropriate given their relationship to an audience; how much distance is appropriate given their relationship to the issue. As a general rule, persuasion occurs more easily when audiences can identify with rhetors. Identification increases as distance decreases.

Intimate Distance = Closer Identification, More Persuasive Potential
Formal Distance = Less Identification, Less Persuasive Potential

Rhetors who know an audience well, or whose audience is quite small, can use an intimate distance (unless some factor in the rhetorical situation prevents this). The distance created in personal letters, for example, is ordinarily quite intimate, whereas that used in business correspondence is more formal because rhetors either do not know their correspondents personally or because convention dictates that such relationships be kept at arm's length, so to speak. However, rhetorical situations can create exceptions to the distance–intimacy equation. Formal language is ordinarily appropriate in a courtroom, for example, even though an attorney, a defendant, and a judge constitute a very small group. In addition, the attorney may know both the judge and the defendant well. Nonetheless, she probably ought to use formal language in her conversations with both, given the official and serious nature of courtroom transactions. And sometimes very large groups are addressed in quite intimate language: performers at concerts and television evangelists, whose audiences number in the thousands or even millions, nonetheless occasionally address their audiences quite personally and intimately.

A rhetor's attitude toward the issue also influences distance. Where rhetors remain as neutral as possible, expressing neither a supportive nor rejecting attitude, distance tends to be greater. On the other hand, rhetors' strong expression of an attitude— approval or disapproval, for example—closes distance.

More Attitude = Intimate Distance
Less Attitude = More Formal Distance

To demonstrate the contrasting effects of distance created by more or less attitude, we examine two accounts of an event. Here is the *New York Times'* account of a shooting in Tucson, Arizona:

> TUCSON — Representative Gabrielle Giffords, an Arizona Democrat, and at least 17 others were shot Saturday morning when a gunman opened fire outside a supermarket where Ms. Giffords was meeting with constituents.
>
> Six of the victims died, among them John M. Roll, the chief judge for the United States District Court for Arizona, and a 9-year-old girl, the Pima County sheriff, Clarence W. Dupnik, said.
>
> Ms. Giffords, 40, whom the authorities called the target of the attack, was in critical condition Sunday morning at the University Medical Center in Tucson, where she was operated on by a team of neurosurgeons on Saturday. Dr. Peter Rhee, medical director of the hospital's trauma and critical care unit, said Saturday that she had been shot once in the head, "through and through," with the bullet going through her brain.
>
> Investigators identified the gunman as Jared Lee Loughner, 22, and said that he was refusing to cooperate with the authorities and had invoked his Fifth Amendment rights. Mr. Loughner was in custody with the Federal Bureau of Investigation on Saturday night, the Pima County sheriff's office said. . . .
>
> Mark Kimble, an aide to Ms. Giffords, said the shooting occurred about 10 a.m. in a small area between an American flag and an Arizona flag. He said that he went into the store for coffee, and that as he came out the gunman started firing.
>
> Ms. Giffords had been talking to a couple about Medicare and reimbursements, and Judge Roll had just walked up to her and shouted "Hi," when the gunman, wearing sunglasses and perhaps a hood of some sort, approached and shot the judge, Mr. Kimble said. "Everyone hit the ground," he said. "It was so shocking."

Traditionally, straight news reporting confines itself to the facts of the matter. No judgments are made, and most of the piece consists of facts and testimony that can be verified. This approach creates a relatively formal tone and increases the rhetorical distance between rhetor and readers.

In contrast, commentators are under no mandate to stick to the facts. Indeed, commentators are obliged to express opinions about events. Inevitably, then, their accounts close up rhetorical distance because they convey attitude. Here is the *Times'* opinion columnist Paul Krugman on the day following the shooting:

> When you heard the terrible news from Arizona, were you completely surprised? Or were you, at some level, expecting something like this atrocity to happen?
>
> Put me in the latter category. I've had a sick feeling in the pit of my stomach ever since the final stages of the 2008 campaign. I remembered the upsurge in political hatred after Bill Clinton's election in 1992—an upsurge that culminated in the Oklahoma City bombing. And you could see, just by watching the crowds at McCain–Palin rallies, that it was ready to happen again.

Krugman begins with two questions, which immediately closes the distance between himself and his readers. The questions are written in second person, directly addressing his readers. Then he makes a personal reference, remembering how he felt back in 1992 and again in 2008. He does not report any facts about the shooting itself, assuming that his readers know those already. This assumption also serves to close the distance between him and his audience. And so the tone of the piece overall is informal, far more so than that in the same newpaper's reporting of the incident.

Grammatical Person

The prominent features of style that affect voice and distance are grammatical person, verb tense and voice, word size, qualifers, and—in written discourse—punctuation. There are three grammatical persons available in English: first person, where the person or persons speaking or writing refer to themselves as "I" or "we"; second person, where the audience is addressed by means of "you"; and third person, where the rhetor mentions agents or issues but does not allude directly to herself or her audience.

First-Person Reference: "I want you to do the dishes today."

Second-Person Address: "Do these dishes today or else."

Third-Person Reference: "Someone must do these dishes today."

Composition textbooks (and teachers) often tell their students never to use first-person ("I" or "we") or second-person ("you") pronouns in the papers they write in school. No doubt teachers adhere to this rule because school writing is supposedly formal in tone, or because they want their students to sound objective—that is, they do not want their students' voices to take center stage in papers written for school. However, we think that this rule is far too simple and inflexible to respond to the great variety of rhetorical situations that people encounter.

Generally, first- and second-person discourse create less distance between a rhetor and an audience than does third-person discourse because the participants in the action are referred to directly. In third-person discourse, the issue or subject is foregrounded instead, and references to the rhetor or her audience tend to disappear. Thus third-person discourse creates the greatest possible rhetorical distance. First- and second-person discourse are used in situations where rhetors are physically proximate to audiences—in conversation, and in more formal speech situations as well. In settings where spoken discourse is used, "I" and "you" actually refer to participants in the situation, even when the audience is very, very large, as it is at football games and open-air concerts. Third person is generally used by speakers only within quite formal contexts, or if convention dictates that it be used—by scientists or engineers, for instance.

First- and Second-Person Discourse   First- and second-person are ordinarily used in speech when small groups of people are conversing. Clarity of pronoun reference is ordinarily not a problem in conversation because the persons to whom the pronouns apply are visible and audible to all participants. To see how important it is to maintain the relatively intimate distance necessary to conversation, try speaking about someone who is present in the third person (use her name; use the pronouns *she* and *her* to refer to her). Third-person pronouns create such a distance that the person so referred to may feel that she has suddenly become invisible.

First- and second-grammatical persons have interesting and complex ethical effects in writing and in electronic discourse because the persons participating in these rhetorical acts are not physically proximate to each other. Here is a fictional example of first-person discourse, from Benjamin Kunkel's novel *Indecision:*

> A week before Quito I was sitting up in bed in New York, the edges of my awareness lapped at by traffic. I was sitting there with one hand holding open the book I was reading, and the other hand placed above the head of sleeping Vaneetha. There I was, pinned in space and time like a specimen in a box.

Here is a version of the passage revised into third-person discourse:

> A week before he was to leave for Quito, Dwight was sitting up in bed in New York, the edges of his awareness lapped at by traffic. He was sitting there with one hand holding open the book he was reading, and the other hand placed above the head of sleeping Vaneetha. There he was, pinned in space and time like a specimen in a box.

The third-person version demonstrates how that choice increases the distance between reader and writer, as well as between readers and the subject of the novel, the post–9/11 "midlife crisis" of twenty-eight-year-old Dwight B. Wilmerding.

Because it is modeled on conversation, first-person discourse always implies the presence of a hearer or a reader, a "you" who is listening or reading, whether that "you" is explicitly mentioned or not. Prose that relies on an "I–you" relation indicates to members of an audience that a rhetor feels close enough to them to include them in a relatively intimate conversation: "Dear folks: I know you may be worried about me, so I'm writing to say that I arrived safely. Please send money. Love, your son." The author of this note gives no details at all about his arrival—when, where, how. He obviously feels so close to his audience that he assumes they need no more information than he supplies.

In relationships that are not intimate, the "I–you" voice has complex ethical effects. Novelist Fyodor Dostoevski's "Underground Man" provides a good instance of the ego-centeredness that may result from the use of first-person discourse, even when the rhetor is a fictional person, as he is in this case:

> I am a sick man . . . I am a spiteful man. I am an unpleasant man. I think my liver is diseased. However, I don't know beans about my disease, and I am not sure what is bothering me. I don't treat it and never have, though I respect medicine and doctors. Besides, I am extremely superstitious, let's say sufficiently so to respect medicine. (I am educated enough not to be superstitious, but I am.) No, I refuse to treat it out of spite. You probably will not understand that. Well, but I understand it. Of course, I can't explain to you just whom I am annoying in this case by my spite. (1)

Here is a complaining neighbor, wrapped so deeply in his own troubles that he seems at first to be engaging in an ego-centered, aimless and self-contradictory monologue. But suddenly he acknowledges the presence of an audience ("you probably will not understand"), a move that establishes a sort of back-fence intimacy. And the final sentence in the passage suggests that the relationship will become "us" against "them" before very long. The intimate "I–you" relationship includes Dostoevski's audience, whether they want to be this man's companion or not.

The ethical possibilities opened by grammatical person are endless. In *Desert Solitaire* Edward Abbey used a combination of third and first persons to separate "us" from "them."

> There may be some among the readers of this book . . . who believe without question that any and all forms of construction and development are intrinsic goods, in the national parks as well as anywhere else, who virtually identify quantity with quality and therefore assume that the greater the quantity of traffic, the higher the value received. There are some who frankly and boldly advocate the eradication of the last remnants of wilderness and the complete subjugation of nature to the requirement of—not man—but industry. This is a courageous view, admirable in its simplicity and power, and with the weight of all modern history behind it. It is also quite insane. I cannot attempt to deal with it here.
>
> There will be other readers, I hope, who share my basic assumption that wilderness is a necessary part of civilization and that it is the primary responsibility of the national park system to preserve intact and undiminished what little still remains. (47)

Abbey referred to those who don't share his opinions in the third person, perhaps because he was pretty sure they wouldn't be among his readers. This tactic created a "we–they" relationship that gave Abbey's readers a sense of being allied with him against those who do not share his position.

We, the plural first-person pronoun, shares in the complex rhetorical effects created by the use of *I. We* may establish a level of intimacy that presumes much in common between rhetor and audience, even when in fact a great power differential exists between them. Here for example, is an excerpt from President Obama's remarks at a memorial service for victims of the Tucson shooting:

> To the families of those we've lost; to all who called them friends; to the students of this university, the public servants gathered tonight, and the people of Tucson and Arizona: I have come here tonight as an American who, like all Americans, kneels to pray with you today, and will stand by you tomorrow.
>
> There is nothing I can say that will fill the sudden hole torn in your hearts. But know this: the hopes of a nation are here tonight. We mourn with you for the fallen. We join you in your grief. And we add our faith to yours that Representative Gabrielle Giffords and the other living victims of this tragedy pull through. (http://tucsoncitizen .com/tc-blog/2011/01/12/citizen-coverage-of-giffords-shooting-memorials/)

Even though he had a worldwide audience for these remarks and had not met most of the people in his immediate audience, Obama chose an intimate distance for this address. The intimate voice is appropriate for consolation, as it is to his assumption that even though most Americans did not know the victims personally, they joined their families in mourning the loss.

We used the first-person plural pronoun, even though to do so is unconventional in textbooks. We did so for three reasons. First of all, this voice seemed to be more honest because much of what we have to say here has developed from our own thinking about the usefulness of ancient rhetoric. As a result, writing in first person was easier for us because we didn't have to go searching for circumlocutions like "in the opinion of the authors" to express what we think. Second, when we took a position on a matter that is debated by scholars of ancient rhetoric, the first-person voice allowed us to take responsibility for that position; third person made flat statements about disputed matters seem far too authoritative and decisive in situations where opinions differ. Third, we hoped that readers would identify more readily with a first-person voice. The material is foreign and difficult, and by itself puts quite a little distance between us and our readers. The use of a third-person voice would only widen that distance.

Our choice of first person did create one problem, one that some readers may have noticed by now. Its use can create an ego-centered voice that excludes an audience. Whether this happens or not depends on the care taken by the rhetor to establish a respectable ethos and on his attitude toward his subject. We worried a good deal that our use of the plural first-person "we" would take on authority we don't mean it to have. That is, we feared it would become the so-called royal we, so called because kings and queens use it when making official announcements.

There is yet another rhetorical problem inherent in the use of a first-person voice. The first-person voice often led us to want to write in second person as well, as in phrases like "Notice how . . ." and "you should do. . . ." Because we wanted to avoid the instructional tone conveyed by the second person, we were often forced to substitute third-person circumlocutions for "you"—"the rhetor," "the writer," "the speaker," and so on.

Second-Person Discourse   Second-person discourse is the province of advertising. "Get Your Second Wind"; "Eat Fresh"; "You're in good hands." Advertisers want their audiences to feel close to the companies they represent and the products they sell.

The cozy second-person voices they establish cover over the fact that every ad gives instructions to its audience: use this, buy that. In other words, a rhetorical problem is potentially inherent in second-person discourse because rhetors who adopt it are giving directions. Obviously, this is true of recipes and directions for using or assembling something: "Add just a pinch of marjoram to the boiling sauce"; "Join tab A to slot B." The person who gives directions assumes a position of superiority to audiences. If readers are ready to be dictated to, as users of recipes usually are, this voice works.

When readers or hearers are not receptive to instruction, use of the second-person pronoun can increase distance rather than closing it. For example, when a chairwoman of the Congressional Black Caucus, Carolyn Cheeks Kirkpatrick, asked television talk-show host Don Imus if he understood that his language was offensive to black women, he responded in the affirmative. Then he said: "I can't get any place with you people." This would be funny if what it reveals weren't so horrible: Imus's use of the second person in the phrase "you people" is a palpable reminder of America's long history of segregation of black people, and its use created an alienating distance between himself and his audience—in this case a powerful black woman.

Third-Person Discourse   Third-person voice establishes the greatest possible distance between writer and reader. Use of this grammatical person announces that its author, for whatever reasons, cannot afford too much intimacy with an audience. Third person is appropriate when a rhetor wishes to establish herself as an authority or when she wishes to efface her voice so that the issue may seem to be presented as objectively as possible. In third-person discourse, the relationship of both rhetor and audience to the issue being discussed is more important than the relation between them.

Here is a passage from Fredrich A. Hayek's *The Constitution of Liberty* that is written in third person:

> The great aim of the struggle for liberty has been equality before the law. This equality under the rules which the state enforces may be supplemented by a similar equality of the rules that men voluntarily obey in the relations with one another. This extension of the principles of equality to the rules of moral and social conduct is the chief expression of what is commonly called the democratic spirit—and probably that aspect of it that does most to make inoffensive the inequalities that liberty necessarily produces. (85)

Hayek did not qualify the generalizations put forward in this paragraph with an "I think" or even with an "Experience shows that. . . ." He may have had several reasons for choosing to write in this distancing fashion: to seem objective, to seem authoritative and therefore forceful, or to keep his subject—equality—in front of readers, rather than his personality. Because Hayek is a very well known political theorist, his status as an authority (his situated ethos) may be such that he doesn't have to qualify his generalizations.

Here's another example of third-person discourse from the first page of *How Institutions Think,* written by a well-known anthropologist, Mary Douglas:

> Writing about cooperation and solidarity means writing at the same time about rejection and mistrust. Solidarity involves individuals being ready to suffer on behalf of the larger group and their expecting other individual members to do as much for them. It is difficult to talk about these questions coolly. They touch on intimate feelings of loyalty and sacredness. Anyone who has accepted trust and demanded sacrifice or willingly given either knows the power of the social bond. Whether there is a commitment to authority or a hatred of tyranny or something between the extremes, the social bond itself is taken to be something above question. Attempts to bring it out into the light of day and to investigate it are resisted. Yet it needs to be examined. Everyone is affected directly by the quality of trust around him or her. (1)

This third-person voice is a bit less distancing than Hayek's, because it does refer to people, rather than to abstractions. However, Douglas takes great pains not to name anyone, even though she is writing about intimate issues ("feelings of loyalty and sacredness"). Use of the third person forces Douglas to put rather vague words in the grammatical subject positions of her sentences: "writing," "solidarity," "it," "they," "anyone." We have revised the passage into first person, making the author ("I") the grammatical subject of most of the sentences:

> If I write about cooperation and solidarity, I must write at the same time about rejection and mistrust. I define "solidarity" as the readiness of individuals to suffer on behalf of the larger group and their expecting other individual members to do as much for them. I have difficulty talking about these questions coolly, because they touch on intimate feelings of loyalty and sacredness. Because I have accepted trust and demanded sacrifice, and have willingly given them as well, I know the power of the social bond. I take the social bond to be above question; my commitment to authority or my hatred of tyranny is irrelevant to this question. Every time I attempt to bring it out into the light of day and to investigate it, people resist my efforts. Yet we need to examine it, because all of us are affected by the quality of trust around us.

We think the revision makes the passage clearer and more lively as well. Use of the first person also forces us to take responsibility for the large generalizations we make, following Douglas, about the touchiness of this question. However, use of first-person discourse does lessen the authority carried by the original passage because the generalizations made in the revision are less sweeping in scope. That is, they apply to "I" rather than to people in general.

Scientists, social scientists, and other scholars use third-person discourse to reinforce the impression that the facts speak for themselves, that human beings have had as little influence in these matters as possible. The warning label on cigarette packages, for example, used to read as follows: "Warning: The Surgeon General Has Determined That Cigarette Smoking Is Dangerous To Your Health." Even though the Surgeon General probably did not conduct the research that discovered the connection between smoking and lung cancer, the message relied on the authority of that office to underscore the seriousness of the message. A later version of this warning reads: "Quitting Smoking Now Greatly Reduces Serious Risks to Your Health." Although the newer version is a bit more specific, it is also firmer because it omits reference to an author and addresses the audience directly. It is probably safe to predict that this warning will never be couched in a first-person voice: "I think that smoking cigarettes is bad for you, and you ought to stop it. Mary Jones, M.D." The intimacy of the first person undermines the authority that this serious message requires.

Our use of alternating male and female pronouns has irritated some of our readers. Some who have complained about this practice would prefer that we stick to a single gender, thus reducing the number of occasions in which gender switches call attention to the rhetoric of our argument and hence distract readers from what we are saying. Other readers assert that consistent use of male pronouns would be less distracting. Calls for consistency in gender reference suggest that readers imagine a rhetorical actor or actors with whom they identify while reading. When that actor's gender is altered, the reader must stop to adjust her picture of the imagined actor (as may happen while you are reading this very sentence). Calls for sole reliance on the male gender, however, seem to us to stem from a commonplace: that rhetorical actors are, or ought to be, male. That is to say, the first objection to our practice is rhetorical; the second is ideological. We adopted the practice of switching the gender of pronouns referring to rhetorical actors to call our readers' attention to both the workings of rhetorical actors and the power of the commonplace. Some of our critics have said our second aim goes beyond our responsibilities as rhetoric teachers. What do you think?

Students often use third person when they write for teachers on the correct assumptions that the formal distance lends authority to their work and that it is appropriate for the rhetorical situation that obtains in most classrooms. A curious thing sometimes happens within third-person prose, however: people write phrases like "the writer of this paper feels" or "in the opinion of this author." If these constructions emerge during the writing process, it may be that the issue demands that the rhetor express some opinions and take responsibility for them. In this case, first-person may be a better choice.

As we noted earlier, third-person statements tend to have an authoritative flavor. When rhetors find themselves trying to add **qualifiers** about their opinions or attitudes, it may be the case that the third-person voice is inappropriate or even dishonest. Of course, dishonesty is disastrous if a reader detects it.

Verb Tense and Voice

The choice of grammatical person is the most influential element in establishing voice and distance. However, other stylistic choices, such as verb tense and voice, affect an ethos as well. Present tense has more immediacy than past tense; use of the present tense gives an audience a sense of participation in events that are occurring at the moment, whereas past tense makes them feel like onlookers in events that have already occurred. Compare your response to the following phrasings:

Present Tense: Quintilian teaches his students to . . .

Past Tense: Quintilian taught his students to . . .

The second example distances readers from Quintilian because it explicitly places his teaching in the past.

In English, verbs may assume one of two "voices"—active and passive. Passive verb constructions betray themselves through an explicit or implicit "by _____" phrase, as in "The door was left open (by _____)." Phasing such a construction in **active voice** requires the rhetor to supply somebody (or some thing) who can act as an agent on the door: John, the dog, the wind, as in "John left the door open." Active verb constructions tend to lessen distance because the rhetor using them is forced to name either herself or somebody or something else as an actor in the sentence; usually this rhetorical subject (the actor) is also the grammatical subject of a sentence with an active verb construction. Passive constructions, on the other hand, tend to create distance between rhetor and issue because the grammatical subject of the sentence is usually not its rhetorical subject.

> ACTIVE VOICE: Mary did the dishes.
>
> PASSIVE VOICE: The dishes were done (by Mary).
>
> ACTIVE VOICE: I take responsibility for these actions.
>
> PASSIVE VOICE: Responsibility must be taken for these actions (by me).

Active constructions force rhetors to betray their presence as creator of the discourse; **active voice** also forces them to take overt responsibility for their assertions. Passive constructions permit rhetors to avoid taking responsibility for their statements. "The police were misled" is a passive construction that avoids mentioning the person who did the misleading.

Sometimes this strategy is useful, depending on the rhetorical situation. If a rhetor does not know what she needs to know, she may want to disguise her ignorance by using passive constructions. Rhetors who do so, however, run the risk of damaging their audience's estimate of their intelligence, honesty, and goodwill. Take this passive sentence, for example: "Sometimes ridiculed for directing their presentation to the nonintellectual, television news coverage is obligated to give a concise, easily understandable, factual news report." In this case, the use of third person creates distance between author and audience because the passive construction allows the rhetor to disappear. She is nowhere in sight. Because nobody is around to take responsibility, readers might wonder just how authoritative this statement is. A reader might wonder: "Well, who obligates television news coverage to be concise, factual, and so on? Who says so? In my experience, Anderson Cooper and Katie Couric and the rest don't always stick to the facts. . . ." If this happens, the rhetor might as well have never written at all, because important aspects of her ethos—that she seem well informed and honest, and that she have her audience's interest in mind—have been compromised. Active voice might have been a better choice, although it requires her to name some names and take some responsibility for her assertions: "Critics sometimes ridicule television news coverage for directing their presentation to the nonintellectual. Newswriters couch the news in simple terms, however, because their duty as journalists obligates them to give a concise, easily understandable, factual news report."

Word Size

Other stylistic resources help to establish voice, as well. Word size seems to affect voice and distance. American audiences tend to assume that polysyllabic words (big words with lots of syllables, like *polysyllabic*) indicate that their user is well educated. Hence they are likely to award authority to a rhetor who uses them. Compare the effect of "It will be my endeavor in this analysis" to that of "Here I will try to analyze. . . ."

When used carefully, polysyllabic words are generally more precise than smaller words: *polysyllabic* is more specific than *large* or *big; deconstructing* is both more impressive and precise than *taking apart; chlorofluorocarbons* is more precise, but less intimate, than *the stuff that causes holes in the ozone layer.* Because of their greater accuracy, larger words tend to appear in formal discourse, whereas rhetors are more concerned with accuracy than with establishing an intimate relation with readers. However, big words can have the disadvantage of making their user sound pompous; too many polysyllabic words can also discourage people from making the effort to plow through them, especially if their meanings are obscure to the intended audience. Here is a brief passage written by philosopher Jacques Derrida:

> On what conditions is a grammatology possible? Its fundamental condition is certainly the undoing of logocentrism. But this condition of possibility turns into a condition of impossibility. In fact it risks upsetting the concept of science as well. Graphematics or grammatography ought no longer to be presented as sciences; their goal should be exorbitant when compared to a grammatological knowledge. (74)

Although Derrida writes simple sentences, he nonetheless litters his pages with polysyllabic terms whose meanings are unfamiliar to many readers because he coined many of them himself. One has to be very committed to read Derrida's work because it takes a long time to learn the meanings of the terms he employs.

Familiar words are effective in informal discursive situations where the audience is on fairly close terms with the rhetor; everyone shares common understanding that lessens the rhetor's obligation to be precise. "Cool!" is an example wherein precision of meaning is absolutely sacrificed to the establishment of intimacy. As you can see, this phrase, which is ordinarily used in conversation, loses much of its effect in print. And while the meaning of *cool* has been readily understood by the readers, we might do better now to substitute another phrase for it such as "*awesome,*" which does (did) similar kinds of work. Laudatory expressions such as these go in and out of fashion very quickly because their utterance is the very mark of cool.

Qualifiers

Qualifiers like *some, most, virtually,* and *all* affect voice and distance. A qualifier is any term (usually an adverb or an adjective) or phrase that alters the degree of force or extent contained in a statement. Compare the relative distance achieved by the use of qualifiers in the following statements:

> All humans are created equal.
>
> It may be that most humans are created equal.
>
> I believe that very few humans are created equal.
>
> Virtually no humans are created equal.

The first statement is quite distant, because it makes a sweeping, authoritative judgment. No authors are present to identify with readers. The other statements are more intimate because they betray the presence of an author, modifying the extent or intensity of her judgment in each case. As a general rule, the more qualifiers, and the more intensity they convey, the more intimate the distance between rhetor and audience. Qualifiers have this effect because they indicate, however subtly, that someone is present, making judgments about degrees of intensity. Compare this unqualified statement to the heavily qualified one that follows it:

UNQUALIFIED: Three months after announcing it had settled a lawsuit filed against it by Bread and Butter Corporation, the City Council of Ourtown made the agreement public today.

HEAVILY QUALIFIED: Three long months after announcing it had tentatively settled one of the most expensive civil lawsuits in the city's history, today the City Council of Ourtown, with some trepidation, made public a proposed agreement between it and the gigantic Bread and Butter Corporation.

The first version creates more distance between author and readers because the writer expresses few judgements about the event under discussion. The author of the second version, on the other hand, is willing to qualify events by using adjectives and adverbs that express degree ("tentatively," "expensive," "gigantic.")

Composition textbooks sometimes caution writers against the use of qualifiers, calling them "weasel words." However, cautious rhetors often find it necessary to use a few qualifiers to represent a position as accurately as possible. (The underlined words in the preceding sentence are qualifiers.) Moreover, qualifiers can be effective in reducing distance between a rhetor and an audience in situations where an intimate distance is more persuasive than a more formal one. As a result, qualifiers can also make your work more interesting, and this effect is enhanced if the qualifiers add interesting detail to an account.

Punctuation

Punctuation is an extremely subtle means of establishing voice and distance in written discourse. The more exotic marks of punctuation work to close distance between writers and readers; they do the work that gestures, facial expressions, tone, and pitch do for speakers. Dashes convey breathlessness or hurry—or a midthought—or an afterthought. Parentheses (like these) decrease distance, because they have the flavor of an interruption, a remark whispered behind the hand. Exclamation points indicate strong emotions at work! Textbooks say that quotation marks are only to be used to represent material that has been quoted from another source, but increasingly quotation marks are being used for emphasis. This example shows them doing both jobs: "We don't "cash" checks." Underlining or **bold** or CAPITAL LETTERS convey emphasis or importance, and all these graphic signals close the distance between rhetor and audience. In electronic discourse, text written in caps is taken as evidence that the user is SHOUTING, and the tactic is considered impolite unless used sparingly and for effect.

If you doubt that such small things do influence distance, note whether you are offended or not the next time you see them in a message e-mailed to you by someone you do not know. Contemporary decorum seems to dictate, in short, that fancy or innovative punctuation should be used in intimate situations, whereas discourse composed for more formal rhetorical situations should feature only the standard punctuation used to mark sentences and indicate possession.

Rhetorical Exercises

1. Go on a trope hunt. Between now and your next class meeting, locate a host of different kinds of tropes. You may wish to consult broadly: popular magazines, newspapers, Web sites, billboards, and advertisements are all fair game. Once you record the trope, use the information in this chapter to name it. Be on the lookout for particularly rare or artful tropes. Be prepared to tell the class why you've categorized the trope as you have.

2. Try your hand at composing figures and tropes. Find a passage of your writing and examine it to see whether you unconsciously used any of the figures or tropes discussed in this chapter. Rewrite any of the sentences in the passage, inserting figures or tropes where they are appropriate. Approach this task systematically over a few days or weeks; your eventual goal is to use each kind of figure or trope discussed in this chapter.

3. Revise a passage you've written in the plain style so that it is appropriate for a more formal rhetorical situation. Use complex sentence constructions, longer words, and lots of figures and tropes. For models of highly ornate prose styles you can turn to the work of composers from earlier periods of history. John Donne's sermons are good examples, as are those composed by American preachers such as Jonathan Edwards or Martin Luther King.

4. Analyze a few pieces of writing in terms of the rhetorical distance created by their authors' voices. Do the authors assume they know readers well, or do they establish a formal distance? How do they achieve this distance? Look at their uses of grammatical person, verb voice and tense, word size, **qualifiers**, and punctuation.

5. We also recommend that rhetors as a practice be on the lookout for professional speakers and writers' uses of the various figures discussed in this chapter. When you find figures or tropes that you admire, write them down in a commonplace book. Practice imitating them. A modern handbook of the figures is a very useful aid to composers. We highly recommend Richard Lanham's *A Handlist of Rhetorical Figures.*

Endnotes

1. Like ancient rhetoricians, we think that correctness and clarity are not truly rhetorical considerations, and so we don't pay much attention to them. We also think that Americans' obsession with correctness and clarity has kept them from studying and enjoying the more complex uses of language that are addressed here.

   There are plenty of good books available that discuss correctness and clarity. We recommend the *Exercise Book for Understanding English Grammar* by Martha Kolln and Robert Funk. Any good handbook for writers will also demonstrate the **correctness rules** of traditional grammar. We recommend *The St. Martin's Handbook* by Andrea Lunsford (6th edition, 2007). Dictionaries of usage are also available; Fowler's *Modern English Usage* is the standard reference work. Writers who are interested in achieving a clearer style can consult Joseph Williams and Gregory Colomb's *Style: Lessons in Clarity and Grace* and/or Martha Kolln and Loretta Gray's *Rhetorical Grammar.* Williams/Colomb and Kolln/Gray also attend to a few beauties of style.

2. Writers who are interested in practicing this kind of stylistic appropriateness can consult the ancient treatises written by Hermogenes of Tarsus, usually called *The Ideas of Style* or *The Types of Style,* as well as that by Demetrius of Phaleron, called *On Style.* These treatises give copious advice about how to achieve such effects as solemnity, vehemence, simplicity, force, and the like.

3. We are indebted in this section to Walker Gibson's *Persona: A Style Study for Readers and Writers* and *Tough, Sweet, and Stuffy: An Essay on Modern American Prose Styles.*

Works Cited

Abbey, Edward. *Desert Solitaire.* Tucson: Arizona UP, 1968. Print.

"Apple: I-Pad is Delicious." <http://www.youtube.com/watch?v=Lpo__xhTSv8&NR=1>. Online.

Boswell, Thomas. "Opportunity, and Paradise, Lost at Open." *The Washington Post* June 10, 2006. <http://www.washingtonpost.com/wp-dyn/content/article/2006/06/18/AR2006061801028.html>.

Chua, Amy. "Why Chinese Mothers Are Superior." *The Wall Street Journal,* U.S. Edition. 01/08/11. <http://online.wsj.com/article/SB10001424052748704111504576059713528698754. html?mod=WSJ_hp_mostpop_read>. Online.

David, Laurie, and Carleton Kendrick. "Please Pass the Civility." *Huffington Post,* 01/17/11. <http://www.huffingtonpost.com/laurie-david/please-pass-the-civility_b_809815.html>. Online.

Derrida, Jacques. *Of Grammatology.* Trans. Gayatri Spivak. Baltimore: John Hopkins UP, 1976. Print.

Dostoyevsky, Fyodor. *Notes from Underground.* New York: E. P. Dutton, 1960. Print.

Douglas, Mary. *How Institutions Think.* Syracuse, New York: Syracuse UP, 1986. Print.

Eddlam, Thomas. "Avatar: A Visually Stunning and Historically Perfect Allegory." *The New American.* 12/21/09. <http://www.thenewamerican.com/index.php/reviews/movies/2599-avalon-a-visually-stunning-and-perfect-historical-allegory>. Online.

Gettleman, Jeffrey. "Southern Liberals Had Lott Moments, Too." *New York Times* 22 December 2002, national edition, sec. 4. Print.

Gettleman, Jeffrey. "The New Somalia: A Grimly Familiar Rerun." *New York Times* 21 February 2007, national edition, sec. A. Print.

Gibson, Walker. *Persona: A Style Study for Readers and Writers.* New York: Random House, 1969. Print.

———. *Tough, Sweet, and Stuffy: An Essay on Modern American Prose Styles.* Bloomington: Indiana UP, 1966. Print.

Giovanni, Nikki. "We Are Virginia Tech." *Americanrhetoric.com.* <http://www.americanrhetoric.com/speeches/nikkigiovannivatechmemorial.htm>. Online.

Graves, Robert. *I, Claudius.* New York: Vintage, 1961. Print.

Krugman, Paul. "Climate of Hate." *The New York Times,* 01/09/11. <http://www.nytimes.com/2011/01/10/opinion/10krugman.html?sq=krugman%20on%20tucson%20shooting&st=Search&adxnnl=1&scp=1&adxnnlx=1295975456-aL5/X80gryBHyS58RARGqA&pagewanted=print>. Online.

Kunkel, Benjamin. *Indecision: A Novel.* New York: Random House, 2006. Print.

Lacey, Mark, and David. M. Herszenhorn. "In Attack's Wake, Political Repercussions." *New York Times* 01/08/11. <http://www.nytimes.com/2011/01/09/us/politics/09giffords.html?_r=1&ref=arizonashooting2011>. Online.

Landrieu, Mitch. "Address at the Katrina 5 Commemoration & Determination Ceremony." Mahalia Jackson Theater, New Orleans, Louisiana 8/29/10. <http://www.americanrhetoric.com/speeches/mitchlandrieukatrina5.htm>.

Mehr, Bob. "In the Beginning Was the Word." *Mojo* June 2007, 90–95. Print.

Rader, Dan. "Palin, Crosshairs, and Semiotics: Signs of the Times." *San Francisco Chronicle* 1/14/11. <http://www.sfgate.com/cgi-bin/blogs/drader/detail?entry_id=80950#ixzz1Bzt42Gsl>.

"The Rise and Fall of Four Loko." *The Week* November 24, 2010. <http://theweek.com/article/index/209434/the-rise-and-fall-of-four-loko#>. Online.

Sharpton, Al. "In MLK's honor, let's strive for dialogue that's passionate but not poisonous." *The Washington Post.* 1/11/11. <http://www.washingtonpost.com/wp-n/content/article/2011/01/11/AR2011011104334.html>. Online.

Wolcott, James. "Feets of Fury." *Vanity Fair Online,* 1/20/11. <http://www.vanityfair.com/online/wolcott/2011/01/dennis-perrin-and-ioz-are.html>. Online.

Wolfe, Tom. *The Kandy-Kolored Tangerine-Flake Streamline Baby.* New York: Bantam, 1999. Print.

SECTION FOUR
Readings on Revision and Reflection

Shitty First Drafts

22

Anne Lamott

Born in San Francisco in 1954, Anne Lamott is a graduate of Goucher College in Baltimore and is the author of six novels, including Rosie *(1983),* Crooked Little Heart *(1997),* All New People *(2000), and* Blue Shoes *(2002). She has also been the food reviewer for California magazine, a book reviewer for* Mademoiselle, *and a regular contributor to* Salon's *"Mothers Who Think." Her nonfiction books include* Operating Instructions: A Journal of My Son's First Year *(1993), in which she describes her adventures as a single parent, and* Tender Mercies: Some Thoughts on Faith *(1999), in which she charts her journey toward faith in God.*

In the following selection, taken from Lamott's popular book about writing, Bird by Bird *(1994), she argues for the need to let go and write those "shitty first drafts" that lead to clarity and sometimes brilliance in our second and third drafts.*

—Joseph Harris

Now, practically even better news than that of short assignments is the idea of shitty first drafts. All good writers write them. This is how they end up with good second drafts and terrific third drafts. People tend to look at successful writers who are getting their books published and maybe even doing well financially and think that they sit down at their desks every morning feeling like a million dollars, feeling great about who they are and how much talent they have and what a great story they have to tell; that they take in a few deep breaths, push back their sleeves, roll their necks a few times to get all the cricks out, and dive in, typing fully formed passages as fast as a court reporter. But this is just the fantasy of the uninitiated. I know some very great writers, writers you love who write beautifully and have made a great deal of money, and not one of them sits down routinely feeling wildly enthusiastic and confident. Not one of them writes elegant first drafts. All right, one of them does, but we do not like her very much. We do not think that she has a rich inner life or that God likes her or can even stand her. (Although when I mentioned this to my priest friend Tom, he said you can safely assume you've created God in your own image when it turns out that God hates all the same people you do.)

Very few writers really know what they are doing until they've done it. Nor do they go about their business feeling dewy and thrilled. They do not type a few stiff warm-up sentences and then find themselves bounding along like huskies across the snow. One writer I know tells me that he sits down every morning and says to himself nicely, "It's not like you don't have a choice, because you do—you can either type, or kill yourself." We all often feel like we are pulling teeth, even those writers whose prose ends up being the most natural and fluid. The right words and sentences just do not come pouring out like ticker tape most of the time. Now, Muriel Spark is said to have felt that she was taking dictation from God every morning—sitting there, one supposes, plugged into a Dictaphone, typing away, humming. But this is a very hostile and aggressive position. One might hope for bad things to rain down on a person like this.

For me and most of the other writers I know, writing is not rapturous. In fact, the only way I can get anything written at all is to write really, really shitty first drafts.

The first draft is the child's draft, where you let it all pour out and then let it romp all over the place, knowing that no one is going to see it and that you can shape it later. You just let this childlike part of you channel whatever voices and visions come through and onto the page. If one of the characters wants to say, "Well, so what, Mr. Poopy Pants?," you let her. No one is going to see it. If the kid wants to get into really sentimental, weepy, emotional territory, you let him. Just get it all down on paper because there may be something great in those six crazy pages that you would never have gotten to by more rational, grown-up means. There may be something in the very last line of the very last paragraph on page six that you just love, that is so beautiful or wild that you now know what you're supposed to be writing about, more or less, or in what direction you might go—but there was no way to get to this without first getting through the first five and a half pages.

I used to write food reviews for *California* magazine before it folded. (My writing food reviews had nothing to do with the magazine folding, although every single review did cause a couple of canceled subscriptions. Some readers took umbrage at my comparing mounds of vegetable puree with various ex-presidents' brains.) These reviews always took two days to write. First I'd go to a restaurant several times with a few opinionated, articulate friends in tow. I'd sit there writing down everything anyone said that was at all interesting or funny. Then on the following Monday I'd sit down at my desk with my notes and try to write the review. Even after I'd been doing this for years, panic would set in. I'd try to write a lead, but instead I'd write a couple of dreadful sentences, XX them out, try again, XX everything out, and then feel despair and worry settle on my chest like an x-ray apron. It's over, I'd think calmly. I'm not going to be able to get the magic to work this time. I'm ruined. I'm through. I'm toast. Maybe, I'd think, I can get my old job back as a clerk-typist. But probably not. I'd get up and study my teeth in the mirror for a while. Then I'd stop, remember to breathe, make a few phone calls, hit the kitchen and chow down. Eventually I'd go back and sit down at my desk, and sigh for the next ten minutes. Finally I would pick up my one-inch picture frame, stare into it as if for the answer, and every time the answer would come: all I had to do was to write a really shitty first draft of, say, the opening paragraph. And no one was going to see it.

So I'd start writing without reining myself in. It was almost just typing, just making my fingers move. And the writing would be terrible. I'd write a lead paragraph that was a whole page, even though the entire review could only be three pages long, and then I'd start writing up descriptions of the food, one dish at a time, bird by bird, and the critics would be sitting on my shoulders, commenting like cartoon characters. They'd be pretending to snore, or rolling their eyes at my overwrought descriptions, no matter how hard I tried to tone those descriptions down, no matter how conscious I was of what a friend said to me gently in my early days of restaurant reviewing. "Annie," she said, "it is just a piece of *chicken*. It is just a bit of *cake*."

But because by then I had been writing for so long, I would eventually let myself trust the process—sort of, more or less. I'd write a first draft that was maybe twice as long as it should be, with a self-indulgent and boring beginning, stupefying descriptions of the meal, lots of quotes from my black-humored friends that made them sound more like the Manson girls than food lovers, and no ending to speak of. The whole thing would be so long and incoherent and hideous that for the rest of the day I'd obsess about getting creamed by a car before I could write a decent second draft. I'd worry that people would read what I'd written and believe that the accident had really been a suicide, that I had panicked because my talent was waning and my mind was shot.

The next day, I'd sit down, go through it all with a colored pen, take out everything I possibly could, find a new lead somewhere on the second page, figure out a kicky place to end it, and then write a second draft. It always turned out fine, sometimes even funny and weird and helpful. I'd go over it one more time and mail it in.

Then, a month later, when it was time for another review, the whole process would start again, complete with the fears that people would find my first draft before I could rewrite it.

Almost all good writing begins with terrible first efforts. You need to start somewhere. Start by getting something—anything—down on paper. A friend of mine says that the first draft is the down draft—you just get it down. The second draft is the up draft—you fix it up. You try to say what you have to say more accurately. And the third draft is the dental draft, where you check every tooth, to see if it's loose or cramped or decayed, or even, God help us, healthy.

■ ■ ■ FOR CLASS DISCUSSION

1. Lamott says that the perceptions most people have of how writers work is different from the reality of the work itself. She refers to this in the first paragraph as "the fantasy of the uninitiated." What does she mean?
2. In the paragraph beginning "But because by then I had been writing for so long . . . ," Lamott refers to a time when, through experience, she "eventually let [herself] trust the process—sort of, more or less." She is referring to the writing process, of course, but why "more or less"? Do you think that her wariness is personal, or is she speaking for all writers in this regard? Explain.
3. From what Lamott has to say, is writing a first draft more about the product or the process? Do you agree in regard to your own first drafts? Explain.

■ ■ ■

23 Revising

Joseph Harris

FIRST DRAFT OF PAPER INADVERTENTLY BECOMES FINAL DRAFT, *EUGENE, OR—The first draft of an English 140 paper by University of Oregon sophomore Marty Blain ultimately became the final draft, Blain re-ported Monday. "I was gonna keep working on it and add a bunch of stuff about how the guy who wrote [The Great Gatsby] was affected by a lot of the stuff going on around him," she said. "But then I was like, fuck it." Blair said that she spent the time that would have been devoted to revision watching* Friends *in her dorm's TV lounge.*

—*The Onion*, September 27, 2000

I'm dying for some action
I'm sick of sitting 'round here trying to
write this book.

—Bruce Springsteen, "Dancing in the Dark"

So far in this book I've offered you four moves for rewriting—for making the words, ideas, and images of others part of your own project as a writer. In this last chapter, I propose some ways of using those moves in *revising*—that is, in rethinking, refining, and developing—your own work-in-progress as writer. *Revising* is thus a particular form of what throughout this book I've called *rewriting*; it names the work of returning to a draft of a text you've written in order to make your thinking in it more nuanced, precise, suggestive, and interesting.

My method here will be to work in the mode of the previous four chapters—to ask what it might mean to come to terms with, forward, counter, or take the approach of your own text-in-progress. My hope is that doing so will allow me offer a view of revising that, on the one hand, doesn't reduce it to a mere fiddling with sentences, to editing for style and correctness, but that also, on the other hand, avoids lapsing into mystical exhortations for risk taking or critical self-awareness or some other vague but evidently desirable quality of mind.

My aim is instead to describe revising as a knowable practice, as a consistent set of questions you can ask of a draft of an essay that you are working on:

- *What's your project?* What do you want to accomplish in this essay? (Coming to Terms)
- *What works?* How can you build on the strengths of your draft? (Forwarding)
- *What else might be said?* How might you acknowledge other views and possibilities? (Countering)
- *What's next?* What are the implications of what you have to say? (Taking an Approach)

While these questions are straightforward, they are not easy. Revising is the sort of thing that is fairly simple to describe but very hard to do well—like playing chess, or serving in tennis, or teaching a class. It is also an activity that tends to be hidden from view. As readers we usually come upon texts in their final form—with many of the hesitations, repetitions, digressions, false starts, alternative phrasings, inconsistencies, speculations, infelicities, and flat-out mistakes of earlier drafts smoothed over, corrected, or erased. Another way to put this is to say that finished texts tend to conceal much of the labor involved in writing them. Since we rarely get to see the early drafts of most published texts, it can often seem as though other writers work, as it were, without ever blotting a line, confidently progressing through their texts from start to finish, paragraph to paragraph, chapter to chapter, as if they were speaking them aloud. This one-draft view of writing is reinforced by most movie and TV depictions of writers at work, as we watch them quickly type perfectly balanced and sequenced sentences until, with a sigh of satisfaction, they pound out THE END or press SEND. It is also a view inculcated by the pace and structure of American schooling, whose frequent exams reward students who can produce quick clean essays on demand. A result is that much of what little instruction that does get offered in writing tends to focus on questions of correctness. Handbooks are filled with advice on proofreading and teachers downgrade for mistakes in grammar and spelling.

But while the moments of both inspiration and correction, of creating a text and fixing its errors, are well marked in our culture, the work of revision, of rethinking and reshaping a text, is rarely noted. With the exception of a few literati who, in anticipation of future biographies and critical editions, seem to save all their papers, early, drafts tend to get cleared off the desk or deleted from the hard drive once a project is finished, or even as it is being written. In fact, one of the few places where you can readily trace how a project evolves from one draft to the next—and thus make the labor of writing it more visible—is in a university writing course. Several of the examples in this chapter are thus drawn, with their permission, from the writings of students in courses I have taught. Each is an example of a student working with—commenting on, analyzing, rethinking—a draft of his or her own writing. For that is perhaps the key challenge of revising, to find a way to step outside of your own thinking and to look at the text you are working on as another reader might. But before looking at strategies for revising in detail, let me briefly distinguish it from two other important forms of work on an academic essay.

Drafting, Revising, Editing

For most academic writers, work on a piece begins long before they sit down at a keyboard or desk and continues well past their first attempts at putting their thoughts into prose. They tend, that is, to imagine a text they are writing less as a performance (which is what an exam calls for) and more as a work-in-progress, as an ongoing project that they can add to and reshape over time. And while the working habits of individual writers are too varied to be generalized into a single process of composing, you can think of the labor of writing as involving:

- Drafting, or generating text.
- Revising, or working with the text you've created, rethinking and reshaping what you want to say.
- Editing, or working on your text as an artifact, preparing the final version of your document.

The three form art intuitive sequence: First, you move from ideas to words on the screen or page; next you reconsider and rework what you've written, often with the help of responses from readers; and, finally, you edit, design, and format your final document. In practice, though, these forms of work tend to be overlapping and recursive: Most writers do some amount of revising and editing as they draft (although it is usually wise not to invest too much time in polishing a passage before you know for sure if you will even include it in the final version of your text); serious revision almost always involves the drafting of some new prose; and the careful editing of a piece can often lead back into a more extensive revising of it.

By far the most elusive of these three forms of work is drafting—or what is sometimes called *invention*. Trying to figure out something to write about has been the frustration of writing students—and their teachers—for decades. Stephen King puts the problem with his usual plainspoken acuity in his novel *Misery*—in which the writer of a popular series of paperback romances is held hostage by a demented fan and forced to write a new book to her liking. (In other words, the novel is about a writing class.) Here are the thoughts of King's captive author as he desperately tries to get started on his new book:

> Another part of him was furiously trying out ideas, rejecting them, trying to combine them, rejecting the combinations. He sensed this going on but had no direct contact with it and wanted none. It was dirty down there in the sweatshops.
>
> He understood what he was doing now as TRYING TO HAVE AN IDEA. TRYING TO HAVE AN IDEA wasn't the same thing as GETTING AN IDEA. GETTING AN IDEA was a more humble way of saying *I am inspired, or Eureka! My muse has spoken!* . . .
>
> This other process—TRYING TO HAVE AN IDEA—was nowhere near as exalted or exalting, but it was every bit as mysterious and every bit as necessary. Because when you were writing a novel you almost always got roadblocked somewhere, and there was no sense in trying to go until you HAD AN IDEA.

> **INTERTEXTS**
>
> Steven King, *Misery* (New York: Signet, 1988), 119–20.

> His usual procedure when it was necessary to HAVE AN IDEA was to put on his coat and go for a walk. He recognized walking as good exercise, but it was boring. If you didn't

have someone to talk to while you walked, a book was a necessity. But if you needed to HAVE AN IDEA, boredom could be to a roadblocked novel what chemotherapy was to a cancer patient.

I can't claim to have all that much to say about how to begin writing an essay. For me, like King, the deep origins of words and ideas seem more often than not mysterious and untraceable. But King does also offer us a number of useful ways of thinking about this mystery. First, he points to the importance of seizing hold of those ideas that do somehow come to you. The volume next to the one you were looking for on the library shelf, the comment from another class that continues to echo in your head, the connection you notice between the papers and books that happen to be sitting on your desk, the song or movie that a text reminds you of-work on an essay often begins with such serendipities. Second, King notes the value of patience, of knowing when you're stalled, when you simply need to take a break. Similarly, he speaks of the usefulness of boredom, of letting ideas percolate. Finally, he suggests that a writer often needs to start not from a moment of inspiration (*eureka!*) but from the need to work through a conceptual problem or roadblock. Indeed, I'd suggest that most academic writing begins with such questions rather than insights, with difficulties in understanding rather than moments of mastery.

What I hope I can tell you more about is how to revise a text you've begun to write, to work with the words you've started to put on the page, or screen. Perhaps the most common mistake that student writers make is to slight the work of revising—either by trying to conceive and draft an entire text from start to end in a single sitting, without pausing to consider alternate (and perhaps more interesting) ways of developing their ideas, or by worrying so much about issues of editing and correctness that they hardly allow themselves to think about anything else at all. (It is only too possible, as any writing teacher can tell you, to create a text that is wonderfully designed, phrased, formatted, edited, and proofread—but that says almost nothing.) Many students enter college without really ever having been asked to rethink their views on an issue or to: restructure the approach they've taken in an essay. They've been trained in how to find and fix mistakes, and perhaps even in how to respond to specific questions about a draft posed by their teacher. But their final drafts are essentially the same as their first ones—only cleaner, smoother, more polished. They have been taught how to edit but not how to revise.

In revising, the changes you make to a text are connected. They form a plan of work. For instance, if in reworking the introduction to an essay, you realize that you also need to change the order of the paragraphs that follow it, then you are revising. Or if dealing with a new example also requires you to adjust some of your key words or concepts, you are revising. Or if in rethinking the implications of your argument at the end of an essay, you also begin to see a stronger way of beginning it, you are revising. And so on. In revising, one change leads to others. You edit sentences; you revise essays.

The changes you make in editing tend to be ad hoc and local. To edit is to fine-tune a document. Proofreading is the extreme case: You simply correct a typo or a mistake in punctuation and move on. Nothing else needs to be done; no other changes need to be made. Similarly, you can often edit for style, recast the wording of a particular sentence to make it more graceful or clear, without having to alter much (or anything) else in the paragraph of which it is part. You can even sometimes insert a sentence or two in a paragraph—to add an example, clarify a point, answer a question—while making few or no other changes to it. Indeed I've seen entire blocks of text dropped into an essay without sending any ripples at all into the paragraphs before or after it, but rather leaving the original flow of ideas serenely undisturbed. The aim of revising is to rethink the ideas and examples that drive your thinking in an essay; the aim of editing is to improve the flow and design of your document. Both forms of work are important. But simply editing a text that needs to be rethought and revised is like waxing a car that needs repairs to its engine.

Tracking Revision

You can begin to see how the work of revising differs from that of editing by mapping the changes you make in moving from one draft of an essay to the next. Most word processing programs have a "track changes" or "compare documents" tool that you can use to record the changes you make in keyboarding a new version of an essay. Using this tool allows you to mark where you

- Add to
- Delete
- Move (cut and paste)
- Rework (select and type over)
- Reformat a text you are working on.

You can of course also note and mark such changes by hand; the software simply cuts down on some of the drudgery involved.

Revising an essay is complex and difficult intellectual work. But it is work not only with ideas but text. You can't just think changes to an essay; you need to *make* them. (This is a lesson I've learned to my chagrin only too many times—as paragraphs that seemed to flow clearly in my mind when I was in the shower or out for a walk with the dogs somehow become muddled and intractable when I sit down to type, them out.) At some point, that is, you have to translate plans and ideas into the material labor of adding, cutting, moving, reworking, or reformatting text. While revising clearly involves more than keyboarding, all of the work you do in rethinking a text will find its final expression in' some combination of those five functions. Tracking the changes you make in keyboarding a new draft of an essay can thus help make the conceptual work you've done in revising more visible.

Let me offer an example. Here is the opening paragraph of the first draft of an essay written by Abhijit Mehta, a student in a writing course, in response to an assignment that asked him to describe some' of the distinctive ways a particular group makes use of language—to reflect on how they give their own spin, as it were, to the meanings of certain words. Abhijit decided to write on the vocabulary of his own field of study, mathematics:

The Strange Language of Math

As our society becomes more dependant on technology, the work of mathematicians and physicists
comes closer to everyday experience. In order to
have a basic understanding of many modern issues

INTERTEXTS

Abhijit Mehta, "the Playful Language
of Math" (1st and 2nd drafts), unpub-
lished essay, Duke University, 2002.

and technologies, people need to become more familiar with the language of, math and
science. However, mathematicians and physicists have a tendency to use common words in
a strange way. In math and physics, *nice, elegant, trivial, well-behaved, charm, flavor, strange,*
and *quark* all have meanings that can be very different from their everyday meanings. Mathematicians and physicists often use common words to express ideas that are very complex.

The rest of the essay follows the plan laid out in this paragraph, as Abhijit goes
on to discuss the particular meanings mathematicians give to each of the terms he
mentions—*nice, elegant, trivial,* and so on—in the order that he lists them. What the
readers of his first draft told Abhijit, though, was that while in creating this catalogue
of odd usages he had assembled the materials for an interesting essay, he hadn't yet
suggested what those specialized uses told us about the culture of math. Indeed, the
problem with the draft is hinted at in its title, which simply says that the language of
math is "strange" but doesn't specify *how*. His readers thus asked Abhijit for a more
precise sense of the attitudes and values that lay behind the usages he discussed. What
kind of "strangeness" connected the ways mathematicians used these words?

Hard questions, but it turned out that Abhijit had answers to them. Here is the
opening of his second and revised draft.

The Playful Language of Math

As our society becomes more dependent on technology, the work of mathematicians and
physicists comes closer to everyday experience. In order to have a basic understanding
of many modern issues and technologies, people need to become more familiar with the
language of math and science. However, mathematicians and physicists have a tendency to
use common words to describe complex things. In math and physics, *nice, elegant, trivial,
well-behaved, charm, flavor, strange,* and *quark* all have meanings that can be very different
from their everyday meanings. The migration of these words from common usage to their
specialized usage conveys some of the playful attitude that mathematicians and physicists
have towards abstract, complex problems.

And here is a version that maps the keyboarding changes between the two paragraphs.
Words ~~deleted~~ from the first draft are struck through; text <u>added</u> to the second draft
is underlined.

The ~~Strange~~ <u>Playful</u> Language of Math

As our society becomes more ~~dependant~~ <u>dependent</u> on technology, the work of mathematicians and physicists comes closer to everyday experience. In order to have a basic understanding of many modern issues and technologies, people need to become more familiar
with the language of math and science. However, mathematicians and physicists have a
~~tendancy~~ <u>tendency</u> to use common words ~~in a strange way~~ <u>to describe complex things</u>. In
math and physics, *nice, elegant, trivial, well-behaved, charm, flavor, strange,* and *quark* all have
meanings that can be very different from their everyday meanings. ~~Mathematicians and~~

~~physicists often use common words to express ideas that are very complex.~~ <u>The migration of these words from common usage to their specialized usage conveys some of the playful attitude that mathematicians and physicists have towards abstract, complex problems.</u>

This map of changes shows that Abhijit was working on at least three different levels in moving from his first to second draft: At the most mundane level, he did some proofreading and corrected the spellings of *dependent* and *tendency*. Such work is simple correction, necessary but uninteresting. On a second level, he also edited for clarity and concision, combining two sentences that say almost the same thing in his first draft (mathematicians have a "tendency to use common words in a strange way" and "often use common words to express ideas that are very complex") into a single briefer statement in the second ("a tendency to use common words to express complex things"). But while such editing helps the flow of this particular paragraph, its impact does not extend beyond it. While intelligent and helpful, it remains a local edit, unconnected to a larger pattern of revision throughout the essay.

The third level of work—what I would call *revision*—involves such a pattern and plan of change. By far the most ambitious change that Abhijit makes in his second draft is to move, in both his revised title and new last sentence, from a nebulous description of the language of math as "strange" to a more precise view of it as *playful*. These two changes signal an important shift in his project as a writer—from offering a simple catalogue of some of the strange ways that mathematicians use words to making an argument about the unexpected playfulness of the field, as evidenced by its vocabulary. In the rest of his revised essay, Abhijit goes on to identify two ways in which the playfulness of mathematicians comes into view—one in their unconventional use of common words like *nice* or *trivial* and the other in their choice of exotic and fanciful terms like *quark* to describe their concepts and discoveries. This allows him to conclude his piece by contesting the cultural stereotype of the math nerd or computer geek as a humorless drone. In short, for Abhijit the notion of play becomes a generative concept, an idea that leads to other ideas, that he uses to structure and develop the revised version of his essay.

When students in the courses I teach hand in a revised draft of an essay, I require them to include with it another copy of their text on which they track all the changes they have made in moving from one draft to the next and, more important, highlight those changes that are central to their plan of revision. I then ask them to refer to this map in writing a brief reflection on their aims and strategies in revising. (See the Projects box "Mapping Your Approach" below in this chapter for the guidelines I offer students for creating this map and reflection.) And so, for instance, a version of Abhijit's opening paragraph that boldfaced changes in **revising** (as contrasted with local proofreading or editing changes) might look something like this:

The ~~Strange~~ **Playful** Language of Math
As our society becomes more ~~dependant~~ <u>dependent</u> on technology, the work of mathematicians and physicists comes closer to everyday experience. In order to have a basic understanding of many modern issues and technologies, people need to become more familiar with the language of math and science. However, mathematicians and physicists have a

~~tendancy~~ <u>tendency</u> to use common words ~~in a strange way~~ <u>to describe complex things</u>. In math and physics, *nice, elegant, trivial, well-behaved, charm, flavor, strange,* and *quark* all have meanings that can be very different from their everyday meanings. ~~Mathematicians and physicists often use common words to express ideas that are very complex.~~ **<u>The migration of these words from common usage to their specialized usage conveys some of the playful attitude that mathematicians and physicists have towards abstract, complex problems.</u>**

Those points throughout the rest of his revised essay where Abhijit returned to and developed the idea of the playful attitude of math would then also be boldfaced.

My aim here is not to denigrate the work of proofreading or editing. There is almost always a moment near the end of work on an essay when the most serious task that remains for you to do is to recheck and format your document with as much thought and care as you can give. (There was yet one more draft of Abhijit's essay to come, for instance, in which he noted in his opening paragraph that he would discuss *two* forms of playfulness in math, as well as made other local refinements to his prose.) Nor am I especially invested in advocating one particular method of mapping revision. What I do hope to have shown here, however, is how the local task of editing sentences and paragraphs differs in tangible and practical ways from the more global work of rethinking an essay. If in tracking the changes you've made to the draft of an essay, you can't point to a series or pattern of changes linked by an idea, then you haven't revised, you've only edited. With this sense of revising as rethinking in mind, then, let me turn to the four questions I proposed earlier.

What's Your Project? Coming to Terms With a Draft

It may seem the most banal of advice to suggest that in composing an essay you should have a good sense of your overall aim in writing, of what you want to achieve in your work, but there are at least two reasons why this truism proves harder to act upon than it might at first appear. First, while academic writers tend to begin with problems that they want to investigate, with texts that intrigue or puzzle or somehow fascinate them, their essays, when completed, need not simply to pose questions but also to respond to them. You may begin work on a project simply with the goal of finding out more about a certain subject or thinking your way through a particular set of issues, but in writing about that subject you need to articulate a stance, to establish a position of your own. The orientation of your work, that is, needs to shift as you make your way through a project. (The writing researcher and teacher Linda Flower has called this moving from *writer-based* to *reader-based* prose.) Second, you will often find that your ideas evolve over the course of writing, particularly when you are at work on an ambitious or complex project. Digressions morph into key lines of argument; examples don't quite seem to work as planned; apercus become central ideas; afterthoughts prove more interesting than the ideas they followed; a reader's comment makes you think about your subject in unexpected ways; a small shift in

> **INTERTEXTS**
>
> Linda Flower, *Problem Solving Strategies for Writing in College and the Community,* 4th ed. (New York: Heinle, 1997).

phrasing leads into unforeseen avenues of thought. These are not problems to be avoided in working on an essay; they are moments to be anticipated and used.

Your project as a writer is thus something you are likely to need to rethink throughout the process of working on an essay. You may find it especially useful to revisit your purposes in writing, when you have completed close to a full draft of an essay. I have often found, in rereading my work at such moments, that I seem to be looking at a different piece than the one I thought I had set out to write. The question, then, is whether to rethink what I've written in order to adhere to my original plan or to revise the plan to better describe what I've ended up writing. The answer is usually some mix of both, as my sense of my project as a whole evolves alongside my attempts to write my way through particular problems and examples.

But to test your project against your draft in such a way you need a precise and detailed account of what your aims in writing actually are. You need, that is, to come to terms with your own work. And, as I suggested in the first chapter, this involves not simply restating something like your "main idea" but rather describing your project in writing—your goals, the materials you're working on, and the moves you make with those materials. I thus often require students in my courses, once they have completed a draft of an essay, to write a brief *abstract* of their work as it then stands. (A version of this assignment appears in the Projects box "Coming to Terms with Your Own Work-in-Progress" at the end of the first chapter.) In writing such an abstract your goal should not be to reintroduce your essay but to summarize its gist for someone who has not read it. You want, that is, to write a piece that describes your essay from the outside, that distills what you have to say into as clear and pointed a form as possible.

For example, if I were to abstract the second section of this chapter—"Drafting, Revising, Editing"—I might say something like this:

> In this section I define three forms of work that go into producing an essay: *drafting, revising,* and *editing.* I suggest that while our culture both romanticizes the labor of drafting and fetishizes the importance of editing for correctness, the work of revision, of rethinking writing, often goes unnoticed and undervalued. After a brief account of the mysteries of drafting (with the help of Stephen King), I argue for distinguishing the local changes of editing from the *global* work of revising.

As my use of italics suggests, one aim of an abstract is to bring forward the key terms and ideas of an essay. And as the main verbs of my sentences indicate ("I define;' "I suggest:' and "I argue"), another goal is to identify its line of thought, the moves its writer makes. (It is up to you as my reader, of course, to decide how well I have managed to catch the gist of the previous section and what aspects of it I may have glossed over or distorted.)

The point of writing an abstract of your own work is to push you to think about the essay you are writing on two levels: (1) your project as a whole; and (2) how you develop your line of thinking. In one sense, of course, it trivializes the complexities of an essay to reduce them to a single page or paragraph, but it's also a problem if you can't offer a lucid overview of your aims in writing. If it simply seems impossible to summarize an essay that you are in the process of drafting, this may be a sign that you haven't yet quite figured out what you want to say in it. On the other hand; you also want there to be a sense of surprise and nuance in how you write out your ideas, from sentence to sentence and paragraph to paragraph, that eludes complete summary—or otherwise there will be no reason for anyone to read through your piece as whole. Forcing yourself to write an abstract of an essay you've drafted can help you move between these levels, to see where your prose advances your project effectively and where it does not. Sometimes you may find that you need to rethink how you talk about your project in order to catch up with the actual work you've done in your draft. And you are also likely to find, on a practical level, that many of the sentences you compose for your abstract end up as part of your next draft, signaling key moves or points in your argument.

PROJECTS   Making a Revising Plan

One reason, I suspect, that many writers end up simply· editing rather than revising their work-in-progress is that they approach the task haphazardly, simply trying to fix mistakes or infelicities in their texts as they happen to come across them, without ever forming a larger sense of what they want to accomplish through making such changes. To counter this tendency to fine-tune rather than rewrite, I ask students in my courses, after they've gotten feedback on a piece they are writing, to form a plan for revising their work-in-progress. We then discuss these plans before they actually begin work on the next draft of their essays. In developing their revising plans, I ask students first to write an abstract of what they have drafted so far and then:

> Offer a brief but specific plan for revision. Try as much as you can at this point to describe the substance or content of the changes you want to make. See if you can answer the following questions as precisely as you can:
>
> - Which comments from your readers—either written on your draft or offered during a workshop—have you found most useful in rethinking your essay?
> - If you plan to add to what you've written so far, what will you say and where will it go?
> - If you now plan to revise your project in writing, how will you do so? If you want to work with any different ideas or examples, what will they be? ■

In coming to terms with a draft, it is also often useful to counterpose the sort of overview of an essay provided by an abstract with the more narrative working through of it offered by a *sentence outline*. To create such an outline, you simply need to go through an essay, summarizing each of its paragraphs or sections in a single sentence. The result should be a kind of quick-paced version of your essay, in which it becomes clear how each of your moves and examples follows upon the other (or, sometimes, where they fail to do so). The trick in writing such a sentence outline is much like that in composing an abstract—you want to write new prose (rather than simply highlighting phrases from your text) and you want to focus less on the topics of your paragraphs than on what you are trying to do in them, on the moves you are making as a writer.

And so, for instance, if I were to outline the previous section of this chapter, "Tracking Revision," I might produce something like this:

> I begin by suggesting that there are five basic types of changes that you can make in revising an essay: adding, deleting, moving, reworking, and reformatting. I then suggest that while revision can't be reduced to keyboarding, tracking keyboarding changes can make the conceptual work that goes into revising more visible. I then offer the first and second drafts of the opening paragraph of Abhijit's essay as an example of how to track changes and think about them. I start by reproducing his first draft and suggesting that there was a problem with the vagueness of "strange" as a descriptor for the language of math. Then I reproduce his second draft, first as plain text (so that readers don't get confused by all those strikeovers and underlines) and then with changes marked. Next I argue that this map of revision shows Abhijit working on three levels: proofreading, editing, and revision. I suggest that revision differs from editing in being *systematic* and *generative*, and reproduce yet one more version of Abhijit's second draft with revising changes boldfaced. Finally, I set up the next sections of the chapter by saying that I will now try to offer four strategies for rewriting (and not simply editing) your own work-in-progress.

I'll again leave it to you as my reader to decide how effective an outline of the preceding section this may be. But even though my example here is of an outline of a section in its final form, I hope you can begin to get a sense of how you could use this technique to identify moments in a text that you might want to rethink and rework. (They would be those points where you find yourself saying something like: "Well, what *am* I really trying to do here?" or "How does *this* sentence or idea follow from *that* one?") I've argued throughout this book that the strong use of the work of other writers needs to be grounded in a generous understanding of their projects. The same principle applies to your own work-in-progress. Before revising an essay, you need to articulate a clear sense of your aims in writing, so you can then assess what is working in your text and what is not.

What Works? Revising as Forwarding

An irony of revising is that writers often become so preoccupied with fixing what isn't going right in a text that they neglect to build on what is. The upshot of such attempts at remediation is often not a more interesting essay but simply one that is a little less weak in revising you want not only to deal with the problems of a draft but also to develop its strengths. And so, when students in my courses read and respond to one another's work, I ask them to mark both those passages that strike them as especially strong and those that they have questions or worries about. (The usual code is a straight line for <u>strengths</u> and a wavy< add wavy line under "wavy"> one for questions. You can, of course, use this system in rereading and marking your own drafts as well as in responding to the work of others.) This simple form of marking a text offers writers a map of their work that identifies those passages that their readers liked, posed questions about, or were simply indifferent toward-that no one made any particular note of. While the instinct of many writers is to let such unmarked passages stand-after all, no one has signaled them out as a problem—this third category of (non-) response more often than not points to passages that they may want to cut or abbreviate, since it is prose that has failed to draw the interest, one way or the other, of any of their readers.

You will probably want to spend most of your time reworking or developing those moments in a text that your readers have marked for either praise or question. Note that it's not always a bad sign for readers to have questions about a certain point or passage in an essay. This often means that there is something there worth thinking about, puzzling over, working through. Indeed, you can sometimes find a section of an essay both compelling and troubling at once—and I have many times seen readers mark some of the most interesting passages in an essay with both straight and wavy lines! The point is to identify those moments that have most drawn the attention of readers and to see how you can build on them, bring them forward in your next draft.

INTERTEXTS

I learned this simple and useful code of commenting on drafts, along with many other strategies of response, from Peter Elbow's remarkable and enduring guide to running a writer's workshop, *Writing without Teachers*, 2nd ed. (New York: Oxford University Press, 2000).

Another question to ask is *where* readers mark a draft as interesting or intriguing. Often enough, you may find that several of your readers seem engaged by a sentence that appears in the middle of a paragraph in a middle page of your essay—that is, in a spot where it might well have been missed.

In revising you may thus want to consider positioning that idea more prominently—perhaps at the start of the paragraph or even shifted to the opening of your essay. Or you may learn that your readers think that your most interesting work comes at the very end of your essay, on its last page or so. In such a case, you may want to see what happens if you begin your next draft with those closing ideas and see where doing so takes your thinking. This is in fact advice that I have given to many writers. The value of writing an early draft of an essay can sometimes lie in the chance it gives you to think your way through to the point, sometimes at the very end of your draft, where you've finally figured out what is you want to say. Often the best way to build on that work is not to try to salvage the fumblings of your first pages but to continue to forge ahead, to begin your next draft from the point where you ended your first.

What Else Might Be Said? Revising as Countering

Writers are often urged to anticipate the questions that readers might ask about their work, usually so that they can then preempt any possible objections to what they are trying to argue. While this advice makes some sense, it suffers from imagining the writing of an essay as the staking out of a position in a pro-con debate, and thus tends to lock a writer into defending a fixed point of view. But there is another, and I think more interesting, way of countering your own work-in-progress, and that is not simply to ask what possible objections might be raised to your work but also what alternative lines of thought you might want to pursue. You want to read a draft of an essay in ways that open up the possibilities of what you might say rather than lock you into a particular perspective. In revising you thus need to learn how to look at your work-in-progress not simply as a finished (or nearly finished) artifact but also as a source of ideas, a starting point for more writing.

Sometimes revising involves reworking existing text, but many other times it consists of following through on an idea or an aside, building on a suggestive turn of phrase, or taking your essay in an unplanned direction. In writing there are often moments when the best thing to do is to start over—except that you won't really be starting over, but rather beginning with an idea that's grabbed you in the midst of your work on an essay, or with a new sense of where you want to go in your thinking, or even with just a few key terms or examples that you've gleaned from the experience of working on your first draft. For instance, here is how Charles Jordan described how he rethought and redrafted an essay he was writing on Thomas Bell's novel *Out of This Furnace* for an undergraduate course in critical reading:

> My paper didn't simply evolve from a mediocre paper to an acceptable one (as I suspect most of my classmates' papers did). Rather, instead of just improving on the same paper, I wrote one with a completely different point. I started out focusing on the cyclic nature of the workers' lives and their experiences, and how the cycle was a perpetual one in which those who were in this class were trapped. However, going from first to second draft, I was asked to find something I could say at the end (or at least the middle) of my analysis that I couldn't say at the beginning. I said that I thought that my analysis validated the statement that the experiences and struggles of those in this working class actually came to define the class of people in this novel. I included something to that effect briefly in my conclusion, and in a few other places throughout the paper. However, I began to realize (not only on my own but also through the help of readers) that my initial argument of the "endless cycle" was weak, and evidence was scarce and hard to find. . . . What started out being an insightful one or two line statement in my paper started seeming more and more like an interesting argument I could make, which would also be stronger (due to more evidence). So, my paper metamorphosed from a paper trying to prove the existence of this cycle into a paper trying to show that Bell tries to define this class of workers by their struggles and sacrifices. So the major change in my paper was that my arguments and examples were then framed to support this new thesis. Also, I reworded a lot of awkward phrases, and added a few more examples. . . . Besides the fact that the main argument in the paper was changed, all the other changes I made were minor, and mostly technical.

> **INTERTEXTS**
>
> Charles Jordan, "Reflection on Writing," unpublished essay, Duke University, 2001. The essay that Charles describes in this reflection was on Thomas Bell, *Out of This Furnace* (Pittsburgh: University of Pittsburgh Press, 1976).

What Charles has to say here reminds me of the passage I quoted earlier by Stephen King. Both contrast the "minor and technical" work of piecing a text together with the more central problem of finding and developing its key ideas—although Charles usefully shows how such ideas can emerge not only through happenstance (as King suggests) but also through a process of talk and revision. But there is a kind of boldness, a willingness to set aside what isn't working and to build on what is, that underlies the views of both writers. Rather than simply trying to pull together evidence for a line of thought that he had begun to realize was mediocre, Charles chose the riskier path of developing another idea. I admire that. The aim of revising should not be simply to fix up or refine a text but to develop and extend what it has to say—to make your writing more precise, nuanced, inventive, and surprising. The best form of countering a work-in-progress allows for new lines of thought to emerge.

What's Next? Revising as Looking Ahead

One of the most difficult problems in writing involves figuring out how to close an essay or chapter or book before you've simply begun to repeat yourself. There's a familiar kind of academic essay that says almost everything it has to say in its first few pages—that begins, as it were, with its conclusions, laying out its thesis so mordantly in its opening paragraphs that its writer is' left with little to do in the rest of the piece but to offer a set of supporting examples for points he or she has already made. The principal aim of such writing sometimes seems to be to ensure that there will be no surprises beyond the first page or two, that everything will follow the initial plan and argument as set out by the writer. The conclusions of such essays thus tend to be almost wholly ornamental, bookends whose task is simply to restate what has come before.

I have no quarrel with the need 'to define a clear plan of work for an essay or book. You want readers to know what your project is, to have a sense of where you're headed in your thinking and what you see as at stake in your writing. (See the Project box "Mapping Your Approach".) But you also want to *develop* a line of thinking in an essay, to explore its contradictions and stuck points and ambiguities, not simply to stake out a fixed position and defend it. You want to be able to say something at the end of an essay that you couldn't say at its start, that your work in the previous pages has made possible.

A good question to ask of a draft of an essay that you are writing, then, is at what point do you simply start to restate what you've said before? For that is where you will want to bring the piece to a close. And if your experience is like mine, you may often find in rereading a draft that you have written several pages past the point where you might have ended it. I have many times found myself wondering how to conclude a piece, only to find that I already had—although without yet realizing it. You want to finish a piece not with a ceremonial flourish, a restatement of what has come before, but with a look ahead, a gesture toward work to come, a new question or idea or insight to be followed.

PROJECTS Mapping Your Approach

You may find the metaphor of a *map* useful in clarifying the approach you want to take in a piece of writing. Think of this map as having two parts: an overview and road signs. The former is a passage near the start of your piece that states where you are headed in your thinking and how you will get there. For example, *In this essay I argue that . . . First, I look at . . . Then I call on . . .* An overview is often a revised version of the sort of abstract I talked about before. Road signs are brief markers throughout your text that indicate the moves you are making as a writer. In a longer piece, road signs may be section headings (as in the chapters of this book). In a shorter essay, they may be signaled by metatextual phrases like *An example of this problem is . . .* or *Some implications of this stance are . . .* or *By way of concluding, let me . . .*

First, read through your text and highlight its overview and road signs. Then, check to see if your overview really describes your essay as it now stands. Sometimes you end up in different place at the end of a piece than you thought you were headed toward at its start. Sometimes you find alternate lines of inquiry. Sometimes you simply wander off track. If your overview and essay don't correspond with each other, decide which you want to change.

Finally, check to see if you have clearly marked the turns of thought throughout your text. If you list your subheads and/or metatextual phrases, these should offer a workable outline of your essay. If not, then you may need to mark the steps of your thinking more clearly. ■

A powerful close to an essay or book responds to two questions: *So what?* and *What's next?* By this I don't mean that such questions are posed! explicitly—they rarely are—but that readers should finish a text with a strong sense of how they have been asked to change what they feel or believe, as well as of what would be involved in continuing to think along the lines 'you have proposed, of what it would mean for them to take on *your* approach. In revising, then, you want to ask yourself the same question as you consider how to close an essay: How might this piece point toward new work, new writing?

It is an ambitious question—and one that you need to work toward answering throughout the whole of your essay and not simply at its conclusion. But it is not an impossible question to ask or answer. For instance, in an early draft of an analysis of the term *sketchy*, an adjective then in common use at both Duke and many other college campuses, Justin Lee concluded with this paragraph:

> Sketchy has become more than a word used in 'context at Duke to refer to unsure ideas. It has become a transformer itself—reshaping people's attitudes and thoughts. As a sort of personal character modifier, *sketchy* is now a powerful integrity-altering word that forms a powerful impact.

While this is not a terrible close to an essay, it failed to get at the idea driving the work that Justin had done throughout his piece—which was that there was something suspect about a term, *sketchy*, that could be used to indicate vague disapproval of almost anything, without ever really indicating what the grounds for that disapproval were. And what could a reader do with the vague idea that sketchy somehow had a "powerful impact" on the "integrity" of its users? What did his analysis point toward? It was hard to say. So this is how Justin revised his closing paragraph:

> *Sketchy* has become more than a word used in context at Duke to refer to unsure ideas. It has become a transformer itself—reshaping people's attitudes and thoughts. As a sort of personal character modifier, *sketchy* is an influential character-altering word that carries a powerful impact. What I have come to discover through the course of this paper is that sketchy is also at times a less than ideal word to use. Ironically, its strength is also its weakness. To see this connection clearly, think about what makes *sketchy* a perfect word sometimes—its vagueness does. *Sketchy* carries an almost deliberate non-committal interpretation, in that it has such a wide range of uses. This means that people can say it without actually "totally taking a side,' so to speak, allowing someone to voice an opinion, but also not requiring that person to "lay all of his cards down." It permits a person to half commit to a conviction without totally coming out. . . . People never really know how strongly a person is using it in context; therefore, people never know what to make of it. For this reason, the word sketchy is itself "sketchy," according to the definition and application it has taken on at Duke University—and should be used with caution.

In this new closing Justin not only offers a pointed criticism of the use of *sketchy* as a way of "half committing" yourself to an opinion but also suggests a self-reflexive mode of analysis in which you apply the values of a term to itself. Is *sketchy* itself sketchy? How cool is cool? Is it shady to call someone else shady? Justin is thus doing new work until the very end of his piece, rather than simply concluding by restating what he has already said (as was the case in his first closing passage). And in doing so, he invites his readers to continue the work he has begun, to take up his approach, to write in his spirit.

> **INTERTEXTS**
>
> Justin Lee, "Sketchy: A Transformer of Personal Character," unpublished essay (2nd and 3rd drafts), Duke University 2002.

You can imagine the work of revision, then, at its most ambitious, as pushing beyond the space of a single essay, as advancing a project whose ideas, aims, and possibilities spill over the bounds of a single piece and point toward further writing. That is what the first four chapters of this book are about: extending and rewriting the work of others. But you can also rewrite your own work in this interesting and difficult sense—to use one essay to fuel the next, to conclude not by wrapping things up but by pointing toward new lines of inquiry, by setting new tasks for yourself as a writer. Here's how another Duke undergraduate, Emily Murphy, put it in reflecting on her work on an essay in which she tried to connect the idea of "cultural capital," as formulated by a number of social theorists, to her own experiences in trying to reach out to people from other social classes. (These experiences included spending a number of days without money or shelter in order to gain some insight into the lives of homeless persons.)

> For some reason, I have a feeling that this is not the final draft of this paper—I imagine that I will revisit it again throughout my life. Therefore, although it is completely "revised" for now, it is doubtful that that is the final version. When the assignment was first given, I

brainstormed lots of semi-related ideas, but I wasn't sure how I could connect them reasonably. I honestly did not think that I would use my homeless story in my piece, but when I told the story to my group, they became fascinated by it. I decided to write about-being homeless and somehow relate it to our educational system, comparing myself with Cary and Kovacic. However, when I wrote the paper, I started discussing "cultural capital"—a term which I had previously just thrown around. I have learned about this term in several classes, but I have never truly considered the "cultural capital" of my high school. Once I started brainstorming, it was difficult to stop. I realized that 'I need to be specific, citing many examples. At this point, I knew that my paper could logically discuss my homeless experience in terms of "cultural capital." The paper began to take shape. When I presented it, I realized that I needed to reword some sentences because

> **INTERTEXTS**
>
> Emily Murphy, "Reflection on Class and Cultural Capital," unpublished essay, Duke University, 2001.

of my tone. I didn't want to appear that I was over-generalizing—after all, I am really just trying to discuss my own situation. Even though I tried to make this clear, I still feel that the paper could be easily criticized for its overgeneralization. Throughout this week, I have continued to think of more examples or semi-related topics. It was difficult for me to actually turn in the final draft because I kept on wanting to add more. Finally, my roommate looked at me and said: "You're obsessing Em, turn it in." At this point, I do like this draft. However, I also know that I will probably write a slightly different draft after my experiences student teaching this summer. This paper will follow me, hopefully expanding and altering through time—it will be interesting to compare drafts. My roommate knows me well—I do obsess.

Emily eloquently describes her essay here as "following" her, its shape and ideas shifting as she herself changes as a person and writer. But you might just as readily describe your project as a writer as something that is always a few steps ahead of you—that is, as something you are always reaching *toward*, only to find, at the very point you think you have at last come to the end of work on an essay or book, that there is still more writing to be done.

I've tried throughout this book to describe rewriting as an active and generous use of the work of others, an attempt to keep the conversation going, *to add* to what other writers and intellectuals have thought and said about a subject. My aim here in this chapter has been to suggest how in revising you might look similarly at your own work-in-progress—that is, to view a draft of an essay not as something to be patched or fixed but as a starting point for new work, for further talk and writing. I've tried, that is, to offer a view of academic writing as a *social* practice, as a form of intellectual work that is always rooted in a set of ongoing conversations, and that is always looking to push such talk another step forward. Even so, I'm aware that I've said fairly little so far about the actual social context in which much of this work takes place—that is, about the college or university writing course. In the afterword, then, I share some of my ideas about designing and teaching courses in academic writing. But while I address this section to my fellow teachers, I hope that my brief sketch of the pace and rhythm, the feel and tone, of the sort of courses I try to teach will be of interest to students as well.

PROJECTS Reflecting on Revision

When students in a course I am teaching are ready to turn in the final version of an essay, I also ask them to reflect on the work they have done over the last several weeks in drafting, revising, and editing their projects. Here is what I ask them to give me:

Along with the revised and final version of your essay, I'd like you to turn in a set of materials that trace the progress of your work in writing it. These materials will take some time and care to get ready. Please submit a folder with the following materials:

- The archival version of your essay.

- A version of your essay on which you highlight the changes you have made in moving from your first to second draft—marking those points where you have added to, cut, shifted, reworked, or reformatted your text. You can use the "compare documents" function in Microsoft Word to do much of this work, but you are likely to find that you also need to use colored pens to mark or clarify certain kinds of changes. Include a key to reading your highlights (e.g., green for added text, blue for cuts, etc.)

- In addition to tracking these changes, you should also identify a series of connected moves that you have made in rethinking your essay—that is, to point to a *pattern* of revision that runs through your piece. Mark this pattern clearly you should be able to point to at least three or four linked changes at various points in your essay and to name the idea that connects them.

- A copy of the previous drafts of your essay, along with the comments of your readers on those drafts.

- Any revising plans you have created during your work on your essay.

- A brief but specific reflection on how your project has developed over the last few weeks. Drawing on the map of changes you've' made, and especially the series of moves in revision you've identified, talk about the aims and strategies that have directed your work in drafting and revising your essay. How did your project in writing evolve over time? How did you come up with and carry through on your plan for revising? What went according to plan and what surprised you? If you have the opportunity to return to this piece, what further work might you want to do on it? ■

24 The Maker's Eye: Revising Your Own Manuscripts

Donald M. Murray

Born in Boston, Massachusetts, in 1924, Donald M. Murray taught writing for many years at the University of New Hampshire, his alma mater. He has served as an editor at Time *magazine, and he won the Pulitzer Prize in 1954 for editorials that appeared in the* Boston Globe. *Murray's published works include novels, short stories, poetry, and sourcebooks for teachers of writing, like* A Writer Teaches Writing *(1968),* The Craft of Revision *(1991), and* Learning by Teaching *(1982), in which he explores aspects of the writing process.* Write to Learn, *(6th ed., 1998), a textbook for college composition courses, is based on Murray's belief that writers learn to write by writing, by taking a piece of writing through the whole process, from invention to revision.*

In the following essay, first published in the Writer *in October 1973 and later revised for this text, Murray discusses the importance of revision to the work of the writer. Most professional writers live by the maxim that "writing is rewriting." And to rewrite or revise effectively, we need to become better readers of our own work, open to discovering new meanings, and sensitive to our use of language. Murray draws on the experiences of many writers to make a compelling argument for careful revising and editing.*

When students complete a first draft, they consider the job of writing done—and their teachers too often agree. When professional writers complete a first draft, they usually feel that they are at the start of the writing process. When a draft is completed, the job of writing can begin.

That difference in attitude is the difference between amateur and professional, inexperience and experience, journeyman and craftsman. Peter F. Drucker, the prolific business writer, calls his first draft "the zero draft"—after that he can start counting. Most writers share the feeling that the first draft, and all of those which follow, are opportunities to discover what they have to say and how best they can say it.

To produce a progression of drafts, each of which says more and says it more clearly, the writer has to develop a special kind of reading skill. In school we are taught to decode what appears on the page as finished writing. Writers, however, face a different category of possibility and responsibility when they read their own drafts. To them the words on the page are never finished.

Each can be changed and rearranged, can set off a chain reaction of confusion or clarified meaning. This is a different kind of reading which is possibly more difficult and certainly more exciting.

Writers must learn to be their own best enemy. They must accept the criticism of others and be suspicious of it; they must accept the praise of others and be even more suspicious of it. Writers cannot depend on others. They must detach themselves from their own pages so that they can apply both their caring and their craft to their own work.

Such detachment is not easy. Science-fiction writer Ray Bradbury supposedly puts each manuscript away for a year to the day and then rereads it as a stranger. Not many writers have the discipline or the time to do this. We must read when our judgment may be at its worst, when we are close to the euphoric moment of creation.

Then the writer, counsels novelist Nancy Hale, "should be critical of everything that seems to him most delightful in his style. He should excise what he most admires, because he wouldn't thus admire it if he weren't . . . in a sense protecting it from criticism." John Ciardi, the poet, adds, "The last act of the writing must be to become one's own reader. It is, I suppose, a schizophrenic process, to begin passionately and to end critically, to begin hot and to end cold; and, more important, to be passion-hot and critic-cold at the same time."

Most people think that the principal problem is that writers are too proud of what they have written. Actually, a greater problem for most professional writers is one shared by the majority of students. They are overly critical, think everything is dreadful, tear up page after page, never complete a draft, see the task as hopeless.

The writer must learn to read critically but constructively, to cut what is bad, to reveal what is good. Eleanor Estes, the children's book author, explains: "The writer must survey his work critically, coolly, as though he were a stranger to it. He must be willing to prune, expertly and hard-heartedly. At the end of each revision, a manuscript may look . . . worked over, torn apart, pinned together, added to, deleted from, words changed and words changed back. Yet the book must maintain its original freshness and spontaneity."

Most readers underestimate the amount of rewriting it usually takes to produce spontaneous reading. This is a great disadvantage to the student writer, who sees only a finished product and never watches the craftsman who takes the necessary step back, studies the work carefully, returns to the task, steps back, returns, steps back, again and again. Anthony Burgess, one of the most prolific writers in the English-speaking world, admits, "I might revise a page twenty times." Roald Dahl, the popular children's writer, states, "By the time I'm nearing the end of a story, the first part will have been reread and altered and corrected at least 150 times. . . . Good writing is essentially rewriting. I am positive of this."

Rewriting isn't virtuous. It isn't something that ought to be done. It is simply something that most writers find they have to do to discover what they have to say and how to say it. It is a condition of the writer's life.

There are, however, a few writers who do little formal rewriting, primarily because they have the capacity and experience to create and review a large number of invisible drafts in their minds before they approach the page. And some writers slowly produce finished pages, performing all the tasks of revision simultaneously, page by page, rather than draft by draft. But it is still possible to see the sequence followed by most writers most of the time in rereading their own work.

Most writers scan their drafts first, reading as quickly as possible to catch the larger problems of subject and form, and then move in closer and closer as they read and write, reread and rewrite.

The first thing writers look for in their drafts is *information*. They know that a good piece of writing is built from specific, accurate, and interesting information. The writer must have an abundance of information from which to construct a readable piece of writing.

Next writers look for *meaning* in the information. The specifics must build to a pattern of significance. Each piece of specific information must carry the reader toward meaning.

Writers reading their own drafts are aware of *audience*. They put themselves in the reader's situation and make sure that they deliver information which a reader wants to know or needs to know in a manner which is easily digested. Writers try to be sure that they anticipate and answer the questions a critical reader will ask when reading the piece of writing.

Writers make sure that the *form* is appropriate to the subject and the audience. Form, or genre, is the vehicle which carries meaning to the reader, but form cannot be selected until the writer has adequate information to discover its significance and an audience which needs or wants that meaning.

Once writers are sure the form is appropriate, they must then look at the *structure,* the order of what they have written. Good writing is built on a solid framework of logic, argument, narrative, or motivation which runs through the entire piece of writing and holds it together. This is the time when many writers find it most effective to outline as a way of visualizing the hidden spine by which the piece of writing is supported.

The element on which writers spend a majority of their time is *development*. Each section of a piece of writing must be adequately developed. It must give readers enough information so that they are satisfied. How much information is enough? That's as difficult as asking how much garlic belongs in a salad. It must be done to taste, but most beginning writers underdevelop, underestimating the reader's hunger for more information.

As writers solve development problems, they often have to consider questions of *dimension*. There must be a pleasing and effective proportion among all the parts of the piece of writing. There is a continual process of subtracting and adding to keep the piece of writing in balance.

Finally, writers have to listen to their own voices. *Voice* is the force which drives a piece of writing forward. It is an expression of the writer's authority and concern. It is what is between the words on the page, what glues the piece of writing together. A good piece of writing is always marked by a consistent, individual voice.

As writers read and reread, write and rewrite, they move closer and closer to the page until they are doing line-by-line editing. Writers read their own pages with infinite care. Each sentence, each line, each clause, each phrase, each word, each mark of punctuation, each section of white space between the type has to contribute to the clarification of meaning.

Slowly the writer moves from word to word, looking through language to see the subject. As a word is changed, cut or added, as a construction is rearranged, all the words used before that moment and all those that follow that moment must be considered and reconsidered.

Writers often read aloud at this stage of the editing process, muttering or whispering to themselves, calling on the ear's experience with language. Does this sound right—or that? Writers edit, shifting back and forth from eye to page to ear to page. I find I must do this careful editing in short runs, no more than fifteen or twenty minutes at a stretch, or I become too kind with myself. I begin to see what I hope is on the page, not what actually is on the page.

This sounds tedious if you haven't done it, but actually it is fun. Making something right is immensely satisfying, for writers begin to learn what they are writing about by writing. Language leads them to meaning, and there is the joy of discovery, of understanding, of making meaning clear as the writer employs the technical skills of language.

Words have double meanings, even triple and quadruple meanings. Each word has its own potential of connotation and denotation. And when writers rub one word against the other, they are often rewarded with a sudden insight, an unexpected clarification.

The maker's eye moves back and forth from word to phrase to sentence to paragraph to sentence to phrase to word. The maker's eye sees the need for variety and balance, for a firmer structure, for a more appropriate form. It peers into the interior of the paragraph, looking for coherence, unity, and emphasis, which make meaning clear.

I learned something about this process when my first bifocals were prescribed. I had ordered a larger section of the reading portion of the glass because of my work, but even so, I could not contain my eyes within this new limit of vision. And I still find myself taking off my glasses and bending my nose toward the page, for my eyes unconsciously flick back and forth across the page, back to another page, forward to still another, as I try to see each evolving line in relation to every other line.

When does this process end? Most writers agree with the great Russian writer Tolstoy, who said, "I scarcely ever reread my published writings, if by chance I come across a page, it always strikes me: all this must be rewritten; this is how I should have written it."

The maker's eye is never satisfied, for each word has the potential to ignite new meaning. This article has been twice written all the way through the writing process [. . .]. Now it is to be republished in a book. The editors made a few small suggestions, and then I read it with my maker's eye. Now it has been re-edited, re-revised, re-read, and re-re-edited, for each piece of writing to the writer is full of potential and alternatives.

A piece of writing is never finished. It is delivered to a deadline, torn out of the typewriter on demand, sent off with a sense of accomplishment and shame and pride and frustration. If only there were a couple more days, time for just another run at it, perhaps then . . .

■ ■ ■ **FOR CLASS DISCUSSION**

1. How does Murray define *information* and meaning? Why is the distinction between the two terms important?

2. According to Murray, at what point(s) in the writing process do writers become concerned about the individual words they are using? What do you think Murray means when he says that "language leads [writers] to meaning"?

3. The phrase "the maker's eye" appears in Murray's title and in several places throughout the essay. What do you suppose he means by this? Consider how the maker's eye could be different from the reader's eye.

4. According to Murray, when is a piece of writing finished? What, for him, is the function of deadlines?

■ ■ ■

Making Meaning Clear: The Logic of Revision

Donald M. Murray

Donald M. Murray. Professor of English at the University of New Hampshire and a Pulitzer Prize editorial writer, has been director of freshman English and now supervises a university-wide composition course. He is the author of A Writer Teaches Writing *as well as articles, poems, novels, and juvenile nonfiction books. He was writing consultant to the Boston* Globe *and is consultant to the Providence* Journal-Bulletin, *the* News Observer *and the Raleigh* Times, *and other newspapers.*

The writer's meaning rarely arrives by room-service, all neatly laid out on the tray. Meaning is usually discovered and clarified as the writer makes hundreds of small decisions, each one igniting a sequence of consideration and reconsideration.

Revision is not just clarifying meaning, it is discovering meaning and clarifying it while it is being discovered. That makes revision a far more complicated process than is usually thought—and a far simpler process at the same time.

It is complicated because the writer cannot just go to the rule book. Revision is not a matter of correctness, following the directions in a manual. The writer has to go back again and again and again to consider what the writing means and if the writer can accept, document, and communicate that meaning. In other words, writing is not what the writer does after the thinking is done; writing is thinking.

This also makes revision simpler. There is a logic to the process. The writer needs only a draft, a pen, and a brain. Each editorial act must relate to meaning. That is the primary consideration that rules each editorial decision. Considerations of audience, structure, tone, pace, usage, mechanics, typography are primarily decided on one issue: do they make the meaning clear?

The process of revision—what the reviser does—is fairly simple. The writer cuts, adds, reorders, or starts over. Each of these acts fits into a sequence most of the time. The writer solves the problems of meaning, and those solutions make it possible to solve the problems of order, and those solutions make it possible to solve the problems of voice.

Unfortunately, many teachers—and, I have discovered recently, many newspaper editors—do not understand the logic of revision and, therefore, do not encourage or even allow revision. They pounce on first draft writing and make corrections.

Since most writers have not discovered their meaning in their first draft, the corrections editors make must come from the editors' own preconception of what the writing should mean. It comes from the editors' own experience, their own research, their own prejudices. They work in ignorance of the writer's intentions and take the writing away from the writer.

When editors or teachers kidnap the first draft, they also remove the responsibility for making meaning from the writer. Writing becomes trivialized, unchallenging, unauthoritative, impersonal, unimportant.

Hemingway told us, "Prose is architecture, not interior decoration. . . . " Premature correction by a teacher or an editor must focus mainly on the decoration, the cosmetics of writing. Of course, writers must spell correctly, must follow the conventions of language that make meaning clear. But the writer must do it in relation to the writer's meaning through the medium of the writer's own voice. Writing is too important to be corrected by the book; it must be corrected in relation to meaning.

When revision is encouraged, not as a punishment but as a natural process in the exploration of the text to discover meaning, then many basic writers become motivated to revise. It is a slow but miraculous process. The basic writers spot a hint of meaning that surprises them. Usually the meaning is in a primitive form at the time it is first shared with a teacher or fellow student. Basic writers are urged on. Soon they do not revise to become correct, they revise to discover their individual meaning, to hear their own voices making those meanings clear, and to hear their readers' delight as an unexpected meaning is recognized as true.

The making of meaning through revision is a logical craft. Once a student has made meaning, the process can be repeated. It is not an act of magic anymore than magic acts are; it is a matter of tuning an engine, kneading dough, sewing a dress, building a shelf. The act of revision allows the writer to take something that was not and make it something that is; it allows the writer to achieve the satisfaction of completion, closure.

Revision can be the most satisfying part of teaching composition if the teacher is willing to let go. The composition teacher must wean the student. The teacher must give the responsibility for the text to the writer, making clear again and again that it is the student, not the teacher, who decides what the writing means.

The best way for teachers to reveal exploration in revision is by writing in public on the blackboard, or by using an overhead projector, allowing the students to see how writing struggles to find what it has to say. The teacher should not consciously write badly; the teacher should write as well as possible. That will produce copy that is quite bad enough to deserve revision.

The teacher who writes in public will expose the fact that writing often does not come clear; in fact, syntax often breaks down just at the point where a new or significant meaning is beginning to break out of its shell. That meaning has an awkward and clumsy time of it, but if the writer listens carefully and nurtures the meaning, it may grow into significance. Or it may not. It may have to be put aside. But first it has to be understood before it can be rejected. Teachers who are willing to share evolving writing will find their class willing to share in a workshop where everyone is trying to help the writer discover and clarify the evolving meaning.

I have internalized a checklist that follows the logic of revision. It may be helpful to consider this checklist, but each teacher should work to develop a new checklist with each class. Neither my checklist nor anyone else's checklist should be taken as gospel. The checklist should be formulated while the class experiences the process of making meaning clear.

The principles that underlie my checklist are:

- *Build on strength.* The writer searches the text for the meaning that is being developed by the writing and looks for what is working to make it work better. Revising is not so much a matter of correction as it is a matter of discovering the strength of the text and extending that strength.
- *Cut what can be cut.* An effective piece of writing has a single dominant meaning, and everything in the text must advance that meaning.
- *Simplicity is best.* This does not mean writing in pidgin English, merely sending a telegram to the reader. It does mean making the writing as simple as it can be for what is being said. The message may be complex, and that may require linguistic or rhetorical complexity, but that complexity should always be the simplest way to communicate the complexity.
- *The writing will tell you how to write.* In revising I do not look to rule books, to models from other writers, to what I have written before, or how I have written it. The answers to the problems of this piece of writing lie in the evolving text. I have faith that if I read carefully—if I listen to my own developing voice—I will discover what I have to say.

My checklist requires at least three different kinds of reading—for focus, form and voice. This does not mean that I read the text three times; it is possible that the readings overlap and I read it only a couple of times. Most times I read it many more times. There is no ideal number of readings. I read it enough times to discover what I have to say.

During each of the readings I keep my eye and my ear on the single dominant meaning that is evolving from the text. A good piece of writing, I believe, says only one thing. Or to put it in a different way, the many things that are said in a piece of writing all add up to a single meaning.

Here is my internal checklist articulated:

Focus. First I read the text as fast as possible, trying to keep my pen capped, trying to see it from a distance the way the reader will so I can ask myself the larger questions of content and meaning. I do not do this "first" reading, of course, until I have the meaning of the writing in mind. In other words, I have to have a focus before I can work on *the* focus. If, in each stage of the reading, the meaning does not become clearer and clearer, I go back and discover a potential meaning that can be brought into focus. The questions I ask are:

- *What does the piece of writing mean?* If it is not clear, I will take the time to write a sentence that makes the meaning clear, that achieves what Virginia Woolf calls, "the power of combination," that contains the tensions within the piece of writing in a single statement.

- *Are all the reader's questions answered?* Many times I will brainstorm the questions that the reader will inevitably ask of the text.
- *Is new information needed?*
- *Is the piece built on undocumented assumptions?* Sometimes I will actually write down my assumptions to see if they make sense or stand up as a firm foundation for the piece.
- *Is the genre appropriate to the meaning?* One of my novels started out as a series of articles. By genre I mean fiction, poetry, or the larger categories of non-fiction—personal narrative, familiar essay, argument, exposition.
- *Are there any tangents that can be cut loose?* I used to have much more trouble getting rid of those wonderful pieces of evidence or examples of writing that really did not relate to the meaning. Hannah Lees taught me how to solve this problem. For years I wrote one paragraph to a page, then played solitaire with these paragraphs, arranging and re-arranging them until they made a single meaning.
- *Is there a section that should be a separate piece of writing?*
- *Is each point supported by convincing evidence?* Sometimes I actually role-play a reader. It is always a specific person I know who does not agree with me and who I believe does not like me. I want to confront my enemies and defeat them before the writing is published.
- *Is the piece long enough to satisfy the reader?* Most writers underwrite, and I am no exception. The tendency is to say it and not to give the reader enough room for the reader to discover the meaning.
- *Is the piece short enough to keep the reader involved?* The piece of writing must develop its own energy, its own momentum. If my mind wanders during this first quick reading, the reader's certainly will.

Form. Next, I read the text again, a bit more slowly, only uncapping my pen when a marginal note is necessary, trying to look at the text as a sequence of chunks of writing, perhaps chunks of meaning. I am no longer looking at the text as a whole, although I am aware of the territory now, and I am trying to keep myself free of the concern with detail, for a premature involvement with the details of language may keep me from evaluating the questions of form. The questions I ask are:

- *Is the title on target?* Years ago when I could put my own heads on editorials, I found that the effort to write a title is worth the trouble. I may draft as many as a hundred titles, for each one is a way of discovering meaning, and I can draft a number of titles in almost slivers of time. At this stage of the revision process I check to make sure that the title relates to the meaning as that meaning has now evolved.
- *Does the lead catch the reader in three seconds—or less?* I hear rumors of good pieces of writing that have poor leads or beginnings, but I have not been able to find any from professional writers. The first few lines of a piece of writing establish the tone, the voice, the direction, the pace, the meaning. I check once more to make sure that the lead will entice the reader.
- *Does the lead deliver on its contract with the reader?* The lead must be honest. It must relate to the meaning that will evolve through the text.

- *Does the piece answer the reader's questions at the point the reader will ask them?* This is the key to effective organization. Again and again I will ask the questions the reader will ask, even if they are the questions I do not want the reader to ask, and then number them in the order the reader will ask them. A good piece of writing does not need transitional phrases. The information arrives when the reader can use it. The reader's questions and their order can be anticipated.
- *How can I get out of the way of the reader and show rather than tell?* Orwell instructed writers that they should be like a pane of glass through which the reader sees the subject. I do not want the reader to be impressed with my writing; my arrogance is greater than that. I want the reader to receive the evidence in such a direct fashion that it will cause the reader to think the way I want the reader to think . I want to show so effectively that the reader will see my meaning as inevitable.
- *Is there an effective variety of documentation?* Most of us fall into a pattern using quotations, citations, anecdotes, statistics, personal experience—whatever we feel comfortable using or whatever we think we do well. The documentation, of course, should be what works best for the point being documented.
- *Does the pace reinforce the meaning?* The reader should be allowed to absorb each point before moving on to the next one. I tend to write and to teach too intensively; I have to remember to give the reader room.
- *Does the pace provide the energy to carry the reader forward?*
- *Are the dimensions appropriate to the meaning?* The size of each section should be in proportion to other sections.
- *Does the end echo the lead and fulfill its promise?*

Voice. At last, I read the text slowly, line by line, my pen uncapped. I usually read the text many times within this category, generally working from the larger issue of voice down to paragraphs to sentences to phrases to single words. This is the most satisfying part of revision. There is a single meaning. It will change and develop and become clearer, but there is a focus, there is an order, and there is the chance to work with language, to combine my voice with the voice that is evolving from the draft. The questions I then ask are:

- *Can the piece be read aloud?* Does it sound as if one person is talking to one person? Reading is a private experience, a human contact from one single person to another single person. I think that effective writing should be conversational. Sometimes the conversation is more formal than others, but it should never be stuffy, pretentious, or incapable of being read aloud by the writer.
- *Are important pieces of specific information at the ends and beginnings of key sentences, paragraphs, sections, and the entire piece itself?* The 2-3-1 principle of emphasis can do as much as anything else to sharpen up prose and make meaning clear: the second most important point of emphasis is at the beginning; the least important piece of emphasis is at the middle, and the greatest point of emphasis is at the end.
- *Does each paragraph make one point?*
- *Does each paragraph carry a full load of meaning to the reader?*

- *Do the paragraphs vary in length in relation to meaning—the shorter the more important the information?*
- *Are the paragraphs in order?* If the reader's questions are answered when they will be asked, formal transitions will not be needed.
- *Does the reader leave each sentence with more information than the reader entered it?*
- *Are there sentences that announce what will be said or sum up what has been said and, therefore, can be cut?*
- *Are most sentences subject-verb-object sentences?* At least most sentences that carry the essence of meaning should be direct sentences. The interesting work done in sentence-combining has too often confused this issue. Of course sentences should be combined, but the strength and vigor of the language still lies in simple, direct subject-verb-object sentences. These are the sentences, short and to the point, that will communicate.
- *Are there clauses that get in the way of meaning?* Many sentences have to be reordered so that the meaning comes clear. This usually means that sentences have to be read aloud again and again until the information in the sentence appears at the moment that the reader can use it.
- *Are the verbs active and strong enough to drive the meaning forward?* The verbs are the engines of meaning, and during revision the writer must give priority to finding verbs that are accurate and provide energy.
- *Has the right word been found?* Many times we try to use two almost right words in the hope that we will trap the meaning between them. That does not work. Mark Twain said, "The difference between the right word and the almost-right word is the difference between lightning and a lightning-bug." He was right. Revision is the search for the exactly right word.
- *Does the meaning depend on verbs and nouns, not adverbs and adjectives?* The right word is rarely an adjective or an adverb. Again, the meaning is not caught best in the crush between adjective and noun, or adverb and verb. I always feel a tiny sense of failure when I use an adjective or an adverb. I have failed to find the right noun or the right verb.
- *Is there sexist or racist language that should be changed?*
- *Can the writing be more specific?*
- *Are there unnecessary -lys, -ings, thats, and woulds that should be cut?* Each writer must develop a list of linguistic interferences with meaning. I find when I do professional ghost-editing that merely cutting the *-lys*, the *-ings*, the *thats*, the *woulds*—and yes, the unnecessary verb *be*—will make an obscure text start to come clear.
- *Is every fact checked?*
- *Is every word spelled correctly?*
- *Is there anything I can do to make the writing simple? clear? graceful? accurate? fair?*

Do I formally ask all of these questions of myself in every piece of writing I do? Of course not. These concerns are internalized, and they overlap. The process is recursive. I discover meaning by language. I work back and forth from meaning to focus to form to voice and from voice to form to focus to meaning.

The process is, however, logical. Everything on the page must reveal meaning. Every word, every space between words, is put on the page or left on the page because it develops the meaning of the piece of writing.

This checklist cannot be dumped on the beginning or the remedial writer, but it can be used by the teacher to establish priorities. The student has to learn that writing is a search for meaning, and once a potential meaning is found, it may be clarified through the process of revision.

There is a simple guiding logic to revision, and every question of spelling, usage, structure, mechanics, style, content, documentation, voice, pace, development, must be answered in terms of meaning.

Think of a workman who moves in close, measuring, marking, sawing, fitting, standing back to examine the job, moving back in close to plane, chisel, mark and fit, standing back again to study the task, moving in close to nail the piece in place, stepping back for another look, moving in close to set the nails, another step back, another look, then in close to hide the nail holes, to sand, stepping back to make sure the sanding is complete, then in close at last to apply the finish.

Actually the workman probably moved in close many more times before finishing the task and certainly stepped back many times to see the job entire. And so does the writer, working between word and meaning.

What the student can discover is that this process is logical; it can be understood. An effective piece of writing is produced by a craft. It is simply a matter of working back and forth between focus, form, and voice until the meaning is discovered and made clear.

26 When We Dead Awaken: Writing as Re-Vision

Adrienne Rich

Ibsen's "When We Dead Awaken" is a play about the use that the male art-ist and thinker—in the process of creating culture as we know it—has made of women, in his life and in his work; and about a woman's slow struggling awakening to the use to which her life has been put. Bernard Shaw wrote in 1900 of this play:

> [Ibsen] shows us that no degradation ever devized or permitted is as disastrous as this degradation; that through it women can die into luxuries for men and yet can kill them; that men and women are becoming conscious of this; and that what remains to be seen as perhaps the most interesting of all imminent social develop-ments is what will happen "when we dead awaken".[1]

It's exhilarating to be alive in a time of awakening consciousness; it can also be confusing, disorienting, and painful. This awakening of dead or sleep-ing consciousness has already affected the lives of millions of women, even those who don't know it yet. It is also affecting the lives of men, even those who deny its claims upon them. The argument will go on whether an oppres-sive economic class system is responsible for the oppressive nature of male/female relations, or whether, in fact, the sexual class system is the original model on which all the others are based. But in the last few years connections have been drawn between our sexual lives and our political institutions, which are inescapable and illuminating. The sleepwalkers are coming awake, and for the first time this awakening has a collective reality; it is no longer such a lonely thing to open one's eyes.

Re-vision—the act of looking back, of seeing with fresh eyes, of entering an old text from a new critical direction—is for us more than a chapter in cultural history: it is an act of survival. Until we can understand the assump-tions in which we are drenched we cannot know ourselves. And this drive to self-knowledge, for woman, is more than a search for identity: it is part of her refusal of the self-destructiveness of male-dominated society. A radical critique of literature, feminist in its impulse, would take the work first of all as a clue to how we live, how we have been living, how we have been led to imagine ourselves, how our language has trapped as well as liberated us; and how we can begin to see—and therefore live—afresh. A change in the concept of sexual identity is essential if we are not going to see the old political order re-assert itself in every new revolution. We need to know the writing of the past, and know it differently than we have ever known it; not to pass on a tradition but to break its hold over us.

For writers, and at this moment for women writers in particular, there is the challenge and promise of a whole new psychic geography to be explored. But there is also a difficult and dangerous walking on the ice, as we try to find language and images for a consciousness we are just coming into, and with little in the past to support us. I want to talk about some aspects of this difficulty and this danger.

Jane Harrison, the great classical anthropologist, wrote in 1914 in a letter to her friend Gilbert Murray:

> By the by, about "Women," it has bothered me often—why do women never want to write poetry about Man as a sex—why is Woman a dream and a terror to man and not the other way around? . . . Is it mere convention and propriety, or something deeper?[2]

I think Jane Harrison's question cuts deep into the myth-making tradition, the romantic tradition; deep into what women and men have been to each other; and deep into the psyche of the woman writer. Thinking about that question, I began thinking of the work of two 20th-century women poets, Sylvia Plath and Diane Wakoski. It strikes me that in the work of both Man appears as, if not a dream, a fascination and a terror; and that the source of the fascination and the terror is, simply, Man's power—to dominate, tyrannize, choose, or reject the woman. The charisma of Man seems to come purely from his power over her and his control of the world by force, not from anything fertile or life-giving in him. And, in the work of both these poets, it is finally the woman's sense of *herself*—embattled, possessed—that gives the poetry its dynamic charge, its rhythms of struggle, need, will, and female energy. Convention and propriety are perhaps not the right words, but until recently this female anger and this furious awareness of the Man's power over her were not available materials to the female poet, who tended to write of Love as the source of her suffering, and to view that victimization by Love as an almost inevitable fate. Or, like Marianne Moore and Elizabeth Bishop, she kept human sexual relationships at a measured and chiselled distance in her poems.

One answer to Jane Harrison's question has to be that historically men and women have played very different parts in each others' lives. Where woman has been a luxury for man, and has served as the painter's model and the poet's muse, but also as comforter, nurse, cook, bearer of his seed, secretarial assistant and copyist of manuscripts, man has played a quite different role for the female artist. Henry James repeats an incident which the writer Prosper Merimee described, of how, while he was living with George Sand,

> he once opened his eyes, in the raw winter dawn, to see his companion, in a dressing-gown, on her knees before the domestic hearth, a candlestick beside her and a red *madras* round her head, making bravely, with her own hands, the fire that was to enable her to sit down betimes to urgent pen and paper. The story represents him as having felt that the spectacle

chilled his ardor and tried his taste; her appearance was unfortunate, her occupation an inconsequence, and her industry a reproof-the result of all of which was a lively irritation and an early rupture."[3]

I am suggesting that the specter of this kind of male judgment, along with the active discouragement and thwarting of her needs by a culture controlled by males, has created problems for the woman writer: problems of contact with her-self, problems of language and style, problems of energy and survival.

In rereading Virginia Woolf's *A Room Of One's Own* for the first time in some years, I was astonished at the sense of effort, of pains taken, of dogged tentative-ness, in the tone of that essay. And I recognized that tone. I had heard it often enough, in myself and in other women. It is the tone of a woman almost in touch with her anger, who is determined not to appear angry, who is *willing* herself to be calm, detached, and even charming in a roomful of men where things have been said which are attacks on her very integrity. Virginia Woolf is addressing an audience of women, but she is acutely conscious—as she always was—of being over-heard by men: by Morgan and Lytton and Maynard Keynes and for that matter by her father, Leslie Stephen. She drew the language out into an exacerbated thread in her determination to have her own sensibility yet protect it from those masculine presences. Only at rare moments in that essay do you hear the passion in her voice; she was trying to sound as cool as Jane Austen, as Olympian as Shakespeare, because that is the way the men of the culture thought a writer should sound.

No male writer has written primarily or even largely for women, or with the sense of women's criticism as a consideration when he chooses his materials, his theme, his language. But to a lesser or greater extent, every woman writer has written for men even when, like Virginia Woolf, she was supposed to be addressing women. If we have come to the point when this balance might begin to change, when women can stop being haunted, not only by "convention and propriety" but by internalized fears of being and saying themselves, then it is an extraordinary moment for the woman writer—and reader.

I have hesitated to do what I am going to do now, which is to use myself as an illustration. For one thing, it's a lot easier and less dangerous to talk about other women writers. But there is something else. Like Virginia Woolf, I am aware of the women who are not with us here because they are washing the dishes and looking after the children. Nearly fifty years after she spoke, that fact remains largely unchanged. And I am thinking also of women whom she left out of the picture altogether—women who are washing other people's dishes and caring for other people's children, not to mention women who went on the streets last night in order to feed their children. We seem to be special women here, we have liked to think of ourselves as special, and we have known that men would tolerate, even romanticize us as special, as long as our words and actions didn't threaten their privilege of tolerating or rejecting us according to *their* ideas of what a special woman ought to be. An important insight of the radical women's movement, for me, has been how divisive and how ultimately destructive is this myth of the special woman, who is also the token woman. Every one of us here in this room has had great luck—we are teachers, writers, academicians; our own gifts could not have been enough, for we all know women whose gifts are buried or aborted. Our struggles can have meaning only if they can help to change the lives of women whose gifts—and whose very being—continue to be thwarted.

My own luck was being born white and middle-class into a house full of books, with a father who encouraged me to read and write. So for about twenty years I wrote for a particular man, who criticized and praised me and made me feel I was indeed "special." The obverse side of this, of course, was that I tried for a long time to please him, or rather, not to displease him. And then of course there were other men—writers, teachers—the Man, who was not a terror or a dream but a literary master and a master in other ways less easy to acknowledge. And there were all those poems about women, written by men: it seemed to be a given that men wrote poems and women frequently inhabited them. These women were almost always beautiful, but threatened with the loss of beauty, the loss of youth—the fate worse than death. Or, they were beautiful and died young, like Lucy and Lenore. Or, the woman was like Maud Gonne, cruel and disastrously mistaken, and the poem reproached her because she had refused to become a luxury for the poet.

A lot is being said today about the influence that the myths and images of women have on all of us who are products of culture. I think it has been a peculiar con-fusion to the girl or woman who tries to write because she is peculiarly susceptible to language. She goes to poetry or fiction looking for *her* way of being in the world, since she too has been putting words and images together; she is looking eagerly for guides, maps possibilities; and over and over in the "words' masculine persuasive force" of literature she comes up against something that negates everything she is about: she meets the image of Woman in books written by men. She finds a terror and a dream, she finds a beautiful pale face, she finds La Belle Dame Sans Merci, she finds Juliet or Tess or Salomé, but precisely what she does not find is that absorbed, drudging, puzzled, sometimes inspired creature, herself, who sits at a desk trying to put words together.

So what does she do? What did I do? I read the older women poets with their peculiar keenness and ambivalence: Sappho, Christina Rossetti, Emily Dickinson, Elinor Wylie, Edna Millay, H.D. I discovered that the woman poet most admired at the time (by men) was Marianne Moore, who was maidenly, elegant, intellectual, discreet. But even in reading these women I was looking in them for the same things I had found in the poetry of men, because I wanted women poets to be the equals of men, and to be equal was still confused with sounding the same.

I know that my style was formed first by male poets: by the men I was reading as an undergraduate—Frost, Dylan Thomas, Donne, Auden, MacNiece, Stevens, Yeats. What I chiefly learned from them was craft. But poems are like dreams: in them you put what you don't know you know. Looking back at poems I wrote before I was 21, I'm startled because beneath the conscious craft are glimpses of the split I even then experienced between the girl who wrote poems, who defined herself in writing poems, and the girl who was to define herself by her relation-ships with men. "Aunt Jennifer's Tigers," written while I was a student, looks with deliberate detachment at this split.

Aunt Jennifer's tigers stride across a screen,
Bright topaz denizens of a world of green.
They do not fear the men beneath the tree;
They pace in sleek chivalric certainty.

Aunt Jennifer's fingers fluttering through her wool
Find even the ivory needle hard to pull.
The massive weight of Uncle's wedding band
Sits heavily upon Aunt Jennifer's hand.

When Aunt is dead, her terrified hands will lie
Still ringed with ordeals she was mastered by.
The tigers in the panel that she made
Will go on striding, proud and unafraid.[4]

In writing this poem, composed and apparently cool as it is, I thought I was creating a portrait of an imaginary woman. But this woman suffers from the opposition of her imagination, worked out in tapestry, and her life-style, "ringed with ordeals she was mastered by." It was important to me that Aunt Jennifer was a person as distinct from myself as possible—distanced by the formalism of the poem, by its objective, observant tone—even by putting the woman in a different generation.

In those years formalism was part of the strategy—like asbestos gloves, it allowed me to handle materials I couldn't pick up barehanded. (A later strategy was to use the persona of a man, as I did in "The Loser.") I finished college, published my first book by a fluke, as it seemed to me, and broke off a love affair. I took a job, lived alone, went on writing, fell in love. I was young, full of energy, and the book seemed to mean that others agreed I was a poet. Because I was also deter-mined to have a "full" woman's life, I plunged in my early twenties into marriage and had three children before I was thirty. There was nothing overt in the environment to warn me: these were the '50's, and in reaction to the earlier wave of feminism, middle-class women were making careers of domestic perfection, working to send their husbands through professional schools, then retiring to raise large families. People were moving out to the suburbs, technology was going to be the answer to everything, even sex; the family was in its glory. Life was extremely private; women were isolated from each other by the loyalties of marriage. I have a sense that women didn't talk to each other much in the fifties—not about their secret emptinesses, their frustrations. I went on trying to write; my second book and first child appeared in the same month. But by the time that book came out I was already dissatisfied with those poems, which seemed to me mere exercises for poems I hadn't written. The book was praised, however, for its "gracefulness"; I had a marriage and a child. If there were doubts, if there were periods of null depression or active despairing, these could only mean that I was ungrateful, insatiable, perhaps a monster.

About the time my third child was born, I felt that I had either to consider myself a failed woman and a failed poet, or to try to find some synthesis by which to understand what was happening to me. What frightened me most was the sense of drift, of being pulled along on a current which called itself my destiny, but in which I seemed to be losing touch with whoever I had been, with the girl who had experienced her own will and energy almost ecstatically at times, walking around a city or riding a train at night or typing in a student room. In a poem about my grandmother I wrote (of myself): "A young girl, thought sleeping, is certified dead."[5] I was writing very little, partly from fatigue, that female fatigue of suppressed anger and the loss of contact with her own being; partly from the discontinuity of female life with its attention to small chores, errands, work that others constantly undo, small children's constant needs. What I did write was unconvincing to me; my anger and frustration were hard to acknowledge in or out of poems because in fact I cared a great deal about my husband and my children. Trying to look back and understand that time I have tried to analyze the real nature of the conflict. Most, if not all, human lives are full of fantasy—passive day-dreaming which need not be acted on. But to write poetry or fiction, or even to think well, is not to fantasize, or to put fantasies on paper. For a poem to coalesce, for a character or an action to take shape, there has to be an imaginative transformation of reality which is in no way passive. And a certain freedom of the mind is needed—freedom to press on, to enter the currents of your thought like a glider pilot, knowing that your motion can be sustained, that the buoyancy of your attention will not be suddenly snatched away. Moreover, if the imagination is to transcend and transform experience it has to question, to challenge, to conceive of alternatives, perhaps to the very life you are living at that moment. You have to be free to play around with the notion that day might be night, love might be hate; nothing can be too sacred for the imagination to turn into its opposite or to call experimentally by another name. For writing is re-naming. Now, to be maternally with small children all day in the old way, to be with a man in the old way of marriage, requires a holding-back, a putting-aside of that imaginative activity, and seems to demand instead a kind of conservatism. I want to make it clear that I am *not* saying that in order to write well, or think well, it is necessary to become unavailable to others, or to become a devouring ego. This has been the myth of the masculine artist and thinker; and I repeat, I do not accept it. But to be a female human being trying to fulfill traditional female functions in a traditional way is in direct conflict with the subversive function of the imagination. The word traditional is important here. There must be ways, and we will be finding out more and more about them, in which the energy of creation and the energy of relation can be united. But in those earlier years I always felt the conflict as a failure of love in myself. I had thought I was choosing a full life: the life available to most men, in which sexuality, work, and parenthood could coexist. But I felt, at 29, guilt toward the people closest to me, and guilty toward my own being.

I wanted, then, more than anything, the one thing of which there was never enough: time to think, time to write. The fifties and early sixties were years of rapid revelations: the sit-ins and marches in the South, the Bay of Pigs, the early anti-war movement, raised large questions—questions for which the masculine world of the academy around me seemed to have expert and fluent answers. But I needed desperately to think for myself—about pacifism and dissent and violence, about poetry and society and about my own relationship to all these things. For about ten years I was reading in fierce snatches, scribbling in notebooks, writing poetry in fragments; I was looking desperately for clues, because if there were no clues than I thought I might be insane. I wrote in a notebook about this time:

> Paralyzed by the sense that there exists a mesh of relationships—e.g. between my anger at the children, my sensual life, pacifism, sex, (I mean sex in its broadest significance, not merely sexual desire)—an interconnectedness which, if I could see it, make it valid, would give me back myself, make it possible to function lucidly and passionately. Yet I grope in and out among these dark webs.

I think I began at this point to feel that politics was not something: "out there" but something "in here" and of the essence of my condition.

In the late '50's I was able to write, for the first time, directly about experiencing myself as a woman. The poem was jotted in fragments during children's naps, brief hours in a library, or at 3 a.m. after rising with a wakeful child. I despaired of doing any continuous work at this time. Yet I began to feel that my fragments and scraps had a common consciousness and a common theme, one which I would have been very unwilling to put on paper at an earlier time because I had been taught that poetry should be "universal," which meant, of course, non-female. Until then I had tried very much *not* to identify myself as a female poet. Over two years I wrote a 10-part poem called "Snapshots of a Daughter-in-Law," in a longer, looser mode than I'd ever trusted myself with before. It was an extraordinary relief to write that poem. It strikes me now as too literary, too dependent on allusion; I hadn't found the courage yet to do without authorities, or even to use the pronoun "I"—the woman in the poem is always "she." One section of it, No. 2, concerns a woman who thinks she is going mad; she is haunted by voices telling her to resist and rebel, voices which she can hear but not obey.

The poem "Orion," written five years later, is a poem of reconnection with a part of myself I had felt I was losing—the active principle, the energetic imagination, the "half-brother" whom I projected, as I had for many years, into the constellation Orion. It's no accident that the words "cold and egotistical" appear in this poem, and are applied to myself. The choice still seemed to be between "love"—womanly, maternal love, altruistic love—a love defined and ruled by the weight of an entire culture; and egotism—a force directed by men into creation, achievement, ambition, often at the expense of others, but justifiably so. For weren't they men, and wasn't that their destiny as womanly love was ours? I know now that the alternatives are false ones-that the word "love" is itself in need of re-vision.

There is a companion poem to "Orion," written three years later, in which at last the woman in the poem and the woman writing the poem become the same person. It is called "Planetarium," and it was written after a visit to a real planetarium, where I read an account of the work of Caroline Herschel, the astronomer, who worked with her brother William, but whose name remained obscure, as his did not.

In closing I want to tell you about a dream I had last summer. I dreamed I was asked to read my poetry at a mass women's meeting, but when I began to read, what came out were the lyrics of a blues song. I share this dream with you because it seemed to me to say a lot about the problems and the future of the woman writer, and probably of women in general. The awakening of consciousness is not like the crossing of a frontier—one step, and you are in another country. Much of woman's poetry has been of the nature of the blues song: a cry of pain, of victimization, or a lyric of seduction. And today, much poetry by women—and prose for that matter—is charged with anger. I think we need to go through that anger, and we will betray our own reality if we try, as Virginia Woolf was trying, for an objectivity, a detachment, that would make us sound more like Jane Austen or Shakespeare. We know more than Jane Austen or Shakespeare knew: more than Jane Austen because our lives are more complex, more than Shakespeare because we know more about the lives of women, Jane Austen and Virginia Woolf included.

Both the victimization and the anger experienced by women are real, and have real sources, everywhere in the environment, built into society. They must go on being tapped and explored by poets, among others. We can neither deny them, nor can we rest there. They are our birth-pains, and we are bearing ourselves. We would be failing each other as writers and as women, if we neglected or denied what is negative, regressive, or Sisyphean in our inwardness.

We all know that there is another story to be told. I am curious and expectant about the future of the masculine consciousness. I feel in the work of the men whose poetry I read today a deep pessimism and fatalistic grief; and I wonder if it isn't the masculine side of what women have experienced, the price of masculine dominance. One thing I am sure of: just as woman is becoming her own mid-wife, creating herself anew, so man will have to learn to gestate and give birth to his own subjectivity—something he has frequently wanted woman to do for him. We can go on trying to talk to each other, we can sometimes help each other, poetry and fiction can show us what the other is going through; but women can no longer be primarily mothers and muses for men: we have our own work cut out for us.

THE LOSER

A man thinks of the woman he once loved: first, after her wedding, and then nearly a decade later.

I
I kissed you, bride and lost, and went
home from that bourgeois sacrament,
your cheek still tasting cold upon
my lips that gave you benison
with all the swagger that they knew—
as losers somehow learn to do.
Your wedding made my eyes ache; soon
the world would be worse off for one
more golden apple dropped to ground
without the least protesting sound,

and you would windfall lie, and we
forget your shimmer on the tree.

Beauty is always wasted: if
not Mignon's song sung to the deaf,
at all events to the unmoved.
A face like yours cannot be loved
long or seriously enough.
Almost, we seem to hold it off.

II
Well, you are tougher than I thought.
Now when the wash with ice hangs taut
this morning of St. Valentine,
I see you strip the squeaking line,
your body weighed against the load,
and all my groans can do no good.

Because you are still beautiful,
though squared and stiffened by the pull
of what nine windy years have done.
You have three daughters, lost a son.
I see all your intelligence
flung into that unwearied stance.

My entry is of no avail.
I turn my head and wish him well
who chafed your beauty into use
and lives forever in a house
lit by the friction of your mind.
You stagger in against the wind.

ADRIENNE RICH 1958[6]

ORION

Far back when I went zig-zagging
through tamarack pastures
you were my genius, you
my cast-iron Viking, my helmed
lion-heart king in prison.
Years later now you're young

my fierce half-brother, staring
down from that simplified west
your breast open, your belt dragged down
by an oldfashioned thing, a sword
the last bravado you won't give over
though it weighs you down as you stride

and the stars in it are dim
and maybe have stopped burning.
But you burn, and I know it;
as I throw back my head to take you in
an old transfusion happens again:
divine astronomy is nothing to it.

Indoors I bruise and blunder,
break faith, leave ill enough
alone, a dead child born in the dark.
Night cracks up over the chimney,
pieces of time, frozen geodes
come showering down in the grate.

A man reaches behind my eyes
and finds them empty
a woman's head turns away
from my head in the mirror
children are dying my death
and eating crumbs of my life.

Pity is not your forte.
Calmly you ache up there
pinned aloft in your crow's nest,
my speechless pirate!
You take it all for granted
 and when I look you back

it's with a starlike eye
shooting its cold and egotistical spear
where it can do least damage.
Breathe deep! No hurt, no pardon
out here in the cold with you
you with your back to the wall.

ADRIENNE RICH 1965[7]

SNAPSHOTS OF A DAUGHTER-IN-LAW

2.
Banging the coffee-pot into the sink
she hears the angels chiding, and looks out
past the raked gardens to the sloppy sky.
Only a week since They said: *Have no patience.*

The next time it was: *Be insatiable.*
Then: *Save yourself; others you cannot save.*
Sometimes she's let the tapstream scald her arm,
a match burn to her thumbnail,

or held her hand above the kettle's snout
right in the woolly steam. They are probably angels,
since nothing hurts her anymore, except
each morning's grit blowing into her eyes.

ADRIENNE RICH 1958–1960[8]

PLANETARIUM

(Thinking of Caroline Herschel, 1750–1848, astronomer, sister of William; and others)

A woman in the shape of a monster
a monster in the shape of a woman
the skies are full of them

a woman   'in the snow
among the Clocks and instruments
or measuring the ground with poles'

in her 98 years to discover
8 comets

she whom the moon ruled
like us
levitating into the night sky
riding the polished lenses

Galaxies of women, there
doing penance for impetuousness

ribs chilled
in those spaces   of the mind

An eye,
  'virile, precise and absolutely certain'
  from the mad webs of Uranisborg

       encountering the NOVA

every impulse of light exploding
from the core
as life flies out of us

  Tycho whispering at last
  'Let me not seem to have lived in vain'

What we see, we see
and seeing is changing

the light that shrivels a mountain
and leaves a man alive

Heartbeat of the pulsar
heart sweating through my body

The radio impulse
pouring in from Taurus

  I am bombarded yet   I stand

I have been standing all my life in the
direct path of a battery of signals
the most accurately transmitted most
untranslateable language in the universe
I am a galactic cloud so deep   so involuted
that a light wave could take 15
years to travel through me   And has
taken   I am an instrument in the shape
of a woman trying to translate pulsations
into images   for the relief of the body
and the reconstruction of the mind.

      ADRIENNE RICH 1968[9]

Notes

1. G. B. Shaw, *The Quintessence of Ibsenism* (Hill and Wang, 1922), p. 139.
2. J. G. Stewart, *Jane Ellen Harrison: A Portrait from Letters* (London, 1959), p. 140.
3. Henry James, "Notes on Novelists" in *Selected Literary Criticism of Henry James*, ed. Morris Shapira (London: Heineman, 1963), pp. 157–58.
4. Adrienne Rich, *A Change of World* (Yale University Press, 1951). Quoted by permission of the author.
5. "Halfway," in *Necessities of Life* (W. W. Norton and Company, 1966), p. 34.
6. *Snapshots of a Daughter-in-Law: Poems, 1954–1962.* Copyright © 1956, 1957, 1958, 1959, 1960, 1961, 1962, 1963, 1967 by Adrienne Rich Conrad. Reprinted by permission of W. W. Norton and Company, Inc.
7. *Leaflets: Poems, 1965–1968.* Copyright © 1969 by W. W. Norton and Company, Inc. Reprinted by permission of W. W. Norton and Company, Inc.
8. *Snapshots of a Daughter-in-Law* (see note 6).
9. *The Will to Change: Poems, 1968–1970.* Copyright © by W. W. Norton and Company, Inc. Reprinted by permission of W. W. Norton and Company, Inc.

Revision Strategies of Student Writers and Experienced Adult Writers

27

Nancy Sommers

Nancy Sommers, formerly Director of Composition at the University of Oklahoma, is now Adjunct Assistant Professor at New York University. She has taught writing at Boston University, the Harvard Graduate School of Business Administration, and the Polaroid Corporation. An NCTE Promising Researcher for her studies of the processes of revising, she is writing a research monograph on revision.

Although various aspects of the writing process have been studied extensively of late, research on revision has been notably absent. The reason for this, I suspect, is that current models of the writing process have directed attention away from revision. With few exceptions, these models are linear; they separate the writing process into discrete stages. Two representative models are Gordon Rohman's suggestion that the composing process moves from prewriting to writing to rewriting and James Britton's model of the writing process as a series of stages described in metaphors of linear growth, conception—incubation—production.[1] What is striking about these theories of writing is that they model themselves on speech: Rohman defines the writer in a way that cannot distinguish him from a speaker ("A writer is a man who . . . puts [his] experience into words in his own mind"—p. 15); and Britton bases his theory of writing on what he calls (following Jakobson) the "expressiveness" of speech.[2] Moreover, Britton's study itself follows the "linear model" of the relation of thought and language in speech proposed by Vygotsky, a relationship embodied in the linear movement "from the motive which engenders a thought to the shaping of the thought, *first* in inner speech, *then* in meanings of words, and *finally* in words" (quoted in Britton, p. 40). What this movement fails to take into account in its linear structure—"first . . . then . . . finally"—is the recursive shaping of thought by language; what it fails to take into account is *revision*. In these linear conceptions of the writing process revision is understood as a separate stage at the end of the process—a stage that comes after the completion of a first or second draft and one that is temporally distinct from the prewriting and writing stages of the process.[3]

The linear model bases itself on speech in two specific ways. First of all, it is based on traditional rhetorical models, models that were created to serve the spoken art of oratory. In whatever ways the parts of classical rhetoric are described, they offer "stages" of composition that are repeated in contemporary models of the writing process. Edward Corbett, for instance, describes the "five parts of a discourse"—*inventio, dispositio, elocutio, memoria, pronuntiatio*—and, disregarding the last two parts since "after rhetoric came to be concerned mainly with written discourse, there was no further need to deal with them,"[4] he produces a model very close to Britton's conception [*inventio*], incubation [*dispositio*], production [*elocutio*]. Other rhetorics also follow this procedure, and they do so not simply because of historical accident. Rather, the process represented in the linear model is based on the irreversibility of speech. Speech, Roland Barthes says, "is irreversible":

> "A word cannot be retracted, except precisely by saying that one retracts it. To cross out here is to add: if I want to erase what I have just said, I cannot do it without showing the eraser itself (I must say: '*or rather. . .*' '*I expressed myself badly. . .*'); paradoxically, it is ephemeral speech which is indelible, not monumental writing. All that one can do in the case of a spoken utterance is to tack on another utterance."[5]

What is impossible in speech is *revision*: like the example Barthes gives, revision in speech is an afterthought. In the same way, each stage of the linear model must be exclusive (distinct from the other stages) or else it becomes trivial and counterproductive to refer to these junctures as "stages."

By staging revision after enunciation, the linear models reduce revision in writing, as in speech, to no more than an afterthought. In this way such models make the study of revision impossible. Revision, in Rohman's model, is simply the repetition of writing; or to pursue Britton's organic metaphor, revision is simply the further growth of what is already there, the "pre-conceived" product. The absence of research on revision, then, is a function of a theory of writing which makes revision both superfluous and redundant, a theory which does not distinguish between writing and speech.

What the linear models do produce is a parody of writing. Isolating revision and then disregarding it plays havoc with the experiences composition teachers have of the actual writing and rewriting of experienced writers. Why should the linear model be preferred? Why should revision be forgotten, superfluous? Why do teachers offer the linear model and students accept it? One reason, Barthes suggests, is that "there is a fundamental tie between teaching and speech," while "writing begins at the point where speech becomes *impossible*."[6] The spoken word cannot be revised. The possibility of revision distinguishes the written text from speech. In fact, according to Barthes, this is the essential difference between writing and speaking. When we must revise, when the very idea is subject to recursive shaping by language, then speech becomes inadequate. This is a matter to which I will return, but first we should examine, theoretically, a detailed exploration of what student writers as distinguished from experienced adult writers *do* when they write and rewrite their work. Dissatisfied with both the linear model of writing and the lack of attention to the process of revision, I conducted a series of studies over the past three years which examined the revision processes of student writers and experienced writers to see what role revision played in their writing processes. In the course of my work the revision process was redefined as *a sequence of changes in a composition—changes which are initiated by cues and occur continually throughout the writing of a work.*

Methodology

I used a case study approach. The student writers were twenty freshmen at Boston University and the University of Oklahoma with SAT verbal scores ranging from 450–600 in their first semester of composition. The twenty experienced adult writers from Boston and Oklahoma City included journalists, editors, and academics. To refer to the two groups, I use the terms *student writers* and *experienced writers* because the principal difference between these two groups is the amount of experience they have had in writing.

Each writer wrote three essays, expressive, explanatory, and persuasive, and rewrote each essay twice, producing nine written products in draft and final form. Each writer was interviewed three times after the final revision of each essay. And each writer suggested revisions for a composition written by an anonymous author. Thus extensive written and spoken documents were obtained from each writer.

The essays were analyzed by counting and categorizing the changes made. Four revision operations were identified: deletion, substitution, addition, and reordering. And four levels of changes were identified: word, phrase, sentence, theme (the extended statement of one idea). A coding system was developed for identifying the frequency of revision by level and operation. In addition, transcripts of the interviews in which the writers interpreted their revisions were used to develop what was called a *scale of concerns* for each writer. This scale enabled me to codify what were the writer's primary concerns, secondary concerns, tertiary concerns, and whether the writers used the same scale of concerns when revising the second or third drafts as they used in revising the first draft.

Revision Strategies of Student Writers

Most of the students I studied did not use the terms *revision* or *rewriting*. In fact, they did not seem comfortable using the word *revision* and explained that revision was not a word they used, but the word their teachers used. Instead, most of the students had developed various functional terms to describe the type of changes they made. The following are samples of these definitions:

> *Scratch Out and Do Over Again:* "I say scratch out and do over, and that means what it says. Scratching out and cutting out. I read what I have written and I cross out a word and put another word in; a more decent word or a better word. Then if there is somewhere to use a sentence that I have crossed out, I will put it there."

Reviewing: "Reviewing means just using better words and eliminating words that are not needed. I go over and change words around."

Reviewing: "I just review every word and make sure that everything is worded right. I see if I am rambling; I see if I can put a better word in or leave one out. Usually when I read what I have written, I say to myself, 'that word is so bland or so trite,' and then I go and get my thesaurus."

Redoing: "Redoing means cleaning up the paper and crossing out. It is looking at something and saying, no that has to go, or no, that is not right."

Marking Out: "I don't use the word rewriting because I only write one draft and the changes that I make are made on top of the draft. The changes that I make are usually just marking out words and putting different ones in."

Slashing and Throwing Out: "I throw things out and say they are not good. I like to write like Fitzgerald did by inspiration, and if I feel inspired then I don't need to slash and throw much out."

The predominant concern in these definitions is vocabulary. The students understand the revision process as a rewording activity. They do so because they perceive words as the unit of written discourse. That is, they concentrate on particular words apart from their role in the text. Thus one student quoted above thinks in terms of dictionaries, and, following the eighteenth century theory of words parodied in *Gulliver's Travels*, he imagines a load of things carried about to be exchanged. Lexical changes are the major revision activities of the students because economy is their goal. They are governed, like the linear model itself, by the Law of Occam's razor that prohibits logically needless repetition: redundancy and superfluity. Nothing governs speech more than such superfluities; speech constantly repeats itself precisely because spoken words, as Barthes writes, are expendable in the cause of communication. The aim of revision according to the students' own description is therefore to clean up speech; the redundancy of speech is unnecessary in writing, their logic suggests, because writing, unlike speech, can be reread. Thus one student said, "Redoing means cleaning up the paper and crossing out." The remarkable contradiction of cleaning by marking might, indeed, stand for student revision as I have encountered it.

The students place a symbolic importance on their selection and rejection of words as the determiners of success or failure for their compositions. When revising, they primarily ask themselves: can I find a better word or phrase? A more impressive, not so cliched, or less hum-drum word? Am I repeating the same word or phrase too often? They approach the revision process with what could be labeled as a "thesaurus philosophy of writing"; the students consider the thesaurus a harvest of lexical substitutions and believe that most problems in their essays can be solved by rewording. What is revealed in the students' use of the thesaurus is a governing attitude toward their writing: that the meaning to be communicated is already there, already finished, already produced, ready to be communicated, and all that is necessary is a better word "rightly worded." One student defined revision as "redoing"; "redoing" meant "just using better words and eliminating words that are not needed." For the students, writing is translating: the thought to the page, the language of speech to the more formal language of prose, the word to its synonym. Whatever is translated, an original text already exists for students, one which need not be discovered or acted upon, but simply communicated.[7]

The students list repetition as one of the elements they most worry about. This cue signals to them that they need to eliminate the repetition either by substituting or deleting words or phrases. Repetition occurs, in large part, because student writing imitates—transcribes—speech: attention to repetitious words is a manner of cleaning speech. Without a sense of the developmental possibilities of revision (and writing in general) students seek, on the authority of many textbooks, simply to clean up their language and prepare to type. What is curious, however, is that students are aware of lexical repetition, but not conceptual repetition. They only notice the repetition if they can "hear" it; they do not diagnose lexical repetition as symptomatic of problems on a deeper level. By rewording their sentences to avoid the lexical repetition, the students solve the immediate problem, but blind themselves to problems on a textual level; although they are using different words, they are sometimes merely restating the same idea with different words. Such blindness, as I discovered with student writers, is the inability to "see" revision as a process: the inability to "review" their work again, as it were, with different eyes, and to start over.

The revision strategies described above are consistent with the students' understanding of the revision process as requiring lexical changes but not semantic changes. For the students, the extent to which they revise is a function of their level of inspiration. In fact, they use the word *inspiration* to describe the ease or difficulty with which their essay is written, and the extent to which the essay needs to be revised. If students feel inspired, if the writing comes easily, and if they don't get stuck on individual words or phrases, then they say that they cannot see any reason to revise. Because students do not see revision as an activity in which they modify and develop perspectives and ideas, they feel that if they know what they want to say, then there is little reason for making revisions.

The only modification of ideas in the students' essays occurred when they tried out two or three introductory paragraphs. This results, in part, because the students have been taught in another version of the linear model of composing to use a thesis statement as a controlling device in their introductory paragraphs. Since they write their introductions and their thesis statements even before they have really discovered what they want to say, their early close attention to the thesis statement, and more generally the linear model, function to restrict and circumscribe not only the development of their ideas, but also their ability to change the direction of these ideas.

Too often as composition teachers we conclude that students do not willingly revise. The evidence from my research suggests that it is not that students are unwilling to revise, but rather that they do what they have been taught to do in a consistently narrow and predictable way. On every occasion when I asked students why they hadn't made any more changes, they essentially replied, "I knew something larger was wrong, but I didn't think it would help to move words around." The students have strategies for handling words and phrases and their strategies helped them on a word or sentence level. What they lack, however, is a set of strategies to help them identify the "something larger" that they sensed was wrong and work from there. The students do not have strategies for handling the whole essay. They lack procedures or heuristics to help them reorder lines of reasoning or ask questions about their purposes and readers. The students view their compositions in a linear way as a series of parts. Even such potentially useful concepts as "unity" or "form" are reduced to the rule that a composition, if it is to have form, must have an introduction, a body, and a conclusion, or the sum total of the necessary parts.

The students decide to stop revising when they decide that they have not violated any of the rules for revising. These rules, such as "Never begin a sentence with a conjunction" or "Never end a sentence with a preposition," are lexically cued and rigidly applied. In general, students will subordinate the demands of the specific problems of their text to the demands of the rules. Changes are made in compliance with abstract rules about the product, rules that quite often do not apply to the specific problems in the text. These revision strategies are teacher-based, directed towards a teacher-reader who expects compliance with rules—with pre-existing "conceptions"—and who will only examine parts of the composition (writing comments about those parts in the margins of their essays) and will cite any violations of rules in those parts. At best the students see their writing altogether passively through the eyes of former teachers or their surrogates, the textbooks, and are bound to the rules which they have been taught.

Revision Strategies of Experienced Writers

One aim of my research has been to contrast how student writers define revision with how a group of experienced writers define their revision processes. Here is a sampling of the definitions from the experienced writers:

Rewriting: "It is a matter of looking at the kernel of what I have written, the content, and then thinking about it, responding to it, making decisions, and actually restructuring it."

Rewriting: "I rewrite as I write. It is hard to tell what is a first draft because it is not determined by time. In one draft, I might cross out three pages, write two, cross out a fourth, rewrite it, and call it a draft. I am constantly writing and rewriting. I can only conceptualize so much in my first draft—only so much information can be held in my head at one time; my rewriting efforts are a reflection of how much information I can encompass at one time. There are levels and agenda which I have to attend to in each draft."

Rewriting: "Rewriting means on one level, finding the argument, and on another level, language changes to make the argument more effective. Most of the time I feel as if I can go on rewriting forever. There is always one part of a piece that I could keep working on. It is always difficult to know at what point to abandon a piece of writing. I like this idea that a piece of writing is never finished, just abandoned."

Rewriting: "My first draft is usually very scattered. In rewriting, I find the line of argument. After the argument is resolved, I am much more interested in word choice and phrasing."

Revising: "My cardinal rule in revising is never to fall in love with what I have written in a first or second draft. An idea, sentence, or even a phrase that looks catchy, I don't trust. Part of this idea is to wait a while. I am much more in love with something after I have written it than I am a day or two later. It is much easier to change anything with time."

Revising: "It means taking apart what I have written and putting it back together again. I ask major theoretical questions of my ideas, respond to those questions, and think of proportion and structure, and try to find a controlling metaphor. I find out which ideas can be developed and which should be dropped. I am constantly chiseling and changing as I revise."

The experienced writers describe their primary objective when revising as finding the form or shape of their argument. Although the metaphors vary, the experienced writers often use structural expressions such as "finding a framework," "a pattern," or "a design" for their argument. When questioned about this emphasis, the experienced writers responded that since their first drafts are usually scattered attempts to define their territory, their objective in the second draft is to begin observing general patterns of development and deciding what should be included and what excluded. One writer explained, "I have learned from experience that I need to keep writing a first draft until I figure out what I want to say. Then in a second draft, I begin to see the structure of an argument and how all the various sub-arguments which are buried beneath the surface of all those sentences are related." What is described here is a process in which the writer is both agent and vehicle. "Writing," says Barthes, unlike speech, "develops like a seed, not a line,"[8] and like a seed it confuses beginning and end, conception and production. Thus, the experienced writers say their drafts are "not determined by time," that rewriting is a "constant process," that they feel as if (they) "can go on forever." Revising confuses the beginning and end, the agent and vehicle; it confuses, *in order to find*, the line of argument.

After a concern for form, the experienced writers have a second objective: a concern for their readership. In this way, "production" precedes "conception." The experienced writers imagine a reader (reading their product) whose existence and whose expectations influence their revision process. They have abstracted the standards of a reader and this reader seems to be partially a reflection of themselves and functions as a critical and productive collaborator—a collaborator who has yet to love their work. The anticipation of a reader's judgment causes a feeling of dissonance when the writer recognizes incongruities between intention and execution, and requires these writers to make revisions on all levels. Such a reader gives them just what the students lacked: new eyes to "review" their work. The experienced writers believe that they have learned the causes and conditions, the product, which will influence their reader, and their revision strategies are geared towards creating these causes and conditions. They demonstrate a complex understanding of which examples, sentences, or phrases should be included or excluded. For example, one experienced writer decided to delete public examples and add private examples when writing about the energy crisis because "private examples would be less controversial and thus more persuasive." Another writer revised his transitional sentences because "some kinds of transitions are more easily recognized as transitions than others." These examples represent the type of strategic attempts these experienced writers use to manipulate the conventions of discourse in order to communicate to their reader.

But these revision strategies are a process of more than communication; they are part of the process of *discovering meaning* altogether. Here we can see the importance of dissonance; at the heart of revision is the process by which writers recognize and resolve the dissonance they sense in their writing. Ferdinand de Saussure has argued that meaning is differential or "diacritical," based on differences between terms rather than "essential" or inherent qualities of terms. "Phonemes," he said, "are characterized not, as one might think, by their own positive quality but simply by the fact that they are distinct."[9] In fact, Saussure bases his entire *Course in General Linguistics* on these differences, and such differences are dissonant; like musical dissonances which gain their significance from their relationship to the "key" of the composition which itself is determined by the whole language, specific language (parole) gains its meaning from the system of language (langue) of which it is a manifestation and part. The musical composition—a "composition" of parts—creates its "key" as in an overall structure which determines the value (meaning) of its parts. The analogy with music is readily seen in the compositions of experienced writers: both sorts of composition are based precisely on those structures experienced writers seek in their writing. It is this complicated relationship between the parts and the whole in the work of experienced writers which destroys the linear model; writing cannot develop "like a line" because each addition or deletion is a reordering of the whole. Explicating Saussure, Jonathan Culler asserts that "meaning depends on difference of meaning."[10] But student writers constantly struggle to bring their essays into congruence with a predefined meaning. The experienced writers do the opposite: they seek to discover (to create) meaning in the engagement with their writing, in revision. They seek to emphasize and exploit the lack of clarity, the differences of meaning, the dissonance, that writing as opposed to speech allows in the possibility of revision. Writing has spatial and temporal features not apparent in speech—words are recorded in space and fixed in time—which is why writing is susceptible to reordering and later addition. Such features make possible the dissonance that both provokes revision and promises, from itself, new meaning.

For the experienced writers the heaviest concentration of changes is on the sentence level, and the changes are predominantly by addition and deletion. But, unlike the students, experienced writers make changes on all levels and use all revision operations. Moreover, the operations the students fail to use—reordering and addition—seem to require a theory of the revision process as a totality—a theory which, in fact, encompasses the *whole* of the composition. Unlike the students, the experienced writers possess a non-linear theory in which a sense of the whole writing both precedes and grows out of an examination of the parts. As we saw, one writer said he needed "a first draft to figure out what to say," and "a second draft to see the structure of an argument buried beneath the surface." Such a "theory" is both theoretical and strategical; once again, strategy and theory are conflated in ways that are literally impossible for the linear model. Writing appears to be more like a seed than a line.

Two elements of the experienced writers' theory of the revision process are the adoption of a holistic perspective and the perception that revision is a recursive process. The writers ask: what does my essay as a *whole* need for form, balance, rhythm, or communication. Details are added, dropped, substituted, or reordered according to their sense of what the essay needs for emphasis and proportion. This sense, however, is constantly in flux as ideas are developed and modified; it is constantly "reviewed" in relation to the parts. As their ideas change, revision becomes an attempt to make their writing consonant with that changing vision.

The experienced writers see their revision process as a recursive process—a process with significant recurring activities—with different levels of attention and different agenda for each cycle. During the first revision cycle their attention is primarily directed towards narrowing the topic and delimiting their ideas. At this point, they are not as concerned as they are later about vocabulary and style. The experienced writers explained that they get closer to their meaning by not limiting themselves too early to lexical concerns. As one writer commented to explain her revision process, a comment inspired by the summer 1977 New York power failure: "I feel like Con Edison cutting off certain states to keep the generators going. In first and second drafts, I try to cut off as much as I can of my editing generator, and in a third draft, I try to cut off some of my idea generators, so I can make sure that I will actually finish the essay." Although the experienced writers describe their revision process as a series of different levels or cycles, it is inaccurate to assume that they have only one objective for each cycle and that each cycle can be defined by a different objective. The same objectives and sub-processes are present in each cycle, but in different proportions. Even though these experienced writers place the predominant weight upon finding the form of their argument during the first cycle, other concerns exist as well. Conversely, during the later cycles, when the experienced writers' primary attention is focused upon stylistic concerns, they are still attuned, although in a reduced way, to the form of the argument. Since writers are limited in what they can attend to during each cycle (understandings are temporal), revision strategies help balance competing demands on attention. Thus, writers can concentrate on more than one objective at a time by developing strategies to sort out and organize their different concerns in successive cycles of revision.

It is a sense of writing as discovery—a repeated process of beginning over again, starting out new—that the students failed to have. I have used the notion of dissonance because such dissonance, the incongruities between intention and execution, governs both writing and meaning. Students do not see the incongruities. They need to rely on their own internalized sense of good writing and to see their writing with their "own" eyes. Seeing in revision—seeing beyond hearing—is at the root of the word *revision* and the process itself; current dicta on revising blind our students to what is actually involved in revision. In fact, they blind them to what constitutes good writing altogether. Good writing disturbs: it creates dissonance. Students need to seek the dissonance of discovery, utilizing in their writing, as the experienced writers do, the very difference between writing and speech—the possibility of revision.

Acknowledgment

The author wishes to express her gratitude to Professor William Smith, University of Pittsburgh, for his vital assistance with the research reported in this article and to Patrick Hays, her husband, for extensive discussions and critical editorial help.

Notes

1. D. Gordon Rohman and Albert O. Wlecke, "Pre-writing: The Construction and Application of Models for Concept Formation in Writing," Cooperative Research Project No. 2174, U.S. Office of Education, Department of Health, Education, and Welfare; James Britton, Anthony Burgess, Nancy Martin, Alex McLeod, Harold Rosen, *The Development of Writing Abilities (11–18)* (London: Macmillan Education, 1975).

2. Britton is following Roman Jakobson, "Linguistics and Poetics," in T. A. Sebeok, *Style in Language* (Cambridge, Mass: MIT Press, 1960).

3. For an extended discussion of this issue see Nancy Sommers, "The Need for Theory in Composition Research," *College Composition and Communication,* 30 (February, 1979), 46–49.

4. *Classical Rhetoric for the Modern Student* (New York: Oxford University Press, 1965), p. 27.

5. Roland Barthes, "Writers, Intellectuals, Teachers," in *Image-Music-Text,* trans. Stephen Heath (New York: Hill and Wang, 1977), pp. 190–191.

6. "Writers, Intellectuals, Teachers," p. 190.

7. Nancy Sommers and Ronald Schleifer, "Means and Ends: Some Assumptions of Student Writers," *Composition and Teaching,* II (in press).

8. *Writing Degree Zero in Writing Degree Zero and Elements of Semiology,* trans. Annette Lavers and Colin Smith (New York: Hill and Wang, 1968), p. 20.

9. *Course in General Linguistics,* trans. Wade Baskin (New York, 1966), p. 119.

10. Jonathan Culler, *Saussure* (Penguin Modern Masters Series; London: Penguin Books, 1976), p. 70.

Thirteen (Lucky!) Strategies for Revision

Academic Writing Program, University of Maryland, 2014

"The beautiful part of writing is that you don't have to get it right the first time, unlike, say, a brain surgeon."

—Robert Cormier

1. Synthesize your feedback from the entire semester.

Gather all the essays you wrote over the course of the semester. Be sure to collect the versions that have your teacher's and peers' comments on them. Take time to read through all of the feedback you got from peers and your teacher, looking for patterns. What keeps popping up? What's consistently strong and what do you consistently need to improve? What issues keep appearing? Make a list of the recurrent themes or issues. You can take time to address each of these issues when you revise.

2. Write a reverse outline of your essay.

- Re-read the essay you plan to revise.
- In the margins of your essay, jot down a one-sentence summary of each paragraph.
- On a separate page, compose a "reverse" outline of your essay by listing the (one-sentence) primary argument for each paragraph.
- Read your reverse outline. As you do so, answer the following: where are ideas out of place? What can you rearrange? Where do your ideas flow logically and where is there a gap in logic? Where do your ideas seem connected and/or disconnected? What seems to be extraneous information that you can omit? Where do you need new material?
- Based on your reverse outline, make a plan for how you can reorganize your essay, what you can omit, what you can expand, etc.
- See "Rewriting" (Joseph Harris, in this collection) for more details on how to compose a reverse outline.

3. Write a plan of action.

Before jumping into your revision, write a plan of action. Include the three main elements or issues you plan to tackle. This might include adding a new section with additional research, starting the conclusion from scratch, or re-writing all of your topic sentences to match your new thesis. Having a pre-determined plan of action will help keep you on track as you try to make substantive revisions.

4. Start a new document file for the revision.

Instead of revising your essay in the same MS Word document, click "Save As" and start a new document. Give it a new title with a draft number and/or date (such as InquiryEssay2 or PositionPaper-11.1.13). This may sound obvious, but saving into a new document will enable you to delete text, copy/paste and make major changes without losing your original work. It is easier to make substantive revisions when you have multiple (similar) versions of your essay saved with different titles.

5. Find a new reader for your essay, one that is NOT in your class.

A new reader can read the essay with fresh eyes, interests, and questions. Think of asking your sibling, friend, roommate, parent, grandparent, colleague, etc., to read your essay. People who aren't in your class sometimes give better feedback about what's missing and what works/doesn't based on their sense of the piece as a whole.

6. Revisit the stases.

Go back to stasis theory. Ask yourself: can I approach this topic and essay more effectively if I argue or inquire in a different stasis? If your first draft argues or inquires in the value stasis, for example, you might try to approach the issue through cause/effect. If you argue about the actions that should be taken to address an issue, you might consider the definition stasis. Think about where the real controversy in your issue lies. How might changing the stasis strengthen your argument or refocus your entire essay?

7. Play "What If."

Review the essay that you plan to revise with the question "what if" in mind. Here are the types of questions you might ask of yourself and your writing:

- What if my conclusion became my introduction?
- What if I made this point my central claim?
- What if I used this source instead of another?
- What if I offered my experience in this way instead of that way?

As you explore these what if questions, you should also consider how the changes would then affect the rest of the essay.

8. Work on thesis and support away from the essay.

Rather than working on the essay itself, focus your attention solely on your thesis statement or central inquiry question. Write your thesis or central question in a new document or on a separate paper. Focusing only on that thesis or question, consider the following: given the stated thesis, what does my audience expect to learn? What is interesting or exciting to me about my thesis? How might I make this more specific? Does this thesis have a worthy counterargument or not? How might I rewrite or reconsider the thesis statement in light of what I have learned since writing the original essay?

9. Identify what's "good" and what you want to keep.

Free-write about what is essentially "good" about your paper. What is it that you want to preserve or save? This may be a central idea or point that forms the "heartbeat" of the paper, or it may be specific passages of text that form a foundation. It's important to know what's worth saving before you start changing things up. Furthermore, identifying this "good" part might also enable you to envision new and better supporting claims or see that the central point of the essay could shift from the previous idea to this new "good" idea. It also makes it easier to delete entire paragraphs or passages, which can be an important part of revision.

10. Return to research and source use.

Now that you are more experienced researchers, can you return to the way that you chose, interpreted, and "forwarded" (to use Joseph Harris's term) your sources? Did you give ample credit when due? Do you need to differentiate more between your ideas and the ideas of others? Is there better evidence, after your extensive research, to support your central question or argument? Are there places where you could do more research and find better sources?

11. Radically rearrange your paper.

Break out the scissors and tape. Cut apart your draft into paragraphs or chunks and tape them back together in a new order. Re-label sections and craft new transitions between them. Consider what happens to the essay if a different part of the essay becomes the introduction—what now needs to go? What could stay? How would this material that remains need to be reframed?

12. Summarize and revise.

Write a one-paragraph summary or abstract of your paper. Then, consider these questions: What's included in the summary? What's left out? After composing your summary and considering your abstract, turn back to your paper and consider what you should keep, emphasize, take out, or restructure to make the argument clearer or more effective.

13. What else? What's next?

Consider the question, what else could happen in this paper? What else could you say about this subject or in support of this argument? Also consider the question, what's next? What's the next level or stage for this paper and how might you take it there?

Reflective Writing and the Revision Process: What Were You Thinking?

29

Sandra L. Giles

"Reflection" and "reflective writing" are umbrella terms that refer to any activity that asks you to think about your own thinking.* As composition scholars Kathleen Blake Yancey and Jane Bowman Smith explain, reflection records a "student's process of thinking about what she or he is doing while in the process of that doing" (170). In a writing class, you may be asked to think about your writing processes in general or in relation to a particular essay, to think about your intentions regarding rhetorical elements such as audience and purpose, or to think about your choices regarding development strategies such as comparison-contrast, exemplification, or definition. You may be asked to describe your decisions regarding language features such as word choice, sentence rhythm, and so on. You may be asked to evaluate or assess your piece of writing or your development as a writer in general. Your instructor may also ask you to perform these kinds of activities at various points in your process of working on a project, or at the end of the semester.

A Writer's Experience

The first time I had to perform reflective writing myself was in the summer of 2002. And it did feel like a performance, at first. I was a doctoral student in Wendy Bishop's Life Writing class at Florida State University, and it was the first class I had ever taken where we English majors actually practiced what we preached; which is to say, we actually put ourselves through the various elements of process writing. Bishop led us through invention exercises, revision exercises, language activities, and yes, reflective writings. For each essay, we had to write what she called a "process note" in which we explained our processes of working on the essay, as well as our thought processes in developing the ideas. We also discussed what we might want to do with (or to) the essay in the future, beyond the class. At the end of the semester, we composed a self-evaluative cover letter for our portfolio in which we discussed each of our essays from the semester and recorded our learning and insights about writing and about the genre of nonfiction.

My first process note for the class was a misguided attempt at good-student-gives-the-teacher-what-she-wants. Our assignment had been to attend an event in town and write about it. I had seen an email announcement about a medium visiting from England who would perform a "reading" at the Unity Church in town. So I went and took notes. And wrote two consecutive drafts. After peer workshop, a third. And then I had to write the process note, the likes of which I had never done before. It felt awkward, senseless. Worse than writing a scholarship application or some other mundane writing task. Like a waste of time, and like it wasn't real writing at all. But it was required.

So, hoop-jumper that I was, I wrote the following: "This will eventually be part of a longer piece that will explore the Foundation for Spiritual Knowledge in Tallahassee, Florida, which is a group of local people in training to be mediums and spirituals healers. These two goals are intertwined." Yeah, right. Nice and fancy. Did I really intend to write a book-length study on those folks? I thought my professor would like the idea, though, so I put it in my note. Plus, my peer reviewers had asked for a longer, deeper piece. That statement would show I was being responsive to their feedback, even though I didn't agree with it. The peer reviewers had also wanted me to put myself into the essay more, to do more with first-person point of view rather than just writing a reporter-style observation piece. I still disagree with them, but what I should have done in the original process note was go into why: my own search for spirituality and belief could not be handled in a brief essay. I wanted the piece to be about the medium herself, and mediumship in general, and the public's reaction, and why a group of snarky teenagers thought they could be disruptive the whole time and come off as superior. I did a better job later—more honest and thoughtful and revealing about my intentions for the piece—in the self-evaluation for the portfolio. That's because, as the semester progressed and I continued to have to write those darned process notes, I dropped the attitude. In a conference about my writing, Bishop responded to my note by asking questions focused entirely on helping me refine my intentions for the piece, and I realized my task wasn't to please or try to dazzle her. I stopped worrying about how awkward the reflection was, stopped worrying about how to please the teacher, and started actually reflecting and thinking. New habits and ways of thinking formed. And unexpectedly, all the hard decisions about revising for the next draft began to come more easily.

And something else clicked, too. Two and a half years previously, I had been teaching composition at a small two-year college. Composition scholar Peggy O'Neill taught a workshop for us English teachers on an assignment she called the "Letter to the Reader." That was my introduction to reflective writing as a teacher, though I hadn't done any of it myself at that point. I thought, "Okay, the composition scholars say we should get our students to do this." So I did, but it did not work very well with my students at the time. Here's why: I didn't come to understand what it could do for a writer, or how it would do it, until I had been through it myself.

After Bishop's class, I became a convert. I began studying reflection, officially called metacognition, and began developing ways of using it in writing classes of all kinds, from composition to creative nonfiction to fiction writing. It works. Reflection helps you to develop your intentions (purpose), figure out your relation to your audience, uncover possible problems with your individual writing processes, set goals for revision, make decisions about language and style, and the list goes on. In a nutshell, it helps you develop more insight into and control over composing and revising processes. And according to scholars such as Chris M. Anson, developing this control is a feature that distinguishes stronger from weaker writers and active from passive learners (69–73).

My Letter to the Reader Assignment

Over recent years, I've developed my own version of the Letter to the Reader, based on O'Neill's workshop and Bishop's class assignments. For each essay, during a revising workshop, my students first draft their letters to the reader and then later, polish them to be turned in with the final draft. Letters are composed based on the following instructions:

> This will be a sort of cover letter for your essay. It should be on a separate sheet of paper, typed, stapled to the top of the final draft. Date the letter and address it to "Dear Reader." Then do the following in nicely developed, fat paragraphs:
>
> 1. Tell the reader what you intend for the essay to do for its readers. Describe its purpose(s) and the effect(s) you want it to have on the readers. Say who you think the readers are.
>   - Describe your process of working on the essay. How did you narrow the assigned topic? What kind of planning did you do? What steps did you go through, what changes did you make along the way, what decisions did you face, and how did you make the decisions?
>   - How did comments from your peers, in peer workshop, help you? How did any class activities on style, editing, etc., help you?
> 2. Remember to sign the letter. After you've drafted it, think about whether your letter and essay match up. Does the essay really do what your letter promises? If not, then use the draft of your letter as a revising tool to make a few more adjustments to your essay. Then, when the essay is polished and ready to hand in, polish the letter as well and hand them in together.

Following is a sample letter that shows how the act of answering these prompts can help you uncover issues in your essays that need to be addressed in further revision. This letter is a mock-up based on problems I've seen over the years. We discuss it thoroughly in my writing classes:

Dear Reader,

    This essay is about how I feel about the changes in the financial aid rules. I talk about how they say you're not eligible even if your parents aren't supporting you anymore. I also talk a little bit about the HOPE scholarship. But my real purpose is to show how the high cost of books makes it impossible to afford college if you can't get on financial aid. My readers will be all college students. As a result, it should make students want to make a change. My main strategy in this essay is to describe how the rules have affected me personally.

    I chose this topic because this whole situation has really bugged me. I did freewriting to get my feelings out on paper, but I don't think that was effective because it seemed jumbled and didn't flow. So I started over with an outline and went on from there. I'm still not sure how to start the introduction off because I want to hook the reader's interest but I don't know how to do that. I try to include many different arguments to appeal to different types of students to make the whole argument seem worthwhile on many levels.

    I did not include comments from students because I want everyone to think for themselves and form their own opinion. That's my main strategy. I don't want the paper to be too long and bore the reader. I was told in peer workshop to include information from other students at other colleges with these same financial aid problems. But I didn't do that because I don't know anybody at another school. I didn't want to include any false information.

Thanks,
(signature)

Notice how the letter shows us, as readers of the letter, some problems in the essay without actually having to read the essay. From this (imaginary) student's point of view, the act of drafting this letter should show her the problems, too. In her first sentence, she announces her overall topic. Next she identifies a particular problem: the way "they" define whether an applicant is dependent on or independent of parents. So far, pretty good, except her use of the vague pronoun "they" makes me hope she hasn't been that vague in the essay itself. Part of taking on a topic is learning enough about it to be specific. Specific is effective; vague is not. Her next comment about the HOPE scholarship makes me wonder if she's narrowed her topic enough. When she said "financial aid," I assumed federal, but HOPE is particular to the state of Georgia and has its own set of very particular rules, set by its own committee in Atlanta. Can she effectively cover both federal financial aid, such as the Pell Grant for example, as well as HOPE, in the same essay, when the rules governing them are different? Maybe. We'll see. I wish the letter would address more specifically how she sorts that out in the essay. Then she says that her "real purpose" is to talk about the cost of books. Is that really her main purpose? Either she doesn't have a good handle on what she wants her essay to do or she's just throwing language around to sound good in the letter. Not good, either way.

When she says she wants the readers to be all college students, she has identified her target audience, which is good. Then this: "As a result, it should make students want to make a change." Now, doesn't that sound more in line with a statement of purpose? Here the writer makes clear, for the first time, that she wants to write a persuasive piece on the topic. But then she says that her "main strategy" is to discuss only her own personal experience. That's not a strong enough strategy, by itself, to be persuasive.

In the second section, where she discusses process, she seems to have gotten discouraged when she thought that freewriting hadn't worked because it resulted in something "jumbled." But she missed the point that freewriting works to generate ideas, which often won't come out nicely organized. It's completely fine, and normal, to use freewriting to generate ideas and then organize them with perhaps an outline as a second step. As a teacher, when I read comments like this in a letter, I write a note to the student explaining that "jumbled" is normal, perfectly fine, and nothing to worry about. I'm glad when I read that sort of comment so I can reassure the student. If not for the letter, I probably wouldn't have known of her unfounded concern. It creates a teaching moment.

Our imaginary student then says, "I'm still not sure how to start the introduction off because I want to hook the reader's interest but don't know how to do that." This statement shows that she's thinking along the right lines—of capturing the reader's interest. But she hasn't quite figured out how to do that in this essay, probably because she doesn't have a clear handle on her purpose. I'd advise her to address that problem and to better develop her overall strategy, and then she would be in a better position to make a plan for the introduction. Again, a teaching moment. When she concludes the second paragraph of the letter saying that she wants to include "many different arguments" for "different types of students," it seems even more evident that she's not clear on purpose or strategy; therefore, she's just written a vague sentence she probably thought sounded good for the letter.

She begins her third paragraph with further proof of the problems. If her piece is to be persuasive, then she should not want readers to "think for themselves and form their own opinion." She most certainly should have included comments from other students, as her peer responders advised. It wouldn't be difficult to interview some fellow students at her own school. And as for finding out what students at other schools think about the issue, a quick search on the Internet would turn up newspaper or newsletter articles, as well as blogs and other relevant sources. Just because the official assignment may not have been to write a "research" paper doesn't mean you can't research. Some of your best material will come that way. And in this particular type of paper, your personal experience by itself, without support, will not likely persuade the reader. Now, I do appreciate when she says she doesn't want to include any "false information." A lot of students come to college with the idea that in English class, if you don't know any information to use, then you can just make it up so it sounds good. But that's not ethical, and it's not persuasive, and just a few minutes on the Internet will solve the problem.

This student, having drafted the above letter, should go back and analyze. Do the essay and letter match up? Does the essay do what the letter promises? And here, does the letter uncover lack of clear thinking about purpose and strategy? Yes, it does, so she should now go back and address these issues in her essay. Without having done this type of reflective exercise, she likely would have thought her essay was just fine, and she would have been unpleasantly surprised to get the grade back with my (the teacher's) extensive commentary and critique. She never would have predicted what I would say because she wouldn't have had a process for thinking through these issues—and might not have known how to begin thinking this way. Drafting the letter should help her develop more insight into and control over the revising process so she can make more effective decisions as she revises.

How It Works

Intentions—a sense of audience and purpose and of what the writer wants the essay to do—are essential to a good piece of communicative writing. Anson makes the point that when an instructor asks a student to verbalize his or her intentions, it is much more likely that the student will have intentions (qtd. in Yancey and Smith 174). We saw this process in mid-struggle with our imaginary student's work (above), and we'll see it handled more effectively in real student examples (below). As many composition scholars explain, reflective and self-assessing activities help writers set goals for their writing. For instance, Rebecca Moore Howard states that "writers who can assess their own prose can successfully revise that prose" (36). This position is further illustrated by Xiaoguang Cheng and Margaret S. Steffenson, who conducted and then reported a study clearly demonstrating a direct positive effect of reflection on student revising processes in "Metadiscourse: A Technique for Improving Student Writing." Yancey and Smith argue that self-assessment and reflection are essential to the learning process because they are a "method for assigning both responsibility and authority to a learner" (170). Students then become independent learners who can take what they learn about writing into the future beyond a particular class rather than remaining dependent on teachers or peer evaluators (171). Anson echoes this idea, saying that reflection helps a writer grow beyond simply succeeding in a particular writing project: "Once they begin thinking about writing productively, they stand a much better chance of developing expertise and working more successfully in future writing situations" (73).

Examples from Real Students

Let's see some examples from actual students now, although for the sake of space we'll look at excerpts. The first few illustrate how reflective writing helps you develop your intentions. For an assignment to write a profile essay, Joshua Dawson described his purpose and audience: "This essay is about my grandmother and how she overcame the hardships of life. [. . .] The purpose of this essay is to show how a woman can be tough and can take anything life throws at her. I hope the essay reaches students who have a single parent and those who don't know what a single parent goes through." Joshua showed a clear idea of what he wanted his essay to do. For a cultural differences paper, Haley Moore wrote about her mission trip to Peru: "I tried to show how, in America, we have everything from clean water to freedom of religion and other parts of the world do not. Also, I would like for my essay to inspire people to give donations or help in any way they can for the countries that live in poverty." Haley's final draft actually did not address the issue of donations and focused instead on the importance of mission work, a good revision decision that kept the essay more focused.

In a Composition II class, Chelsie Mathis wrote an argumentative essay on a set of controversial photos published in newspapers in the 1970s which showed a woman falling to her death during a fire escape collapse. Chelsie said,

> The main purpose of this essay is to argue whether the [newspaper] editors used correct judgment when deciding to publish such photos. The effect that I want my paper to have on the readers is to really make people think about others' feelings and to make people realize that poor judgment can have a big effect. [. . .] I intend for my readers to possibly be high school students going into the field of journalism or photojournalism.

Chelsie demonstrated clear thinking about purpose and about who she wanted her essay to influence. Another Comp II student, Daniel White, wrote, "This essay is a cognitive approach of how I feel You-Tube is helping our society achieve its dreams and desires of becoming stars." I had no idea what he meant by "cognitive approach," but I knew he was taking a psychology class at the same time. I appreciated that he was trying to integrate his learning from that class into ours, trying to learn to use that vocabulary. I was sure that with more practice, he would get the hang of it. I didn't know whether he was getting much writing practice at all in psychology, so I was happy to let him practice it in my class. His reflection showed learning in process.

My students often resist writing about their composing processes, but it's good for them to see and analyze how they did what they did, and it also helps me know what they were thinking when they made composing decisions. Josh Autry, in regards to his essay on scuba diving in the Florida Keys at the wreck of the Spiegel Grove, said, "Mapping was my preferred method of outlining. It helped me organize my thoughts, go into detail, and pick the topics that I thought would be the most interesting to the readers." He also noted, "I choose [sic] to write a paragraph about everything that can happen to a diver that is not prepared but after reviewing it I was afraid that it would scare an interested diver away. I chose to take that paragraph out and put a few warnings in the conclusion so the aspiring diver would not be clueless." This was a good decision that did improve the final draft. His earlier draft had gotten derailed by a long discussion of the dangers of scuba diving in general. But he came to this realization and decided to correct it without my help—except that I had led the class through reflective revising activities. D'Amber Walker wrote, "At first my organization was off because I didn't know if I should start off with a personal experience which included telling a story or start with a statistic." Apparently, a former teacher had told her not to include personal experiences in her essays. I reminded her that in our workshop on introductions, we had discussed how a personal story can be a very effective hook to grab the reader's attention. So once again, a teaching moment. When Jonathan Kelly said, "I probably could have given more depth to this paper by interviewing a peer or something but I really felt unsure of how to go about doing so," I was able to scold him gently. If he really didn't know how to ask fellow students their opinions, all he had to do was ask me. But his statement shows an accurate assessment of how the paper could have been better. When Nigel Ellington titled his essay "If Everything Was Easy, Nothing Would Be Worth Anything," he explained, "I like this [title] because it's catchy and doesn't give too much away and it hooks you." He integrated what he learned in a workshop on titles. Doing this one little bit of reflective thinking cemented that learning and gave him a chance to use it in his actual paper.

How It Helps Me (the Instructor) Help You

Writing teachers often play two roles in relation to their students. I am my students' instructor, but I am also a fellow writer. As a writer, I have learned that revision can be overwhelming. It's tempting just to fiddle with words and commas if I don't know what else to do. Reflection is a mechanism, a set of procedures, to help me step back from a draft to gain enough distance to ask myself, "Is this really what I want the essay (or story or poem or article) to do? Is this really what I want it to say? Is this the best way to get it to say that?" To revise is to re-vision or re-see, to re-think these issues, but you have to create a critical distance to be able to imagine your piece done another way. Reflection helps you create that distance. It also helps your instructor better guide your work and respond to it.

The semester after my experience in Bishop's Life Writing Class, I took a Fiction Writing Workshop taught by Mark Winegardner, author of *The Godfather Returns* and *The Godfather's Revenge*, as well as numerous other novels and short stories. Winegardner had us create what he called the "process memo." As he indicated in an interview, he uses the memo mainly as a tool to help the workshop instructor know how to respond to the writer's story. If a writer indicates in the memo that he knows something is still a problem with the story, then the instructor can curtail lengthy discussion of that issue's existence during the workshop and instead prompt peers to provide suggestions. The instructor can give some pointed advice, or possibly reassurance, based on the writer's concerns that, without being psychic, the instructor would not otherwise have known about. Composition scholar Jeffrey Sommers notes that reflective pieces show teachers what your intentions for your writing actually are, which lets us respond to your writing accurately, rather than responding to what we think your intentions might be ("Enlisting" 101–2). He also points out that we can know how to reduce your anxiety about your writing appropriately ("Behind" 77). Thus, without a reflective memo, your teacher might pass right over the very issue you have been worried about.

The Habit of Self-Reflective Writing

One of the most important functions of reflective writing in the long run is to establish in you, the writer, a habit of self-reflective thinking. The first few reflective pieces you write may feel awkward and silly and possibly painful. You might play the teacher-pleasing game. But that's really not what we want (see Smith 129). Teachers don't want you to say certain things, we want you to think in certain ways. Once you get the hang of it and start to see the benefits in your writing, you'll notice that you've formed a habit of thinking reflectively almost invisibly. And not only will it help you in writing classes, but in any future writing projects for biology class, say, or even further in the future, in writing that you may do on the job, such as incident reports or annual reports for a business. You'll become a better writer. You'll become a better thinker. You'll become a better learner. And learning is what you'll be doing for the rest of your life. I recently painted my kitchen. It was a painful experience. I had a four-day weekend and thought I could clean, prep, and paint the kitchen, breakfast nook, and hallway to the garage in just four days, not to mention painting the trim and doors white. I pushed myself to the limit of endurance. And when I finished the wall color (not even touching the trim), I didn't like it. The experience was devastating. A very similar thing had happened three years before when I painted my home office a color I now call "baby poop." My home office is still "baby poop" because I got so frustrated I just gave up. Now, the kitchen was even worse. It was such a light green it looked like liver failure and didn't go with the tile on the floor. Plus, it showed brush marks and other flaws. What the heck?

But unlike three years ago, when I had given up, I decided to apply reflective practices to the situation. I decided to see it as time for revision- type thinking. Why had I wanted green to begin with? (Because I didn't want blue in a kitchen. I've really been craving that hot dark lime color that's popular now. So yes, I still want it to be green.) Why hadn't I chosen a darker green? (Because I have the darker, hotter color into the room with accessories. The lighter green has a more neutral effect that I shouldn't get sick of after six months. Perhaps I'll get used to it, especially when I get around to painting the trim white.) What caused the brush strokes? (I asked an expert. Two factors: using satin finish rather than eggshell, and using a cheap paintbrush for cut-in-areas.) How can they be fixed? (Most of the brush strokes are just in the cut-in areas and so they can be redone quickly with a better quality brush. That is, if I decide to keep this light green color.) Is the fact that the trim is still cream-colored rather than white part of the problem? (Oh, yes. Fix that first and the other problems might diminish.) What can I learn about timing for my next paint project? (That the cleaning and prep work take much longer than you think, and that you will need two coats, plus drying time. And so what if you didn't finish it in four days? Relax! Allow more time next time.) Am I really worried about what my mother will say? (No, because I'm the one who has to look at it every day.) So the solution? Step one is to paint the trim first and then re-evaluate. Using a method of reflection to think back over my "draft" gives me a method for proceeding with "revision." At the risk of sounding like a pop song, when you stop to think it through, you'll know what to do.

Revision isn't just in writing. These methods can be applied any time you are working on a project—of any kind—or have to make decisions about something. Establishing the habit of reflective thinking will have far-reaching benefits in your education, your career, and your life. It's an essential key to success for the life-long learner.

■ ■ ■   FOR CLASS DISCUSSION

1. Define what metacognitive or reflective writing is. What are some of the prompts or "topics" for reflective writing?
2. Have you ever been asked to do this type of writing? If so, briefly discuss your experience.
3. Why does reflective writing help a student learn and develop as a better writer? How does it work?
4. Draft a Letter to the Reader for an essay you are working on right now. Analyze the letter to see what strengths or problems it uncovers regarding your essay.

■ ■ ■

Works Cited

Anson, Chris M. "Talking About Writing: A Classroom-Based Study of Students' Reflections on Their Drafts." Smith and Yancey 59–74.

Bishop, Wendy. "Life Writing." English Department. Florida State University, Tallahassee, FL. Summer 2002. Lecture.

Cheng, Xiaoguang, and Margaret S. Steffenson. "Metadiscourse: A Technique for Improving Student Writing." *Research in the Teaching of English* 30.2 (1996): 149–81. Print.

Howard, Rebecca Moore. "Applications and Assumptions of Student Self-Assessment." Smith and Yancey 35–58.

O'Neill, Peggy. "Reflection and Portfolio Workshop." Humanities Division. Abraham Baldwin Agricultural College, Tifton, GA. 25 January 2000. Lecture, workshop.

Smith, Jane Bowman. "'Know Your Knowledge': Journals and Self-Assessment." Smith and Yancey 125–38.

Smith, Jane Bowman, and Kathleen Blake Yancey, eds. *Self-Assessment and Development in Writing: A Collaborative Inquiry.* Cresskill, NJ: Hampton, 2000. Print.

Sommers, Jeffrey. "Behind the Paper: Using the Student-Teacher Memo." *College Composition and Communication* 39.1 (1988): 77–80. Print.

———. "Enlisting the Writer's Participation in The Evaluation Process." *Journal of Teaching Writing* 4.1 (1985): 95–103. Print.

Winegardner, Mark. Personal interview. 3 February 2003.

Yancey, Kathleen Blake, and Jane Bowman Smith. "Reflections on Self-Assessment." Smith and Yancey 169–76.

SECTION FIVE

An Anthology of Arguments

In this panel from the cartoon *Zits*, cartoonists Jim Borgman and Jerry Scott target parents' misunderstanding of their Generation Y children, who are often characterized as multitasking digital natives, skilled with—but also dependent on—their technology and its social networks.

Taken from *Writing Arguments: A Rhetoric with Readings*, Ninth Edition
by John D. Ramage, John C. Bean, and June Johnson

Digital Literacies

30

Lightning-fast technological innovation and change have become predictable constants in our fast-paced lives. No sooner do we acquire the latest must-have gadget than it becomes obsolete, supplanted by a newer, updated model with greater capacity and more speed. Such terms as "4G," "Android," and "1080p" spin out from advertising media, while television commercials satirize the hapless consumer lost in the whirlwind of change, trying to make sense of it all. More often than not, that hapless consumer is a parent of a certain age, struggling to comprehend what seems to be an entirely new language spoken by his or her children.

Technological change is so rapid, in fact, that institutions—especially educational institutions, which are inherently slow to change—must struggle to keep up. Educators had no sooner recognized the value of the Internet as an information source and the importance of integrating it into their teaching than they were forced to grapple with Web 2.0, which permitted user-generated content to be shared by audiences worldwide. Suddenly social networks, blogs, and tweets demanded a place in teachers' lesson plans as educators, parents, and students contemplated their value—and their dangers. Smart phones and text messaging have created additional challenges. Indeed, these technologies have altered every facet of our lives, from the way we acquire information to the way we communicate with friends and family. The impact is still being sorted out.

One fact is certain: We are now witnessing the first generation of children raised with digital technologies as constants in their lives. From the cradle, these young people have had access to computers, phones, and other technologies that provide them with instant access to information and connections to friends and family 24/7/365. To some, it feels as though the "digital generation" lives in a world apart, strange and daunting to their elders. In 2001 writer Marc Prensky dubbed them "Digital Natives"— "native speakers" of the digital languages in which they have been immersed since birth. Prensky and others have posited that such immersion in digital activity has actually resulted in a difference in brain function, and experts contemplate the existence and implications of a "digital divide" between "digital natives" and "digital immigrants," for whom these technologies constitute a type of foreign language or culture.

The readings that follow ask you to consider the issues and questions raised by the perceived digital divide: Does the divide, in fact, exist? What does the research tell us? What are the implications of ubiquitous technologies for interpersonal relationships, for education, and for society? What benefits do these technologies bring—and what risks? Are the alarms raised by some about the impact of digital technologies merited, or are they similar in kind to alarms raised over innovations throughout human history?

Digital Natives and Immigrants: What Brain Research Tells Us

NANCY K. HERTHER

Nancy K. Herther is Librarian for Sociology, Anthropology, American Studies, and Asian American Studies at the University of Minnesota. She has been a columnist for the journals Database *and* Online. *The following article appeared in the November/December 2009 issue of* Online. *In 2010 she received the Outstanding Reviewer Award from Emerald for her work on The Electronic Library.*

Technological advances and saturation-level promotion for every type of computer-based product explode around us daily. The focus is clearly on the younger generations—Digital Natives—who form the most avid consumer group, worldwide, for technology-based products. From cell phones to iPods, computers to gaming systems, the sales of digital products to young people dwarf the acceptance rates of other market segments. However, how does this fascination with and adoption of technology relate to brain development? Is brain power generationally defined?

Every generation is influenced by the events, major personalities, and trends of its time. For these newest generations, it's technology and social networking. In their book, *Born Digital: Understanding the First Generation of Digital Natives* (New York: Basic Books, 2008), Harvard's John Palfrey and Urs Gasser describe the generation this way: "These kids are different. They study, work, write, and interact with each other in ways that are very different from the ways that you did growing up. . . . And they're connected to one another by a common culture. Major aspects of their lives—social interactions, friendships, civic activities—are mediated by digital technologies. And they've never known any other way of life."

Digital Natives

These kids aren't just different, they've been dubbed with differing designations: Born Digital, Digital Youth, Millennials, Next Generation, Echo Boomers, Net Gen, Screenagers, Bebo Generation, Google Generation, MySpace Generation, Gen Y, First Digitals, Generation Z, Generation I, Internet Generation, or iGeneration. But the labeling that seems to bring up the greatest number of hits in the literature—and sparked the most controversy—is Digital Natives.

Don Tapscott, author of *Growing Up Digital: The Rise of the Net Generation* (New York: McGraw Hill, 1999) and *Grown Up Digital: How the Net Generation Is Changing Your World* (New York: McGraw Hill, 2008), and game designer and consultant Marc Prensky have been perhaps the most influential in defining the latest youth generation. The literature of education and library/information science in recent years has embraced the notion of Digital Natives to describe this generation (defined by Tapscott as those born since 1980) and the impact they are having (or should have) in defining the future of our institutions, programs, and profession. Many of the core arguments, particularly as promoted by Prensky, contain some very incendiary, broad-brush assumptions. In "Digital Natives, Digital Immigrants," *On the Horizon*, Vol. 9. No. 5, pp. 1–2, October 2001 (www.marcprensky.com/writing/Prensky%20%20Digital%20Natives,%20Digital%20Immigrants%20-%20Part1.pdf), he says:

5   "But this is not just a joke. It's very serious, because the single biggest problem facing education today is that *our Digital Immigrant instructors, who speak an outdated language (that of the pre-digital age), are struggling to teach a population that speaks an entirely new language.*

"This is obvious to the Digital Natives—school often feels pretty much as if we've brought in a population of heavily accented, unintelligible foreigners to lecture them. They often can't understand what the Immigrants are saying."

Digital Immigrants and Beyond

Believers in Prensky's theories also promote that definition of older generations—nonnatives—as "Digital Immigrants," technology users older than 30 who can use technology but in frameworks and ways that reveal their nondigital roots. Others have built from this theory. An article titled "Digital Denizens" from Richard Stockton College's (N.J.) Instructional Technology Resources (www.stockton.edu/-intech/spotlight-digital-denizens.htm) suggests additional categories, scaled by technology acceptance and facility.

- *Digital recluse*: use of technology is a result of the need to function in the current environment, not used by choice; computers are prohibited at home
- *Digital refugee*: unwillingly forced to use technology: prefers hard copies, does not trust electronic resources; seeks assistance; may have grown up with technology or adopted it as an adult
- *Digital immigrant*: willingly uses technology, but not familiar with its potential; believes technology can be used successfully for some tasks; may have grown up with technology or adopted it as an adult
- *Digital native*: chooses to use technology for numerous tasks; adapts as the tools change; may have grown up with technology or adopted it as an adult
- *Digital explorer*: uses technology to push the envelope; seeks new tools that can do more and work both faster and easier
- *Digital innovator*: adapts and changes old tools for new tasks; creates new tools
- *Digital addict*: dependent on technology; will go through withdrawal when technology is not available

In a rush to better serve this upcoming generation, many librarians have set out to re-examine the very purpose, value, and efficiency of our institutions, services, and profession. The assumption that existing ideas, philosophies, and methods are as antiquated as anyone older than some magical age seems to underlie much of the contemporary discourse. Are these statements and assertions based on solid, scientifically validated facts or are they feeding off of the concerns and, perhaps, panic felt by most people (of any age) due to the constant onslaught of new technological gizmos and possibilities?

Recently, we've seen a more research-oriented approach that looks at contemporary society and education—warts and all—and works to better understand the role of technology as both a tool for learning and a stimulator for more general cultural change. In one recent evaluation of the educational literature, Sue Bennett and her colleagues at the University of Wollongong in Australia found little empirical evidence to support the claims being made today about Digital Natives and concluded that "the debate can be likened to an academic form of a 'moral panic'" ("The Digital Natives Debate: A Critical Review of the Evidence," *British Journal of Educational Technology*, Vol. 39, No. 5, pp. 775–786, 2008).

Just What *Is* a Generation

10 Soon after his on-campus arrest for soliciting contributions without permission for a civil rights cause on Oct. 1, 1964, Jack Weinberg, a University of California–Berkeley graduate student, famously proclaimed. "You can't trust anyone over 30." This quickly became one of the many slogans of the 1960s, reflecting the belief that anyone older than 30 wasn't to be trusted; that to do so was to buy into the status quo. It is interesting to see that, this time around, it's the people older than 30 who are claiming that their own generation is hopelessly over the hill.

Merriam-Webster defines a generation as "A group of individuals born and living contemporaneously." Perhaps it is too soon to understand the full character or common themes of the current generation;

however, according to Prensky, Digital Natives include anyone who grew up with digital technology from birth. They "have not just changed *incrementally* from those of the past, nor simply changed their slang, clothes, body adornments, or styles, as has happened between generations previously. A really big *discontinuity* has taken place."

However, if you look at timelines of technology introduction or acceptance over the past 50 years or so, you see a far more nuanced landscape.

The ISI citation indexes and MEDLARS went online in 1963, ORBIT and Dialog in 1972. Many online searchers have been using computers, with various search protocols, throughout their professional lives—and those early computer systems required far more technological savvy than today's plug-and-play systems. My first computer, which dated from the mid-1970s, was a KIM-2 single-board computer from MOS Technology—which required that you solder in the chips yourself. You had no inherent storage memory or input/output devices.

Although Digital Natives buy and use technological products, there is little if any evidence that they have any interest or deep knowledge about what's inside these "black boxes," or that, as a generation, today's kids are actively *changing* technology or using it in *unique* ways to change our world. If anything, research seems to be showing that technology usage is increasingly changing our kids.

15   With the rise of the neurosciences and the use of functional magnetic resonance imaging (fMRIs) to diagnose problems and to watch the brain in action, are we truly finding some type of digital divide by chronological age? Does experience and facility with technology mean anything? Can we potentially rewire our brains to gain more brain power? Can we exercise our gray matter to stay in optimal brain shape? I wanted to find out for myself, so I interviewed some brain research experts.

Neuroscientic Studies of the Brain on Internet

Data from the University of California–Los Angeles' (UCLA) Semel Institute for Neuroscience and Human Behavior found that the brains of Digital Natives were more actively engaged while the subject was navigating a web-page as opposed to reading printed text. This garnered attention in the popular press. The conclusions and hype surrounding this finding were compelling.

Gary Small, director of the Semel Institute and UCLA's Parlow-Solomon Chair on Aging, led the study. Author of both scholarly articles and popular books on neuroscience topics, particularly *iBrain: Surviving the Technological Alteration of the Modern Mind* (New York: Collins Living, 2008). Small believes that due to both age and experience, youth have different experiences and acceptance for technology.

"To me," Small explains, "the 'digital native' construct is a shorthand for combining one's age group—which tells us something about their biological development at a certain stage of life, the age in which they were introduced to technology—and other features of their life styles." He sees the age differential as "a gradual process and not so timebound. There are many digital immigrants who spend just as much time with technology as do digital natives. I would say that, today, nearly all kids are digital natives. They buy and constantly use all sorts of technology, and they spend less time in face-to-face conversations. Their skills are great but their social contact skills could use some work."

Does this spell generation gap at some biological level? No. Small sees the brain as intrinsically flexible and eminently trainable. In February 2009, Small and his colleagues published a study ("Your Brain on Google: Patterns of Cerebral Activation During Internet Searching." *American Journal of Geriatric Psychiatry*, Vol. 17, No. 2, pp. 116–126) that assessed the effect of internet searching on brain activity among volunteers between the ages of 55 and 76. Half of them were well-practiced in searching; the other half were not. Using fMRIs to scan the subjects' brains while they surfed the web, they found that the brains of the web-savvy group reflected about twice as much brain activity compared to the brains of those who were not web-savvy.

20   "We found that people with prior Internet experience had a much greater activation in their brain when they searched online than those who had never searched online and it was also much greater than for reading a book page," Small explains. "The frontal lobe was particularly activated, that's the thinking, decision-making part of the brain. Searching the Internet involved decision-making, which the frontal activity may have reflected."

The really important part of the study followed. After a week's training the less-savvy group was retested. The results? "Just after a week of searching online, the Internet Naïve subjects showed brain neural circuitry similar to those of the experienced Internet searcher. That is very rapid adaptation that likely occurs as we learn new technologies." If something can be remediated in as little as a week, can this really be a generational crisis or is it an issue of experience and choice? Small opts for the latter explanation.

The Brain Rules

Recent findings in cognitive neuroscience are providing educators with fresh new insights on cognition, learning intelligence, memory, and emotion. Questions remain about how memories are stored and retrieved, the varieties of learning, and whether the adult brain can regrow tissue.

John Medina, author of the popular book *Brain Rules: 12 Principles for Surviving and Thriving at Work, Home, and School* (Seattle: Pear Press, 2009), is a developmental molecular biologist on the faculty at the University of Washington and director of the Brain Center for Applied Learning Research at Seattle Pacific University.

Does Medina believe there really can be such a huge, generational difference—or any real difference at all—between the brains of Digital Natives and those of their parents or grandparents? "I take with a grain of salt the notion of 'if-you-are-born-at-a-certain-date' then you are imbued with a certain suite of behaviors. It seems to me that this is the same intellectual framework upon which astrology is based, snooty as that might sound," Medina notes.

"Real evolutionary changes that resulted from specific neuroanatomical alterations whose origins percolated up from the germ line take hundreds of thousands of years to accomplish in humans."

25   Should we be concerned that fMRIs may show differences in the brain behaviors of younger and older computer users? "There is no question that digital natives will have their brains wired differently in response to specific types of media exposure than others not so exposed," Medina explains, "but that is also true if this generation never saw a computer, spoke French instead of English, or spoke English but one person learned tennis and the other learned pinball. The brain is in the business of reacting to its environment by continuously rewiring itself in response to external experience."

Gary Marcus, New York University psychology professor and author of *Kluge: The Haphazard Evolution of the Human Mind* (New York: Houghton Mifflin, 2008) notes, "I was born in 1970 and would clearly classify myself as a digital native. In general, it's quite difficult to decouple the effect of age from the effects of experience."

"I seriously doubt that there is any significant difference in the genetic makeup of people born before and after 1980," Marcus continues, "but experience can indeed radically alter our cognitive capabilities—that's why we send people to school!" Marcus' studies indicate that "overall, the genetics of the brain are unlikely to have changed in recent times, although kids with lots of exposure to computers probably do think about them differently than at least some adults who only start using computers later in life. But there are lots of older folks who have become perfectly comfortable with computers, so it's not an absolute thing."

Apostolos Georgopoulos, University of Minnesota regents professor and director of the university's Center for Cognitive Sciences, takes this even further. He told me, "There is absolutely no scientific basis for claiming that young people's brains have changed in recent times or that there is such a major difference between the brain at different ages. There isn't a shred of scientific evidence to back up these claims. This is totally unfounded. All of this is really a form of 'just so' stories. People say something that they feel speaks to their beliefs and others listen and believe it too, but it has no basis in fact. Brains change but not in the way implied by those statements."

A Growing Brain Power Marketplace

Clearly, the dominance of technology in culture and products continues. Technology is ever-present, and, as in the past, technologies that are proven useful are quickly integrated into existing systems and processes. You can call it progress. In just the past few years, we have electronic voting systems, YouTube and Facebook campaigning, and instant news. We are also seeing the rise of a new technologically enabled science that is increasingly helping us learn more about our brains, thinking, and learning. This is spawning a new marketplace for products and services designed to help us all improve and maintain brain function.

30   SharpBrains, a market research firm covering this emerging industry, estimates that the market grew from $5 million to $80 million between 2005 and 2007. "Cognitive health care is more and more being integrated into general health care," notes SharpBrains' co-founder and CEO Alvaro Fernandez (Fernandez., Alvaro and Goldberg, Elkhonon; "The State of the Brain Fitness Software Market 2009," San Francisco; SharpBrains, 2009). "Consumers are starting to demand that their insurance companies, retirement homes, and other services provide these types of services."

Fernandez notes two major factors that have moved the industry forward: first, the release of Nintendo's Brain Age game, which ignited over-the-counter sales; second, the publication in the *Journal of the American Medical Association* (*JAMA*) of the results of a follow-up study showing that even 5 years after a computer-based cognition intervention study, the subjects who received cognitive training *continued* to have better function than the control group (Willis, S.L., et al., "Long-Term Effects of

Cognitive Training on Everyday Functional Outcomes in Older Adults," *JAMA*, Vol. 296. No. 23. pp. 2,805–2,814, Dec. 20, 2006).

The Flexible Brain at Any Age

We all age. Yet age seems less an issue for neuroscience today. "The brain is completely flexible, we never lose the ability to adapt, to learn, and even to generate new neurons," Fernandez explains. "This is precisely why cognitive training technology is of such interest to baby boomers and others. There is no research coming out of neuroscience that would support ideas that digital natives are any better equipped; however, they may certainly be more experienced—but experience is something that can be overcome with training. Age is less predictive of health and functioning than it was perhaps a hundred years ago. Today age is less important than attitude, behavior, and habit in terms of mental functioning and learning."

Fernandez noted three recent studies that support this perspective:

1. Improved Driver Safety at Any Age

Allstate Insurance Company studied 85,000 drivers older than 50 who were given computer-based programs designed to enhance driving safety. It found cognitive training resulted in reduced risk factors leading to safer driving.

35 ### 2. Computer Training Benefits Older People More Than Youth

Arthur Kramer and colleagues compared cognitive performance in two groups playing video games: one group in their 20s and the other in their 60s. They found significant cognitive benefits in the older group—but *not* in the younger subjects. (Basak, C., et al., "Can Training in a Real-Time Strategy Video Game Attenuate Cognitive Decline in Older Adults?" *Psychology and Aging* 2008; DOI: 10.1037/a0013494. Boot, W.R.; Kramer, A.F.; Simons, D.J.; Fabiani, M.; and Gratton, G.: "The Effects of Video Game Playing on Attention. Memory, and Executive Control," *Acta Psychologica*, Vol. 129, No. 3, pp. 387–398, 2008)

3. You Can Train Your Working Memory

Torkel Klingberg's book. *The Overflowing Brain: Information Overload and the Limits of Working Memory* (Oxford: Oxford University Press, 2008), reports on a 2-year study showing that it is possible to increase working-memory capacity. Fernandez believes this is critically important research: "This improvement is not just confined to the task for which they trained, but generalizable to other cognitive tasks," he says. For all of us facing "information overload," this is good news indeed.

Protecting *Your* Gray Matter

Exercising the brain has similarities to physical fitness. Fernandez observes, "The exercises you would use to develop your biceps are very different than what you would use to improve your abs."

As new research appears and products flood the market, how can we select the best products for our needs? The marketplace is already giving us many options. Here's a quick tour of just a few options.

Sparks of Genius

Rohn Kessler, founder and CEO of Sparks of Genius (www.sparksofgenius.com) in Boca Raton, Fla., opened his doors in 2002, initially serving a population split between children needing educational remediation and aging consumers facing dementia and Alzheimer's disease. "Science shows that, just like going to the gym for your physical health, there is benefit to continuing to work on training and maintaining your cognitive health," Kessler notes. "We do targeted brain fitness prescriptions using proprietary computer software to improve cognitive skills such as memory, concentration, processing speed, organizing, reasoning, impulse control, and executive function skills."

40 What does he advise for busy online searchers? "The most important thing is that people need to continuously involve themselves in activities that are new, stimulating, and challenging. Most people don't do *new* things. If you spend most of your time online, maybe you need to find things beyond the computer. You need to work on physical health as well. Every time the heart beats, 15%–20% of the blood needs to go to the brain to bring it the oxygen it needs. So you need to get out of your chair and work out!"

'Health Club for Your Brain'

San Francisco-based vibrantBrains (www.vibrantbrains.com) calls itself a "health club for your brain," a place where you can grab a brain-boosting snack, test out new equipment, attend lectures, sign up for classes, or just work out on the various equipment, computer-based programs and other service programs of the club. "Our goal is to provide our clients with a true brain fitness community," notes co-founder Lisa Schoonerman. "We use scientifically developed cognitive exercises and have a Scientific Advisory Board to provide us with advice and critical information in this dynamic area. Studies show that regular mental workouts are WD-40 for the brain," Schoonerman said.

Maintaining Your Marbles

If you find yourself in the Chicago loop area, you may want to stop in at Marbles: The Brain Store (http://marblesthebrainstore.com). "A first-of-its kind retail concept that focuses on products designed to stimulate and strengthen the brain," Marbles has been in operation since October 2008 and is already expanding with two more stores in the area. The store offers the assistance of well-trained sales staff members who are experienced with the store's products; it also offers opportunities to try out the software, games, and other items for yourself before you buy.

The Future

Technology has given us "just-in-time" learning and information, has made communication truly mobile, and has allowed everyone to be both consumers and producers of information and entertainment. We are developing communities of practice, communities of learning, and other social networks that we couldn't have imagined possible just a few decades ago. We can now share information, simulate options, and have realtime, web-based interactions across the globe.

We all need a commitment to ongoing learning to keep up. Gary Small notes that "since iBrain was published there was some interesting research done that looked at one idea from the book: That too much tech time takes away from developing other communication skills. The scientists looked at about 200 digital natives, between the ages of 17 and 23. They were given the task of recognizing emotional expression as a face morphed from a neutral to either a happy face or an angry face. They found there was a happy face advantage, meaning the volunteers could recognize the happy face faster. But if the volunteers played a violent video game before the face expression task, they lost the happy face advantage. It just seems to make sense intuitively that, if you aren't spending a lot of time in face-to-face communication, those kinds of abilities weaken without practice, while other mental skills might strengthen. A basic principle of brain stimulation is that when a mental activity is repeated, the neural networks controlling it strengthen." So even those natives have something to learn.

45   Are there *real* generational differences? I hope so—without it there is no change. A recent Pew Research Center poll showed that the differences in values between young and older Americans are now forming "the largest generation gap since divisions 40 years ago over Vietnam, civil rights and women's liberation." Paul Taylor, director of the Pew Research Center's Social and Demographic Trends Project, noted that today's generation gap appears to be more tepid in nature than it was in the 1960s: "Today, it's more of a general outlook, a different point of view, a general set of moral values," he explained, with more tolerant views on gay marriage, interracial relationships, and other issues.

I see a world in which we are *all* struggling to keep up, to multitask, despite knowing that the strains of trying to serve so many masters weakens our efforts and lessens our intellectual product. I also see myself in a profession that, regardless of the available format, seeks to find the *best* available information for our users and seeks to help clients become more-informed creators as well as users of that information. In academe, this role also includes seeing that our communities learn how to do *quality* research themselves—going far beyond the Google search—to become the *best* in their fields. Being willing to accept less, from ourselves or our clients, is suicidal. Rather than worrying about a serious generation gap, what we really seem to need is more intergenerational sharing.

Bibliography/References

Basak C, et al. "Can training in a real-time strategy video game attenuate cognitive decline in older adults?" *Psychology and Aging* 2008; DOI: 10.1037/a0013494.

Bennett, Sue, Karl Maton and Lisa Kervin. "The 'digital natives' debate: A critical review of the evidence," *British Journal of Educational Technology* 39(5): 775–86, 2008.

Boot, W. R., Kramer, A. F., Simons, D. J., Fabianl, M. & Gratton, G. "The effects of video game playing on attention, memory, and executive control," *Acta Psychologica*, 129, 387–398, 2008.

Stockton College. "Digital Denizens" from *Instructional Technology Resources*, no date. Available online (www.stockton.edu/-Intech/spolfight-digital-denizens.htm).

Fernandez, Alvaro & Elkhonon Goldberg. *The SharpBrains Guide to Brain Fitness: 18 Interviews with Scientists, Practical Advice, and Product Reviews, to Keep your Brain Sharp.* San Francisco: SharpBrains, 2009.

Fernandez, Alvaro & Elkhonon Goldberg. *The State of the Brain Fitness Software Market 2009.* San Francisco: SharpBrains, 2009.

Klingberg, Torkel. *The Overflowing Brain: Information Overload and the Limits of Working Memory.* Oxford: Oxford University Press, 2008.

Marcus, Gary. *Kluge: The Haphazard Construction of the Human Mind.* New York: Houghton Mifflin, 2008.

Medina, John. *Brain Rules: 12 Principles for Surviving and Thriving at Work, Home, and School.* Seattle, WA: Pear Press, 2009.

Palfrey, John & Urs Gasser. *Bom Digital: Understanding the First Generation of Digital Natives,* New York: Basic Books, 2008.

Pew Research Center. *Growing Old in America: Expectations vs. Reality.* 2009 Available online (http://pewsocialtrends.org/puos/736/getting-old-in-america).

Prensky, Marc. "Digital Natives, Digital Immigrants," *On the Horizon* 9(5):1–2, October 2001 (www.marcprensky.com/writing/Prensky%20%20Digital%20Natives,%20Digital%20Immigrants%20-%20Part1.pdf).

Prensky, Marc. "Digital Natives, Digital Immigrants: Do they really *think differently?*" *On the Horizon* 9(6), October 2001 (www.scribd.com/doc/2902912/Prensky-Digital-Natives-Digital-Immigrants-Part2).

Small, Gary. *iBrain: Surviving the Technological Alteration of the Modern Mind.* New York: Collins Living, 2008.

Small, Gary, et al. "Your brain on Google: Patterns of cerebral activation during internet searching," *American Journal of Geriatric Psychiatry* 17(2): 116–126, February 2009.

Tapscott, Don. *Growing Up Digital: The Rise of the Net Generation.* New York: McGrawHill, 1999.

Tapscott, Don. *Grown Up Digital: How the Net Generation is Changing Your World.* New York: McGrawHill, 2008.

Willis, S.L., et al. "Long-term effects of cognitive training on everyday functional outcomes in older adults," *JAMA* 296(23): 2805–14, December 20, 2006.

Digital Demands: The Challenges of Constant Connectivity

AN INTERVIEW WITH SHERRY TURKLE

Sherry Turkle, Director of MIT's Initiative on Technology and Self, is a scholar, researcher, and longtime observer of technology's impact on people. Her 2011 book, Alone Together: Why We Expect More from Technology and Less from Each Other, *posits a potential downside to human reliance on digital technologies and poses the question: Is our perpetual connectedness actually making us feel more alone? The following interview is excerpted from a PBS Frontline TV/Web report "Digital Nation."*

SHERRY TURKLE: What I'm seeing is a generation that says consistently, "I would rather text than make a telephone call." Why? It's less risky. I can just get the information out there. I don't have to get all involved; it's more efficient. I would rather text than see somebody face to face.

There's this sense that you can have the illusion of companionship without the demands of friendship. The real demands of friendship, of intimacy, are complicated. They're hard. They involve a lot of negotiation. They're all the things that are difficult about adolescence. And adolescence is the time when people are using technology to skip and to cut corners and to not have to do some of these very hard things. One of the things I've found with continual connectivity is there's an anxiety of disconnection; that these teens have a kind of panic. They say things like, "I lost my iPhone; it felt like somebody died, as though I'd lost my mind." The technology is already part of them.

And with the constant possibility of connectivity, one of the things that I see is a very subtle movement from "I have a feeling. I want to make a call" to "I want to have a feeling. I need to make a call"—

in other words, people almost feeling as if they can't feel their feeling unless they're connected. I'm hearing this all over now so it stops being pathological if it becomes a generational style.

FRONTLINE: Some would say most of the [university] lectures, most of the classes, most of the books are unnecessarily long and boring, and the stuff that's great you could fit in a couple of hands, and that's the stuff they should really commit to and memorize and study. The rest of it is better short and quick and to the point. Look at haiku. It's much harder to do something quickly than it is to do something for hours. And who's to say that it's better to take your time and not be distracted?

5 **TURKLE:** The ability to trace complicated themes through a literary work, through a poem, through a play—these pleasures will be lost to us because they become pleasures through acquired skills. You need to learn how to listen to a poem, read a [Fyodor] Dostoevsky novel, read a Jane Austen novel. These are pleasures of reading that demand attention to things that are long and woven and complicated. And this is something that human beings have cherished and that have brought tremendous riches. And to just say, "Well, we're of a generation that now likes it short and sweet and haiku. Why? Just because the technology makes it easy for us to have things that are short and sweet and haiku." In other words, it's an argument about sensibility and aesthetics that's driven by what technology wants.

I don't really care what technology wants. It's up to people to develop technologies, see what affordances the technology has. Very often these affordances tap into our vulnerabilities. I would feel bereft if, because technology wants us to read short, simple stories, we bequeath to our children a world of short, simple stories. What technology makes easy is not always what nurtures the human spirit.

I've been an MIT professor for 30 years; I've seen the losses. There's no one who's been teaching for 25 years and doesn't think that our students aren't different now than they were then. They need to be stimulated in ways that they didn't need to be stimulated

before. No, that's not good. You want them to think about hard things. You want them to think about complicated things. When you have the ability to easily do showy, fabulous things, you want to believe they're valuable because that would be great. I think that we always have to ask ourselves, when technology makes something easy, when its affordances allow us to do certain things, is this valuable? What are the human purposes being served? And in the classroom, what are the educational purposes being served?

One of the most distressing things to me in looking at K–12 is the use of PowerPoint in the schools. I believe that PowerPoint is one of the most frequently used pieces of software in classrooms. Students are taught how to make an argument—to make it in bullets, to add great photos, to draw from the popular culture, and show snippets of movies and snippets of things that [he or she] can grab from the Web, and funny cartoons and to kind of make a mélange, a pastiche of cropped cultural images and animations and to make a beautiful PowerPoint. And that's their presentation.

10 PowerPoints are about simple, communicable ideas illustrated by powerful images, and there's a place for that. But that isn't the same as critical thinking. Great books are not fancied-up PowerPoint presentations. Great books take you through an argument, show how the argument is weak, meet objections, and show a different point of view. By the time you're through with all that, you're way beyond the simplicities of PowerPoint.

Computers are seductive; computers are appealing. There's no harm in using the seductive and appealing to draw people in, to get them in their seats, and to begin a conversation. The question is, what happens after that?

FRONTLINE: What about multitasking?

TURKLE: Because technology makes it easy, we've all wanted to think it is good for us, a new kind of thinking, an expansion of our ability to reason and cycle through complicated things—do more and be more efficient. Unfortunately, the new research is coming in that says when you multitask, everything gets done a little worse; there's a degradation of all functions. Did we need to really go through 10 years of drinking the Kool-Aid on the educational wonders of multitasking and forgetting about everything we knew about what it takes to really accomplish something hard?

At MIT, I teach the most brilliant students in the world. But they have done themselves a disservice by drinking the Kool-Aid and believing that a multitasking learning environment will serve their best purposes because they need to be taught how to make a sustained, complicated argument on a hard, cultural, historical, psychological point. Many of them were trained that a good presentation is a PowerPoint presentation—you know, bam-bam-bam—it's very hard for them to have a kind of quietness, a stillness in their thinking where one thing can actually lead to another and build and build and build and build. There are just some things that are not amenable to being thought about in conjunction with 15 other things. And there are some kinds of arguments you cannot make unless you're willing to take something from beginning to end.

15   We're becoming quite intolerant of letting each other think complicated things. I don't think this serves our human needs because the problems we're facing are quite complicated. To hear someone else out, you need to be able to be still for a while and pay attention to something other than your immediate needs. So if we're living in a moment when you can be in seven different places at once, and you can have seven different conversations at once on a back channel here, on a phone here, on a laptop, how do we save stillness? How threatened is it? How do we regain it?

Erik Erikson is a psychologist who wrote a great deal about adolescence and identity, and he talks about the need for stillness in order to fully develop and to discover your identity and become who you need to become and think what you need to think. And I think stillness is one of the great things in jeopardy.

[Henry David] Thoreau, in writing about Walden Pond, lists the three things that he feels the experience is teaching him to develop fully as the man he wants to become. He wants to live deliberately; he wants to live in his life; and he wants to live with no sense of resignation. But on all of those dimensions, I feel that we're taking away from ourselves the things that Thoreau thought were so essential to discovering an identity.

We're not deliberate; we're bombarded. We have no stillness; we have resignation.

Kids say: "Well, it has to be this way; we have no other way to live. We're not living fully in our lives. We're living a little in our lives and a little bit in our Facebook lives." You know, you put up a different life, you put up a different person. So it's not to be romantic about Thoreau, but I think he did write, as Erikson wrote, about the need for stillness; to be deliberate; to live in your life and to never feel that you're just resigned to how things need to be.

20   When we're texting, on the phone, doing e-mail, getting information, the experience is of being filled up. That feels good. And we assume that it is nourishing in the sense of taking us to a place we want to go. And I think that we are going to start to learn that in our enthusiasms and in our fascinations, we can also be flattened and depleted by what perhaps was once nourishing us but which can't be a steady diet. If all I do is my e-mail, my calendar, and my searches, I feel great; I feel like a master of the universe. And then it's the end of the day, I've been busy all day, and I haven't thought about anything hard, and I have been consumed by the technologies that were there and that had the power to nourish me.

The point is we're really at the very beginning of learning how to use this technology in the ways that are the most nourishing and sustaining. We're going to slowly find our balance, but I think it's going to take time. So I think the first discipline is to think of us as being in the early days so that we're not so quick to yes, no, on, off, good, good, and to just kind of take it slowly and not feel that we need to throw out the virtues of deliberateness, living in life, stillness, solitude.

There is a wonderful Freudian formulation, which is that loneliness is failed solitude. In many ways we are forgetting the intellectual and emotional value of solitude. You're not lonely in solitude. You're only lonely if you forget how to use solitude to replenish yourself and to learn. And you don't want a generation that experiences solitude as loneliness. And that is something to be concerned about, because if kids feel that they need to be connected in order to be themselves, that's quite unhealthy. They'll always feel lonely, because the connections that they're forming are not going to give them what they seek.

Diagnosing the Digital Revolution: Why It's So Hard to Tell if It's Really Changing Us

ALISON GOPNICK

Alison Gopnick, a professor of psychology and affiliate professor of philosophy at the University of California at Berkeley, is a widely recognized researcher and scholar in the field of children's learning and development. She has published many books and articles in these areas, including The Philosophical Baby: What Children's Minds Tell Us about Love, Truth, and the Meaning of Life. *In this article, published in* Slate *in February 2011, she examines and questions some of Sherry Turkle's pessimistic claims for the impact of technology on young people.*

They gave her The Device when she was only 2 years old. It sent signals along the optic nerve that swiftly transported her brain to an alternate universe—a captivating other world. By the time she was 7 she would smuggle it into school and engage it secretly under her desk. By 15 the visions of The Device—a girl entering a ballroom, a man dying on the battlefield—seemed more real than her actual adolescent life. She would sit with it, motionless, oblivious to everything around her, for hours on end. Its addictive grip was so great that she often stayed up half the night, unable to put it down.

When she grew up, The Device dominated her house: no room was free from it, no activity, not even eating or defecating, was carried on without its aid. Even when she made love it was the images of The Device that filled her mind. Psychologists showed that she literally could not disengage from it—if The Device could reach the optic nerve, she would automatically and inescapably be in its grip. Neuroscientists demonstrated that large portions of her brain, parts that had once been devoted to understanding the real world, had been co-opted by The Device.

A tale of the dystopian technological future? No, just autobiography. The Device is, of course, the printed book and I've been its willing victim all my life. But this might be how Sherry Turkle would describe it in her new book, *Alone Together*, and, in some ways, she'd be right.

The story illustrates why it's so hard to know how new technologies will affect us. Some technologies really have reshaped our lives, minds, and societies. Print did change everything. So did the telegraph. Information had always traveled at the speed of a fast horse; suddenly, it traveled at the speed of electricity, from 10 miles an hour to millions. (The old movie newspaper clichés "Get me rewrite!" "Tear up the afternoon edition!" seem like part of a timeless past, but they actually reflect the elaborate and ingenious technologies that took advantage of telegraphic immediacy—"Extra, extra!" was a ping and a pop-up.)

5   But other changes that seemed equally profound at the time have turned out, in retrospect, to be minor. The radio was an improvement on the telegraph but it didn't have the same exponential, transformative effect. How do we know when and

how changing your technology will change your life?

Sherry Turkle has been chronicling the impact of the digital revolution for some 20 years. In her *Alone Together* she focuses on two developments, social robots and Internet communications (texting, Second Life, e-mail, Facebook). Her method is ethnographic—she interviews people, especially children and adolescents, at length about how they feel about those technologies. Turkle is a sensitive interviewer and an elegant writer, and her book captures the anxiety and ambivalence that children and adolescents (and adults, too) feel about the new developments. Her general conclusion is that those anxieties are justified. Both robots and the Web will have a profound, and bad, effect on human psychology. Technology will lead to devalued and alienated lives rather than enriched ones.

When the ethnographic "clinical interview" method is done well, as Turkle does it, it can give us an excellent picture of what people think about the effects of technology. The trouble is that it doesn't tell us what those effects actually are. The children she talks to are remarkably thoughtful, but they are also contradictory: Robots are sort of people, but then again they're just machines; cell phones make parents more intrusive, or maybe more distant. Turkle quotes Niels Bohr's statement that the opposite of a profound truth is sometimes another profound truth, but fails to mention his preamble that the opposite of a fact is a falsehood. Facts about the effects of technology are thin on the ground. For example, there are remarkably few firm scientific conclusions from 50 years of psychological research on children and television.

There is also the problem of what psychologists call the "cultural ratchet effect." We learn differently as children than as adults. For grown-ups, learning a new skill is painful, attention-demanding, and slow. Children learn unconsciously and effortlessly. Because of this, each new generation rapidly acquires all the accumulated innovations of the past without even knowing it. The story of The Device is startling because we were born with print. The new

10

generation, in turn, will consciously alter those earlier practices and invent new ones. They can take the entire past for granted as they move toward the future.

These generational shifts are the engine of cultural innovation, and they are particularly relevant for technological change—our children will talk digital as a native language, while we speak it haltingly with an immigrant accent. But generational shifts go beyond technology. They also produce entirely arbitrary changes, like the historical changes from Elizabethan words or dances or dresses to ours. Even in the Neolithic period, pottery decorations changed over generations. These changes can feel significant even though they actually don't alter much of anything. The telegraph really did mean The End of Civilization As We Knew It, but the waltz and the crinoline caused just as much angst.

This immediate generational transformation, the click of the ratchet, is so vivid that the long historical changes and constancies are hard to see. The year before you were born looks like Eden, the year after your children were born looks like Mad Max.

Which of the effects that Turkle and other digital pessimists attribute to technology really are radical transformations, and which are relatively small changes magnified by the ratchet effect? Is the Internet the telegraph or just the crinoline? Some of the stories Turkle tells seem awfully like false nostalgia. A young woman feels guilty because she surreptitiously writes e-mail while she is Skyping (for hours!) with her distant grandmother. A teenager complains that her mother is distracted by her cell phone when she picks her up from school. Did we really once listen to our grandmothers with undivided attention? Were adolescent girls delighted by the rich and meaningful conversations they had with their mothers? Is the teenager who comes home from school and IMs her friends while she updates her Facebook page really much worse off than the one who came home and watched Gilligan's Island reruns? (More autobiography there.)

Turkle and her interviewees sometimes seem to treat minor variations on human nature like threatening psychological revolutions. For example, Turkle and many of her subjects worry that people might interact with nonhuman simulacra, like robots, as if they were people, and might lose themselves in imaginary worlds like Second Life.

But, after all, a majority of young children communicate extensively with imaginary companions, creatures who are even more elusive than robots since they don't exist at all. All normal children become immersed in unreal pretend worlds. And their elders do the same. Is the Turklean child who cries over a Furby really all that different from the Dickensian one who weeps for a doll? Is the lonely widow who talks to a robot really all that different than the one who talks to her dead husband's picture? Or religiously follows the lives of soap opera characters? Is a Second Life romance all that different from a Harlequin one?

And what about the fact that we communicate through highly abstract signals, rather than face to face? Take texting, surely the most baffling technological success of our age. We've harnessed vast computational power to let us write telegrams with our thumbs. Turkle and the teenagers contrast texting nostalgically, not only with live conversation, but with that day-before-yesterday Eden of the telephone—a technology that once seemed equally threatening.

15   But, at least since writing began, perhaps even since language itself began, human beings have conducted their most intimate lives through abstract, digital symbols. Bertrand Russell and Lady Ottoline Morrell carried on their love affair through the London post, writing several times a day, and Proust used the equally rapid and frequent pneumatic petits bleus of Paris. London letters were delivered 12 times a day and a petit bleu arrived two hours after it was sent (not much more slowly than an AT&T connection and probably more reliably). The Henry James story "The Great Good Place" is a utopian fantasy about unhooking from the grid and begins with a bitter lament at the inundation of telegrams and overflow of obligations that will be familiar to anyone with a bulging inbox.

Another worry is about attention. It is certainly true that by the time we're adults attention is a limited resource and attentional patterns are hard to change. But the exaggerated highlyfocused attention we consider appropriate in a contemporary classroom is itself a recent cultural invention, and one with costs as well as benefits. Guatemalan Mayan mothers successfully teach their children to divide their attention, as Western mothers teach children to focus theirs.

Despite all this, Turkle and the digital pessimists may be on to something. There is something about the Internet that seems genuinely different—a telegraphlike transformation. But it isn't the result of changes in the speed or character of communications. Texts and e-mails travel no faster than phone calls and telegrams, and their content isn't necessarily richer or poorer.

Turkle may be right, though, that there is a transformative difference in how many people we interact with, though it would be nice to have some objective evidence. There is an anthropological observation that most of us can keep track of only a couple of hundred people—a village-worth. The rise of cities just led us to define that village sociologically instead of geographically. City dwellers learn not to acknowledge, or even see, most of the people they pass on the street, a skill that seems baffling and obnoxious to rural visitors. The post and the petit bleu connected a relatively small urban literary circle.

The Web expands that circle exponentially. When we do a Google search we aren't consulting a brilliant computer, but the aggregated opinions of millions of other people. Facebook, which began as a way of digitally defining your social network, rapidly increases it beyond recognition. On the Web we communicate with the planet relying on a psychology that was designed for the village. You used to listen to your friends and Walter Cronkite, and, unless you were Walter, you could assume that your friends were the ones listening to you. Now it's much harder to tell whom we should listen to and who is listening to us, or at least we haven't yet figured out how to do it. We can edit out the obnoxious guy on the street more easily than the anonymous flame on the blog. On the Web we all become small-town visitors lost in the big city.

20 Even these reactions aren't completely new, though. City dwellers never entirely succeeded in turning Manhattan into Peoria, and they didn't really want to. The contradictory emotions Turkle describes are the characteristic urban emotions— excitement, novelty, and possibility balanced against loneliness, distraction, and alienation, and they seem to have arisen almost as soon as cit-

ies themselves. We were alone together in ancient Rome and 11th-century Kyoto. Long before even the printed book, Horace and Lady Murasaki re-acted to the life of their physical cities by yearning for simplicity, mindfulness, and meaning. Turkle's children also seem to yearn for a digital version of the classical pastoral retreat, or the Buddhist monastery. Maybe that would do us all some good. But the villa and the monastery would be much less appealing if we didn't have the big city and the Web of the wide world to return to.

Social Networking, Then and Now

MIKE KEEFE

Mike Keefe is a long-time editorial cartoonist for The Denver Post *and a syndicated cartoonist whose work has appeared in publications on three continents. Winner of numerous awards for his work, Keefe is past president of the Association of American Editorial Cartoonists and has served as a juror for the Pulitzer Prizes in Journalism. Keefe's books include* Running Awry, Keefe-Kebab, *and* The Ten-Speed Commandments.

Living and Learning with New Media: Summary of Findings from the Digital Youth Project

MIZUKO ITO, HEATHER HORST, MATTEO BITTANTI, DANAH BOYD, BECKY HERR-
STEPHENSON, PATRICIA G. LANGE, C.J. PASCOE, AND LAURA ROBINSON WITH SONJA
BAUMER, RACHEL CODY, DILAN MAHENDRAN, KATYNKA MARTÍNEZ, DAN PERKEL,
CHRISTO SIMS, AND LISA TRIPP

The Digital Youth Project was a three-year ethnographic study undertaken by research-ers at the University of Southern California and the University of California at Berkeley. Funded by the MacArthur Foundation as a component of its Digital Media and Learning Project, the study is the most extensive examination to date of how young people in the United States use digital and new media. According to its Web site, the study focused on the following two questions: "How are new media being integrated into youth practices and agendas? How do these practices change the dynamics of youth–adult negotiations over literacy, learning, and authoritative knowledge?" A brief research summary is printed here. Links to the summary and the final report are available at http://digitalyouth.ischoo l.berkeley.edu/report.

Research Summary

Over three years, University of California, Irvine researcher Mizuko Ito and her team interviewed over 800 youth and young adults and conducted over 5000 hours of online observations as part of the most extensive U.S. study of youth media use.

They found that social network and video-sharing sites, online games, and gadgets such as iPods and mobile phones are now fixtures of youth culture. The research shows that today's youth may be coming of age and struggling for autonomy and identity amid new worlds for communication, friendship, play, and self-expression.

Many adults worry that children are wasting time online, texting, or playing video games. The researchers explain why youth find these activities compelling and impor-tant. The digital world is creating new opportunities for youth to grapple with social norms, explore interests, develop technical skills, and experiment with new forms of self-expression. These activities have captured teens' attention because they provide avenues for extending social worlds, self-directed learning, and independence.

Major Findings

YOUTH USE ONLINE MEDIA TO EXTEND FRIENDSHIPS AND INTERESTS.

Most youth use online networks to extend the friendships that they navigate in the familiar contexts of school, religious organizations, sports, and other local activities. They can be "always on," in constant contact with their friends through private com-munications like instant messaging or mobile phones, as well as in public ways through social network sites such as MySpace and Facebook. With these "friendship-driven" practices, youth are almost always associating with people they already know in their offline lives. The majority of youth use new media to "hang out" and extend existing friendships in these ways.

5   A smaller number of youth also use the online world to explore interests and find information that goes beyond what they have access to at school or in their local community. Online groups enable youth to connect to peers who share specialized and niche interests of various kinds, whether that is online gaming, creative writing, video editing, or other artistic endeavors. In these interest-driven networks, youth may find new peers outside the boundaries of their local community. They can also find opportunities to publicize and distribute their work to online audiences, and to gain new forms of visibility and reputation.

YOUTH ENGAGE IN PEER-BASED, SELF-DIRECTED LEARNING ONLINE.

In both friendship-driven and interest-driven online activity, youth create and navigate new forms of expression and rules for social behavior. By exploring new interests, tinkering, and "messing around" with new forms of media, they acquire various forms of technical and media literacy. Through trial and error, youth add new media skills to their repertoire, such as how to create a video or game, or customize their MySpace page. Teens then share their creations and receive feedback from others online. By its immediacy and breadth of information, the digital world lowers barriers to self-directed learning.

Some youth "geek out" and dive into a topic or talent. Contrary to popular images, geeking out is highly social and engaged, although usually not driven primarily by local friendships. Youth turn instead to specialized knowledge groups of both teens and adults from around the country or world, with the goal of improving their craft and gaining reputation among expert peers. While adults participate, they are not automatically the resident experts by virtue of their age. Geeking out in many respects erases the traditional markers of status and authority.

New media allow for a degree of freedom and autonomy for youth that is less apparent in a classroom setting. Youth respect one another's authority online, and they are often more motivated to learn from peers than from adults. Their efforts are also largely self-directed, and the outcome emerges through exploration, in contrast to classroom learning that is oriented by set, predefined goals.

Implications

New media forms have altered how youth socialize and learn, and raise a new set of issues that educators, parents, and policymakers should consider.

ADULTS SHOULD FACILITATE YOUNG PEOPLE'S ENGAGEMENT WITH DIGITAL MEDIA.

10   Contrary to adult perceptions, while hanging out online, youth are picking up basic social and technical skills they need to fully participate in contemporary society. Erecting barriers to participation deprives teens of access to these forms of learning. Participation in the digital age means more than being able to access serious online information and culture. Youth could benefit from educators being more open to forms of experimentation and social exploration that are generally not characteristic of educational institutions.

GIVEN THE DIVERSITY OF DIGITAL MEDIA, IT IS PROBLEMATIC TO DEVELOP A STANDARDIZED SET OF BENCHMARKS AGAINST WHICH TO MEASURE YOUNG PEOPLE'S TECHNICAL AND NEW MEDIA LITERACY.

Friendship-driven and interest-driven online participation have very different kinds of social connotations. For example, whereas friendship-driven activities center upon peer culture, adult participation is more welcomed in the latter more "geeky" forms of learning. In addition, the content, behavior, and skills that youth value are highly variable depending on with which social groups they associate.

IN INTEREST-DRIVEN PARTICIPATION, ADULTS HAVE AN IMPORTANT ROLE TO PLAY.

Youth using new media often learn from their peers, not teachers or adults. Yet adults can still have tremendous influence in setting learning goals, particularly on the interest-driven side where adult hobbyists function as role models and more experienced peers.

TO STAY RELEVANT IN THE 21ST CENTURY, EDUCATION INSTITUTIONS NEED TO KEEP PACE WITH THE RAPID CHANGES INTRODUCED BY DIGITAL MEDIA.

Youths' participation in this networked world suggests new ways of thinking about the role of education. What, the authors ask, would it mean to really exploit the potential of the learning opportunities available through online resources and networks? What would it mean to reach beyond traditional education and civic institutions and enlist the help of others in young people's learning? Rather than assuming that education is primarily about preparing for jobs and careers, they question what it would mean to think of it as a process guiding youths' participation in public life more generally.

More Information

More information about the study and the MacArthur Foundation's digital media and learning initiative can be found online at www.digitallearning.macfound.org/ethnography [www.macfound.org].

Designing Learning from "End-to-End"

CATHY DAVIDSON

Cathy Davidson is Ruth F. DeVarney Professor of English and John Hope Franklin Humanities Institute Professor of Interdisciplinary Studies at Duke University. She is co-founder of the Humanities, Arts, Sciences, and Technology Advanced Collaboratory—HASTAC (pronounced "haystack"). This cross-disciplinary network of researchers and institutions is dedicated to exploring new possibilities for teaching and learning, within and outside the academy, made possible by digital technologies. In the following essay, Professor Davidson considers a new metaphor to guide the future of learning.

When Tim Berners-Lee and a handful of colleagues began developing the World Wide Web, they did so without a blueprint but with something better: a principle. What if all the world's knowledge could easily be transferred between us without going through a central node controlling the shape of that information? What if my computer could abide by certain kinds of communication protocols, could send out packets of information, and then any other computer in the world set up to understand those protocols could receive it? What if we all, the human community, could exchange our ideas without a publisher, without asking anyone's permission, without an editor, without a censor or an inspector or a digital traffic cop making it happen? The principle is called the "end-to-end" network principle. It goes back to the late 1970s when David Clark, David Reed, and Jerome Saltzer began advocating a new end-to-end form of systems design. For a succinct explanation of how the principle works, check out our friend Howard Rheingold's YouTube video "Understanding How Networks Work is a 21st Century Literacy."

Learning as Assembly Line

Let's think about the end-to-end principle as a key metaphor for designing learning futures. The end-to-end principle is the opposite of the "assembly line" principle of linear product development. In an assembly line, raw material is developed into a specific, pre-designed product as it is passed from set station to station down a line where each person on that line performs a pre-assigned function with a supervisor standing over the whole operation making sure everything proceeds at exactly the right, predetermined pace in order to arrive at the predetermined end-product. Every single person and every thing has a place and a function, and all of it is timed for maximum efficiency. That's what Taylorist labor is.

What I've been researching for the last decade is how disciplines, fields, majors, minors, graduate schools, professional schools, certification, I.Q. tests, multiple choice tests, MBA programs, skyscrapers (the modern office with its hierarchy of corner offices and cubicles arranged along long corridors with centralizing elevators—a vertical corridor), educational standards, blueprints, spreadsheets, statistics, standard deviation, the "two cultures" divide of the sciences versus the human and social sciences and arts, brain cartography (assigning specific functions to specific subsections of the brain), evolutionary sociobiology (where the human body is evolved from the beasts), evolutionary neuroscience (where the human brain is a machine), developmental psychology, disabilities (learning and otherwise), eugenic and racialist ideas, gender essentialism, and even our ideas about human aging are all derived from the assembly metaphor and model of systems design. *Really.*

You go back into the archives (I've found the papers, for example, of the guy who first conceived of the multiple choice test in 1914) and you see that the metaphor of efficiency motivated and inspired the modern (i.e. twentieth century) ways of thinking. The steam engine, the assembly line, and the Model T are *the ne plus ultra* upon which the "learning futures" of the twentieth century were designed.

Why Everything Must Change

5   What happens when the end-to-end principle is the systems metaphor for knowledge in the 21st century? What happens when you don't control the outcome, the functions, the end-design, the specific roles assigned to who will make it? What happens when you do not assign specific individuals to the process of creation but encourage self-forming groups to

innovate together? What happens if what you provide is a learning platform, with minimal controls? What if you allow anyone who wants to participate the opportunity to do so? What if you make the point of entry participation rather than a Ph.D. or certification or a blueprint or statistical measures to assess what they contribute or how? What happens? *Everything changes.*

As David Theo Goldberg and I have argued in the two-year long collaborative and participatory project that resulted in *The Future of Thinking*, the institutions that support all of us in our transformative learning are only now beginning to change. I don't see this as a problem. On the contrary, we are right on time. It was about 15 years into the machine age that all of the educational institutions, tools, and concepts of the Industrial Age began to be institutionalized. We are at that place now in the digital age.

Crowdsourced, Interactive

This week, at the Designing Learning Futures conference in Long Beach, Calif., more than 500 of us will be exploring how this revolutionary principle, the end-to-end principle of the World Wide Web, can work in designing our learning futures.

I know that sounds vague and abstract, so here's one concrete example of what we're up to. On Saturday afternoon (Mar. 5), just as the conference is winding down, on one of the last panels on the last day, I'll be joining a face-to-face panel of HASTAC Scholars, including the doctoral student who directs the HASTAC Scholars program (Fiona Barnett) and two of HASTAC Scholars (Dixie Ching and Jade Davis). But it won't be just the four of us. We'll be joined by whoever in the world is on the end of the social media flowing into our panel for a crowdsourced interactive session. What does that mean? We don't know exactly but we look forward to seeing what participation at a crowdsourced panel might look like.

Creating Knowledge and Networking It

In practical terms, there are almost 200 HASTAC Scholars—undergraduate and graduate students from more than 75 institutions in North America and abroad who are part of a loose network with very open community rules and requirements. Any HASTAC Scholar (as with anyone who joins HASTAC, admission is open to anyone who registers to be a member) one can blog at any time on any subject of relevance to digital media, interaction, social movements, communication, the arts, programming, or learning. And beyond. Four or so times a year, the HASTAC Scholars hold Forums on heady topics where the comments section reads like scholarly books, hundreds of pages if we printed them out. It's not just about contributing to knowledge but networking it, so that the knowledge itself isn't an end product but an end-to-end networked system. In that way, topics ranging from "Feel the Noise" to "Critical Code Studies" to "Race, Ethnicity, and Diaspora in the Digital Age," to the all-time most active topic, "Queer and Feminist New Media Spaces," change and morph, feed into new alliances, future dissertations, new conferences and panels, new modes of inquiry, new tools and new partners.

10   For an NSF grant we are writing now, we were asked to tally how many people (actual unique visitors) had visited these Forums. We were blown away by the number: 350,000.

You read that right. *350,000*! This is at a time when education is being devalued and de-funded, when humanistic thinking is thought to be on the wane. A student-run forum, of the highest intellectual caliber, has been joined by 350,000 people. We do not know who they are. Those 350,000—anonymous and eager to participate with whatever access to comput-ing or mobile device that allows them to be part of the World Wide Web—are central to any learning future we design together (*because* they are distributed and decentralized). They will be the unseen but present participants at our panel on Saturday (Mar. 5).

It's not just about the 500 people at Designing Learning Futures. If we are doing it right, if we are rethinking open learning and participation for the twenty-first century, if our idea of "design" is based not on the time-and-space-bound assembly line systems model but on the open end-to-end network principle, then our efforts we'll be joined by a good 350,000 . . . and counting!

Youthful Indiscretions: Should Colleges Protect Social Network Users from Themselves and Others?

DANA L. FLEMING

Dana L. Fleming is a Boston-area attorney specializing in labor and employment and higher education law. The following article appeared in the Winter 2008 issue of the New England Journal of Higher Education.

Counting members in the hundreds of millions, online social networking communities such as *MySpace* and *Facebook* may prove nearly as transformative as the 1876 inven-tion of the telephone. Creating a *MySpace* or *Facebook* profile is free and making online "friends" is easy—if you're under 30. But students' online identities and friendships come at a price, as job recruiters, school administrators, law enforcement officers and sexual predators sign on and start searching.

MySpace is routinely ranked among the top three most popular websites in America. The site was founded in 2003 by Tom Anderson, a graduate student at UCLA. Two years later, Rupert Murdoch's News Corp. purchased *MySpace* for a reported $327 million. Be-yond its financial success, *MySpace* boasts an international audience with more users than any other networking site in the world.

In New England, however, *Facebook* is a local favorite among college students and recent graduates, perhaps because it was founded in the region, by then Harvard sopho-more Mark Zuckerberg. The first month the site went "live" in 2004, half of Harvard's undergraduates signed up. Its popularity spread to other Boston-area campuses including MIT, Boston University and Boston College. By December 2004, the number of registered *Facebook* users surpassed one million. *Facebook* began by catering to undergraduates and for many years restricted membership by requiring all users to have a ".edu" email ac-count. In recent years, *Facebook* has opened its site to a wider audience in order to serve the growing demand for online social networking. Yet, *Facebook* remains the most popular site among New England college students.

Other sites such as *Friendster*, *LiveJournal* and *YouTube* offer additional means for users to "broadcast" their innermost thoughts and secrets across the World Wide Web. To join, a user needs only an email address and a willingness to share his or her "profile" with other users. Profiles usually include pictures and personal descriptions, music and video clips, plus information about the user's relationship status, school affiliations, interests and hometown. "Friending" someone (yes, it's a verb now) is as easy as searching for a name and clicking on it. This automatically sends a "friend request" to the other user, which that user can then accept, simply by clicking on the request. Perhaps not surprisingly, it is commonplace for users to have hundreds, even thousands of friends. Thirty percent of students report accepting "friend" requests from total strangers.

5   Joining or forming groups on these networks is easy too. With just a few clicks, users can join "Drunks United," "Sexy and Single on MySpace," or "My B.A.C. is Higher Than Your GPA." All of these groups have memberships in the tens of thousands. While privacy settings allow users to restrict who may view their profiles and group affiliations, such settings are rarely enabled by the user. Even when access is restricted to a user's so-called "friends," when students have hundreds or even thousands of "friends," anonymity can be hard to come by.

The explosion in online social networking sites and attendant loss of anonymity carries a cost. One University of Chicago student ruined his chances at a summer internship when an executive from the company viewed his *Facebook* profile, only to discover that his interests included "smoking blunts" (cigars stuffed with marijuana), shooting people, and obsessive sex. A chemical engineering major sabotaged his career in a similar manner by confessing in his online bio that he liked to "blow things up."

Recruiters are not the only ones checking up on students' profiles. In May 2005, two swimmers at Louisiana State University lost athletic scholarships for making disparaging comments about their coach on *Facebook*. In October 2005, a student at Boston's Fisher College was reportedly expelled for defaming a college police officer on *Facebook*. In an ongoing dispute at Millersville University in Pennsylvania, a young woman was denied her teaching degree after a fellow student brought one of her *MySpace* photos to the attention of school administrators. The photo, which has spurred a lawsuit, features the young woman wearing a pirate hat, drinking from an opaque plastic cup. The photo is suggestively captioned "Drunken Pirate."

A private Christian university in Virginia got creative when it found out that one of its law students posted an unflattering video of the school's founder, Pat Robertson, on *Facebook* and *YouTube*. (In the video, Pat Robertson appears to scratch his face with his middle finger.) The university has demanded that the law student publicly apologize for the posting or submit a legal brief defending it as satire protected under the First Amendment. Reports indicate that the student has chosen the latter punishment.

The dangers of online social networking transcend disciplinary actions and reputational harm. A 17-year-old Rhode Island girl was reportedly drugged and raped by three men she befriended on *MySpace*. Detectives in Colorado recently used *MySpace* to identify six men involved in the brutal rape and robbery of one of their online "friends." And the parents of a 13-year-old girl from Texas blame *MySpace* for their daughter's sexual assault and tried unsuccessfully to sue the company for negligence. The girl, "Julie Doe," lied about her age on her *MySpace* profile, then agreed to meet one of her "friends" in a restaurant parking lot where her friend, a 19-year-old male, sexually assaulted her. A U.S. District Court Judge dismissed the suit, stating: "If anyone had a duty to protect Julie Doe, it was her parents, not *MySpace.*"

10   Parents groups, attorneys general and legislators are grappling with how to protect young users from other users and, still more challenging, how to protect young users from themselves. Forty-five attorneys general are pushing *MySpace* to adopt more parental controls and an age-verification system. For example, Connecticut Attorney General Richard Blumenthal wants to see *MySpace* raise its minimum age limit from 14 to 16. Several bills in Congress have included provisions barring schools and libraries that receive federal funding from allowing minors to access networking sites like *MySpace* and *Facebook.*

Like lawmakers, college administrators have not yet determined how to handle the unique issues posed by the public display of their students' indiscretions. While some are starting to develop very thoughtful policies about these sites, many still wonder what all the fuss is about. Some schools use material from *MySpace* and *Facebook* in their judiciary proceedings while others turn a blind eye to the site. Some address the risks associated with these sites during freshman orientation, while others let students proceed at their own risk.

The office of student affairs at the University of Maine warns that while "the administrators are not monitoring *Facebook,*" they may act on any violations of law or University policy if it is brought to their attention. As the school candidly puts it: "Just because you don't want them [the administrators] to look at your page doesn't mean they can't or won't." Norwich University offers this reminder to its students: "As an institution of higher learning, Norwich University recognizes the importance of free speech and the use of information technology in the pursuit of educational goals. Nonetheless . . . we are all expected to behave—on campus, in public and online—in a manner consistent with the University's Honor Code and Guiding Values."

The Norwich policy, like many others across the country, is followed by a series of practical tips for online networkers, such as: "Don't post anything you wouldn't be comfortable with your grandmother seeing." Good advice, to be sure, but even a cursory perusal of these sites suggests that many students are not listening.

There is no practical way for colleges to monitor the content of these sites, as students' profiles and postings are changing constantly. It would take a full-time staff working around the clock to scratch the surface of a single network. An aggressive monitoring approach can also backfire. When students find out that a network is being monitored by administrators, they frequently change networks, password-protect their profile or group or post misleading information to confuse and frustrate administrators, (e.g., one student advertised a frat party at a specific dorm room, only to leave a "gotcha" note for campus police).

15   While a blanket monitoring approach is unfeasible, if not counterproductive, a targeted review of online social networking sites can be a good thing. For example, when a student exhibits signs of distress, a review of his or her online profile or blog may be appropriate. A review of a student's profile may also be appropriate where that student is involved in a disciplinary proceeding. Courts treat people's online postings as evidence in criminal proceedings, and college and university lawyers routinely check students' online profiles. It stands to reason then, that schools are free to use content from these sites in their own judiciary proceedings. Colleges that wish to create a policy specially tailored to online social networking policies should review Cornell's University's "Thoughts on *Facebook*," which cautions students about the personal risks and legal ramifications of online social networking, while at the same time acknowledging the benefits and popular appeal of such sites. In this era of aggressive date-mining and total information access, students' privacy is in peril. Advertisers are particularly interested in students' personal information, as they try to tailor ads to individual users. For example, a restaurant may create an online advertisement based not only on the student's geographic location, but also by noting that one of their "friends" is a regular customer. This type of targeted advertising helps to explain the financial success of sites like *MySpace* and *Facebook* where online advertisers can pay as much for online advertising space as they do for commercial slots on primetime TV.

    Under the Family Educational Rights and Privacy Act (FERPA), colleges have a responsibility not to divulge students' personal information, sell their names, phone numbers and email addresses to advertisers or otherwise violate their privacy rights. But when students post their most intimate secrets online, how can schools protect students' privacy?

    Though many students believe that the information they post online is "private," it's not—and the simplest way to address the liabilities posed by these sites is to treat them like any other university activity, subject to the school's code of conduct and applicable state and federal laws.

I Can't Wait . . .

PAUL NOTH

Paul Noth's cartoons appear regularly in the New Yorker *and other publications, including* The Wall Street Journal. *He has been a writer for* Late Night with Conan O'Brien *and* CBS's The Late Late Show *and is working on a graphic novel,* The Milwaukee Apocalypse. *View his Web site at www.paulnoth.com.*

"I can't wait to see what you're like online."

◼ ◼ ◼ FOR CLASS DISCUSSION Digital Literacies

1. Think about the articles in this chapter as well as your own experiences with digital technologies. In what specific ways do you think these technologies affect interpersonal relationships, for better or worse? What claims of danger or harm are made in these readings? What arguments can you identify that counter these claims? Which arguments are most convincing, and why?

2. Log your own use of communication technologies over twenty-four hours—social networking, emailing, texting, tweeting, talking over a device, web surfing, TV watching. Come to class prepared to discuss the ways in which you use these various technologies (e.g., social interaction, information or news gathering, education, movies or television, music, gaming, consumer activity, business communication, work, other). Do the findings of the Digital Youth Project, reported in "Living and Learning with New Media," accurately reflect your digital consumption? Which of the activities you have identified help to improve your literacy skills? Which of these activities, if any, impede or interfere with your learning or literacy?

3. As a class, brainstorm and make a list of the ways you or your teachers have used or are using digital or other technological applications in the classroom. Then

review Cathy Davidson's suggestion that our current model of learning is out-moded. Are there areas of incompatibility between current school models and technological applications? How might education, on Davidson's model, change the way schools look, or the way students learn? What other models or metaphors for schools or learning can you imagine?

4. Much has been made in the mainstream media about the dangers of revealing too much personal information on social networking sites such as *Facebook* and *MySpace*. Discuss your own experiences of identity sharing on social networking spaces: What do you reveal? What do you conceal? What responsibility, if any, do schools or colleges and universities have to ensure the safety of students who post personal information over their servers? Do you agree with Dana L. Fleming that "a targeted review of [students'] social networking sites can be a good thing"? Should students be required to make their social networking sites conform to a school's code of conduct?

WRITING ASSIGNMENT   Researched Argument

If your school has published any guidelines for using social networking spaces, review their policy. Such information might be available on your school's "information technology" or "computer services" Web site or in the student handbook, or you might have to contact your school's computer center or Dean of Students office. Conduct some research to find such policies at other schools; for example, see "Thoughts on Facebook" on the Cornell University Web site, http://www.cit.cornell.edu/policy/memos/facebook.html. You might also want to review recommendations for safe use of such sites at onguardonline.gov/socialnetworking.html or at http://www.ftc.gov/bcp/edu/pubs/consumer/tech/tec13.shtm. Then, write a researched argument for or against school oversight of students' publicly posted content, or write a set of guidelines appropriate for use by your school. ■

For additional writing, reading, and research resources, go to
www.mycomplab.com

Immigration in the Twenty-First Century

31

We are accustomed to discussing immigration as a political issue. Candidates for public office and politicians debate immigration policy or strategies for stopping the flow of illegal immigrants across our borders. We are also accustomed to media coverage of marches and protests by illegal immigrants petitioning for rights—to drive, to receive an education, to obtain health care—and we are well aware of efforts to stem the flow of Mexican citizens into the United States. Immigration reform is an ongoing issue in national politics with many stakeholders, including immigrant students. Of particular interest is the DREAM (Development, Relief, and Education for Alien Minors) Act, a bill that has been introduced in Congress several times in the last few years. The DREAM Act would provide a path to citizenship for illegal immigrants who arrived in the U.S. by the age of 15 either through the completion of a college degree or military service. In 2010, the bill passed the House of Representatives but not the Senate. Advocates in Congress and beyond have pledged to continue their support until a version of the DREAM legislation can be enacted.

Legal immigrants make headlines less regularly, but the fact is that streams of immigrants, many of them young people, continue to arrive in the United States through legal as well as illegal means. U.S. Census data from 2009 showed that there are 2.64 million foreign-born U.S. residents under age eighteen. As the articles in this chapter suggest, there is tremendous national, ethnic, and cultural diversity within this population. Nor do these census figures account for the vast numbers of first-generation Americans, the children of immigrants. By virtue of the 14th Amendment, whether their parents arrived in the United States by legal or illegal means, children born on U.S. soil are citizens. They are being educated in American schools but may go home to families whose first language is not English and whose religious and cultural practices are outside the American mainstream.

The readings in this chapter (as well as those in Chapter 2) ask you to consider the issues and challenges of immigration in a country that prides itself on its immigrant origins but sometimes has trouble welcoming people with unfamiliar appearances, languages, and practices. In particular, this chapter asks you to consider the following questions: How well is the United States accommodating its immigrant populations? What are the particular issues and challenges facing immigrant youth? To what extent should immigrants be expected to adapt or acculturate to a new country? Is it possible, or even advisable, for immigrants to preserve elements of their home culture while adapting to their new culture?

A Note to Young Immigrants

MITALI PERKINS

Mitali Perkins was born in India and emigrated to the United States when she was six years old. At first she lived in New York, but later, as a seventh-grader in a California suburb, Perkins was the only person in her class who was not white and not born in America. This experience, of living in what she calls the "strange space between cultures," has inspired her fiction, including Monsoon Summer *and* The Not-So-Star-Spangled Life of Sunita Sen. *Mitali Perkins maintains a blog on* MySpace *that includes a "fire escape," which, she hopes, is "a safe place to think, chat, and read about life between cultures." This article appeared in the magazine* Teaching Tolerance *in the Fall of 2005.*

Be ready: You lose a lot once you're tossed into the mainstream. You lose a place that feels like home, a community where the basics are understood, where conversations can begin at a deeper level. No easy havens await you, no places to slip into with a sigh of relief, saying, "At last, a place where everybody is like me." In the neighborhood, you're like a pinch of chili tossed into a creamy pot. You lose the sharpness of your ethnic flavor quickly but find that you can never fully dissolve.

You lose the ability to forget about race. You're aware of it everywhere in town, like a woman aware of her gender in a roomful of men. You dodge stereotypes at school by underperforming or over-achieving. You wonder if you're invisible to the opposite sex because you're foreign or because you're unattractive.

You lose a language. You still speak your parents' language, but it will soon begin to feel foreign to lips, pen and mind. Your heart won't forget as quickly; it will reserve a space for this mother tongue, your instructor of emotion, whispered in love and hurled in anger. Your heart language will speak words that tremble through tears; it will join you with others in the camaraderie of uncontrollable laughter. In your new language, English, you enjoy the lyrical cadence of poetry and glimpse the depth of ancient epics, but your heart will remain insatiable.

You lose the advantage of parents who can interpret the secrets of society. Your friends learn the art of conversation, the habits of mealtimes, the nuances of relationships, even the basics of bathroom behavior, from their parents. Your own parents' social etiquette sometimes leads to confusion or embarrassment in the outside world. You begin to take on the responsibility of buffering your parents from a culture that is even more foreign to them. You translate this new world's secrets for them.

5   You lose the stabilizing power of traditions. The year is not punctuated by rituals your grandmother and great-grandmother celebrated. Holidays in this new place lack the power to evoke nostalgia and renew childlike wonder. Your parents' feasts of celebration fall on days when you have to go to school.

You lose the chance to disappear into the majority anywhere in your new world. In the new neighborhood, you draw reactions common to minorities—outright racism, patronizing tokenism, enthusiasm from curious culture-seekers. If you travel across the seas to neighborhoods where your parents grew up, you're greeted with curious, appraising stares. You're too tall or too short; you move your arms and hips differently when you walk; you smile too often or not often enough; you employ the confusing nonverbal gestures from another world.

But don't get discouraged. In fact, you should feel quite the opposite. There is good news about life in the melting pot. There are gains to offset the losses, if you manage not to melt away altogether. You're boiled down, refined to your own distinctiveness.

You realize early that virtues are not the property of one heritage; you discover a self powerful enough to balance the best of many worlds.

A part of you rises above the steamy confusion of diversity to glimpse the common and universal. You recognize the ache that makes us all feel like strangers, even in the middle of comfortable homogeneity. You understand the soul's craving for a real home because yours is never sated with a counterfeit version.

So take time to mourn your losses, but remember to revel in the gains. Learn to embrace a litany of genuine labels—words like *stranger, pilgrim, sojourner, wayfarer*. Stride past the lure of false destinations, intent on traveling to a place where, at last, everyone can feel at home.

Miss or Diss?

SCARF ACE

This excerpt is taken from the blog Scarf Ace: Wearing a Muslim Head Scarf in America, *whose masthead describes the subject matter as follows: "An American Muslim wears the Islamic headscarf in middle America. Issues: Hijab, Modesty, Religion, Law, Faith, and Beauty." The blogger's profile identifies her as "a Pakistani-American Muslim mother" and lists her interests as "Islam, Muslims, Women's rights, America, and Motherhood."*

May 24, 2008

So it's been a year with the scarf. The weather is getting so hot and humid now, it's a big ordeal to get dressed and go out, especially being all covered up. I apologize in advance if this post is offensive, hurtful, confusing, etc. to anyone who loves wearing a headscarf. I started this blog as a way to cope with all the frustrations involved in starting hijab. And having an outlet has helped me to keep it on. Also, since I'm not an "all or nothing" type of person, getting comments from people that tell me that it is understandable to wear it while at the same time still have doubts and struggle and dislike for it also has helped me keep it on. Being able to be open and honest about my mental rumblings helps me feel less "two-faced" when it comes to wearing the headscarf, since the general assumption is that a hijabi has it all figured out in a very solid, committed way. It makes me think, what comes first, the chicken or the egg? In other words, should a Muslim girl wear the headscarf AFTER she's got her beliefs all figured out, or BEFORE as a way to help her solidify her beliefs? Anyhoo . . .

I miss the relief of cool breezes on my neck.

I miss having a good hair day and/or a great fitting outfit showing off whatever's left of my decreasing physical assets to get that ego boost.

5 I miss not wondering what other people are thinking when they see me.

If it weren't for 2 main things, I think I would have stopped wearing it by now:

1. My husband's high regard for hijab
2. Being a stay-at-home mom, I have the freedom to choose when and where I go (unlike at work or school).

When I struggle, these are the voices I hear in my head:

GOD: It's OK. I am Most Merciful, Gracious, Oft Forgiving. Remember Me and I will remember you.

HIJABI POLICE: She really should figure out who she is. What is her point?

10 NON-MUSLIM, IGNORANT: 1. I should watch her/stare at her/glance at her to figure her out. 2. I've got her figured out and it ain't good.

NON-MUSLIM, ENLIGHTENED: 1. There is a woman with a scarf. Perhaps she is Muslim. 2. It's refreshing to see diversity!

And, what I don't miss about not wearing a scarf: that nagging feeling of inconsistency when I thought about being all covered up to pray but not when out in public.

Sometimes when I'm sitting in traffic at an intersection, watching all the cars buzz by me, looking inside them to see people who dress nothing like me, I wonder, "Why am I here?" Shouldn't I be somewhere where the people, the women, dress like me, with headscarves and covered-up-ness? Why do I live here? Is there anywhere I can go and not feel like odd-man out all the time? Yup, sure, Iran, Pakistan, Indonesia, India . . . Dearborn, Michigan? . . . places where covered heads are the norm. So why did my family and other families come to America? Hmm . . . But I know that this kind of attitude is dangerous for America, it leads to the "Love it or Leave it" thing or "Go home!" or "Act like an American!" There is a part of America that says there is no one way to *look like* an American. But then there's another part that says, yes there is, and it doesn't include a Muslim headscarf, a Sikh turban, or a Hindu dot on the forehead. But it does seem to include a Nun's Habit. Hmm . . . It's interesting. It reminds me of how in some parts of Pakistani culture, the words, "American" and "Christian" are interchangeable.

I saw this Christian channel program in which they were sponsoring a "return the Jews to Israel" campaign, showing clips of people saying, "As a Christian, I feel very connected to my Jewish brothers." I thought . . . what about your Muslim brothers? Why is there no brotherly love for us?! I'm not going to get into the political problems/history of this issue here, but my point is that I was insecure for a moment, imagining a world with Jews and Christians against the Muslims, but then I felt this strength inside, a sort of "Well, if it's us against them, then, I will go down with this ship," which is a sort of nice feeling to have, instead of the insecure one I often feel when I think of those people who would rather not have Muslims around . . .

Anyway, back to my point about being in traffic. I'm just desperate to see some other hijabis when I go out, especially if it was a common thing to always see headscarves wherever I go.

Scarfing It Down

FATEMEH FAKHRAIE

Fatemeh Fakhraie maintains a Web site called Muslimah Media Watch: Looking at Muslim Women in the Media and in Pop Culture, *a forum for critiquing images of Muslim women. "We're tired," says the site, "of seeing ourselves portrayed in the media in ways that are one-dimensional and misleading." She has also been a regular contributor to the blog* Racialicious.com. *Her research interests revolve around identity, appearance, and style, especially regarding Islamic attire.*

Even before Pakistani-Canadian teen Aqsa Parvez was killed by her father last December because of her alleged refusal to wear hijab, provinces in Canada were hopping on the headscarf-banning bandwagon set in motion by countries like France and Turkey where women in hijab are not allowed in public institutions like schools and government buildings. Exclusionary rulings have also affected non-governmental entities: Many female sports teams (in both Canada and the United States) with members who wear hijab have been subject to short- or long-term rulings by sports federations banning them from playing on the basis that hijab is unsafe, despite the development of sport-safe hijabs. This past January, Washington, D.C. high-school track competitor Juashaunna Kelly was disqualified from a meet after officials deemed her custom-made uniform unfit for competition—even though she'd worn it the previous three seasons.

The idea of banning the hijab is an exclusionary and ignorant one. But a good share of the ignorance comes as much from the media's coverage of these bans as from those implementing them. News stories on hijab bans are always ready to skew the issue by focusing on the hijab ban as a "freedom of religion" issue. More important, the stories nearly always take away the voices of those who should have a say in these bans—namely, Muslim women themselves. How can we know what a particular person or group thinks about something that concerns them if we don't talk to them about it?

Another problem with the coverage is that the stories often call the hijab "a traditional Muslim garment" or "an Islamic obligation." While many Muslims do see hijab as a mandatory obligation, others do not. There are many devout women who don't observe hijab for whatever reason, and decrying hijab bans on the pretext of religious freedom leaves these women out—are they not Muslims, despite the fact that they don't wear a headscarf?

When you get right down to it, banning a headscarf is banning an item of clothing, which is an issue of personal, not religious, freedom. But banning the hijab specifically targets women. It's kind of like not allowing women to wear long-sleeved shirts; or, if you want to add a religious dimension to it, it's like banning Christmas sweaters. (A tempting idea sometimes, but not one most people would take seriously.)

5   So the next time you hear about a hijab ban (and sadly, there will be a next time), think about your best pair of jeans or your faded t-shirt with the logo of your favorite band. Then think about being forbidden by law to wear them.

Sophia's Choice: Problems Faced by Female Asylum-Seekers and Their U.S. Citizen Children

ANITA ORTIZ MADDALI

Anita Ortiz Maddali is a visiting clinical assistant professor at the Children and Family Justice Center at Northwestern University School of Law. She represents women and children seeking asylum or other forms of immigration relief, as well as non-citizen youth with criminal problems. This article appeared in the journal Feminist Studies *in Spring 2008.*

The United States is a beacon of hope for many who seek refuge from persecution in their home countries. As the plaque on the Statue of Liberty reads, "Give me your tired, your poor, / your huddled masses, yearning to breathe free, / the wretched refuse of your teeming shore. / Send these, the homeless, tempest-tost to me, / I lift my lamp beside the golden door."[1] Despite the high ideals embodied by these words, the politics of immigration and changing values have made immigration difficult, including for those fleeing persecution and seeking asylum in the United States. People from around the world come to the United States—from our neighbors in Latin America to as far away as Africa—to seek refuge from persecution by applying for asylum in the United States, yet the process of applying for asylum is full of pitfalls and challenges.[2]

This commentary focuses on the challenges that women seeking asylum endure, particularly when they give birth to children after arriving in the United States. It springs from my experience at the Children and Family Justice Center at Northwestern University School of Law in Chicago. We represent women and children from various countries fleeing different forms of persecution who are seeking asylum in the United States. By no means does this commentary encompass the entire spectrum of problems faced by immigrants or asylum-seekers—only the particular problems that I have witnessed while representing asylum-seekers at the Children and Family Justice Center.

Clients we have represented include women from Guatemala and Tanzania fleeing domestic abuse, a young woman from Central America targeted by drug traffickers, children from Honduras and Guatemala fleeing street gangs, and a young woman from China who owed $60,000 to the smugglers who forcibly brought her to the United States.

Women applying for asylum face an uphill legal battle as they seek to remain in the United States. In contrast, children born in the United States to these women are automatically classified as citizens because of the location of their birth. Thus, if a woman is denied asylum and forced to return to her homeland, this result not only has serious consequences for her but also for her U.S.-citizen child. Having fled persecution, returning poses a difficult, if not impossible choice for asylum-seekers—bringing their children back to the homeland and possibly exposing them to persecution there, or leaving them, in some cases, in the arms of strangers in the United States. In this commentary, I share some of my experiences and thoughts regarding these women, their children, and the difficult choices engendered by U.S. immigration policy.

5   A toughening of immigration standards has become a focus of debate in the United States. This debate is not new, but rather a resurfacing of a contentious and long-standing issue with real world consequences. The rigid enforcement of tougher immigration policies results in great uncertainty and fear among large groups of individuals living in the United States. Facing deportation, people without legal status deal with the choice of taking their children back to their homeland or leaving them in the United States. The *New York Times* told the story of the Mancia family who came to the United States from Honduras. The family left Honduras to escape growing gang violence; the mother's sister was killed by gang members while traveling on a public bus. The mother applied for asylum, but her claim was denied. She was eventually deported to Honduras, and the father, still in the United States, is facing his own deportation. He and his wife have two sons, one of whom,

because he was born in the United States, is a citizen. "If forced to depart, he [the father] will weigh whether to leave his sons with friends in New Bedford to get a quality of schooling he believes they will not have in Honduras."[3] Thus the fear of deportation affects not only those considered "illegal" but also "innocent" U.S. citizens.

According to a recent Pew Hispanic Center study, over three million U.S.-citizen children have undocumented parents.[4] Proponents of tougher immigration reform have referred to the children in this category as "anchor babies," a pejorative term implying that mothers have conceived these children so that the child's U.S.-citizen status can "anchor" the parents by allowing them to remain in the United States.[5] The anchor argument stems from an immigration provision that allows a U.S.-citizen child age 21 or older to petition for her/his undocumented parents to become legal permanent residents.

Brief Background on Asylum

Individuals fleeing persecution are entitled to apply for a form of immigration relief called asylum. The international community came together and developed standards for the treatment of refugees after the horrors of World War II. These standards were incorporated into the 1951 Convention Relating to the Status of Refugees. They were later expanded upon in the 1967 Protocol Relating to the Status of Refugees, which the United States acceded to on November 1, 1968. Later, as part of the Refugee Act of 1980, the United States developed asylum regulations to conform to its international obligations under the 1967 Protocol.[6]

A person applying for asylum must demonstrate that she has suffered or fears persecution on account of one of five protected grounds—race, religion, nationality, political opinion, and/or membership in a particular social group. An applicant must also show that she is unable or unwilling to return or avail herself of the protection of her country because of the persecution.

The women we represent at the Children and Family Justice Center come to the United States seeking protection. Sometimes they come alone; other times they come with their children. Assuming they are aware of asylum, they apply for this relief once they come to the United States. Applying for asylum immediately, however, does not signify that their cases are resolved expeditiously. With immigration courts burdened by heavy caseloads, it can take as long as three years before a person's asylum case is adjudicated. During this lengthy waiting period, an asylum-seeker must adjust to life in the United States. Sometimes asylum-seekers have children while awaiting resolution of their cases. These children automatically become U.S. citizens because they are born on U.S. soil. In contrast to her child's, the mother's immigration status remains in limbo. In this situation, a woman must not only deal with the anxiety of applying for asylum, but she must also worry about her children's future in the event that she loses her asylum case and is deported. Through our representation, I have witnessed these women struggle with the uncertainty of their children's fates. I have seen the strain placed on families as they deal with the possibility of separation.

10   In some instances the immigration rules and policies seem to acknowledge the inherent complexity involved in dealing with families. For instance, if an asylum-seeker is granted

asylum, the asylum-seeker's children who are unmarried and under the age of 21 at the time the application was filed can obtain derivative relief through the parent who has been granted asylum. An applicant's children, whether within or outside the United States, can be beneficiaries of the law on asylum. Thus, immigration policy on asylum seems to embrace the unification of the family unit by providing for such benefits. Going against the principle of uniting families, however, immigration laws prohibit a child from petitioning for her parents to obtain status. In contrast to the situation described above, a child who has been granted asylum cannot petition for her parents to be a beneficiary of her asylum grant.

Similarly, a U.S.-citizen child cannot petition for her parents to obtain legal immigration status. In the event that an asylum applicant loses her asylum case, the applicant's U.S.-citizen child, if under the age of 21, cannot petition for her to obtain legal status in the United States. In such cases, the mother must return to her country of origin, although the U.S. government cannot deport the U.S.-citizen child because that child possesses all of the benefits that citizenship entails. A parent must then decide whether to leave the child behind in the United States or bring her U.S.-citizen child into a potentially harmful situation in her country of origin.

Sophia's Story

Sophia left Guatemala, where domestic abuse is a serious problem, to escape the physical and emotional abuse she endured at the hands of her husband.[7] Sophia's husband beat her routinely, hospitalizing her on numerous occasions. Hospital officials never reported the abuse to local authorities, and Sophia had nowhere to seek help. Although Guatemalan law prohibits domestic abuse, it does not establish prison sentences for the abuse. According to the research by the U.S. Department of State, in Guatemala abusers are charged with assault only when bruises resulting from the abuse remain visible for at least ten days.[8]

At the time that Sophia became pregnant with her second child, her husband's beatings intensified. Her husband was angry that Sophia was pregnant. In an effort to protect herself and her children, Sophia, still pregnant, fled to the United States with her five-year-old son. Shortly after arriving in the United States, Sophia gave birth to her baby girl in Chicago. She and her children found a community in Chicago where they could reside. Sophia worked as a nanny to support herself and her two children. Her son attended school and began adjusting to his new life.

Sophia and her son remained undocumented. Two and a half years after arriving in the United States, Sophia received an order of removal. Sophia's daughter was classified as a U.S. citizen because of the location of her birth. Looking for legal representation, Sophia immediately contacted a nonprofit agency that referred her to the Children and Family Justice Center for legal assistance. We agreed to represent her.

15   After extensive interviews with Sophia, we filed an asylum claim on her behalf. Sophia's asylum case presented many challenges. First, Sophia's persecution occurred at the hands of a private actor—her husband. Asylum claims based on persecution by private actors are difficult to argue because the original asylum framework aimed to protect individuals

who were being persecuted by their government.[9] The situation today is different. Now, women and children constitute the majority of refugees, and the harms they flee often occur within the private sphere.[10] Thus, in order to work within the original framework, an asylum-seeker must show some type of government action or inaction. Specifically, when the persecution occurred at the hands of a private actor, the applicant must demonstrate that the government was unable or unwilling to control the persecutor.[11]

We also needed to demonstrate that her husband persecuted her on account of one of the five protected grounds mentioned above. Again, the international community did not anticipate the types of claims that would be brought by women so there is no protected ground for persecution based on gender. Therefore, under the asylum framework, many of the claims brought by women, especially those involving domestic violence, are argued under the "membership in a particular social group" ground.[12]

The definition of "membership in a particular social group" is amorphous. Courts, however, have provided some guidance. In the Seventh Circuit (the federal appeals court in which the Chicago immigration court resides and whose precedent the Chicago immigration court is required to follow), members of a particular social group must share certain common and immutable characteristics that a person cannot change or should not be required to change.[13] Although one can argue that "women" or "gender" can fit within this construction, case law has instructed that the social group cannot be all encompassing because the courts are often concerned about opening the floodgates by enlarging the pool of applicants eligible for asylum.[14] We cannot argue, for example, that all women from a certain country are targeted for female genital mutilation (FGM) because they are women. The social group needs to be narrowed even further. For instance, a proper social group would be women from a specific ethnic group, who are targeted by individuals performing FGM and who oppose the practice. In Sophia's case, we needed to construct her social group with particularity, so as not to argue that all victims of domestic violence in Guatemala are eligible for asylum.

Sophia fears returning to Guatemala. Sophia's husband has continued making threats to her family members, stating that he will take the children away from Sophia if she returns. Sophia fears that he will abuse the children if they are living with him. Sophia cannot imagine leaving her daughter in the United States if she is deported.

If Sophia is denied asylum, not only will she and her son, who is a derivative on her asylum application, be forced to return to a dangerous, potentially life-threatening situation, her U.S.-citizen daughter's fate will be precarious as well. The government cannot deport the U.S.-citizen child, but to remain in the United States will mean separation from her mother and brother. If Sophia brings her daughter to Guatemala, her daughter will be subjected to violence from an abusive father. Sophia has no real choice. Each option is devastating, and each option more likely than not will result in harm to Sophia's daughter.

20   Sophia's story is not unique. Many women flee their homeland because of some type of persecution. Sophia did not have her daughter to anchor her in the United States. Instead, Sophia came to the United States, as a pregnant woman, to protect herself and her children from abuse.

Aisha's Story

Aisha was one of the thousands of black Mauritanians forcibly expelled in 1989 from her country of Mauritania and brought to Senegal.[15] On the day that she was taken, soldiers came to Aisha's house in Mauritania and dragged her and her husband by force into military trucks. Soldiers brought Aisha to a military camp, but left her husband in the truck. She never saw him again.

During the night, while in the camp, two soldiers entered the barracks where she was sleeping and raped her. She could not see their faces as they wore scarves, which are customary and used to prevent desert sands from entering their eyes. A couple of hours later, the soldiers returned and raped her yet again. Pregnant at the time, the force of the rape caused Aisha to lose her baby.

The next day soldiers brought Aisha, along with a group of other black Mauritanians, across the border into Senegal. Placed in a refugee camp, Aisha had no money and no choice but to live her life in Senegal. She worked in a market selling goods but was never able to officially settle in Senegal.

While in Senegal, Aisha met Ibrahim, a Senegalese citizen. Ibrahim visited Aisha quite often at the market, and they spoke a great deal during these visits. After developing a strong friendship, Aisha revealed the circumstances that led to her coming to Senegal. From these conversations, Ibrahim knew that Aisha wanted to leave, and over the course of time he helped Aisha obtain an airline ticket and false documents to come to the United States.

25 After receiving these documents, Aisha immediately left for the United States. She arrived at JFK airport, managed to get through customs, and took a Greyhound bus to Indianapolis to stay with a Senegalese couple Ibrahim had known.

Aisha immediately applied for asylum after coming to the United States, but an asylum officer referred her case to an immigration judge. At this point, Aisha was placed in removal proceedings, so she contacted a legal service agency who referred her case to the Children and Family Justice Center.

Aisha, like so many in similar situations, did not know what the future would hold. She worked seven days a week braiding hair. Aisha was haunted by her past, struggled in her present to support herself, and feared for the future.

About a year after arriving, Aisha met a man from Mauritania who had also been expelled from his country and who was applying for asylum. What started initially as a friendship eventually developed into a romantic relationship. Aisha became pregnant with their baby, and five months before her asylum hearing she gave birth to a baby girl. Aisha continued working in the braid shop, but now she braided hair with her baby daughter strapped to her back.

After the immigration hearing, the immigration judge believed Aisha's story and granted Aisha asylum because of the persecution she suffered on account of her race and her ethnic group—black Mauritanians. A year later, the baby's father also obtained asylum. Aisha and her partner are still together, and they are raising their daughter. Had Aisha been denied asylum, not only would the family's life circumstances have changed, but so too would their daughter's. Aisha faced the possibility of being returned to a country from which she was forcibly expelled. She could have been faced with the prospect of bringing her daughter into the same country where she and her partner faced persecution because of their race and ethnicity or of leaving her child motherless in the United States.

Courts Weigh in on the Issue

30 The two cases discussed below provide some insight into a court's analysis of asylum law within this context. Although these cases involve women from Nigeria who fear that their children will be subjected to female genital mutilation, women with children from around the globe who are fleeing different types of harms must not only worry about their own safety if they are returned to their countries but also about their children's safety.

In Oforji v. Ashcroft, a Seventh Circuit case, a Nigerian woman feared that her U.S.-citizen daughters would be subjected to female genital mutilation if she were deported to Nigeria. The mother felt that she would have to bring her children with her if she were deported. Oforji asked for derivative asylum relief under the Convention against Torture, which is an alternative form of relief for people who demonstrate that it is more likely than not that they will be tortured if returned to their country of origin. The court did not grant Oforji relief. It reasoned that the mother could choose to leave her children in comparative safety in the United States. Because they were U.S. citizens, they could not be deported. The mother herself did not face persecution or torture, as she had already been subjected to FGM.[16]

The court stated, "Oforji will be faced with the unpleasant dilemma of permitting her citizen children to remain in this country under the supervision of the state of Illinois or an otherwise suitable guardian, or taking her children back to Nigeria to face the potential threat of FGM. Congress has foreseen such difficult choices, but has opted to leave the choice with the illegal immigrant, not the courts." The court went on to say, "[u]nder the present law a woman who is otherwise a deportable alien does not have any incentive to bear a child (who automatically becomes a citizen) whose rights to stay are separate from the mother's obligation to depart."[17]

In a later Seventh Circuit case, Olowo v. Ashcroft, the court found that the mother did not actually have a choice. Olowo argued that if she was deported to Nigeria, she would have to bring her lawful permanent resident daughters with her. In Nigeria, these daughters would face the threat of FGM. Using the same reasoning as Oforji, the court found that because the mother had already undergone FGM, she did not demonstrate that she would be subjected to persecution. Although she feared that her daughters would be subjected to FGM, they legally did not have to go to Nigeria with their mother because they were legal permanent residents. Moreover, the daughters' father was a legal permanent resident and the children could stay with him—circumstances that factored heavily into the court's reasoning. The mother argued that her husband would have to go with the family to Nigeria because he could not care for the girls on his own. The court stated, "[b]oth of Ms. Olowo's daughters are legal permanent residents, as is their father, and when there is a parent who is available to care for the daughters in the United States, they are under no compulsion to leave." In contrast to Oforji where the court seemed to imply that the mother had a choice, the court told the Clerk of the court to forward a copy of the court's opinion to the Illinois

Department of Children and Family Services because the mother's choice would not be in the best interest of her children. The court stated, "The notion that Ms. Olowo's daughters will be removed to Nigeria and subjected to this brutal procedure offends our sense of decency, and allowing Ms. Olowo to make this decision unilaterally disregards the legal rights of the children."[18]

The Need for Immigration Reform

The statements of anti-immigrant advocates minimize the consequences that certain policies have on immigrant children. Reflecting this attitude is a statement by the executive director of the Center for Immigration Studies, a group striving to limit immigration: "Kids often pay for the bad decisions of their parents. If you do something wrong that sends you to jail, well, your kids suffer for that. If you are careless with your mortgage and lose your house, your kids suffer along with you. . . . [The parents] knew what they were doing when they had kids here, knowing that they were still illegal immigrants."[19] Sharing this sentiment, Rosemary Jenks of NumbersUSA, a group whose goal is to limit immigration, believes that the parents bear the responsibility for any negative effects deportation may have on their children.[20]

35   However, the U.S. Supreme Court stated in a landmark case, Plyer v. Doe, that children should not be penalized for the actions of their parents. This case involved a class action lawsuit that was brought in 1977 on behalf of "certain school-age children of Mexican origin residing in Smith County, Texas, who could not establish that they had been legally admitted into the United States." The lawsuit was a response to an action taken by the state legislature in 1975 that revised its education laws to withhold state funds to school districts for the education of children who were not legally admitted in the United States. Local school districts were also able to deny enrollment to children under this revision. The case was eventually argued before the U.S. Supreme Court in 1981. The Supreme Court held that such an action on the part of the state violated the Equal Protection Clause of the Fourteenth Amendment. The Court made clear that children cannot control the actions of their parents. "Even if the State found it expedient to control the conduct of adults by acting against their children, legislation directing the onus of a parent's misconduct against his children does not comport with fundamental conceptions of justice." According to the Court, penalizing the child for a parent's actions is fundamentally unjust.[21]

Family separation can have a significant impact on children. Research demonstrates that family separation in the context of immigration can be quite traumatic. During the course of one study, researchers interviewed a 14-year-old girl from the Dominican Republic who left her country to come to the United States. In speaking with the researchers, she stated, "The day I left my mother I felt like my heart was staying behind. Because she was the only person I trusted—she was my life. I felt as if a light had extinguished. I still have not been able to get used to living without her."[22] The separation of children from their mothers can disrupt a child's own development and inhibit a "secure attachment bond," which can lead to emotional disturbances in a child's development.[23]

The psychological traumas of separation impact parents as well. According to one woman who had been in the United States for ten years while her asylum and Temporary

Protected Status (TPS) application remained pending, she worried daily about her children left behind in El Salvador. She told the researcher:

> I live ansustiada [anguished] because I don't know if they eat or not, if they are clothed or not, if they get sick, will they get good treatment? [her voice breaking] It's the most horrible torture for a human being, not knowing how your children are, if they're suffering. Sometimes I want to abandon everything and go home to see my boys. But then I think, I have a daughter here too, and I have put up with this life for a while already, so I better stay put, so that they can, God willing, benefit more in the future. It's my only consolation.[24]

Immigration policy is complicated, and a thorough discussion of solutions to this problem is beyond the scope of this commentary. One area of reform, however, would be to change the cancellation of removal provisions, which are a form of immigration relief available to nonpermanent residents who are inadmissible or deportable.[25] A person applying for cancellation of removal must meet certain requirements. One of these requirements is to demonstrate that the person's deportation would cause exceptional and extremely unusual hardship to her lawful permanent resident or U.S.-citizen spouse, child, or parent. Another requirement is to show continuous presence in the United States for at least ten years. Prior to 1997, the continuous presence period was seven years, but the Illegal Immigration Reform and Immigrant Responsibility Act of 1996 changed the time requirement to ten years.[26] This arbitrary number disqualifies many immigrants from obtaining cancellation of removal. Many of these immigrants are valuable and productive members of society. Judge Posner, in his concurring opinion in Oforji v. Ashcroft, stated that "[t]he seven-year (or ten-year) rule is irrational viewed as a device for identifying those cases in which the hardship to an alien's children should weigh against forcing her to leave the country."[27]

Conclusion

40   The mothers with whom I have worked want the best for their children, and their actions indicate that their only goal is to provide for, care for, and protect their children. We should strive for a society in which our U.S.-citizen children live in a supportive family environment, enabling them to thrive and become productive members of society. Thus, Congress should consider the importance of the familial unit while enacting immigration legislation. As the justices in Plyler v. Doe recognized, children should not be penalized for the perceived "sins" of their parents. Reforming immigration laws to keep innocent children in mind would comport with the U.S. ideals of human rights, justice, and opportunity.

Footnotes

I would like to thank my husband Chaitanya Maddali who has taught me to dream without making dreams my master.

1 Emma Lazarus, "The New Colossus," 1885, lines 10–14.

2 Obtaining asylum is no easy task. For instance, from 2001 through 2005, 60–63 percent of defensive asylum applications were denied on the merits, and approximately 80 percent of all defensive asylum

applications, not just those considered on the merits, were denied. In terms of the numbers of those actually granted asylum, one out of five defensive applicants are granted asylum in immigration court. TRAC Immigration, "The Asylum Process," Transnational Records Access Clearing house (TRAC) Reports, http://trac.syr.edu/immigration/reports/159.

3 Julia Preston, "As Deportation Pace Rises, Illegal Immigrants Dig In," New York Times, Sec. A, 1 May 2007; www.nytimes.com/2007/05/01/us/01deport, html?ref= todayspaper.

4 Jeffrey S. Passel, Estimates of the Size and Characteristics of the Undocumented Population (Washington, D.C.: Pew Hispanic Center, 2005), http://pewhispanic.org/files/reports/44.pdf.

5 Federation for American Immigration Reform, "Anchor Babies: The Children of Illegal Aliens," www.fairus.org/site/PageServer?pagename=iic%5fimmigrationissuecenters 4608.

6 Convention Relating to the Status of Refugees, 189 United Nations' Treaty Series (U.N.T.S.) 137, adopted 28 July 1951, entered into force 22 Apr. 1954; Protocol of 1967 Relating to the Status of Refugees, 606 U.N.T.S. 267, entered into force 4 Oct. 1967; Edward M. Kennedy, "Refugee Act of 1980," International Migration Review 15, no. 1/2 (1981): 141–56.

7 Many of the facts, including the name and country, have been changed to protect the identity of the client. The facts in this story are an amalgamation of different clients we have represented.

8 U.S. Department of State, Guatemala: Country Reports on Human Rights Practices, Bureau of Democracy, Human Rights and Labor 2006, www.state.gov/g/drl/rls/hrrpt/2006/ 78751.htm.

9 Judith Kumin, "Gender: Persecution in the Spotlight," Refugees 2, no. 123 (2001): 13, www.unhcr.org/home/PUBL/3b5e90ea0.pdf.

10 Bela Hovy, "Building a Gender and Age-Sensitive Approach to Refugee Protection," Migration Information Source 2003, www.migrationinformation.org/Feature/display. cfm?id=104.

11 In Re Fauziya Kasinga, 21 Immigration and Naturalization (I&N) Dec. 357, 365 (Board of Immigration Appeals [BIA] 1996).

12 Kumin, "Gender: Persecution in the Spotlight," 12.

13 Lwin v. INS, 144 F.3d 505, 512 (7th Cir. 1998) (following the reasoning in Matter of Acosta, 19 I&N Dec. 211,233 [BIA 1985]).

14 Escobar v. Gonzales, 417 F.3d 363, 368-69 (3rd Cir. 2005) (arguing that "[P]overty, homelessness, and youth are far too vague and all encompassing . . . " to constitute characteristics that define a social group).

15 The facts, including the name, have been changed. Moreover, in an effort to protect the privacy of clients, this story combines the facts from two clients' cases.

16 Oforji v. Ashcroft, 354 F.3d 609, 616, 615 (7th Cir. 2003).

17 Oforji v. Ashcroft, 354 F.3d 618 (7th Cir. 2003).

18 Olowo v. Ashcroft, 368 F.3d 692, 697–698, 700–701, 703–704 (7th Cir. 2004).

19 N.C. Aizenman, "Pleading to Stay a Family: Raids on Illegal Immigrants Have Their U.S.-Born Children Fearing Separation—and Some Are Lobbying Capitol Hill," Washington Post, A2, 2 Apr. 2007, www.washingtonpost.com/wpdyn/content/article/ 2007/04/01/AR2007040101181.html.

20 Preston, "As Deportation Pace Rises."

21 Plyler v. Doe, 457 U.S. 202, 206, 205, 202, 220 (1982).

22 Cerda Suarez-Orozco, Irina L.G. Todorova, and Josephine Lovie, "Making Up for Lost Time: The Experience of Separation and Reunification among Immigrant Families," Family Process 41, no. 4 (2002): 634.

23 Victoria B. Mitrani, Daniel A. Santisteban, and Joan A. Muir, "Addressing Immigration-Related Separations in Hispanic Families with a Behavior-Problem Adolescent," American Journal of Orthopsychiatry 74, no. 3 (2004): 220, 221.

24 Cecilia Menjivar, "Liminal Legality: Salvadoran and Guatemalan Immigrants' Lives in the United States," American Journal of Sociology 111, no. 4 (2006): 1022.

25 There is also a cancellation or removal provision for legal permanent residents. The requirements, however, differ from those for nonpermanent residents.

26 National Immigration Law Center, "BIA Issues Decisions Interpreting Hardship Standards in Suspension and Cancellation Cases," Immigrants' Rights Update 15, no. 4 (2001), www.nilc.org/immlawpolicy/removpsds/removpsds067.htm.

27 Oforji, 354 F.3d at 620.

Born in the U.S.A.

KEVIN CLARKE

Kevin Clarke is an associate editor for America *magazine with a Master of Arts in International Studies from DePaul University. He has been recognized by the Associated Church Press and the Catholic Press Association for his opinion and feature writing, and by Catholic Relief Services for his reporting on international issues. As a senior editor for* U.S. Catholic *magazine, in which this commentary first appeared in October 2010, his writing focused on social justice issues including poverty in America and across the globe, universal health care, and the role of the Internet in protests in Africa and the Middle East.*

The birther movement is at it again. No I'm not talking about the fringe group that insists, in defiance of all evidence to the contrary, that President Barack Obama is not a native-born citizen.

The birther movement I'm talking about is fixed on repealing the 14th Amendment, a Civil War-era addition to the Constitution clarifying the citizenship of freed slaves that confers instant citizenship on any person born in the United States or any of its territories, military bases, or assorted colonial leftovers. The birth prohibitionists fixate on reports of a gazillion or so migrants each year scheduling U.S. visits to coincide with due dates so their children become so-called anchor babies, offering a toe-hold for undocumented parents and siblings.

If that were actually the case, maybe we should just be gratified that there are folks who have such a high esteem for U.S. citizenship, entrepreneurial instincts, and acute long-term planning skills (anchor babies' citizenship doesn't "pay off" until age 21) and leave it at that. But there's plenty of reason to doubt the veracity of the "drop and leave" migrant delivery South Carolina Senator Lindsey Graham so charmingly describes and plenty more reason not to use sociological myth-making to screw up what has been one of the hallmarks of the promise and generosity of American life.

Birthright citizenship in truth is practiced by a minority of nations around the world, but it's a civic tradition in the United States that is rooted in English Common Law and long predates the 14th Amendment's codification. Were it not for our acceptance of birthright citizenship, a great many "Americans" born in the 18th and 19th centuries to economic migrants from European backwaters like Ireland and Germany would not have been able to become citizens. After decades of accepting citizenship by birth, this tradition has suddenly become controversial. What's changed?

5   Increased socio-economic uncertainty always brings out the worst in America's nativist impulses, now unironically adopted by the children and grandchildren of immigrants. Politicians looking for editorial traction have settled on the issue as a public relations winner. But something uglier is also at work. You don't have to venture too far into the cyber underbelly of the 14th Amendment repealers before an atavistic ugliness becomes obvious—and odious.

We already know what stratified citizenship looks like. Generations of Japanese born to Korean parents are still marked as less than equal. Without fail, such gradations of citizenship lead to structural discrimination, labor exploitation, and frequently outright physical violence against the diminished partner in nationhood. The notion of degraded citizenship can lead to a permanent underclass and generations of unresolved tension and resentment.

That's why America's insta-citizenship, which confers not only the rights and privileges of U.S. citizenship on the native-born but also the responsibilities and obligations, shines so brightly as a beacon of human dignity. Using native birth as a standard for citizenship is eminently reasonable. It is fortuitously uncomplicated; it speaks to our best traditions as a republic. This clear principle inoculates American democracy from unseemly and potentially hazardous debates about how to define "real Americans."

Catholic teaching can contribute to this conversation before it becomes too overwrought. We refuse to condemn those who migrate out of economic or political necessity. We acknowledge our scriptural obligation to protect and support the sojourner and the vulnerable. We embrace and defend the sacredness of life.

The anchor baby prohibitionists can certainly find anecdotal evidence to support their broad suspicions, but most of the people having children in America, whatever their legal or visa status, do so because they are open to life and want to be a family together. Our tradition has been to welcome that life into the world with them.

10 Welcoming, not denigrating the newcomer, has made us a stronger nation and a better people. That will continue to be true no matter how much rhetorical heat the 14th Amendment revisionists are able to generate before November.

Anchor Babies Away

This editorial appeared in the August 13, 2010, edition of The Washington Times, *a Washington, D.C.–based newspaper founded in 1982 by the Reverend Sun Myung Moon, founder of the Unification Church. The newspaper is known for its conservative point of view and has "an eye toward upholding traditional values and principles while keeping politicians and officials of all parties and persuasions honest."*

Eight percent of babies born in U.S. hospitals in 2008 had mothers who were illegal aliens, according to a report released Wednesday by the Pew Research Center. Such newborns bring significant societal costs. Because their parents are poor, the families contribute little in taxes while at the same time relying heavily on government services.

For example, with $593 billion spent at the federal and state level on public elementary and secondary schools, boosting enrollment by

8 percent would likely represent $47 billion in additional costs. Given the language barriers, these new entrants undoubtedly represent an above-average expense. Subsidizing these costs brings to mind the dilemma raised by the late Milton Friedman, who warned that free immigration and a welfare state should never be combined.

The problem is growing, and Republicans like House Minority Leader John Boehner of Ohio think one of the solutions that should at least be on the table for

discussion is ending the birthright citizenship that has created the so-called "anchor baby" phenomenon. Even Senate Majority Leader Harry Reid, Nevada Democrat, at one time recognized this as a problem.

The current practice of granting automatic citizen status to children born in the United States to non-citizen parents derives from a disputed provision of the 14th Amendment which states, "All persons born or naturalized in the United States, and subject to the jurisdiction thereof, are citizens of the United States and the States wherein they reside." The precise meaning of the phrase "subject to the jurisdiction" opens a question of whether amending the Constitution is needed to end the practice.

5   A plurality of Americans, 49 percent, are willing to do just that, according to a new CNN/Opinion Research poll. However, such an effort only addresses a symptom of problems that run much deeper. First, our borders are hopelessly insecure. Until the ease of entry into this country is fixed, the steady flow of illegal immigrants will continue. Second, our overly generous welfare state provides financial incentives for people to leave Mexico and come to the United States. Amending the Constitution takes immense effort, and the most recent efforts to modify this governing document have failed. Neither securing the border nor curbing the welfare state requires the effort of a constitutional amendment. We will not solve our immigration problems until we first tackle the two core issues.

"Oh, Great, An Anchor Baby"

LEE JUDGE

Lee Judge is an editorial cartoonist whose work has appeared in hundreds of newspapers and magazines, including The New York Times, The Washington Post, The Chicago Sun-Times, The National Review, *and the* Kansas City Star, *where he was the staff cartoonist for 27 years. His work has also been featured on* Good Morning America *and* C-SPAN.

"OH, GREAT, AN ANCHOR BABY."

My Life in the Shadows

REYNA WENCES

Reyna Wences was brought to the United States illegally from Mexico as a child. When this essay appeared in the New York Times Upfront *in January 2011, Wences was 19. She is the co-founder of the Immigrant Youth Justice League, a Chicago-based organization led by undocumented youth "working for immigrant rights through education, resource-gathering, and youth mobilization." Their blog can be found at iyjl.org.*

I'll never forget the day I left Mexico for the last time. I was nine, and my mother, three-year-old brother, and I abandoned our apartment in Mexico City. We boarded a bus heading north to the border city of Nogales to meet up with a "coyote"—a guide who helps smuggle people into the United States.

We had paid the coyote $6,000, borrowing most of the money from relatives. All we could take with us that morning in July 2000 was a small bag with a change of clothes and water. The sun was hot, and I remember praying we wouldn't have to travel through the desert, where temperatures can reach 120°F and many people die from dehydration.

To my surprise, getting across the border and to our final destination proved uneventful: We didn't see any guards and just walked into Arizona, to a city also called Nogales. From there, a driver hired by the coyote took us to Chicago to join my stepfather, an engineer who had entered the U.S. a year earlier on a three-month work visa but stayed after the visa expired.

Even as a young girl, I understood why he chose to remain in the U.S. illegally, and why my mother wanted us to join him: In Mexico, my parents often had to choose between paying the rent and buying food. Like most immigrants, they came to the U.S. seeking a better life for their family.

No Social Security Number

5   But growing up undocumented has meant living in limbo, with opportunities only half open to me. I was fortunate to have gone to Walter Payton College Prep school in Chicago, and I got into several top-tier colleges. But without a Social Security number, I was ineligible for the financial aid I needed to be able to go to many of them.

I'm likely to be in a similar situation in the working world because without a Social Security number, employers can't legally hire me. So although I'm now a freshman at the University of Illinois at Chicago studying sociology, I may never be able to work in my field. Without legal status, I'll have no better options than my stepfather, who fixes factory machinery, or my mom, a former teacher who works as a cashier in a fast-food restaurant.

I understand why many people are upset about the 11 million undocumented people in the U.S. Some fear that immigrants will take their jobs or think the U.S. shouldn't reward those who came here illegally.

The DREAM Act

But I would also ask that people try to understand my situation. As a child, I didn't have a say in my parents' decision to bring me to the U.S., and this country is now my home. Without legal status, however, I'll be relegated to the margins and will never be a fully engaged member of American society.

The DREAM Act, which was introduced in Congress in 2009, may be my best hope, although its prospects for passage are uncertain. It would provide a provisional path to citizenship for undocumented immigrants who were brought here before age 16, have graduated from a U.S. high school, and have completed or are on course to complete at least two years of college or military service.

10   On March 10, 2010, along with seven other undocumented students and hundreds of supporters, I marched to Chicago's Federal Plaza to raise awareness of the DREAM Act and the need for immigration reform, sparking a week of "coming out" marches across the country.

When it was my turn to speak, I revealed my immigration status: "My name is Reyna Wences," I announced, "and I am undocumented." I knew I risked deportation, but it was worth it.

I was tired of living in the shadows.

DREAM On

MARK KRIKORIAN

Mark Krikorian is executive director of the Center for Immigration Studies and the author of The New Case Against Immigration, Both Legal and Illegal *(2008). He is also a contributor to the* National Review Online, *a source for "Republican/conservative news, commentary, and opinion," where this commentary appeared in December 2010.*

Harry Reid and Nancy Pelosi have pledged a vote as early as this week on the DREAM Act (Development, Relief and Education for Alien Minors), a bill that would legalize illegal aliens who arrived here before the age of 16 and who comply with certain educational or military-service requirements.

The core principle behind this amnesty proposal is that it is aimed at those who have grown up here and are, psychologically and emotionally, Americans. In the words of America's Voice, a hard-left open-borders group, the beneficiaries of the measure are "patriotic young Americans in all but paperwork."

There's no doubt that this is the most sympathetic group of illegal immigrants. That is precisely why DREAM has been dangled as bait for the more general amnesty proposals described as "comprehensive immigration reform," with amnesty advocates brandishing the situation of these young people as justification for a broader amnesty. (Though no one seems to have stopped to ask: If such a comprehensive bill would provide amnesty for all illegals, then why would we need DREAM?)

Nonetheless, now that the amnesty crowd has belatedly decided to move ahead on DREAM as a standalone measure, many in the public and

Congress are open to the idea of addressing the situation of such young people. But the DREAM Act, in every one of its iterations over the years, has four fatal flaws.

5   1. The act is billed as legalizing those brought as infants or toddlers, and yet it covers people brought here up to age 16. The examples used by advocates are nearly always people who were brought here very young. The student-body president at Fresno State University, Pedro Ramirez—who was "coincidentally" revealed to be an illegal alien just as the DREAM Act lame-duck effort got under way—came here at age three. Harvard student Eric Balderas was brought here at age four. Yves Gomes was brought here at 14 months, Juan Gomez at two years, Marie Gonzalez at five, Dan-el Padilla at four, and so on.

So why set the age cutoff at 16? If the point is to provide amnesty to those whose identity was formed here, then you'd need a much lower age cutoff. I have a 15-year-old, and if I took him to live illegally in Mexico (and living illegally is a lot harder to do there than here), he would always remain, psychologically, an American, because his identity is already formed. The Roman Catholic Church and English common law set the age of reason at seven. That, combined with a requirement of at least ten years' continuous residence here, seems like a much more defensible place to draw the line. Unless, of course, you're just using those who came as young children to bootstrap a larger amnesty.

2. Next, all amnesties have at least three harmful consequences, and the DREAM Act ignores all three. The first of these is massive fraud. Perhaps one-fourth of those legalized under the 1986 Immigration Reform and Control Act received amnesty fraudulently, including Mahmud Abouhalima, a leader of the first World Trade Center attack. The fraud in that first big amnesty program was so pervasive as to be almost comical, with people claiming work histories here that included picking watermelons from trees and digging cherries out of the ground.

And yet what does the DREAM Act say about fraud? As Sen. Jeff Sessions (R., Ala.) points out in "Ten Things You Need To Know about S-3827, the DREAM Act," the measure "prohibits using any of the information contained in the amnesty application (name, address, length of illegal presence that the alien admits to, etc.) to initiate a removal proceeding or investigate or prosecute fraud in the application process." This is like playing a slot machine without having to put any money in—any illegal alien can apply, and if he wins, great, but if he loses, he can't be prosecuted *even if he lied through his teeth about everything*. No amnesty proposal can be taken seriously unless applicants are made to understand, right up front, that any lies, no matter how trivial, will result in arrest and imprisonment.

3. Another problem with DREAM, which all amnesties share, is that it will attract new illegal immigration. Prospective illegal immigrants, considering their options, are more likely to opt to come if they see that their predecessors eventually hit the jackpot. In 1986, we had an estimated 5 million illegals, 3 million of whom were legalized. We now have more than twice as many as before the

last amnesty, and they've been promised repeatedly that if they hold out a little longer they'll be able to stay legally. Any new amnesty, even if only for those brought here as children, will attract further illegal immigration.

There's really no way to prevent this, but to minimize it, you need stringent enforcement measures. This was the logic of the 1986 law and the recent "comprehensive immigration reform" proposals. The critique of such "grand bargains" has been that the illegals get their amnesty but the promised enforcement never materializes—and that critique remains valid. But if the sponsors of DREAM were serious about addressing the plight of people brought here as infants and toddlers, they would include muscular enforcement measures as proof of their bona fides. These would include mandatory use of E-Verify for all new hires, explicit authorization of state and local governments to enforce civil immigration law, and full implementation of an exit-tracking system for all foreign visitors, for starters. And the legal status of all the amnesty beneficiaries would remain provisional until the enforcement measures were up and running and passed judicial muster. Even these might not be sufficient to turn back a new wave of illegal immigration sparked by the amnesty, but the lack of such measures speaks volumes about the real intentions of the DREAM Act's sponsors.

4. Finally, all amnesties reward illegal immigrants—in this case, both those brought here as children *and* the adults who subjected them to this limbo. Any serious proposal to legalize young people brought here as infants or toddlers would need to prevent the possibility that their parents and other adults responsible for bringing them here illegally would ever receive any benefit from the amnesty, namely, future sponsorship as legal immigrants. This could be done in two ways: Either the amnesty recipients would not be put on a "path to citizenship" at all, but instead be given a time-limited work visa, indefinitely renewable so long

as they stay out of trouble. This would mean they could not petition for any relatives to immigrate in the future. Alternatively, the amnesty beneficiaries could receive green cards and eventual citizenship, but we would abolish all the legal-immigration categories for family members other than spouses and minor children of U.S. citizens. Either way, the adults who knew what they were doing would never be rewarded.

A DREAM Act 2.0 that addressed these problems—that prosecuted fraud, implemented enforcement, prevented downstream legal immigration, and focused much more narrowly on those who came very young—would possibly be something that even I, were I a congressman, might be able to vote for. But the lack of these elements is clear proof that the amnesty crowd isn't interested in fixing the specific problem of a sympathetic but small group of people; rather, these young people are simply poster children who have been used for years to try to justify a general amnesty for all illegal aliens. And when the DREAM Act fails, as it will, Pedro Ramirez and his fellows will need to ask the pro-amnesty politicians and lobbying groups why they were sacrificed on the altar of "comprehensive immigration reform."

■ ■ ■ **FOR CLASS DISCUSSION** Immigration in the Twenty-First Century

1. Mitali Perkins, Scarf Ace, and Fatemeh Fakhraie refer to aspects of their cultures and beliefs that mark them as different from the mainstream, and each imagines the assumptions and reactions of others to their differences. How does the media give us insight into other cultures, yet also create perceptions that may distance us from truly understanding the lived experience of someone from that culture?

2. Besides headscarves, what other items of clothing or body adornment mark a person as a member of a religious, ethnic, cultural, or other group? Which of these go largely unnoticed in mainstream American society? Which are controversial, and why?

3. Anita Ortiz Maddali, Kevin Clarke, Lee Judge, and the editorial writers from the *Washington Times* provide different scenarios for the circumstances under which first-generation citizens may be born and use different terms to describe these children. What is the rhetorical effect of these competing definitions? How might the intended audience for each piece feel more or less sympathetic toward these children and their families?

4. Read Mark Krikorian's essay, "DREAM On," as both a believer and a doubter. Working in small groups or as a class, discuss: What are the warrants for *believing* his argument—that is, what other beliefs or values must one hold in order to buy his contentions about the consequences of granting amnesty to illegal immigrants? What beliefs and values would enable one to *doubt* Krikorian's argument?

5. What activities or privileges do citizens of the United States take for granted that might be difficult or impossible for illegal immigrants or their children? How might these barriers perpetuate or even create some of the problems stemming from illegal immigration in the United State?

WRITING ASSIGNMENT   White Paper Summarizing the Arguments about a Policy Proposal

Although not all of the readings in this chapter deal specifically with U.S. immigration laws and policies, the people discussed in these readings are affected by those policies on a daily basis. Research one recent proposal to change federal or state immigration laws (such as the federal DREAM Act or Arizona's SB 1070, which allows law enforcement officers to demand proof of legal immigration status from anyone they stop) and read about it in three to five sources. Identify and characterize the stakeholders in the debate: Who are they? What do they stand to gain or lose? Then analyze the arguments used by these stakeholders. What are their strengths and weaknesses? Finally, write a white paper in which you summarize the proposal and the arguments for and against it for a citizen wanting to be better informed. You might find the following resources helpful as a starting place: the White House Web site on immigration reform at http://www.whitehouse.gov/infocus/immigration, the Federation for American Immigration Reform site at www.fairus.org, the National Immigration Law Center at www.nilc.org, or the League of Women Voters Immigration Study at www.lwv.org. ∎

For additional writing, reading, and research resources, go to www.mycomplab.com

32 The Value(s) of Higher Education in a Changing Economy

As many students know from firsthand experience, the costs of a college education continue to rise while the job market for recent college graduates reels from a global recession. This growing economic insecurity has led to increased scrutiny of the decision to seek a higher education. More than ever, students must carefully weigh the costs and benefits of attending college. In the process, students face pressures to define their educational goals and values, choose institutions likely to lead to their vocational paths, and consider alternatives to attending college altogether. Some argue that the price of college exceeds future rewards. Others argue that higher education gains value when it more intentionally prepares students for the demands of a more competitive job market. Still others maintain that a commitment to a liberal arts education has the lifelong benefit of developing students intellectually, ethically, and emotionally rather than emphasizing narrow vocational goals. Most arguments, however, tend to acknowledge the complexity of the issues.

This chapter offers a range of voices in the conversations about attending college and the decisions students face if they choose to enroll. With volatile economic changes providing an explicit and implicit context for the perspectives in this chapter, these readings engage the vital questions facing prospective, current, and recently graduated college students. Across different genres, from a valedictorian's speech to a think tank's policy analysis, the readings explore related questions: To what extent does college affordably provide access to in-demand skills? What makes education valuable beyond economic incentive? What tensions exist between a focus on the future rewards of a college degree and education as an end in itself? Does higher education put too much emphasis on producing workers? How can the values of a liberal arts education actually complement a more vocationally minded education?

Learning by Degrees

REBECCA MEAD

As a staff writer for The New Yorker *since 1997 and author of* One Perfect Day: The Selling of the American Wedding, *Rebecca Mead has explored a wide variety of journalistic subjects. From the infertility egg industry to God-based diets, Mead carefully analyzes cultural phenomena. In this comment, published in the Talk of the Town section of* The New Yorker *on June 10, 2010, Mead addresses the cultural trend of viewing college for its financial benefits rather than for its impact on self-worth.*

A member of the Class of 2010—who this season dons synthetic cap and gown, listens to the inspirational words of David Souter (Harvard), Anderson Cooper (Tulane), or Lisa Kudrow (Vassar), and collects a diploma—need not be a statistics major to know that the odds of stepping into a satisfying job, or, indeed, any job, are lower now than might have been imagined four long years ago, when the first posters were hung on a dorm-room wall, and having a .edu e-mail address was still a novelty. Statistically speaking, however, having an expertise in statistics may help in getting a job: according to a survey conducted by the National Association of Colleges and Employers, graduates with math skills are more likely than their peers in other majors to find themselves promptly and gainfully employed.

The safest of all degrees to be acquiring this year is in accounting: forty-six percent of graduates in that discipline have already been offered jobs. Business majors are similarly placed: forty-four percent will have barely a moment to breathe before undergoing the transformation from student to suit. Engineers of all stripes—chemical, computer, electrical, mechanical, industrial, environmental—have also fared relatively well since the onset of the recession: they dominate a ranking, issued by Payscale.com, of the disciplines that produce the best-earning graduates. Particular congratulations are due to aerospace engineers, who top the list, with a starting salary of just under sixty thousand dollars—a figure that, if it is not exactly stratospheric, is twenty-five thousand dollars higher than the average starting salary of a graduate in that other science of the heavens, theology.

Economics majors aren't doing badly, either: their starting salary averages about fifty thousand a year, rising to a mid-career median of a hundred and one thousand. Special note should be taken of the fact that if you have an economics degree you can, eventually, make a living proposing that other people shouldn't bother going to college. This, at least, is the approach of Professor Richard K. Ved-

der, of Ohio University, who is the founder of the Center for College Affordability and Productivity. According to the *Times*, eight out of the ten job categories that will add the most employees during the next decade—including home-health aide, customer-service representative, and store clerk—can be performed by someone without a college degree. "Professor Vedder likes to ask why fifteen percent of mail carriers have bachelor's degrees," the paper reported.

The argument put forth by Professor Vedder (Ph.D., University of Illinois) is, naturally, economic: of those overly schooled mail carriers, he said, "Some of them could have bought a house for what they spent on their education." Another economist, Professor Robert I. Lerman, of American University (Ph.D., M.I.T.), told the *Times* that high schools, rather than readying all students for college, should focus on the acquisition of skills appropriate to the workplace. According to the *Times*, these include the ability to "solve problems and make decisions," "resolve conflict and negotiate," "cooperate with others," and "listen actively."

5   It may be news that the academy is making a case for the superfluity of the academy, but skepticism about the value of college, and of collegians, is hardly novel. Within the sphere of business, a certain romance attaches to the figure of the successful college dropout, like Steve Jobs, who was enrolled at Reed for only a semester, or Bill Gates, who started at Harvard in 1973 but didn't get his degree until it was granted, honorarily, thirty-four years later. On the political stage, too, having spent excessive hours in seminar rooms and libraries is widely regarded as a liability. *Vide* Peggy Noonan's celebration, during the 2004 Presidential campaign, of George W. Bush's lack of cerebration. "He's not an intellectual," Noonan wrote in the *Wall Street Journal*. "Intellectuals start all the trouble in the world."

The candidates' education, or the insufficiency thereof, came up again during the most recent Presidential election. Sarah Palin told Katie Couric that she was "not one of those who maybe came from a background of, you know, kids who perhaps graduate college and their parents get them a passport and give them a backpack and say go off and travel the world"—even though Palin evidently considered college important enough to have tried out five different ones within three years. Meanwhile, Barack Obama's degrees from prestigious universities were, to his critics, evidence of his unfitness for office. "The last thing we need are more pointy-headed intellectuals running the government," the political scientist Charles Murray (B.A., Harvard; Ph.D., M.I.T.) said during the closing months of the campaign. As President, Obama has rightly noted that too many Americans are already skipping college or dropping out, even without economists having advised them to do so; within weeks of the Inauguration, he pledged to increase the national graduation rate, which is significantly lower than that of many other developed nations, including Canada, Japan, and Korea.

The skip-college advocates' contention—that, with the economic downturn, a college degree may not be the best investment—has its appeal. Given the high cost of attending college in the United States, the question of whether a student is getting his or her money's worth tends to loom large with whoever is paying the tuition fees and the meal plan bills. Even so, one needn't necessarily be a liberal-arts graduate to regard as distinctly and speciously utilitarian the idea that higher education is, above all, a route to economic advancement. Un-addressed in that calculus is any question of what else an education might be for: to nurture critical thought; to expose individuals to the signal accomplishments of humankind; to develop in them an ability not just to listen actively but to respond intelligently.

All these are habits of mind that are useful for an engaged citizenry, and from which a letter carrier, no less than a college professor, might derive a sense of self-worth. For who's to say in what direction a letter carrier's thoughts might, or should, turn, regardless of the job's demands? Consider Stephen Law, a professor of philosophy at the University of London, who started his working life delivering mail for the British postal service, began reading works of philosophy in his spare time, decided that he'd like to know more, and went on to study the discipline at City University, in London, and at Oxford University. (A philosophy graduate in the Class of 2010, by the way, stands to earn an average starting salary of forty thousand dollars a year, rising to a lifetime median of seventy-six thousand. Not exactly statistician money, but something to think about.) Indeed, if even a professionally oriented college degree is no longer a guarantee of easily found employment, an argument might be made in favor of a student's pursuing an education that is less, rather than more, pragmatic. (More theology, less accounting.) That way, regardless of each graduate's ultimate path, all might be qualified to be carriers of arts and letters, of which the nation can never have too many.

How Much Is That Bachelor's Degree Really Worth? The Million Dollar Misunderstanding

MARK SCHNEIDER

Along with writing about many issues involving education, Mark Schneider has served as a commissioner of the U.S. Department of Education's National Center for Education Statistics. He is currently a visiting scholar at the American Enterprise Institute (AEI). His book Choosing Schools: Consumer Choice and the Quality of American Schools *makes a* *statistical case for parental choice in public schools. In "How Much Is That Bachelor's Degree Really Worth? The Million Dollar Misunderstanding," an "Outlook" policy analysis put out by AEI, Schneider statistically challenges the idea that a college graduate makes $1,000,000 more in a lifetime than a non-college graduate.*

Many claim that a college degree is worth a million dollars, but like so many other "facts" about higher education in the United States, it is not quite right. Indeed, using a set of reasonable assumptions that factors in school selectivity, the cost of a college education, and foregone wages, I show that the million dollar figure is grossly inflated, and may be three times too high.

Imagine that your daughter is a junior in high school and continually complains, "I don't want to go to college. I'm sick of school. Why do I have to go?" You refrain from blurting out, "Because I want you out of the house so I can turn your bedroom into a media room." Instead, you say, "So you can get a good job and make more money." If your child were an economist-in-waiting, she might demand to know, "How much more?" And you would probably repeat the figure you read everywhere: "A million dollars!"

The figure has become a commonplace, used by parents, colleges and universities, and, yes, even insurance companies. Arizona State University used it in 2007 to justify a tuition increase:

> The portion of the cost of a college education paid through tuition is the best investment that a student can make in his or her future. Unlike disposable items such as food, fuel, or even a car—items that are consumed or depreciate in value over time—college education lasts a lifetime. Average annual earnings of individuals with a bachelor's degree are more than 75 percent higher than the earnings of high school graduates. These additional earnings sum to more than $1 million over a lifetime.[1]

5 State Farm used the number to argue that a college education is an "investment for a lifetime" and that parents should therefore buy into one of its 529 funds:

> A college education has the potential to earn a student much more than just a diploma—it could be the single most important tool to compete in the global marketplace of the future. According to the College Board, college graduates earn 80 percent more on average than high school graduates. Over the course of your child's life, the difference in earning potential between a high school graduate and a college graduate is more than $1 million. A child's education could be one of the largest investments you'll make in your lifetime. But it may also provide you with the highest return: a child's successful future. The State Farm® College Savings Plan sponsored by the State of Nebraska helps make college investing simple, affordable, and convenient.[2]

The million dollar number is also used by politicians and others interested in postsecondary education. Doug Lederman of Inside Higher Ed described the commonplace use of this number: "Go ahead—just try to find an instance in the last few years in which someone trying to make the case that going to college matters hasn't trotted out the statistic that the average college graduate earns $1 million more over the course of a lifetime than a high school graduate does."[3]

As in the State Farm citation, the College Board is the source most often cited by those promulgating the million dollar number, but the number actually traces back to U.S. Census Bureau calculations developed by Jennifer Cheeseman Day and Eric C. Newburger in 2002.[4] They wrote, "Over a work-life, individuals who have a bachelor's degree would earn on average $2.1 million—about one third more than workers who did not finish college, and nearly twice as much as workers with only a high school diploma."[5] These data have been updated by Mark Kantrowitz, who shows that, since the Census report, the added value of a bachelor's degree over a high school diploma or GED had increased to $1.2 million in 2005 from $910,000 in 1997–99.[6]

There have been arguments over this million dollar number. Perhaps the most pointed came from Charles Miller, who headed former U.S. secretary of education Margaret Spellings's Commission on the Future of Higher Education. In April 2008, Miller released a public letter to College Board president Gaston Caperton accusing him of misleading the public by repeating the million dollar number in the College Board's *Education Pays* reports. In his letter, Miller argues that by replacing some assumptions used by the College Board with other, perhaps more reasonable, ones (for example, including those who took six years to graduate instead of four and deducting tuition costs from lifetime earnings), the present value of the lifetime earnings differential is only $279,893 for a bachelor's degree versus a high school degree. Miller wrote, "It is reasonable to conclude that a college degree is not as valuable as has been claimed."

10   Miller's letter touched off a testy exchange about how prominently the million dollar number is actually displayed in the College Board reports. (In the latest, the number appears in footnotes with many caveats.) The argument over the size of the payoff for attending college is far from over. A recent report by the National Association of State Universities and Land Grant Colleges (NASULGC) presents an estimate of the payoff for a college degree that is much closer to Miller's than to a million dollars.[7] The report estimates the net present value of the difference between a college education and a high school degree at only $121,539.[8] Even though this is far below the million dollar payoff—and less than half of what Miller estimated—the authors still claim that "earning the bachelor's degree pays handsomely."

Indeed, careful economic analysis consistently shows positive rates of return to college education—and even the low numbers presented by Miller or NASULGC are still "handsome" rates of return. According to Pedro Carneiro, in the United States, the increase in earnings is, on average, around 10 percent per year of higher educational schooling. There is also a "sheepskin effect"—meaning that the returns are likely to be even higher if you earn a bachelor's degree rather than simply taking the return to a year of education multiplied by four. Carneiro concludes that education is a "very productive investment" that may, in fact, outperform most other investments.[9]

Clearly, there is a serious debate about assumptions, discount rates, how to handle the cost of tuition, lost earnings, and the like. The debate will continue, but in this *Outlook,* I look at the return to postsecondary education from a different angle.

Current debates over the million dollar payoff have focused on an *average* return for all college graduates, ranging from Harvard-educated hedge fund managers who (used to) make hundreds of millions per year to a graduate from Bob's College, who, as a result of his degree, was promoted from assistant manager to manager of a retail store at the mall. But the rates of return to attending different calibers or types of colleges or universities may vary dramatically. The NASULGC report did note, "While data demonstrate significantly higher annual and lifetime earnings for those who earn a bachelor's degree, there is no data that reliably shows that earnings bear a predictable relationship to the institution from which an individual earns the bachelor's degree."[10] But this point is rarely addressed in any systematic way.

The goal of this *Outlook* is a modest step in that direction. Adding a finer grain to the ongoing debate about the returns to college education, I show that there is variation in the lifetime earnings of students graduating from different types of schools—variation that is hidden by focusing on the average increase in earnings reported in most analyses.

15   The ideal analysis would pinpoint variations in the rate of return at the campus level, which would help students figure out in which college to enroll. Even more so, we would want a "value added" model to account for the highly stratified nature of schools. (There is a sorting process in which highly qualified students go to the most selective schools, and their higher lifetime earnings may have less to do with the quality of their education than with their innate intellectual capacities.) While we await such models and analyses, the purpose here is to illustrate the range in the variance in the payoff to higher education and to see if graduates from particular types of colleges or universities are more or less likely to reach the million dollar payoff.

To do this, I have adopted the Census approach to developing synthetic estimates of work-life earnings as updated by Kantrowitz, who kindly shared the spreadsheets he developed. In this analysis, rather than treating all bachelor's degrees as equal and measuring the average gain in earnings, I seed the estimates with actual salary data observed for graduates from different types of colleges and universities ten years after graduation.

Specifically, I use data from the U.S. Department of Education's 2003 follow-up to the 1993 *Baccalaureate and Beyond Longitudinal Study* (B&B)[11] to generate the starting salaries for the synthetic estimates of work-life earnings. In the 2003 B&B follow-up, over eleven thousand college graduates were interviewed and supplied data about their work experiences since graduation, including current income. Instead of simply using the overall average salary for this sample of graduates, I take information about the institution from which the respondent graduated in 1993 and classify that school by sector (private nonprofit or public) and by five levels of selectivity, ranging from the most selective (the Ivy Leagues) to open admissions schools.[12]

Cross-classifying sector and selectivity creates ten categories of postsecondary institutions, and I compute the average salary for respondents in each category. Nearly all the students in this study were in their midthirties.[13] With the average salary for each of these ten types of schools, and knowing student age, I have the information to feed into the Census models, as further refined by Kantrowitz, to generate synthetic estimates of lifetime earnings for students in each category of school.

Variation in Rates of Return

Figure 1 presents the estimates of work-life earnings of the 1993 class of college graduates in each of the ten categories of colleges and universities. These initial estimates do not take into account tuition costs or lost years of earnings while a student pursued a college degree.

20   These data show a substantial return on the bachelor's degree regardless of the type of institution from which a person graduated: the million dollar payoff is evident across all students taken together and for graduates from colleges in six of the ten categories. A seventh comes in just under the million dollar payoff. The lowest payoff is still over $700,000.[14]

Let's return to your conversation with your daughter. You show her figure 1 and say, "I told you so. Go to college, and you're more than likely to earn an extra million dollars!" Remember, your daughter is an economist-in-waiting, and she replies, "You forgot to account for opportunity costs associated with getting that degree. And what about discounting these future earnings into a present value?" You admit that she is right and go back to your spreadsheets.

Estimating Discounted Returns to College Education

Figure 2 shows a radically different picture than the estimates of Figure 1. Once we account for tuition payments and discount earnings streams, the payoff falls dramatically. Except for the exceptionally high payoff for attending the most selective nonprofit institutions

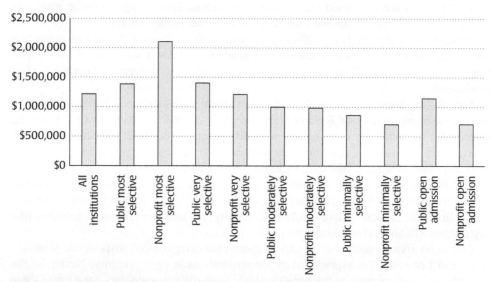

FIGURE 1 INITIAL ESTIMATES OF LIFETIME DIFFERENCE IN EARNINGS, BACHELOR'S DEGREE VERSUS HIGH SCHOOL GRADUATE, BY INSTITUTION TYPE

SOURCE: Author's calculations.

Sources and Assumptions for the Estimates in Figure 1

In Kantrowitz's model, there is an observed mean income from the Census Bureau for individuals in ten-year age groups: twenty-five to thirty-four, thirty-five to forty-four, forty-five to fifty-four, and fifty-five to sixty-four (all the numbers in this analysis are based on 2003 data, the year in which the B&B follow-up was conducted).

A growth rate in annual income is estimated for individuals in each of these cohorts based on their level of education. For high school graduates in the thirty-five to forty-four cohort, the rate of growth is 2.64 percent; for bachelor's degree holders, the rate is 3.02 percent. Note that the growth rate for high school graduates is about the same as the average growth in GDP, while the bachelor's degree holder exceeds this by about a third of a percent.

Kantrowitz uses these growth rates and the values observed by the Census to compute the added value of a bachelor's degree. His "raw" estimate is around $1.2 million, which is almost the exact same number reported as the average for all students in Figure 1.

However, since I wanted to disaggregate the results by the ten categories of higher education institutions, and since the BB study reports respondent incomes at one point in time, I had to modify Kantrowitz's method. Specifically, Kantrowitz has the observed values for the mean income of every age group, while I have the mean only for thirty-five-year-olds. I have taken the ratio of the income of each of the other age cohorts observed in the Census data and applied those ratios to estimate the mean income for the other age cohorts based on the values observed in the BB. For example, in the 2003 Census data, the average income of workers age twenty-five to thirty-four was 76 percent of the mean income of workers age thirty-five to forty-four. In the BB follow-up, the 2003 income of graduates from the most selective nonprofit institutions is just over $70,000. Using a 3.02 percent growth rate for the next nine years, the average income of these graduates age thirty-five to forty-four is about $80,000, and the computed average for workers age twenty-five to thirty-four with these degrees is 76 percent of this, or $61,000.

To estimate the income of eighteen- to twenty-four-year-olds, I take the growth rates calculated by Kantrowitz and work backwards from the observed incomes of BB. In the first set of estimates presented in Figure 1, income for college graduates between the ages of eighteen and twenty-two is set to zero.

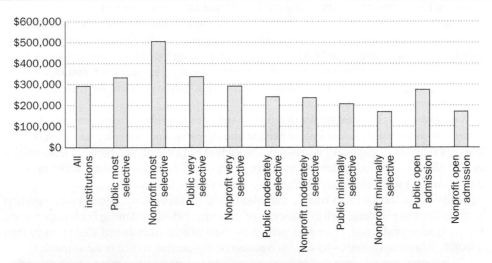

FIGURE 2 THE DIFFERENCE BETWEEN WORK-LIFE EARNINGS, BACHELOR'S DEGREE VERSUS HIGH SCHOOL GRADUATE, 2003 DOLLARS, ADJUSTING FOR TUITION, BY INSTITUTION TYPE

SOURCE: Author's calculations.

Sources and Assumptions for the Estimates in Figure 2

Figure 2 takes tuition into account. To estimate tuition costs, I used the 1989 and 1993 Integrated Postsecondary Education Data System data sets to calculate the average tuition cost that students in each of these categories of institutions paid. This ranged from around $15,000 for students in the most selective nonprofits to around $2,000 for students attending less selective public institutions. For the earnings stream from ages eighteen to twenty-two, tuition is counted against lifetime earnings. Note the tuition is "sticker price" and not net price. We know that many students do not pay full price, so there may be an upward bias in this number. But the tuition number we use does not include the full costs of attendance either—fees, books, room and board, etc. Finally, since this is based on in-state tuition, it understates the costs that out-of-state students paid in public institutions. Clearly, refinements of these estimates are needed in the future. The earnings stream is discounted to 2003 dollars, using a 4.8 percent discount rate, which is roughly the average rate of long-term Treasury bills. The calculation takes into account federal income taxes as computed by Kantrowitz and applied to the income estimates for graduates in each of the ten categories of schools, as well as all students taken together.

and the low payoff for attending less selective ones, statistically, the results are roughly the same. Furthermore, even among the graduates of the most selective nonprofit institutions (the graduates who do the best by far in any of the ten categories), their superior earning power still falls far short of the magic million.[15]

You remind your daughter that it is not for nothing that economics is called the dismal science. In return she asks, "Okay, but these are still averages, and we all know that averages can hide lots of variation. Clearly, I should go to an Ivy League school if I can get in. But if I can't, where should I go?"

Here you have a serious parent–child discussion about the paucity of good data and your inability to answer this perfectly reasonable question. You note that other people have been struggling with this question. You show her a copy of a recent edition of *SmartMoney* magazine, which undertook an analysis of salary returns for fifty institutions in a piece entitled "The Best Colleges for Making Money." Examining the salaries that graduates from fifty of the most expensive four-year colleges earn in early and midcareer, and factoring in the cost of tuition and fees, *SmartMoney* calculated a "payback" ratio for each school. To use their word, the results are "jarring."[16]

SmartMoney's analysis shows that public colleges are often giving students a much   25 better return than their better-known private counterparts. For example, the University of Georgia delivers a "payback" nearly three times that of Harvard, and both the Universities of Delaware and Rhode Island outperform every Ivy League institution in the ranking. *SmartMoney's* institution-level analysis is a step in the right direction.

Students not only choose a college; they also choose a field of study. There is wide variation in the salaries that students earn as a function of their career choices. Among B&B respondents, ten years after graduation, those who were in the field of education earned slightly more than $30,000, while respondents who were in business or engineering earned twice as much.

To measure the returns to attending one college versus another more precisely and to help students and their families judge how well different programs are doing, the nation needs more comprehensive student unit record systems, especially ones that link student higher education records to earnings after college. Approximately forty states currently have student-based data systems, but they are of varying quality and coverage. Further, these databases are designed and maintained by state higher education agencies without much concern for interoperability with other state systems. Most important, very few of these systems link to postgraduation databases (such as state unemployment insurance systems), making computation of the variation in employment outcomes and income by school and by program virtually impossible.

Even with such systems, debates will continue about the appropriate methods for calculating returns to a bachelor's degree, but without them, studies such as this, the recent NASULGC study, and *SmartMoney*'s report are at best dim flashlights shining light into a fundamentally important but dark corner of America's system of postsecondary education.

As you develop these points, your daughter is now rolling her eyes and wanting to return to her Facebook-YouTube-Twitter world. You are beginning to fear she will decide not to go to college, and your dreams of turning her bedroom into a media room for your brand-new sixty-five-inch HDTV with five-channel surround sound are fading. But you have the responsibility to be honest with your daughter, so your final words should be something like, "Honey, you'll still get a better job and make more money if you go to college, but that million dollar payoff you keep hearing about? Forget about it."

Mr. Schneider thanks Stuart Elliott for his help in calculating these returns and Mark Kantrowitz, who provided comments and generously shared his spreadsheets, which were modified to produce these results.

Notes

1 Arizona State University, "ASU Proposes Tuition Increase," news release, November 14, 2007, available at http://asunews.asu.edu/20071108_Tuition (accessed April 23, 2009).

2 State Farm Insurance, "College Education: An Investment of a Lifetime," available at www.statefarm .com/mutual/sc/invest_know/investforlife.asp (accessed April 23, 2009).

3 Doug Lederman, "College Isn't Worth a Million Dollars," Inside Higher Ed, April 7, 2008, available at www.insidehighered.com/news/2008/04/07/miller (accessed April 23, 2009).

4 Jennifer Cheeseman Day and Eric C. Newburger, *The Big Payoff: Educational Attainment and Synthetic Estimates of Work–Life Earnings* (Washington, DC: U.S. Census Bureau, July 2002), available at www.census.gov/prod/2002pubs/p23-210.pdf (accessed April 23, 2009).

5 Ibid., 4.

6 Mark Kantrowitz, "The Financial Value of a Higher Education," *NASFAA Journal of Student Financial Aid* 37, no. 1 (2007): 19–27.

7 National Association of State Universities and Land Grant Colleges (NASULGC), *University Tuition, Consumer Choice and College Affordability: Strategies for Addressing a Higher Education Affordability Challenge* (Washington, DC: NASULGC, November 2008).

8 There are some errors and questionable assumptions in this analysis. For example, the $37,100 figure cited in appendix A for a high school diploma is actually the figure for "some college, no degree" rather than for "high school graduate," which is $31,500. See College Board, *Education Pays 2007*, figure 1.1, available at www.collegeboard.com/prod_downloads/about/news_info/trends/ed_pays_2007.pdf

(accessed April 23, 2009). The report uses a thirty-five-year work life, not forty, and uses medians, not means. That said, I show that using some of the same needed adjustments to income flows as used in this report (most notably discounting and tuition), estimates of work-life earnings are closer to this estimate than to the magic million dollar number.

9 Pedro Carneiro, "If the BA Is the Work of the Devil, It's Not His Best Work," Cato Unbound, October 8, 2008, available at www.cato-unbound.org/2008/10/08/pedro-carneiro/if-the-ba-is-the-work-of-the-devil-its-not-his-best-work (accessed April 23, 2009).

10 NASULGC, *University Tuition, Consumer Choice and College Affordability: Strategies for Addressing a Higher Education Affordability Challenge,* 10.

11 U.S. Department of Education, National Center for Education Statistics, *Baccalaureate and Beyond Longitudinal Study* (B&B) (Washington, DC: Department of Education, 2003), available at http://nces.ed.gov/surveys/b&b/ (accessed April 29, 2009).

12 The selectivity of postsecondary institutions was calculated using the methods published in the National Postsecondary Student Aid Survey of 2000. My thanks to Ted Socha of the National Center for Education Statistics for calculating this selectivity measure for the 2003 data.

13 The average age of the respondents in this ten-year follow-up survey of the 1993 B&B study was thirty-five. While the Kantrowitz and Cheeseman Day and Newburger papers are based on work-life estimates from age twenty-five through sixty-four, the estimates in this *Outlook* begin at age eighteen to account for the costs of attaining a college degree. These costs are in terms of lost income (a high school graduate has had an income during the four years that the college graduate was in school). In addition, the college graduate had to spend money on tuition to obtain the degree.

14 Note that this approach does not take into account student quality—the high payoff for students graduating from the most selective nonprofits may reflect students' innate skills as much as or more than the quality of the education they received while attending Harvard or Yale. But that is a far more complicated argument than the one addressed by the synthetic cohort approach.

15 There are some computational issues in this analysis to keep in mind. It sidesteps the issue of the non-monetary rewards to higher education that accrue to both the individual and to society. It also neglects any financial aid that the student may have received and may overestimate lost wages, since many students may work while in college. It uses a 4.8 percent discount rate, which is roughly equivalent to the historical rate for longterm Treasury bills, but that is a choice that can change the outcomes of the analysis (the lower the discount rate, the higher the returns). The income data are based on a sample; therefore, there is error associated with the starting estimates of income.

16 Neil Parmar, "The Best Colleges for Making Money," *SmartMoney,* December 16, 2008, available at www.smartmoney.com/Personal-Finance/College-Planning/The-Best-Colleges-For-Making-Money (accessed April 23, 2009).

"It's a Bachelor of Arts Double Major"

JESSE SPRINGER

Jesse Springer is a graphic artist based in Eugene, Oregon. Mainly addressing local issues, Springer's editorial cartoons regularly appear in The Eugene Register-Guard *and other state newspapers. You can find more of Springer's work on his Web site www .springercreative.com.*

What Do You Do with a B.A. in History?

KEN SAXON

Ken Saxon, a graduate of Princeton and Stanford's Graduate School of Business, has been both an entrepreneur and a leader in the non-profit sector for more than 20 years. He currently heads Courage to Lead, a leadership and support program for executives of non-profit organizations based in California. He also serves on the board of several non-profit organizations. Saxon delivered this speech in 2010 to the freshman class of the University of California, Santa Barbara. A transcript of the speech can be found on Andy Chan's blog The Heart of the Matter.

"What do you do with a B.A. in English,
What is my life going to be?
Four years of college and plenty of knowledge,
Have earned me this useless degree.
I can't pay the bills yet,
'Cause I have no skills yet,
The world is a big scary place."

That's a cute song in a funny Broadway show, Avenue Q. But it sends a message that's quite different from what I've experienced in my own life. I went off to college, and unencumbered by personal or parental concerns that I come out with a professional skill, I majored in History.

What did I do with a BA in European History?

I got myself a job in corporate finance at the largest real estate company in America.

5   I attended Stanford Business School.

I started and built a company that stores business files and records and expanded it up and down the West Coast.

I sold the business, and got deeply involved with community nonprofit organizations.

I founded and run a leadership and renewal program for nonprofit executive directors, and I became Chairman of the Board of a local foundation working on global development issues, and recently went to Kenya visiting health clinics serving the poorest of the poor.

None of this journey (none of it!) was even a glimmer in my mind's eye when I was sitting in a lecture hall in my freshman year at college. Life journeys are rarely predictable, and they inevitably have lots of twists and turns. It doesn't hurt at all to head out in a certain direction—as a matter of fact, clear goals and ambition are a good thing—but to act with high confidence that you will end up where you plan to at the start of college is folly.

10   So if you buy into my premise about life's uncertainty, what consequence does this have for how you approach your four or so years at a university like UCSB? Well my talk this evening will explore the benefits of taking a liberal arts approach to college. And if you already feel confident what your professional path will be, I'm going to encourage you to broadly explore a lot of other academic fields during your time here.

In this talk, I'm going to focus on three things:

1. The purpose of a college education, and what the liberal arts is all about,
2. The downside of focusing on college as a pre-professional or technical education experience, and
3. I want to talk about some questions I think are fundamental to your education, and how a liberal arts approach to college can help you get some answers.

First, let's talk about what college is for. I think our society does many young people a disservice. Kids constantly get the message that if they want to get at what life has to offer, they need to go to college. Supposedly, according to the data, your income will be higher, you'll be more likely to have a successful marriage, and more likely to live a happy life.

But then tons of young people head off to college—record numbers in the last decade—without really thinking about why, and what they want out of it. That was certainly the case for me. In my family, it was just expected that I go to college. And I went to the best one I got into—Princeton.

15   So what would I say that the purpose of a college education is? I'd start by saying that it's about discovering who you are, what you're passionate about, what's important to you, and what doesn't interest you in the slightest. Answering such questions is a life-long journey. But the fact is that this is a unique moment in your life. [READ SLOWLY] Compared to your time here at UCSB, there will likely be no other time in your life when it will be easier to try so many interesting things, to find out what you like and don't like, and be influenced by so many incredible potential mentors.

To me, college is a time for experimentation and paying attention. I can't think of any way better to do all of this than by taking a liberal arts approach to college.

According to Wikipedia—and as a liberal arts guy, I love Wikipedia, that giant storehouse of general knowledge—"the term liberal arts denotes a curriculum that imparts general knowledge and develops the student's rational thought and intellectual capabilities, unlike a professional, vocational, technical curricula emphasizing specialization."

So let's pick that apart. First of all, it makes clear what liberal arts is not:

- professional, vocational, technical curricula emphasizing specialization. I think they're talking about a couple things here. One is a type of curriculum—like pre-med or engineering—that focuses on specific learning to prepare for a certain kind of career. The other part of this is specialization—a narrow approach to education, as opposed to a broad approach. If you think about it, grad school is 100 percent specialized or focused in a certain discipline. In college, in contrast, you have a choice as to whether you go narrow or broad.

20   In terms of what the liberal arts IS, the definition also says a few things. First, it says that the approach imparts general knowledge—once again, broad over narrow. But it says something else that's really important, that it develops the student's rational thought and intellectual capabilities.

So, what's that all about? I think they're talking about things like critical thinking, analytical reasoning, and creativity. They're talking about complexity, and the ability to learn and adapt.

There's no question a liberal arts education is a great place to develop your critical faculties, taking in a lot of information and making informed judgments about complex questions. This is a skill-set that is integral to succeeding in the broader world, and certainly in my world of business and of leadership.

Now I know many of you are hearing other messages that really conflict with the liberal arts approach. The University of California, as you know better than anyone, has gotten ridiculously expensive, and some of you may feel pressure—either personally, or from your parents—to get a good return on that investment by pretty quickly getting a good paying job. And, of course, there are student loans to repay. I also know what the economy is like right now, and that you may be more focused on developing marketable skills than you may have been just a few years ago.

But even if you want to go out and quickly make a good amount of money, I have some cautions about a pre-professional approach to college.

25   First of all, how can you be sure you know where the better paying fields are going to be in five years? From my experience at Stanford Business School, I can't tell you how many times I've seen that the industry that everyone wants to get into one year is headed for a fall the next. All the students in the late 80s that wanted to get into real estate development. CRASH! The flood of students in the late 90s that wanted to go into Internet startups. OUCH! How about the house flippers of a few years ago? It all looked like easy money. But that's how markets work—tons of people and money follow such bullish signals, leading to a glut of that kind of business, leading to a hyper-competitive market, and then a crash. It's the nature of markets, and it has happened since the beginning of time. So the question here is—even if you wanted to, how could you know the best fields for making money in the future? Even pre-med students today can't be sure of what the career path of a doctor will look like in the more than a decade it will take until they finish their residency.

Now, let's say you want to go into business one day, as I ultimately did. What would be the best preparation for that? I can tell you that as a hiring employer, here are things I looked for:
Evidence of:

Initiative and leadership,
Work ethic,
Communication skills, and
Emotional intelligence and interpersonal skills.
None of those is linked to a specific line of study.

It is true that there are some prospective employers who will be searching for narrow lines of study in their hiring. But many, many do not. When I applied as a senior in college for a newly created finance job at the world's largest real estate development company based in Dallas, Texas, I don't know what they thought when they saw I was a European History major from Princeton. But I do know that something in my letter and resume led them to want to interview me, and somehow I was able to stand out from the six finalists they flew down to Dallas. You can try to predict such things, but everyone's different, and you just never know. I found out later that the hiring manager—a high-level executive in a Texas-based global real estate company—graduated college with a B.A. in English. Go figure.

30   I also want to ask how can you know what you like at this point in your life? My experience is that people who like what they do, who love what they do, are much more likely to be successful at it, in addition to being happier. And if you're going to spend a third of your life working, why not like what you do? Seems like a no-brainer to me.

So to pick the bulk of your curriculum now based upon your guess as to what you might want to do in the working world, when you really haven't tried that many things and don't likely know what will make you happy later in life, seems foolhardy to me. If it turns out you're wrong, you may have wasted a big opportunity. Tons of my friends changed their majors, and tons have changed careers. One of my best friends in business school went through med school first, only to discover that he hated it. He didn't want to quit, so he graduated—and then went to business school. This stuff happens, and it may happen to you.

And so often the best things that happen to you, the things that make all the difference, happen by chance, or result from failure—not the result of careful planning.

I want to play something for you. Who here has seen on the Internet the commencement speech that Steve Jobs gave at Stanford in 2005? It's really quite an extraordinary talk, and I encourage you to watch the whole 15-minute Steve Jobs video sometime. He tells three stories of his life, and I want to play the first one for you.

> I dropped out of Reed College after the first 6 months, but then stayed around as a drop-in for another 18 months or so before I really quit. So why did I drop out?
>
> It started before I was born. My biological mother was a young, unwed college graduate student, and she decided to put me up for adoption. She felt very strongly that I should be adopted by college graduates, so everything was all set for me to be adopted at birth by a lawyer and his wife. Except that when I popped out they decided at the last minute that they really wanted a girl. So my parents, who were on a waiting list, got a call in the middle of the night asking: "We have an unexpected baby boy; do you want him?" They said: "Of course." My biological mother later found out that my mother had never graduated from college and that my father had never graduated from high school. She refused to sign the final adoption papers. She only relented a few months later when my parents promised that I would someday go to college.
>
> And 17 years later I did go to college. But I naively chose a college that was almost as expensive as Stanford, and all of my working-class parents' savings were being spent on my college tuition. After six months, I couldn't see the value in it. I had no idea what I wanted to do with my life and no idea how college was going to help me figure it out. And here I was spending all of the money my parents had saved their entire life. So I decided to drop out and trust that it would all work out OK. It was pretty scary at the time, but looking back it was one of the best decisions I ever made. The minute I dropped out I could stop taking the required classes that didn't interest me, and begin dropping in on the ones that looked interesting.
>
> It wasn't all romantic. I didn't have a dorm room, so I slept on the floor in friends' rooms, I returned coke bottles for the 5¢ deposits to buy food with, and I would walk the 7 miles across town every Sunday night to get one good meal a week at the Hare Krishna temple. I loved it. And much of what I stumbled into by following my curiosity and intuition turned out to be priceless later on. Let me give you one example:
>
> Reed College at that time offered perhaps the best calligraphy instruction in the country. Throughout the campus every poster, every label on every drawer, was beautifully hand calligraphed. Because I had dropped out and didn't have to take the normal classes, I decided to take a calligraphy class to learn how to do this. I learned about serif and san serif typefaces, about varying the amount of space between different letter combinations, about what makes great typography great. It was beautiful, historical, artistically subtle in a way that science can't capture, and I found it fascinating.
>
> None of this had even a hope of any practical application in my life. But ten years later, when we were designing the first Macintosh computer, it all came back to me. And we designed it all into the Mac. It was the first computer with beautiful typography. If I had never dropped in on

35

that single course in college, the Mac would have never had multiple typefaces or proportionally spaced fonts. And since Windows just copied the Mac, its likely that no personal computer would have them. If I had never dropped out, I would have never dropped in on this calligraphy class, and personal computers might not have the wonderful typography that they do. Of course it was impossible to connect the dots looking forward when I was in college. But it was very, very clear looking backwards ten years later.

40   Again, you can't connect the dots looking forward; you can only connect them looking backwards. So you have to trust that the dots will somehow connect in your future. You have to trust in something—your gut, destiny, life, karma, whatever. This approach has never let me down, and it has made all the difference in my life."

I shared this story with you NOT to encourage you to drop out of college—although it shows that that's not necessarily the end of the world. I mean, I've been to one of Steve Jobs houses, and I can assure you he's no longer eating at the Hare Krishna temple. No, I shared this story with you because it embodies an important point—that we can't always understand or explain the practical purpose of our choices to others as we go along. All we can do is listen to our hearts, follow our instincts and make the best judgments we can. It's all part of the experience of getting to know ourselves.

And that leads us back to some of what I suggested were the important life questions to make some progress answering while you're in college?

Who am I?

What am I passionate about?

45   What's important to me?

What doesn't interest me at all?

For me, embracing a liberal arts education was a great way to find some answers.

As part of putting this talk together, I did something I haven't done in decades—I pulled out my college transcript. It turns out I took courses in 16 different academic departments at Princeton. Clearly, I took the liberal arts seriously!

So let me share a few examples of how these experiences in the liberal arts helped me learn about myself.

50   From studying philosophy, I learned that abstract theories were intellectually interesting to me, but not so satisfying. Turns out, I'm a doer, an entrepreneur. I had the same experience with mathematics. Though I was good at it, once the classes got too deep into the abstract realm and I couldn't figure out the real world application, I lost interest.

From working week after week with a pigeon in a Psychology lab, I learned about Behaviorism, where our habits and behaviors came from and how they can be molded. It turns out that I love figuring out people, how they think and make decisions, and how to motivate them and bring out their best. My studies of Psychology and the brain have helped me be a better employer, a better negotiator, and a better parent—and they've helped me better understand myself.

From studying history, I learned that every struggle my society and I are going through is not new, that I am part of a story much larger than myself, and I learned humility about my role in that story. Interestingly to me, when I lost my bearings when the Twin Towers fell on 9/11, it was from history that I regained my sense of perspective—reading about how other societies survived much greater horrors over the centuries. It helped get me out of my own grief, and reminded me of the power of human resilience.

By writing a senior thesis and doing historical research leafing through primary source material in national archives in London and in Washington, I learned about how hard it is to understand the "truth" when relying on secondhand sources, like books and newspapers (and now on the Internet), where everything is filtered through other people's perspectives and biases. I also learned I was capable of original research, and of finding my own voice. And just like the marathons I've run, writing a 130-page thesis built endurance and expanded my sense of my own capabilities.

And what of studying music and art and architecture and literature? They helped me learn about what I find beautiful, and how that enhances my life. A couple years ago, I finally got to Barcelona, Spain [to] see the Gaudi-designed buildings whose pictures amazed me in Architecture class almost 30 years ago. It was a personal thrill.

55 Each academic subject is a window, a lens, through which to see the world. As you broaden yourself, you will notice things you wouldn't have noticed—you will appreciate things you would have completely missed—and you will meet and connect with more interesting people, possibly because you may be a more interesting person yourself!

And I don't know if you all will value this or not, but as you broaden yourself, you will be able to be a much more productive citizen. One of our biggest national problems is that we have become more self-focused as a people, and less able and willing to understand and care about others. Taking a liberal arts education—for example, my classes in Politics, East Asian Studies, Religion and Sociology—made me a less provincial and more worldly person. And the more connected you become to the world, the more you know and the more you care.

And by the way, one of the ways your generation is way ahead of mine is how global you are. Many times more of you will study abroad than my peers did in college. Were I in your seat right now, I would definitely study abroad, and I think it's one of the most encouraging indicators in our country that so many more American students do so today.

One more suggestion—take classes from the best teachers you can find, no matter what they teach. My experience is that they are the classes you will remember. Every college has iconic professors who know who they are, why they are teaching, and who love to open young minds. At Princeton, if you ask me the classes that most impacted how I see the world, they were not in my major. One of them was a Civil Engineering class. Why did I, a History major with no professional interest in science and engineering, take a Civil Engineering class? Because fellow students I respected told me to. They said David Billington was an incredible teacher. Billington loved how structures like buildings and bridges, when designed well, could come to symbolize a place and its people. His course "Structures and the Urban Environment" filled a 400-person lecture hall each spring. One of our homework assignments was to walk across his favorite built American structure—the Brooklyn Bridge—and write about our experience of it. Billington had a big impact on how I see my surroundings. Now I don't know who they are, but I know there are teachers like this at UCSB. Find them and spend time with them. They are the professors you will remember, and who will impact how you view yourself and the world.

Personally, I happen to be someone who loves to learn, so for me getting exposed by excellent teachers to varied subjects was a lot of fun. One last encouragement for each of you, no matter what your field of study, is to go through the course offerings and take something off the wall that just sounds fun to you—not because it's easy, not because you think it might get you a job, but just because it piques your interest. This is the time to do it. You are very privileged to be here at UCSB, and you have a unique opportunity.

60 Think forward. In 15 or 20 years, many of you will be buried in responsibilities—work, family. You may have a desire to expand yourself, to be a more stimulated and interesting person, to expose yourself to the new. At that point in your life, it's not impossible, but it's really hard.

Here, it's easy. It's right at your fingertips. Don't take it for granted. This opportunity will be gone before you know it.

Good wishes to each of you on your journey.

How to Get a Real Education at College

SCOTT ADAMS

Scott Adams is best known as the cartoonist of the widely published comic strip Dilbert, *which humorously characterizes a white-collar business office. While publishing the first* Dilbert *cartoon in 1989, Adams worked at Pacific Bell. His workplace experiences inspired his comic strip and also this commentary piece. Published on April 9, 2011, in* The Wall Street Journal, *Adams uses his business experience in college as the basis for arguing that the majority of students should focus on practical and life skills, such as entrepreneurship, while in college.*

I understand why the top students in America study physics, chemistry, calculus and classic literature. The kids in this brainy group are the future professors, scientists, thinkers and engineers who will propel civilization forward. But why do we make B students sit through these same classes? That's like trying to train your cat to do your taxes—a waste of time and money. Wouldn't it make more sense to teach B students something useful, like entrepreneurship?

I speak from experience because I majored in entrepreneurship at Hartwick College in Oneonta, N.Y. Technically, my major was economics. But the unsung advantage of attending a small college is that you can mold your experience any way you want.

There was a small business on our campus called The Coffee House. It served beer and snacks, and featured live entertainment. It was managed by students, and it was a money-losing mess, subsidized by the college. I thought I could make a difference, so I applied for an opening as the so-called Minister of Finance. I landed the job, thanks to my impressive interviewing skills, my can-do attitude and the fact that everyone else in the solar system had more interesting plans.

The drinking age in those days was 18, and the entire compensation package for the managers of The Coffee House was free beer. That goes a long way toward explaining why the accounting system consisted of seven students trying to remember where all the money went. I thought we could do better. So I proposed to my accounting professor that for three course credits I would build and operate a proper accounting system for the business. And so I did. It was a great experience. Meanwhile, some of my peers were taking courses in art history so they'd be prepared to remember what art looked like just in case anyone asked.

5 One day the managers of The Coffee House had a meeting to discuss two topics. First, our Minister of Employment was recommending that we fire a bartender, who happened to be one of my best friends. Second, we needed to choose a leader for our group. On the first question, there was a general consensus that my friend lacked both the will and the potential to master the bartending arts. I reluctantly voted with the majority to fire him.

But when it came to discussing who should be our new leader, I pointed out that my friend—the soon-to-be-fired bartender—was tall, good-looking and so gifted at b.s. that he'd be the perfect leader. By the end of the meeting I had persuaded the group to fire the worst bartender that any of us had ever seen . . . and ask him if he would consider being our leader. My friend nailed the interview and became our Commissioner. He went on to do a terrific job. That was the year I learned everything I know about management.

Turning the Classroom Upside Down

At about the same time, this same friend, along with my roommate and me, hatched a plan to become the student managers of our dormitory and to get paid to do it. The idea involved replacing all of the professional staff, including the resident assistant, security guard and even the cleaning crew, with students who would be paid to do the work. We imagined forming a dorm government to manage elections for various jobs, set out penalties for misbehavior and generally take care of business. And we imagined that the three of us, being the visionaries for this scheme, would run the show.

We pitched our entrepreneurial idea to the dean and his staff. To our surprise, the dean said that if we could get a majority of next year's dorm residents to agree to our scheme, the college would back it.

It was a high hurdle, but a loophole made it easier to clear. We only needed a majority of students who said they *planned* to live in the dorm next year. And we had plenty of friends who were happy to plan just about anything so long as they could later change their minds. That's the year I learned that if there's a loophole, someone's going to drive a truck through it, and the people in the truck will get paid better than the people under it.

10 The dean required that our first order of business in the fall would be creating a dorm constitution and getting it ratified. That sounded like a nightmare to organize. To save time, I wrote the constitution over the summer and didn't mention it when classes resumed. We held a constitutional convention to collect everyone's input, and I listened to two hours of diverse opinions. At the end of the meeting I volunteered to take on the daunting task of crafting a document that reflected all of the varied and sometimes conflicting opinions that had been aired. I waited a week, made copies of the document that I had written over the summer, presented it to the dorm as their own ideas and watched it get approved in a landslide vote. That was the year I learned everything I know about getting buy-in.

For the next two years my friends and I each had a private room at no cost, a base salary and the experience of managing the dorm. On some nights I also got paid to do overnight security, while also getting paid to clean the laundry room. At the end of my security shift I would go to The Coffee House and balance the books.

My college days were full of entrepreneurial stories of this sort. When my friends and I couldn't get the gym to give us space for our informal games of indoor soccer, we considered our options. The gym's rule was that only organized groups could reserve time. A few days later we took another run at it, but this time we were an organized soccer club, and I was the president. My executive duties included filling out a form to register the club and remembering to bring the ball.

By the time I graduated, I had mastered the strange art of transforming nothing into something. Every good thing that has happened to me as an adult can be traced back to that training. Several years later, I finished my MBA at Berkeley's Haas School of Business. That was the fine-tuning I needed to see the world through an entrepreneur's eyes.

If you're having a hard time imagining what an education in entrepreneurship should include, allow me to prime the pump with some lessons I've learned along the way.

15   **Combine Skills.** The first thing you should learn in a course on entrepreneurship is how to make yourself valuable. It's unlikely that any average student can develop a world-class skill in one particular area. But it's easy to learn how to do several different things fairly well. I succeeded as a cartoonist with negligible art talent, some basic writing skills, an ordinary sense of humor and a bit of experience in the business world. The "Dilbert" comic is a combination of all four skills. The world has plenty of better artists, smarter writers, funnier humorists and more experienced business people. The rare part is that each of those modest skills is collected in one person. That's how value is created.

Fail Forward. If you're taking risks, and you probably should,

you can find yourself failing 90% of the time. The trick is to get paid while you're doing the failing and to use the experience to gain skills that will be useful later. I failed at my first career in banking. I failed at my second career with the phone company. But you'd be surprised at how many of the skills I learned in those careers can be applied to almost any field, including cartooning. Students should be taught that failure is a process, not an obstacle.

Find the Action. In my senior year of college I asked my adviser   20
how I should pursue my goal of being a banker. He told me to figure out where the most innovation in banking was happening and to move there. And so I did. Banking didn't work out for me, but the advice still holds: Move to where the action is. Distance is your enemy.

Attract Luck. You can't manage luck directly, but you can manage your career in a way that makes it easier for luck to find you. To succeed, first you must *do* something. And if that doesn't work, which can be 90% of the time, do something else. Luck finds the doers. Readers of the *Journal* will find this point obvious. It's not obvious to a teenager.

Conquer Fear. I took classes in public speaking in college and a few more during my corporate days. That training was marginally useful for learning how to mask nervousness in public. Then I took the Dale Carnegie course.

It was life-changing. The Dale Carnegie method ignores speaking technique entirely and trains you instead to enjoy the experience of speaking to a crowd. Once you become relaxed in front of people, technique comes automatically. Over the years, I've given speeches to hundreds of audiences and enjoyed every minute on stage. But this isn't a plug for Dale Carnegie. The point is that people can be trained to replace fear and shyness with enthusiasm. Every entrepreneur can use that skill.

Write Simply. I took a two-day class in business writing that taught me how to write direct sentences and to avoid extra words. Simplicity makes ideas powerful. Want examples? Read anything by Steve Jobs or Warren Buffett.

Learn Persuasion. Students of entrepreneurship should learn the art of persuasion in all its forms, including psychology, sales, marketing, negotiating, statistics and even design. Usually those skills are sprinkled across several disciplines. For entrepreneurs, it makes sense to teach them as a package.

That's my starter list for the sort of classes that would serve B students well. The list is not meant to be complete. Obviously an entrepreneur would benefit from classes in finance, management and more.

Remember, children are our future, and the majority of them are B students. If that doesn't scare you, it probably should.

Coxsackie-Athens Valedictorian Speech 2010: Here I Stand

ERICA GOLDSON

Erica Goldson was the 2010 valedictorian of Coxsackie-Athens High School in Cox-sackie, New York. After graduation, she attended the University at Buffalo for a se-mester but withdrew, somewhat disappointed with her college experience, to travel. She is currently chronicling her travels across the United States on her blog America Via Erica. *She describes herself on her blog as "forming her own path" rather than "submit[ting] to the unfulfilling mainstream version of success." Goldson delivered this unconventional speech at her graduation in June 2010. It can be found both on her blog and on YouTube.*

There is a story of a young but earnest Zen student who approached his teacher and asked the Master, "If I work very hard and diligently, how long will it take for me to find Zen?" The Master thought about this, then replied, "Ten years." The student then said, "But what if I work very, very hard and really apply myself to learn fast—how long then?" Replied the Master, "Well, twenty years." "But, if I *really, really* work at it, how long then?" asked the student. "Thirty years," replied the Master. "But, I do not understand," said the disappointed student. "At each time that I say I will work harder, you say it will take me longer. Why do you say that?" Replied the Master, "When you have one eye on the goal, you only have one eye on the path."

This is the dilemma I've faced within the American education system. We are so fo-cused on a goal, whether it be passing a test, or graduating as first in the class. However, in this way, we do not really learn. We do whatever it takes to achieve our original objective.

Some of you may be thinking, "Well, if you pass a test, or become valedictorian, didn't you learn something?" Well, yes, you learned something, but not all that you could have. Perhaps, you only learned how to memorize names, places, and dates to later on forget in order to clear your mind for the next test. School is not all that it can be. Right now, it is a place for most people to determine that their goal is to get out as soon as possible.

I am now accomplishing that goal. I am graduating. I should look at this as a positive experience, especially being at the top of my class. However, in retrospect, I cannot say that I am any more intelligent than my peers. I can attest that I am only the best at doing what I am told and working the system. Yet, here I stand, and I am supposed to be proud that I have completed this period of indoctrination. I will leave in the fall to go on to the next phase expected of me, in order to receive a paper document that certifies that I am capable of work. But I contest that I am a human being, a thinker, an adventurer—not a worker. A worker is someone who is trapped within repetition—a slave of the system set up before him. But now, I have successfully shown that I was the best slave. I did what I was told to the extreme. While others sat in class and doodled to later become great artists, I sat in class to take notes and become a great test-taker. While others would come to class without their homework done because they were reading about an interest of theirs, I never missed an assignment. While others were creating music and writing lyrics, I decided to do extra credit, even though I never needed it. So, I wonder, why did I even want this position? Sure, I earned it, but what will come of it? When I leave educational institutionalism, will I be successful or forever lost? I have no clue about what I want to do with my life; I have no interests because I saw every subject of study as work, and I excelled at every subject just for the purpose of excelling, not learning. And quite frankly, now I'm scared.

5   John Taylor Gatto, a retired school teacher and activist critical of compulsory schooling, asserts, "We could encourage the best qualities of youthfulness—curiosity, adventure, resilience, the capacity for surprising insight simply by being more flexible about time, texts, and tests, by introducing kids into truly competent adults, and by giving each student what autonomy he or she needs in order to take a risk every now and then. But we don't do that." Between these cinderblock walls, we are all expected to be the same. We are trained to ace every standardized test, and those who deviate and see light through a different lens are worthless to the scheme of public education, and therefore viewed with contempt.

H. L. Mencken wrote in *The American Mercury* for April 1924 that the aim of public education is not

> to fill the young of the species with knowledge and awaken their intelligence. . . . Nothing could be further from the truth. The aim . . . is simply to reduce as many individuals as possible to the same safe level, to breed and train a standardized citizenry, to put down dissent and originality. That is its aim in the United States. (Gatto)

To illustrate this idea, doesn't it perturb you to learn about the idea of "critical thinking"? Is there really such a thing as "uncritically thinking?" To think is to process information in order to form an opinion. But if we are not critical when processing this information, are we really thinking? Or are we mindlessly accepting other opinions as truth?

This was happening to me, and if it wasn't for the rare occurrence of an avant-garde tenth grade English teacher, Donna Bryan, who allowed me to open my mind and ask questions before accepting textbook doctrine, I would have been doomed. I am now enlightened, but my mind still feels disabled. I must retrain myself and constantly remember how insane this ostensibly sane place really is.

10   And now here I am in a world guided by fear, a world suppressing the uniqueness that lies inside each of us, a world where we can either acquiesce to the inhuman nonsense of corporatism and materialism or insist on change. We are not enlivened by an educational system that clandestinely sets us up for jobs that could be automated, for work that need not be done, for enslavement without fervency for meaningful achievement. We have no choices in life when money is our motivational force. Our motivational force ought to be passion, but this is lost from the moment we step into a system that trains us, rather than inspires us.

We are more than robotic bookshelves, conditioned to blurt out facts we were taught in school. We are all very special, every human on this planet is so special, so aren't we all deserving of something better, of using our minds for innovation, rather than memorization, for creativity, rather than futile activity, for rumination rather than stagnation? We are not here to get a degree, to then get a job, so we can consume industry-approved placation after placation. There is more, and more still.

The saddest part is that the majority of students don't have the opportunity to reflect as I did. The majority of students are put through the same brainwashing techniques in order to create a complacent labor force working in the interests of large corporations and secretive government, and worst of all, they are completely unaware of it. I will never be able to turn back these 18 years. I can't run away to another country with an education system meant to enlighten rather than condition. This part of my life is over, and I want to make sure that no other child will have his or her potential suppressed by powers meant to exploit and control. We are human beings. We are thinkers, dreamers, explorers, artists, writers, engineers. We are anything we want to be—but only if we have an educational system that supports us rather than holds us down. A tree can grow, but only if its roots are given a healthy foundation.

For those of you out there that must continue to sit in desks and yield to the authoritarian ideologies of instructors, do not be disheartened. You still have the opportunity to stand up, ask questions, be critical, and create your own perspective. Demand a setting that will provide you with intellectual capabilities that allow you to expand your mind instead of directing it. Demand that you be interested in class. Demand that the excuse, "You have to learn this for the test" is not good enough for you. Education is an excellent tool, if used properly, but focus more on learning rather than getting good grades.

For those of you that work within the system that I am condemning, I do not mean to insult; I intend to motivate. You have the power to change the incompetencies of this system. I know that you did not become a teacher or administrator to see your students bored. You cannot accept the authority of the governing bodies that tell you what to teach, how to teach it, and that you will be punished if you do not comply. Our potential is at stake.

15   For those of you that are now leaving this establishment, I say, do not forget what went on in these classrooms. Do not abandon those that come after you. We are the new future and we are not going to let tradition stand. We will break down the walls of corruption to let a garden of knowledge grow throughout America. Once educated properly, we will have the power to do anything, and best of all, we will only use that power for good, for we will be cultivated and wise. We will not accept anything at face value. We will ask questions, and we will demand truth.

So, here I stand. I am not standing here as valedictorian by myself. I was molded by my environment, by all of my peers who are sitting here watching me. I couldn't have accomplished this without all of you. It was all of you who truly made me the person I am today. It was all of you who were my competition, yet my backbone. In that way, we are all valedictorians.

I am now supposed to say farewell to this institution, those who maintain it, and those who stand with me and behind me, but I hope this farewell is more of a "see you later" when we are all working together to rear a pedagogic movement. But first, let's go get those pieces of paper that tell us that we're smart enough to do so!

■ ■ ■ **FOR CLASS DISCUSSION** Higher Education in a Changing Economy

1. Many of these readings attempt to challenge commonly held beliefs, assumptions, and values about education. For example, Erica Goldson questions goal-oriented incentive structures in education. Mark Schneider challenges the claim that college graduates earn substantially more over their lifetimes than noncollege graduates. As you read, ask yourself: What are the stated and unstated assumptions about education that each author is challenging? Keep a list of the commonly held beliefs, assumptions, and values that these readings engage and note similarities and differences among the readings.

2. After reading Ken Saxon and Rebecca Mead, summarize Saxon's and Mead's definitions of a liberal arts education. Where do Saxon's and Mead's ideas differ? How would you define the features and supposed benefits of a liberal-arts education? Now reread Saxon and Mead and consider how your understanding of a liberal-arts education has changed or deepened. How have your own attitudes towards a liberal-arts education changed or become reinforced in your readings?

3. Scott Adams asks why "B students" should focus on more abstract disciplines such as literature, calculus, chemistry, and physics. Adams claims that it is a waste of time and money akin to "trying to train your cat to do your taxes." Do you agree that the more average students in these hard subjects should focus instead on more "useful" areas? If so, what other more useful focuses can you think of besides entrepreneurship? Be specific about the kinds of practical subject areas you would propose. If you do not agree, how might these, and other traditional academic subjects, benefit students not performing particularly well in them? Be specific when describing those benefits.

4. Erica Goldson's speech does not specifically address college, yet it critically examines many foundations of educational practices. How can you extend Goldson's thinking to the practices and values of higher education? How might Goldson question, for example, Schneider or Springer?

5. What does the setting of Springer's cartoon—the pawn shop—suggest he thinks about the value of a liberal-arts degree? What do other authors in this section, such as Saxon and Schneider, believe we should think about education in relationship to money? In light of these various arguments, do you think that students should think about their degrees as exchangeable for money or goods? Why or why not?

■ ■ ■

WRITING ASSIGNMENT   Speech to a Graduating High School Class

Imagine that you have been asked to speak at a public high-school commencement about attending college. Your purpose is to make a strong claim about the value (or lack thereof) of higher education. Drawing on both the readings from this chapter and your own experience as a college student, propose a way for students to think about the importance college. Be sure to address opposing arguments from these readings as you advocate for your own. ■

For additional writing, reading, and research resources, go to
www.mycomplab.com

33 Women in Math and Science

The puzzling relationship between biology and culture in the formation of gender identity has triggered extensive research with important consequences for parents, educators, and each of us individually as we try to make sense of our own gendered lives. Why do girls tend to play with dolls and boys with trucks? Are boys who push and shove each other in junior high school halls ramped up on testosterone or simply acting out cultural expectations for males? Are little girls who hold tea parties for their teddy bears imitating cultural stereotypes or living out some kind of biological hardwiring? Some research points heavily toward "nature" (gendered behavior is influenced by sex differences in genes, brain structure, hormone production, and exposure to prenatal hormones in utero), while other research points just as heavily toward "nurture" (boys and girls are socialized into different gender roles). Most scientists resist choosing either nature or nurture as the sole determinate of gendered behavior; they point rather to complex interactions between biology and the environment. Science writer Deborah Blum uses the metaphor of radio signals to suggest this relationship: biology produces "faint signals" that get "amplified by culture."[1]

The readings in this chapter and in Chapter 12 connect the nature/nurture controversy about gender differences to the phenomenon that women are currently underrepresented in the career fields of mathematics, physics, and engineering. The nature/nurture controversy exploded into an international debate following the January 2005 remarks of Lawrence Summers, then president of Harvard University, at an economics conference on diversifying the engineering and science workforce. Summers hypothesized that the underrepresentation of female professors on tenured faculties in math, science, and engineering at prestigious universities might be caused by innate differences between the sexes (nature) rather than by patterns of discrimination and socialization that discouraged women from entering these fields (nurture). Summers's remarks made instant headlines, serving as the kairotic moment for the debate that followed. Op-ed writers and bloggers voiced their views on Summers' hypothesis, often reflecting their own political perspectives on feminism, family values, and women's roles in society.

The first six readings in this chapter represent the reactions of scientists and science writers to Summers's speech. The last reading is a scientific research report showing how an engineering professor and a team of psychologists designed a study to investigate stereotype threat and women's performance in engineering.

[1]Blum, Deborah. "The Gender Blur." *Utne Reader* Sept.–Oct. 1998: 45–48.

Solving for XX

DEBORAH BLUM

Deborah Blum is a professor of journalism at the University of Wisconsin and a past president of the National Association of Science Writers. She won the 1992 Pulitzer prize for her book The Monkey Wars *on the ethical dilemmas of primate research. Her 1998 book* Sex on the Brain *was named a* New York Times *Notable Book of the Year. The following article appeared in the* Boston Globe *on January 23, 2005.*

Some time back, when I began reporting on the science of sex differences, I had the privilege of interviewing Richard Lynn, an Irish scientist whose views on mental differences between the races had been enshrined in a then-bestseller titled "The Bell Curve."

We had an unspoken contest going throughout the conversation. He was trying to make me lose my temper. I was trying to keep it. I won, sort of.

Even when he informed me that women lacked the brains to perform sophisticated math calculations and to handle strategy, I simply wrote it down. When he used the example of his daughter—she would never be able to beat him in chess, she lacked the necessary intellectual equipment—I merely pointed out that some people would find that statement offensive.

No matter what he said, I politely continued asking my questions. Apparently, however, I was polite in an increasingly loud voice because afterward people from across the newsroom stopped to tell me that I did the most *interesting* interviews.

5   OK, perhaps we should call that contest a draw.

This is not meant to yoke Lynn with Harvard president Lawrence H. Summers, who received international attention last week for his speculation, made at an academic conference, that a difference in "innate ability" might be one reason that women still lag substantially in the field of science and math.

Summers later explained that he intended only to be provocative, not to imply that women were, well, dumb. But for many women—including myself—the first reaction to these remarks was a sense of dismayed deja vu.

Spend any time at all studying the biology of behavior and you will find it riddled with similar, nature-based defenses of the often less-than-perfect status quo. In the days before women were admitted to college, male scientists insisted that girls were born too fragile and emotional to even handle higher education. Only a few weeks ago, a University of Michigan study concluded that men are less attracted to assertive and successful women, which the authors called a natural biological response.

As Marlene Zuk, a University of California-Riverside biologist specializing in sex-linked behaviors, wearily said to me this week: "I don't find Summers's statements either offensive or provocative—they trot out the same old lines we've heard for decades if not centuries, and they just aren't supported by good data."

10   But before considering the data, I'd like to begin on a note of superficial agreement with Summers.

According to a number of irate women who heard the speech, Harvard's president used a particular anecdote to illustrate the case for sex-specific biology. He'd once given his young daughter a pair of toy trucks as a gift. She turned them into a rather charming single-parent truck family, naming them "Daddy Truck" and "Baby Truck." I can't claim to be offended by that story since I tell the same kind of tales on my two sons, although mine tend to involve dismembering Barbies. There's nothing like being the parent of a small child to convince you that biology is a powerful influence on behavior—and vice versa.

The research to support the latter idea is getting better all the time. There are some terrific studies from the National Institutes of Health showing that parenting style itself can affect the way behavioral genes are expressed; countless others demonstrate that the way we behave helps shape both the structure and function of our brain. Behavioral researchers have found, for instance, that constant anxiety can alter pathways in the brain that produce stress hormones, raising the levels to such an extent that the body resets into a constant nervous state. Further, the compounds produced in that stress-chain reaction can cause damage to certain parts of the brain, such as the hippocampus, which helps regulate memory. In other words, if you suffer from memory problems during stress, chances are it's because stress has altered your brain.

So, nature impacts nurture—and vice versa. They dance together throughout our lives, so closely intertwined in their particular waltz, that it becomes simplistic to argue that a behavior is just one or the other.

But according to members of his audience, Summers took the simplistic approach, using his truck anecdote to imply that little girls' lack of interest in the mechanical aspects of toy trucks preordained their future failure in the analytical world of math and science. This, he said, helps explain the fact that while women make up 35 percent of the faculty in American universities, they constitute only 20 percent of the science and engineering departments.

15   He's right about those numbers, and it's to his credit that he sees them as a problem. It's also true that there are some good studies on childhood play, which indicate that hormones, such as testosterone, contribute to the stereotypical rough-and-tumble style of boys. Other research shows that girls with unusually high levels of testosterone often play rough, disdain dolls, and prefer trucks to be trucks.

But I've never seen research showing that those girls all became brilliant scientists—or that testosterone-influenced play has anything to do with math ability. In fact, comparable male-female math ability has been well documented for many years. In 1990, University of Wisconsin psychologist Janet Hyde and her colleagues did the first national meta-analysis showing that adolescent boys and girls were barely a few percentage points apart in average math performance—a conclusion that has been repeatedly confirmed. Hyde later found that most "gender effect differences" in all areas, from math or verbal ability to musical talent—fall in the small or "close to zero" range.

There is a twist to those average results—one actually raised by Summers. Although overall scores in math, for instance, are comparable, males seem to cluster at the high and low ends of the results, and women more consistently in the middle. For decades, psychologists have been puzzled over this "male variability"; the first papers pointing it out surfaced in 1914. No one knows for sure what those results mean. Do men have more potential for genius or failure? Or more of a tendency to test extremely badly or extremely well? In any case, almost everyone agrees that this is an area deserving of more research.

Hyde points out that some of the mythologies of gender difference—such as the myth about math-challenged women perpetuated by Summers—can and do influence performance. Surveys have found that both parents and teachers admit that they expect more from boys, based on the impression of greater talent. Not surprisingly, she finds Summers's foray into gender biology unimpressive: "Offensive and stupid, both. Worse, with his level of education and intelligence, he has no excuse."

That is, unless we want to argue that the male brain, due to some innate failure of ability, just cannot quite grasp the complex interaction between nature and nurture. In the interest of fairness, that could make a good story; kind of provocative, don't you think? I might enjoy doing the interviews—and I could promise to keep my voice down during the process.

The Science of Difference: Sex Ed

STEVEN PINKER

In this article published in the New Republic Online *in February 2005, psychologist Steven Pinker argues that research from cognitive science and evolutionary biology supports Lawrence Summers's hypothesis that innate differences between males and females can influence mathematical aptitude. Pinker is the Johnstone Family Professor of Psychology at Harvard and has also served on the faculty at MIT. He is a leading authority on language acquisition in children and is especially interested in the neural basis of consciousness.*

When I was an undergraduate in the early 1970s, I was assigned a classic paper published in *Scientific American* that began: "There is an experiment in psychology that you can perform easily in your home. . . . Buy two presents for your wife, choosing things . . . she will find equally attractive." Just ten years after those words were written, the author's blithe assumption that his readers were male struck me as comically archaic. By the early '70s, women in science were no longer an oddity or a joke but a given. Today, in my own field, the study of language development in children, a majority of the scientists are women. Even in scientific fields with a higher proportion of men, the contributions of women are so indispensable that any talk of turning back the clock would be morally heinous and scientifically ruinous.

Yet to hear the reaction to Harvard President Lawrence Summers's remarks at a conference on gender imbalances in science, in which he raised the possibility of innate sex differences, one might guess that he had proposed exactly that. Nancy Hopkins, the eminent MIT biologist and advocate for women in science, stormed out of the room to avoid, she said, passing out from shock. An engineering dean called his remarks "an intellectual tsunami," and, with equal tastelessness, a *Boston Globe* columnist compared him to people who utter racial epithets or wear swastikas. Alumnae threatened to withhold donations, and the National Organization of Women called for his resignation. Summers

was raked in a letter signed by more than 100 Harvard faculty members and shamed into issuing serial apologies.

Summers did not, of course, say that women are "natively inferior," that "they just can't cut it," that they suffer "an inherent cognitive deficit in the sciences," or that men have "a monopoly on basic math ability," as many academics and journalists assumed. Only a madman could believe such things. Summers's analysis of why there might be fewer women in mathematics and science is commonplace among economists who study gender disparities in employment, though it is rarely mentioned in the press or in academia when it comes to discussions of the gender gap in science and engineering. The fact that women make up only 20 percent of the workforce in science, engineering, and technology development has at least three possible (and not mutually exclusive) explanations. One is the persistence of discrimination, discouragement, and other barriers. In popular discussions of gender imbalances in the workforce, this is the explanation most mentioned. Although no one can deny that women in science still face these injustices, there are reasons to doubt they are the only explanation. A second possibility is that gender disparities can arise in the absence of discrimination as long as men and women differ, on average, in their mixture of talents, temperaments, and interests—whether this difference is the result of biology, socialization, or an interaction of the two. A third explanation is that child-rearing, still disproportionately shouldered by women, does not easily co-exist with professions that demand Herculean commitments of time. These considerations speak against the reflex of attributing every gender disparity to gender discrimination and call for research aimed at evaluating the explanations.

The analysis should have been unexceptionable. Anyone who has fled a cluster of men at a party debating the fine points of flat-screen televisions can appreciate that fewer women than men might choose engineering, even in the absence of arbitrary barriers. (As one female social scientist noted in *Science Magazine,* "Reinventing the curriculum will not make me more interested in learning how my dishwasher works.") To what degree these and other differences originate in biology must be determined by research, not fatwa. History tells us that how much we want to believe a proposition is not a reliable guide as to whether it is true.

5   Nor is a better understanding of the causes of gender disparities inconsequential. Overestimating the extent of sex discrimination is not without costs. Unprejudiced people of both sexes who are responsible for hiring and promotion decisions may be falsely charged with sexism. Young women may be pressured into choosing lines of work they don't enjoy. Some proposed cures may do more harm than good; for example, gender quotas for grants could put deserving grantees under a cloud of suspicion, and forcing women onto all university committees would drag them from their labs into endless meetings. An exclusive focus on overt discrimination also diverts attention from policies that penalize women inadvertently because of the fact that, as the legal theorist Susan Estrich has put it, "Waiting for the connection between gender and parenting to be broken is waiting for Godot." A tenure clock that conflicts with women's biological clocks, and family-unfriendly demands like evening seminars and weekend retreats, are obvious examples. The regrettably low proportion of women who have received tenured job offers from Harvard during

Summers's presidency may be an unintended consequence of his policy of granting tenure to scholars early in their careers, when women are more likely to be bearing the full burdens of parenthood.

Conservative columnists have had a field day pointing to the Harvard hullabaloo as a sign of runaway political correctness at elite universities. Indeed, the quality of discussion among the nation's leading scholars and pundits is not a pretty sight. Summers's critics have repeatedly mangled his suggestion that innate differences might be one cause of gender disparities (a suggestion that he drew partly from a literature review in my book, *The Blank Slate*) into the claim that they must be the only cause. And they have converted his suggestion that the statistical distributions of men's and women's abilities are not identical to the claim that all men are talented and all women are not—as if someone heard that women typically live longer than men and concluded that every woman lives longer than every man. Just as depressing is an apparent unfamiliarity with the rationale behind political equality, as when Hopkins sarcastically remarked that, if Summers were right, Harvard should amend its admissions policy, presumably to accept fewer women. This is a classic confusion between the factual claim that men and women are not indistinguishable and the moral claim that we ought to judge people by their individual merits rather than the statistics of their group.

Many of Summers's critics believe that talk of innate gender differences is a relic of Victorian pseudoscience, such as the old theory that cogitation harms women by diverting blood from their ovaries to their brains. In fact, much of the scientific literature has reported numerous statistical differences between men and women. As I noted in *The Blank Slate,* for instance, men are, on average, better at mental rotation and mathematical word problems; women are better at remembering locations and at mathematical calculation. Women match shapes more quickly, are better at reading faces, are better spellers, retrieve words more fluently, and have a better memory for verbal material. Men take greater risks and place a higher premium on status; women are more solicitous to their children.

Of course, just because men and women are different does not mean that the differences are triggered by genes. People develop their talents and personalities in response to their social milieu, which can change rapidly. So some of today's sex differences in cognition could be as culturally determined as sex differences in hair and clothing. But the belief, still popular among some academics (particularly outside the biological sciences), that children are born unisex and are molded into male and female roles by their parents and society is becoming less credible. Many sex differences are universal across cultures (the twentieth-century belief in sex-reversed tribes is as specious as the nineteenth-century belief in blood-deprived ovaries), and some are found in other primates. Men's and women's brains vary in numerous ways, including the receptors for sex hormones. Variations in these hormones, especially before birth, can exaggerate or minimize the typical male and female patterns in cognition and personality. Boys with defective genitals who are surgically feminized and raised as girls have been known to report feeling like they are trapped in the wrong body and to show characteristically male attitudes and interests. And a meta-analysis of 172 studies by psychologists Hugh Lytton and David Romney in 1991 found virtually no consistent difference in the way contemporary Americans socialize their sons and daughters. Regardless of whether it explains the gender disparity in science, the idea that some sex differences have biological roots cannot be dismissed as Neanderthal ignorance.

Since most sex differences are small and many favor women, they don't necessarily give an advantage to men in school or on the job. But Summers invoked yet another difference that may be more consequential. In many traits, men show greater variance than women, and are disproportionately found at both the low and high ends of the distribution. Boys are more likely to be learning disabled or retarded but also more likely to reach the top percentiles in assessments of mathematical ability, even though boys and girls are similar in the bulk of the bell curve. The pattern is readily explained by evolutionary biology. Since a male can have more offspring than a female—but also has a greater chance of being childless (the victims of other males who impregnate the available females)—natural selection favors a slightly more conservative and reliable baby-building process for females and a slightly more ambitious and error-prone process for males. That is because the advantage of an exceptional daughter (who still can have only as many children as a female can bear and nurse in a lifetime) would be canceled out by her unexceptional sisters, whereas an exceptional son who might sire several dozen grandchildren can more than make up for his dull childless brothers. One doesn't have to accept the evolutionary explanation to appreciate how greater male variability could explain, in part, why more men end up with extreme levels of achievement.

10 What are we to make of the breakdown of standards of intellectual discourse in this affair—the statistical innumeracy, the confusion of fairness with sameness, the refusal to glance at the scientific literature? It is not a disease of tenured radicals; comparable lapses can be found among the political right (just look at its treatment of evolution). Instead, we may be seeing the operation of a fascinating bit of human psychology.

The psychologist Philip Tetlock has argued that the mentality of taboo—the belief that certain ideas are so dangerous that it is sinful even to think them—is not a quirk of Polynesian culture or religious superstition but is ingrained into our moral sense. In 2000, he reported asking university students their opinions of unpopular but defensible proposals, such as allowing people to buy and sell organs or auctioning adoption licenses to the highest-bidding parents. He found that most of his respondents did not even try to refute the proposals but expressed shock and outrage at having been asked to entertain them. They refused to consider positive arguments for the proposals and sought to cleanse themselves by volunteering for campaigns to oppose them. Sound familiar?

The psychology of taboo is not completely irrational. In maintaining our most precious relationships, it is not enough to say and do the right thing. We have to show that our heart is in the right place and that we don't weigh the costs and benefits of selling out those who trust us. If someone offers to buy your child or your spouse or your vote, the appropriate response is not to think it over or to ask how much. The appropriate response is to refuse even to consider the possibility. Anything less emphatic would betray the awful truth that you don't understand what it means to be a genuine parent or spouse or citizen. (The logic of taboo underlies the horrific fascination of plots whose protagonists are agonized by unthinkable thoughts, such as *Indecent Proposal* and *Sophie's Choice*.) Sacred and tabooed

beliefs also work as membership badges in coalitions. To believe something with a perfect faith, to be incapable of apostasy, is a sign of fidelity to the group and loyalty to the cause. Unfortunately, the psychology of taboo is incompatible with the ideal of scholarship, which is that any idea is worth thinking about, if only to determine whether it is wrong.

At some point in the history of the modern women's movement, the belief that men and women are psychologically indistinguishable became sacred. The reasons are understandable: Women really had been held back by bogus claims of essential differences. Now anyone who so much as raises the question of innate sex differences is seen as "not getting it" when it comes to equality between the sexes. The tragedy is that this mentality of taboo needlessly puts a laudable cause on a collision course with the findings of science and the spirit of free inquiry.

Male Scientist Writes of Life as Female Scientist

SHANKAR VEDANTAM

Shankar Vedantam, staff writer for the Washington Post, *is the author of* The Hidden Brain: How Our Unconscious Minds Elect Presidents, Control Markets, Wage Wars, and Save Our Lives *(2010). He is also a national radio and TV commentator on issues related to science, religion, and human behavior. The following article, which appeared in the* Washington Post *in July 2006, reports on the views of several scientists favoring the nurture side of the nature/nurture debate, including those of transgendered Stanford neurobiologist Ben Barres.*

Neurobiologist Ben Barres has a unique perspective on former Harvard president Lawrence Summers's assertion that innate differences between the sexes might explain why many fewer women than men reach the highest echelons of science.

That's because Barres used to be a woman himself.

In a highly unusual critique published yesterday, the Stanford University biologist—who used to be Barbara—said his experience as both a man and a woman had given him an intensely personal insight into the biases that make it harder for women to succeed in science.

After he underwent a sex change nine years ago at the age of 42, Barres recalled, another scientist who was unaware of it was heard to say, "Ben Barres gave a great seminar today, but then his work is much better than his sister's."

5 And as a female undergraduate at MIT, Barres once solved a difficult math problem that stumped many male classmates, only to be told by a professor: "Your boyfriend must have solved it for you."

"By far," Barres wrote, "the main difference I have noticed is that people who don't know I am transgendered treat me with much more respect" than when he was a woman. "I can even complete a whole sentence without being interrupted by a man."

Barres said the switch had given him access to conversations that would have excluded him previously: "I had a conversation with a male surgeon and he told me he had never met a woman surgeon who was as good as a man."

Barres's salvo, bolstered with scientific studies, marks a dramatic twist in a controversy that began with Summers's suggestion last year that "intrinsic aptitude" may explain why there are relatively few tenured female scientists at Harvard. After a lengthy feud with the Faculty of Arts and Sciences, Summers resigned earlier this year.

The episode triggered a fierce fight between those who say talk of intrinsic differences reflects sexism that has held women back and those who argue that political correctness is keeping scientists from frankly discussing the issue.

10 While there are men and women on both sides of the argument, the debate has exposed fissures along gender lines, which is what makes Barres so unusual. Barres said he has realized from personal experience that many men are unconscious of the privileges that come with being male, which leaves them unable to countenance talk of glass ceilings and discrimination.

Barres's commentary was published yesterday in the journal Nature. The scientist has also recently taken his argument to the highest reaches of American science, crusading to make access to prestigious awards more equitable.

In an interview, Nancy Andreasen, a well-known psychiatrist at the University of Iowa, agreed with Barres. She said it took her a long time to convince her husband that he got more respect when he approached an airline ticket counter than she did. When she stopped sending out research articles under her full name and used the initials N.C. Andreasen instead, she said, the acceptance rate of her publications soared.

Andreasen, one of the comparatively few women who have won the National Medal of Science,

said she is still regularly reminded she is female. "Often, I will be standing in a group of men, and another person will come up and say hello to all the men and just will not see me, because in a professional setting, men are not programmed to see women," she said. "Finally, one of the men will say, 'I guess you haven't met Nancy Andreasen,' and then the person will turn bright red and say, 'Oh Nancy, nice to see you!' "

Summers did not respond to a request for an interview. But two scientists Barres lambasted along with Summers said the Stanford neurobiologist had misrepresented their views and unfairly tarred those who disagree with crude assertions of racism and sexism. Harvard cognitive scientist Steven Pinker and Peter Lawrence, a biologist at Britain's Laboratory of Molecular Biology in Cambridge, said convincing data show there are differences between men and women in a host of mental abilities.

15 While bias could be a factor in why there were fewer women at the pinnacles of science, both argued that this was not a primary factor.

Pinker, who said he is a feminist, said experiments have shown, on average, that women are better than men at mathematical calculation and verbal fluency, and that men are better at spatial visualization and mathematical reasoning. It is hardly surprising, he said, that in his own field of language development, the number of women outstrips men, while in mechanical engineering, there are far more men.

"Is it essential to women's progress that women be indistinguishable from men?" he asked. "It confuses the issue of fairness with sameness. Let's say the data shows sex differences. Does it become okay to discriminate against women? The moral issue of treating individuals fairly should be kept separate from the empirical issues."

Lawrence said it is a "utopian" idea that "one fine day, there will be an equal number of men and women in all jobs, including those in scientific research."

He said a range of cognitive differences could partly account for stark disparities, such as at his own institute, which has 56 male and six female scientists. But even as he played down the role of sexism, Lawrence said the "rat race"

in science is skewed in favor of pushy, aggressive people—most of whom, he said, happen to be men.

20 "We should try and look for the qualities we actually need," he said. "I believe if we did, that we would choose more women and more gentle men. It is gentle people of all sorts who are discriminated against in our struggle to survive."

Barres and Elizabeth Spelke, a Harvard psychologist who has publicly debated Pinker on the issue, say they have little trouble with the idea that there are differences between the sexes, although some differences, especially among children, involve biases among adults in interpreting the same behavior in boys and girls.

And both argue it is difficult to tease apart nature from nurture. "Does anyone doubt if you study harder you will do better on a test?" Barres asked. "The

mere existence of an IQ difference does not say it is innate. . . . Why do Asian girls do better on math tests than American boys? No one thinks they are innately better."

In her debate with Pinker last year, Spelke said arguments about innate differences as explanations for disparities become absurd if applied to previous eras. "You won't see a Chinese face or an Indian face in 19th-century science," she said. "It would have been tempting to apply this same pattern of statistical reasoning and say, there must be something about European genes that give rise to greater mathematical talent than Asian genes."

"I think we want to step back and ask, why is it that almost all Nobel Prize winners are men today?" she concluded. "The answer to that question may be the same reason why all the great scientists in Florence were Christian."

Girls = Boys at Math

DAVID MALAKOFF

David Malakoff is a freelance science writer and occasional contributor to ScienceNow Daily News, *an online daily news service for the prestigious peer-reviewed journal* Science. *This brief article, posted in July 2008, summarizes a technical research report from the University of Wisconsin, which contains data that may undermine Summers' views.*

At school, girls and boys show similar levels of ability in the sciences.

Zip. Zilch. Nada. There's no real difference between the scores of U.S. boys and girls on common math tests, according to a massive new study. Educators hope the finding will finally dispel lingering perceptions that girls don't measure up to boys when it comes to crunching numbers.

"This shows there's no issue of intellectual ability—and that's a message we still need to get out to some of our parents and teachers," says Henry "Hank" Kepner, president of the National Council of Teachers of Mathematics in Reston, Virginia.

It won't be a new message. Nearly 20 years ago, a large-scale study led by psychologist Janet Hyde of the University of Wisconsin, Madison, found a "trivial" gap in math test scores between boys and girls in elementary and middle school. But it did suggest that boys were better at solving more complex problems by the time they got to high school.

Now, even that small gap has disappeared, Hyde reports in tomorrow's issue of *Science*. Her team sifted through scores from standardized tests taken in 2005, 2006, and 2007 by nearly 7 million students in 10 states. Overall, the researchers found "no gender difference" in scores among children in grades two through 11. Among students with the highest test scores, the team did find that white boys outnumbered white girls by about two to one. Among Asians, however, that result was nearly reversed. Hyde says that suggests that cultural and social factors, not gender alone, influence how well students perform on tests.

5   Another portion of the study did confirm that boys still tend to outscore girls on the mathematics section of the SAT test taken by 1.5 million students interested in attending college. In 2007, for instance, boys' scores were about 7% higher on average than girls'. But Hyde's team argues that the gap is a statistical illusion, created by the fact that more girls take the test. "You're dipping farther down into the distribution of female talent,

which brings down the score," Hyde says. It's not clear that statisticians at the College Board, which produces the SAT, will agree with that explanation. But Hyde says it's good news, because it means the test isn't biased against girls.

The study's most disturbing finding, the authors say, is that neither boys nor girls get many tough math questions on state tests now required to measure a school district's progress under the 2002 federal No Child Left Behind law. Using a four-level rating scale, with level one being easiest, the authors said that they found no challenging level-three or -four questions on most state tests. The authors worry that means that teachers may start dropping harder math from their curriculums, because "more teachers are gearing their instruction to the test."

The results "essentially confirm" earlier studies—and they should finally put to rest the idea that girls aren't going into technical fields because they can't do the math, says Ann Gallagher, a psychologist who studies testing at the Law School Admission Council in Newtown, Pennsylvania. But she still thinks there may be cultural or psychological reasons for why girls still tend to lag behind boys on high-stakes tests such as the SAT. Among students she's observed, she says "the boys tend to be a little more idiosyncratic in solving problems, the girls more conservative in following what they've been taught."

Daring to Discuss Women in Science

JOHN TIERNEY

John Tierney writes science columns for the New York Times, *where the following article appeared in 2010, five years after Lawrence Summers' controversial speech. Here Tierney re-examines Summers's speech in light of new research on gender differences in science and math including the University of Wisconsin study cited by Malakoff.*

The House of Representatives has passed what I like to think of as Larry's Law. The official title of this legislation is "Fulfilling the potential of women in academic science and engineering," but nothing did more to empower its advocates than the controversy over a speech by Lawrence H. Summers when he was president of Harvard.

This proposed law, if passed by the Senate, would require the White House science adviser to oversee regular "workshops to enhance gender equity." At the workshops, to be attended by researchers who receive federal money and by the heads of science and engineering departments at universities, participants would be given before-and-after "attitudinal surveys" and would take part in "interactive discussions or other activities that increase the awareness of the existence of gender bias."

I'm all in favor of women fulfilling their potential in science, but I feel compelled, at the risk of being shipped off to one of these workshops, to ask a couple of questions:

1) Would it be safe during the "interactive discussions" for someone to mention the new evidence supporting Dr. Summers's controversial hypothesis about differences in the sexes' aptitude for math and science?

5   2) How could these workshops reconcile the "existence of gender bias" with careful studies that show that female scientists fare as well as, if not better than, their male counterparts in receiving academic promotions and research grants?

Each of these questions is complicated enough to warrant a 10 column, so I'll take them one at a time, starting this week with the issue of sex differences.

When Dr. Summers raised the issue to fellow economists and other researchers at a conference in 2005, his hypothesis was caricatured in the press as a revival of the old notion that "girls can't do math." But Dr. Summers said no such thing. He acknowledged that there were many talented female scientists and discussed ways to eliminate the social barriers they faced.

Yet even if all these social factors were eliminated, he hypothesized, the science faculty composition at an elite school like Harvard might still be skewed by a biological factor: the greater variability observed among men in intelligence test scores and various traits. Men and women might, on average, have equal mathematical ability, but there could still be disproportionately more men with very low or very high scores.

These extremes often don't matter much because relatively few people are involved, leaving the bulk of men and women clustered around the middle. But a tenured physicist at a leading university,

Dr. Summers suggested, might well need skills and traits found in only one person in 10,000: the top 0.01 percent of the population, a tiny group that would presumably include more men because it's at the extreme right tail of the distribution curve.

"I would like nothing bet- 10 ter than to be proved wrong," Dr. Summers told the economists, expressing the hope that gender imbalances could be rectified simply by eliminating social barriers. But he added, "My guess is that there are some very deep forces here that are going to be with us for a long time."

Dr. Summers was pilloried for even suggesting the idea, and the critics took up his challenge to refute the hypothesis. Some have claimed he was proved wrong by recent reports of girls closing the gender gap on math scores in the United States and other countries. But even if those reports (which have been disputed) are accurate, they involve closing the gap only for average math scores—not for the extreme scores that Dr. Summers was discussing.

Some scientists and advocates 15 for gender equity have argued that the remaining gender gap in extreme scores is rapidly shrinking and will disappear. It was called "largely an artifact of changeable sociocultural factors" last year by two researchers at the University of Wisconsin, Janet S. Hyde and Janet E. Mertz. They noted evidence of the gap narrowing and

concluded, "Thus, there is every reason to believe that it will continue to narrow in the future."

But some of the evidence for the disappearing gender gap involved standardized tests that aren't sufficiently difficult to make fine distinctions among the brighter students. These tests, like the annual ones required in American public schools, are limited by what's called the ceiling effect: If you're measuring people in a room with a six-foot ceiling, you can't distinguish among the ones taller than six feet.

Now a team of psychologists at Duke University has looked at the results of tests with more headroom. In an article in a forthcoming issue of the journal Intelligence, they analyze the test scores of students in the United States who took college admissions tests while they were still in the seventh grade. As part of an annual talent search since 1981, the SAT and ACT tests have been given to more than 1.6 million gifted seventh graders, with roughly equal numbers of boys and girls participating.

The Duke researchers—Jona- 15 than Wai, Megan Cacchio, Martha Putallaz and Matthew C. Makel—focused on the extreme right tail of the distribution curve: people ranking in the top 0.01 percent of the general population, which for a seventh grader means scoring above 700 on the SAT math test. In the early 1980s, there were 13 boys for every girl in that group, but by 1991 the gender gap had narrowed to four to one, presumably because of sociocultural factors like encouragement and instruction in math offered to girls.

Since then, however, the math gender gap hasn't narrowed, despite the continuing programs to encourage girls. The Duke researchers report that there are still four boys for every girl at the extreme right tail of the scores for the SAT math test. The boy-girl ratio has also remained fairly constant, at about three to one, at the right tail of the ACT tests of both math and science reasoning. Among the 19 students who got a perfect score on the ACT science test in the past two decades, 18 were boys.

Meanwhile, the seventh-grade girls outnumbered the boys at the right tail of tests measuring verbal reasoning and writing ability. The Duke researchers report in Intelligence, "Our data clearly show that there are sex differences in cognitive abilities in the extreme right tail, with some favoring males and some favoring females."

The researchers say it's impossible to predict how long these math and science gender gaps will last. But given the gaps' stability for two decades, the researchers conclude, "Thus, sex differences in abilities in the extreme right tail should not be dismissed as no longer part of the explanation for the dearth of women in math-intensive fields of science."

Other studies have shown that these differences in extreme test scores correlate with later achievements in science and academia. Even when you consider only members of an elite group like the top percentile of the seventh grad-

20 ers on the SAT math test, someone at the 99.9 level is more likely than someone at the 99.1 level to get a doctorate in science or to win tenure at a top university.

Of course, a high score on a test is hardly the only factor important for a successful career in science, and no one claims that the right-tail disparity is the sole reason for the relatively low number of female professors in math-oriented sciences. There are other potentially more important explanations, both biological and cultural, including possible social bias against women.

But before we accept Congress's proclamation of bias, before we start re-educating scientists at workshops, it's worth taking a hard look at the evidence of bias against female scientists. That will be the subject of another column.

"Daring to Discuss Women in Science": A Response to John Tierney

CAROLYN SIMARD

Carolyn Simard, who has a Ph.D. in communication studies from Stanford, is the vice president of research and executive programs at the Anita Borg Institute for Women and Technology in Palo Alto, California. The following article is a blog posted June 9, 2010, on the Huffington Post *technology site Huffpost Tech.*

On Monday, John Tierney of the *New York Times* published a provocative article, "Daring to Discuss Women in Science" in which he argues that biology may be a factor to explain why women are not reaching high-level positions. He suggests that boys are innately more gifted at math and science and that the dearth of women in science may point to simple biological differences. If this is the case, why would we waste our time trying to get more women in science?

Mr. Tierney, let's indeed discuss women in science.

First, let me start by saying that I applaud the discussion—all potential explanations for a complex issue and all evidence need to be considered, even the ones that are not popular in the media or not "politically correct." I also believe that Larry Summer's now infamous comments about the possibility that biological differences account for the dearth of women scientists and technologists was, similarly, in the spirit of intellectual debate.

The problem with the biology argument that "boys are just more likely to be born good at math and science" isn't that it's not "politically correct"—it's that it assumes that we can take away the power of societal influences, which have much more solid evidence than the biology hypothesis. Tierney makes the point himself in his article—in order provide evidence for biological differences, he cites a longitudinal Duke study which shows that the highest achievers in SAT math tests (above 700), which counted 13 boys for every girl in the early 80s, became a ratio of 4 boys to 1 girls in 1991, "presumably because of sociocultural factors." Hmm, isn't this actual evidence that biology is not what is at play here? If it is possible to reduce the gender achievement gap in math by 3 thanks to "sociocultural factors," I rest my case, sociocultural factors are indeed extremely powerful.

5   The Duke study also notes that the 4/1 achievement gap at the highest score hasn't changed in the last 20 years despite ongoing programs to encourage girls in math and science, whereas the highest achievers in writing ability (SAT above 700) shows a ratio of 1.2 girls for every boy, slightly favoring girls. However, if the premise is that boys are inherently "better" at math, and girls are inherently better at writing, why would the achievement gap be so large in math and negligible in writing? The stagnant 4 to 1 ratio is not evidence that there is an innate biological difference in math aptitude, but rather confirmation that persistent sociocultural barriers remain—that is, science and math are still thought of as male domains.

Research shows that math and science are indeed thought of as stereotypically male domains. Project Implicit at Harvard University studied half a million participants in 34 countries and found that that 70 percent of respondents worldwide have implicit stereotypes associating science with male more than with female. Years of research by Claude Steele and Joshua Aronson and their colleagues shows that implicit stereotypes affect girls' performance in math—a phenomenon called "stereotype threat." When girls receive cues that "boys are better at math," their scores in math suffer; one study in a classroom setting showed that the difference in performance between boys and girls in math SAT scores was eliminated by simply having a mentor telling them that math is learned over time rather than "innate."

The problem is, girls are routinely getting the message that they don't belong in math and science, further undermining their performance (and Mr. Tierney's article isn't exactly helping in changing the stereotype for the general public). The result of this implicit (unconscious) stereotype is that parents, teachers, and school counselors are less likely to encourage girls to pursue math and science than they are boys. These girls are then less likely to seek advanced math classes and would be unlikely, without those opportunities, to make it to the above 700 SAT math score regardless of innate ability.

Anecdotally, I had this experience with my daughter a couple of years ago. At age 10, she had somehow decided that she wasn't good at math (despite being raised in a household with 2 PhDs). With her self-confidence plummeting, math homework became very painful in our household. When I dug deeper, I found that she mistakenly believed that you were either born with math ability or you weren't—that this was an innate biological ability as opposed to something you could learn, and that somehow she hadn't been "born with it." Once I actively dispelled that notion and provided her with additional mentoring, her math performance significantly improved. I never hear her say that she isn't good at math anymore, and her math homework is flawless.

The Duke article, and Tierney, raises an important question about preference, however, that research suggests that boys are more interested in "things" and girls are more interested in "people," and thus gravitate towards fields reflecting that interest. In this research too, there is debate about what in this difference is "nature" versus "nurture"— there are powerful socialization forces at play. Regardless, we have to dispel the notion that science is only about "things" and not about people or somehow disconnected from all social relevance. Indeed, some of the most successful interventions to increase girls' interest in math and science have been to reframe the curriculum to provide examples and projects that are grounded in the interests of a diverse population of students. The EPICS program at Purdue University is a great example of grounding engineering disciplines in socially relevant contexts and has been shown to engage a diversity of students.

10   What we need, to put this debate to rest, is to replicate these findings in a country where science and math is not viewed as stereotypically male. The most recent cross-national comparison study, published in 2010 in Psychological Bulletin by Nicole Else-Quest and her colleagues and comparing 43 countries, shows that the achievement difference in math between girls and boys varies broadly across countries.

Their research shows that country by country variation is correlated with gender differences in self-confidence in math, which is compounded by stereotype threat. One of the strongest predictors of the gender gap in math achievement is a given country's level of gender equity in science jobs, consistent with socialization arguments: "if girls' mothers, aunts, and sisters do not have STEM careers, they will perceive that STEM is a male domain and thus feel anxious about math, lack the confidence to take challenging math courses, and underachieve on math tests."

Until girls stop getting the signal that math is for boys, the 4 to 1 gender ratio in highest achievement categories of math and science will persist. This has nothing to do with innate ability.

Mr. Tierney, I look forward to your subsequent articles on this issue. Let's indeed dare to discuss women in science and continue to bring to bear the most relevant research on this issue.

Stereotype Threat and Women's Performance in Engineering

AMY E. BELL, STEVEN J. SPENCER, EMMA ISERMAN, AND CHRISTINE E. R. LOGEL

In this scientific report, published in the Journal of Engineering Education *in October 2003, an engineering professor from Virginia Tech and three psychologists from the University of Waterloo in Canada examine the effect of "stereotype threat" on women's performance in an engineering exam. Parts of the "results" section of this article depend for full comprehension on readers' knowledge of statistics, but the rest of the article should be understandable to a nonscientific audience.*

Abstract

Recent research has demonstrated that stereotype threat—the concern that others will judge one negatively due to a stereotype that exists about one's group—interferes with women's performance on standardized math and engineering exams. In the current research we find that when a shortened version of the Fundamental of Engineering Exam is described as a test that is diagnostic of ability (i.e., when stereotype threat is high) women perform worse than men on the test. When stereotype threat is reduced, however (by characterizing the test as non-diagnostic or as not producing gender differences), women do just as well as men. The implication of these results for improving the engineering education environment is discussed.

I. Introduction

A. Persistent Under-representation of Women in Engineering

Of the bachelor's degrees awarded in science and engineering in the U.S. in 1996, 47 percent were awarded to women (up from 38 percent in the mid-1980s). However, the percentages differ greatly by field. For instance, in 1996, women earned the following percentages of bachelor's degrees by field: 73 percent psychology; 50 percent biological and agricultural sciences; 51 percent social sciences; 37 percent physical sciences; 33 percent earth, atmospheric, and ocean sciences; 46 percent mathematics; 27 percent computer science; and, 18 percent engineering [1]. The percentages of master's and doctoral engineering degrees awarded to women in 1996 were 17 percent and 12 percent, respectively [1].

The U.S. engineering bachelor's degree figures have steadily improved for women from 15.4 percent in 1990 to 18.6 percent in 1998 to 21 percent in 2001 [1–3]. However, there is a disparity across the various engineering disciplines. For instance, women earned only 14 percent of the electrical, computer and mechanical engineering bachelor's degrees in 2001, but they earned 34 percent, 36 percent and 39 percent of the industrial, chemical and biomedical engineering bachelor's degrees, respectively [3]. The overall figure of 21 percent is evidence that electrical, computer and mechanical engineering represent the majority (52 percent) of bachelor engineering degrees awarded [3].

Not only do women earn a disproportionately lower share of the awarded engineering degrees, they also have lower retention rates than men. Table 1 shows the nationwide retention rates for women and men at three points in the undergraduate engineering pipeline for a 1982–1993 cohort. This data illustrates that the retention rates of women are lower at every point in the undergraduate engineering pipeline.

Paradoxically, although the degree completion rate for women is significantly lower than the rate for men, the grade point averages (GPAs) of women and men were nearly identical (GPA = 2.98, standard deviation = for women; GPA = 2.88, standard deviation = 0.561 for men) [4].

Many studies have investigated the reasons why women remain persistently under-represented in science, mathematics, and engineering. Some of the primary reasons that are given to explain this phenomenon include: women's loss of confidence/lower self-confidence [5]; a chilly classroom/learning environment for women [6]; gender-role socialization [7]; and women's innate inability (relative to men's) in science and mathematics [8, 9].

An innovative approach to understanding the lower performance of women on difficult math tests offers a new perspective on the performance and retention of women in fields that require a significant amount of mathematics, like engineering. This new approach suggests that—in addition to lower/loss of self-confidence, chilly climate factors and socialization effects—the differences in women's performance and retention may be explained, at least in part, by the influence of stereotypes and prejudice on their performance. This influence has been characterized as *stereotype threat.*

B. Stereotype Threat Defined

Research on stereotype threat examines the experience of being in a situation where one risks being judged negatively due to a commonly held devaluing stereotype that exists about one's group [10–16]. The primary hypothesis of stereotype threat research is that when one is in a situation in which a negative stereotype exists about one's group, then the concern with being judged or of self-fulfilling the stereotype interferes with one's performance. This predicament of being in a situation in which one faces judgment based on societal stereotypes begins with a prejudice that is widely known—even among people who do not believe the stereotype. For instance, our society alleges women have inferior math abilities compared to men. So when a woman finds herself in a situation in which her math skills are being tested (e.g., a formal test or answering a question in math class), she experiences a pressure that may degrade her performance. This is a predicament that others, not stereotyped in this way, do not face. Stereotype threat hypothesizes that this predicament creates a pressure that leads to performance degradation.

C. Stereotype Threat Example

Consider the following illustration of stereotype threat and performance [16]. A study examined black and white men's performance on a golf putting task. The participants were randomly separated into two groups. The first group performed the putting task after being instructed that the task was a measure of athletic ability; the second group performed the task after being instructed that it was a measure of sports intelligence. The black men outperformed the white men when the task was characterized as testing athletic ability. However, the white men outperformed the black men when the task was characterized as testing sports intelligence. How the test was represented to the participants affected their

TABLE 1 **Retention rates of women and men in undergraduate engineering at three points in the pipeline: 1982–1993 cohort [4].**

Gender	Percent retained after completing only threshold courses in engineering	Percent retained after taking engineering courses beyond threshold, but before degree	Percent completed bachelor's degree
Women	77.3%	64.6%	41.9%
Men	81.7%	80.0%	61.6%

"Threshold" courses roughly include the mathematics and 1–2 introductory engineering courses encountered in the first 2–4 academic semesters of an engineering curriculum; see [4] for a description of "threshold" courses.

performance. The characterization of the test as a measure of athletic ability induced stereotype threat for the white men while the characterization of the test as a measure of sports intelligence induced stereotype threat for the black men. Ironically, this simple putting task tested neither athletic ability nor sports intelligence.

D. Stereotype Threat Elaborated

Stereotype threat is not tied to one particular group; it is likely that everyone experiences it in various situations throughout her or his life. The strength of stereotype threat varies with the situation; for instance, a woman may suffer from its effects in her math class, but not in her elementary education class. Stereotype threat is not an internalized belief in the stereotype or a fear that it may be true. Nor is stereotype threat a belief that others will be prejudiced against you. It is a threat that is "in the air [13]." Stereotype threat can be experienced even if one does not believe the stereotype or worry that the stereotype could be true about oneself. A person can have high self-confidence and still suffer from the effects of stereotype threat; indeed, past research indicates that stereotype threat effects are largest among the best students who are most identified with the subject matter [10, 14].

An important difference between the stereotype threat explanation for women's underperformance on math tests and the explanation based on lower self-confidence is that stereotype threat only occurs in specific situations—situations in which the negative stereotype applies (i.e. when a woman is taking a difficult math test). In contrast, the self-confidence explanation is intrinsic to the person—it is felt in all situations. Furthermore, the stereotype threat explanation does not imply that there is something wrong with the women; however, a lack of self-confidence insinuates that the women need to "fix themselves" and improve their poor self-image.

The present research further evaluates the impact of stereotype threat on women's performance on standardized engineering tests. Section II outlines the previous, germane research on stereotype threat and gender. Section III describes a new study on stereotype threat in engineering: the design, participants, procedure, scoring, and results are presented. Section IV discusses the implications of these new results.

II. Background
A. Stereotype Threat and Women's Math Performance

Previous research has demonstrated the dramatic impact of stereotype threat on women's performance on math tests. From a stereotype threat perspective, a student's concern about being stereotyped by others should be highest when two factors are at play: (i) the student is performing poorly (e.g., the questions are difficult); and, (ii) a stereotype might be applied to the student (e.g., the stereotype that women are not good at math). Based on previous research, it is in this situation that differences between men and women's performance should emerge. In one study, women with strong math backgrounds performed worse than men with similar backgrounds on difficult tests—yet women performed equally well on easy tests [10]. Although stereotype threat is the purported cause of the performance differential, other interpretations remain. For example, one could argue that women's lesser math capabilities only become evident on more advanced material.

15   Another study examined the performance of highly selected women and men on a difficult math test when the relevance of the stereotype was manipulated by how the test was characterized. In the "relevant" stereotype threat condition, participants were told that the test had shown gender differences in the past. Conversely, in the "irrelevant" stereotype threat condition, participants were told that the test had never shown gender differences. There are two important points to note. First, in the relevant stereotype condition, it was not stated that men had outperformed women in the past, just that there had been gender differences. Second, in the irrelevant stereotype condition, the validity of the stereotype was not attacked; instead, the *particular* math test was characterized as having shown no gender differences in the past. The results showed that men significantly outperformed women in the relevant stereotype condition and women and men performed equally well in the irrelevant stereotype condition [10]. Since the women's performance improved and equaled the men's when the difficult test was characterized as having shown no gender differences in the past, it suggests that there was something in the testing situation that was responsible for the difference. After all, if the women were less mathematically capable, then a different test characterization would have no impact on their performance. Thus, there is strong evidence that women's underperformance on the difficult tests resulted from stereotype threat and not from innate inability.

In addition to explaining differences in performance, stereotype threat may also illuminate the lower retention rates of women in math-related fields. Researchers have argued that the stereotype threat that women experience in math-related domains may cause them to "disidentify" with the domain [13]. In other words, women drop out of math in order to avoid the evaluative threat that they sometimes feel in this domain. Indeed, one study indicated that women expressed less interest in pursuing academic majors and careers involving high levels of mathematics after watching stereotypic TV commercials [12].

B. Stereotype Threat and Women's Engineering Performance

Similar to the prejudice that women are inferior to men in mathematical ability, there exists a societal stereotype that women are less capable than men in engineering ability. In a previous study, we showed that stereotype threat undermines women's performance on engineering exams [15]. Eighteen women and thirty men, engineering sophomores and juniors at Virginia Tech, participated in the experiment. The test questions were a subset of questions from the general portion of the standardized Fundamentals of Engineering Exam (FEE) [17]. One-half of the participants were randomly assigned to take an easy version of the engineering test and the other half took a difficult version of the engineering test. We only selected participants for the studies who indicated that they had a relatively high grade point average (GPA) in engineering, and who stated that they were good in engineering and that it was important for them to be good in engineering. The test directions, called the "diagnostic" directions (see Figure 1), were the same for both the easy and difficult tests. The diagnostic directions increased the stereotype threat for women with its assertion of being able to distinguish the good engineers from the bad.

Our hypothesis was twofold. First, we anticipated no difference in the performance between women and men on the easy exam since the stereotype threat would be eliminated (or severely mitigated) by positive performance. Second, we expected a gender difference to emerge on the difficult exam in which the stereotype threat condition was "high" (difficult questions and diagnostic directions). Our results indicated that women and men performed equally on the easy engineering exam (57 percent score for both women and men), whereas men performed significantly better than women on the difficult engineering exam (21 percent score for women, 34 percent score for men) [15]. This difference remained statistically significant even when controlling for GPA and self-reported competence and importance of engineering.

III. Description of the Study
A. Design

The previous research on stereotype threat's impact on women's performance on engineering tests does not conclusively rule out inherent gender differences on the difficult test [15]. For example, one might argue that women's lesser engineering capabilities only become apparent on more advanced material. However, this seems unlikely for two reasons. The results of the previous study indicated no gender differences in GPA, easy test performance, self-reported engineering competence, and self-reported importance of engineering. Also, the difficult test questions were hard due to a lack of familiarity, not complexity; it is unlikely that only unfamiliar questions would reveal innate gender differences.

20   To further investigate whether stereotype threat—and not inherent gender differences—is the explanation for differences in performance, we designed a study to directly assess the effects of stereotype threat on women's engineering performance. All participants took the difficult engineering test; however, we manipulated the relevance of stereotype threat with three sets of directions that characterized the test differently. In the "relevant" stereotype condition, the diagnostic directions represented the test as being able to discriminate between capable and incapable engineers; this induced a high stereotype threat condition for the women (similar to the previous study [15]). In the non-diagnostic directions condition we reduced stereotype threat by characterizing the test as being unable to judge a person's engineering competence; this mitigated the stereotype threat for the women since the test is unable to judge their performance. Finally in the gender-fair directions condition we reduced stereotype threat by characterizing the test

Diagnostic	Non-Diagnostic	Gender-Fair
This test has been shown to be an excellent indicator of engineering aptitude and ability in a large number of settings and across a wide spectrum of students. *This test is especially effective at assessing people's engineering limitations in problem areas.*	The problem set you will be working on today was specifically designed to present you with problems varying in their degree of difficulty so that we might be able to get an accurate picture of which problems should be included or excluded on our future version of this test. *We are not interested in your overall score on the test, and, in fact, the problems are in such an early stage of development that we could not say what a particular score would signify.*	This test has been shown to be an excellent indicator of engineering aptitude and ability in a large number of settings and across a wide spectrum of students. The test is especially effective at assessing people's engineering limitations in problem areas. *Prior use of these problems has shown them to be gender-fair—that is, men and women perform equally well on these problems.*

FIGURE 1 PERTINENT EXCERPTS FROM TEST DIRECTIONS. ITALICS ADDED FOR EMPHASIS; ITALICS DID NOT APPEAR IN THE ACTUAL TEST DIRECTIONS.

as one in which no-gender differences have been found. Figure 1 highlights the germane passages from these two sets of directions.

We developed the difficult engineering test from questions available as practice tests for the general portion of the FEE. We reduced the number of questions and shortened the duration, but maintained the proportions of questions for each of the various engineering areas. The composition (and ordering) of the eighteen questions were as follows: six math, two electric circuits, two statics, two chemistry, and one each for thermodynamics, dynamics, material science, computers, ethics, and engineering economics.

B. Participants

The participants were recruited to take part in the study through email and in-class announcements. We only selected participants who indicated that they had a relatively high grade point average (GPA) in engineering, and who stated that they were good in engineering and that it was important for them to be good in engineering (GPA scores were subsequently verified by official university records). We selected participants using these criteria because previous stereotype threat studies have indicated that stereotype threat effects are largest among the best students who are most identified with the subject matter [10,14]. Nine women and 18 men took the test in the diagnostic condition, 11 women and 18 men took the test in the non-diagnostic condition, and 9 women and 18 men took the test in the gender-fair condition.

C. Procedure

The participants reported to each testing session in small, mixed gender groups; students were randomly assigned to the three test conditions. To begin, the students read the engineering test directions—either diagnostic, non-diagnostic, or gender-fair (these labels were not available to the students). They then took the difficult engineering test that was computerized (a paper copy was also distributed for working out the problems); they were given 30 minutes to complete it. Upon completion of the test the participants were reassured that no one was expected to do well since the advanced test material was beyond their current level. The participants were thanked for their time and paid $15.

D. Scoring

In scoring the answers we separated the math questions from the engineering questions. Our previous study demonstrated that the difficult math questions were relatively easy for our participants even with the diagnostic instructions (there were no significant differences between the women's and men's math scores).

In calculating a participant's score for the engineering part of the exam we did not include questions that were directly related to the participant's major. The engineering major (i.e., expertise area) for each question is sometimes ambiguous. For instance, industrial and systems engineering (ISE) students take a materials science (MSE) course in their junior year; however, MSE is not an ISE expertise area. The final categorizations were determined by the required courses in only the freshman and sophomore years of each engineering department. For example, the two electric circuit questions were not included in the score calculation for electrical and computer engineering majors. However, the computers and ethics questions were included in the score calculation for all engineering majors. We did this because we reasoned that the questions in a student's major would not be difficult for her or him. We refer to this calculated engineering score as the "non-expert engineering score." Moreover, we controlled for guessing in the non-expert engineering score by subtracting one-fourth of a point for each wrong answer. This normalized a chance performance to zero instead of twenty-five percent; it also implied that the scores were not inflated by random guessing.

E. Hypothesis

We expect that in the diagnostic instructions condition in which stereotype threat is high, women will under-perform compared to men on the engineering test. However, in the non-diagnostic instructions and gender-fair instructions conditions, we anticipate that the women will perform equally with the men.

F. Results

We tested for differences in the data using focused comparisons that tested the specific hypotheses we predicted and further examined our findings by testing for differences between specific means.[1] We compared means using the F statistic which is computed as

---

[1] Our study was designed to replicate the results of previous research on the effect of stereotype threat on women's math performance [10, 11]; we wanted to determine whether similar variables influenced women's engineering performance. Thus, we tested our hypotheses using focused comparisons in analysis of variance; this analysis provides a more sensitive test of our results than a standard ANOVA (a two-way ANOVA in this case). Rosenthal and Rosnow provide a detailed description of these procedures and a complete explanation of their proper use [18].

TABLE 2 **Non-expert engineering score (in percentage and controlled for guessing) by gender and test instructions condition. Means with different subscripts differ at $p < .0.5$.**

	Instructions Condition		
	Diagnostic	Gender-Fair	Non-Diagnostic
Women	9_a	28_b	$21_{a,b}$
Men	30_b	36_b	$21_{a,b}$

the ratio of the variability due to differences between the mean scores of the conditions to the variability due to differences between the data and mean score within each condition. For each computed F statistic, a corresponding p-value is also calculated; it describes the level of statistical significance (p is a function of F; as F increases, p decreases). Small values of p, typically [p < 0.05] or [p < 0.1], indicate that the mean scores across the conditions being compared are significantly different.

A focused contrast of our prediction that women who took the test with diagnostic instructions (high stereotype threat) would perform worse than people in the other five conditions (women/non-diagnostic, women/gender-fair, men/diagnostic, men/non-diagnostic, men/gender-fair) was significant. The F statistic testing this comparison was 4.42; the probability that such a large F value occurred by chance is less than 5 percent [(p < .05)]. Thus, we conclude that women's performance is significantly lower when stereotype threat is high. The means for each condition are reported in Table 2 and also illustrated in Figure 2.

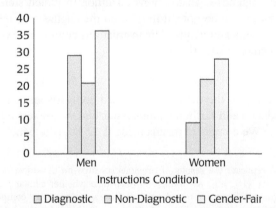

FIGURE 2 NON-EXPERT ENGINEERING SCORE (IN PERCENTAGE AND CONTROLLED FOR GUESSING) BY GENDER AND TEST INSTRUCTIONS CONDITION.

A comparison of women and men's performance in each of the three conditions was also conducted. Women (mean score = 9 percent) performed worse than men (mean score = 30 percent) in the diagnostic instructions condition ($F = 4.92$, $p < 0.05$). However, women performed about as well as men in the gender-fair instructions condition (mean score = 28 percent for women and 36 percent for men, $F = 0.622$, $p > 0.40$) and women performed as well as men in the non-diagnostic instructions condition (mean score = 21 percent for both women and men, $F = 0$, $p > 0.90$). It is interesting that the performance of both men and women tended to drop in the non-diagnostic instructions condition compared to the gender-fair condition. Perhaps the participants took the test less seriously and thus did not perform as well when the test was described as non-diagnostic.

In addition, the effect of the different conditions on each gender's performance was examined. Women in the diagnostic instructions condition performed worse than women in the gender-fair instructions condition (mean score = 9 percent and 28 percent respectively, $F = 3.93$, $p = 0.05$) and women in the diagnostic instructions condition tended to perform worse than women in the non-diagnostic instructions condition, but this difference did not reach statistical significance (mean score = 9 percent and 21 percent respectively, $F = 1.71$, $p = 0.20$). Among men there was a tendency for men to score lower in the non-diagnostic condition than in the other conditions, but none of these differences reached statistical significance (mean score = 30 percent in diagnostic condition, 21 percent in non-diagnostic condition, and 36 percent in the gender-fair condition; all F values < 3.5 and all p values > 0.05).

An analysis of performance on the math questions revealed that, consistent with our previous research [15], these questions were indeed relatively easy for all of the participants and there were no significant differences between women and men's scores in any of the conditions. The mean math scores for women (W) and men (M) were: 56 percent (W) and 46 percent (M) in the diagnostic condition; 50 percent (W) and 57 percent (M) in the non-diagnostic condition; and, 50 percent (W) and 49 percent (M) in the gender-fair condition.

IV. Conclusion

The results of this study extend previous research and further support the idea that stereotype threat undermines women's performance on engineering exams [15].

As part of the stereotype that women are less capable than men in engineering ability, there is a commonly held belief (particularly among engineering educators) that students have to be "tough" in order to succeed in engineering and that the women students tend to not be as tough as the men students. One can almost imagine their interpretation of the results of this research: "If the women's performance is going to depend on the phrasing of one or two sentences in the test directions, then they are too sensitive and not tough enough to be good engineers." Is this true—are the women too weak? Consider the following. A group of white men with strong math backgrounds took a difficult math test [14]. One-half of the participants took the test after it had been suggested that, in general, Asians were better at math than whites (the stereotype threat condition). The remaining participants took the test when there was no mention of Asian-white math ability differences (the control group). The white men who took the test under the stereotype threat condition significantly under-performed the white men in the control group. Can it be concluded that the under-performing white men are too sensitive and not tough enough; after all, it was only *one* mention in *one* test. Unlike the women in math and engineering, white men are not burdened by a history of stereotypes regarding their lesser abilities. Of course, the answer is that the men are no more weak or sensitive than the women. Human nature—and not a lack of "toughness"—prompts us to be affected by the prejudices that exist about our group.

The current study strongly suggests that stereotype threat may be a more important impediment to women's success and persistence in engineering than has been realized. Furthermore, a recent, comprehensive study collected and analyzed data from students, faculty and administrators at 53 universities; one of the primary conclusions of the study was that the classroom and department climates were significant factors in the women students' persistence in engineering [19]. However, there may be hope even despite the rather depressing statistics reviewed earlier. If stereotype threat is undermining women's success in engineering then there are tractable ways to reduce stereotype threat, improve the climate, and increase women's success.

25   In creating classrooms and learning environments low in stereotype threat and warm in climate, it is not enough to just avoid negative behaviors—positive efforts must also be made. When stereotype threat is the remaining barrier for a student, Steele has suggested several "wise" strategies that a teacher can employ to mitigate the impact of threatening stereotypes [13]. The recommended wise strategies include the following:

- expressing optimism about the student's potential to achieve and succeed;
- assigning challenging—not trivial—work at a challenging, not overwhelming, pace;
- affirming the student's belongingness based on her or his intellectual potential; and,
- valuing multiple perspectives and approaches to the academic content.

Hall and Sandler have provided a comprehensive list of action items for administrators, faculty and students on warming up the climate for women students [6]. Among the negative behaviors for teachers to avoid are: making seemingly helpful comments that imply women are not as competent as men; disparaging women in general, women's intellectual abilities, or women's professional potential; and, using sexist humor as a classroom device. Some recommended positive behaviors for teachers to adopt are: use terminology that includes both men and women; call directly on women students as well as men students in class; and, ask women and men qualitatively similar questions (critical and factual questions).

If engineering educators can create environments in which stereotype threat is low then more women should succeed and persist. Perhaps in such an environment, in which many of the obstacles to women's success are removed, each woman would be able to achieve the same level of success as her male colleagues. The current research suggests that creating such environments in our engineering programs may be an important way to reduce the under-representation of women in our field.

Acknowledgments

The authors would like to thank Mr. Satyabrata Rout for his assistance in collecting the data in this experiment. This work was supported by a grant from the Alfred P. Sloan Foundation.

References

[1] National Science Foundation, "Women, Minorities, and Persons with Disabilities in Science and Engineering: 2000," Arlington, VA, 2000 (NSF 00–327).

[2] Engineering Workforce Commission of the AAES, "Engineering and Technology Enrollments," American Association of Engineering Societies (AAES), Washington, D.C., 1998 and 1999.

[3] "Databytes," *American Society of Engineering Education Prism,* September 2001.

[4] Adelman, C., "Women and Men of the Engineering Path: A Model for Analyses of Undergraduate Careers," U.S. Department of Education and the National Institute for Science Education, Washington, D.C., 1998.

[5] Seymour, E., and N.M. Hewitt, *Talking About Leaving: Why Undergraduates Leave the Sciences,* Westview Press, 1997.

[6] Hall, R.M., and B.R. Sandler, "The Classroom Climate: A Chilly One for Women?," Project on the Status and Education of Women, Association of American Colleges, Washington, D.C., 1982.

[7] Meece, J.L., J.S. Eccles, C.M. Kaczala, S.B. Goff, and R. Futterman, "Sex Differences in Math Achievement: Towards a Model of Academic Choice," *Psychological Bulletin,* Vol. 91, 1982, pp. 324–348.

[8] Benbow, C.P., and J.C. Stanley, "Sex Differences in Mathematical Reasoning Ability: More Facts," *Science,* Vol. 222, 1983, pp. 1029–1031.

[9] Benbow, C.P., and J.C. Stanley, "Sex Differences in Mathematical Ability: Fact or Artifact?," *Science,* Vol. 210, 1980, pp. 1262–1264.

[10] Spencer, S.J., C.M. Steele, and D.M. Quinn, "Stereotype Threat and Women's Math Performance," *Journal of Experimental and Social Psychology,* Vol. 1999, 35, pp. 4–28.

[11] Quinn, D.M., and S.J. Spencer, "How Stereotype Threat Interferes with Women's Math Performance," *Journal of Social Issues,* Vol. 57, 2001, pp. 55–71.

[12] Davies, P.G., S.J. Spencer, D.M. Quinn, and R. Gerhardstein, "All Consuming Images: How Demeaning Commercials that Elicit Stereotype Threat can Restrain Women Academically and Professionally," *Personality and Social Psychology Bulletin,* Vol. 28, 2002, pp. 1615–1628.

[13] Steele, C.M., "A Threat in the Air: How Stereotypes Shape Intellectual Identity and Performance," *American Psychologist,* Vol. 52, No. 6, June 1997, pp. 613–629.

[14] Aronson, J., M.J. Lustina, C. Good, and K. Keough, "When White Men Can't Do Math: Necessary and Sufficient Factors in Stereotype Threat," *Journal of Experimental Social Psychology,* Vol. 35, 1999, pp. 29–46.

[15] Bell, A.E. and S.J. Spencer, "The Effect of Stereotype Threat on Women's Performance on the Fundamentals of Engineering Exam," *Proceedings of the American Society of Engineering Education Annual Conference,* Montreal, Canada, June 2002.

[16] Stone, J., C. I. Lynch, M. Sjomeling, and J.M. Darley, "Stereotype Threat Effects on Black and White Athletic Performance," *Journal of Personality and Social Psychology,* Vol. 77, 1999, pp. 1213–1227.

[17] National Society of Professional Engineers, <http://www/nspe/org>, accessed July 7, 2003.

[18] Rosenthal, R., and R.L. Rosnow, *Contrast Analysis: Focused Comparisons in the Analysis of Variance,* Cambridge University Press, Cambridge, England, 1985.

[19] Goodman, I.F., C.M. Cunningham, C. Lachapelle, M. Thompson, K. Bittinger, R.T. Brennan, and M. Delci, "The Women's Experiences in College Engineering (WECE) Project," Goodman Research Group Inc., April 2002.

Authors' Biographies

Amy E. Bell is an Assistant Professor in the Department of Electrical and Computer Engineering at Virginia Tech. She received her Ph.D. in electrical engineering from the University of Michigan. Bell conducts research in wavelet image compression, embedded systems, and bioinformatics. She is the recipient of a 1999 National Science Foundation CAREER award, a 2002 National Science Foundation Information Technology Research award, and two awards for teaching excellence.

Address: 340 Whittemore Hall, Electrical and Computer Engineering, Virginia Tech, Blacksburg, VA, 2406–0111; telephone: 540–231–2940; fax: 540–231–8292; e-mail: abell@vt.edu.

Steve Spencer is an Associate Professor in the Department of Psychology at the University of Waterloo. He has conducted numerous studies on the effect of stereotype threat on women's math performance.

Address: 200 University Avenue West, Psychology Department, University of Waterloo, Waterloo, ON, N2L 3G1; e-mail: sspencer@watarts.uwaterloo.ca.

Emma Iserman is a graduate student at the University of Waterloo.

Address: 200 University Avenue West, Psychology Department, University of Waterloo, Waterloo, ON, N2L 3G1; e-mail: eciserma@watarts.uwaterloo.ca.

Christine E.R. Logel is a graduate student at the University of Waterloo.

Address: 200 University Avenue West, Psychology Department, University of Waterloo, Waterloo, ON, N2L 3G1; e-mail: c3robins@watarts.uwaterloo.ca.

■ ■ ■ **FOR CLASS DISCUSSION** Women in Math and Science

1. The writers in this chapter, besides expressing their own views about the nature/nurture controversy and the relation of gender to mathematical ability, refer to previous empirical studies addressing these questions. Working in small groups or as a whole class, try to place these studies in one of three columns:

   a. Research studies/experiments that support the nature hypothesis

   b. Research studies/experiments that support the nurture hypothesis

   c. Research studies/experiments that are ambiguous or open to different interpretations

2. From a broad cultural perspective, what is at stake in the controversy over Summers's speech?

   a. What important values and beliefs are reinforced or threatened by different positions on this controversy?

   b. What ideologies or world views makes some commentators apt to accept Summers's biological hypothesis and others apt to oppose it?

   c. Where do you stand and why?

WRITING ASSIGNMENT Argument on Summers's Biological Hypothesis

In June 2006, Lawrence Summers resigned as president of Harvard, having received votes of "no confidence" from the faculty. One of the contributing causes of the no-confidence vote was the accusation of sexism stemming from his innate-differences speech. Conservative media commentators accused the liberal Harvard faculty of railroading Summers from office, preferring political correctness over truth-seeking inquiry. Drawing on evidence from the readings in this chapter along with your own personal experiences, write your own argument defending or attacking Summers' biological explanation for the underrepresentation of women on elite research faculties in math, science, and engineering. In some cases, you might need to do further research into the scientific controversy on gender differences. An example of a student paper on this issue is Julee Christianson's "Why Lawrence Summers Was Wrong: Culture Rather Than Biology Explains the Under-Representation of Women in Science and Mathematics" on pp. 273–280. ■

For additional writing, reading, and research resources, go to
www.mycomplab.com

34 Choices for a Sustainable World

Since the publication of the U.N. Intergovernmental Panel on Climate Change's report, *Climate Change 2007*, which affirms the scientific conclusion that human-influenced climate change threatens our global environment, much of the public debate has shifted from arguing about causes of global warming to arguing about potential consequences and solutions. The dominant question is no longer whether climate change is happening but what actions we should take in view of its impact. What choices should we make as a society? What actions should we expect of our leaders? What life choices should we make as ethical members of society when we consider how our individual actions affect both our close neighbors and those who live around the globe? What actions can we hope, or even demand, that others make? Can we fight climate change without causing an economic collapse?

These discussions on climate change reveal many points of view: Some want to increase domestic production of oil; others seek alternative sources of energy; more broadly, others ask how we might live in a more sustainable manner. A memorable definition of *sustainability* has been expressed in these words: "Leave the world better than you found it, take no more than you need, try not to harm [the] life of the environment, make amends if you do" (from Fifth Town Artisan Cheese Company). When people focus on sustainability, they recognize that the earth's resources are limited, that these resources are being overdrawn, and that some countries such as the United States and China are responsible for a much larger percentage of environmental damage than others. Awareness of the suffering caused by environmental damage to the poor in today's world and of the potential suffering that may be inflicted on our children and grandchildren leads us to reevaluate the traditional choices we have made in using the world's resources.

Furthermore, as climate change, alternative sources of energy, and sustainability have gained traction as important issues, the words "environmentally friendly," "green," and "sustainable" have become trendy concepts and useful marketing tools, prompting many to call for more stringent environmental regulations. The verbal and visual arguments in this chapter invite you to enter these controversies as you explore these questions: Who should take responsibility for the effects of climate change? What sources of energy and which environmental practices appear to be the most sustainable? How will our individual choices interconnect to make a powerful social response to the threat of climate change?

Our Gas Guzzlers, Their Lives

NICHOLAS KRISTOF

Nicholas D. Kristof, a two-time Pulitzer Prize–winning journalist who writes regular columns for the New York Times, *is known for his eloquence about human suffering in third-world countries. Kristof, a world traveler and reporter, authored, with his wife Sheryl WuDunn, also a journalist,* China Wakes: The Struggle for the Soul of a Rising Power *(1994),* Thunder from the East: Portrait of a Rising Asia *(2000), and* Half the Sky: Turning Oppression into Opportunity for Women Worldwide *(2009). Each year he takes a student and a teacher, winners of an essay contest, on a reporting trip. In this op-ed piece, written during the 2007 trip, Kristof employs his knowledge of Africa and world economics to build a case for greater environmental responsibility on the part of wealthy countries.*

BUJUMBURA, Burundi—If we need any more proof that life is unfair, it is that subsistence villagers here in Africa will pay with their lives for our refusal to curb greenhouse gas emissions.

When we think of climate change, we tend to focus on Alaskan villages or New Orleans hurricanes. But the people who will suffer the worst will be those living in countries like this, even though they don't contribute at all to global warming.

My win-a-trip journey with a student and a teacher has taken us to Burundi, which the World Bank's latest report shows to be the poorest country in the world. People in Burundi have an annual average income of $100, nearly one child in five dies before the age of five, and life expectancy is 45.

Against that grim backdrop, changing weather patterns in recent years have already caused crop failures—and when the crops fail here, people starve. In short, our greenhouse gases are killing people here.

5 "If the harvest fails in the West, then you have stocks and can get by," said Gerard Rusuku, an agriculture scientist here who has been studying the impact of global warming in Africa. "Here, we're much more vulnerable. If climate change causes a crop failure here, there's famine."

Guillaume Foliot of the World Food Program notes that farmers here overwhelmingly agree that the weather has already become more erratic, leading to lost crops. And any visitor can see that something is amiss: Africa's "great lakes" are shrinking.

Burundi is on Lake Tanganyika, which is still a vast expanse of water. But the shoreline has retreated 50 feet in the last four years, and ships can no longer reach the port.

"Even the hippos are unhappy," said Alexander Mbarubukeye, a fisherman on the lake, referring to the hippos that occasionally waddled into town before the lake retreated.

The biggest of Africa's great lakes, Lake Victoria, was dropping by a vertical half-inch a day for much of last year. And far to the north, once enormous Lake Chad has nearly vanished. The reasons for the dipping lake levels seem to include climate change.

10 Greenhouse gases actually have the greatest impact at high latitudes—the Arctic and Antarctica. But the impact there isn't all bad (Canada will gain a northwest passage), and the countries there are rich enough to absorb the shocks.

In contrast, the Intergovernmental Panel on Climate Change warned this year that the consequences for Africa will be particularly harsh because of the region's poverty and vulnerability.

It foresees water shortages and crop failures in much of Africa.

"Projected reductions in yield in some countries could be as much as 50 percent by 2020, and crop net revenues could fall as much as 90 percent," the panel warned. It also cautioned that warming temperatures could lead malaria to spread to highland areas. Another concern is that scarcities of food and water will trigger wars. More than five million lives have already been lost since 1994 in wars in Rwanda, Burundi and Congo, and one factor was competition for scarce resources.

"It seems to me rather like pouring petrol onto a burning fire," Jock Stirrup, the chief of the British defense staff, told a meeting in London this month. He noted that climate change could cause weak states to collapse.

Yoweri Museveni, Uganda's president, describes climate change as "the latest form of aggression" by rich countries against Africa. He has a point. Charles Ehrhart, a Care staff member in Kenya who works full time on climate-change issues, says that the negative impact of the West's carbon emissions will overwhelm the positive effects of aid.

15 "It's at the least disastrous and quite possibly catastrophic," Mr. Ehrhart said of the climate effects on Africa. "Life was difficult, but with climate change it turns deadly."

"That's what hits the alarm bells for an organization like Care," he added. "How can we ever achieve our mission in this situation?"

All this makes it utterly reckless that we fail to institute a carbon tax or at least a cap-and-trade system for emissions. The cost of our environmental irresponsibility will be measured in thousands of children dying of hunger, malaria and war.

Pain at the Pump? We Need More

DANIEL C. ESTY AND MICHAEL E. PORTER

Daniel C. Esty and Michael E. Porter, widely recognized and published authors in their fields, emphasize business concerns as an essential aspect of sustainability. As commissioner of Connecticut's Department of Energy and Environmental Protection with a background as Professor of Law and Environmental Policy at Yale University, Daniel Esty plans to integrate environmental, energy, and economic policies. Michael E. Porter, who holds a prestigious professorship at Harvard Business School, introduced ideas on competitive strategy that are now taught in business schools worldwide and is considered the world's most influential thinker on management and competitiveness. In this op-ed piece, published in the New York Times *on April 28, 2011, they examine the positive effects an emissions charge would have on innovation in American business.*

Gasoline prices are above $4 per gallon in much of the country, a reminder that our dependence on oil carries a great cost. President Obama has promised that the Justice Department will be

vigilant in pursuing price-gouging at the pump, but what we really need is to address the full set of energy-related problems, with a focus on spurring clean energy innovation.

Our trade deficit arises in large measure from the hundreds of billions of dollars we pay for foreign oil. The imbalances threaten America's economic stability and national security. Our consumption of fossil fuels and our energy inefficiency are a drag on our competitiveness and increase air pollution and the threat of climate change.

To compete globally, we need to encourage clean energy innovation while letting the market decide which particular technologies prevail. Experience in fields like information technology and telecommunications suggests that creating demand for innovation is far more effective than subsidizing company-specific research projects or providing incentives for particular technologies. Governments just aren't good at picking winners; witness the billions wasted on corn-based ethanol subsidies.

The best way to drive energy innovation would be an emissions charge of $5 per ton of greenhouse gases beginning in 2012, rising to $100 per ton by 2032. The low initial charge, starting next year, would make the short-term burden on consumers and businesses almost negligible.

5 An emissions charge is not a radical idea; making people pay for the harm they cause lies at the heart of property rights. European countries participate in a cap-and-trade system that effectively imposes a carbon charge. Even China is pushing to shut down inefficient coal-burning plants by imposing emissions charges. Thus, instituting a carbon charge would have only a minimal impact on American competitiveness—

and might even improve it as the incentive for efficiency and innovation kicked in.

Our proposal would apply to all greenhouse gas emissions, so that everybody, and every fossil-fuel-dependent form of energy, would be included. Coal-burning power plants would pay based on the emissions measured at their smokestacks. Oil companies would pay for every gallon of gas or oil delivered. Yes, these costs would be passed on to consumers, but this is what motivates changes in behavior and technological investments.

Some will say that even the modest emissions charge we propose is politically impossible, given the death of the cap-and-trade bill that the House passed in 2009. But the ballooning federal deficit has created a new political imperative. A modest emissions charge will look attractive compared with raising individual income taxes or burdening the economy with new corporate or payroll taxes.

Let's be clear: the main goal is not to raise revenue. It is to create a powerful incentive for a gradual but steady shift toward clean and sustainable energy sources. In the short term, an emissions charge would create a major impetus for a move from oil and coal to natural gas, with its much lower carbon content. Gas would likely become the preferred fuel for new power generation, and by extension, for transportation, as electric vehicles

become cost-effective alternatives to internal combustion cars.

Technological advances have made vast quantities of domestic shale gas accessible. The shift to gas as a transitional fuel would allow the United States to cut greenhouse-gas emissions by up to 50 percent over the next decade. In the longer term, the prospect of a steadily rising emissions charge would focus the private sector's attention on energy-saving and carbon-reducing innovations. The calculus for investments would immediately change. Anyone pursuing an energy-consuming project, like a power plant, would factor in the rising long-term charge into their choice of technology. People buying new cars would have an added incentive to think about fuel economy.

10 Entrepreneurial spirit would be unleashed in companies from multinational enterprises to back-of-the-garage inventors. By stimulating major gains in energy productivity and renewable energy, our approach would help stimulate global growth and free up resources to meet other pressing needs.

In tackling our trade imbalance, budget deficit, competitiveness challenges and oil-related vulnerability—not to mention climate change—our plan has a powerful logic. And because it harnesses our capacity for innovation and entrepreneurship, it could attract broad support, and a bipartisan majority in Congress.

Carbon-Neutral Is Hip, but Is It Green?

ANDREW C. REVKIN

Andrew C. Revkin has authored three books about environmental issues: The Burning Season *(1990) about an Amazon rain forest activist who was killed;* Global Warming: Understanding the Forecast *(1992); and most recently,* The North Pole Was Here: Puzzles and Perils at the Top of the World *(2006). An environmental reporter for the* New York Times, *Revkin has won the American Association for the Advancement of Science Journalism Award, and he holds degrees in biology and journalism. This exploratory piece, which was first published in the* New York Times *on April 29, 2007, questions the effectiveness of carbon-neutral practices. The carbon-neutral movement seeks to cut the carbon emissions of individuals and businesses largely by encouraging activities and purchases that in some way cancel out the negative effects of burning carbons: for example, buying and planting trees to counter the emissions caused by flying in jets or driving cars.*

In addition to the celebrities—Leo, Brad, George—politicians like John Edwards and Hillary Clinton are now running, at least part of the time, carbon-neutral campaigns. A lengthening list of big businesses—international banks, London's taxi fleet, luxury airlines—also claim "carbon neutrality." Silverjet, a plush new trans-Atlantic carrier, bills itself as the first fully carbon-neutral airline. It puts about $28 of each round-trip ticket into a fund for global projects that, in theory, squelch as much carbon dioxide as the airline generates—about 1.2 tons per passenger, the airline says.

Also, a largely unregulated carbon-cutting business has sprung up. In this market, consultants or companies estimate a person's or company's output of greenhouse gases. Then, these businesses sell "offsets," which pay for projects elsewhere that void or sop up an equal amount of emissions—say, by planting trees or, as one new company proposes, fertilizing the ocean so algae can pull the gas out of the air. Recent counts by *Business Week* magazine and several environmental watchdog groups tally the trade in offsets at more than $100 million a year and growing blazingly fast.

But is the carbon-neutral movement just a gimmick?

On this, environmentalists aren't neutral, and they don't agree. Some believe it helps build support, but others argue that these purchases don't accomplish anything meaningful—other than giving someone a slightly better feeling (or greener reputation) after buying a 6,000-square-foot house or passing the million-mile mark in a frequent-flier program. In fact, to many environmentalists, the carbon-neutral campaign is a sign of the times—easy on the sacrifice and big on the consumerism.

5   As long as the use of fossil fuels keeps climbing—which is happening relentlessly around the world—the emission of greenhouse gases will keep rising. The average American, by several estimates, generates more than 20 tons of carbon dioxide or related gases a year; the average resident of the planet about 4.5 tons.

At this rate, environmentalists say, buying someone else's squelched emissions is all but insignificant.

"The worst of the carbon-offset programs resemble the Catholic Church's sale of indulgences back before the Reformation," said Denis Hayes, the president of the Bullitt Foundation, an environmental

grant-making group. "Instead of reducing their carbon footprints, people take private jets and stretch limos, and then think they can buy an indulgence to forgive their sins."

"This whole game is badly in need of a modern Martin Luther," Mr. Hayes added.

Some environmental campaigners defend this marketplace as a legitimate, if imperfect, way to support an environmental ethic and political movement, even if the numbers don't all add up.

10 "We can't stop global warming with voluntary offsets, but they offer an option for individuals looking for a way to contribute to the solution in addition to reducing their own emissions and urging their elected representatives to support good policy," said Daniel

A. Lashof, the science director of the climate center at the Natural Resources Defense Council.

But he and others agree that more oversight is needed. Voluntary standards and codes of conduct are evolving in Europe and the United States to ensure that a ton of carbon dioxide purchased is actually a ton of carbon dioxide avoided.

The first attempt at an industry report card, commissioned by the environmental group Clean Air/Cool Planet (which has some involvement in the business), gave decidedly mixed reviews to the field, selecting eight sellers of carbon offsets that it concluded were reasonably reliable.

But the report, "A Consumer's Guide to Retail Carbon-Offset

Providers," concluded that this market was no different than any other, saying, "if something sounds too good to be true, it probably is."

Prices vary widely for offsetting the carbon dioxide tonnage released by a long plane flight, S.U.V. commute or energy-hungry house. The report suggested that the cheapest offsets may not be legitimate.

15 For example, depending on where you shop for carbon credits, avoiding the ton of carbon dioxide released by driving a midsize car about 2,000 miles could cost $5 or $25, according to data in the report.

Mr. Hayes said there were legitimate companies and organizations that help people and companies measure their emissions and find ways to cut them, both directly and indirectly by purchasing certain kinds of credits. But overall, he said, an investment in such credits—given the questions about their reliability—should be looked at more as conven-tional charity (presuming you check to be sure the projects are real) and less as something like a license to binge on private jet travel.

Save the Planet, Let Someone Else Drill

CHARLES KRAUTHAMMER

A well-known psychiatrist in his earlier life, Charles Krauthammer has become a Pulitzer Prize-winning columnist who writes for the Washington Post, Time *magazine, and* The New Republic. *He is known as a conservative policy analyst whose articulate commentaries influence national affairs, from foreign policy to bioethics. His columns are widely reprinted in U.S. newspapers and around the world. In this op-ed piece, which appeared in the* Washington Post *on August 1, 2008, Krauthammer contends that opening up the Arctic National Wildlife Refuge in northern Alaska for oil drilling is more environmentally sustainable than using oil produced in foreign countries.*

WASHINGTON—House Speaker Nancy Pelosi opposes lifting the moratorium on drilling in the Arctic National Wildlife Refuge and on the Outer Continental Shelf. She won't even allow it to come to a vote.

With $4 gas having massively shifted public opinion in favor of domestic production, she wants to protect her Democratic members from having to cast an antidrilling election-year vote. Moreover, given the public mood, she might even lose. This cannot be permitted. Why? Because as she explained to Politico: "I'm trying to save the planet; I'm trying to save the planet."

A lovely sentiment. But has Pelosi actually thought through the moratorium's actual effects on the planet?

Consider: 25 years ago, nearly 60 percent of U.S. petroleum was produced domestically. Today it's 25 percent. From its peak in 1970, U.S. production has declined a staggering 47 percent. The world consumes 86 million barrels a day; the United States, roughly 20 million. We need the stuff to run our cars and planes and economy. Where does it come from?

5   Places like Nigeria, where chronic corruption, environmental neglect and resulting unrest and instability lead to pipeline explosions, oil spills and illegal siphoning by the poverty-stricken population—which leads to more spills and explosions. Just last week, two Royal Dutch Shell pipelines had to be shut down because bombings by local militants were causing leaks into the ground.

Compare the Niger Delta to the Gulf of Mexico, where deepsea U.S. oil rigs withstood Hurricanes Katrina and Rita without a single undersea well suffering a significant spill.

The United States has the highest technology to ensure the safest drilling. Today, directional drilling—essentially drilling down, then sideways—allows access to oil that in 1970 would have required a surface footprint more than three times as large. Additionally, the U.S. has one of the most extensive and least corrupt regulatory systems on the planet.

Does Pelosi imagine that with so much of America declared off-limits, the planet is less injured as drilling shifts to Kazakhstan and Venezuela and Equatorial Guinea? That Russia will be more environmentally scrupulous than we in drilling in *its* Arctic?

The net environmental effect of Pelosi's no-drilling willfulness is *negative*. Outsourcing U.S. oil production does nothing to lessen worldwide environmental despoliation. It simply exports it to more corrupt, less efficient, more unstable parts of the world—thereby increasing net planetary damage.

10   Democrats want no oil from the American OCS or ANWR. But of course they do want more oil. From OPEC. From where Americans don't vote. From places Democratic legislators can't see.

On May 13, Sen. Chuck Schumer—deeply committed to saving just those pieces of the planet that might have huge reserves of American oil—demanded that the Saudis increase production by a million barrels a day. It doesn't occur to him that by eschewing the slightest disturbance of the mating habits of the Arctic caribou, he is calling for the further exploitation of the pristine deserts of Arabia. In the name of the planet, mind you.

The other panacea, yesterday's rage, is biofuels: We can't drill our way out of the crisis, it seems, but we can greenly grow 15 our way out. By now, however, it is blindingly obvious even to Democrats that biofuels are a devastating force for environmental degradation. It has led to the rape of "lungs of the world" rainforests in Indonesia and Brazil as huge tracts have been destroyed to make room for palm oil and sugar plantations.

Here in the U.S., one out of every three ears of corn is stuffed into a gas tank (by way of ethanol), causing not just food shortages abroad and high prices at home, but intensive increases in farming with all of the attendant environmental problems (soil erosion, insecticide pollution, water consumption, etc.).

This to prevent drilling on an area in the Arctic one-sixth the size of Dulles Airport that leaves untouched a refuge one-third the size of Britain.

There are a dizzying number of economic and national-security arguments for drilling at home: a $700 billion oil balance-of-payment deficit, a gas tax (equivalent) levied on the paychecks of American workers and poured into the treasuries of enemy and terror-supporting regimes, growing dependence on unstable states of the Persian Gulf and Caspian basin. Pelosi and the Democrats stand athwart shouting: We don't care. We come to save the planet!

They seem blissfully unaware that the argument for their drill-there-not-here policy collapses on its own environmental terms.

Fuel for Thought: All Biofuels Are Not Created Equal

DAVID TILMAN AND JASON HILL

David Tilman is Regents Professor and McKnight Presidential Professor of Ecology at the University of Minnesota. In his academic biographical sketch, Tilman describes his interest in "the benefits that society receives from natural and managed ecosystems, and in the ways to assure environmental and social sustainability in the face of global increases in human consumption and population." He has written numerous scholarly articles and books on resource and plant competition and on biofuels. At the same university, Jason Hill is Assistant Professor in Bioproducts and Biosystems engineering, where his research currently centers on how the global biofuels industry will affect climate change, land use, biodiversity, and human well being. This editorial, which was published in the Seattle Times *on April 15, 2007, shows Tilman and Hill in the role of public intellectuals, translating their research into understandable terms for general readers.*

The world has come full circle. A century ago our first transportation biofuels—the hay and oats fed to our horses—were replaced by gasoline. Today, ethanol from corn and biodiesel from soybeans have begun edging out gasoline and diesel.

This has been hailed as an overwhelmingly positive development that will help us reduce the threat of climate change and ease our dependence on foreign oil. In political circles, ethanol is the flavor of the day, and presidential candidates have been cycling through Iowa extolling its benefits. Lost in the ethanol-induced euphoria, however, is the fact that three of our most fundamental needs—food, energy, and a livable and sustainable environment—are now in direct conflict. Moreover, our recent analyses of the full costs and benefits of various biofuels, performed at the University of Minnesota, present a markedly different and more nuanced picture than has been heard on the campaign trail.

Some biofuels, if properly produced, do have the potential to provide climate-friendly energy, but where and how can we grow them? Our most fertile lands are already dedicated to food production. As demand for both food and energy increases, competition for fertile lands could raise food prices enough to drive the poorer third of the globe into malnourishment. The destruction of rainforests and other ecosystems to make new farmland would threaten the continued existence of countless animal and plant species and would increase the amount of climate-changing carbon dioxide in the atmosphere.

Finding and implementing solutions to the food, fuel and environment conflict is one of the greatest challenges facing humanity. But solutions will be neither adopted nor sought until we understand the interlinked problems we face.

5   Fossil-fuel use has pushed atmospheric carbon dioxide higher than at any time during the past half-million years. The global population has increased threefold in the past century and will increase by half again, to 9 billion people, by 2050. Global food and fossil energy consumption are on trajectories to double by 2050.

Biofuels, such as ethanol made from corn, have the potential to provide us with cleaner energy. But because of how corn ethanol currently is made, only about 20 percent of each gallon is "new" energy. That is because it takes a lot of "old" fossil energy to make it: diesel to run tractors, natural gas to make fertilizer and, of course, fuel to run the refineries that convert corn to ethanol.

For this reason, if every one of the 70 million acres on which corn was grown in 2006 was used for ethanol, the amount produced would displace only 12 percent of the U.S. gasoline market. Moreover, the "new" (non-fossil) energy gained would be very small—just 2.4 percent of the market. Car tune-ups and proper tire air pressure would save more energy.

There is another problem with relying on a food-based biofuel, such as corn ethanol, as the poor of Mexico can attest. In recent months, soaring corn prices, sparked by demand from ethanol plants, have doubled the price of tortillas, a staple food. Tens of thousands of Mexico City's poor recently protested this "ethanol tax" in the streets.

In the United States, the protests have also begun—in Congress. Representatives of the dairy, poultry and livestock industries, which rely on corn as a principal animal feed, are seeking an end to subsidies for corn ethanol in the hope of stabilizing corn prices. (It takes about three pounds of corn to produce a pound of chicken, and seven or eight pounds to grow a pound of beef.) Profit margins are being squeezed, and meat prices are rising.

10   U.S. soybeans, which are used to make biodiesel, may be about to follow corn's trajectory, escalating the food-vs.-fuel conflict. The National Biodiesel Board recently reported that 77 biodiesel production plants are under construction and that eight established plants are expanding capacity.

In terms of environmental impact, all biofuels are not created equal. Ethanol is the same chemical product no matter what its source. But ethanol made from prairie grasses, from corn grown in Illinois and from sugar cane grown on newly cleared land in Brazil have radically different impacts on greenhouse gases.

Corn, like all plants, is a natural part of the global carbon cycle. The growing crop absorbs carbon dioxide from the atmosphere, so burning corn ethanol does not directly create any additional carbon. But that is only part of the story. All of the fossil fuels used to grow corn and change it into ethanol release new carbon dioxide and other greenhouse gases. The net effect is that ethanol from corn grown in the Corn Belt does increase atmospheric greenhouse gases, and this increase is only about 15 percent less than the increase caused by an equivalent amount of gasoline. Soybean biodiesel does better, causing a greenhouse-gas increase that is about 40 percent less than that from petroleum diesel.

In Brazil, Sugar Cane

In Brazil, ethanol made from sugar cane produces about twice as much ethanol per acre as corn. Brazilian ethanol refineries get their power from burning cane residue, in effect recycling carbon from the atmosphere. The environmental benefit is large. Sugarcane ethanol grown on established soils releases 80 percent less greenhouse gases than gasoline.

But that isn't the case for sugarcane ethanol or soybean biodiesel from Brazil's newly cleared lands,

15 including tropical forests and savannas. Clearing land releases immense amounts of greenhouse gases into the air, because much of the material in the plants and soil is broken down into carbon dioxide.

Plants and soil contain three times more carbon than the atmosphere. The trees and soil of an acre of rainforest—which, once cleared, is suitable for growing soybeans—contain about 120 tons of organic carbon. An acre of tropical woodland or savanna, suitable for sugar cane, contains about half this amount. About a fourth of the carbon in an ecosystem is released to the atmosphere as carbon dioxide when trees are clear-cut, brush and branches are burned or rot, and roots decay. Even more is lost during the first 20 to 50 years of farming, as soil carbon decomposes into carbon dioxide and as wood products are burned or decay.

This means that when tropical woodland is cleared to produce sugar cane for ethanol, the greenhouse gas released is about 50 percent greater than what occurs from the production and use of the same amount of gasoline. And that statistic holds for at least two decades.

20 Simply being "renewable" does not automatically make a fuel better for the atmosphere than the fossil fuel it replaces, nor guarantee that society gains any new energy by its production. The European Union was recently shocked to learn that some of its imported biodiesel, derived from palm trees planted on rain-forest

lands, was more than twice as bad for climate warming as petroleum diesel. So much for the "benefits" of that form of biodiesel.

Although current Brazilian ethanol is environmentally friendly, the long-term environmental implications of buying more ethanol and biodiesel from Brazil, a possibility raised recently during President Bush's trip to that country, are cloudy. It could be harmful to both the climate and the preservation of tropical plant and animal species if it involved, directly or indirectly, additional clearing of native ecosystems.

Concerns about the environmental effects of ethanol production are starting to be felt in the United States as well. It appears that American farmers may add 10 million acres of corn this year to meet booming demand for ethanol. Some of this land could come from millions of acres now set aside nationwide for conservation under a government-subsidized program. Those uncultivated acres absorb atmospheric carbon, so farming them and converting the corn into ethanol could release more carbon dioxide into the air than would burning gasoline.

Alternative Crops

There are biofuel crops that can be grown with much less energy and chemicals than the food crops we currently use for biofuels. And they can be grown on our less fertile land, especially land that has been degraded by farming. This would decrease competition between food and biofuel. The United States has about 60 million acres of such land—in the Conservation Reserve Program, road edge rights-of-way and abandoned farmlands.

In a 10-year experiment reported in Science magazine in December, we explored how much bioenergy could be produced by 18 different native prairie plant species grown on highly degraded and infertile soil. We planted 172 plots in central Minnesota with various combinations of these species, randomly chosen. We found, on this highly degraded land, that the plots planted with mixtures of many native prairie perennial species yielded 238 percent more bioenergy than those planted with single species. High plant diversity led to high productivity, and little fertilizer or chemical weed or pest killer was required.

The prairie "hay" harvested from these plots can be used to create high-value energy sources. For instance, it can be mixed with coal and burned for electricity generation. It can be "gasified," then chemically combined to make ethanol or synthetic gasoline. Or it can be burned in a turbine engine to make electricity. A technique that is undergoing rapid development involves bioengineering enzymes that digest parts of plants (the cellulose) into sugars that are then fermented into ethanol.

Whether converted into electricity, ethanol or synthetic gasoline, the high-diversity hay from infertile land produced as much or more new usable energy per acre as did fertile land planted with corn for ethanol. And it could be harvested year after year.

Even more surprising were the greenhouse-gas benefits. When high-diversity mixtures of native plants are grown on degraded soils, they remove carbon dioxide from the air. Much of this carbon ends up stored in the soil. In essence, mixtures of native plants gradually restore the carbon levels that degraded soils had before being cleared and farmed. This benefit lasts for about a century.

25   Across the full process of growing high-diversity prairie hay, converting it into an energy source and using that energy, we found a net removal and storage of about a ton and a half of atmospheric carbon dioxide per acre. The net effect is that ethanol or synthetic gasoline produced from high-diversity prairie hay grown on degraded land can provide energy that actually reduces atmospheric levels of carbon dioxide.

Carbon-Negative Biofuels

When one of these carbon-negative biofuels is mixed with gasoline, the resulting blend releases less carbon dioxide than traditional gasoline.

Biofuels, if used properly, can help us balance our need for food, energy and a habitable and sustainable environment. To help this happen, though, we need a national biofuels policy that favors our best options. We must determine the carbon impacts of each method of making these fuels, then mandate fuel blending that achieves a prescribed greenhouse-gas reduction. We have the knowledge and technology to start solving these problems.

The U.S. Energy Story in Numbers: Energy Supply and Disposition by Type of Fuel, 1960–2009

U.S. ENERGY INFORMATION ADMINISTRATION

The table on pages 635–636 tells a wealth of stories about energy production and consumption in the United States. Note how the table lets you track the growth of energy consumption from 1960 to 2009 or compute the growing gap between domestic production of energy and domestic consumption.

TABLE 919 Energy Supply and Disposition by Type of Fuel: 1960 to 2009

Year	Production					Renewable energy[4]					Net imports, total[8]	Consumption					
	Total[1]	Crude oil[2]	Dry natural gas	Coal[3]	Nuclear electric power	Total[1,5]	Hydro-electric power[6]	Biofuel[7]	Solar/ photo-voltaic	Wind		Total[1]	Petro-leum[9]	Dry natural gas[10]	Coal	Nuclear power	Renewable energy,[4] total
1960	42.80	14.93	12.66	10.82	0.01	2.93	1.61	1.32	(NA)	(NA)	2.71	45.09	19.92	12.39	9.84	0.01	2.93
1970	63.50	20.40	21.67	14.61	0.24	4.08	2.63	1.43	(NA)	(NA)	5.71	67.84	29.52	21.79	12.26	0.24	4.08
1975	61.36	17.73	19.64	14.99	1.90	4.72	3.15	1.50	(NA)	(NA)	11.71	72.00	32.73	19.95	12.66	1.90	4.72
1980	67.23	18.25	19.91	18.60	2.74	5.49	2.90	2.48	(NA)	(NA)	12.10	78.12	34.20	20.24	15.42	2.74	5.49
1984	68.92	18.85	18.01	19.72	3.55	6.52	3.39	2.97	(Z)	(Z)	8.68	76.71	31.05	18.39	17.07	3.55	6.52
1985	67.80	18.99	16.98	19.33	4.08	6.19	2.97	3.02	(Z)	(Z)	7.58	76.49	30.92	17.70	17.48	4.08	6.19
1986	67.18	18.38	16.54	19.51	4.38	6.22	3.07	2.93	(Z)	(Z)	10.13	76.76	32.20	16.59	17.26	4.38	6.22
1987	67.66	17.67	17.14	20.14	4.75	5.74	2.63	2.88	(Z)	(Z)	11.59	79.17	32.87	17.64	18.01	4.75	5.74
1988	69.03	17.28	17.60	20.74	5.59	5.57	2.33	3.02	(Z)	(Z)	12.93	82.82	34.22	18.45	18.85	5.59	5.57
1989[11]	69.48	16.12	17.85	21.36	5.60	6.39	2.84	3.16	0.06	0.02	14.11	84.94	34.21	19.60	19.07	5.60	6.39
1990	70.87	15.57	18.33	22.49	6.10	6.21	3.05	2.74	0.06	0.03	14.06	84.65	33.55	19.60	19.17	6.10	6.21
1991	70.53	15.70	18.23	21.64	6.42	6.24	3.02	2.78	0.06	0.03	13.19	84.61	32.85	20.03	18.99	6.42	6.24
1992	70.13	15.22	18.38	21.69	6.48	5.99	2.62	2.93	0.06	0.03	14.44	85.96	33.53	20.71	19.12	6.48	5.99
1993	68.49	14.49	18.58	20.34	6.41	6.26	2.89	2.91	0.07	0.03	17.01	87.60	33.74	21.23	19.84	6.41	6.26
1994	70.89	14.10	19.35	22.20	6.69	6.15	2.68	3.03	0.07	0.04	18.33	89.26	34.56	21.73	19.91	6.69	6.15
1995	71.32	13.89	19.08	22.13	7.08	6.70	3.21	3.10	0.07	0.03	17.75	91.17	34.44	22.67	20.09	7.08	6.70
1996	72.64	13.72	19.34	22.79	7.09	7.17	3.59	3.16	0.07	0.03	19.07	94.17	35.67	23.08	21.00	7.09	7.17
1997	72.63	13.66	19.39	23.31	6.60	7.18	3.64	3.11	0.07	0.03	20.70	94.76	36.16	23.22	21.45	6.60	7.18
1998	73.04	13.24	19.61	24.05	7.07	6.66	3.30	2.93	0.07	0.03	22.28	95.18	36.82	22.83	21.66	7.07	6.65

Year																
1999	71.90	12.45	19.34	23.30	7.61	6.68	3.27	2.97	0.07	0.05	23.54	96.81	37.84	22.91	21.62	7.61	6.68
2000	71.49	12.36	19.66	22.74	7.86	6.26	2.81	3.01	0.07	0.06	24.97	98.97	38.26	23.82	22.58	7.86	6.26
2001	71.88	12.28	20.17	23.55	8.03	5.31	2.24	2.62	0.07	0.07	26.39	96.32	38.19	22.77	21.91	8.03	5.31
2002	70.93	12.16	19.44	22.73	8.15	5.89	2.69	2.71	0.06	0.11	25.74	97.85	38.23	23.56	21.90	8.15	5.89
2003	70.20	12.03	19.63	22.09	7.96	6.14	2.82	2.81	0.06	0.11	27.01	98.13	38.81	22.83	22.32	7.96	6.14
2004	70.35	11.50	19.07	22.85	8.22	6.24	2.69	3.00	0.06	0.14	29.11	100.31	40.29	22.91	22.47	8.22	6.25
2005	69.59	10.96	18.56	23.19	8.16	6.39	2.70	3.10	0.07	0.18	30.15	100.45	40.39	22.56	22.80	8.16	6.41
2006	70.96	10.80	19.02	23.79	8.22	6.77	2.87	3.23	0.07	0.26	29.81	99.79	39.96	22.22	22.45	8.22	6.82
2007	71.61	10.72	19.83	23.49	8.46	6.71	2.45	3.49	0.08	0.34	29.24	101.53	39.77	23.70	22.75	8.46	6.72
2008	73.42	10.51	20.83	23.85	8.43	7.38	2.51	3.87	0.10	0.55	25.94	99.40	37.28	23.79	22.39	8.43	7.37
2009[12]	72.97	11.24	21.50	21.58	8.35	7.76	2.68	3.90	0.11	0.70	22.85	94.58	35.27	23.36	19.76	8.35	7.74

[In quadrillion British thermal units (Btu) (42.80 represents 42,800,000,000,000,000).]
NA Not available. Z Less than 5 trillion. [1]Includes other types of fuel, not shown separately. [2]Includes lease condensate. [3]Beginning 1989, includes waste coal supplied. Beginning 2001, also includes a small amount of refuse recovery. [4]Electricity net generation from conventional hydroelectric power, geothermal, solar, and wind; consumption of electricity from wood, waste, and alcohol fuels; geothermal heat pump and direct use energy; and solar thermal direct use energy. [5]Production equals consumption for all renewable energy sources except biofuels. [6]Conventional hydroelectricity net generation. [7]Wood and wood-derived fuels, biomass waste, fuel ethanol, and biodiesel. [8]Imports minus exports. [9]Petroleum products supplied, including natural gas plant liquids and crude oil burned as fuel. [10]Includes supplemental gaseous fuels. [11]There is a discontinuity in this time series between 1989 and 1990. [12]Preliminary.
Source: U.S. Energy Information Administration, *Annual Energy Review 2009,* August 2010. See also <http://www.eia.doe.gov/emeu/aer/overview.html>.

The Problem Is the Solution: Cultivating New Traditions Through Permaculture

JASON POWERS

Jason Powers wrote this article for Clamor, *a small independent magazine in the alternative press. Published largely through volunteer efforts for the seven years of its existence,* Clamor *was nominated by* Utne Reader *for its Independent Press awards each year of its existence, first in the category of Best New Title and subsequently in the category of Culture/ Social Coverage. Permaculture, the topic of this article, engages the values of* Clamor, *in that it promotes change based on action of those without political or governmental power. The article was published in the May/June 2006 issue.*

Irresponsible traditions of waste, conquest, and over-consumption have dominated much of human history, leading to the collapse of many past societies. History has shown us that a civilization that undermines its land and resource base through wasteful and exploitative habits eventually will collapse. Today, the destruction hinges upon our wasteful and exploitative economy, based on perpetual growth, and the fossil fuel–dependent industrial agriculture that strips our soils and poisons our waters. Agribusiness corporations are consolidating ownership of the world's seed stock, while the genetically altered organisms they produce silently embed themselves into the wild gene pool, with yet unknown consequences for global food security and biodiversity. Oil and natural gas production, the cheap energy that our agriculture, industry, and transportation systems depend on, has most likely peaked and begun to regress. Extinction of species is drastically increasing due to pollution, ecological devastation, and weather change. Extinction of cultures due to conquest—euphemistically termed, "development"—and resource extraction is likewise increasing.

In many ways shielded from the effects of the global economy by our relative wealth, most in the "developed" world live unaware of the effects of our lifestyle, not knowing or caring where our food, water, energy, and consumer products come from, nor what is done to bring us these things. Even as we imagine progress and technological salvation, our systems and the culture they've created perpetuate denial.

Clearly, whether we choose to change or not, we will have to eventually. It's just a matter of when we're able to leave denial behind and look honestly at how we live. From this we will hopefully (re)develop skills and traditions that teach us to value and care for what sustains us: the land, our communities, and our relationships.

Permaculture arose from the realization that prevailing agricultural systems were fundamentally unsustainable and creating worldwide catastrophe. Based on observations of the sustainable systems of nature, as well as many of the traditions of indigenous cultures, permaculture was developed and applied in the 1970s by Australians Bill Mollison, a forestry worker and scientist, and David Holmgren, then a 20-year-old student. As initially conceived, "Permaculture is the conscious design and maintenance of agriculturally productive ecosystems which have the diversity, stability, and resilience of natural ecosystems. It is the harmonious integration of landscape and people providing their food, energy, shelter, and other material and non-material needs in a sustainable way," according to Mollison's Designers' Manual, the "bible" of permaculture.

5   Originally an attempt to return to systems of small-scale intensive gardens, permaculture now

incorporates numerous techniques for ecologically sustainable living: grey water, recycling, solar energy, rainwater catchment, natural building, and local food networks. "You could say it's a rational man's approach to not shitting in his bed . . . a framework that never ceases to move, but that will accept information from anywhere," explained co-founder Mollison in an interview with In Context. Coined in 1976 as a conjunction of "permanent agriculture," the word permaculture has evolved to signify a "permanent culture," one that has since spread into a de-centralized global movement, adapted and implemented by peoples in nearly every ecosystem, and socioeconomic level, by rural and urban, rich and poor.

Toby Hemenway, a permaculture teacher, designer and author of *Gaia's Garden: A Guide to Home-Scale Permaculture* likens permaculture to "a toolbox that helps organize [techniques] and helps you decide when to use them." Aiding this are four simple ethical tenets: caring for the earth, caring for people, limiting growth and consumption, and sharing surplus (goods, energy, time, etc.). Design principles derived from these tenets incorporate no-till and perennial gardening, use of natural patterns, energy efficiency, and intelligent use of space and resources. As in nature, stability is created through diversity and the relationships between the elements in the system. "The philosophy behind permaculture is one of working with, rather than against, nature; of protracted and thoughtful observation rather than protracted and thoughtless action; of looking at systems in all their functions, rather than asking only one yield of them; and of allowing systems to demonstrate their own evolutions," Mollison writes. Practitioners try to integrate the different elements into harmonious relationships where cooperation and mutual support are encouraged, multiple functions are filled by one element, and multiple elements fill one function. This is seen in the "guild," a permaculture-specific technique which uses vertical space to stack and layer mutually beneficial plants.

To be sustainable, a system must create as much or more energy than it consumes, so closing energy and resource loops becomes very important. Problems are reframed as solutions and waste is redirected as inputs for other processes. "I have become increasingly aware of how the output/waste of my activities can be reused as inputs useful in other activities," admits Leopoldo Rodriguez, an economics professor at Portland State University with three years of permaculture experience. "I think a lot more about the placement of different elements in the process of putting a garden together, planting a tree in the yard or building a chicken coop." Beyond understanding one's own systemic impact, permaculture bolsters people's self-sufficiency. "Grow food or learn how to forage wild food yourself. The empowerment of this one act will have a great effect on you," says courthouse clerk Carla Bankston, an eight-year permaculture devotee.

In addition to this focus on sustainability and DIY [do it yourself] practicality, successful application of permaculture depends on continuous feedback, adjustment and involvement with the design. "One key aspect is to reassess at every step and make sure that you're still in line with what your original goals were," Hemenway says. "You stay with the project for long after it's up and running because it's always going to change. It creates a long-term relationship which will in the long run wind up being cheaper." He contrasts that with how things are typically done. "Our culture does a cost benefit analysis where we say 'Okay, this is the cheapest way to do it so let's do it like that.' It makes it very difficult to [do] anything resembling what sustainable cultures do."

Always site and system specific, permaculture is incredibly versatile. Its principles are broad enough to be applied to various systems—economics, home building, human relationships, and food distribution systems. Mayans in Guatemala, post-Soviet Cubans, and villagers in rural Zimbabwe have all successfully bolstered their communities' food security by ceasing to use expensive chemical-based processes. Instead they combine production-intensive and energy-saving permaculture techniques like mulching, composting and water harvesting with their traditional farming methods, concentrating once again on subsistence rather than producing commodities for export. City Repair in Portland, Oregon, applies it to urban planning with community-guided creation of public spaces and the integration of natural building into the cityscape. The Permaculture Credit Union in New Mexico invests in their community rather than destructive companies, offering loan discounts for fuel-efficient automobiles and second mortgages for energy efficient upgrades on houses. "I've seen businesses and organizations where people have applied permaculture principles that have helped them get a lot more functional," says Hemenway, "It works with so-called invisible structures as well as with visible things like landscapes or buildings."

10 "[Permaculture] involves rediscovering a lot of things we have lost," Linda Hendrickson, a Portland weaver and recent permaculturist, says. While it is true the philosophy challenges many of our modern habits, it is by no means anachronistic. "You look at the inputs and the outputs and embedded energy," explains Hemenway. "What did it take to build that solar panel? Is there more energy being consumed in the creation of it than you're going to get back from its use? I don't rule out any technology simply because it's technology, but we look at it as how much really does it cost to be using this, and who gets hurt by it." Rather than reject modern know-how, permaculture examines both negative and positive impact, a more conscientious approach than our current mass delusion of "progress" as endless and thoughtless expansion.

This broad integration of technique and application, as well as the inclusion of ethics in design originally captivated Hemenway. While leaving his job at a biotech company, he stumbled across Bill Mollison's *Designers' Manual* at the public library.

"I leafed through the pages and said, 'This is it. This is everything I've ever wanted to do. This is ecology and appropriate technology and design and gardening. It puts it all together.'"

It's easy to be overwhelmed by the many facets of permaculture design at first. Karen Tilou, who applies permaculture techniques to the orchard she manages, explains, "There's so much you can do, so people end up feeling like 'Wow, I'm not doing anything if I'm not doing all of it.'" To avoid this, "Find what aspect of permaculture's ethics and principles you can apply to what you really love. It doesn't have to be about gardens or solar energy."

Ultimately, permaculture is responsible to earth and home, wherever that may be. Joseph and Jacqueline Freeman, who live and garden on a ten-acre farm, advise, "Start paying attention to the small things, like where your water comes from and where it goes. Keep your septic outflow nontoxic by using low-impact detergent when you wash clothes. Be aware of packaging when you make purchases. Develop relationships with elders and others of like mind so you can keep adding to your knowledge. Build community in whatever ways you can." Though nice to have the space rural areas offer, permaculture is especially important in urban areas. "The cities and suburbia are the places where the resources are being consumed," Hemenway observes. "It's where everybody lives in this country. If those places can't change then we're not going to get there."

By no means the solution, permaculture offers a valuable approach to restructuring our lives and counters the deleterious habits of our society by simultaneously looking forward to new technology and backward to older agricultural traditions and indigenous wisdom. In contrast to our current pathologies of short-term profit, waste, perpetual growth, oversimplification and reductionism, permaculture teaches us to slow down, observe, evaluate our actions and consumption patterns, to value the land, the local and relationships.

The Soil vs. the Sensex

VANDANA SHIVA

Vandana Shiva is an internationally known voice for environmentalism and social justice, espousing the rights of the third-world poor who suffer at the hands of international corporations. With a doctorate in physics, she has expertise in both scientific and social issues and writes regularly on political, economic, and environmental topics. Her most recent books are Staying Alive: Women, Ecology, and Development *(2010),* Soil Not Oil: Environmental Justice in a Time of Climate Crisis *(2008),* Earth Democracy: Justice, Sustainability, and Peace *(2005), and* Water Wars: Privatization, Pollution and Profit *(2002). Shiva's article, "The Soil vs. the Sensex" reflects her concern for the farmer who works the land as opposed to powerful business interests represented by the Sensex, which is India's stock exchange. It was published in the October 2010 issue of* India Currents.

The earth, the source of all nourishment and sustenance, is seen as a mother in most cultures. She is Terra Madre and Gaia, Dharti, and Vasundhara. Even today, in parts of India not destroyed by the Green Revolution, tribals and peasants apologize to the earth at the beginning of every agriculture season for hurting her with their plough, and promise [to] take no more than their need.

But the culture of the sacred earth is under severe threat, and this threat looms over the communities who depend on the land. As India grows at 9 percent, and the Sensex (the stock exchange index in Mumbai) becomes the measure of the state of the people and the state of the land, the rich and the privileged often forget that the majority in India depends neither on the Sensex nor the state. They depend on the Maati Ma (Mother Earth). Yet the dominant culture of the land and the earth is being marginalized; our biodiversity and cultural diversity are at risk; our very future is threatened.

The war against the land is cultural and material. The culture of the sacred earth is one of nonviolence and restraint, of compassion and care for all life that the earth creates and supports. The bird and the tree, the earthworm and the elephant, all have their space and their share in the gifts of Mother Earth. We referred to this culture as Vasundhaiva Kutumbkam. I call it Earth Democracy.

Materially a sacred earth invites us to create technologies and economies that sustain the fertility and productivity of the soil and the land. An agrarian economy is a highly evolved economy in the yardstick of the sacred earth because it is the only economy in which humans can give back to the earth. Every other economy—urban, industrial—is an economy of taking. All that urban and industrial society gives back to the land is waste and pollution.

5   The earth is no longer seen as the source of soil fertility. Instead synthetic fertilizers made in chemical factories are viewed as the source of soil fertility, even though they kill soil fauna and flora, the real creators of fertility. The farmers and the earth are no longer seen as the source of food. Nestle and Cargill, Lever and ITC become the "food providers." The farmer is no longer the annadata (grain provider, giver of food). Food is no longer the sacred gift that creates and maintains life. It is just another commodity.

Maximization of profits, not maximization of well being, determines what we eat. No wonder there is increasing hunger and malnutrition of the poor, who do not get enough food, and the malnutrition of the rich, who live on junk food and processed food. India is emerging as the epicenter of the diabetes epidemic. Changes in food cultures and diets have a lot to do with these new diseases.

The farmer is no longer seen as the source of seed—the 200,000 rice varieties we have grown, or the 15,000 mangoes, or the 15,000 banana varieties disappear from science and from the earth. Monsanto becomes the "inventor" of seed, the "owner" of life through intellectual property and patents. It does not matter if 200,000 Indian farmers commit suicide because they have been pushed into debt by costly, unreliable, nonrenewable seed and the related destruction of their seed sovereignty and seed freedom. All that matters is that the profits of seed corporations keep increasing.

Farmers who have tilled the land for generations, and want to continue taking care of the earth, refuse to be uprooted. The new rich, the big corporations, think that they have the right to dispossess every tribal and every farmer of their land and resources, bury the soil under the concrete jungle of new luxury townships, and literally kill the earth. From the perspective of Maati Ma, this is matricide. And no society can flourish if it destroys the very source of its sustenance.

The Sensex will rise and fall. The earth has sustained life for billions of years and can continue to do so. While wealthy Indians are high on the recent climb of the stock market they need to remember the collapse of the financial markets in South East Asia in 1997.

10 We as a society and as a civilization based on the sacred earth are on the threshold of destroying our very ecological foundation by worshipping money and markets. These are becoming the new sacred. And false sacred emerge when society loses its anchor.

We need to re-anchor ourselves in the earth. We need to stop uprooting those who are anchored in the land, our peasants and tribals.

We need to return to the Earth, our mother.

■ ■ ■ ■ **FOR CLASS DISCUSSION** Choices for a Sustainable World

1. In this chapter, many of the arguments are causal arguments. Working individually or in a group, choose one of the arguments that rely heavily on causal reasoning. Trace the causal chain the writer constructs. How well does the writer support each link in the chain? Where might readers challenge this causal reasoning? What do you see as the most persuasive part of this argument and why?

2. As the readings in this chapter illustrate, the problem of reducing and replacing the use of fossil fuels is complex. Andrew Revkin questions the effectiveness of carbon trading. Tilman and Hill call for a rethinking of biofuel. Esty and Porter advocate a tax on carbon emissions. On a different path, Shiva and Powers propose making citizens, not corporations, responsible for the care of the earth and the harvest of its abundance. After reconstructing the main claim and reasons in each argument, discuss what you think each argument contributes to the search for sustainability.

3. Charles Krauthammer's "Save the Planet, Let Someone Else Drill" and Esty and Porter's "Pain at the Pump? We Need More" argue from a business perspective yet arrive at quite different proposals. Contrast their arguments. What assumptions underlie their arguments? What are their reasons and evidence? What audience would be most receptive to each argument?

4. Kristof, Shiva, and Powers present ethical arguments. What reasons do they use in appealing to the reader? What rhetorical strategies do they use to influence the reader? What values do they appeal to in their audience?

5. The table on pages 635–636 tells many energy stories. Find one that you found surprising, unexpected, or particularly troubling. Tell the story vividly in a graph (line graph, pie chart, bar graph) and share your graphic with classmates. ■ ■ ■

WRITING ASSIGNMENT Rhetorical Analysis or Rogerian Response to an Argument

Option 1: Rhetorical Analysis of an Argument. Write a thesis-driven analysis of one of the arguments in this chapter in which you analyze the writer's appeals to *logos, ethos,* and *pathos.* Consider how the writer's angle of vision shapes the argument and how persuasive this argument is for a general audience.

Option 2: Rogerian Response to an Argument. Write a Rogerian response addressed to the writer of one of the readings in this chapter with which you particularly disagree. Begin your argument by setting up the problem the writer is addressing. Then write an accurate summary of the writer's argument and identify the values you share with the writer to establish common ground. ■

> For additional writing, reading, and research resources, go to
> www.mycomplab.com

Argument Classics

In this chapter we present five arguments that have been particularly effective at influencing public opinion, presenting uncomfortable truths to their audiences, and demonstrating powerful strategies of persuasion. Each of these arguments has made a difference in the world, either because it has persuaded people of the justice of its claims or has evoked powerful resistance and counterargument. Each of these arguments is also richly suitable for classroom analysis. Widely reprinted in anthologies, each argument has achieved classic status in its ability to engage students in discussion, promote critical thinking about important issues, and move students and teachers alike to introspection and to agreement or dissent.

Letter from Birmingham Jail

MARTIN LUTHER KING, JR.

Martin Luther King's "Letter from a Birmingham Jail," is one of the world's most famous arguments. It accelerated the U.S. civil rights movement in the 1960s and inspired protests against racism and oppression throughout the world. On April 3, 1963, Dr. King, as leader of the Southern Christian Leadership Conference, helped organize a series of sit-ins in Birmingham, Alabama, to protest segregation. On April 6 and 7, the demonstrations escalated when 45 protesters were arrested and two police dogs attacked and mauled a 19-year-old protester. The city then obtained an injunction forbidding King from organizing more demonstrations. When King refused to call off the demonstrations, he was arrested on Good Friday, April 12, and placed in solitary confinement in the Birmingham jail. While in jail he read a newspaper ad "A Call for Unity" signed by eight Alabama clergymen, urging demonstrators to make their case in the courts, not on the streets. These eight clergymen comprise the immediate audience for King's open letter, which he began writing in the margins of the newspaper and later finished on a yellow pad provided by a friendly jailer. "Letter from Birmingham Jail" elegantly illustrates the power of audience-based reasons.

Newspaper Ad that Inspired King's Letter: "A Call for Unity"
12 April 1963
We the undersigned clergymen are among those who, in January, issued "An Appeal for Law and Order and Common Sense," in dealing with racial problems in Alabama. We expressed understanding that honest convictions in racial matters could properly

be pursued in the courts, but urged that decisions of those courts should in the meantime be peacefully obeyed.

Since that time there had been some evidence of increased forbearance and a willingness to face facts. Responsible citizens have undertaken to work on various problems which cause racial friction and unrest. In Birmingham, recent public events have given indication that we will have opportunity for a new constructive and realistic approach to racial problems.

However, we are now confronted by a series of demonstrations by some of our Negro citizens, directed and led in part by outsiders. We recognize the natural impatience of people who feel that their hopes are slow in being realized. But we are convinced that these demonstrations are unwise and untimely.

We agree rather with certain local Negro leadership which has called for honest and open negotiation of racial issues in our area. And we believe this kind of facing of issues can best be accomplished by citizens of our own metropolitan area, white and Negro, meeting with their knowledge and experience of the local situation. All of us need to face that responsibility and find proper channels for its accomplishment.

5   Just as we formerly pointed out that "hatred and violence have no sanction in our religious and political traditions," we also point out that such actions as incite to hatred and violence, however technically peaceful those actions may be, have not contributed to the resolution of our local problems. We do not believe that these days of new hope are days when extreme measures are justified in Birmingham.

We commend the community as a whole, and the local news media and law enforcement officials in particular, on the calm manner in which these demonstrations have been handled. We urge the public to continue to show restraint should the demonstrations continue, and the law enforcement officials to remain calm and continue to protect our city from violence.

We further strongly urge our own Negro community to withdraw support from these demonstrations, and to unite locally in working peacefully for a better Birmingham. When rights are consistently denied, a cause should be pressed in the courts and in negotiations among local leaders, and not in the streets. We appeal to both our white and Negro citizenry to observe the principles of law and order and common sense.

Signed by:
C.C.J. Carpenter, D.D., LL.D., Bishop of Alabama
Joseph A. Durick, D.D., Auxiliary Bishop, Diocese of Mobile-Birmingham
Rabbi Milton L. Grafman, Temple Emanu-El, Birmingham, Alabama
Bishop Paul Hardin, Bishop of the Alabama-West Florida Conference of the Methodist
      Church
Bishop Nolan B. Harmon, Bishop of the North Alabama Conference of the Methodist
      Church
George M. Murray, D.D., LL.D., Bishop Coadjutor, Episcopal Diocese of Alabama
Edward V. Ramage, Moderator, Synod of the Alabama Presbyterian Church in the United
      States
Earl Stallings, Pastor, First Baptist Church, Birmingham, Alabama

Letter from Birmingham Jail
16 April 1963

My Dear Fellow Clergymen:

While confined here in the Birmingham city jail, I came across your recent statement calling my present activities "unwise and untimely." Seldom do I pause to answer criticism of my work and ideas. If I sought to answer all the criticisms that cross my desk, my secretaries would have little time for anything other than such correspondence in the course of the day, and I would have no time for constructive work. But since I feel that you are men of genuine good will and that your criticisms are sincerely set forth, I want to try to answer your statement in what I hope will be patient and reasonable terms.

I think I should indicate why I am here in Birmingham, since you have been influenced by the view which argues against "outsiders coming in." I have the honor of serving as president of the Southern Christian Leadership Conference, an organization operating in every southern state, with headquarters in Atlanta, Georgia. We have some eighty-five affiliated organizations across the South, and one of them is the Alabama Christian Movement for Human Rights. Frequently we share staff, educational and financial resources with our affiliates. Several months ago the affiliate here in Birmingham asked us to be on call to engage in a nonviolent direct-action program if such were deemed necessary. We readily consented, and when the hour came we lived up to our promise. So I, along with several members of my staff, am here because I was invited here. I am here because I have organizational ties here.

But more basically, I am in Birmingham because injustice is here. Just as the prophets of the eighth century B.C. left their villages and carried their "thus saith the Lord" far beyond the boundaries of their home towns, and just as the Apostle Paul left his village of Tarsus and carried the gospel of Jesus Christ to the far corners of the Greco-Roman world, so am I compelled to carry the gospel of freedom beyond my own home town. Like Paul, I must constantly respond to the Macedonian call for aid.

Moreover, I am cognizant of the interrelatedness of all communities and states. I cannot sit idly by in Atlanta and not be concerned about what happens in Birmingham. Injustice anywhere is a threat to justice everywhere. We are caught in an inescapable network of mutuality, tied in a single garment of destiny. Whatever affects one directly, affects all indirectly. Never again can we afford to live with the narrow, provincial "outside agitator" idea. Anyone who lives inside the United States can never be considered an outsider anywhere within its bounds.

5   You deplore the demonstrations taking place in Birmingham. But your statement, I am sorry to say, fails to express a similar concern for the conditions that brought about the demonstrations. I am sure that none of you would want to rest content with the superficial kind of social analysis that deals merely with effects and does not grapple with underlying causes. It is unfortunate that demonstrations are taking place in Birmingham, but it is even more unfortunate that the city's white power structure left the Negro community with no alternative.

In any nonviolent campaign there are four basic steps: collection of the facts to determine whether injustices exist; negotiation; self-purification; and direct action. We have gone through all these steps in Birmingham. There can be no gainsaying the fact that racial injustice engulfs this community. Birmingham is probably the most thoroughly segregated city in the United States. Its ugly record of brutality is widely known. Negroes have experienced grossly unjust treatment in the courts. There have been more unsolved bombings of Negro homes and churches in Birmingham than in any other city in the nation. These are the hard, brutal facts of the case. On the basis of these conditions, Negro leaders sought to negotiate with the city fathers. But the latter consistently refused to engage in good-faith negotiation.

Then, last September, came the opportunity to talk with leaders of Birmingham's economic community. In the course of the negotiations, certain promises were made by the merchants—for example, to remove the stores' humiliating racial signs. On the basis of these promises, the Reverend Fred Shuttlesworth and the leaders of the Alabama Christian Movement for Human Rights agreed to a moratorium on all demonstrations. As the weeks and months went by, we realized that we were the victims of a broken promise. A few signs, briefly removed, returned; the others remained.

As in so many past experiences, our hopes had been blasted, and the shadow of deep disappointment settled upon us. We had no alternative except to prepare for direct action, whereby we would present our very bodies as a means of laying our case before the conscience of the local and the national community. Mindful of the difficulties involved, we decided to undertake a process of self-purification. We began a series of workshops on nonviolence, and we repeatedly asked ourselves: "Are you able to accept blows without retaliating?" "Are you able to endure the ordeal of jail?" We decided to schedule our direct-action program for the Easter season, realizing that except for Christmas, this is the main shopping period of the year. Knowing that a strong economic-withdrawal program would be the by-product of direct action, we felt that this would be the best time to bring pressure to bear on the merchants for the needed change.

Then it occurred to us that Birmingham's mayoral election was coming up in March, and we speedily decided to postpone action until after election day. When we discovered that the Commissioner of Public Safety, Eugene "Bull" Connor, had piled up enough votes to be in the run-off, we decided again to postpone action until the day after the run-off so that the demonstrations could not be used to cloud the issues. Like many others, we waited to see Mr. Connor defeated, and to this end we endured postponement after postponement. Having aided in this community need, we felt that our direct-action program could be delayed no longer.

10 You may well ask: "Why direct action? Why sit-ins, marches and so forth? Isn't negotiation a better path?" You are quite right in calling for negotiation. Indeed, this is the very purpose of direct action. Nonviolent direct action seeks to create such a crisis and foster such a tension that a community which has constantly refused to negotiate is forced to confront the issue. It seeks so to dramatize the issue that it can no longer be ignored. My citing the creation of tension as part of the work of the nonviolent-resister may sound

rather shocking. But I must confess that I am not afraid of the word "tension." I have earnestly opposed violent tension, but there is a type of constructive, nonviolent tension which is necessary for growth. Just as Socrates felt that it was necessary to create a tension in the mind so that individuals could rise from the bondage of myths and half-truths to the unfettered realm of creative analysis and objective appraisal, so must we see the need for nonviolent gadflies to create the kind of tension in society that will help men rise from the dark depths of prejudice and racism to the majestic heights of understanding and brotherhood.

The purpose of our direct-action program is to create a situation so crisis-packed that it will inevitably open the door to negotiation. I therefore concur with you in your call for negotiation. Too long has our beloved Southland been bogged down in a tragic effort to live in monologue rather than dialogue.

One of the basic points in your statement is that the action that I and my associates have taken in Birmingham is untimely. Some have asked: "Why didn't you give the new city administration time to act?" The only answer that I can give to this query is that the new Birmingham administration must be prodded about as much as the outgoing one, before it will act. We are sadly mistaken if we feel that the election of Albert Boutwell as mayor will bring the millennium to Birmingham. While Mr. Boutwell is a much more gentle person than Mr. Connor, they are both segregationists, dedicated to maintenance of the status quo. I have hope that Mr. Boutwell will be reasonable enough to see the futility of massive resistance to desegregation. But he will not see this without pressure from devotees of civil rights. My friends, I must say to you that we have not made a single gain in civil rights without determined legal and nonviolent pressure. Lamentably, it is an historical fact that privileged groups seldom give up their privileges voluntarily. Individuals may see the moral light and voluntarily give up their unjust posture; but, as Reinhold Niebuhr has reminded us, groups tend to be more immoral than individuals.

We know through painful experience that freedom is never voluntarily given by the oppressor; it must be demanded by the oppressed. Frankly, I have yet to engage in a direct-action campaign that was "well timed" in the view of those who have not suffered unduly from the disease of segregation. For years now I have heard the word "Wait!" It rings in the ear of every Negro with piercing familiarity. This "Wait" has almost always meant "Never." We must come to see, with one of our distinguished jurists, that "justice too long delayed is justice denied."

We have waited for more than 340 years for our constitutional God-given rights. The nations of Asia and Africa are moving with jetlike speed toward gaining political independence, but we still creep at horse-and-buggy pace toward gaining a cup of coffee at a lunch counter. Perhaps it is easy for those who have never felt the stinging darts of segregation to say, "Wait." But when you have seen vicious mobs lynch your mothers and fathers at will and drown your sisters and brothers at whim; when you have seen hate-filled policemen curse, kick, and even kill your black brothers and sisters; when you see the vast majority of your twenty million Negro brothers smothering in an airtight cage of poverty in the midst of an affluent society; when you suddenly find your tongue twisted and your speech stammering as you seek to explain to your six-year-old daughter why she can't go to the public amusement park that has just been advertised on television, and see tears welling up in her eyes when she is told that Funtown is closed to colored children, and see ominous clouds of inferiority beginning to form in her little mental sky, and see her beginning to distort her personality by developing an unconscious bitterness toward white people; when you have to concoct an answer for a five-year-old son who is asking: "Daddy, why do white people treat colored people so mean?"; when you take a cross-country drive and find it necessary to sleep night after night in the uncomfortable corners of your automobile because no motel will accept you; when you are humiliated day in and day out by nagging signs reading "white" and "colored"; when your first name becomes "nigger," your middle name becomes "boy" (however old you are) and your last name becomes "John," and your wife and mother are never given the respected title "Mrs."; when you are harried by day and haunted by night by the fact that you are a Negro, living constantly at tip-toe stance, never quite knowing what to expect next, and are plagued with inner fears and outer resentments; when you are forever fighting a degenerating sense of "nobodi-ness"—then you will understand why we find it difficult to wait. There comes a time when the cup of endurance runs over, and men are no longer willing to be plunged into the abyss of despair. I hope, sirs, you can understand our legitimate and unavoidable impatience.

15   You express a great deal of anxiety over our willingness to break laws. This is certainly a legitimate concern. Since we so diligently urge people to obey the Supreme Court's decision of 1954 outlawing segregation in the public schools, at first glance it may seem rather paradoxical for us consciously to break laws. One may well ask: "How can you advocate breaking some laws and obeying others?" The answer lies in the fact that there are two types of laws: just and unjust. I would be the first to advocate obeying just laws. One has not only a legal but a moral responsibility to obey just laws. Conversely, one has a moral responsibility to disobey unjust laws. I would agree with St. Augustine that "an unjust law is no law at all."

Now, what is the difference between the two? How does one determine whether a law is just or unjust? A just law is a man-made code that squares with the moral law or the law of God. An unjust law is a code that is out of harmony with the moral law. To put it in the terms of St. Thomas Aquinas: An unjust law is a human law that is not rooted in eternal law and natural law. Any law that uplifts human personality is just. Any law that degrades human personality is unjust. All segregation statutes are unjust because segregation distorts the soul and damages the personality. It gives the segregator a false sense of superiority and the segregated a false sense of inferiority. Segregation, to use the terminology of the Jewish philosopher Martin Buber, substitutes an "I–it" relationship for an "I–thou" relationship and ends up relegating persons to the status of things. Hence, segregation is not only politically, economically and sociologically unsound, it is morally wrong and sinful. Paul Tillich has said that sin is separation. Is not segregation an existential expression of man's tragic separation, his awful estrangement, his terrible sinfulness? Thus it is that I can urge men to obey the 1954 decision of the Supreme

Court, for it is morally right; and I can urge them to disobey segregation ordinances, for they are morally wrong.

Let us consider a more concrete example of just and unjust laws. An unjust law is a code that a numerical or power majority group compels a minority group to obey but does not make binding on itself. This is *difference* made legal. By the same token, a just law is a code that a majority compels a minority to follow and that it is willing to follow itself. This is *sameness* made legal.

Let me give another explanation. A law is unjust if it is inflicted on a minority that, as a result of being denied the right to vote, had no part in enacting or devising the law. Who can say that the legislature of Alabama which set up that state's segregation laws was democratically elected? Throughout Alabama all sorts of devious methods are used to prevent Negroes from becoming registered voters, and there are some counties in which, even though Negroes constitute a majority of the population, not a single Negro is registered. Can any law enacted under such circumstances be considered democratically structured?

Sometimes a law is just on its face and unjust in its application. For instance, I have been arrested on a charge of parading without a permit. Now, there is nothing wrong in having an ordinance which requires a permit for a parade. But such an ordinance becomes unjust when it is used to maintain segregation and to deny citizens the First-Amendment privilege of peaceful assembly and protest.

20   I hope you are able to see the distinction I am trying to point out. In no sense do I advocate evading or defying the law, as would the rabid segregationist. That would lead to anarchy. One who breaks an unjust law must do so openly, lovingly, and with a willingness to accept the penalty. I submit that an individual who breaks a law that conscience tells him is unjust, and who willingly accepts the penalty of imprisonment in order to arouse the conscience of the community over its injustice, is in reality expressing the highest respect for law.

Of course, there is nothing new about this kind of civil disobedience. It was evidenced sublimely in the refusal of Shadrach, Meshach and Abednego to obey the laws of Nebuchadnezzar, on the ground that a higher moral law was at stake. It was practiced superbly by the early Christians, who were willing to face hungry lions and the excruciating pain of chopping blocks rather than submit to certain unjust laws of the Roman Empire. To a degree, academic freedom is a reality today because Socrates practiced civil disobedience. In our own nation, the Boston Tea Party represented a massive act of civil disobedience.

We should never forget that everything Adolf Hitler did in Germany was "legal" and everything the Hungarian freedom fighters did in Hungary was "illegal." It was "illegal" to aid and comfort a Jew in Hitler's Germany. Even so, I am sure that, had I lived in Germany at the time, I would have aided and comforted my Jewish brothers. If today I lived in a Communist country where certain principles dear to the Christian faith are suppressed I would openly advocate disobeying that country's antireligious laws.

I must make two honest confessions to you, my Christian and Jewish brothers. First, I must confess that over the past few years I have been gravely disappointed with the white moderate. I have almost reached the regrettable conclusion that the Negro's great stumbling block in his stride toward freedom is not the White Citizen's Counciler or the Ku Klux Klanner, but the white moderate, who is more devoted to "order" than to justice; who prefers a negative peace which is the presence of tension to a positive peace which is the presence of justice; who constantly says, "I agree with you in the goal you seek, but I cannot agree with your methods of direct action"; who paternalistically believes he can set the timetable for another man's freedom; who lives by a mythical concept of time and who constantly advises the Negro to wait for a "more convenient season." Shallow understanding from people of good will is more frustrating than absolute misunderstanding from people of ill will. Lukewarm acceptance is much more bewildering than outright rejection.

I had hoped that the white moderate would understand that law and order exist for the purpose of establishing justice and that when they fail in this purpose they become the dangerously structured dams that block the flow of social progress. I had hoped that the white moderate would understand that the present tension in the South is a necessary phase of the transition from an obnoxious negative peace, in which the Negro passively accepted his unjust plight, to a substantive and positive peace, in which all men will respect the dignity and worth of human personality. Actually, we who engage in nonviolent direct action are not the creators of tension. We merely bring to the surface the hidden tension that is already alive. We bring it out in the open, where it can be seen and dealt with. Like a boil that can never be cured so long as it is covered up but must be opened with all its ugliness to the natural medicines of air and light, injustice must be exposed, with all the tension its exposure creates, to the light of human conscience and the air of national opinion before it can be cured.

25   In your statement you assert that our actions, even though peaceful, must be condemned because they precipitate violence. But is this a logical assertion? Isn't this like condemning a robbed man because his possession of money precipitated the evil act of robbery? Isn't this like condemning Socrates because his unswerving commitment to truth and his philosophical inquiries precipitated the act by the misguided populace in which they made him drink hemlock? Isn't this like condemning Jesus because his unique God-consciousness and never-ceasing devotion to God's will precipitated the evil act of crucifixion? We must come to see that, as the federal courts have consistently affirmed, it is wrong to urge an individual to cease his efforts to gain his basic constitutional rights because the quest may precipitate violence. Society must protect the robbed and punish the robber.

I had also hoped that the white moderate would reject the myth concerning time in relation to the struggle for freedom. I have just received a letter from a white brother in Texas. He writes: "All Christians know that the colored people will receive equal rights eventually, but it is possible that you are in too great a religious hurry. It has taken Christianity almost two thousand years to accomplish what it has. The teachings of Christ take time to come to earth." Such an attitude stems from a tragic misconception of time, from the strangely irrational notion that there is something in the very flow of time that will inevitably cure all ills. Actually, time itself is neutral; it can be used either destructively or constructively. More and more I feel that the people of ill will have used time much more effectively than have the people of good will. We will have to repent in this generation not merely for the hateful words and actions of the bad people but for the appalling silence of the good people. Human progress never rolls in on wheels of inevitability; it comes through the tireless efforts of men willing to be co-workers with God, and without this hard work, time itself becomes an ally of the forces of social stagnation. We must use time creatively, in the knowledge that the time is always ripe to do right. Now is the time to make real the promise of democracy and transform our pending national elegy into a creative psalm of brotherhood. Now is the time to lift our national policy from the quicksand of racial injustice to the solid rock of human dignity.

You speak of our activity in Birmingham as extreme. At first I was rather disappointed that fellow clergymen would see my nonviolent efforts as those of an extremist. I began thinking about the fact that I stand in the middle of two opposing forces in the Negro community. One is a force of complacency, made up in part of Negroes who, as a result of long years of oppression, are so drained of self-respect and a sense of "somebodiness" that they have adjusted to segregation; and in part of a few middle-class Negroes who, because of a degree of academic and economic security and because in some ways they profit by segregation, have become insensitive to the problems of the masses. The other force is one of bitterness and hatred, and it comes perilously close to advocating violence. It is expressed in the various black nationalist groups that are springing up across the nation, the largest and best-known being Elijah Muhammad's Muslim movement. Nourished by the Negro's frustration over the continued existence of racial discrimination, this movement is made up of people who have lost faith in America, who have absolutely repudiated Christianity, and who have concluded that the white man is an incorrigible "devil."

I have tried to stand between these two forces, saying that we need emulate neither the "do-nothingism" of the complacent nor the hatred and despair of the black nationalist. For there is the more excellent way of love and nonviolent protest. I am grateful to God that, through the influence of the Negro church, the way of nonviolence became an integral part of our struggle.

If this philosophy had not emerged, by now many streets of the South would, I am convinced, be flowing with blood. And I am further convinced that if our white brothers dismiss as "rabble-rousers" and "outside agitators" those of us who employ nonviolent direct action, and if they refuse to support our nonviolent efforts, millions of the Negroes will, out of frustration and despair, seek solace and security in black-nationalist ideologies—a development that would inevitably lead to a frightening racial nightmare.

30   Oppressed people cannot remain oppressed forever. The yearning for freedom eventually manifests itself, and that is what has happened to the American Negro. Something within has reminded him of his birthright of freedom, and something without has reminded him that it can be gained. Consciously or unconsciously, he has been caught up by the *Zeitgeist*, and with his black brothers of Africa and his brown and yellow brothers of Asia, South America and the Caribbean, the United States Negro is moving with a sense of great urgency toward the promised land of racial justice. If one recognizes this vital urge that has engulfed the Negro community, one should readily understand why public demonstrations are taking place. The Negro has many pent-up resentments and latent frustrations, and he must release them. So let him march; let him make prayer pilgrimages to the city hall; let him go on freedom rides—and try to understand why he must do so. If his repressed

emotions are not released in nonviolent ways, they will seek expression through violence; this is not a threat but a fact of history. So I have not said to my people: "Get rid of your discontent." Rather, I have tried to say that this normal and healthy discontent can be channeled into the creative outlet of nonviolent direct action. And now this approach is being termed extremist.

But though I was initially disappointed at being categorized as an extremist, as I continued to think about the matter I gradually gained a measure of satisfaction from the label. Was not Jesus an extremist for love: "Love your enemies, bless them that curse you, and persecute you." Was not Amos an extremist for justice: "Let justice roll down like waters and righteousness like an ever-flowing stream." Was not Paul an extremist for the Christian gospel: "I bear in my body the marks of the Lord Jesus." Was not Martin Luther an extremist: "Here I stand; I cannot do otherwise, so help me God." And John Bunyan: "I will stay in jail to the end of my days before I make a butchery of my conscience." And Abraham Lincoln: "This nation cannot survive half slave and half free." And Thomas Jefferson: "We hold these truths to be self-evident, that all men are created equal . . . ." So the question is not whether we will be extremists, but what kind of extremists we will be. Will we be extremists for hate or for love? Will we be extremists for the preservation of injustice or for the extension of justice? In that dramatic scene on Calvary's hill three men were crucified. We must never forget that all three were crucified for the same crime—the crime of extremism. Two were extremists for immorality, and thus fell below their environment. The other, Jesus Christ, was an extremist for love, truth and goodness, and thereby rose above his environment. Perhaps the South, the nation and the world are in dire need of creative extremists.

I had hoped that the white moderate would see this need. Perhaps I was too optimistic; perhaps I expected too much. I suppose I should have realized that few members of the oppressor race can understand the deep groans and passionate yearnings of the oppressed race, and still fewer have the vision to see that injustice must be rooted out by strong, persistent and determined action. I am thankful, however, that some of our white brothers in the South have grasped the meaning of this social revolution and committed themselves to it. They are still all too few in quantity, but they are big in quality. Some—such as Ralph McGill, Lillian Smith, Harry Golden, James McBride Dabbs, Ann Braden and Sarah Patton Boyle—have written about our struggle in eloquent and prophetic terms. Others have marched with us down nameless streets of the South. They have languished in filthy, roach-infested jails, suffering the abuse and brutality of policemen who view them as "dirty nigger-lovers." Unlike so many of their moderate brothers and sisters, they have recognized the urgency of the moment and sensed the need for powerful "action" antidotes to combat the disease of segregation.

Let me take note of my other major disappointment. I have been so greatly disappointed with the white church and its leadership. Of course, there are some notable exceptions. I am not unmindful of the fact that each of you has taken some significant stands on this issue. I commend you, Reverend Stallings, for your Christian stand on this past Sunday, in welcoming Negroes to your worship service on a nonsegregated basis. I commend the Catholic leaders of this state for integrating Spring Hill College several years ago.

But despite these notable exceptions, I must honestly reiterate that I have been disappointed with the church. I do not say this as one of those negative critics who can always find something wrong with the church. I say this as a minister of the gospel, who loves the church; who was nurtured in its bosom; who has been sustained by its spiritual blessings and who will remain true to it as long as the cord of life shall lengthen.

35   When I was suddenly catapulted into the leadership of the bus protest in Montgomery, Alabama, a few years ago, I felt we would be supported by the white church. I felt that the white ministers, priests and rabbis of the South would be among our strongest allies. Instead, some have been outright opponents, refusing to understand the freedom movement and misrepresenting its leaders; all too many others have been more cautious than courageous and have remained silent behind the anesthetizing security of stained-glass windows.

In spite of my shattered dreams, I came to Birmingham with the hope that the white religious leadership of this community would see the justice of our cause and, with deep moral concern, would serve as the channel through which our just grievances could reach the power structure. I had hoped that each of you would understand. But again I have been disappointed.

I have heard numerous southern religious leaders admonish their worshipers to comply with a desegregation decision because it is the law, but I have longed to hear white ministers declare: "Follow this decree because integration is morally right and because the Negro is your brother." In the midst of blatant injustices inflicted upon the Negro, I have watched white churchmen stand on the sideline and mouth pious irrelevancies and sanctimonious trivialities. In the midst of a mighty struggle to rid our nation of racial and economic injustice, I have heard many ministers say: "Those are social issues, with which the gospel has no real concern." And I have watched many churches commit themselves to a completely otherworldly religion which makes a strange, un-Biblical distinction between body and soul, between the sacred and the secular.

I have traveled the length and breadth of Alabama, Mississippi and all the other southern states. On sweltering summer days and crisp autumn mornings I have looked at the South's beautiful churches with their lofty spires pointing heavenward. I have beheld the impressive outlines of her massive religious-education buildings. Over and over I have found myself asking: "What kind of people worship here? Who is their God? Where were their voices when the lips of Governor Barnett dripped with words of interposition and nullification? Where were they when Governor Wallace gave a clarion call for defiance and hatred? Where were their voices of support when bruised and weary Negro men and women decided to rise from the dark dungeons of complacency to the bright hills of creative protest?"

Yes, these questions are still in my mind. In deep disappointment I have wept over the laxity of the church. But be assured that my tears have been tears of love. There can be no deep disappointment where there is not deep love. Yes, I love the church. How could I do otherwise? I am in the rather unique position of being the son, the grandson, and the great-grandson of preachers. Yes, I see the church as the body of Christ. But, oh! How we have blemished and scarred that body through social neglect and through fear of being nonconformists.

40   There was a time when the church was very powerful—in the time when the early Christians rejoiced at being deemed worthy to suffer for what they believed. In those days the church was not merely a thermometer that recorded the ideas and principles of popular opinion; it was a thermostat that transformed the mores of society. Whenever the early Christians entered a town, the people in power became disturbed and immediately sought to convict the Christians for being "disturbers of the peace" and "outside agitators." But the Christians pressed on, in the conviction that they were "a colony of heaven," called to obey God rather than man. Small in number, they were big in commitment. They were too God-intoxicated to be "astronomically intimidated." By their effort and example they brought an end to such ancient evils as infanticide and gladiatorial contests.

Things are different now. So often the contemporary church is a weak, ineffectual voice with an uncertain sound. So often it is an archdefender of the status quo. Far from being disturbed by the presence of the church, the power structure of the average community is consoled by the church's silent—and often even vocal—sanction of things as they are.

But the judgment of God is upon the church as never before. If today's church does not recapture the sacrificial spirit of the early church, it will lose its authenticity, forfeit the loyalty of millions, and be dismissed as an irrelevant social club with no meaning for the twentieth century. Every day I meet young people whose disappointment with the church has turned into outright disgust.

Perhaps I have once again been too optimistic. Is organized religion too inextricably bound to the status quo to save our nation and the world? Perhaps I must turn my faith to the inner spiritual church, the church within the church, as the true *ekklesia* and the hope of the world. But again I am thankful to God that some noble souls from the ranks of organized religion have broken loose from the paralyzing chains of conformity and joined us as active partners in the struggle for freedom. They have left their secure congregations and walked the streets of Albany, Georgia, with us. They have gone down the highways of the South on tortuous rides for freedom. Yes, they have gone to jail with us. Some have been dismissed from their churches, have lost the support of their bishops and fellow ministers. But they have acted in the faith that right defeated is stronger than evil triumphant. Their witness has been the spiritual salt that has preserved the true meaning of the gospel in these troubled times. They have carved a tunnel of hope through the dark mountain of disappointment.

I hope the church as a whole will meet the challenge of this decisive hour. But even if the church does not come to the aid of justice, I have no despair about the future. I have no fear about the outcome of our struggle in Birmingham, even if our motives are at present misunderstood. We will reach the goal of freedom in Birmingham and all over the nation, because the goal of America is freedom. Abused and scorned though we may be, our destiny is tied up with America's destiny. Before the pilgrims landed at Plymouth, we were here. Before the pen of Jefferson etched the majestic words of the Declaration of Independence across the pages of history, we were here. For more than two centuries our forebears labored in this country without wages; they made cotton king; they built the homes of their masters while suffering gross injustice and shameful humiliation—and yet out of a bottomless vitality they continued to thrive and develop. If the inexpressible cruelties of slavery could not stop us, the opposition we now face will surely fail. We will win our freedom because the sacred heritage of our nation and the eternal will of God are embodied in our echoing demands.

45   Before closing I feel impelled to mention one other point in your statement that has troubled me profoundly. You warmly commended the Birmingham police force for keeping "order" and "preventing violence." I doubt that you would have so warmly commended the police force if you had seen its dogs sinking their teeth into unarmed, nonviolent Negroes. I doubt that you would so quickly commend the policemen if you were to observe their ugly and inhumane treatment of Negroes here in the city jail; if you were to watch them push and curse old Negro women and young Negro girls; if you were to see them slap and kick old Negro men and young boys; if you were to observe them, as they did on two occasions, refuse to give us food because we wanted to sing our grace together. I cannot join you in your praise of the Birmingham police department.

It is true that police have exercised a degree of discipline in handling the demonstrators. In this sense they have conducted themselves rather "nonviolently" in public. But for what purpose? To preserve the evil system of segregation. Over the past few years I have consistently preached that nonviolence demands that the means we use must be as pure as the ends we seek. I have tried to make clear that it is wrong to use immoral means to attain moral ends. But now I must affirm that it is just as wrong, or perhaps even more so, to use moral means to preserve immoral ends. Perhaps Mr. Connor and his policemen have been rather nonviolent in public, as was Chief Pritchett in Albany, Georgia, but they have used the moral means of nonviolence to maintain the immoral end of racial injustice. As T. S. Eliot has said: "The last temptation is the greatest treason: To do the right deed for the wrong reason."

I wish you had commended the Negro sit-inners and demonstrators of Birmingham for their sublime courage, their willingness to suffer and their amazing discipline in the midst of great provocation. One day the South will recognize its real heroes. They will be the James Merediths, with the noble sense of purpose that enables them to face jeering and hostile mobs, and with the agonizing loneliness that characterizes the life of the pioneer. They will be old, oppressed, battered Negro women, symbolized in a seventy-two-year-old woman in Montgomery, Alabama, who rose up with a sense of dignity and with her people decided not to ride segregated buses, and who responded with ungrammatical profundity to one who inquired about her weariness: "My feets is tired, but my soul is at rest." They will be the young high school and college students, the young ministers of the gospel and a host of their elders, courageously and nonviolently sitting in at lunch counters and willingly going to jail for conscience' sake. One day the South will know that when these disinherited children of God sat down at lunch counters, they were in reality standing up for what is best in the American dream and for the most sacred values in our Judaeo-Christian heritage, thereby bringing our nation back to those great wells of democracy which were dug deep by the founding fathers in their formulation of the Constitution and the Declaration of Independence.

Never before have I written so long a letter. I'm afraid it is much too long to take your precious time. I can assure you that it would have been much shorter if I had been writing from a comfortable desk, but what else can one do when he is alone in a narrow jail cell, other than write long letters, think long thoughts and pray long prayers?

If I have said anything in this letter that overstates the truth and indicates an unreasonable impatience, I beg you to forgive me. If I have said anything that understates the truth and indicates my having a patience that allows me to settle for anything less than brotherhood, I beg God to forgive me.

50   I hope this letter finds you strong in faith. I also hope that circumstances will soon make it possible for me to meet each of you, not as an integrationist or a civil-rights leader but as a fellow clergyman and a Christian brother. Let us all hope that the dark clouds of racial prejudice will soon pass away and the deep fog of misunderstanding will be lifted from our fear-drenched communities, and in some not too distant tomorrow the radiant stars of love and brotherhood will shine over our great nation with all their scintillating beauty.

Yours for the cause of Peace and Brotherhood
MARTIN LUTHER KING, JR.

Lifeboat Ethics: The Case Against Aid That Does Harm

GARRETT HARDIN

Garrett Hardin's "Lifeboat Ethics: The Case Against Aid That Does Harm" is not as widely known as King's "Letter from Birmingham Jail," but it has been influential in changing the debate about foreign aid, in stimulating new thinking about the causes of poverty and about ways to combat it, and in promoting wider understanding of the "tragedy of the commons." It has also sparked dozens of impassioned counterarguments. Based on an unflinching analysis of consequences, Hardin presents his anti-liberal thesis against foreign aid and open borders. Rhetorically, Hardin's argument is famous for its extended use of analogy—in this case a lifeboat filled with people representing rich countries and an ocean of swimmers (poor countries) clamoring to get in the boat. The article was originally published in Psychology Today *in 1974.*

Environmentalists use the metaphor of the earth as a "spaceship" in trying to persuade countries, industries and people to stop wasting and polluting our natural resources. Since we all share life on this planet, they argue, no single person or institution has the right to destroy, waste, or use more than a fair share of its resources.

But does everyone on earth have an equal right to an equal share of its resources? The spaceship metaphor can be dangerous when used by misguided idealists to justify suicidal policies for sharing our resources through uncontrolled immigration and foreign aid. In their enthusiastic but unrealistic generosity, they confuse the ethics of a spaceship with those of a lifeboat.

A true spaceship would have to be under the control of a captain, since no ship could possibly survive if its course were determined by committee. Spaceship Earth certainly has no captain; the United Nations is merely a toothless tiger, with little power to enforce any policy upon its bickering members.

If we divide the world crudely into rich nations and poor nations, two thirds of them are desperately poor, and only one third comparatively rich, with the United States the wealthiest of all. Metaphorically each rich nation can be seen as a lifeboat full of comparatively rich people. In the ocean outside each lifeboat swim the poor of the world, who would like to get in, or at least to share some of the wealth. What should the lifeboat passengers do?

5   First, we must recognize the limited capacity of any lifeboat. For example, a nation's land has a limited capacity to support a population and as the current energy crisis has shown us, in some ways we have already exceeded the carrying capacity of our land.

Adrift in a Moral Sea

So here we sit, say 50 people in our lifeboat. To be generous, let us assume it has room for 10 more, making a total capacity of 60. Suppose the 50 of us in the lifeboat see 100 others swimming in the water outside, begging for admission to our boat or for handouts. We have several options: we may be tempted to try to live by the Christian ideal of being "our brother's keeper," or by the Marxist ideal of "to each according to his needs." Since the needs of all in the water are the same, and since they can all be seen as "our brothers," we could take them all into our boat, making a total of 150 in a boat designed for 60. The boat swamps, everyone drowns. Complete justice, complete catastrophe.

Since the boat has an unused excess capacity of 10 more passengers, we could admit just 10 more to it. But which 10 do we let in? How do we choose? Do we pick the best 10, "first come, first served"? And what do we say to the 90 we exclude? If we do let an extra 10 into our lifeboat, we will have lost our "safety factor," an engineering principle of critical importance. For example, if we don't leave room for excess capacity as a safety factor in our country's agriculture, a new plant disease or a bad change in the weather could have disastrous consequences.

Suppose we decide to preserve our small safety factor and admit no more to the lifeboat. Our survival is then possible although we shall have to be constantly on guard against boarding parties.

While this last solution clearly offers the only means of our survival, it is morally abhorrent to many people. Some say they feel guilty about their good luck. My reply is simple: "Get out and yield your place to others." This may solve the problem of the guilt-ridden person's conscience, but it does not change the ethics of the lifeboat. The needy person to whom the guilt-ridden person yields his place will not himself feel guilty about his good luck. If he did, he would not climb aboard. The net result of conscience-stricken people giving up their unjustly held seats is the elimination of that sort of conscience from the lifeboat.

10   This is the basic metaphor within which we must work out our solutions. Let us now enrich the image, step by step, with substantive additions from the real world, a world that must solve real and pressing problems of overpopulation and hunger.

The harsh ethics of the lifeboat become even harsher when we consider the reproductive differences between the rich nations and the poor nations. The people inside the lifeboats are doubling in numbers every 87 years; those swimming around outside are doubling, on the average, every 35 years, more than twice as fast as the rich. And since the world's resources are dwindling, the difference in prosperity between the rich and the poor can only increase.

As of 1973, the U.S. had a population of 210 million people, who were increasing by 0.8 percent per year. Outside our lifeboat, let us imagine another 210 million people (say the combined populations of Colombia, Ecuador, Venezuela, Morocco, Pakistan, Thailand and the Philippines) who are increasing at a rate of 3.3 percent per year. Put differently, the doubling time for this aggregate population is 21 years, compared to 87 years for the U.S.

The harsh ethics of the lifeboat become harsher when we consider the reproductive differences between rich and poor.

Multiplying the Rich and the Poor

Now suppose the U.S. agreed to pool its resources with those seven countries, with everyone receiving an equal share. Initially the ratio of Americans to non-Americans in this model would be one-to-one. But consider what the ratio would be after 87 years, by which time the Americans would have doubled to a population of 420 million. By then, doubling every 21 years, the other group would have swollen to 3.54 billion. Each American would have to share the available resources with more than eight people.

15   But, one could argue, this discussion assumes that current population trends will continue, and they may not. Quite so. Most likely the rate of population increase will decline much faster in the U.S. than it will in the other countries, and there does not seem to be much we can do about it. In sharing with "each according to his needs," we must recognize that needs are determined by population size, which is determined by the rate of reproduction, which at present is regarded as a sovereign right of every nation, poor or not. This being so, the philanthropic load created by the sharing ethic of the spaceship can only increase.

The Tragedy of the Commons

The fundamental error of spaceship ethics, and the sharing it requires, is that it leads to what I call "the tragedy of the commons." Under a system of private property, the men who own property recognize their responsibility to care for it, for if they don't they will eventually suffer. A farmer, for instance, will allow no more cattle in a pasture than its carrying capacity justifies. If he overloads

it, erosion sets in, weeds take over, and he loses the use of the pasture.

If a pasture becomes a commons open to all, the right of each to use it may not be matched by a corresponding responsibility to protect it. Asking everyone to use it with discretion will hardly do, for the considerate herdsman who refrains from overloading the commons suffers more than a selfish one who says his needs are greater. If everyone would restrain himself, all would be well; but it takes only one less than everyone to ruin a system of voluntary restraint. In a crowded world of less than perfect human beings, mutual ruin is inevitable if there are no controls. This is the tragedy of the commons.

One of the major tasks of education today should be the creation of such an acute awareness of the dangers of the commons that people will recognize its many varieties. For example, the air and water have become polluted because they are treated as commons. Further growth in the population or per-capita conversion of natural resources into pollutants will only make the problem worse. The same holds true for the fish of the oceans. Fishing fleets have nearly disappeared in many parts of the world, technological improvements in the art of fishing are hastening the day of complete ruin. Only the replacement of the system of the commons with a responsible system of control will save the land, air, water and oceanic fisheries.

The World Food Bank

In recent years there has been a push to create a new commons called a World Food Bank, an international depository of food reserves to which nations would contribute according to their abilities and from which they would draw according to their needs. This humanitarian proposal has received support from many liberal international groups, and from such prominent citizens as Margaret Mead, U.N. Secretary General Kurt Waldheim, and Senators Edward Kennedy and George McGovern.

20   A world food bank appeals powerfully to our humanitarian impulses. But before we rush ahead with such a plan, let us recognize where the greatest political push comes from, lest we be disillusioned later. Our experience with the "Food for Peace program,"or Public Law 480, gives us the answer. This program moved billions of dollars worth of U.S. surplus grain to food-short, population-long countries during the past two decades. But when P.L. 480 first became law, a headline in the business magazine *Forbes* revealed the real power behind it: "Feeding the World's Hungry Millions: How It Will Mean Billions for U.S. Business."

And indeed it did. In the years 1960 to 1970, U.S. taxpayers spent a total of $7.9 billion on the Food for Peace program. Between 1948 and 1970, they also paid an additional $50 billion for other economic-aid programs, some of which went for food and food-producing machinery and technology. Though all U.S. taxpayers were forced to contribute to the cost of P.L. 480 certain special interest groups gained handsomely under the program. Farmers did not have to contribute the grain; the Government or rather the taxpayers, bought it from them at full market prices. The increased demand raised prices of farm products generally. The manufacturers of farm machinery, fertilizers and pesticides benefited by the farmers' extra efforts to grow more food. Grain elevators profited from storing the surplus until it could be shipped. Railroads made money hauling it to ports, and shipping lines profited from carrying it overseas. The implementation of P.L. 480 required the creation of a vast Government bureaucracy, which then acquired its own vested interest in continuing the program regardless of its merits.

Extracting Dollars

Those who proposed and defended the Food for Peace program in public rarely mentioned its importance to any of these special interests. The public emphasis was always on its humanitarian effects. The combination of silent selfish interests and highly vocal humanitarian apologists made a powerful and successful lobby for extracting money from taxpayers. We can expect the same lobby to push now for the creation of a World Food Bank.

However great the potential benefit to selfish interests, it should not be a decisive argument against a truly humanitarian program. We must ask if such a program would actually do more good than harm, not only momentarily but also in the long run. Those who propose the food bank usually refer to a current "emergency" or "crisis" in terms of world food supply. But what is an emergency? Although they may be infrequent and sudden, everyone knows that emergencies will occur from time to time. A well-run family, company, organization or country prepares for the likelihood of accidents and emergencies. It expects them, it budgets for them, it saves for them.

Learning the Hard Way

What happens if some organizations or countries budget for accidents and others do not? If each country is solely responsible for its own well-being, poorly managed ones will suffer. But they can learn from experience. They may mend their ways, and learn to budget for infrequent but certain emergencies. For example, the weather varies from year to year, and periodic crop failures are certain. A wise and competent government saves out of the production of the good years in anticipation of bad years to come. Joseph taught this policy to Pharaoh in Egypt more than 2,000 years ago. Yet the great majority of the governments in the world today do not follow such a policy. They lack either the wisdom or the competence, or both. Should those nations that do manage to put something aside be forced to come to the rescue each time an emergency occurs among the poor nations?

25   "But it isn't their fault!" Some kind-hearted liberals argue. "How can we blame the poor people who are caught in an emergency? Why must they suffer for the sins of their governments?" The concept of blame is simply not relevant here. The real question is, what are the operational consequences of establishing a world food bank? If it is open to every country every time a need develops, slovenly rulers will not be motivated to take Joseph's advice. Someone will always come to their aid. Some countries will deposit food in the world food bank, and others will withdraw it. There will be almost no overlap. As a result of such solutions to food shortage emergencies, the poor countries will not learn to mend their ways, and will suffer progressively greater emergencies as their populations grow.

Population Control the Crude Way

On the average poor countries undergo a 2.5 percent increase in population each year; rich countries, about 0.8 percent. Only rich countries have anything in the way of food reserves set aside, and even they do not have as much as they should. Poor countries have none. If poor countries received no food from the outside, the rate of their population growth would be periodically 30 checked by crop failures and famines. But if they can always draw on a world food bank in time of need, their population can continue to grow unchecked, and so will their "need" for aid. In the short run, a world food bank may diminish that need, but in the long run it actually increases the need without limit.

Without some system of worldwide food sharing, the proportion of people in the rich and poor nations might eventually stabilize. The overpopulated poor countries would decrease in numbers, while the rich countries that had room for more people would increase. But with a well-meaning system of sharing, such as a world food bank, the growth differential between the rich and the poor countries will not

only persist, it will increase. Because of the higher rate of population growth in the poor countries of the world, 88 percent of today's children are born poor, and only 12 percent rich. Year by year the ratio becomes worse, as the fast-reproducing poor outnumber the slow-reproducing rich.

A world food bank is thus a commons in disguise. People will have more motivation to draw from it than to add to any common store. The less provident and less able will multiply at the expense of the abler and more provident, bringing eventual ruin upon all who share in the commons. Besides, any system of "sharing" that amounts to foreign aid from the rich nations to the poor nations will carry the taint of charity, which will contribute little to the world peace so devoutly desired by those who support the idea of a world food bank.

As past U.S. foreign-aid programs have amply and depressingly demonstrated, international charity frequently inspires mistrust and antagonism rather than gratitude on the part of the recipient nation [see "What Other Nations Hear When the Eagle Screams,"by Kenneth J. and Mary M. Gergen, PT, June].

Chinese Fish and Miracle Rice

The modern approach to foreign aid stresses the export of technology and advice, rather than money and food. As an ancient Chinese proverb goes: "Give a man a fish and he will eat for a day; teach him how to fish and he will eat for the rest of his days." Acting on this advice, the Rockefeller and Ford Foundations have financed a number of programs for improving agriculture in the hungry nations. Known as the "Green Revolution," these programs have led to the development of "miracle rice" and "miracle wheat," new strains that offer bigger harvests and greater resistance to crop damage. Norman Borlaug, the Nobel Prize winning agronomist who, supported by the Rockefeller Foundation, developed "miracle wheat," is one of the most prominent advocates of a world food bank.

Whether or not the Green Revolution can increase food production as much as its champions claim is a debatable but possibly irrelevant point. Those who support this well-intended humanitarian effort should first consider some of the fundamentals of human ecology. Ironically, one man who did was the late Alan Gregg, a vice president of the Rockefeller Foundation. Two decades ago he expressed strong doubts about the wisdom of such attempts to increase food production. He likened the growth and spread of humanity over the surface of the earth to the spread of cancer in the human body, remarking that "cancerous growths demand food; but, as far as I know, they have never been cured by getting it."

Overloading the Environment

Every human born constitutes a draft on all 35 aspects of the environment: food, air, water, forests, beaches, wildlife, scenery and solitude. Food can, perhaps, be significantly increased to meet a growing demand. But what about clean beaches, unspoiled forests, and solitude? If we satisfy a growing population's need for food, we necessarily decrease its per capita supply of the other resources needed by men.

India, for example, now has a population of 600 million, which increases by 15 million each year. This population already puts a huge load on a relatively impoverished environment. The country's forests are now only a small fraction of what they were three centuries ago and floods and erosion continually destroy the insufficient farmland that remains. Every one of the 15 million new lives added to India's population puts an additional burden on the environment, and increases the economic and social costs of crowding. However humanitarian our intent, every Indian life saved through medical or nutritional assistance from abroad diminishes the quality of life for those who remain, and for subsequent generations. If rich countries make it possible, through foreign aid, for

600 million Indians to swell to 1.2 billion in a mere 28 years, as their current growth rate threatens, will future generations of Indians thank us for hastening the destruction of their environment? Will our good intentions be sufficient excuse for the consequences of our actions?

My final example of a commons in action is one for which the public has the least desire for rational discussion—immigration. Anyone who publicly questions the wisdom of current U.S. immigration policy is promptly charged with bigotry, prejudice, ethnocentrism, chauvinism, isolationism or selfishness. Rather than encounter such accusations, one would rather talk about other matters leaving immigration policy to wallow in the crosscurrents of special interests that take no account of the good of the whole, or the interests of posterity.

Perhaps we still feel guilty about things we said in the past. Two generations ago the popular press frequently referred to Dagos, Wops, Polacks, Chinks and Krauts in articles about how America was being "overrun" by foreigners of supposedly inferior genetic stock [see "The Politics of Genetic Engineering: Who Decides Who's Defective?" PT, June]. But because the implied inferiority of foreigners was used then as justification for keeping them out, people now assume that restrictive policies could only be based on such misguided notions. There are other grounds.

A Nation of Immigrants

Just consider the numbers involved. Our Government acknowledges a net inflow of 400,000 immigrants a year. While we have no hard data on the extent of illegal entries, educated guesses put the figure at about 600,000 a year. Since the natural increase (excess of births over deaths) of the resident population now runs about 1.7 million per year, the yearly gain from immigration amounts to at least 19 percent of the total annual increase, and may be as much as 37 percent if we include the estimate for illegal immigrants. Considering the growing use of

birth-control devices, the potential effect of educa- 40
tion campaigns by such organizations as Planned
Parenthood Federation of America and Zero Population Growth, and the influence of inflation and
the housing shortage, the fertility rate of American
women may decline so much that immigration
could account for all the yearly increase in population. Should we not at least ask if that is what we
want?

For the sake of those who worry about whether
the "quality" of the average immigrant compares
favorably with the quality of the average resident, let
us assume that immigrants and native-born citizens
are of exactly equal quality, however one defines
that term. We will focus here only on quantity; and
since our conclusions will depend on nothing else, all
charges of bigotry and chauvinism become irrelevant.

Immigration vs. Food Supply

World food banks move food to the people, hastening the exhaustion of the environment of the
poor countries. Unrestricted immigration, on the
other hand, moves people to the food, thus speed-
ing up the destruction of the environment of the
rich countries. We can easily understand why poor
people should want to make this latter transfer, but
why should rich hosts encourage it?

As in the case of foreign-aid programs, immigration receives support from selfish interests
and humanitarian impulses. The primary selfish
interest in unimpeded immigration is the desire of employers for cheap labor, particularly in
industries and trades that offer degrading work.
In the past, one wave of foreigners after another
was brought into the U.S. to work at wretched
jobs for wretched wages. In recent years the Cubans, Puerto Ricans and Mexicans have had this
dubious honor. The interests of the employers of
cheap labor mesh well with the guilty silence of
the country's liberal intelligentsia. White Anglo-
Saxon Protestants are particularly reluctant to call
for a closing of the doors to immigration for fear
of being called bigots.

But not all countries have such reluctant
leadership. Most educated Hawaiians, for example, are keenly aware of the limits of their environment, particularly in terms of population growth.
There is only so much room on the islands, and
the islanders know it. To Hawaiians, immigrants
from the other 49 states present as great a threat
as those from other nations. At a recent meeting
of Hawaiian government officials in Honolulu, I
had the ironic delight of hearing a speaker who
like most of his audience was of Japanese ancestry,
ask how the country might practically and constitutionally close its doors to further immigration.
One member of the audience countered: "How
can we shut the doors now? We have many friends
and relatives in Japan that we'd like to bring here
some day so that they can enjoy Hawaii too." The
Japanese-American speaker smiled sympathetically
and answered: "Yes, but we have children now,
and someday we'll have grandchildren too. We can
bring more people here from Japan only by giving away some of the land that we hope to pass on
to our grandchildren some day. What right do we
have to do that?"

At this point, I can hear U.S. liberals asking:
"How can you justify slamming the door once
you're inside? You say that immigrants should
be kept out. But aren't we all immigrants, or the
descendants of immigrants? If we insist on staying, must we not admit all others?" Our craving for
intellectual order leads us to seek and prefer sym-
metrical rules and morals: a single rule for me and
everybody else; the same rule yesterday, today and
tomorrow. Justice, we feel, should not change with
time and place.

We Americans of non-Indian ancestry can look
upon ourselves as the descendants of thieves who
are guilty morally, if not legally, of stealing this land
from its Indian owners. Should we then give back
the land to the now living American descendants of
those Indians? However morally or logically sound
this proposal may be, I, for one, am unwilling to
live by it and I know no one else who is. Besides, the

logical consequence would be absurd. Suppose that, intoxicated with a sense of pure justice, we should decide to turn our land over to the Indians. Since all our other wealth has also been derived from the land, wouldn't we be morally obliged to give that back to the Indians too?

Pure Justice vs. Reality

Clearly, the concept of pure justice produces an infinite regression to absurdity. Centuries ago, wise men invented statutes of limitations to justify the rejection of such pure justice, in the interest of preventing continual disorder. The law zealously defends property rights, but only relatively recent property rights. Drawing a line after an arbitrary time has elapsed may be unjust, but the alternatives are worse.

We are all the descendants of thieves, and the world's resources are inequitably distributed. But we must begin the journey to tomorrow from the point where we are today. We cannot remake the past. We cannot safely divide the wealth equitably among all peoples so long as people reproduce at different rates. To do so would guarantee that our grandchildren and everyone else's grandchildren, would have only a ruined world to inhabit.

45 To be generous with one's own possessions is quite different from being generous with those of posterity. We should call this point to the attention of those who from a commendable love of justice and equality, would institute a system of the commons, either in the form of a world food bank, or of unrestricted immigration. We must convince them if we wish to save at least some parts of the world from environmental ruin.

Without a true world government to control reproduction and the use of available resources, the sharing ethic of the spaceship is impossible. For the foreseeable future, our survival demands that we govern our actions by the ethics of a lifeboat, harsh though they may be. Posterity will be satisfied with nothing less.

Guernica

PABLO PICASSO

On April 26, 1937, two years before the German Nazis rolled across Poland at the beginning of World War II, Hitler sent a contingent of airplanes on a practice run over the small market town of Guernica, a Basque village in northern Spain, to test their effectiveness at bombing a city into oblivion. Hitler had two goals: to support the right wing army of Generalissimo Francisco Franco in overthrowing the existing Spanish government and to perfect techniques of aerial bombardment needed in its planned blitzkrieg across Europe. The utter destruction of Guernica has come to symbolize the atrocity of modern warfare. Pablo Picasso, who had been commissioned by the Spanish Government to create a mural for Spain's exhibition building at the 1937 World's Fair in Paris, chose the horror of Guernica as his theme. Picasso's huge (11 feet by 26 feet), black and white, oil-on-canvas painting has become perhaps the world's most famous visual argument against war.

The Obligation to Endure

RACHEL CARSON

"The Obligation to Endure" is the second chapter of Rachel Carson's influential book The Silent Spring. *A marine biologist, meticulous researcher, and powerful writer, Carson is regarded as one of the world's most influential environmentalists.* The Silent Spring *(1962) exposed the subtle, insidious dangers of DDT, a pesticide that since its discovery in the 1940s had been hailed as a miracle substance that could wipe out mosquitoes and other disease-bearing or crop-destroying insects. According to the National Resource Defense Council, whose Web site contains an inspiring story about Carson's work,* The Silent Spring *"eloquently questioned humanity's faith in technological progress and helped set the stage for the environmental movement." In "The Obligation to Endure," which precedes the more technical portions of the book, Carson presents her causal argument showing how apparently beneficial chemicals can have disastrous unanticipated consequences. Her work was strenuously attacked by the chemical industry, which argued that if we followed Carson's recommendations we would return to the dark ages of insect-borne diseases and famine from failed agriculture. But Carson's carefully documented research defended her against the charges of the chemical industry. According to the National Resource Defense Council, the "threats Carson had outlined—the contamination of the food chain, cancer, genetic damage, the deaths of entire species—were too frightening to ignore. For the first time, the need to regulate industry in order to protect the environment became widely accepted, and environmentalism was born."*

The history of life on earth has been a history of interaction between living things and their surroundings. To a large extent, the physical form and the habits of the earth's vegetation and its animal life have been molded by the environment. Considering the whole span of earthly time, the opposite effect, in which life actually modifies its surroundings, has been relatively slight. Only within the moment of time represented by the present century has one species—man—acquired significant power to alter the nature of his world.

During the past quarter century this power has not only increased to one of disturbing magnitude but it has changed in character. The most alarming of all man's assaults upon the environment is the contamination of air, earth, rivers, and sea with dangerous and even lethal materials. This pollution is for the most part irrecoverable; the chain of evil it initiates not only in the world that must support life but in living tissues is for the most part irreversible. In this now universal contamination of the environment, chemicals are the sinister and little-recognized partners of radiation in changing the very nature of the world—the very nature of its life. Strontium 90, released through nuclear explosions into the air, comes to earth in rain or drifts down as fallout, lodges in soil, enters into the grass or corn or wheat grown there, and in time takes up its abode in the bones of a human being, there to remain until his death. Similarly, chemicals sprayed on croplands or forests or gardens lie long in soil, entering into living organisms, passing from one to another in a chain of poisoning and death. Or they pass mysteriously by underground streams until they emerge and, through the alchemy of air and sunlight, combine into new forms that kill vegetation, sicken cattle, and work unknown harm on those who drink from once pure wells. As Albert Schweitzer has said, "Man can hardly even recognize the devils of his own creation."

It took hundreds of millions of years to produce the life that now inhabits the earth—eons of time in which that developing and evolving and diversifying life reached a state of adjustment and balance with its surroundings. The environment, rigorously shaping and directing the life it supported, contained elements that were hostile as well as supporting. Certain rocks gave out dangerous radiation; even within the light of the sun, from which all life draws its energy, there were short-wave radiations with power to injure. Given time—time not in years but in millennia—life adjusts, and a balance has been reached. For time is the essential ingredient; but in the modern world there is no time.

The rapidity of change and the speed with which new situations are created follow the impetuous and heedless pace of man rather than the deliberate pace of nature. Radiation is no longer merely the background radiation of rocks, the bombardment of cosmic rays, the ultraviolet of the sun that have existed before there was any life on earth; radiation is now the unnatural creation of man's tampering with the atom. The chemicals to which life is asked to make its adjustment are no longer merely the calcium and silica and copper and all the rest of the minerals washed out of the rocks and carried in rivers to the sea; they are the synthetic creations of man's inventive mind, brewed in his laboratories, and having no counterparts in nature.

5   To adjust to these chemicals would require time on the scale that is nature's; it would require not merely the years of a man's life but the life of generations. And even this, were it by some miracle possible, would be futile, for the new chemicals come from our laboratories in an endless stream; almost five hundred annually find their way into actual use in the United States alone. The figure is staggering and its implications are not easily grasped—500 new chemicals to which the bodies of men and animals are required somehow to adapt each year, chemicals totally outside the limits of biologic experience.

Among them are many that are used in man's war against nature. Since the mid-1940's over 200 basic chemicals have been created for use in killing insects, weeds, rodents, and other organisms described in the modern vernacular as "pests"; and they are sold under several thousand different brand names.

These sprays, dusts, and aerosols are now applied almost universally to farms, gardens, forests, and homes—nonselective chemicals that have the power to kill every insect, the "good" and the "bad," to still the song of birds and the leaping of fish in the streams, to coat the leaves with a deadly film, and to linger on in soil—all this though the intended target may be only a few weeds or insects. Can anyone believe it is possible to lay down such a barrage of poisons on the surface of the earth without making it unfit for all life? They should not be called "insecticides," but "biocides."

The whole process of spraying seems caught up in an endless spiral. Since DDT was released for civilian use, a process of escalation has been going on in which ever more toxic materials must be found. This has happened because insects, in a triumphant vindication of Darwin's principle of the survival of the fittest, have evolved super races immune to the particular insecticide used, hence a deadlier one has always to be developed—and then a deadlier one than that. It has happened also because, for reasons to be described later, destructive insects often undergo a "flareback," or resurgence, after spraying, in numbers greater than before. Thus the chemical war is never won, and all life is caught in its violent crossfire.

Along with the possibility of the extinction of mankind by nuclear war, the central problem of our age has therefore become the contamination of man's total environment with such substances of incredible potential for harm—substances that accumulate in the tissues of plants and animals and even penetrate the germ cells to shatter or alter the very material of heredity upon which the shape of the future depends.

10　Some would-be architects of our future look toward a time when it will be possible to alter the human germ plasm by design. But we may easily be doing so now by inadvertence, for many chemicals, like radiation, bring about gene mutations. It is ironic to think that man might determine his own future by something so seemingly trivial as the choice of an insect spray.

All this has been risked—for what? Future historians may well be amazed by our distorted sense of proportion. How could intelligent beings seek to control a few unwanted species by a method that contaminated the entire environment and brought the threat of disease and death even to their own kind? Yet this is precisely what we have done. We have done it, moreover, for reasons that collapse the moment we examine them. We are told that the enormous and expanding use of pesticides is necessary to maintain farm production. Yet is our real problem not one of *overproduction*? Our farms, despite measures to remove acreages from production and to pay farmers *not* to produce, have yielded such a staggering excess of crops that the American taxpayer in 1962 is paying out more than one billion dollars a year as the total carrying cost of the surplus-food storage program. And is the situation helped when one branch of the Agriculture Department tries to reduce production while another states, as it did in 1958, "It is believed generally that reduction of crop acreages under provisions of the Soil Bank will stimulate interest in use of chemicals to obtain maximum production on the land retained in crops."

All this is not to say there is no insect problem and no need of control. I am saying, rather, that control must be geared to realities, not to mythical situations, and that the methods employed must be such that they do not destroy us along with the insects.

The problem whose attempted solution has brought such a train of disaster in its wake is an accompaniment of our modern way of life. Long before the age of man, insects inhabited the earth—a group of extraordinarily varied and adaptable beings. Over the course of time since man's advent, a small percentage of the more than half a million species of insects have come into conflict with human welfare in two principal ways: as competitors for the food supply and as carriers of human disease.

Disease-carrying insects become important where human beings are crowded together, especially under conditions where sanitation is poor, as in time of natural disaster or war or in situations of extreme poverty and deprivation. Then control of some sort becomes necessary. It is a sobering fact, however, as we shall presently see, that the method of massive chemical control has had only limited success, and also threatens to worsen the very conditions it is intended to curb.

15   Under primitive agricultural conditions the farmer had few insect problems. These arose with the intensification of agriculture—the devotion of immense acreages to a single crop. Such a system set the stage for explosive increases in specific insect populations. Single-crop farming does not take advantage of the principles by which nature works; it is agriculture as an engineer might conceive it to be. Nature has introduced great variety into the landscape, but man has displayed a passion for simplifying it. Thus he undoes the built-in checks and balances by which nature holds the species within bounds. One important natural check is a limit on the amount of suitable habitat for each species. Obviously then, an insect that lives on wheat can build up its population to much higher levels on a farm devoted to wheat than on one in which wheat is intermingled with other crops to which the insect is not adapted.

The same thing happens in other situations. A generation or more ago, the towns of large areas of the United States lined their streets with the noble elm tree. Now the beauty they hopefully created is threatened with complete destruction as disease sweeps through the elms, carried by a beetle that would have only limited chance to build up large populations and to spread from tree to tree if the elms were only occasional trees in a richly diversified planting.

Another factor in the modern insect problem is one that must be viewed against a background of geologic and human history: the spreading of thousands of different kinds of organisms from their native homes to invade new territories. This worldwide migration has been studied and graphically described by the British ecologist Charles Elton in his recent book *The Ecology of Invasions.* During the Cretaceous Period, some hundred million years ago, flooding seas cut many land bridges between continents and living things found themselves confined in what Elton calls "colossal separate nature reserves." There, isolated from others of their kind, they developed many new species. When some of the land masses were joined again, about 15 million years ago, these species began to move out into new territories—a movement that is not only still in progress but is now receiving considerable assistance from man.

The importation of plants is the primary agent in the modern spread of species, for animals have almost invariably gone along with the plants, quarantine being a comparatively recent and not completely effective innovation. The United States Office of Plant Introduction alone has introduced almost 200,000 species and varieties of plants from all over the world. Nearly half of the 180 or so major insect enemies of plants in the United States are accidental imports from abroad, and most of them have come as hitchhikers on plants.

In new territory, out of reach of the restraining hand of the natural enemies that kept down its numbers in its native land, an invading plant or animal is able to become enormously abundant. Thus it is no accident that our most troublesome insects are introduced species.

20   These invasions, both the naturally occurring and those dependent on human assistance, are likely to continue indefinitely. Quarantine and massive chemical campaigns are only extremely expensive ways of buying time. We are faced, according to Dr. Elton, "with a life-and-death need not just to find new technological means of suppressing this plant or that animal"; instead we need the basic knowledge of animal populations and their relations to their surroundings that will "promote an even balance and damp down the explosive power of outbreaks and new invasions."

Much of the necessary knowledge is now available but we do not use it. We train ecologists in our universities and even employ them in our governmental agencies but we seldom take their advice. We allow the chemical death rain to fall as though there were no alternative, whereas in fact there are many, and our ingenuity could soon discover many more if given opportunity.

Have we fallen into a mesmerized state that makes us accept as inevitable that which is inferior or detrimental, as though having lost the will or the vision to demand that which is good? Such thinking, in the words of the ecologist Paul Shepard, "idealizes life with only its head out of water, inches above the limits of toleration of the corruption of its own environment . . . Why should we tolerate a diet of weak poisons, a home in insipid surroundings, a circle of acquaintances who are not quite our enemies, the noise of motors with just enough relief to prevent insanity? Who would want to live in a world which is just not quite fatal?"

Yet such a world is pressed upon us. The crusade to create a chemically sterile, insect-free world seems to have engendered a fanatic zeal on the part of many specialists and most of the so-called control agencies. On every hand there is evidence that those engaged in spraying operations exercise a ruthless power. "The regulatory entomologists . . . function as prosecutor, judge and jury, tax assessor and collector and sheriff to enforce their own orders," said Connecticut entomologist Neely Turner. The most flagrant abuses go unchecked in both state and federal agencies.

It is not my contention that chemical insecticides must never be used. I do contend that we have put poisonous and biologically potent chemicals indiscriminately into the hands of persons largely or wholly ignorant of their potentials for harm. We have subjected enormous numbers of people to contact with these poisons, without their consent and often without their knowledge. If the Bill of Rights contains no guarantee that a citizen shall be secure against lethal poisons distributed either by private individuals or by public officials, it is surely only because our forefathers, despite their considerable wisdom and foresight, could conceive of no such problem.

25 I contend, furthermore, that we have allowed these chemicals to be used with little or no advance investigation of their effect on soil, water, wildlife, and man himself. Future generations are unlikely to condone our lack of prudent concern for the integrity of the natural world that supports all life.

There is still very limited awareness of the nature of the threat. This is an era of specialists, each of whom sees his own problem and is unaware of or intolerant of the larger frame into which it fits. It is also an era dominated by industry, in which the right to make a dollar at whatever cost is seldom challenged. When the public protests, confronted with some obvious evidence of damaging results of pesticide applications, it is fed little tranquilizing pills of half truth. We urgently need an end to these false assurances, to the sugar coating of unpalatable facts. It is the public that is being asked to assume the risks that the insect controllers calculate. The public must decide whether it wishes to continue on the present road, and it can do so only when in full possession of the facts. In the words of Jean Rostand, "The obligation to endure gives us the right to know."

A Modest Proposal: For Preventing the Children of Poor People in Ireland, from Being a Burden on Their Parents or Country, and for Making Them Beneficial to the Public

JONATHAN SWIFT

"A Modest Proposal," by Jonathan Swift—a political journalist, satirist, clergyman in the Anglican Church, and Dean of St. Patrick's Cathedral in Dublin—was first published as a pamphlet in 1729. It remains one of the most famous satirical arguments in western literature. In this argument, which has the problem-solution structure of a practical proposal, Swift addresses the ruling classes in both England and Ireland, attacking the political and economic policies that are starving the lower classes in Ireland including bans on Irish industries and exports. Satire is a rhetorical vehicle of exposure and critique with the intent of rendering its object ridiculous or shocking in order to inspire reform. One of the main tools of satire is verbal irony, in which the speaker means something quite different from what is actually said. In this satirical argument, Swift, speaking in the persona of what critics have variously identified as an eighteenth century humanitarian or an economist, proposes a solution to the suffering of the Irish poor—a solution that pretends to be rational and pragmatic. Note how the speaker gives the problem presence, offers a pragmatic (but ironic) solution, justifies his solution with reasons and evidence, and engages with opposing views.

It is a melancholy object to those who walk through this great town or travel in the country, when they see the streets, the roads, and cabin doors, crowded with beggars of the female sex, followed by three, four, or six children, all in rags and importuning every passenger for an alms. These mothers, instead of being able to work for their honest livelihood, are forced to employ all their time in strolling to beg sustenance for their helpless infants: who as they grow up either turn thieves for want of work, or leave their dear native country to fight for the Pretender in Spain, or sell themselves to the Barbadoes.

I think it is agreed by all parties that this prodigious number of children in the arms, or on the backs, or at the heels of their mothers, and frequently of their fathers, is in the present deplorable state of the kingdom a very great additional grievance; and, therefore, whoever could find out a fair, cheap, and easy method of making these children sound, useful members of the commonwealth, would deserve so well of the public as to have his statue set up for a preserver of the nation.

But my intention is very far from being confined to provide only for the children of professed beggars; it is of a much greater extent, and shall take in the whole number of infants at a certain age who are born of parents in effect as little able to support them as those who demand our charity in the streets.

As to my own part, having turned my thoughts for many years upon this important subject, and maturely weighed the several schemes of other projectors, I have always found them grossly mistaken in the computation. It is true, a child just dropped from its dam may be supported by her milk for a solar year, with little other nourishment; at most not above the value of 2s., which the mother may certainly get, or the value in scraps, by her lawful occupation of begging; and it is exactly at one year old that I propose to provide for them in such a manner as instead of being a charge upon their parents or the parish, or wanting food and raiment for the rest of their lives, they shall on the contrary contribute to the feeding, and partly to the clothing, of many thousands.

5   There is likewise another great advantage in my scheme, that it will prevent those voluntary abortions, and that horrid practice of women murdering their bastard children, alas! too frequent among us! sacrificing the poor innocent babes I doubt more to avoid the expense than the shame, which would move tears and pity in the most savage and inhuman breast.

The number of souls in this kingdom being usually reckoned one million and a half, of these I calculate there may be about two hundred thousand couple whose wives are breeders; from which number I subtract thirty thousand couples who are able to maintain their own children, although I apprehend there cannot be so many, under the present distresses of the kingdom; but this being granted, there will remain an hundred and seventy thousand breeders. I again subtract fifty thousand for those women who miscarry, or whose children die by accident or disease within the year. There only remains one hundred and twenty thousand children of poor parents annually born. The question therefore is, how this number shall be reared and provided for, which, as I have already said, under the present situation of affairs, is utterly impossible by all the methods hitherto proposed. For we can neither employ them in handicraft or agriculture; we neither build houses (I mean in the country) nor cultivate land: they can very seldom pick up a livelihood by stealing, till they arrive at six years old, except where they are of towardly parts, although I confess they learn the rudiments much earlier, during which time, they can however be properly looked upon only as probationers, as I have been informed by a principal gentleman in the county of Cavan, who protested to me that he never knew above one or two instances under the age of six, even in a part of the kingdom so renowned for the quickest proficiency in that art.

I am assured by our merchants, that a boy or a girl before twelve years old is no salable commodity; and even when they come to this age they will not yield above three pounds, or three pounds and half-a-crown at most on the exchange; which cannot turn to account either to the parents or kingdom, the charge of nutriment and rags having been at least four times that value.

I shall now therefore humbly propose my own thoughts, which I hope will not be liable to the least objection.

I have been assured by a very knowing American of my acquaintance in London, that a young healthy child well nursed is at a year old a most delicious, nourishing, and wholesome food, whether stewed, roasted, baked, or boiled; and I make no doubt that it will equally serve in a fricassee or a ragout.

10   I do therefore humbly offer it to public consideration that of the hundred and twenty thousand children already computed, twenty thousand may be reserved for breed, whereof only one-fourth part to be males; which is more than we allow to sheep, black cattle or swine; and my reason is, that these children are seldom the fruits of marriage, a circumstance not much regarded by our savages, therefore one male will be sufficient to serve four females. That the remaining hundred thousand may, at a year old, be offered in the sale to the persons of quality and fortune through the kingdom; always advising the mother to let them suck plentifully in the last month, so as to render them plump and fat for a good table. A child will make two dishes at an entertainment for friends; and when the family dines alone, the fore or hind quarter will make a reasonable dish, and seasoned with a little pepper or salt will be very good boiled on the fourth day, especially in winter.

I have reckoned upon a medium that a child just born will weigh 12 pounds, and in a solar year, if tolerably nursed, increaseth to 28 pounds.

I grant this food will be somewhat dear, and therefore very proper for landlords, who, as they have already devoured most of the parents, seem to have the best title to the children.

Infant's flesh will be in season throughout the year, but more plentiful in March, and a little before and after; for we are told by a grave author, an eminent French physician, that fish being a prolific diet, there are more children born in Roman Catholic countries about nine months after Lent than at any other season; therefore, reckoning a year after Lent, the markets will be more glutted than usual, because the number of popish infants is at least three to one in this kingdom: and therefore it will have one other collateral advantage, by lessening the number of papists among us.

I have already computed the charge of nursing a beggar's child (in which list I reckon all cottagers, laborers, and four-fifths of the farmers) to be about two shillings per annum, rags included; and I believe no gentleman would repine to give ten shillings for the carcass of a good fat child, which, as I have said, will make four dishes of excellent nutritive meat, when he hath only some particular friend or his own family to dine with him. Thus the squire will learn to be a good landlord, and grow popular among his tenants; the mother will have eight shillings net profit, and be fit for work till she produces another child.

15   Those who are more thrifty (as I must confess the times require) may flay the carcass; the skin of which artificially dressed will make admirable gloves for ladies, and summer boots for fine gentlemen.

As to our city of Dublin, shambles may be appointed for this purpose in the most convenient parts of it, and butchers we may be assured will not be wanting; although I rather recommend buying the children alive, and dressing them hot from the knife, as we do roasting pigs.

A very worthy person, a true lover of his country, and whose virtues I highly esteem, was lately pleased in discoursing on this matter to offer a refinement upon my scheme. He said that many gentlemen of this kingdom, having of late destroyed their deer, he conceived that the want of venison might be well supplied by the bodies of young lads and maidens, not exceeding fourteen years of age nor under twelve; so great a number of both sexes in every country being now ready to starve for want of work and service; and these to be disposed of by their parents, if alive, or otherwise by their nearest relations. But with due deference to so excellent a friend and so deserving a patriot, I cannot be altogether in his sentiments; for as to the males, my American acquaintance assured me, from frequent experience, that their flesh was generally tough and lean, like that of our schoolboys by continual exercise, and their taste disagreeable; and to fatten them would not answer the charge. Then as to the females, it would, I think, with humble submission be a loss to the public, because they soon would become breeders themselves; and besides, it is not improbable that some scrupulous people might be apt to censure such a practice (although indeed very unjustly), as a little bordering upon cruelty; which, I confess, hath always been with me the strongest objection against any project, however so well intended.

But in order to justify my friend, he confessed that this expedient was put into his head by the famous Psalmanazar, a native of the island Formosa, who came from thence to London above twenty years ago, and in conversation told my friend, that in his country when any young person happened to be put to death, the executioner sold the carcass to persons of quality as a prime dainty; and that in his time the body of a plump girl of fifteen, who was crucified for an attempt to poison the emperor, was sold to his imperial majesty's prime minister of state, and other great mandarins of the court, in joints from the gibbet, at four hundred crowns. Neither indeed can I deny, that if the same use were made of several plump young girls in this town, who without one single groat to their fortunes cannot stir abroad without a chair, and appear at playhouse and assemblies in foreign fineries which they never will pay for, the kingdom would not be the worse.

Some persons of a desponding spirit are in great concern about that vast number of poor people, who are aged, diseased, or maimed, and I have been desired to employ my thoughts what course may be taken to ease the nation of so grievous an encumbrance. But I am not in the least pain upon that matter, because it is very well known that they are every day dying and rotting by cold and famine, and filth and vermin, as fast as can be reasonably expected. And as to the young laborers, they are now in as hopeful a condition; they cannot get work, and consequently pine away for want of nourishment, to a degree that if at any time they are accidentally hired to common labor, they have not strength to perform it; and thus the country and themselves are happily delivered from the evils to come.

20 I have too long digressed, and therefore shall return to my subject. I think the advantages by the proposal which I have made are obvious and many, as well as of the highest importance.

For first, as I have already observed, it would greatly lessen the number of papists, with whom we are yearly overrun, being the principal breeders of the nation as well as our most dangerous enemies; and who stay at home on purpose with a design to deliver the kingdom to the Pretender, hoping to take their advantage by the absence of so many good protestants, who have chosen rather to leave their country than stay at home and pay tithes against their conscience to an episcopal curate.

Secondly, The poorer tenants will have something valuable of their own, which by law may be made liable to distress and help to pay their landlord's rent, their corn and cattle being already seized, and money a thing unknown.

Thirdly, Whereas the maintenance of an hundred thousand children, from two years old and upward, cannot be computed at less than ten shillings a-piece per annum, the nation's stock will be thereby increased fifty thousand pounds per annum, beside the profit of a new dish introduced to the tables of all gentlemen of fortune in the kingdom who have any refinement in taste. And the money will circulate among ourselves, the goods being entirely of our own growth and manufacture.

Fourthly, The constant breeders, beside the gain of eight shillings sterling per annum by the sale of their children, will be rid of the charge of maintaining them after the first year.

25   Fifthly, This food would likewise bring great custom to taverns; where the vintners will certainly be so prudent as to procure the best receipts for dressing it to perfection, and consequently have their houses frequented by all the fine gentlemen, who justly value themselves upon their knowledge in good eating: and a skilful cook, who understands how to oblige his guests, will contrive to make it as expensive as they please.

Sixthly, This would be a great inducement to marriage, which all wise nations have either encouraged by rewards or enforced by laws and penalties. It would increase the care and tenderness of mothers toward their children, when they were sure of a settlement for life to the poor babes, provided in some sort by the public, to their annual profit instead of expense. We should see an honest emulation among the married women, which of them could bring the fattest child to the market. Men would become as fond of their wives during the time of their pregnancy as they are now of their mares in foal, their cows in calf, their sows when they are ready to farrow; nor offer to beat or kick them (as is too frequent a practice) for fear of a miscarriage.

Many other advantages might be enumerated. For instance, the addition of some thousand carcasses in our exportation of barreled beef, the propagation of swine's flesh, and improvement in the art of making good bacon, so much wanted among us by the great destruction of pigs, too frequent at our tables; which are no way comparable in taste or magnificence to a well-grown, fat, yearling child, which roasted whole will make a considerable figure at a lord mayor's feast or any other public entertainment. But this and many others I omit, being studious of brevity.

Supposing that one thousand families in this city, would be constant customers for infants flesh, besides others who might have it at merry meetings, particularly at weddings and christenings, I compute that Dublin would take off annually about twenty thousand carcasses; and the rest of the kingdom (where probably they will be sold somewhat cheaper) the remaining eighty thousand.

I can think of no one objection, that will possibly be raised against this proposal, unless it should be urged, that the number of people will be thereby much lessened in the kingdom. This I freely own, and 'twas indeed one principal design in offering it to the world. I desire the reader will observe, that I calculate my remedy for this one individual Kingdom of Ireland, and for no other that ever was, is, or, I think, ever can be upon Earth. Therefore let no man talk to me of other expedients: Of taxing our absentees at five shillings a pound: Of using neither cloaths, nor houshold furniture, except what is of our own growth and manufacture: Of utterly rejecting the materials and instruments that promote foreign luxury: Of curing the expensiveness of pride, vanity, idleness, and gaming in our women: Of introducing a vein of parsimony, prudence and temperance: Of learning to love our country, wherein we differ even from Laplanders, and the inhabitants of Topinamboo: Of quitting our animosities and factions, nor acting any longer like the Jews, who were murdering one another at the very moment their city was taken: Of being a little cautious not to sell our country and consciences for nothing: Of teaching landlords to have at least one degree of mercy towards their tenants. Lastly, of putting a spirit of honesty, industry, and skill into our shop-keepers, who, if a resolution could now be taken to buy only our native goods, would immediately unite to cheat and exact upon us in the price, the measure, and the goodness, nor could ever yet be brought to make one fair proposal of just dealing, though often and earnestly invited to it.

30   Therefore I repeat, let no man talk to me of these and the like expedients, 'till he hath at least some glympse of hope, that there will ever be some hearty and sincere attempt to put them into practice.

But, as to my self, having been wearied out for many years with offering vain, idle, visionary thoughts, and at length utterly despairing of success, I fortunately fell upon this proposal, which, as it is wholly new, so it hath something solid and real, of no expence and little trouble, full in our own power, and whereby we can incur no danger in disobliging England. For this kind of commodity will not bear exportation, and flesh being of too tender a consistence, to admit a long continuance in salt, although perhaps I could name a country, which would be glad to eat up our whole nation without it.

After all, I am not so violently bent upon my own opinion as to reject any offer proposed by wise men, which shall be found equally innocent, cheap, easy, and effectual. But before something of that kind shall be advanced in contradiction to my scheme, and offering a better, I desire the author or authors will be pleased maturely to consider two points. First, as things now stand, how they will be able to find food and raiment for an hundred thousand useless mouths and backs. And secondly, there being a round million of creatures in human figure throughout this kingdom, whose whole subsistence put into a common stock would leave them in debt two millions of pounds sterling, adding those who are beggars by profession to the bulk of farmers, cottagers, and laborers, with their wives and children who are beggars in effect: I desire those politicians who dislike my overture, and may perhaps be so bold as to attempt an answer, that they will first ask the parents of these mortals, whether they would not at this day think it a great happiness to have been sold for food, at a year old in the manner I prescribe, and thereby have avoided such a perpetual scene of misfortunes as they have since gone through by the oppression of landlords, the impossibility of paying rent without money or trade, the want of common sustenance, with neither house nor clothes to cover them from the inclemencies of the weather, and the most inevitable prospect of entailing the like or greater miseries upon their breed for ever.

I profess, in the sincerity of my heart, that I have not the least personal interest in endeavoring to promote this necessary work, having no other motive than the public good of my country, by advancing our trade, providing for infants, relieving the poor, and giving some pleasure to the rich. I have no children by which I can propose to get a single penny; the youngest being nine years old, and my wife past child-bearing.

■ ■ ■ **FOR CLASS DISCUSSION** Argument Classics

1. Each of the arguments in this chapter is trying to persuade its audience toward the writer's (or the artist's) position or angle of vision on a major problem. Working in small groups or as a whole class, explore your answers to the following questions for one of the arguments selected by your instructor:

   a. What is the question or problem addressed by the writer (artist)?

   b. What is the writer's (artist's) position or angle of vision?

   c. What positions or views is the writer (artist) pushing against or opposing?

   d. What is at stake?

2. Working in small groups or as a whole class, choose an argument and analyze the rhetorical strategies used by the writer (or artist) to persuade his or her audience. Then evaluate the effectiveness of these strategies. To generate ideas for this discussion, use the "Questions for Rhetorical Analysis" in Chapter 8, pages 161–162. ■ ■ ■

WRITING ASSIGNMENT   Rhetorical Analysis

Write a thesis-driven rhetorical analysis of one of the classic arguments chosen by your professor. Follow the instructions and guidelines for a rhetorical analysis essay as explained in Chapter 8, pages 170–171. ■

> For additional writing, reading, and research resources, go to
> www.mycomplab.com

Credits

Section One—Inventing Arguments

Chapters 1–14 taken from *Writing Arguments: A Rhetoric with Readings*, Ninth Edition by John D. Ramage, John C. Bean, and June Johnson.

Page 7. "Let the Facts Decide, Not Fear: Ban AB 1108," by Louis W. Sullivan. Reprinted by permission of the author.

Page 18. "College Athletes in Tangled Web," by Brent Schrotenboer, reprinted by permission from the *San Diego Union Tribune*, May 24, 2006.

Page 18. "Homeless Hit Street to Protest Proposed Ban," by Linda Keene, reprinted by permission from the *Seattle Times*, August 28, 1993.

Page 40. "Amnesty?" by John F. Kavanaugh from *America*, March 10, 2008, by permission of America Press.

Page 47. "Why Blame Mexico?" by Fred Reed, from *The American Conservative*, March 10, 2008, by permission of The American Conservative.

Page 132. "Recycling Is Garbage," by John Tierney, from *New York Times Magazine*, June 30, 1996. Reprinted by permission of the author.

Page 138. "Islam in Two Americas," by Ross Douthat, reprinted by permission from the *New York Times*, August 15, 2010.

Page 163. "Egg Heads," by Kathryn Jean Lopez, from *National Review*, September 1, 1998, pp. 26–28, by permission of National Review.

Page 172. "Womb for Rent, For a Price," by Ellen Goodman, reprinted by permission from the *Seattle Times*, April 11, 2008.

Page 222. "All That Noise for Nothing," by Aaron Friedman, reprinted by permission from the *New York Times*, December 11, 2003.

Page 254. "Toon Offensive," by Beth Reis, from *Seattle Times*, June 20, 2008. Reprinted by permission of the author.

Page 280. "Different but (Probably) Equal," by Olivia Judson, reprinted by permission from the *New York Times*, January 23, 2005.

Page 310. "Giving Life After Death Row," by Christian Longo, reprinted by permission from the *New York Times*, March 5, 2011.

Page 311. "A Death Row Donation of Organs?" (Letter to the Editor) by Dr. Kenneth Prager, from the *New York Times*, March 12, 2011. Reprinted by permission of the author.

Page 346. "The Six-Legged Meat of the Future," by Marcel Dicke and Arnold Van Huis, reprinted from the *Wall Street Journal*, February 19, 2011, by permission of Dow Jones & Company, Inc.

Section Two—Rhetoric Supplement

Page 359, Chapter 15. "Inquiry and Argument," taken from *From Inquiry to Argument* by Linda McMeniman.

Page 370, Chapter 16. "Exigence," reprinted by permission of the Academic Writing Program, University of Maryland.

Page 374, Chapter 17. "Using the Five Canons of Rhetoric as Steps in the Process of Writing," reprinted by permission of the Academic Writing Program, University of Maryland.

Page 380, Chapter 18. "Invention—Generating Ideas with Stasis Theory," reprinted by permission of the Academic Writing Program, University of Maryland.

Page 382, Chapter 19. "Writing a Rhetorical Analysis," reprinted by permission of the Academic Writing Program, University of Maryland.

Page 382. "Should High Schools Permit Gay-Straight Alliance Clubs?" by Jim Anderson and Peter LaBarbera, reprinted from *The CQ Researcher* 10, no. 14 (April 14, 2000), by permission of Congressional Quarterly, Inc.

Page 392, Chapter 20. "Stasis Theory—Identifying the Issues and Joining the Debate," reprinted by permission of the Academic Writing Program, University of Maryland.

Section Three—Style: Composition and Ornament

Page 397, Chapter 21. "Style: Composition and Ornament," taken from *Ancient Rhetorics for Contemporary Students,* Fifth Edition by Sharon Crowley and Debra Hawhee.

Section Four—Readings on Revision and Reflection

Page 449, Chapter 22. "Shitty First Drafts," by Anne Lamott, reprinted from *Bird by Bird* (1995), by permission of Random House, Inc.

Page 452, Chapter 23. "Revising," by Joseph Harris, reprinted from *Rewriting: How to Do Things with Texts* (2006), by permission of Utah State University Press.

Page 470, Chapter 24. "The Maker's Eye: Revising Your Own Manuscripts," by Donald M. Murray, reprinted from *The Writer* (1973), by permission of The Rosenberg Group.

Page 475, Chapter 25. "Making Meaning Clear: The Logic of Revision," by Donald M. Murray, reprinted by permission from the *Journal of Basic Writing* 3.3 (fall, winter 1981).

Page 482, Chapter 26. "When We Dead Awaken: Writing as Re Vision," by Adrienne Rich, reprinted from *On Lies, Secrets, and Silence: Selected Prose 1966–1978* (1995), by permission of W.W. Norton & Company, Inc.

Page 495, Chapter 27. "Revision Strategies of Student Writers and Experienced Adult Writers," by Nancy Sommers, reprinted from *College Composition and Communication,* Edition 31.4 (1980), by permission of the National Council of Teachers of English.

Page 505, Chapter 28. "Thirteen (Lucky!) Strategies for Revision," reprinted by permission of the Academic Writing Program, University of Maryland.

Page 509, Chapter 29. "Reflective Writing and the Revision Process: What Were You Thinking?" by Sandra L. Giles, reprinted from *Writing Spaces: Readings on Writing,* Volume 1, edited by Charles Lowe and Pavel Zemliansky (2010), by permission of Parlor Press.

Section Five—An Anthology of Arguments

Chapters 30–35 taken from *Writing Arguments: A Rhetoric with Readings,* Ninth Edition by John D. Ramage, John C. Bean, and June Johnson.

Page 522. "Digital Natives and Immigrants: What Brain Research Tells Us," by Nancy K. Herther, from *Online,* November/December 2009, 33.6. Copyright © 2009 by Nancy K. Herther. First published by Information Today, Inc. www.infotoday.com. Reprinted by permission of the author.

Page 529. "Digital Demands: The Challenges of Constant Connectivity," interview with Sherry Turkel, from *Frontline*'s "Digital Nation." Copyright © 1995–2011 by WGBH Educational Foundation, by permission of FRONTLINE/WGBH, Boston.

Page 532. "Diagnosing the Digital Revolution: Why it's so hard to tell whether it's really changing us," by Alison Gopnik, reprinted by permission from *Slate,* February 7, 2011.

Page 536. "Living and Learning with New Media: Summary of Findings from the Digital Youth Project," by Mizuko Ito (November 2008), by permission of The MIT Press.

Page 538. "Designing Learning," from 'End-to-End' by Cathy Davidson, March 4, 2011 from http://dmlcentral.net/blog/cathy-davidson/designing-learning-end-end. Reprinted by permission of DMLcentral.net.

Page 541. "Youthful Indiscretions: Should Colleges Protect Social Network Users from Themselves and Others?" by Dana L. Fleming, *The New English Journal of Higher Education,* winter 2008, Vol. 22.4, pp. 27–29. Copyright © 2008 by Dana L. Fleming. Reprinted by permission of The New English Journal of Higher Education.

Page 548. "A Note to Young Immigrants," by Mitali Perkins, from *Teaching Tolerance,* fall 2005, Vol. 28. Copyright © 2005 Teaching Tolerance. www.tolerance.org

Page 549. "Miss or Diss?" from http://scarfacewearingheadscarfinamerica.blogspot.com by Umma Ali. Copyright © 2008 by Umma Ali. Reprinted by permission of the author.

Page 551. "Scarfing It Down," by Fatemeh Fakhraie, from *Bitch: Feminist Response to Pop Culture,* Edition 39, spring 2008, pp. 15–16. Copyright © 2008 by Fatemeh Fakhraie. Reprinted by permission of the author.

Page 552. "Sophia's Choice: Problems Faced by Female Asylum Seekers and Their U.S. Citizen Children," by Anita Ortiz Maddali, reprinted by permission from *Feminist Studies* 34, no. 1/2 Edition, (spring summer 2008).

Page 562. "Born in the USA," by Kevin Clarke, from *U.S. Catholic,* October 2010, 75.10, p. 39. Copyright © 2010 by U.S. Catholic. Reproduced by permission of U.S. Catholic. Subscriptions: $22/year from 205 West Monroe, Chicago, IL 60606; Call 1-800-328-6515 for subscription information or visit http://www.uscatholic.org/.

Page 563. "Anchor Babies Away," by David Mastio, from *The Washington Times,* August 13, 2010. Copyright © 2010 by David Mastio. Reprinted by permission of the author.

Page 565. "My Life in the Shadows," by Reyna Wences. Reprinted from the *New York Times Upfront* 143, by permission of Scholastic, Inc.

Page 566. "DREAM On," by Mark Krikorian, from *National Review Online,* December 1, 2010. Copyright © 2010 by Mark Krikorian. Reprinted by permission of National Review.

Page 570. "Learning by Degrees," by Rebecca Mead, reprinted from *The New Yorker,* June 7, 2010, Conde Nast Publications, Inc.

Page 572. "How Much Is That Bachelor's Degree Really Worth? The Million Dollar Misunderstanding," by Mark Schneider, from *Education Outlook,* May 2005. Copyright © 2005 by Mark Schneider. Reprinted by permission of the American Enterprise Institute for Public Policy Research, Washington, D.C.

Page 581. "What Do You Do with a B.A. in History?" by Ken Saxon, from *The Heart of the Matter* by Andy Chan. Reprinted by permission of the author.

Page 588. "How to Get a Real Education at College," by Scott Adams, reprinted by permission from the *Wall Street Journal,* April 9, 2011.

Page 591. "Coxsackie-Athens Valedictorian Speech 2010: Here I Stand," by Erica Goldson, from *America via Erica,* July 7, 2010. Copyright © 2010 by Erica Goldson. Used by permission of the author.

Page 597. "Solving for XX," by Deborah Blum, from *The Boston Globe,* January 23, 2005. Copyright © 2008 by Deborah Blum. Reprinted by permission of the author.

Page 599. "Sex Ed," by Steven Pinker, from *The New Republic,* February 2005. Copyright © 2005 by Steven Pinker. Reprinted by permission of The New Republic.

Page 602. "Male Scientist Writes of Life as Female Scientist," by Shankar Vendantam, reprinted by permission from the *Washington Post,* July 13, 2006.

Page 606. "Daring to Discuss Women in Science," by John Tierney, reprinted by permission from the *New York Times,* June 7, 2010.

Page 608. Response to Tierney by Caroline Simard, from *Huffington Post* Copyright © 2010 by Caroline Simard. Used by permission of the author.

Page 611. "Stereotype Threat and Women's Performance in Engineering," by Amy E. Bell, Emma Iserman, Christine E. R. Logel, Steven J. Spencer, from *Journal of Engineering Education,* October 2003. Copyright © 2003 by Amy E. Bell, Emma Iserman, Christine E. R. Logel, Steven J. Spencer. Reprinted by permission from American Society of Engineering Education.

Images

Page 120. Image Courtesy of The Advertising Archives

Page 140. Jessica Rinaldi/Reuters

Page 141. Don Emmert/AFP/Getty Images

Page 142 (top). AP Images/Seth Wenig

Page 142 (bottom). Jessica Rinaldi/Reuters

Page 157. Image Courtesy of The Advertising Archives

Page 177. Courtesy John of Bean

Page 181. Seattle Field Division of the Drug Enforcement Agency

Page 182. Common Sense for Drug Policy

Page 186. Ad Council

Page 187. Earthjustice/www.earthjustice.org

Page 190. (Figure 9.6) © Nissan North America Inc./Getty Images; (Figure 9.7) © Nissan North America Inc./Framepool Inc.; (Figures 9.8–9.10) © Nissan North America Inc./BBC Motion Gallery; (Figure 9.11) Sterling Artist Management Inc./© Nissan North America Inc.

Page 193 (top). AP Images/Laura Rauch

Page 193 (bottom). Peter Silva/ZUMA Press/Newscom

Page 194 (left). Sean Cockerham/MCT/Newscom

Page 194 (right). AP Images/Alex Brandon

Page 195. Courtesy Brave New Films

Page 196. Army Game Project. Used with permission.

Page 197. Army Game Project. Used with permission.

Page 200. Mark Guthrie/www.cartoonstock.com

Page 203. txtresponsibly.org

Page 213. AP Images/Pat Sullivan

Page 224. By Permission of Michael Ramirez and Creators Syndicate, Inc.

Page 227 (left). Andy Marlette/andymarlette.com

Page 227 (right). By Pat Bagely, www.politicalcartoons.com

Page 254. Clay Bennett Editorial Cartoon used by the permission of Clay Bennett, the Washington Post Writers Group and the Cartoonist Group. All rights reserved.

Page 263. Saatchi & Saatchi/Pedestrian Council of Australia

Page 287. courtesy Everett Collection

Page 292. AP Images/Carolyn Kaster

Page 309. Adey Bryant/www.cartoonstock.com

Page 313. Courtesy of Devito/Verdi New York, NY

Page 321. Courtesy of John Bean

Page 326. Endangered Wildlife Trust

Page 342. Courtesy Mount Sinai Center for Children's Health and the Environment and Fenton Communication

Page 344. (Figure 14.2) YinYang/istockphoto; (Figure 14.5) Peter Essick/Aurora Photos/Alamy; (Figure 14.7) Simon Belcher/Alamy

Page 347. Gavriel Jecan/Photodisc/Getty Images

Page 535. By Mike Keefe, www.politicalcartoons.com

Page 545. Paul Noth/The New Yorker Collection/www.cartoonbank.com

Page 550. Julija Sapic/istockphoto.com

Index